Computer Algorithms
String Pattern Matching Strategies

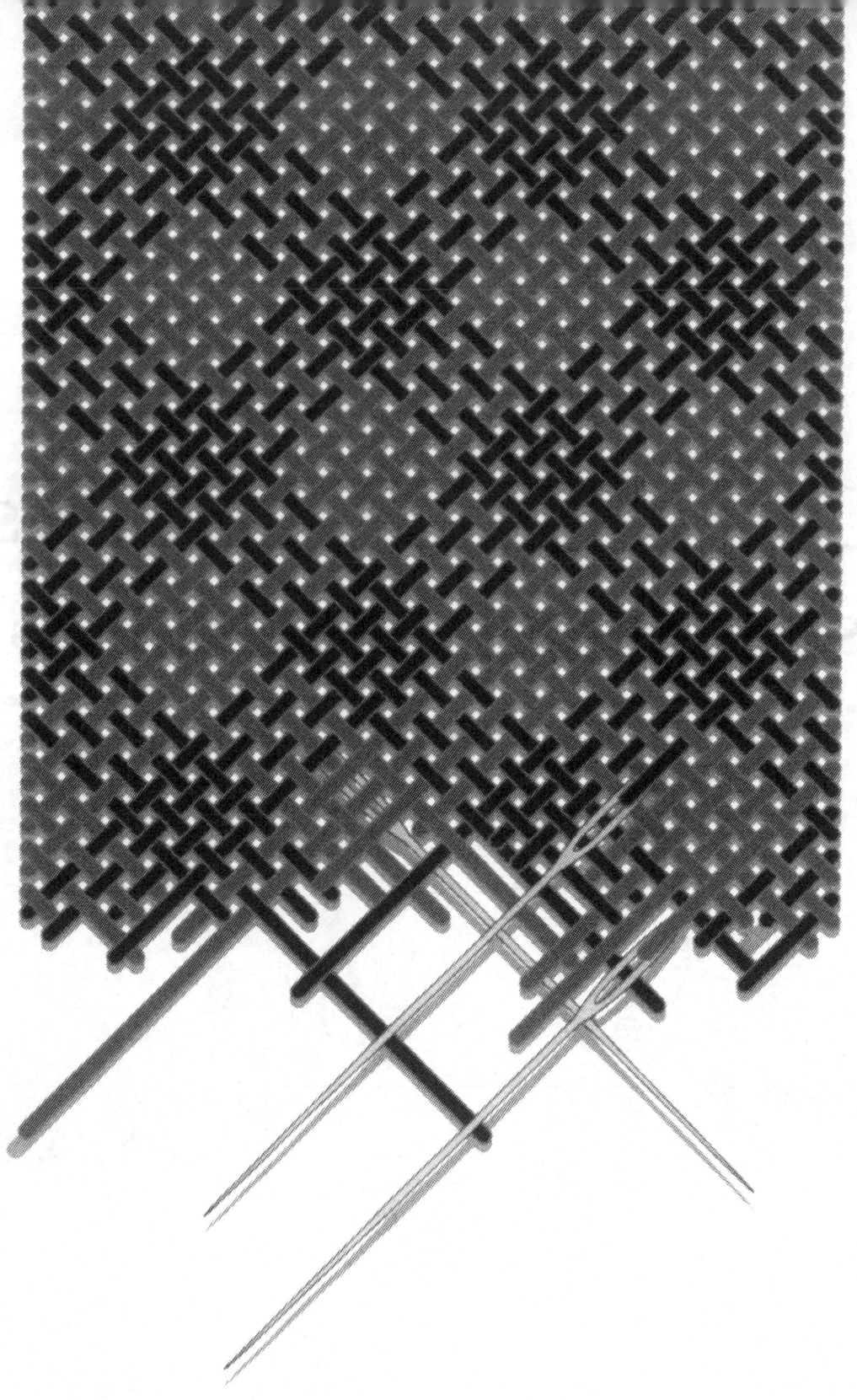

Computer Algorithms
String Pattern Matching Strategies

Jun-ichi Aoe
University of Tokushima, Japan

IEEE Computer Society Press
Los Alamitos, California

Washington • Brussels • Tokyo

Computer Algorithms: string pattern matching strategies / [edited by]
Jun-ichi Aoe.
        p.   cm.
Includes bibliographical references and index.
ISBN 0-8186-5461-9 (m/f). -- ISBN 0-8186-5462-7 (case). -- ISBN
0-8186-5460-0 (paper)
        1. Computer algorithms.   I. Aoe, Jun-ichi, 1951-
QA76.9.A43C67   1994
005.1--dc20
                                                                    93-40355
                                                                    CIP

IEEE Computer Society Press
10662 Los Vaqueros Circle
P.O. Box 3014
Los Alamitos, CA 90720-1264

IEEE Computer Society Press Order Number 5462-05
IEEE Catalog Number 94EH0389-7
Library of Congress Number 93-40355
ISBN 0-8186-5461-9 (microfiche)
ISBN 0-8186-5462-7 (case)

Additional copies may be ordered from:

IEEE Computer Society Press
Customer Service Center
10662 Los Vaqueros Circle
P.O. Box 3014
Los Alamitos, CA 90720-1264
Tel: +1-714-821-8380
Fax: +1-714-821-4641
Email: cs.books@computer.org

IEEE Service Center
445 Hoes Lane
P.O. Box 1331
Piscataway, NJ 08855-1331
Tel: +1-908-981-1393
Fax: +1-908-981-9667

IEEE Computer Society
13, Avenue de l'Aquilon
B-1200 Brussels
BELGIUM
Tel: +32-2-770-2198
Fax: +32-2-770-8505

IEEE Computer Society
Ooshima Building
2-19-1 Minami-Aoyama
Minato-ku, Tokyo 107
JAPAN
Tel: +81-3-3408-3118
Fax: +81-3-3408-3553

Technical Editor: Ajit Singh
Editorial production by Bob Werner
Cover art design and production by Alexander Torres

The Institute of Electrical and Electronics Engineers, Inc.

Contents

Preface

String pattern matching is an important component of many areas of science and information processing. It occurs naturally as part of data processing, text editing, symbol manipulation, term-rewriting, lexical analysis, code generation, spelling correction, bibliographic search, text retrieval, and natural language processing. String pattern matching techniques can be also applied to the recognition of patterns such as shapes, pictures, scenes, and so on. In biology, string pattern matching problems arise in the analysis of protein sequences and nucleic acids and in the investigation of molecular phylogeny. String pattern matching is the most time-consuming part of many programs, and the substitution of a poor matching method by a good one often leads to a substantial increase in speed. Therefore, a fast methodology should be selected. The aim of this volume is to introduce the basic concepts and characteristics of string pattern matching strategies and to provide numerous references for further reading.

The pattern matcher is a program that takes as input the text string x and produces as output the locations in x at which patterns, or keywords, appear as substrings. The simplest patterns are single keywords that match themselves. A somewhat broader class of patterns would be sets of keywords. There are two important variants of pattern-matching problems. One is approximate string matching problems, in which one must find all substrings in a text that are close to a pattern according to some measure of closeness. Another is multidimensional matching problems for finding patterns in higher-dimensional structures such as trees and graphs. In recent years some types of pattern matching algorithms have been implemented on hardware based on the finite state automata and signature files in order to improve processing efficiency. In this book, string pattern matching strategies are classified into the following five chapters.

- Single keyword matching
- Matching sets of keywords
- Approximate string matching
- Multidimensional matching
- Hardware matching

As an introduction to each chapter, my survey article describes the basic concepts of classification mentioned above. Fifteen papers have been selected to further illustrate these concepts. Also, I have made considerable efforts to find a large number of corresponding references and to organize them.

Most of the string matching techniques are treated in detail, with mathematical analyses and suggestions for practical applications, in the books and articles cited throughout the book. The references [Aho, 80], [Aho, 90], [Apostolico et al., 85], [Gonnet et al., 85], and [Sankoff et al., 83] are good surveys for general string pattern matching techniques. The six books [Aho et al., 74], [Frakes et al., 92], [Knuth, 73], [Mehlhorn, 84], [Sedgewick, 86], and [Standish, 80] are useful for the corresponding basic data structures and algorithms.

Chapter 1: Single Keyword Matching

Introduction

Single keyword matching means locating all occurrences of a given pattern in the input text string. It occurs naturally as part of data processing, text editing, text retrieval, and so on. Many text editors and programming languages have facilities for matching strings. The simplest technique is called the brute-force (BF), or naive, algorithm. This approach scans the text from left to right and checks the characters of the pattern character by character against the substring of the text string beneath it. Let m and n be the lengths of the pattern and the text, respectively. In the BF approach, the longest (worst-case) time required for determining that the pattern does not occur in the text is $O(mn)$.

Three major pattern matching algorithms for the improvement of efficiency over the BF technique exist. One of them is the KMP algorithm, developed by Knuth, Morris, and Pratt. The KMP algorithm scans the text from left to right, using knowledge of the previous characters compared to determine the next position of the pattern to use. The algorithm first reads the pattern and in $O(m)$ time constructs a table, called the *next function*, that determines the number of characters to slide the pattern to the right in case of a mismatch during the pattern matching process. The expected theoretical behavior of the KMP algorithm is $O(n+m)$, and the next function takes $O(m)$ space.

The next algorithm, the BM algorithm, was proposed by Boyer and Moore. The BM approach is the fastest pattern matching algorithm for a single keyword in both theory and practice. The BM algorithm compares characters in the pattern from right to left. If a mismatch occurs, the algorithm computes a shift, that is, the amount by which the pattern is moved to the right before a new matching is attempted. It also preprocesses the pattern in order to produce the shift tables. The expected theoretical behavior of the BM algorithm is equal to that of the KMP algorithm, but many experimental results show that the BM algorithm is faster than the KMP algorithm.

The last approach is the KR algorithm, presented by Karp and Rabin. The KR algorithm uses extra memory to advantage by treating each possible m-character section (where m is the pattern length) of the text string as a keyword in a standard hash table, computing the hash function of it, and checking whether it equals the hash function of the pattern. Although the KR algorithm is linear in the number of references to the text string per characters passed, the substantially higher running time of this algorithm makes it unfeasible for pattern matching in strings.

In the rest of the chapter, many improvements, including parallel approaches, and variants of the basic single keyword matching algorithms introduced above are discussed along with the corresponding references.

In order to introduce these typical single keyword matching techniques, I have selected the three papers Knuth, Morris, and Pratt (1977), Boyer and Moore (1977), and Davies and Bowsher (1986). The first two papers are the original papers of the KMP and BM algorithms, respectively. The third paper includes comprehensive descriptions and useful empirical evaluation of the BF, KMP, BM, and KR algorithms. Good surveys of single keyword matching are in [Baeza-Yates, 89a], [Baeza-Yates, 92], and [Pirkldauer, 92].

Brute-force (BF) algorithm

This approach scans the text from left to right and checks the characters of the pattern character by character against the substring of the text string beneath it. When a mismatch occurs, the pattern is shifted to the right one character. Consider the following example.

```
Pattern:      text
Text:         In this example the algorithm searches in the text ...
```

In this example the algorithm searches in the text for the first character of the pattern (indicated by underline). It continues for every character of the pattern, abandoning the search as soon as a mismatch occurs; this happens if an initial substring of the pattern occurs in the text and is known as a *false start*. It is not difficult to see that the worst-case execution time occurs if, for every possible starting position of the pattern in the text, all but the last character of the pattern matches the corresponding character in the text. For pattern $a^{m-1}b$ and for text a^n with $n \gg m$, $O(mn)$ comparisons are needed to determine that the pattern does not occur in the text.

Knuth-Morris-Pratt (KMP) algorithm

The KMP algorithm scans the text from left to right, using knowledge of the previous characters compared, to determine the next position of the pattern to use. The algorithm first reads the pattern and in $O(m)$ time constructs a table, called the next function, that determines how many characters to slide the pattern to the right in case of a mismatch during the pattern matching process. Consider the following example.

```
Position:   1   2   3   4   5
Pattern:    a   b   a   a   a
next:       0   1   0   2   2
```

By using this next function, the text scanning is as follows:

```
          i   1   2   3   4   5
Pattern:      a   b   a   a   a
Text:         a   b   a   b   a   a   b   a   a   a
          j   1   2   3   4   5   7   8   9   10  11
```

Let i and j be the current positions for the pattern and the text, respectively. In the position $j=4$, which is a b in the text, matching becomes unsuccessful in the same position, $i=4$, which is an a in the pattern. By adjusting $i=$next[4]$=2$ to $j=4$, the pattern is shifted 2 characters to the right as follows:

```
              i   1   2   3   4   5
Pattern:          a   b   a   a   a
Text:         a   b   a   b   a   a   b   a   a   a
          j   1   2   3   4   5   7   8   9   10  11
```

After aa is matched, a mismatch is detected in the comparison of a in the pattern with b in the text. Then, the pattern is shifted 3 characters to the right by adjusting $i=$next[5]$=2$ to $j=8$, and then the algorithm finds a successful match as follows:

						i	1	2	3	4	5
Pattern:							a	b	a	a	a
Text:		a	b	a	b	a	a	b	a	a	a
	j	1	2	3	4	5	7	8	9	10	11

Summarizing, the expected theoretical behavior of the KMP algorithm is O($n+m$), and takes O(m) space for the next function. Note that the running time of the KMP algorithm is independent of the size of the alphabet.

Variants that compute the next function are presented by [Bailey et al., 80], [Barth, 81], and [Takaoka, 86]. Barth ([Barth, 84] and [Barth, 85]) has used Markov-chain theory to derive analytical results on the expected number of character comparisons made by the BF and KMP algorithms on random strings.

Boyer and Moore (BM) algorithm

The BM approach is the fastest pattern matching algorithm for a single keyword in both theory and practice. In the KMP algorithm the pattern is scanned from left to right, but the BM algorithm compares characters in the pattern from right to left. If mismatch occurs, then the algorithm computes a shift; that is, it computes the amount by which the pattern is moved to the right before a new matching attempt is undertaken. The shift can be computed using two heuristics. The *match* heuristic is based on the idea that when the pattern is moved to the right, it has to match over all the characters previously matched and bring a *different* character over the character of the text that caused the mismatch. The *occurrence* heuristic uses the fact that we must bring over the character of the text that caused the mismatch the first character of the pattern that matches it. Consider the following example of [Boyer et al., 77].

Pattern:	A T - T H A T̲
Text:	W H I CH - F̲ I N A L L Y - H A L T S · - - A T - T H A T - P O I N T

At the start, comparing the seventh character, F, of the text with the last character, T, fails. Since F is known not to appear anywhere in the pattern, the text pointer can be automatically incremented by 7.

Pattern:	A T - T H A T̲
Text:	W H I CH - F I N A L L Y ̲- H A L T S · - - A T - T H A T - P O I N T

The next comparison is of the hyphen in the text with the rightmost character in the pattern, T. They mismatch, and the pattern includes a hyphen, so the pattern can be moved down 4 positions to align the two hyphens.

Pattern:	A T - T H A̲ T
Text:	W H I CH - F I N A L L Y - H A L̲ T S · - - A T - T H A T - P O I N T

After *T* is matched, comparing *A* in the pattern with *L* in the text fails. The text pointer can be moved to the right by 7 positions, since the character causing the mismatch, *L*, does not occur anywhere in the pattern.

Pattern:	AT - T<u>HA</u>T
Text:	WHI CH- F I NAL L Y - HAL T S . - <u>-</u> A T - T HA T - P OI N T

After *AT* is matched, a mismatch is detected in the comparison of *H* in the pattern with the hyphen in the text. The text pointer can be moved to the right by 7 places, so as to align the discovered substring *AT* with the beginning of the pattern.

Pattern:	AT - THAT
Text:	WHI CH- F I NAL L Y - HAL T S . - - A T - T HA T - P OI N T

Karp and Rabin (KR) algorithm

An algorithm developed in [Karp et al., 87] is an improvement of the brute-force approach to pattern matching. This algorithm is a probabilistic algorithm that adapts hashing techniques to string searching. It uses extra memory to advantage by treating each possible *m*-character section of the text string (where *m* is the pattern length) as a key in a standard hash table, computing the hash function of it, and checking whether it equals the hash function of the pattern. Similar approaches using signature files will be discussed in chapter 5.

Here the hash function is defined as follows:

$$h(k) = k \bmod q, \text{ where } q \text{ is a large prime number.}$$

A large value of *q* makes it unlikely that a collision will occur. We translate the *m*-character into numbers by packing them together in a computer word, which we then treat as the integer *k* in the function above. This corresponds to writing the characters as numbers in a radix *d* number system, where *d* is the number of possible characters. The number *k* corresponding to the *m*-character section text[*i*]...text[*i+m*-1] is

$$k = \text{text}[i] \times d^{m-1} + \text{text}[i+1] \times d^{m-2} + \cdots + \text{text}[i+m-1]$$

Shifting one position to the right in the text string simply corresponds to replacing *k* by

$$(k - \text{text}[i] \times d^{m-1}) \times d + \text{text}[i+m]$$

Consider the example shown in Figure 1 of the KR algorithm based on [Cormen et al., 90]. Each character is a decimal digit, and the hashed value in computed by modulo 11. In Figure 1a the same text string with values computed modulo 11 for each possible position of a section of length 6. Assuming the pattern *k*=163479, we look for sections whose value modulo 11 is 8, since h(*k*)=163479 mod 11=8. Two such sections for 163479 and 123912 are found. The first, beginning at text position 8,

4

is indeed an occurrence of the pattern, and the second, beginning at text position 14, is spurious. In Figure 1b we are computing the value for a section in constant time, given the value for the previous section. The first section has value 163479. Dropping the high-order digit 1 gives us the new value 634791. All computations are performed modulo 11, so the value of the first section is 8 and the value computed of the new section is 3.

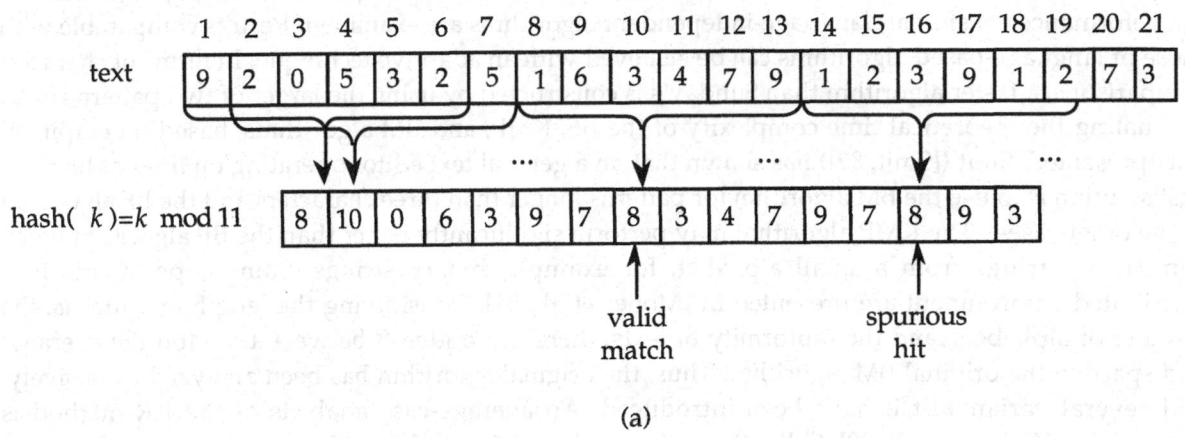

(a)

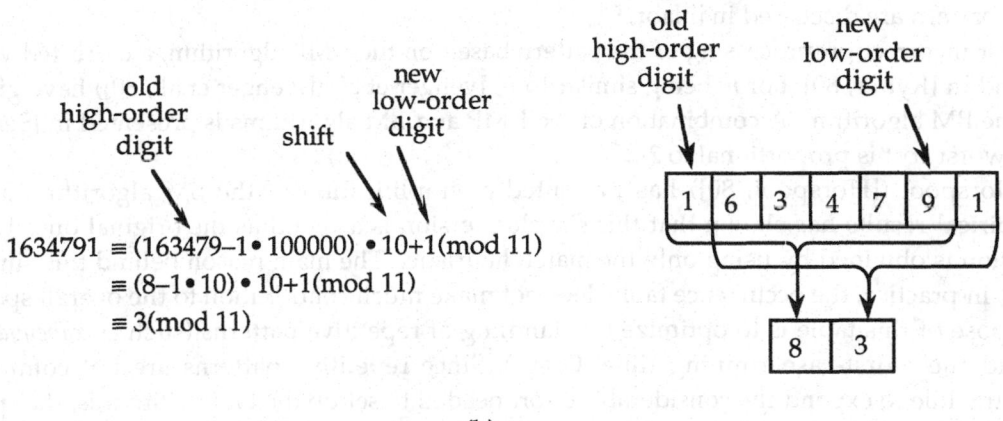

$$1634791 \equiv (163479 - 1 \cdot 100000) \cdot 10 + 1 \pmod{11}$$
$$\equiv (8 - 1 \cdot 10) \cdot 10 + 1 \pmod{11}$$
$$\equiv 3 \pmod{11}$$

(b)

Figure 1. Illustrations of the KR algorithm

Evaluations of single keyword matching algorithms

Rivest ([Rivest, 77]) has shown that any algorithm for finding a keyword in a string must examine at least $n-m+1$ of the characters in the string in the worst case, and Yao ([Yao, 79]) has shown that the minimum average number of characters needed to be examined in looking for a pattern in a random text string is $O(n\lceil \log_A m \rceil / m)$ for $n > 2m$, where A is the alphabet size. The upper bound and lower bound time complexities of single pattern matching are discussed in [Galil et al., 91] and [Galil et al., 92].

The minimum number of character comparisons needed to determine all occurrences of a keyword is an interesting theoretical question. It has been considered by [Galil, 79] and [Guibas et al., 80], and they have discussed some improvements to the BM algorithm for its worst-case behavior. Apostolico et al. ([Apostolico et al., 84] and [Apostolico et al., 86]) have presented a variant of the BM algorithm in which the number of character comparisons is at most $2n$, regardless of the number of occurrences of the pattern in the string. Sunday ([Sunday, 90]) has devised string matching methods that are generally faster than the BM algorithm. His faster method uses statistics of the language being scanned to determine the order in which character pairs are to be compared. In the paper [Smith, 91] the peformances of similar, language-independent algorithms are examined. Results comparable with those of language-based algorithms can be achieved with an adaptive technique. In terms of character comparisons, a faster algorithm than Sunday's is constructed by using the larger of two pattern shifts. Evaluating the theoretical time complexity of the BF, KMP, and BM algorithms, based on empirical data presented, Smit ([Smit, 82]) has shown that, in a general text editor operating on lines of text, the best solution is to use the BM algorithm for patterns longer than three characters and the BF algorithm in the other cases. The KMP algorithm may perform significantly better than the BF algorithm when comparing strings from a small alphabet, for example, binary strings. Some experiments in a distributed environment are presented in [Moller et al., 84]. Considering the length of patterns, the number of alphabets, and the uniformity of texts, there is a trade-off between time (on the average) and space in the original BM algorithm. Thus, the original algorithm has been analyzed extensively, and several variants of it have been introduced. An average-case analysis of the KR method is discussed in [Gonnet et al., 90]. Other theoretical and experimental considerations for single keyword matching are in [Arikawa, 81], [Collussi et al., 90], [Li, 84], [Liu, 81], [Miller et al., 88], [Slisenko, 80], [Waterman, 84], and [Zhu et al., 87]. Preprocessing and string matching techniques for a given text and pattern are discussed in [Naor, 91].

For incorrect preprocessing of the pattern based on the KMP algorithm, a corrected version can be found in [Rytter, 80]. For m being similar to n, Iyenger et al. ([Iyenger et al., 80]) have given a variant of the BM algorithm. A combination of the KMP and BM algorithms is presented in [Semba, 85], and the worst cost is proportional to $2n$.

Horspool ([Horspool, 80]) has presented a simplification of the BM algorithm, and based on empirical results has shown that this simpler version is as good as the original one. The simplified version is obtained by using only the match heuristic. The main reason behind this simplification is that, in practice, the occurrence table does not make much contribution to the overall speed. The only purpose of this table is to optimize the handling of repetitive patterns (such as $xabcyyabc$) and so to avoid the worst-case running time, O(mn). Since repetitive patterns are not common, it is not worthwhile to expend the considerable effort needed to set up the table. With this, the space depends only on the size of the alphabet (almost always fixed) and not on the length of the pattern (variable).

Baeza-Yates ([Baeza-Yates, 89b]) has improved the average time of the BM algorithm using extra space. This improvement is accomplished by applying a transformation that practically increases the size of the alphabet in use. The improvement is such that for long patterns an algorithm more than 50 percent faster than the original can be obtained. In this paper different heuristics are discussed that improve the search time based on the probability distribution of the symbols in the alphabet used. Schaback ([Schaback, 88]) has also analyzed the expected performance of some variants of the BM algorithm.

Horspool's implementation performs extremely well when we search for a random pattern in a random text. In practice, however, neither the pattern nor the text is random; there exist strong dependencies between successive symbols. Raita ([Raita, 92]) has suggested that it is not profitable to compare the pattern symbols strictly from right to left; if the last symbol of the pattern matches the corresponding text symbol, we should next try to match the first pattern symbol, because the dependencies are weakest between these two. His resulting code runs 25 percent faster than the best currently known routine.

Davies et al. ([Davies et al., 86]) have described four algorithms (BF, KMP, BM, and KR) of varying complexity used for pattern matching; and have investigated their behavior. Concluding from the empirical evidence, the KMP algorithm should be used with a binary alphabet or with small patterns drawn from any other alphabet. The BM algorithm should be used in all other cases. Use of the BM algorithm may not be advisable, however, if the frequency at which the pattern is expected to be found is small, since the preprocessing time is in that case significant; similarly with the KMP algorithm, so the BF algorithm is better in that situation. Although the KR algorithm is linear in the number of references to the text string per characters passed, its substantially higher running time makes it unfeasible for pattern matching in strings. The advantage of this algorithm over the other three lies in its extension to two-dimensional pattern matching. It can be used for pattern recognition and image processing and thus in the expanding field of computer graphics. The extension will be discussed in Section 4.

Related problems

Cook ([Cook, 71]) has shown that a linear-time pattern matching algorithm exists for any set of strings that can be recognized by a two-way deterministic push-down automaton (2DPDA), even though the 2DPDA may spend more than linear time recognizing the set of strings. The string matching capabilities of other classes of automata, especially k-head finite automata, have been of theoretical interest to [Apostolico et al., 85], [Chrobak et al., 87], [Galil et al., 83], and [Li et al., 86].

Schemes in [Bean et al., 85], [Crochemore et al., 91], [Duval, 83], [Guibas et al., 81a], [Guibas et al., 81b], and [Lyndon et al., 62] have added new vigor to the study of periods and overlaps in strings and to the study of the combinatorics of patterns in strings. [Crochemore et al., 91] presents a new algorithm that can be viewed as an intermediate between the standard algorithms of the KMP and the BM. The algorithm is linear in time and uses constant space like the algorithm of [Galil et al., 83]. The algorithm relies on a previously known result in combinatorics on words, the critical factorization theorem, which relates the global period of a word to its local repetitions of blocks. The following results are presented in [Crochemore et al., 91].

1. It is linear in time $O(n+m)$, as KMP and BM, with a maximum number of letter comparisons bounded by $2n+5m$ compared to $2n+2m$ for KMP and $2n+f(m)$ for BM, where f depends on the version of their algorithm.

2. The minimum number of letter comparisons used during the search phase (executing the preprocessing of the pattern) is $2n/m$ compared to n for KMP and n/m for BM.

3. The memory space used, additional to the locations of the text and the pattern, is constant instead of $O(m)$ for both KMP and BM.

Parallel approaches of string matching are discussed in [Galil, 85], and an $O(\log \log n)$ time parallel algorithm improving Galil's method is presented in [Breslauer et al., 90]. The paper [Breslauer et al., 92] describes the parallel complexity of the string matching problem using p processors for general alphabets. The other parallel matching algorithms are discussed in [Barkman et al., 89], [Kedam et al., 89], and [Viskin, 85].

FAST PATTERN MATCHING IN STRINGS*

DONALD E. KNUTH†, JAMES H. MORRIS, JR.‡ AND VAUGHAN R. PRATT¶

Abstract. An algorithm is presented which finds all occurrences of one given string within another, in running time proportional to the sum of the lengths of the strings. The constant of proportionality is low enough to make this algorithm of practical use, and the procedure can also be extended to deal with some more general pattern-matching problems. A theoretical application of the algorithm shows that the set of concatenations of even palindromes, i.e., the language $\{\alpha \alpha^R\}^*$, can be recognized in linear time. Other algorithms which run even faster on the average are also considered.

Key words. pattern, string, text-editing, pattern-matching, trie memory, searching, period of a string, palindrome, optimum algorithm, Fibonacci string, regular expression

Text-editing programs are often required to search through a string of characters looking for instances of a given "pattern" string; we wish to find all positions, or perhaps only the leftmost position, in which the pattern occurs as a contiguous substring of the text. For example, *c a t e n a r y* contains the pattern *t e n*, but we do not regard *c a n a r y* as a substring.

The obvious way to search for a matching pattern is to try searching at every starting position of the text, abandoning the search as soon as an incorrect character is found. But this approach can be very inefficient, for example when we are looking for an occurrence of *a a a a a a a b* in *a a a a a a a a a a a a a a a b*. When the pattern is $a^n b$ and the text is $a^{2n} b$, we will find ourselves making $(n+1)^2$ comparisons of characters. Furthermore, the traditional approach involves "backing up" the input text as we go through it, and this can add annoying complications when we consider the buffering operations that are frequently involved.

In this paper we describe a pattern-matching algorithm which finds all occurrences of a pattern of length m within a text of length n in $O(m+n)$ units of time, without "backing up" the input text. The algorithm needs only $O(m)$ locations of internal memory if the text is read from an external file, and only $O(\log m)$ units of time elapse between consecutive single-character inputs. All of the constants of proportionality implied by these "O" formulas are independent of the alphabet size.

Reprinted with permission from the **SIAM Journal on Computing**, Vol. 6, No. 2, June 1977, pp. 323-350. Copyright 1977 by the Society for Industrial and Applied Mathematics, Philadelphia, Pennsylvania. All rights reserved.

* Received by the editors August 29, 1974, and in revised form April 7, 1976.

† Computer Science Department, Stanford University, Stanford, California 94305. The work of this author was supported in part by the National Science Foundation under Grant GJ 36473X and by the Office of Naval Research under Contract NR 044-402.

‡ Xerox Palo Alto Research Center, Palo Alto, California 94304. The work of this author was supported in part by the National Science Foundation under Grant GP 7635 at the University of California, Berkeley.

¶ Artificial Intelligence Laboratory, Massachusetts Institute of Technology, Cambridge, Massachusetts 02139. The work of this author was supported in part by the National Science Foundation under Grant GP-6945 at University of California, Berkeley, and under Grant GJ-992 at Stanford University.

We shall first consider the algorithm in a conceptually simple but somewhat inefficient form. Sections 3 and 4 of this paper discuss some ways to improve the efficiency and to adapt the algorithm to other problems. Section 5 develops the underlying theory, and § 6 uses the algorithm to disprove the conjecture that a certain context-free language cannot be recognized in linear time. Section 7 discusses the origin of the algorithm and its relation to other recent work. Finally, § 8 discusses still more recent work on pattern matching.

1. Informal development. The idea behind this approach to pattern matching is perhaps easiest to grasp if we imagine placing the pattern over the text and sliding it to the right in a certain way. Consider for example a search for the pattern $a\,b\,c\,a\,b\,c\,a\,c\,a\,b$ in the text $b\,a\,b\,c\,b\,a\,b\,c\,a\,b\,c\,a\,a\,b\,c\,a\,b\,c\,a\,b\,c\,a\,c\,a\,b\,c$; initially we place the pattern at the extreme left and prepare to scan the leftmost character of the input text:

```
a b c a b c a c a b
b a b c b a b c a b c a a b c a b c a b c a c a b c
↑
```

The arrow here indicates the current text character; since it points to b, which doesn't match that a, we shift the pattern one space right and move to the next input character:

```
  a b c a b c a c a b
b a b c b a b c a b c a a b c a b c a b c a c a b c
  ↑
```

Now we have a match, so the pattern stays put while the next several characters are scanned. Soon we come to another mismatch:

```
  a b c a b c a c a b
b a b c b a b c a b c a a b c a b c a b c a c a b c
        ↑
```

At this point we have matched the first three pattern characters but not the fourth, so we know that the last four characters of the input have been $a\,b\,c\,x$ where $x \neq a$; we don't have to remember the previously scanned characters, since *our position in the pattern yields enough information to recreate them*. In this case, no matter what x. is (as long as it's not a), we deduce that the pattern can immediately be shifted four more places to the right; one, two, or three shifts couldn't possibly lead to a match.

Soon we get to another partial match, this time with a failure on the eighth pattern character:

```
          a b c a b c a c a b
b a b c b a b c a b c a a b c a b c a b c a c a b c
                      ↑
```

Now we know that the last eight characters were $a\,b\,c\,a\,b\,c\,a\,x$, where $x \neq c$. The pattern should therefore be shifted three places to the right:

$$a\,b\,c\,a\,b\,c\,a\,c\,a\,b$$
$$b\,a\,b\,c\,b\,a\,b\,c\,a\,b\,c\,a\,a\,b\,c\,a\,b\,c\,a\,b\,c\,a\,c\,a\,b\,c$$
$$\uparrow$$

We try to match the new pattern character, but this fails too, so we shift the pattern four (not three or five) more places. That produces a match, and we continue scanning until reaching *another* mismatch on the eighth pattern character:

$$a\,b\,c\,a\,b\,c\,a\,c\,a\,b$$
$$b\,a\,b\,c\,b\,a\,b\,c\,a\,b\,c\,a\,a\,b\,c\,a\,b\,c\,a\,b\,c\,a\,c\,a\,b\,c$$
$$\uparrow$$

Again we shift the pattern three places to the right; this time a match is produced, and we eventually discover the full pattern:

$$a\,b\,c\,a\,b\,c\,a\,c\,a\,b$$
$$b\,a\,b\,c\,b\,a\,b\,c\,a\,b\,c\,a\,a\,b\,c\,a\,b\,c\,a\,b\,c\,a\,c\,a\,b\,c$$
$$\uparrow$$

The play-by-play description for this example indicates that the pattern-matching process will run efficiently if we have an auxiliary table that tells us exactly how far to slide the pattern, when we detect a mismatch at its jth character $pattern[j]$. Let $next[j]$ be the character position in the pattern which should be checked next after such a mismatch, so that we are sliding the pattern $j - next[j]$ places relative to the text. The following table lists the appropriate values:

$j =$	1	2	3	4	5	6	7	8	9	10
$pattern[j] =$	a	b	c	a	b	c	a	c	a	b
$next[j] =$	0	1	1	0	1	1	0	5	0	1

(Note that $next[j] = 0$ means that we are to slide the pattern all the way *past* the current text character.) We shall discuss how to precompute this table later; fortunately, the calculations are quite simple, and we will see that they require only $O(m)$ steps.

At each step of the scanning process, we move either the text pointer or the pattern, and each of these can move at most n times; so at most $2n$ steps need to be performed, after the *next* table has been set up. Of course the pattern itself doesn't really move; we can do the necessary operations simply by maintaining the pointer variable j.

2. Programming the algorithm. The pattern-match process has the general form

```
place pattern at left;
while pattern not fully matched
    and text not exhausted do
    begin
        while pattern character differs from
            current text character
            do shift pattern appropriately;
        advance to next character of text;
    end;
```

For convenience, let us assume that the input text is present in an array $text[1:n]$, and that the pattern appears in $pattern[1:m]$. We shall also assume that $m > 0$, i.e., that the pattern is nonempty. Let k and j be integer variables such that $text[k]$ denotes the current text character and $pattern[j]$ denotes the corresponding pattern character; thus, the pattern is essentially aligned with positions $p+1$ through $p+m$ of the text, where $k = p+j$. Then the above program takes the following simple form:

```
j := k := 1;
while j ≤ m and k ≤ n do
    begin
        while j > 0 and text[k] ≠ pattern[j]
            do j := next[j];
        k := k+1; j := j+1;
    end;
```

If $j > m$ at the conclusion of the program, the leftmost match has been found in positions $k-m$ through $k-1$; but if $j \leq m$, the text has been exhausted. (The **and** operation here is the "conditional and" which does not evaluate the relation $text[k] \neq pattern[j]$ unless $j > 0$.) The program has a curious feature, namely that the inner loop operation "$j := next[j]$" is performed no more often than the outer loop operation "$k := k+1$"; in fact, the inner loop is usually performed somewhat *less* often, since the pattern generally moves right less frequently than the text pointer does.

To prove rigorously that the above program is correct, we may use the following invariant relation: "Let $p = k-j$ (i.e., the position in the text just preceding the first character of the pattern, in our assumed alignment). Then we have $text[p+i] = pattern[i]$ for $1 \leq i < j$ (i.e., we have matched the first $j-1$ characters of the pattern, if $j > 0$); but for $0 \leq t < p$ we have $text[t+i] \neq pattern[i]$ for some i, where $1 \leq i \leq m$ (i.e., there is no possible match of the entire pattern to the left of p)."

The program will of course be correct only if we can compute the *next* table so that the above relation remains invariant when we perform the operation $j := next[j]$. Let us look at that computation now. When the program sets

$j := next[j]$, we know that $j > 0$, and that the last j characters of the input up to and including $text[k]$ were

$$pattern[1] \dots pattern[j-1] \, x$$

where $x \neq pattern[j]$. What we want is to find the least amount of shift for which these characters can possibly match the shifted pattern; in other words, we want $next[j]$ to be the largest i less than j such that the last i characters of the input were

$$pattern[1] \dots pattern[i-1] \, x$$

and $pattern[i] \neq pattern[j]$. (If no such i exists, we let $next[j] = 0$.) With this definition of $next[j]$ it is easy to verify that $text[t+1] \dots text[k] \neq pattern[1] \dots pattern[k-1]$ for $k - j \leq t < k - next[j]$; hence the stated relation is indeed invariant, and our program is correct.

Now we must face up to the problem we have been postponing, the task of calculating $next[j]$ in the first place. This problem would be easier if we didn't require $pattern[i] \neq pattern[j]$ in the definition of $next[j]$, so we shall consider the easier problem first. Let $f[j]$ be the largest i less than j such that $pattern[1] \dots pattern[i-1] = pattern[j-i+1] \dots pattern[j-1]$; since this condition holds vacuously for $i = 1$, we always have $f[j] \geq 1$ when $j > 1$. By convention we let $f[1] = 0$. The pattern used in the example of § 1 has the following f table:

$$j = 1 \quad 2 \quad 3 \quad 4 \quad 5 \quad 6 \quad 7 \quad 8 \quad 9 \quad 10$$
$$pattern[j] = a \quad b \quad c \quad a \quad b \quad c \quad a \quad c \quad a \quad b$$
$$f[j] = 0 \quad 1 \quad 1 \quad 1 \quad 2 \quad 3 \quad 4 \quad 5 \quad 1 \quad 2.$$

If $pattern[j] = pattern[f[j]]$ then $f[j+1] = f[j]+1$; but if not, we can use essentially the same pattern-matching algorithm as above to compute $f[j+1]$, with $text = pattern$! (Note the similarity of the $f[j]$ problem to the invariant condition of the matching algorithm. Our program calculates the largest j less than or equal to k such that $pattern[1] \dots pattern[j-1] = text[k-j+1] \dots text[k-1]$, so we can transfer the previous technology to the present problem.) The following program will compute $f[j+1]$, assuming that $f[j]$ and $next[1]$, $\dots$, $next[j-1]$ have already been calculated:

```
t := f[j];
while t > 0 and pattern[j] ≠ pattern[t]
    do t := next[t];
f[j+1] := t+1;
```

The correctness of this program is demonstrated as before; we can imagine two copies of the pattern, one sliding to the right with respect to the other. For example, suppose we have established that $f[8] = 5$ in the above case; let us consider the computation of $f[9]$. The appropriate picture is

$$a \; b \; c \; a \; b \; c \; a \; c \; a \; b$$
$$a \; b \; c \; a \; b \; c \; a \; c \; a \; b$$
$$\uparrow$$

Since $pattern[8] \neq b$, we shift the upper copy right, knowing that the most recently scanned characters of the lower copy were $a\ b\ c\ a\ x$ for $x \neq b$. The $next$ table tells us to shift right four places, obtaining

$$
\begin{array}{l}
a\ b\ c\ a\ b\ c\ a\ c\ a\ b \\
a\ b\ c\ a\ b\ c\ a\ c\ a\ b \\
\uparrow
\end{array}
$$

and again there is no match. The next shift makes $t = 0$, so $f[9] = 1$.

Once we understand how to compute f, it is only a short step to the computation of $next[j]$. A comparison of the definitions shows that, for $j > 1$,

$$
next[j] = \begin{cases} f[j], & \text{if } pattern[j] \neq pattern[f[j]]; \\ next[f[j]], & \text{if } pattern\ [j] = pattern[f[j]]. \end{cases}
$$

Therefore we can compute the $next$ table as follows, without ever storing the values of $f[j]$ in memory.

$$j := 1;\ t := 0;\ next[1] := 0;$$
while $j < m$ **do**
begin comment $t = f[j]$;
    while $t > 0$ **and** $pattern[j] \neq pattern[t]$
      do $t := next[t]$;
    $t := t + 1;\ j := j + 1$;
    if $pattern[j] = pattern[t]$
    then $next[j] := next[t]$
    else $next[j] := t$;
end.

This program takes $O(m)$ units of time, for the same reason as the matching program takes $O(n)$: the operation $t := next[t]$ in the innermost loop always shifts the upper copy of the pattern to the right, so it is performed a total of m times at most. (A slightly different way to prove that the running time is bounded by a constant times m is to observe that the variable t starts at 0 and it is increased, $m - 1$ times, by 1; furthermore its value remains nonnegative. Therefore the operation $t := next[t]$, which always decreases t, can be performed at most $m - 1$ times.)

To summarize what we have said so far: Strings of text can be scanned efficiently by making use of two ideas. We can precompute "shifts", specifying how to move the given pattern when a mismatch occurs at its jth character; and this precomputation of "shifts" can be performed efficiently by using the same principle, shifting the pattern against itself.

3. Gaining efficiency. We have presented the pattern-matching algorithm in a form that is rather easily proved correct; but as so often happens, this form is not very efficient. In fact, the algorithm as presented above would probably not be competitive with the naive algorithm on realistic data, even though the naive algorithm has a worst-case time of order m times n instead of m plus n, because the chance of this worst case is rather slim. On the other hand, a well-implemented form of the new algorithm should go noticeably faster because there is no backing up after a partial match.

It is not difficult to see the source of inefficiency in the new algorithm as presented above: When the alphabet of characters is large, we will rarely have a partial match, and the program will waste a lot of time discovering rather awkwardly that $text[k] \neq pattern[1]$ for $k = 1, 2, 3, \ldots$. When $j = 1$ and $text[k] \neq pattern[1]$, the algorithm sets $j := next[1] = 0$, then discovers that $j = 0$, then increases k by 1, then sets j to 1 again, then tests whether or not 1 is $\leq m$, and later it tests whether or not 1 is greater than 0. Clearly we would be much better off making $j = 1$ into a special case.

The algorithm also spends unnecessary time testing whether $j > m$ or $k > n$. A fully-matched pattern can be accounted for by setting $pattern[m+1] = $ "@" for some impossible character @ that will never be matched, and by letting $next[m+1] = -1$; then a test for $j < 0$ can be inserted into a less-frequently executed part of the code. Similarly we can for example set $text[n+1] = $ "$\perp$" (another impossible character) and $text[n+2] = pattern[1]$, so that the test for $k > n$ needn't be made very often. (See [17] for a discussion of such more or less mechanical transformations on programs.)

The following form of the algorithm incorporates these refinements.

```
        a := pattern[1];
        pattern[m + 1] := '@' ; next[m + 1] := -1;
        text[n + 1] := '⊥' ; text[n + 2] := a;
        j := k := 1;
get started: comment j = 1;
        while text[k] ≠ a do k := k + 1;
        if k > n then go to input exhausted;
char matched: j := j + 1; k := k + 1;
loop:  comment j > 0;
        if text[k] = pattern[j] then go to char matched;
        j := next[j];
        if j = 1 then go to get started;
        if j = 0 then
            begin
                j := 1; k := k + 1;
                go to get started;
            end;
        if j > 0 then go to loop;
        comment text[k − m] through text[k − 1] matched;
```

This program will usually run faster than the naive algorithm; the worst case occurs when trying to find the pattern $a\,b$ in a long string of a's. Similar ideas can be used to speed up the program which prepares the *next* table.

In a text-editor the patterns are usually short, so that it is most efficient to translate the pattern directly into machine-language code which implicitly contains the *next* table (cf. [3, Hack 179] and [24]). For example, the pattern in § 1 could be compiled into the machine-language equivalent of

$$
\begin{aligned}
&\text{L0:} \quad k := k+1; \\
&\text{L1:} \quad \textbf{if } text[k] \neq a \textbf{ then go to } \text{L0}; \\
&\qquad\quad k := k+1; \\
&\qquad\quad \textbf{if } k > n \textbf{ then go to } \text{input exhausted}; \\
&\text{L2:} \quad \textbf{if } text[k] \neq b \textbf{ then go to } \text{L1}; \\
&\qquad\quad k := k+1; \\
&\text{L3:} \quad \textbf{if } text[k] \neq c \textbf{ then go to } \text{L1}; \\
&\qquad\quad k := k+1; \\
&\text{L4:} \quad \textbf{if } text[k] \neq a \textbf{ then go to } \text{L0}; \\
&\qquad\quad k := k+1; \\
&\text{L5:} \quad \textbf{if } text[k] \neq b \textbf{ then go to } \text{L1}; \\
&\qquad\quad k := k+1; \\
&\text{L6:} \quad \textbf{if } text[k] \neq c \textbf{ then go to } \text{L1}; \\
&\qquad\quad k := k+1; \\
&\text{L7:} \quad \textbf{if } text[k] \neq a \textbf{ then go to } \text{L0}; \\
&\qquad\quad k := k+1; \\
&\text{L8:} \quad \textbf{if } text[k] \neq c \textbf{ then go to } \text{L5}; \\
&\qquad\quad k := k+1; \\
&\text{L9:} \quad \textbf{if } text[k] \neq a \textbf{ then go to } \text{L0}; \\
&\qquad\quad k := k+1; \\
&\text{L10:} \quad \textbf{if } text[k] \neq b \textbf{ then go to } \text{L1}; \\
&\qquad\quad\; k := k+1;
\end{aligned}
$$

This will be slightly faster, since it essentially makes a special case for *all* values of j.

It is a curious fact that people often think the new algorithm will be slower than the naive one, even though it does less work. Since the new algorithm is conceptually hard to understand at first, by comparison with other algorithms of the same length, we feel somehow that a computer will have conceptual difficulties too—we expect the machine to run more slowly when it gets to such subtle instructions!

4. Extensions. So far our programs have only been concerned with finding the leftmost match. However, it is easy to see how to modify the routine so that all matches are found in turn: We can calculate the *next* table for the extended pattern of length $m+1$ using $pattern[m+1] = $ "@", and then we set $resume := next[m+1]$ before setting $next[m+1]$ to -1. After finding a match and doing whatever action is desired to process that match, the sequence

$$j := resume; \textbf{go to } \text{loop};$$

will restart things properly. (We assume that *text* has not changed in the meantime. Note that *resume* cannot be zero.)

Another approach would be to leave $next[m+1]$ untouched, never changing it to -1, and to define integer arrays $head[1:m]$ and $link[1:n]$ initially zero, and to insert the code

$$link[k] := head[j]; head[j] := k;$$

at label "char matched". The test "**if** $j > 0$ **then**" is also removed from the program. This forms linked lists for $1 \le j \le m$ of all places where the first j characters of the pattern (but no more than j) are matched in the input.

Still another straightforward modification will find the longest initial match of the pattern, i.e., the maximum j such that $pattern[1] \ldots pattern[j]$ occurs in *text*.

In practice, the text characters are often packed into words, with say b characters per word, and the machine architecture often makes it inconvenient to access individual characters. When efficiency for large n is important on such machines, one alternative is to carry out b independent searches, one for each possible alignment of the pattern's first character in the word. These searches can treat *entire words* as "supercharacters", with appropriate masking, instead of working with individual characters and unpacking them. Since the algorithm we have described does not depend on the size of the alphabet, it is well suited to this and similar alternatives.

Sometimes we want to match two or more patterns in sequence, finding an occurrence of the first followed by the second, etc.; this is easily handled by consecutive searches, and the total running time will be of order n plus the sum of the individual pattern lengths.

We might also want to match two or more patterns in parallel, stopping as soon as any one of them is fully matched. A search of this kind could be done with multiple *next* and *pattern* tables, with one j pointer for each; but this would make the running time kn plus the sum of the pattern lengths, when there are k patterns. Hopcroft and Karp have observed (unpublished) that our pattern-matching algorithm can be extended so that the running time for simultaneous searches is proportional simply to n, plus the alphabet size times the sum of the pattern lengths. The patterns are combined into a "trie" whose nodes represent all of the initial substrings of one or more patterns, and whose branches specify the appropriate successor node as a function of the next character in the input text. For example, if there are four patterns $\{a\,b\,c\,a\,b, a\,b\,a\,b\,c, b\,c\,a\,c, b\,b\,c\}$, the trie is shown in Fig. 1.

node	substring	if a	if b	if c
0		1	7	0
1	a	1	2	0
2	$a\,b$	5	10	3
3	$a\,b\,c$	4	7	0
4	$a\,b\,c\,a$	1	$a\,b\,c\,a\,b$	$b\,c\,a\,c$
5	$a\,b\,a$	1	6	0
6	$a\,b\,a\,b$	5	10	$a\,b\,a\,b\,c$
7	b	1	10	8
8	$b\,c$	9	7	0
9	$b\,c\,a$	1	2	$b\,c\,a\,c$
10	$b\,b$	1	10	$b\,b\,c$

FIG. 1

Such a trie can be constructed efficiently by generalizing the idea we used to calculate $next[j]$; details and further refinements have been discussed by Aho and Corasick [2], who discovered the algorithm independently. (Note that this algorithm depends on the alphabet size; such dependence is inherent, if we wish to keep the coefficient of n independent of k, since for example the k patterns might each consist of a single unique character.) It is interesting to compare this approach to what happens when the LR(0) parsing algorithm is applied to the regular grammar $S \to a\,S\,|\,b\,S\,|\,c\,S\,|\,a\,b\,c\,a\,b\,|\,a\,b\,a\,b\,c\,|\,b\,c\,a\,c\,|\,b\,b\,c$.

5. Theoretical considerations. If the input file is being read in "real time", we might object to long delays between consecutive inputs. In this section we shall prove that the number of times $j := next[j]$ is performed, before k is advanced, is bounded by a function of the approximate form $\log_\phi m$, where $\phi = (1 + \sqrt{5})/2 \approx 1.618 \ldots$ is the golden ratio, and that this bound is best possible. We shall use lower case Latin letters to represent characters, and lower case Greek letters $\alpha, \beta, \ldots$ to represent strings, with ε the empty string and $|\alpha|$ the length of α. Thus $|a| = 1$ for all characters a; $|\alpha\beta| = |\alpha| + |\beta|$; and $|\varepsilon| = 0$. We also write $\alpha[k]$ for the kth character of α, when $1 \leq k \leq |\alpha|$.

As a warmup for our theoretical discussion, let us consider the *Fibonacci strings* [14, exercise 1.2.8–36], which turn out to be especially pathological patterns for the above algorithm. The definition of Fibonacci strings is

$$(1) \qquad \phi_1 = b, \quad \phi_2 = a; \quad \phi_n = \phi_{n-1}\phi_{n-2} \quad \text{for } n \geq 3.$$

For example, $\phi_3 = a\,b$, $\phi_4 = a\,b\,a$, $\phi_5 = a\,b\,a\,a\,b$. It follows that the length $|\phi_n|$ is the nth Fibonacci number F_n, and that ϕ_n consists of the first F_n characters of an infinite string ϕ_∞ when $n \geq 2$.

Consider the pattern ϕ_8, which has the functions $f[j]$ and $next[j]$ shown in Table 1.

TABLE 1

$j =$	1	2	3	4	5	6	7	8	9	10	11	12	13	14	15	16	17	18	19	20	21
$pattern[j] =$	a	b	a	a	b	a	b	a	a	b	a	a	b	a	b	a	a	b	a	b	a
$f[j] =$	0	1	1	2	2	3	4	3	4	5	6	7	5	6	7	8	9	10	11	12	8
$next[j] =$	0	1	0	2	1	0	4	0	2	1	0	7	1	0	4	0	2	1	0	12	0

If we extend this pattern to ϕ_∞, we obtain infinite sequences $f[j]$ and $next[j]$ having the same general character. It is possible to prove by induction that

$$(2) \qquad f[j] = j - F_{k-1} \quad \text{for } F_k \leq j < F_{k+1},$$

because of the following remarkable near-commutative property of Fibonacci strings:

$$(3) \qquad \phi_{n-2}\phi_{n-1} = c(\phi_{n-1}\phi_{n-2}), \quad \text{for } n \geq 3,$$

where $c(\alpha)$ denotes changing the two rightmost characters of α. For example, $\phi_6 = a\,b\,a\,a\,b \cdot a\,b\,a$ and $c(\phi_6) = a\,b\,a \cdot a\,b\,a\,a\,b$. Equation (3) is obvious when $n = 3$; and for $n > 3$ we have $c(\phi_{n-2}\phi_{n-1}) = \phi_{n-2}c(\phi_{n-1}) = \phi_{n-2}\phi_{n-3}\phi_{n-2} = \phi_{n-1}\phi_{n-2}$ by induction; hence $c(\phi_{n-2}\phi_{n-1}) = c(c(\phi_{n-1}\phi_{n-2})) = \phi_{n-1}\phi_{n-2}$.

Equation (3) implies that

$$(4) \qquad next[F_k - 1] = F_{k-1} - 1 \quad \text{for } k \geq 3.$$

Therefore if we have a mismatch when $j = F_8 - 1 = 20$, our algorithm might set $j := next[j]$ for the successive values 20, 12, 7, 4, 2, 1, 0 of j. Since F_k is $(\phi^k/\sqrt{5})$ rounded to the nearest integer, it is possible to have up to $\sim \log_\phi m$ consecutive iterations of the $j := next[j]$ loop.

We shall now show that Fibonacci strings actually are the worst case, i.e., that $\log_\phi m$ is also an upper bound. First let us consider the concept of *periodicity* in strings. We say that p is a *period* of α if

$$(5) \qquad \alpha[i] = \alpha[i + p] \quad \text{for } 1 \leq i \leq |\alpha| - p.$$

It is easy to see that p is a period of α if and only if

$$(6) \qquad \alpha = (\alpha_1 \alpha_2)^k \alpha_1$$

for some $k \geq 0$, where $|\alpha_1 \alpha_2| = p$ and $\alpha_2 \neq \varepsilon$. Equivalently, p is a period of α if and only if

$$(7) \qquad \alpha \theta_1 = \theta_2 \alpha$$

for some θ_1 and θ_2 with $|\theta_1| = |\theta_2| = p$. Condition (6) implies (7) with $\theta_1 = \alpha_2 \alpha_1$ and $\theta_2 = \alpha_1 \alpha_2$. Condition (7) implies (6), for we define $k = \lfloor |\alpha|/p \rfloor$ and observe that if $k > 0$, then $\alpha = \theta_2 \beta$ implies $\beta \theta_1 = \theta_2 \beta$ and $\lfloor |\beta|/p \rfloor = k - 1$; hence, reasoning inductively, $\alpha = \theta_2^k \alpha_1$ for some α_1 with $|\alpha_1| < p$, and $\alpha_1 \theta_1 = \theta_2 \alpha_1$. Writing $\theta_2 = \alpha_1 \alpha_2$ yields (6).

The relevance of periodicity to our algorithm is clear once we consider what it means to shift a pattern. If $pattern[1] \ldots pattern[j-1] = \alpha$ ends with $pattern[1] \ldots pattern[i-1] = \beta$, we have

$$(8) \qquad \alpha = \beta \theta_1 = \theta_2 \beta$$

where $|\theta_1| = |\theta_2| = j - i$, so the amount of shift $j - i$ is a period of α.

The construction of $i = next[j]$ in our algorithm implies further that $pattern[i]$, which is the first character of θ_1, is unequal to $pattern[j]$. Let us assume that β itself is subsequently shifted leaving a residue γ, so that

$$(9) \qquad \beta = \gamma \psi_1 = \psi_2 \gamma$$

where the first character of ψ_1 differs from that of θ_1. We shall now prove that

$$(10) \qquad |\alpha| > |\beta| + |\gamma|.$$

If $|\beta| + |\gamma| \geq |\alpha|$, there is an overlap of $d = |\beta| + |\gamma| - |\alpha|$ characters between the occurrences of β and γ in $\beta \theta_1 = \alpha = \theta_2 \psi_2 \gamma$; hence the first character of θ_1 is $\gamma[d + 1]$. Similarly there is an overlap of d characters between the occurrences of β and γ in $\theta_2 \beta = \alpha = \gamma \psi_1 \theta_1$; hence the first character of ψ_1 is $\beta[d + 1]$. Since these characters are distinct, we obtain $\gamma[d + 1] \neq \beta[d + 1]$, contradicting (9). This establishes (10), and leads directly to the announced result:

THEOREM. *The number of consecutive times that $j := next[j]$ is performed, while one text character is being scanned, is at most $1 + \log_\phi m$.*

Proof. Let L_r be the length of the shortest string α as in the above discussion such that a sequence of r consecutive shifts is possible. Then $L_1 = 0$, $L_2 = 1$, and we have $|\beta| \geq L_{r-1}$, $|\gamma| \geq L_{r-2}$ in (10); hence $L_2 \geq F_{r+1} - 1$ by induction on r. Now if r shifts occur we have $m \geq F_{r+1} \geq \phi^{r-1}$. $\square$

18

The algorithm of § 2 would run correctly in linear time even if $f[j]$ were used instead of $next[j]$, but the analogue of the above theorem would then be false. For example, the pattern a^n leads to $f[j]=j-1$ for $1\le j\le m$. Therefore if we matched a^m to the text $a^{m-1}b\alpha$, using $f[j]$ instead of $next[j]$, the mismatch $text[m]\ne pattern[m]$ would be followed by m occurrences of $j:=f[j]$ and $m-1$ redundant comparisons of $text[m]$ with $pattern[j]$, before k is advanced to $m+1$.

The subject of periods in strings has several interesting algebraic properties, but a reader who is not mathematically inclined may skip to § 6 since the following material is primarily an elaboration of some additional structure related to the above theorem.

LEMMA 1. *If p and q are periods of α, and $p+q\le|\alpha|+\gcd(p,q)$, then $\gcd(p,q)$ is a period of α.*

Proof. Let $d=\gcd(p,q)$, and assume without loss of generality that $d<p<q=p+r$. We have $\alpha[i]=\alpha[i+p]$ for $1\le i\le|\alpha|-p$ and $\alpha[i]=\alpha[i+q]$ for $1\le i\le|\alpha|-q$; hence $\alpha[i+r]=\alpha[i+q]=\alpha[i]$ for $1+r\le i+r\le|\alpha|-p$, i.e.,

$$\alpha[i]=\alpha[i+r] \quad \text{for } 1\le i\le|\alpha|-q.$$

Furthermore $\alpha=\beta\theta_1=\theta_2\beta$ where $|\theta_1|=p$, and it follows that p and r are periods of β, where $p+r\le|\beta|+d=|\beta|+\gcd(p,r)$. By induction, d is a period of β. Since $|\beta|=|\alpha|-p\ge q-d\ge q-r=p=|\theta_1|$, the strings θ_1 and θ_2 (which have the respective forms $\beta_2\beta_1$ and $\beta_1\beta_2$ by (6) and (7)) are substrings of β; so they also have d as a period. The string $\alpha=(\beta_1\beta_2)^{k+1}\beta_1$ must now have d as a period, since any characters d positions apart are contained within $\beta_1\beta_2$ or $\beta_1\beta_1$. $\square$

The result of Lemma 1 but with the stronger hypothesis $p+q\le|\alpha|$ was proved by Lyndon and Schützenberger in connection with a problem about free groups [19, Lem. 4]. The weaker hypothesis in Lemma 1 turns out to give the best possible bound: If $\gcd(p,q)<p<q$ we can find a string of length $p+q-\gcd(p,q)-1$ for which $\gcd(p,q)$ is *not* a period. In order to see why this is so, consider first the example in Fig. 2 showing the most general strings of lengths 15 through 25 having both 11 and 15 as periods. (The strings are "most general" in the sense that any two character positions that can be different *are* different.)

```
a b c d e f g h i j k a b c d
a b c d a f g h i j k a b c d a
a b c d a b g h i j k a b c d a b
a b c d a b c h i j k a b c d a b c
a b c d a b c d i j k a b c d a b c d
a b c d a b c d a j k a b c d a b c d a
a b c d a b c d a b k a b c d a b c d a b
a b c d a b c d a b c a b c d a b c d a b c
a b c a a b c a a b c a b c a a b c a a b c a
a a c a a a c a a a c a a c a a a c a a a c a a
a a a a a a a a a a a a a a a a a a a a a a a a a
```

FIG. 2

Note that the number of degrees of freedom, i.e., the number of distinct symbols, decreases by 1 at each step. It is not difficult to prove that the number cannot decrease by *more* than 1 as we go from $|\alpha|=n-1$ to $|\alpha|=n$, since the only new relations are $\alpha[n] = \alpha[n-q] = \alpha[n-p]$; we decrease the number of distinct symbols by one if and only if positions $n-q$ and $n-p$ contain distinct symbols in the most general string of length $n-1$. The lemma tells us that we are left with at most $\gcd(p, q)$ symbols when the length reaches $p+q-\gcd(p, q)$; on the other hand we always have exactly p symbols when the length is q. Therefore each of the $p - \gcd(p, q)$ steps *must* decrease the number of symbols by 1, and the most general string of length $p + q - \gcd(p, q) - 1$ must have exactly $\gcd(p, q) + 1$ distinct symbols. In other words, the lemma gives the best possible bound.

When p and q are relatively prime, the strings of length $p+q-2$ on two symbols, having both p and q as periods, satisfy a number of remarkable properties, generalizing what we have observed earlier about Fibonacci strings. Since the properties of these pathological patterns may prove useful in other investigations, we shall summarize them in the following lemma.

LEMMA 2. *Let the strings $\sigma(m, n)$ of length n be defined for all relatively prime pairs of integers $n \geq m \geq 0$ as follows:*

$$\sigma(0, 1) = a, \quad \sigma(1, 1) = b, \quad \sigma(1, 2) = ab;$$

(11)
$$\left. \begin{array}{l} \sigma(m, m+n) = \sigma(n \bmod m, m)\sigma(m, n) \\ \sigma(n, m+n) = \sigma(m, n)\sigma(n \bmod m, m) \end{array} \right\} \text{ if } 0 < m < n.$$

These strings satisfy the following properties:
(i) $\sigma(m, qm+r)\sigma(m-r, m) = \sigma(r, m)\sigma(m, qm+r)$, *for $m > 2$;*
(ii) $\sigma(m, n)$ *has period m, for $m > 1$;*
(iii) $c(\sigma(m, n)) = \sigma(n-m, n)$, *for $n > 2$.*
(The function $c(\alpha)$ was defined in connection with (3) above.)

Proof. We have, for $0 < m < n$ and $q \geq 2$,

$$\sigma(m+n, q(m+n)+m) = \sigma(m, m+n)\,\sigma(m+n, (q-1)(m+n)+m),$$

$$\sigma(m+n, q(m+n)+n) = \sigma(n, m+n)\,\sigma(m+n, (q-1)(m+n)+n),$$

$$\sigma(m+n, 2m+n) = \sigma(m, m+n)\,\sigma(n \bmod m, m),$$

$$\sigma(m+n, m+2n) = \sigma(n, m+n)\,\sigma(m, n);$$

hence, if $\theta_1 = \sigma(n \bmod m, m)$ and $\theta_2 = \sigma(m, n)$ and $q \geq 1$,

(12) $\quad \sigma(m+n, q(m+n)+m) = (\theta_1\theta_2)^q\theta_1, \quad \sigma(m+n, q(m+n)+n) = (\theta_2\theta_1)^q\theta_2.$

It follows that

$$\sigma(m+n, q(m+n)+m)\sigma(n, m+n) = \sigma(m, m+n)\,\sigma(m+n, q(m+n)+m),$$

$$\sigma(m+n, q(m+n)+n)\sigma(m, m+n) = \sigma(n, m+n)\,\sigma(m+n, q(m+n)+n),$$

which combine to prove (i). Property (ii) also follows immediately from (12), except for the case $m = 2$, $n = 2q+1$, $\sigma(2, 2q+1) = (ab)^qa$, which may be verified directly. Finally, it suffices to verify property (iii) for $0 < m < \frac{1}{2}n$, since $c(c(\alpha)) = \alpha$; we must show that

$$c(\sigma(m, m+n)) = \sigma(m, n)\,\sigma(n \bmod m, m) \quad \text{for } 0 < m < n.$$

When $m \le 2$ this property is easily checked, and when $m > 2$ it is equivalent by induction to

$$\sigma(m, m+n) = \sigma(m, n)\, \sigma(m - (n \bmod m), m) \quad \text{for } 0 < m < n, \quad m > 2.$$

Set $n \bmod m = r$, $\lfloor n/m \rfloor = q$, and apply property (i). $\square$

By properties (ii) and (iii) of this lemma, $\sigma(p, p+q)$ minus its last two characters is the string of length $p+q-2$ having periods p and q. Note that Fibonacci strings are just a very special case, since $\phi_n = \sigma(F_{n-1}, F_n)$. Another property of the σ strings appears in [15]. A completely different proof of Lemma 1 and its optimality, and a completely different definition of $\sigma(m, n)$, were given by Fine and Wilf in 1965 [7]. These strings have a long history going back at least to the astronomer Johann Bernoulli in 1772; see [25, § 2.13] and [21].

If α is any string, let $P(\alpha)$ be its shortest period. Lemma 1 implies that all periods q which are not multiples of $P(\alpha)$ must be greater than $|\alpha| - P(\alpha) + \gcd(q, P(\alpha))$. This is a rather strong condition in terms of the pattern matching algorithm, because of the following result.

LEMMA 3. *Let $\alpha = pattern[1] \ldots pattern[j-1]$ and let $a = pattern[j]$. In the pattern matching algorithm, $f[j] = j - P(\alpha)$, and $next[j] = j - q$, where q is the smallest period of α which is not a period of αa. (If no such period exists, $next[j] = 0$.) If $P(\alpha)$ divides $P(\alpha a)$ and $P(\alpha a) < j$, then $P(\alpha) = P(\alpha a)$. If $P(\alpha)$ does not divide $P(\alpha a)$ or if $P(\alpha a) = j$, then $q = P(\alpha)$.*

Proof. The characterizations of $f[j]$ and $next[j]$ follow immediately from the definitions. Since every period of αa is a period of α, the only nonobvious statement is that $P(\alpha) = P(\alpha a)$ whenever $P(\alpha)$ divides $P(\alpha a)$ and $P(\alpha a) \ne j$. Let $P(\alpha) = p$ and $P(\alpha a) = mp$; then the (mp)th character from the right of α is a, as is the $(m-1)p$th, $\ldots$, as is the pth; hence p is a period of αa. $\square$

Lemma 3 shows that the $j := next[j]$ loop will almost always terminate quickly. If $P(\alpha) = P(\alpha a)$, then q must not be a multiple of $P(\alpha)$; hence by Lemma 1, $P(\alpha) + q \ge j + 1$. On the other hand $q > P(\alpha)$; hence $q > \frac{1}{2}j$ and $next[j] < \frac{1}{2}j$. In the other case $q = P(\alpha)$, we had better not have q too small, since q will be a period in the residual pattern after shifting, and $next[next[j]]$ will be $< q$. To keep the loop running it is necessary for new small periods to keep popping up, relatively prime to the previous periods.

6. Palindromes. One of the most outstanding unsolved questions in the theory of computational complexity is the problem of how long it takes to determine whether or not a given string of length n belongs to a given context-free language. For many years the best upper bound for this problem was $O(n^3)$ in a general context-free language as $n \to \infty$; L. G. Valiant has recently lowered this to $O(n^{\log_2 7})$. On the other hand, the problem isn't known to require more than order n units of time for any particular language. This big gap between $O(n)$ and $O(n^{2.81})$ deserves to be closed, and hardly anyone believes that the final answer will be $O(n)$.

Let Σ be a finite alphabet, let Σ^* denote the strings over Σ, and let

$$P = \{\alpha \alpha^R \mid \alpha \in \Sigma^*\}.$$

Here α^R denotes the reversal of α, i.e., $(a_1 a_2 \ldots a_n)^R = a_n \ldots a_2 a_1$. Each string π in P is a *palindrome* of even length, and conversely every even palindrome over

Σ is in P. At one time it was popularly believed that the language P^* of "even palindromes starred", namely the set of *palstars* $\pi_1 \ldots \pi_n$ where each π_i is in P, would be impossible to recognize in $O(n)$ steps on a random-access computer.

It isn't especially easy to spot members of this language. For example, $a\,a\,b\,b\,a\,b\,b\,a$ is a palstar, but its decomposition into even palindromes might not be immediately apparent; and the reader might need several minutes to decide whether or not

$$b\,a\,a\,b\,b\,a\,b\,b\,a\,a\,b\,a\,b\,b\,a\,a\,b\,b\,a\,b\,b\,a\,b\,a\,a$$

$$b\,b\,a\,b\,b\,a\,b\,b\,a\,b\,b\,a\,a\,b\,a\,b\,a\,b\,b\,a\,b\,b\,a\,a\,b$$

is in P^*. We shall prove, however, that palstars can be recognized in $O(n)$ units of time, by using their algebraic properties.

Let us say that a nonempty palstar is *prime* if it cannot be written as the product of two nonempty palstars. A prime palstar must be an even palindrome $\alpha\alpha^R$ but the converse does not hold. By repeated decomposition, it is easy to see that every palstar β is expressible as a product $\beta_1 \ldots \beta_t$ of prime palstars, for some $t \geq 0$; what is less obvious is that such a decomposition into prime factors is unique. This "fundamental theorem of palstars" is an immediate consequence of the following basic property.

LEMMA 1. *A prime palstar cannot begin with another prime palstar.*

Proof. Let $\alpha\alpha^R$ be a prime palstar such that $\alpha\alpha^R = \beta\beta^R\gamma$ for some nonempty even palindrome $\beta\beta^R$ and some $\gamma \neq \varepsilon$; furthermore, let $\beta\beta^R$ have minimum length among all such counterexamples. If $|\beta\beta^R| > |\alpha|$ then $\alpha\alpha^R = \beta\beta^R\gamma = \alpha\delta\gamma$ for some $\delta \neq \varepsilon$; hence $\alpha^R = \delta\gamma$, and $\beta\beta^R = (\beta\beta^R)^R = (\alpha\delta)^R = \delta^R\alpha^R = \delta^R\delta\gamma$, contradicting the minimality of $|\beta\beta^R|$. Therefore $|\beta\beta^R| \leq |\alpha|$; hence $\alpha = \beta\beta^R\delta$ for some δ, and $\beta\beta^R\gamma = \alpha\alpha^R = \beta\beta^R\delta\delta^R\beta\beta^R$. But this implies that γ is the palstar $\delta\delta^R\beta\beta^R$, contradicting the primality of $\alpha\alpha^R$. $\square$

COROLLARY (Left cancellation property.) *If $\alpha\beta$ and α are palstars, so is β.*

Proof. Let $\alpha = \alpha_1 \ldots \alpha_r$ and $\alpha\beta = \beta_1 \ldots \beta_s$ be prime factorizations of α and $\alpha\beta$. If $\alpha_1 \ldots \alpha_r = \beta_1 \ldots \beta_r$, then $\beta = \beta_{r+1} \ldots \beta_s$ is a palstar. Otherwise let j be minimal with $\alpha_j \neq \beta_j$; then α_j begins with β_j or vice versa, contradicting Lemma 1. $\square$

LEMMA 2. *If α is a string of length n, we can determine the length of the longest even palindrome $\beta \in P$ such that $\alpha = \beta\gamma$, in $O(n)$ steps.*

Proof. Apply the pattern-matching algorithm with *pattern* $= \alpha$ and *text* $= \alpha^R$. When $k = n+1$ the algorithm will stop with j maximal such that *pattern*$[1] \ldots$ *pattern* $[j-1] = text[n+2-j] \ldots text[n]$. Now perform the following iteration:

$$\textbf{while } j \geq 3 \textbf{ and } j \text{ even } \textbf{do } j := f(j).$$

By the theory developed in § 3, this iteration terminates with $j \geq 3$ if and only if α begins with a nonempty even palindrome, and $j - 1$ will be the length of the largest such palindrome. (Note that $f[j]$ must be used here instead of $next[j]$; e.g. consider the case $\alpha = a\,a\,b\,a\,a\,b$. But the pattern matching process takes $O(n)$ time even when $f[j]$ is used.) $\square$

THEOREM. *Let L be any language such that L^* has the left cancellation property and such that, given any string α of length n, we can find a nonempty $\beta \in L$*

such that α begins with β or we can prove that no such β exists, in $O(n)$ steps. Then we can determine in $O(n)$ time whether or not a given string is in L^*.

Proof. Let α be any string, and suppose that the time required to test for nonempty prefixes in L is $\leq Kn$ for all large n. We begin by testing α's initial subsequences of lengths $1, 2, 4, \ldots, 2^k, \ldots$, and finally α itself, until finding a prefix in L or until establishing that α has no such prefix. In the latter case, α is not in L^*, and we have consumed at most $(K+K_1)+(2K+K_1)+(4K+K_1)+\cdots+(|\alpha|K+K_1)<2Kn+K_1\log_2 n$ units of time for some constant K_1. But if we find a nonempty prefix $\beta \in L$ where $\alpha = \beta\gamma$, we have used at most $4|\beta|K+K(\log_2|\beta|)$ units of time so far. By the left cancellation property, $\alpha \in L^*$ if and only if $\gamma \in L^*$, and since $|\gamma| = n - |\beta|$ we can prove by induction that at most $(4K+K_1)n$ units of time are needed to decide membership in L^*, when $n > 0$. $\square$

COROLLARY. *P^* can be recognized in $O(n)$ time.*

Note that the related language

$$P_1^* = \{\pi \in \Sigma^* \mid \pi = \pi^R \text{ and } |\pi| \geq 2\}^*$$

cannot be handled by the above techniques, since it contains both $a\,a\,a\,b\,b\,b$ and $a\,a\,a\,b\,b\,b\,b\,a$; the fundamental theorem of palstars fails with a vengeance. It is an open problem whether or not P_1^* can be recognized in $O(n)$ time, although we suspect that it can be done.[1] Once the reader has disposed of this problem, he or she is urged to tackle another language which has recently been introduced by S. A. Greibach [11], since the latter language is known to be as hard as possible; no context-free language can be harder to recognize except by a constant factor.

7. Historical remarks. The pattern-matching algorithm of this paper was discovered in a rather interesting way. One of the authors (J. H. Morris) was implementing a text-editor for the CDC 6400 computer during the summer of 1969, and since the necessary buffering was rather complicated he sought a method that would avoid backing up the text file. Using concepts of finite automata theory as a model, he devised an algorithm equivalent to the method presented above, although his original form of presentation made it unclear that the running time was $O(m+n)$. Indeed, it turned out that Morris's routine was too complicated for other implementors of the system to understand, and he discovered several months later that gratuitous "fixes" had turned his routine into a shambles.

In a totally independent development, another author (D. E. Knuth) learned early in 1970 of S. A. Cook's surprising theorem about two-way deterministic pushdown automata [5]. According to Cook's theorem, any language recognizable by a two-way deterministic pushdown automaton, in *any* amount of time, can be recognized on a random access machine in $O(n)$ units of time. Since D. Chester had recently shown that the set of strings beginning with an even palindrome could be recognized by such an automaton, and since Knuth couldn't imagine how to recognize such a language in less than about n^2 steps on a conventional computer, Knuth laboriously went through all the steps of Cook's construction as applied to Chester's automaton. His plan was to "distill off" what

---

[1] (Note added April, 1976.) Zvi Galil and Joel Seiferas have recently resolved this conjecture affirmatively.

was happening, in order to discover why the algorithm worked so efficiently. After pondering the mass of details for several hours, he finally succeeded in abstracting the mechanism which seemed to be underlying the construction, in the special case of palindromes, and he generalized it slightly to a program capable of finding the longest prefix of one given string that occurs in another.

This was the first time in Knuth's experience that automata theory had taught him how to solve a real programming problem better than he could solve it before. He showed his results to the third author (V. R. Pratt), and Pratt modified Knuth's data structure so that the running time was independent of the alphabet size. When Pratt described the resulting algorithm to Morris, the latter recognized it as his own, and was pleasantly surprised to learn of the $O(m+n)$ time bound, which he and Pratt described in a memorandum [22]. Knuth was chagrined to learn that Morris had already discovered the algorithm, *without* knowing Cook's theorem; but the theory of finite-state machines had been of use to Morris too, in his initial conceptualization of the algorithm, so it was still legitimate to conclude that automata theory had actually been helpful in this practical problem.

The idea of scanning a string without backing up while looking for a pattern, in the case of a two-letter alphabet, is implicit in the early work of Gilbert [10] dealing with comma-free codes. It also is essentially a special case of Knuth's LR(0) parsing algorithm [16] when applied to the grammar

$$S \to aS, \qquad \text{for each } a \text{ in the alphabet,}$$
$$S \to \alpha,$$

where α is the pattern. Diethelm and Roizen [6] independently discovered the idea in 1971. Gilbert and Knuth did not discuss the preprocessing to build the *next* table, since they were mainly concerned with other problems, and the preprocessing algorithm given by Diethelm and Roizen was of order m^2. In the case of a binary (two-letter) alphabet, Diethelm and Roizen observed that the algorithm of § 3 can be improved further: we can go immediately to "char matched" after $j := next[j]$ in this case if $next[j] > 0$.

A conjecture by R. L. Rivest led Pratt to discover the $\log_\phi m$ upper bound on pattern movements between successive input characters, and Knuth showed that this was best possible by observing that Fibonacci strings have the curious properties proved in § 5. Zvi Galil has observed that a real-time algorithm can be obtained by letting the text pointer move ahead in an appropriate manner while the j pointer is moving down [9].

In his lectures at Berkeley, S. A. Cook had proved that P^* was recognizable in $O(n \log n)$ steps on a random-access machine, and Pratt improved this to $O(n)$ using a preliminary form of the ideas in § 6. The slightly more refined theory in the present version of § 6 is joint work of Knuth and Pratt. Manacher [20] found another way to recognize palindromes in linear time, and Galil [9] showed how to improve this to real time. See also Slisenko [23].

It seemed at first that there might be a way to find the *longest common substring* of two given strings, in time $O(m+n)$; but the algorithm of this paper does not readily support any such extension, and Knuth conjectured in 1970 that such efficiency would be impossible to achieve. An algorithm due to Karp, Miller, and Rosenberg [13] solved the problem in $O((m+n)\log(m+n))$ steps, and this tended to support the conjecture (at least in the mind of its originator). However, Peter Weiner has recently developed a technique for solving the longest common substring problem in $O(m+n)$ units of time with a fixed alphabet, using tree structures in a remarkable new way [26]. Furthermore, Weiner's algorithm has the following interesting consequence, pointed out by E. McCreight: a text file can be processed (in linear time) so that it is possible to determine exactly how much of a pattern is necessary to identify a position in the text uniquely; as the pattern is being typed in, the system can be interrupt as soon as it "knows" what the rest of the pattern must be! Unfortunately the time and space requirements for Weiner's algorithm grow with increasing alphabet size.

If we consider the problem of scanning finite-state languages in general, it is known [1 § 9.2] that the language defined by any regular expression of length m is recognizable in $O(mn)$ units of time. When the regular expression has the form

$$\Sigma^*(\alpha_{1,1}+\cdots+\alpha_{1,s(1)})\Sigma^*(\alpha_{2,1}+\cdots+\alpha_{2,s(2)})\Sigma^* \ldots \Sigma^*(\alpha_{r,1}+\cdots+\alpha_{r,s(r)})\Sigma^*$$

the algorithm we have discussed shows that only $O(m+n)$ units of time are needed (considering Σ^* as a character of length 1 in the expression). Recent work by M. J. Fischer and M. S. Paterson [8] shows that regular expressions of the form

$$\Sigma^*\alpha_1\Sigma\alpha_2\Sigma \ldots \Sigma\alpha_r\Sigma^*,$$

i.e., patterns with "don't care" symbols, can be identified in $O(n \log m \log \log m \log q)$ units of time, where q is the alphabet size and $m = |\alpha_1\alpha_2 \ldots \alpha_r|+r$. The constant of proportionality in their algorithm is extremely large, but the existence of their construction indicates that efficient new algorithms for general pattern matching problems probably remain to be discovered.

A completely different approach to pattern matching, based on hashing, has been proposed by Malcolm C. Harrison [12]. In certain applications, especially with very large text files and short patterns, Harrison's method may be significantly faster than the character-comparing method of the present paper, on the average, although the redundancy of English makes the performance of his method unclear.

8. Postscript: Faster pattern matching in strings.[2] In the spring of 1974, Robert S. Boyer and J. Strother Moore and (independently) R. W. Gosper noticed that there is an even faster way to match pattern strings, by skipping more rapidly over portions of the text that cannot possibly lead to a match. Their idea was to look first at $text[m]$, instead of $text[1]$. If we find that the character $text[m]$ does not appear in the pattern at all, we can immediately shift the pattern right m places. Thus, when the alphabet size q is large, we need to inspect only about n/m characters of the text, on the average! Furthermore if $text[m]$ does occur in the pattern, we can shift the pattern by the minimum amount consistent with a match.

---

[2] This postscript was added by D. E. Knuth in March, 1976, because of developments which occurred after preprints of this paper were distributed.

Several interesting variations on this strategy are possible. For example, if $text[m]$ does occur in the pattern, we might continue the search by looking at $text[m-1]$, $text[m-2]$, etc.; in a random file we will usually find a small value of r such that the substring $text[m-r] \ldots text[m]$ does not appear in the pattern, so we can shift the pattern $m-r$ places. If $r = \lfloor 2 \log_q m \rfloor$, there are more than m^2 possible values of $text[m-r] \ldots text[m]$, but only $m-r$ substrings of length $r+1$ in the pattern, hence the probability is $O(1/m)$ that $text[m-r] \ldots text[m]$ occurs in the pattern; If it doesn't, we can shift the pattern right $m-r$ places; but if it does, we can determine all matches in positions $<m-r$ in $O(m)$ steps, shifting the pattern $m-r$ places by the method of this paper. Hence the expected number of characters examined among the first $m - \lfloor 2 \log_q m \rfloor$ is $O(\log_q m)$; this proves the existence of a linear worst-case algorithm which inspects $O(n(\log_q m)/m)$ characters in a random text. This upper bound on the average running time applies to all patterns, and there are some patterns (e.g., a^m or $(a b)^{m/2}$) for which the expected number of characters examined by the algorithm is $O(n/m)$.

Boyer and Moore have refined the skipping-by-m idea in another way. Their original algorithm may be expressed as follows using our conventions:

```
k := m;
while k ≤ n do
    begin
        j := m;
        while j > 0 and text[k] = pattern[j] do
            begin
                j := j − 1; k := k − 1;
            end;
        if j = 0 then
            begin
                match found at (k);
                k := k + m + 1
            end else
                k := k + max (d[text[k]], dd[j]);
    end;
```

This program calls *match found at* (k) for all $0 \leq k \leq n - m$ such that $pattern[1] \ldots pattern[m] = text[k+1] \ldots text[k+m]$. There are two precomputed tables, namely

$$d[a] = \min \{s \,|\, s = m \text{ or } (0 \leq s < m \text{ and } pattern[m-s] = a)\}$$

for each of the q possible characters a, and

$$dd[j] = \min \{s + m - j \,|\, s \geq 1 \text{ and } ((s \geq 1 \text{ or } pattern[i-s] = pattern[i]) \text{ for } j < i \leq m)\},$$

for $1 \leq j \leq m$.

The d table can clearly be set up in $O(q+m)$ steps, and the dd table can be precomputed in $O(m)$ steps using a technique analogous to the method in § 2 above, as we shall see. The Boyer–Moore paper [4] contains further exposition of the algorithm, including suggestions for highly efficient implementation, and gives both theoretical and empirical analyses. In the remainder of this section we shall show how the above methods can be used to resolve some of the problems left open in [4].

First let us improve the original Boyer–Moore algorithm slightly by replacing $dd[j]$ by

$$dd'[j] = \min \{s + m - j \mid s \geqq 1 \text{ and } (s \geqq j \text{ or } pattern[j-s] \neq pattern[j])$$
$$\text{and } ((s \geqq i \text{ or } pattern[i-s] = pattern[i]) \text{ for } j < i \leqq m)\}.$$

(This is analogous to using $next[j]$ instead of $f[j]$; Boyer and Moore [4] credit the improvement in this case to Ben Kuipers, but they do not discuss how to determine dd' efficiently.) The following program shows how the dd' table can be precomputed in $O(m)$ steps; for purposes of comparison, the program also shows how to compute dd, which actually turns out to require slightly *more* operations than dd':

```
for k := 1 step 1 until m do dd[k] := dd'[k] := 2 × m − k;
j := m; t := m + 1;
while j > 0 do
    begin
        f[j] := t;
        while t ≦ m and pattern[j] ≠ pattern[t] do
            begin
                dd'[t] := min (dd'[t], m − j);
                t := f[t];
            end;
        t := t − 1; j := j − 1;
        dd[t] := min (dd[t], m − j);
    end;
for k := 1 step 1 until t do
    begin
        dd[k] := min (dd[k], m + t − k);
        dd'[k] := min (dd'[k], m + t − k);
    end;
```

In practice one would, of course, compute only dd', suppressing all references to dd. The example in Table 2 illustrates most of the subtleties of this algorithm.

TABLE 2

$j =$	1	2	3	4	5	6	7	8	9	10	11
$pattern[j] =$	b	a	d	b	a	c	b	a	c	b	a
$f[j] =$	10	11	6	7	8	9	10	11	11	11	12
$dd[j] =$	19	18	17	16	15	8	7	6	5	4	1
$dd'[j] =$	19	18	17	16	15	8	13	12	8	12	1

To prove correctness, one may show first that $f[j]$ is analogous to the $f[j]$ in § 2, but with right and left of the pattern reversed; namely $f[m] = m + 1$, and for $j < m$ we have

$$f[j] = \min \{i \mid j < i \leq m \text{ and}$$
$$pattern[i+1] \ldots pattern[m] = pattern[j+1] \ldots pattern[m+j-i]\}.$$

Furthermore the final value of t corresponds to $f[0]$ in this definition; $m - t$ is the maximum overlap of the pattern on itself. The correctness of $dd[j]$ and $dd'[j]$ for all j now follows without much difficulty, by showing that the minimum value of s in the definition of $dd[j_0]$ or $dd'[j_0]$ is discovered by the algorithm when $(t, j) = (j_0, j_0 - s)$.

The Boyer–Moore algorithm and its variants can have curiously anomalous behavior in unusual circumstances. For example, the method discovers more quickly that the pattern $a\,a\,a\,a\,a\,a\,a\,c\,b$ does not appear in the text $(a\,b)^n$ if it suppresses the d heuristic entirely, i.e., if $d[t]$ is set to $-\infty$ for all t. Likewise, dd actually turns out to be better than dd' when matching $a^{15}\,b\,c\,b\,a\,b\,a\,b$ in $(b\,a\,a\,b\,a\,b)^n$, for large n.

Boyer and Moore showed that their algorithm has quadratic behavior in the worst case; the running time can be essentially proportional to pattern length times text length, for example when the pattern $c\,a\,(b\,a)^m$ occurs together with the text $(x^{2m}\,a\,a\,(b\,a)^m)^n$. They observed that this particular example was handled in linear time when Kuiper's improvement (dd' for dd) was made; but they left open the question of the true worst case behavior of the improved algorithm.

There are trivial cases in which the Boyer–Moore algorithm has quadratic behavior, when matching all occurrences of the pattern, for example when matching the pattern a^m in the text a^n. But we are probably willing to accept such behavior when there are so many matches; the crucial issue is how long the algorithm takes in the worst case to scan over a text that does *not* contain the pattern at all. By extending the techniques of § 5, it is possible to show that the modified Boyer–Moore algorithm is *linear* in such a situation:

THEOREM. *If the above algorithm is used with dd' replacing dd, and if the text does not contain any occurrences of the pattern, the total number of characters matched is at most $6n$.*

Proof. An execution of the algorithm consists of a series of *stages*, in which m_k characters are matched and then the pattern is shifted s_k places, for $k = 1, 2, \ldots$. We want to show that $\sum m_k \leq 6n$; the proof is based on breaking this cost into three parts, two of which are trivially $O(n)$ and the third of which is less obviously so.

Let $m_k' = m_k - 2s_k$ if $m_k > 2s_k$; otherwise let $m_k' = 0$. When $m_k' > 0$, we will say that the leftmost m_k' text characters matched during the kth stage have been "tapped". It suffices to prove that the algorithm taps characters at most $4n$ times, since $\sum m_k \leq \sum m_k' + 2 \sum s_k$ and $\sum s_k \leq n$. Unfortunately it is possible for some characters of the text to be tapped roughly $\log m$ times, so we need to argue carefully that $\sum m_k' \leq 4n$.

Suppose the rightmost m_k'' of the m_k' text characters tapped during the kth stage are matched again during some later stage, but the leftmost $m_k' - m_k''$ are being matched for the last time. Clearly $\sum (m'_k - m''_k) \leq n$, so it remains to show that $\sum m''_k \leq 3n$.

Let p_k be the amount by which the pattern would shift after the kth stage if the $d[a]$ heuristic were not present ($d[a] = -\infty$); then $p_k \leq s_k$, and p_k is a period of the string matched at stage k.

Consider a value of k such that $m''_k > 0$, and suppose that the text characters matched during the kth stage form the string $\alpha = \alpha_1 \alpha_2$ where $|\alpha| = m_k$ and $|\alpha_2| = m''_k + 2s_k$; hence the text characters in α_1 are matched for the last time. Since the pattern does not occur in the text, it must end with $x\alpha$ and the text scanned so far must end with $z\alpha$, where $x \neq z$. At this point the algorithm will shift the pattern right s_k positions and will enter stage $k + 1$. We distinguish two cases: (i) The pattern length m exceeds $m_k + p_k$. Then the pattern can be written $\theta \beta \alpha$, where $|\beta| = p_k$; the last character of β is x and the last character of θ is $y \neq x$, by definition of dd'. Otherwise (ii) $m \leq m_k + p_k$; the pattern then has the form $\beta \alpha$, where $|\beta| \leq p_k \leq s_k$. By definition of m''_k and the assumption that the pattern does not occur in the text, we have $|\beta \alpha| > s_k + |\alpha_2|$, i.e., $|\beta| > s_k - |\alpha_1|$. In both cases (i) and (ii), p_k is a period of $\beta \alpha$.

Now consider the first subsequent stage k' during which the *leftmost* of the m''_k text characters tapped during stage k is matched again; we shall write $k \to k'$ when the stages are in this relation. Suppose the mismatch occurs this time when text character z' fails to match pattern character x'. If z' occurs in the text within α_1, regarding α as fixed in its stage k position, then x' cannot be within $\beta \alpha$ where $\beta \alpha$ now occurs in the stage k' position of the pattern, since p_k is a period of $\beta \alpha$ and the character p_k positions to the right of x' is a z' (it matches a z' in the text). Thus x' now appears within θ. On the other hand, if z' occurs to the left of α, we must have $|\alpha_1| = 0$, since the characters of α_1 are never matched again. In either event, case (ii) above proves to be impossible. Hence case (i) always occurs when $m''_k > 0$, and x' always appears within θ.

To complete the argument, we shall show that $\sum_{k \to k'} m''_k$, for all fixed k', is at most $3s_{k'}$. Let $p' = p_{k'}$ and let α' denote the pattern matched at stage k'. Let $k_1 < \cdots < k_r$ be the values of k such that $k \to k'$. If $|\alpha'| + p' \leq m$, let $\beta' \alpha'$ be the rightmost $p' + |\alpha'|$ characters of the pattern. Otherwise let α'' be the leftmost $|\alpha'| + p' - m$ characters of α'; and let $\beta' \alpha'$ be α'' followed by the pattern. Note that in both cases α' is an initial substring of $\beta' \alpha'$ and $|\beta'| = p'$. In both cases, the actions of the algorithm during stages $k_1 + 1$ through k' are completely known if we are given the pattern and β', and if we know z' and the place within β' where stage $k_1 + 1$ starts matching. This follows from the fact that β' by itself determines the text, so that if we match the pattern against the string $z' \beta' \beta' \beta' \ldots$ (starting at the specified place for stage $k_1 + 1$) until the algorithm first tries to match z' we will know the length of α'. (If $|\alpha'| < p'$ then β' begins with α' and this statement holds trivially; otherwise, α' begins with β' and has period p'; hence $\beta' \beta' \beta' \ldots$ begins with α'.) Note that the algorithm cannot begin two different stages at exactly the same position within β', for then it would loop indefinitely, contradicting the fact that it does terminate. This property will be out key tool for proving the desired result.

Let the text strings matched during stages $k_1, \ldots, k_r$ be $\alpha_1, \ldots, \alpha_r$, and let their periods determined as in case (i) be $p_1, \ldots, p_r$, respectively; we have $p_j < \frac{1}{2}|\alpha_j|$

for $1 \leqq j \leqq r$. Suppose that during stage k_j the mismatch of $x_j \neq z_j$ implies that the pattern ends with $y_j \beta_j \alpha_j$, where $|\beta_j| = p_j$. We shall prove that $|\alpha_1| + \cdots + |\alpha_r| \leqq 3p'$. First let us prove that $|\alpha_j| < p'$ for all j: We have observed that x' always occurs within θ_j; hence $y_j \beta_j \alpha_j$ occurs as a rightmost substring of $x'\alpha'$. If $|\alpha_j| \geqq p'$ then $p_j + p' \leqq |\beta_j \alpha_j|$; hence the character p_j positions to the right of y_j in $x'\alpha'$ is x_j, as is the character $p_j + p'$ positions to the right of y_j. But the character p' positions to the right of y_j in $x'\alpha'$ is a y_j, since p' is a period of $x'\alpha'$; hence the character $p' + p_j$ positions to the right of y_j is also y_j, contradicting $x_j \neq y_j$.

Since $|\alpha_j| < p'$, each string α_j for $j \geqq 2$ appears somewhere within β', when β' is regarded as a cyclic string, joined end-for-end. (It follows from the definition of $k \to k'$ that $z_j \alpha_j$ is a substring of α' for $j \geqq 2$.) We shall prove that the rightmost halves of these strings, namely the rightmost $\lceil \frac{1}{2}|\alpha_j|\rceil$ characters as they appear in β', are disjoint. This implies that $\frac{1}{2}|\alpha_2| + \cdots + \frac{1}{2}|\alpha_r| \leqq p'$, and the proof will be complete (since $|\alpha_1| \leqq p'$).

Suppose therefore that the right half of the appearance of α_i overlaps the right half of the appearance of α_j within β', for some $i \neq j \geqq 2$, where the rightmost character of α_i is within α_j. This means that the algorithm at stage k_i begins to match characters starting within α_j at least p_j characters to the right of z_j where $z_j \alpha_j$ appears in β', when the text α' is treated modulo p'. (Recall that $p_j < \frac{1}{2}|\alpha_j|$.) The pattern ends with $x_j \alpha_j$, and p_j is a period of $x_j \alpha_j$. The algorithm must work correctly when the text equals the pattern, so there must come a stage, before shifting the pattern to the right of the appearance of α_j, where the algorithm scans left until hitting z_j. At this point, call it stage k'', there must be a mismatch of $z_j \neq x_j$, since p_j or more characters have been matched. (The character p_j positions to the right of z_j is x_j, by periodicity.) Hence $k'' < k'$; and it follows that $k'' = k_i$. (If $k'' > k_i$ we have $z_i \alpha_i$ entirely contained within α'', but then $k_i \to k'$ implies that $k'' = k'$.) Now $k'' = k_i$ implies that $z_j = z_i$ and $x_j = x_i$. We shall obtain a contradiction by showing that the algorithm "synchronizes" its stage $k_i + 1$ behavior with its stage $k_j + 1$ behavior, modulo p', causing an infinite loop as remarked above. The main point is that the dd' table will specify shifting the pattern p_j steps, so that y_j is brought into the position corresponding to z_j, in stage k_i as well as in stage k_j. (Any lesser shift brings an x_j into position p_j spaces to the right of z_j; hence it puts $y_i = x_j$ into the position corresponding to z_j, by periodicity, contradicting $x_i \neq y_i$.) The amount of shift depends on the maximum of the d and dd' entries, and the d entry will be chosen (in either k_i or k_j) if and only if z_j is not a character of β_j; but in this case, the d entry will also specify the same shift both for stage k_i and stage k_j. $\quad\square$

The constant 6 in the above theorem is probably much too large, and the above proof seems to be much too long; the reader is invited to improve the theorem in either or both respects. An interesting example of the rather complex behavior possible with this algorithm occurs when the pattern is $b\psi_r$ and the text is $\psi_r a \psi_r$, for large r, where

$$\psi_0 = a, \qquad \psi_{n+1} = \psi_n \psi_n b \psi_n.$$

COROLLARY. *The worst case running time of the Boyer–Moore algorithm with dd' replacing dd is $O(n + rm)$ character comparisons, if the pattern occurs r times in the text.*

Proof. Let $T(n, r)$ be the worst case running time as a function of n and r, when m is fixed. The theorem implies that $T(n, 0) \leqq 7n$, counting the mismatched characters as well as the matched ones. Furthermore, if $r > 0$ and if the first appearance of the pattern ends at position n_0 we have $T(n, r) \leqq 7(n_0 - 1) + m + T(n - n_0 + m - 1, r - 1)$. It follows that $T(n, r) \leqq 7n + 8rm - 14r$. $\square$

When the Boyer–Moore algorithm implicitly shifts the pattern to the right, it forgets all it "knows" about characters already matched; this is why the linearity theorem is not trivial. A more complex algorithm can be envisaged, with a finite number of states corresponding to which text characters are known to match the pattern in its current position; when in state q we fetch the character $x := text[k - t[q]]$, then we set $k := k + s[q, x]$ and go to state $q'[q, x]$. For example, consider the pattern $a\, b\, a\, c\, b\, a\, b\, a$, and the specification of t, s, and q' in Table 3; exactly 41 distinguishable states can arise. An asterisk (*) in that table shows where the pattern has been fully matched.

The number of states in this generalization of the Boyer–Moore algorithm can be rather large, as the example shows, but the patterns which occur most often in practice probably do not imply many states. The number of states is always less than 2^m, and perhaps a much smaller upper bound is possible; it is unclear which patterns of a given length lead to the most states, and it does not seem obvious that this maximum number of states is exponential in m.

If the characters of the pattern are distinct, say $a_1 a_2 \ldots a_m$, this generalization of the Boyer–Moore algorithm leads to exactly $\frac{1}{2}(m^2 + m)$ states. (Namely, all states of the form $\bullet \ldots \bullet\, a_k \bullet \ldots \bullet\, a_{j+1} \ldots a_m$ for $0 \leqq k < j \leqq m$, with a_k suppressed if $k = 0$.) By merging several of these states we obtain the following simple algorithm, which uses a table $c[x]$ where

$$c[x] = \begin{cases} m - j, & \text{if } x = a_j; \\ -1, & \text{if } x \notin \{a_1, \ldots, a_m\}. \end{cases}$$

The algorithm works only when all pattern characters are distinct, but it improves slightly on the Boyer–Moore technique in this important special case.

```
        j := k := m;
    while k ≦ n do
        begin i := c[text[k]];
            if i < 0 then j := m
            else if i = 0 then
            begin for i := 1 step 1 until m − 1 do
                if text[k − i] ≠ pattern[m − i] then go to nomatch;
                match found at (k − m);
            nomatch: j := m;
            end else if i + j ≧ m then j := i else j := m;
            k := k + j;

        end;
```

Let us close this section by making a preliminary investigation into the question of "fastest" pattern matching in strings, i.e., *optimum* algorithms. What algorithm minimizes the number of text characters examined, over all conceivable algorithms for the problem we have been considering? In order to make this question nontrivial, we shall ask for the minimum *average* number of characters examined when finding *all* occurrences of the pattern in the text, where the average is taken uniformly with respect to strings of length n over a given alphabet. (The minimum worst case number of characters examined is of no interest, since it is between $n - m$ and n for all patterns[3]; therefore we ask for the minimum average number. It might be argued that the minimum average number, taken over random strings, is of little interest, since people rarely search in random strings; they usually search for patterns that actually appear. However, the random-string model is a reasonable approximation when we consider those stretches of text that do not contain the pattern, and the algorithm obviously must examine every character in those places where the pattern does occur.)

The case of patterns of length 2 can be solved exactly; it is somewhat surprising to find that the analysis is not completely trivial even in this case. Consider first the pattern $a\,b$ where $a \neq b$. Let q be the alphabet size, $q \geq 2$. Let $f(n)$ denote the minimum average number of characters examined by an algorithm which finds all occurrences of the pattern in a random text of length n; and let $g(n)$ denote the minimum average number of characters examined in a random text of length $n+1$ which is known to begin with a, not counting the examination of the known first character. These functions can be computed by the following recurrence relations:

$$f(0) = f(1) = g(0) = 0, \qquad g(1) = 1.$$

$$f(n) = 1 + \min_{1 \leq k \leq n} \left(\frac{1}{q}(f(k-1) + g(n-k)) + \frac{1}{q}(g(k-1) + f(n-k)) \right.$$
$$\left. + \left(1 - \frac{2}{q}\right)(f(k-1) + f(n-k)) \right),$$

$$g(n) = 1 + \frac{1}{q}g(n-1) + \left(1 - \frac{1}{q}\right)f(n-1), \qquad n \geq 2.$$

The recurrence for f follows by considering which character is examined first; the recurrence for g follows from the fact that the second character must be examined in any case, so it can be examined first without loss of efficiency. It can be shown that the minimum is always assumed for $k = 2$; hence we obtain the closed form solution

$$f(n) = \frac{n(q^2 + q - 1)}{q(2q-1)} - \frac{(q-1)(q^2 + 2q - 1)}{q(2q-1)^2} + \frac{(1-q)^n}{q^{n-3}(q-1)(2q-1)^2},$$

$$g(n) = \frac{n(q^2 + q - 1)}{q(2q-1)} + \frac{(q-1)(q^2 - 3q + 1)}{q(2q-1)^2} - \frac{(1-q)^n}{q^{n-2}(2q-1)^2}, \qquad n \geq 1.$$

(To prove that these functions satisfy the stated recurrences reduces to showing that the minimum of

$$\left(\frac{1-q}{q}\right)^{k-1} + \left(\frac{1-q}{q}\right)^{n-k}$$

for $1 \leq k \leq n$ occurs for $k = 2$, whenever $n \geq 2$ and $q \geq 2$.)

---

[3] This is clear when we must find *all* occurrences of the pattern; R. L. Rivest has recently proved it also for algorithms which stop after finding *one* occurrence. (*Information Processing Letters*, to appear.)

TABLE 3

state q	known characters	t[q]	s[q, x], q'[q, x]			
			x = a	x = b	x = c	other x
0	• • • • • • • • •	0	0, 1	1, 8	4, 9	8, 0
1	• • • • • • • • a	1	7, 10	0, 2	7, 10	7, 10
2	• • • • • • • b a	2	0, 3	7, 10	2, 11	7, 10
3	• • • • • • a b a	3	5, 12	0, 4	5, 12	5, 12
4	• • • • • b a b a	4	5, 12	5, 12	0, 5	5, 12
5	• • • • c b a b a	5	0, 6	5, 12	5, 12	5, 12
6	• • • a c b a b a	6	5, 12	0, 7	5, 12	5, 12
7	• • b a c b a b a	7	*5, 12	5, 12	5, 12	5, 12
8	• • • • • • • b •	0	0, 2	8, 0	8, 0	8, 0
9	• • • c • • • •	0	0, 13	6, 14	4, 9	8, 0
10	a • • • • • • • •	0	0, 15	1, 8	4, 9	8, 0
11	• • • c b a • •	0	0, 16	6, 14	8, 0	8, 0
12	a b a • • • • • •	0	0, 17	3, 18	4, 9	8, 0
13	• • • c • • • a	1	7, 10	0, 19	7, 10	7, 10
14	• b • • • • • •	0	0, 20	3, 18	4, 9	8, 0
15	a • • • • • • a	1	7, 10	0, 21	7, 10	7, 10
16	• • • c b a • a	1	7, 10	0, 5	7, 10	7, 10
17	a b a • • • • a	1	7, 10	0, 22	7, 10	7, 10
18	• • • • • b • • •	0	0, 23	3, 24	8, 0	8, 0
19	• • • c • • b a	2	0, 25	7, 10	7, 10	7, 10
20	• b • • • • • a	1	7, 10	0, 26	7, 10	7, 10
21	a • • • • • b a	2	0, 27	7, 10	2, 11	7, 10
22	a b a • • • b a	2	0, 28	7, 10	2, 29	7, 10
23	• • • • b • • a	1	7, 10	0, 30	7, 10	7, 10
24	• b • • b • • •	0	0, 31	3, 24	8, 0	8, 0
25	• • • c • a b a	3	5, 12	0, 5	5, 12	5, 12
26	• b • • • • b a	2	0, 32	7, 10	2, 11	7, 10
27	a • • • • a b a	3	5, 12	0, 33	5, 12	5, 12
28	a b a • • a b a	3	5, 12	0, 34	5, 12	5, 12
29	a • • c b a • •	0	0, 35	6, 14	8, 0	8, 0
30	• • • • • b • b a	2	0, 4	7, 10	7, 10	7, 10
31	• b • • b • • a	1	7, 10	0, 36	7, 10	7, 10
32	• b • • • a b a	3	5, 12	0, 37	5, 12	5, 12
33	a • • • b a b a	4	5, 12	5, 12	0, 38	5, 12
34	a b a • b a b a	4	5, 12	5, 12	*5, 12	5, 12
35	a • • c b a • a	1	7, 10	0, 38	7, 10	7, 10
36	• b • • b • b a	2	0, 37	7, 10	7, 10	7, 10
37	• b • • b a b a	4	5, 12	5, 12	0, 39	5, 12
38	a • • c b a b a	5	0, 40	5, 12	5, 12	5, 12
39	• b • c b a b a	5	0, 7	5, 12	5, 12	5, 12
40	a • a c b a b a	6	5, 12	*5, 12	5, 12	5, 12

If the pattern is $a\,a$, the recurrence for f changes to

$$f(n) = 1 + \min_{1 \le k \le n} \left(\frac{1}{q}(g(k-1) + g(n-k)) + \left(1 - \frac{1}{q}\right)(f(k-1) + f(n-k)) \right), \qquad n \ge 2;$$

but this is actually no change!

Hence the following is an optimum algorithm for all patterns of length 2, in the sense of minimum average text characters inspected to find all matches in a random string:

```
    k := 2;
        while k ≦ n do
            begin c := text[k];
                    if c = pattern[2] and text[k − 1] = pattern[1]
                    then match found at (k − 2);
                    while c = pattern[1] do
                        begin k := k + 1; c := text[k];
                                if c = pattern[2] then match found at (k − 2);
                        end;
                    k := k + 2;
        end;
```

For patterns of length 3 the recurrence relations become more complex; they depend on more than simply the length of the strings and knowledge about characters at the boundaries. The determination of an optimum strategy in this case remains an open problem. The algorithm sketched at the beginning of this section shows that an average of $O(n(\log m)/m)$ bit inspections suffices over a binary alphabet. Clearly $\lfloor n/m \rfloor$ is a lower bound, since the algorithm must inspect at least one bit in any block of n consecutive bits. The pattern a^m can be handled with $O(n/m)$ bit inspections on the average; but it seems reasonable to conjecture that patterns of length m exist for arbitrarily large m, such that an average of at least $cn(\log m)/m$ bits must be inspected for all large n. Here c denotes a positive constant, independent of m and n.

Acknowledgment. Robert S. Boyer and J. Strother Moore suggested many important improvements to early drafts of this postscript, especially in connection with errors in the author's first attempts at proving the linearity theorem.

REFERENCES

[1] ALFRED V. AHO, JOHN E. HOPCROFT AND JEFFREY D. ULLMAN, *The Design and Analysis of Computer Algorithms*, Addison-Wesley, Reading, Mass., 1974.

[2] ALFRED V. AHO AND MARGARET J. CORASICK, *Efficient string matching: An aid to bibliographic search*, Comm. ACM, 18 (1975), pp. 333–340.

[3] M. BEELER, R. W. GOSPER AND R. SCHROEPPEL, *HAKMEM*, Memo No. 239, M.I.T. Artificial Intelligence Laboratory, Cambridge, Mass., 1972.

[4] ROBERT S. BOYER AND J. STROTHER MOORE, *A fast string searching algorithm*, manuscript dated December 29, 1975; Stanford Research Institute, Menlo Park, Calif., and Xerox Palo Alto Research Center, Palo Alto, Calif.

[5] S. A. COOK, *Linear time simulation of deterministic two-way pushdown automata*, Information Processing 71, North-Holland, Amsterdam, 1972, pp. 75–80.

[6] PASCAL DIETHELM AND PETER ROIZEN, *An efficient linear search for a pattern in a string*, unpublished manuscript dated April, 1972; World Health Organization, Geneva, Switzerland.

[7] N. J. FINE AND H. S. WILF, *Uniqueness theorems for periodic functions*, Proc. Amer. Math. Soc., 16 (1965), pp. 109–114.

[8] MICHAEL J. FISCHER AND MICHAEL S. PATERSON, *String matching and other products*, SIAM-AMS Proc., vol. 7, American Mathematical Society, Providence, R.I., 1974, pp. 113–125.

[9] ZVI GALIL, *On converting on-line algorithms into real-time and on real-time algorithms for string-matching and palindrome recognition*, SIGACT News, 7 (1975), No. 4, pp. 26–30.

[10] E. N. GILBERT, *Synchronization of binary messages*, IRE Trans. Information Theory, IT-6 (1960), pp. 470–477.

[11] SHEILA A. GREIBACH, *The hardest context-free language*, this Journal, 2 (1973), pp. 304–310.

[12] MALCOLM C. HARRISON, *Implementation of the substring test by hashing*, Comm. ACM, 14 (1971), pp. 777–779.

[13] RICHARD M. KARP, RAYMOND E. MILLER AND ARNOLD L. ROSENBERG, *Rapid identification of repeated patterns in strings, trees, and arrays*, ACM Symposium on Theory of Computing, vol. 4, Association for Computing Machinery, New York, 1972, pp. 125–136.

[14] DONALD E. KNUTH, *Fundamental Algorithms, The Art of Computer Programming*, Vol. 1, Addison-Wesley, Reading, Mass., 1968; 2nd edition 1973.

[15] ———, *Sequences with precisely $k+1$ k-blocks*, Solution to problem E2307, Amer. Math. Monthly, 79 (1972), pp. 773–774.

[16] ———, *On the translation of languages from left to right*, Information and Control, 8 (1965), pp. 607–639.

[17] ———, *Structured programming with* **go to** *statements*, Computing Surveys, 6 (1974), pp. 261–301.

[18] DONALD E. KNUTH, JAMES H. MORRIS, JR. AND VAUGHAN R. PRATT, *Fast pattern matching in strings*, Tech. Rep. CS440, Computer Science Department, Stanford Univ., Stanford, Calif., 1974.

[19] R. C. LYNDON AND M. P. SCHÜTZENBERGER, *The equation $a^M = b^N c^P$ in a free group*, Michigan Math. J., 9 (1962), pp. 289–298.

[20] GLENN MANACHER, *A new linear-time on-line algorithm for finding the smallest initial palindrome of a string*, J. Assoc. Comput. Mach., 22 (1975), pp. 346–351.

[21] A. MARKOFF, *Sur une question de Jean Bernoulli*, Math. Ann., 19 (1882), pp. 27–36.

[22] J. H. MORRIS, JR. AND VAUGHAN R. PRATT, *A linear pattern-matching algorithm*, Tech. Rep. 40, Univ. of California, Berkeley, 1970.

[23] A. O. SLISENKO, *Recognition of palindromes by multihead Turing machines*, Dokl. Steklov Math. Inst., Akad. Nauk SSSR, 129 (1973), pp. 30–202. (In Russian.)

[24] KEN THOMPSON, *Regular expression search algorithm*, Comm. ACM, 11 (1968), pp. 419–422.

[25] B. A. VENKOV, *Elementary Number Theory*, Wolters-Noordhoff, Groningen, the Netherlands, 1970.

[26] PETER WEINER, *Linear pattern matching algorithms*, IEEE Symposium on Switching and Automata Theory, vol. 14, IEEE, New York, 1973, pp. 1–11.

Programming Techniques

G. Manacher, S.L. Graham
Editors

A Fast String Searching Algorithm

Robert S. Boyer
Stanford Research Institute

J Strother Moore
Xerox Palo Alto Research Center

An algorithm is presented that searches for the location, "*i*," of the first occurrence of a character string, "*pat*," in another string, "*string*." During the search operation, the characters of *pat* are matched starting with the last character of *pat*. The information gained by starting the match at the end of the pattern often allows the algorithm to proceed in large jumps through the text being searched. Thus the algorithm has the unusual property that, in most cases, not all of the first *i* characters of *string* are inspected. The number of characters actually inspected (on the average) decreases as a function of the length of *pat*. For a random English pattern of length 5, the algorithm will typically inspect *i*/4 characters of *string* before finding a match at *i*. Furthermore, the algorithm has been implemented so that (on the average) fewer than *i* + *patlen* machine instructions are executed. These conclusions are supported with empirical evidence and a theoretical analysis of the average behavior of the algorithm. The worst case behavior of the algorithm is linear in *i* + *patlen*, assuming the availability of array space for tables linear in *patlen* plus the size of the alphabet.

Key Words and Phrases: bibliographic search, computational complexity, information retrieval, linear time bound, pattern matching, text editing
CR Categories: 3.74, 4.40, 5.25

Reprinted from *Communications of the ACM*, Volume 20, No. 10, October 1977, pp. 62-72. Copyright 1977, Association for Computing Machinery, Inc., reprinted by permission.

Authors' present addresses: R.S. Boyer, Computer Science Laboratory, Stanford Research Institute, Menlo Park, CA 94025. This work was partially supported by ONR Contract N00014-75-C-0816; JS. Moore was in the Computer Science Laboratory, Xerox Palo Alto Research Center, Palo Alto, CA 94304, when this work was done. His current address is Computer Science Laboratory, SRI International, Menlo Park, CA 94025.

1. Introduction

Suppose that *pat* is a string of length *patlen* and we wish to find the position *i* of the leftmost character in the first occurrence of *pat* in some string *string*:

```
pat:      AT-THAT
string:  ... WHICH-FINALLY-HALTS.--AT-THAT-POINT ...
i:                                  ↑
```

The obvious search algorithm considers each character position of *string* and determines whether the successive *patlen* characters of *string* starting at that position match the successive *patlen* characters of *pat*. Knuth, Morris, and Pratt [4] have observed that this algorithm is quadratic. That is, in the worst case, the number of comparisons is on the order of $i * patlen$.[1]

Knuth, Morris, and Pratt have described a linear search algorithm which preprocesses *pat* in time linear in *patlen* and then searches *string* in time linear in *i* + *patlen*. In particular, their algorithm inspects each of the first *i* + *patlen* − 1 characters of *string* precisely once.

We now present a search algorithm which is usually "sublinear": It may not inspect each of the first *i* + *patlen* − 1 characters of *string*. By "usually sublinear" we mean that the expected value of the number of inspected characters in *string* is $c * (i + patlen)$, where $c < 1$ and gets smaller as *patlen* increases. There are patterns and strings for which worse behavior is exhibited. However, Knuth, in [5], has shown that the algorithm is linear even in the worst case.

The actual number of characters inspected depends on statistical properties of the characters in *pat* and *string*. However, since the number of characters inspected on the average decreases as *patlen* increases, our algorithm actually speeds up on longer patterns.

Furthermore, the algorithm is sublinear in another sense: It has been implemented so that on the average it requires the execution of fewer than *i* + *patlen* machine instructions per search.

The organization of this paper is as follows: In the next two sections we give an informal description of the algorithm and show an example of how it works. We then define the algorithm precisely and discuss its efficient implementation. After this discussion we present the results of a thorough test of a particular machine code implementation of our algorithm. We compare these results to similar results for the Knuth, Morris, and Pratt algorithm and the simple search algorithm. Following this empirical evidence is a theoretical analysis which accurately predicts the performance measured. Next we describe some situations in which it may not be advantageous to use our algorithm. We conclude with a discussion of the history of our algorithm.

---

[1] The quadratic nature of this algorithm appears when initial substrings of *pat* occur often in *string*. Because this is a relatively rare phenomenon in string searches over English text, this simple algorithm is *practically* linear in *i* + *patlen* and therefore acceptable for most applications.

2. Informal Description

The basic idea behind the algorithm is that more information is gained by matching the pattern from the right than from the left. Imagine that *pat* is placed on top of the left-hand end of *string* so that the first characters of the two strings are aligned. Consider what we learn if we fetch the *patlen*th character, *char*, of *string*. This is the character which is aligned with the *last* character of *pat*.

Observation 1. If *char* is known not to occur in *pat*, then we know we need not consider the possibility of an occurrence of *pat* starting at *string* positions 1, 2, . . . or *patlen*: Such an occurrence would require that *char* be a character of *pat*.

Observation 2. More generally, if the last (rightmost) occurrence of *char* in *pat* is *delta₁* characters from the right end of *pat*, then we know we can slide *pat* down *delta₁* positions without checking for matches. The reason is that if we were to move *pat* by less than *delta₁*, the occurrence of *char* in *string* would be aligned with some character it could not possibly match: Such a match would require an occurrence of *char* in *pat* to the right of the rightmost.

Therefore unless *char* matches the last character of *pat* we can move past *delta₁* characters of *string* without looking at the characters skipped; *delta₁* is a function of the character *char* obtained from *string*. If *char* does not occur in *pat*, *delta₁* is *patlen*. If *char* does occur in *pat*, *delta₁* is the difference between *patlen* and the position of the rightmost occurrence of *char* in *pat*.

Now suppose that *char* matches the last character of *pat*. Then we must determine whether the previous character in *string* matches the second from the last character in *pat*. If so, we continue backing up until we have matched all of *pat* (and thus have succeeded in finding a match), or else we come to a mismatch at some new *char* after matching the last *m* characters of *pat*.

In this latter case, we wish to shift *pat* down to consider the next plausible juxtaposition. Of course, we would like to shift it as far down as possible.

Observation 3(a). We can use the same reasoning described above—based on the mismatched character *char* and *delta₁*—to slide *pat* down *k* so as to align the two known occurrences of *char*. Then we will want to inspect the character of *string* aligned with the last character of *pat*. Thus we will actually shift our attention down *string* by $k + m$. The distance *k* we should slide *pat* depends on where *char* occurs in *pat*. If the rightmost occurrence of *char* in *pat* is to the right of the mismatched character (i.e. within that part of *pat* we have already passed) we would have to move *pat* backwards to align the two known occurrences of *char*. We would not want to do this. In this case we say that *delta₁* is "worthless" and slide *pat* forward by $k = 1$ (which is always sound). This shifts our attention down *string* by $1 + m$. If the rightmost occurrence of *char* in

pat is to the left of the mismatch, we can slide forward by $k = delta_1(char) - m$ to align the two occurrences of *char*. This shifts our attention down *string* by $delta_1(char) - m + m = delta_1(char)$.

However, it is possible that we can do better than this.

Observation 3(b). We know that the next *m* characters of *string* match the final *m* characters of *pat*. Let this substring of *pat* be *subpat*. We also know that this occurrence of *subpat* in *string* is preceded by a character (*char*) which is different from the character preceding the terminal occurrence of *subpat* in *pat*. Roughly speaking, we can generalize the kind of reasoning used above and slide *pat* down by some amount so that the discovered occurrence of *subpat* in *string* is aligned with the rightmost occurrence of *subpat* in *pat* which is not preceded by the character preceding its terminal occurrence in *pat*. We call such a reoccurrence of *subpat* in *pat* a "plausible reoccurrence." The reason we said "roughly speaking" above is that we must allow for the rightmost plausible reoccurrence of *subpat* to "fall off" the left end of *pat*. This is made precise later.

Therefore, according to Observation 3(b), if we have matched the last *m* characters of *pat* before finding a mismatch, we can move *pat* down by *k* characters, where *k* is based on the position in *pat* of the rightmost plausible reoccurrence of the terminal substring of *pat* having *m* characters. After sliding down by *k*, we want to inspect the character of *string* aligned with the last character of *pat*. Thus we actually shift our attention down *string* by $k + m$ characters. We call this distance *delta₂*, and we define *delta₂* as a function of the position *j* in *pat* at which the mismatch occurred. *k* is just the distance between the terminal occurrence of *subpat* and its rightmost plausible reoccurrence and is always greater than or equal to 1. *m* is just $patlen - j$.

In the case where we have matched the final *m* characters of *pat* before failing, we clearly wish to shift our attention down *string* by $1 + m$ or $delta_1(char)$ or $delta_2(j)$, according to whichever allows the largest shift. From the definition of *delta₂* as $k + m$ where *k* is always greater than or equal to 1, it is clear that *delta₂* is at least as large as $1 + m$. Therefore we can shift our attention down *string* by the maximum of just the two *delta*s. This rule also applies when $m = 0$ (i.e. when we have not yet matched any characters of *pat*), because in that case $j = patlen$ and $delta_2(j) \geq 1$.

3. Example

In the following example we use an " ↑ " under *string* to indicate the current *char*. When this "pointer" is pushed to the right, imagine that it drags the right end of *pat* with it (i.e. imagine *pat* has a hook on its right end). When the pointer is moved to the left, keep *pat* fixed with respect to *string*.

```
pat:          AT-THAT
string:  ... WHICH-FINALLY-HALTS.--AT-THAT-POINT ...
              ↑
```

Since "F" is known not to occur in *pat*, we can appeal to Observation 1 and move the pointer (and thus *pat*) down by 7:

```
pat:                 AT-THAT
string:  ... WHICH-FINALLY-HALTS.--AT-THAT-POINT ...
                ↑
```

Appealing to Observation 2, we can move the pointer down 4 to align the two hyphens:

```
pat:                     AT-THAT
string:  ... WHICH-FINALLY-HALTS.--AT-THAT-POINT ...
                    ↑
```

Now *char* matches its opposite in *pat*. Therefore we step left by one:

```
pat:                     AT-THAT
string:  ... WHICH-FINALLY-HALTS.--AT THAT POINT ...
                   ↑
```

Appealing to Observation 3(a), we can move the pointer to the right by 7 positions because "L" does not occur in *pat*.[2] Note that this only moves *pat* to the right by 6.

```
pat:                          AT-THAT
string:  ... WHICH-FINALLY-HALTS.--AT-THAT-POINT ...
                         ↑
```

Again *char* matches the last character of *pat*. Stepping to the left we see that the previous character in *string* also matches its opposite in *pat*. Stepping to the left a second time produces:

```
pat:                          AT-THAT
string:  ... WHICH-FINALLY-HALTS.--AT-THAT-POINT ...
                        ↑
```

Noting that we have a mismatch, we appeal to Observation 3(b). The *delta*₂ move is best since it allows us to push the pointer to the right by 7 so as to align the discovered substring "AT" with the beginning of *pat*.[3]

```
pat:                          AT-THAT
string:  ... WHICH-FINALLY-HALTS.--AT-THAT-POINT ...
                              ↑
```

This time we discover that each character of *pat* matches the corresponding character in *string* so we have found the pattern. Note that we made only 14 references to *string*. Seven of these were required to confirm the final match. The other seven allowed us to move past the first 22 characters of *string*.

---

[2] Note that *delta*₂ would allow us to move the pointer to the right only 4 positions in order to align the discovered substring "T" in *string* with its second from last occurrence at the beginning of the word "THAT" in *pat*.

[3] The *delta*₁ move only allows the pointer to be pushed to the right by 4 to align the hyphens.

4. The Algorithm

We now specify the algorithm. The notation $pat(j)$ refers to the jth character in *pat* (counting from 1 on the left).

We assume the existence of two tables, $delta_1$ and $delta_2$. The first has as many entries as there are characters in the alphabet. The entry for some character *char* will be denoted by $delta_1(char)$. The second table has as many entries as there are character positions in the pattern. The jth entry will be denoted by $delta_2(j)$. Both tables contain non-negative integers.

The tables are initialized by preprocessing *pat*, and their entries correspond to the values $delta_1$ and $delta_2$ referred to earlier. We will specify their precise contents after it is clear how they are to be used.

Our search algorithm may be specified as follows:

```
        stringlen ← length of string.
        i ← patlen.
top:    if i > stringlen then return false.
        j ← patlen.
loop:   if j = 0 then return i + 1.
        if string(i) = pat(j)
           then
              j ← j − 1.
              i ← i − 1.
           goto loop.
           close;
        i ← i + max(delta₁ (string(i)), delta₂ (j)).
        goto top.
```

If the above algorithm returns false, then *pat* does not occur in *string*. If the algorithm returns a number, then it is the position of the left end of the first occurrence of *pat* in *string*.

The $delta_1$ table has an entry for each character *char* in the alphabet. The definition of $delta_1$ is:

$delta_1(char)$ = If *char* does not occur in *pat*, then *patlen*; else *patlen* $- j$, where j is the maximum integer such that $pat(j) = char$.

The $delta_2$ table has one entry for each of the integers from 1 to *patlen*. Roughly speaking, $delta_2(j)$ is (a) the distance we can slide *pat* down so as to align the discovered occurrence (in *string*) of the last *patlen*$-j$ characters of *pat* with its rightmost plausible reoccurrence, plus (b) the additional distance we must slide the "pointer" down so as to restart the process at the right end of *pat*. To define $delta_2$ precisely we must define the rightmost plausible reoccurrence of a terminal substring of *pat*. To this end let us make the following conventions: Let $ be a character that does not occur in *pat* and let us say that if i is less than 1 then $pat(i)$ is $. Let us also say that two sequences of characters $[c_1 \ldots c_n]$ and $[d_1 \ldots d_n]$ "unify" if for all i from 1 to n either $c_i = d_i$ or $c_i = $ or $d_i = $.

Finally, we define the position of the rightmost plausible reoccurrence of the terminal substring which starts at position $j + 1$, $rpr(j)$, for j from 1 to *patlen*, to be the greatest k less than or equal to *patlen* such that

$[pat(j + 1) \ldots pat(patlen)]$ and $[pat(k) \ldots pat(k + patlen - j - 1)]$ unify and either $k \leq 1$ or $pat(k - 1) \neq pat(j)$.[4] (That is, the position of the rightmost plausible reoccurrence of the substring *subpat*, which starts at $j + 1$, is the rightmost place where *subpat* occurs in *pat* and is not preceded by the character $pat(j)$ which precedes its terminal occurrence — with suitable allowances for either the reoccurrence or the preceding character to fall beyond the left end of *pat*. Note that $rpr(j)$ may be negative because of these allowances.)

Thus the distance we must slide *pat* to align the discovered substring which starts at $j + 1$ with its rightmost plausible reoccurrence is $j + 1 - rpr(j)$. The distance we must move to get back to the end of *pat* is just $patlen - j$. $delta_2(j)$ is just the sum of these two. Thus we define $delta_2$ as follows:

$$delta_2(j) = patlen + 1 - rpr(j).$$

To make this definition clear, consider the following two examples:

j:	1	2	3	4	5	6	7	8	9
pat:	A	B	C	X	X	X	A	B	C
$delta_2(j)$:	14	13	12	11	10	9	11	10	1

j:	1	2	3	4	5	6	7	8	9
pat:	A	B	Y	X	C	D	E	Y	X
$delta_2(j)$:	17	16	15	14	13	12	7	10	1

5. Implementation Considerations

The most frequently executed part of the algorithm is the code that embodies Observations 1 and 2. The following version of our algorithm is equivalent to the original version provided that $delta_0$ is a table containing the same entries as $delta_1$ except that $delta_0(pat(patlen))$ is set to an integer *large* which is greater than $stringlen + patlen$ (while $delta_1(pat(patlen))$ is always 0).

```
            stringlen ← length of string.
            i ← patlen.
            if i > stringlen then return false.
fast:       i ← i + delta₀(string(i)).
            if i ≤ stringlen then goto fast.
undo:       if i ≤ large then return false.
            i ← (i − large) − 1.
            j ← patlen − 1.
slow:       if j = 0 then return i + 1.
            if string(i) = pat(j)
              then
                j ← j − 1.
                i ← i − 1.
                goto slow.
              close;
            i ← i + max(delta₁(string(i)), delta₂(j)).
            goto fast.
```

[4] Note that when $j = patlen$, the two sequences $[pat(patlen + 1) \ldots pat(patlen)]$ and $[pat(k) \ldots pat(k - 1)]$ are empty and therefore unify. Thus, $rpr(patlen)$ is simply the greatest k less than or equal to $patlen$ such that $k \leq 1$ or $pat(k - 1) \neq pat(patlen)$.

Of course we do not actually have two versions of $delta_1$. Instead we use only $delta_0$, and in place of $delta_1$ in the *max* expression we merely use the $delta_0$ entry unless it is *large* (in which case we use 0).

Note that the *fast* loop just scans down *string*, effectively looking for the last character $pat(patlen)$ in *pat*, skipping according to $delta_1$. ($delta_2$ can be ignored in this case since no terminal substring has yet been matched, i.e. $delta_2(patlen)$ is always less than or equal to the corresponding $delta_1$.) Control leaves this loop only when i exceeds *stringlen*. The test at *undo* decides whether this situation arose because all of *string* has been scanned or because $pat(patlen)$ was hit (which caused i to be incremented by *large*). If the first case obtains, *pat* does not occur in *string* and the algorithm returns false. If the second case obtains, then i is restored (by subtracting *large*) and we enter the *slow* loop which backs up checking for matches. When a mismatch is found we skip ahead by the maximum of the original $delta_1$ and $delta_2$ and reenter the *fast* loop. We estimate that 80 percent of the time spent in searching is spent in the *fast* loop.

The *fast* loop can be coded in four machine instructions:

```
fast:   char ← string(i).
        i ← i + delta₀(char).
        skip the next instruction if i > stringlen.
        goto fast.
undo: . . . .
```

We have implemented this algorithm in PDP-10 assembly language. In our implementation we have reduced the number of instructions in the *fast* loop to three by translating i down by *stringlen*; we can then test i against 0 and conditionally jump to *fast* in one instruction.

On a byte addressable machine it is easy to implement "$char \leftarrow string(i)$" and "$i \leftarrow i + delta_0(char)$" in one instruction each. Since our implementation was in PDP-10 assembly language we had to employ byte pointers to access characters in *string*. The PDP-10 instruction set provides an instruction for incrementing a byte pointer by one but not by other amounts. Our code therefore employs an array of 200 indexing byte pointers which we use to access characters in *string* in one indexed instruction (after computing the index) at the cost of a small (five-instruction) overhead every 200 characters. It should be noted that this trick only makes up for the lack of direct byte addressing; one can expect our algorithm to run somewhat faster on a byte-addressable machine.

6. Empirical Evidence

We have exhaustively tested the above PDP-10 implementation on random test data. To gather the test patterns we wrote a program which randomly selects a substring of a given length from a source string. We used this program to select 300 patterns of length *patlen*, for each *patlen* from 1 to 14. We then used our algorithm to search for each of the test patterns in its source string, starting each search in a random position somewhere in the first half of the source string. All of the characters for both the patterns and the strings were in primary memory (rather than a secondary storage medium such as a disk).

We measured the cost of each search in two ways: the number of references made to *string* and the total number of machine instructions that actually got executed (ignoring the preprocessing to set up the two tables).

By dividing the number of references to *string* by the number of characters $i - 1$ passed before the pattern was found (or *string* was exhausted), we obtained the number of references to *string* per character passed. This measure is independent of the particular implementation of the algorithm. By dividing the number of instructions executed by $i - 1$, we obtained the average number of instructions spent on each character passed. This measure depends upon the implementation, but we feel that it is meaningful since the implementation is a straightforward encoding of the algorithm as described in the last section.

We then averaged these measures across all 300 samples for each pattern length.

Because the performance of the algorithm depends upon the statistical properties of *pat* and *string* (and hence upon the properties of the source string from which the test patterns were obtained), we performed this experiment for three different kinds of source strings, each of length 10,000. The first source string consisted of a random sequence of 0's and 1's. The second source string was a piece of English text obtained from an online manual. The third source string was a random sequence of characters from a 100-character alphabet.

In Figure 1 the average number of references to *string* per character in *string* passed is plotted against the pattern length for each of three source strings. Note that the number of references to *string* per character passed is less than 1. For example, for an English pattern of length 5, the algorithm typically inspects 0.24 characters for every character passed. That is, for every reference to *string* the algorithm passes about 4 characters, or, equivalently, the algorithm inspects only about a quarter of the characters it passes when searching for a pattern of length 5 in an English text string. Furthermore, the number of references per character drops as the patterns get longer. This evidence supports the conclusion that the algorithm is "sublinear" in the number of references to *string*.

For comparison, it should be noted that the Knuth, Morris, and Pratt algorithm references *string* precisely 1 time per character passed. The simple search algorithm references *string* about 1.1 times per character passed (determined empirically with the English sample above).

Fig. 1.

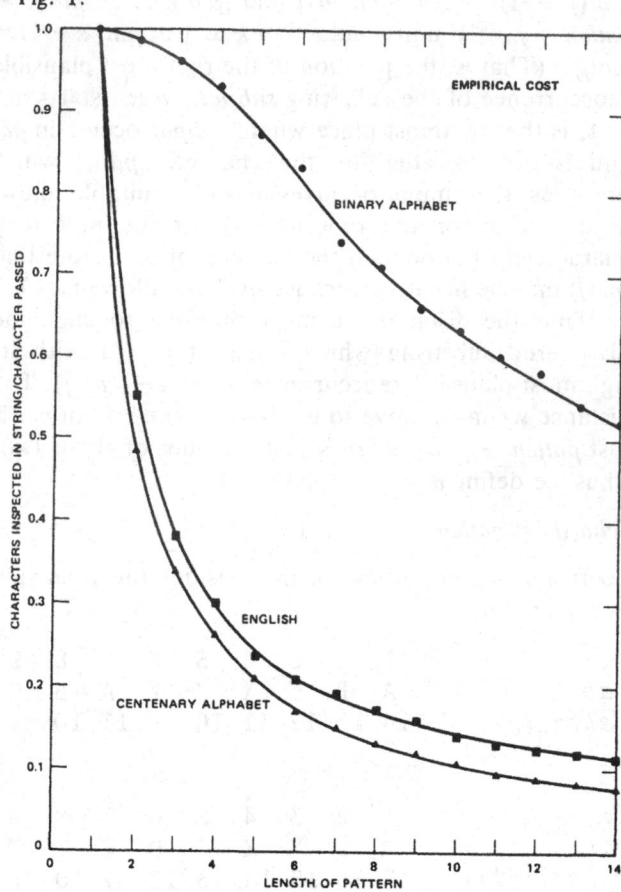

Fig. 2

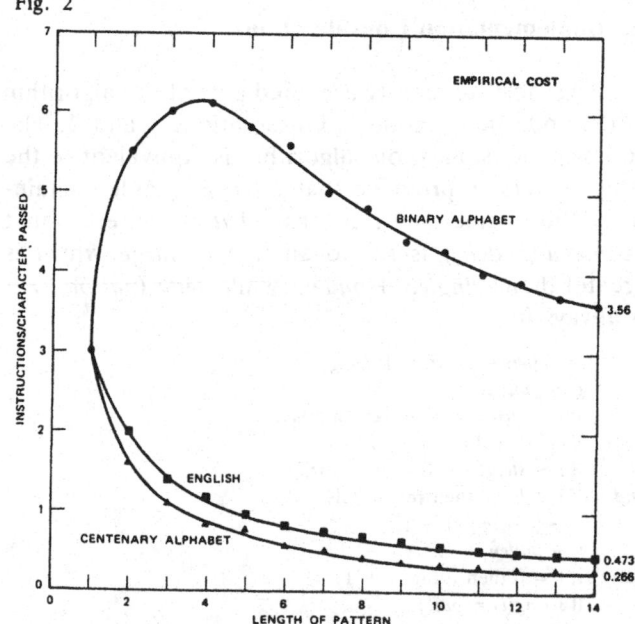

In Figure 2 the average number of instructions executed per character passed is plotted against the pattern length. The most obvious feature to note is that the search speeds up as the patterns get longer. That is, the total number of instructions executed in order to pass over a character decreases as the length of the pattern increases.

Figure 2 also exhibits a second interesting feature of our implementation of the algorithm: For sufficiently large alphabets and sufficiently long patterns the algorithm executes fewer than 1 instruction per character passed. For example, in the English sample, less than 1 instruction per character is executed for patterns of length 5 or more. Thus this implementation is "sublinear" in the sense that it executes fewer than $i + patlen$ instructions before finding the pattern at i. This means that no algorithm which references each character it passes could *possibly* be faster than ours in these cases (assuming it takes at least one instruction to reference each character).

The best alternative algorithm for finding a single substring is that of Knuth, Morris, and Pratt. If that algorithm is implemented in the extraordinarily efficient way described in [4, pp. 11–12] and [2, Item 179],[5] then the cost of looking at a character can be expected to be at least $3 - p$ instructions, where p is the probability that a character just fetched from *string* is equal to a given character of *pat*. Hence a horizontal line at $3 - p$ instructions/character represents the best (and, practically, the worst) the Knuth, Morris, and Pratt algorithm can achieve.

The simple string searching algorithm (when coded with a 3-instruction fast loop[6]) executes about 3.3 instructions per character (determined empirically on the English sample above).

As noted, the preprocessing time for our algorithm (and for Knuth, Morris, and Pratt) has been ignored. The cost of this preprocessing can be made linear in *patlen* (this is discussed further in the next section) and is trivial compared to a reasonably long search. We made no attempt to code this preprocessing efficiently. However, the average cost (in our implementation) ranges from 160 instructions (for strings of length 1) to about 500 instructions (for strings of length 14). It should be explained that our code uses a block transfer instruction to clear the 128-word $delta_1$ table at the beginning of the preprocessing, and we have counted this single instruction as though it were 128 instructions. This accounts for the unexpectedly large instruction count for preprocessing a one-character pattern.

7. Theoretical Analysis

The preprocessing for $delta_1$ requires an array the size of the alphabet. Our implementation first initializes all entries of this array to *patlen* and then sets up

$delta_1$ in a linear scan through the pattern. Thus our preprocessing for $delta_1$ is linear in *patlen* plus the size of the alphabet.

At a slight loss of efficiency in the search speed one could eliminate the initialization of the $delta_1$ array by storing with each entry a key indicating the number of times the algorithm has previously been called. This approach still requires initializing the array the first time the algorithm is used.

To implement our algorithm for extremely large alphabets, one might implement the $delta_1$ table as a hash array. In the worst case, accessing $delta_1$ during the search itself could require order *patlen* instructions, significantly impairing the speed of the algorithm. Hence the algorithm as it stands almost certainly does not run in time linear in $i + patlen$ for infinite alphabets.

Knuth, in analyzing the algorithm, has shown that it still runs in linear time when $delta_1$ is omitted, and this result holds for infinite alphabets. Doing this, however, will drastically degrade the performance of the algorithm on the average. In [5] Knuth exhibits an algorithm for setting up $delta_2$ in time linear in *patlen*.

From the preceding empirical evidence, the reader can conclude that the algorithm is quite good in the average case. However, the question of its behavior in the worst case is nontrivial. Knuth has recently shed some light on this question. In [5] he proves that the execution of the algorithm (after preprocessing) is linear in $i + patlen$, assuming the availability of array space linear in *patlen* plus the size of the alphabet. In particular, he shows that in order to discover that *pat* does not occur in the first i characters of *string*, at most $6 * i$ characters from *string* are matched with characters in *pat*. He goes on to say that the constant 6 is probably much too large, and invites the reader to improve the theorem. His proof reveals that the linearity of the algorithm is entirely due to $delta_2$.

We now analyze the average behavior of the algorithm by presenting a probabilistic model of its performance. As will become clear, the results of this analysis will support the empirical conclusions that the algorithm is usually "sublinear" both in the number of references to *string* and the number of instructions executed (for our implementation).

The analysis below is based on the following simplifying assumption: Each character of *pat* and *string* is an independent random variable. The probability that a character from *pat* or *string* is equal to a given character of the alphabet is p.

Imagine that we have just moved *pat* down *string* to a new position and that this position does not yield a match. We want to know the expected value of the ratio between the cost of discovering the mismatch and the distance we get to slide *pat* down upon finding the mismatch. If we define the cost to be the total number of references made to *string* before discovering the mismatch, we can obtain the expected value of the average number of references to string per character

---

[5] This implementation automatically compiles *pat* into a machine code program which implicitly has the skip table built in and which is executed to perform the search itself. In [2] they compile code which uses the PDP-10 capability of fetching a character and incrementing a byte address in one instruction. This compiled code executes at least two or three instructions per character fetched from *string*, depending on the outcome of a comparison of the character to one from *pat*.

[6] This loop avoids checking whether *string* is exhausted by assuming that the first character of *pat* occurs at the end of *string*. This can be arranged ahead of time. The loop actually uses the same three instruction codes used by the above-referenced implementation of the Knuth, Morris, and Pratt algorithm.

41

passed. If we define the cost to be the total number of machine instructions executed in discovering the mismatch, we can obtain the expected value of the number of instructions executed per character passed.

In the following we say "only the last m characters of pat match" to mean "the last m characters of pat match the corresponding m characters in $string$ but the $(m + 1)$-th character from the right end of pat fails to match the corresponding character in $string$."

The expected value of the ratio of cost to characters passed is given by:

$$\left(\sum_{m=0}^{patlen-1} cost(m) * prob(m) \right) \Bigg/ \left(\sum_{m=0}^{patlen-1} prob(m) * \left(\sum_{k=1}^{patlen} skip(m, k) * k \right) \right)$$

where $cost(m)$ is the cost associated with discovering that only the last m characters of pat match; $prob(m)$ is the probability that only the last m characters of pat match; and $skip(m, k)$ is the probability that, supposing only the last m characters of pat match, we will get to slide pat down by k.

Under our assumptions, the probability that only the last m characters of pat match is:

$$prob(m) = p^m(1 - p)/(1 - p^{patlen}).$$

(The denominator is due to the assumption that a mismatch exists.)

The probability that we will get to slide pat down by k is determined by analyzing how i is incremented. However, note that even though we increment i by the maximum max of the two $deltas$, this will actually only slide pat down by $max - m$, since the increment of i also includes the m necessary to shift our attention back to the end of pat. Thus when we analyze the contributions of the two $deltas$ we speak of the amount by which they allow us to slide pat down, rather than the amount by which we increment i. Finally, recall that if the mismatched character $char$ occurs in the already matched final m characters of pat, then $delta_1$ is worthless and we always slide by $delta_2$. The probability that $delta_1$ is worthless is just $(1 - (1 - p)^m)$. Let us call this $probdelta_1worthless(m)$.

The conditions under which $delta_1$ will naturally let us slide forward by k can be broken down into four cases as follows: (a) $delta_1$ will let us slide down by 1 if $char$ is the $(m + 2)$-th character from the righthand end of pat (or else there are no more characters in pat) and $char$ does not occur to the right of that position (which has probability $(1 - p)^m *$ (if $m + 1 = patlen$ then 1 else p)). (b) $delta_1$ allows us to slide down k, where $1 < k < patlen - m$, provided the rightmost occurrence of $char$ in pat is $m + k$ characters from the right end of pat (which has probability $p * (1 - p)^{k+m-1}$). (c) When $patlen - m > 1$, $delta_1$ allows us to slide past $patlen - m$ characters if $char$ does not occur in pat at all (which has probability $(1 - p)^{patlen-1}$ given that we know $char$ is not the $(m + 1)$-th character from

the right end of pat). Finally, (d) $delta_1$ never allows a slide longer than $patlen - m$ (since the maximum value of $delta_1$ is $patlen$).

Thus we can define the probability $probdelta_1(m, k)$ that when only the last m characters of pat match, $delta_1$ will allow us to move down by k as follows:

$probdelta_1(m, k) =$ if $k = 1$
  then
    $(1 - p)^m *$ (if $m + 1 = patlen$ then 1 else p);
  elseif $1 < k < patlen - m$ then $p * (1 - p)^{k+m-1}$;
  elseif $k = patlen - m$ then $(1 - p)^{patlen-1}$;
  else (i.e. $k > patlen - m$) 0.

(It should be noted that we will not put these formulas into closed form, but will simply evaluate them to verify the validity of our empirical evidence.)

We now perform a similar analysis for $delta_2$; $delta_2$ lets us slide down by k if (a) doing so sets up an alignment of the discovered occurrence of the last m characters of pat in $string$ with a plausible reoccurrence of those m characters elsewhere in pat, and (b) no smaller move will set up such an alignment. The probability $probpr(m, k)$ that the terminal substring of pat of length m has a plausible reoccurrence k characters to the left of its first character is:

$probpr(m, k) =$ if $m + k < patlen$
  then $(1 - p) * p^m$
  else $p^{patlen-k}$

Of course, k is just the distance $delta_2$ lets us slide provided there is no earlier reoccurrence. We can therefore define the probability $probdelta_2(m, k)$ that, when only the last m characters of pat match, $delta_2$ will allow us to move down by k recursively as follows:

$probdelta_2(m, k)$

$$= probpr(m, k) \left(1 - \sum_{n=1}^{k-1} probdelta_2(m, n) \right).$$

We slide down by the maximum allowed by the two $deltas$ (taking adequate account of the possibility that $delta_1$ is worthless). If the values of the $deltas$ were independent, the probability that we would actually slide down by k would just be the sum of the products of the probabilities that one of the $deltas$ allows a move of k while the other allows a move of less than or equal to k.

However, the two moves are not entirely independent. In particular, consider the possibility that $delta_1$ is worthless. Then the $char$ just fetched occurs in the last m characters of pat and does not match the $(m + 1)$-th. But if $delta_2$ gives a slide of 1 it means that sliding these m characters to the left by 1 produces a match. This implies that all of the last m characters of pat are equal to the character $m + 1$ from the right. But this character is known not to be $char$. Thus $char$ cannot occur in the last m characters of pat, violating the hypothesis that $delta_1$ was worthless. Therefore if $delta_1$ is worthless, the probability that $delta_2$ specifies a skip of 1 is 0 and the probability that it specifies one of the larger skips is correspondingly increased.

This interaction between the two *delta*s is also felt (to a lesser extent) for the next m possible $delta_2$'s, but we ignore these (and in so doing accept that our analysis may predict slightly worse results than might be expected since we allow some short $delta_2$ moves when longer ones would actually occur).

The probability that $delta_2$ will allow us to slide down by k when only the last m characters of *pat* match, assuming that $delta_1$ is worthless, is:

$$probdelta_2'(m, k) = \text{ if } k = 1$$
$$\text{then } 0$$
$$\text{else}$$
$$probpr(m, k) \left(1 - \sum_{n=2}^{k-1} probdelta_2'(m, n) \right).$$

Finally, we can define $skip(m, k)$, the probability that we will slide down by k if only the last m characters of *pat* match:

$$skip(m, k) = \text{ if } k = 1$$
$$\text{then } probdelta_1(m, 1) * probdelta_2(m, 1)$$
$$\text{else } probdelta_1worthless(m) * probdelta_2'(m, k)$$
$$+ \sum_{n=1}^{k-1} probdelta_1(m, k) * probdelta_2(m, n)$$
$$+ \sum_{n=1}^{k-1} probdelta_1(m, n) * probdelta_2(m, k)$$
$$+ probdelta_1(m, k) * probdelta_2(m, k).$$

Now let us consider the two alternative *cost* functions. In order to analyze the number of references to *string* per character passed over, $cost(m)$ should just be $m + 1$, the number of references necessary to confirm that only the last m characters of *pat* match.

In order to analyze the number of instructions executed per character passed over, $cost(m)$ should be the total number of instructions executed in discovering that only the last m characters of *pat* match. By inspection of our PDP-10 code:

$$cost(m) = \text{ if } m = 0 \text{ then } 3 \text{ else } 12 + 6m.$$

We have computed the expected value of the ratio of cost per character skipped by using the above formulas (and both definitions of *cost*). We did so for pattern lengths running from 1 to 14 (as in our empirical evidence) and for the values of p appropriate for the three source strings used: For a random binary string p is 0.5, for an arbitrary English string it is (approximately) 0.09, and for a random string over a 100-character alphabet it is 0.01. The value of p for English was determined using a standard frequency count for the alphabetic characters [3] and empirically determining the frequency of space, carriage return, and line feed to be 0.23, 0.03, and 0.03, respectively.[7]

In Figure 3 we have plotted the theoretical ratio of references to *string* per character passed over against

_____
[7] We have determined empirically that the algorithm's performance on truly random strings where $p = 0.09$ is virtually identical to its performance on English strings. In particular, the reference count and instruction count curves generated by such random strings are almost coincidental with the English curves in Figures 1 and 2.

Fig. 3.

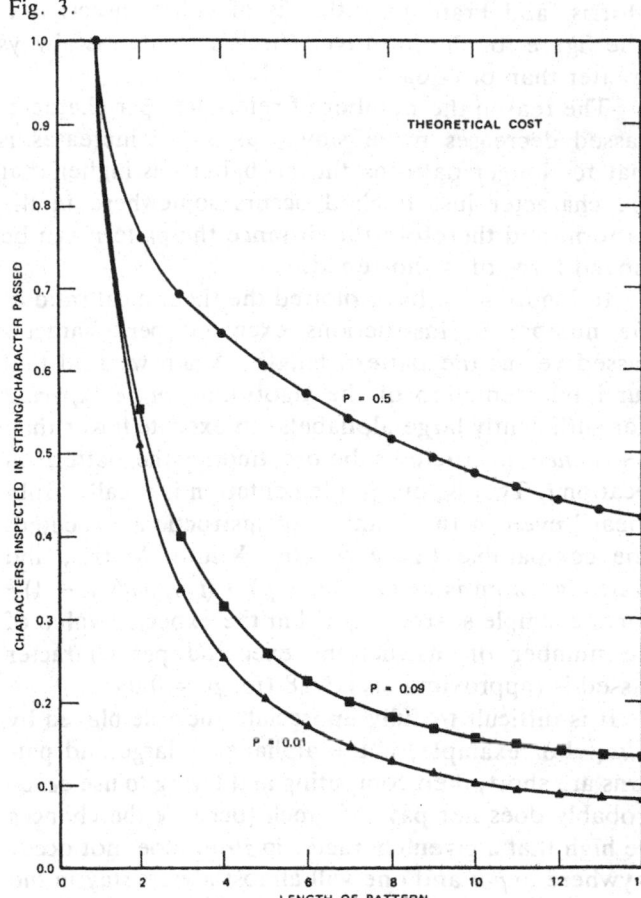

Fig. 4.

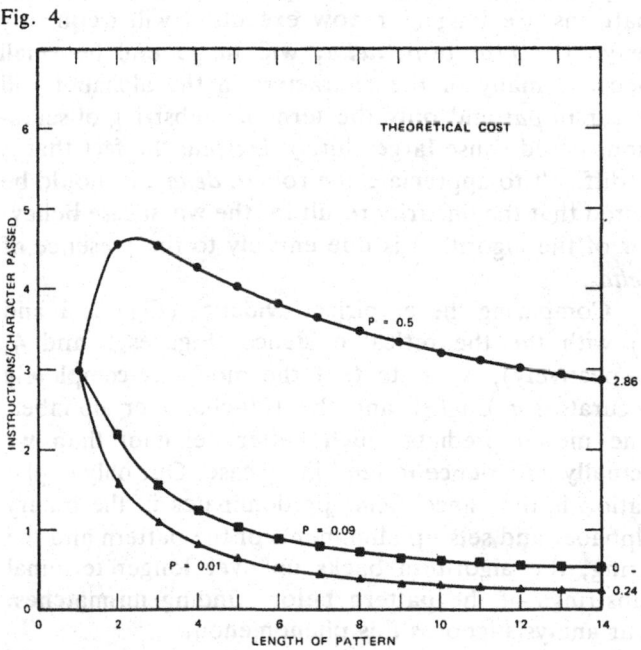

the pattern length. The most important fact to observe in Figure 3 is that the algorithm *can be expected* to make fewer than $i + patlen$ references to *string* before finding the pattern at location i. For example, for English text strings of length 5 or greater, the algorithm may be expected to make less than $(i + 5)/4$ references to *string*. The comparable figure for the Knuth,

Morris, and Pratt algorithm is of course precisely i. The figure for the intuitive search algorithm is always greater than or equal to i.

The reason the number of references per character passed decreases more slowly as *patlen* increases is that for longer patterns the probability is higher that the character just fetched occurs somewhere in the pattern, and therefore the distance the pattern can be moved forward is shortened.

In Figure 4 we have plotted the theoretical ratio of the number of instructions executed per character passed versus the pattern length. Again we find that our implementation of the algorithm *can be expected* (for sufficiently large alphabets) to execute fewer than $i + patlen$ instructions before finding the pattern at location i. That is, our implementation is usually "sublinear" even in the number of instructions executed. The comparable figure for the Knuth, Morris, and Pratt algorithm is at best $(3 - p) * (i + patlen - 1)$.[8] For the simple search algorithm the expected value of the number of instructions executed per character passed is (approximately) 3.28 (for $p = 0.09$).

It is difficult to fully appreciate the role played by $delta_2$. For example, if the alphabet is large and patterns are short, then computing and trying to use $delta_2$ probably does not pay off much (because the chances are high that a given character in *string* does not occur anywhere in *pat* and one will almost always stay in the *fast* loop ignoring $delta_2$).[9] Conversely, $delta_2$ becomes very important when the alphabet is small and the patterns are long (for now execution will frequently leave the *fast* loop; $delta_1$ will in general be small because many of the characters in the alphabet will occur in *pat* and only the terminal substring observations could cause large shifts). Despite the fact that it is difficult to appreciate the role of $delta_2$, it should be noted that the linearity result for the worst case behavior of the algorithm is due entirely to the presence of $delta_2$.

Comparing the empirical evidence (Figures 1 and 2) with the theoretical evidence (Figures 3 and 4, respectively), we note that the model is completely accurate for English and the 100-character alphabet. The model predicts much better behavior than we actually experience in the binary case. Our only explanation is that since $delta_2$ predominates in the binary alphabet and sets up alignments of the pattern and the string, the algorithm backs up over longer terminal substrings of the pattern before finding mismatches. Our analysis ignores this phenomenon.

However, in summary, the theoretical analysis supports the conclusion that on the average the algorithm is sublinear in the number of references to *string* and, for sufficiently large alphabets and patterns, sublinear in the number of instructions executed (in our implementation).

8. Caveat Programmer

It should be observed that the preceding analysis has assumed that *string* is entirely in primary memory and that we can obtain the ith character in it in one instruction after computing its byte address. However, if *string* is actually on secondary storage, then the characters in it must be read in.[10] This transfer will entail some time delay equivalent to the execution of, say, w instructions per character brought in, and (because of the nature of computer I/O) all of the first $i + patlen - 1$ characters will eventually be brought in whether *we* actually reference all of them or not. (A representative figure for w for paged transfers from a fast disk is 5 instructions/character.) Thus there may be a hidden cost of w instructions per character passed over.

According to the statistics presented above one might expect our algorithm to be approximately three times faster than the Knuth, Morris, and Pratt algorithm (for, say, English strings of length 6) since that algorithm executes about three instructions to our one. However, if the CPU is idle for the w instructions necessary to read each character, the actual ratios are closer to $w + 3$ instructions than to $w + 1$ instructions. Thus for paged disk transfers our algorithm can only be expected to be roughly $4/3$ faster (i.e. $5 + 3$ instructions to $5 + 1$ instructions) if we assume that we are idle during I/O. Thus for large values of w the difference between the various algorithms diminishes if the CPU is idle during I/O.

Of course, in general, programmers (or operating systems) try to avoid the situation in which the CPU is idle while awaiting an I/O transfer by overlapping I/O with some other computation. In this situation, the chances are that our algorithm will be I/O bound (we will search a page faster than it can be brought in), and indeed so will that of Knuth, Morris, and Pratt if $w > 3$. Our algorithm will require that fewer CPU cycles be devoted to the search itself so that if there are other jobs to perform, there will still be an overall advantage in using the algorithm.

---

[8] Although the Knuth, Morris, and Pratt algorithm will fetch each of the first $i + patlen - 1$ characters of *string* precisely once, sometimes a character is involved in several tests against characters in *pat*. The number of such tests (each involving three instructions) is bounded by $\log_\Phi(patlen)$, where Φ is the golden ratio.

[9] However, if the algorithm is implemented without $delta_2$, recall that, in exiting the *slow* loop, one must now take the *max* of $delta_1$ and $patlen - j + 1$ to allow for the possibility that $delta_1$ is worthless.

[10] We have implemented a version of our algorithm for searching through disk files. It is available as the subroutine FFILEPOS in the latest release of INTERLISP-10. This function uses the TENEX page mapping capability to identify one file page at a time with a buffer area in virtual memory. In addition to being faster than reading the page by conventional methods, this means the operating system's memory management takes care of references to pages which happen to still be in memory, etc. The algorithm is as much as 50 times faster than the standard INTERLISP-10 FILEPOS function (depending on the length of the pattern).

There are several situations in which it may not be advisable to use our algorithm. If the expected penetration i at which the pattern is found is small, the preprocessing time is significant and one might therefore consider using the obvious intuitive algorithm.

As previously noted, our algorithm can be most efficiently implemented on a byte-addressable machine. On a machine that does not allow byte addresses to be incremented and decremented directly, two possible sources of inefficiency must be addressed: The algorithm typically skips through *string* in steps larger than 1, and the algorithm may back up through *string*. Unless these processes are coded efficiently, it is probably not worthwhile to use our algorithm.

Furthermore, it should be noted that because the algorithm can back up through *string*, it is possible to cross a page boundary more than once. We have not found this to be a serious source of inefficiency. However, it does require a certain amount of code to handle the necessary buffering (if page I/O is being handled directly as in our FFILEPOS). One beauty of the Knuth, Morris, and Pratt algorithm is that it avoids this problem altogether.

A final situation in which it is unadvisable to use our algorithm is if the string matching problem to be solved is actually more complicated than merely finding the first occurrence of a single substring. For example, if the problem is to find the first of several possible substrings or to identify a location in *string* defined by a regular expression, it is much more advantageous to use an algorithm such as that of Aho and Corasick [1].

It may of course be possible to design an algorithm that searches for multiple patterns or instances of regular expressions by using the idea of starting the match at the right end of the pattern. However, we have not designed such an algorithm.

9. Historical Remarks

Our earliest formulation of the algorithm involved only *delta₁* and implemented Observations 1, 2, and 3(a). We were aware that we could do something along the lines of *delta₂* and Observation 3(b), but did not precisely formulate it. Instead, in April 1974, we coded the *delta₁* version of the algorithm in Interlisp, merely to test its speed. We considered coding the algorithm in PDP-10 assembly language but abandoned the idea as impractical because of the cost of incrementing byte pointers by arbitrary amounts.

We have since learned that R.W. Gosper, of Stanford University, simultaneously and independently discovered the *delta₁* version of the algorithm (private communication).

In April 1975, we started thinking about the implementation again and discovered a way to increment byte pointers by indexing through a table. We then formulated a version of *delta₂* and coded the algorithm

more or less as it is presented here. This original definition of *delta₂* differed from the current one in the following respect: If only the last m characters of *pat* (call this substring *subpat*) were matched, *delta₂* specified a slide to the second from the rightmost occurrence of *subpat* in *pat* (allowing this occurrence to "fall off" the left end of *pat*) but without any special consideration of the character preceding this occurrence.

The average behavior of that version of the algorithm was virtually indistinguishable from that presented in this paper for large alphabets, but was somewhat worse for small alphabets. However, its worst case behavior was quadratic (i.e. required on the order of $i * patlen$ comparisons). For example, consider searching for a pattern of the form $CA(BA)^r$ in a string of the form $((XX)^r(AA)(BA)^r)^*$ (e.g. $r = 2$, *pat* = "CABABA," and *string* = "XXXXAABA-BAXXXXAABABA . . ."). The original definition of *delta₂* allowed only a slide of 2 if the last "BA" of *pat* was matched before the next "A" failed to match. Of course in this situation this only sets up another mismatch at the same character in *string*, but the algorithm had to reinspect the previously inspected characters to discover it. The total number of references to *string* in passing i characters in this situation was $(r + 1) * (r + 2) * i/(4r + 2)$, where $r = (patlen - 2)/2$. Thus the number of references was on the order of $i * patlen$.

However, on the average the algorithm was blindingly fast. To our surprise, it was several times faster than the string searching algorithm in the Tenex TECO text editor. This algorithm is reputed to be quite an efficient implementation of the simple search algorithm because it searches for the first character of *pat* one full word at a time (rather than one byte at a time).

In the summer of 1975, we wrote a brief paper on the algorithm and distributed it on request.

In December 1975, Ben Kuipers of the M.I.T. Artificial Intelligence Laboratory read the paper and brought to our attention the improvement to *delta₂* concerning the character preceding the terminal substring and its reoccurrence (private communication). Almost simultaneously, Donald Knuth of Stanford University suggested the same improvement and observed that the improved algorithm could certainly make no more than order $(i + patlen) * log(patlen)$ references to *string* (private communication).

We mentioned this improvement in the next revision of the paper and suggested an additional improvement, namely the replacement of both *delta₁* and *delta₂* by a single two-dimensional table. Given the mismatched *char* from *string* and the position j in *pat* at which the mismatch occurred, this table indicated the distance to the last occurrence (if any) of the substring $[char, pat(j + 1), . . . , pat(patlen)]$ in *pat*. The revised paper concluded with the question of whether this improvement or a similar one produced an algorithm which was at worst linear and on the average "sublinear."

In January 1976, Knuth [5] proved that the simpler improvement in fact produces linear behavior, even in the worst case. We therefore revised the paper again and gave $delta_2$ its current definition.

In April 1976, R.W. Floyd of Stanford University discovered a serious statistical fallacy in the first version of our formula giving the expected value of the ratio of cost to characters passed. He provided us (private communication) with the current version of this formula.

Thomas Standish, of the University of California at Irvine, has suggested (private communication) that the implementation of the algorithm can be improved by fetching larger bytes in the *fast* loop (i.e. bytes containing several characters) and using a hash array to encode the extended $delta_1$ table. Provided the difficulties at the boundaries of the pattern are handled efficiently, this could improve the behavior of the algorithm enormously since it exponentially increases the effective size of the alphabet and reduces the frequency of common characters.

Acknowledgments. We would like to thank B. Kuipers, of the M.I.T. Artificial Intelligence Laboratory, for his suggestion concerning $delta_2$ and D. Knuth, of Stanford University, for his analysis of the improved algorithm. We are grateful to the anonymous reviewer for *Communications* who suggested the inclusion of evidence comparing our algorithm with that of Knuth, Morris, and Pratt, and for the warnings contained in Section 8. B. Mont-Reynaud, of the Stanford Research Institute, and L. Guibas, of Xerox Palo Alto Research Center, proofread drafts of this paper and suggested several clarifications. We would also like to thank E. Taft and E. Fiala of Xerox Palo Alto Research Center for their advice regarding machine coding the algorithm.

Received June 1975; revised April 1976

References
1. Aho, A.V., and Corasick, M.J. Fast pattern matching: An aid to bibliographic search. *Comm. ACM 18,* 6 (June, 1975), 333–340.
2. Beeler, M., Gosper, R.W., and Schroeppel, R. Hakmem. Memo No. 239, M.I.T. Artificial Intelligence Lab., M.I.T., Cambridge, Mass., Feb. 29, 1972.
3. Dewey, G. *Relativ Frequency of English Speech Sounds.* Harvard U. Press, Cambridge, Mass., 1923, p. 185.
4. Knuth, D.E., Morris, J.H., and Pratt, V.R. Fast pattern matching in strings. TR CS-74-440, Stanford U., Stanford, Calif., 1974.
5. Knuth, D.E., Morris, J.H., and Pratt, V.R. Fast pattern matching in strings. (to appear in *SIAM J. Comput.*).

Algorithms for Pattern Matching

G. DAVIES AND S. BOWSHER

Faculty of Mathematics, The Open University, Walton Hall, Milton Keynes, MK7 6AA, U.K.

SUMMARY

This paper describes four algorithms of varying complexity used for pattern matching, and investigates their behaviour. The algorithms are tested using patterns of varying length from several alphabets. It is concluded that although there is no overall 'best' algorithm, the more complex algorithms are worth considering as they are generally more efficient in terms of number of comparisons made and execution time.

KEY WORDS String searching Pattern matching Text editing Information retrieval

INTRODUCTION

Pattern matching is an integral part of many text editing, data retrieval, symbol manipulation, and word and data processing problems. Text editing programs are often required to search through a string of characters looking for instances of a given 'pattern' string—we wish to find the position at which the pattern occurs as a contiguous substring of the text.

In general, given a string of text, $S_1, S_2 . . . S_n$, it is required to find an occurrence, if it exists, of a pattern. $P_1 P_2 . . . P_m$ in the string; such an occurrence is identified by the value i such that the characters $S_i S_{i+1} . . . S_{i-1+m}$ match the characters in the pattern $P_1 P_2 . . . P_m$. There may be more than one occurrence of the pattern in the string and hence more than one value for i.

This paper investigates four algorithms for finding the value of i for the first (leftmost) occurrence of the patterns.

Algorithm 1 is the 'brute-force' method, the obvious solution to the pattern matching problem, where the algorithm considers each character position of the text string being searched and determines whether the successive 'pattern-length' characters of the 'string' starting at that position match the successive 'pattern-length' characters of the pattern.

Algorithm 2 is based on work done by Knuth, Morris and Pratt.[1] It involves the preprocessing of the pattern to be located to create a table which is then used to tell us where to resume matching after a character mismatch has occurred.

Algorithm 3 was developed by R. S. Boyer and J. Strother Moore.[2] The algorithm uses the fact that more information can be gained by matching the pattern from the right than from the left. It also involves preprocessing of the pattern to produce tables that are used to compute the failure jumps, i.e. how far to skip along in the text after a mismatch has occurred.

Algorithm 4 is an algorithm developed by O. M. Rabin and R. M. Karp.[3] It is another brute-force approach to string searching which uses a large memory to advantage by treating each possible m-character section (where m is the pattern length) of the text as a

Reprinted from *Software – Practice and Experience*,
Volume 16, No. 6, June 1986, pp. 575-601. Copyright
1986 by John Wiley & Sons, Ltd.

key in a standard hash table. The algorithm simply computes the hash function for each of the possible m-character sections of the text and checks if it is equal to the hash function of the pattern. It is not necessary to keep a whole hash table in memory since only one key is being sought. The algorithm really only finds an m-character section in the text which has the same hash value as the pattern, so to be extra sure a direct comparison of the text and pattern is made.

AIMS

The purpose of the investigation was to examine four different algorithms of varying complexity used for pattern matching in strings. Four algorithms are discussed and both their theoretical and actual behaviours are looked at.

The investigation aimed to compare and contrast the four algorithms and to answer such questions as:

1. How do the actual performances of the four algorithms compare under test conditions?
2. How does the predicted theoretical behaviour compare with the actual performance on test data?
3. Do variables such as the size of the alphabet or the size of the pattern being searched for have any effect on the performances of the algorithms. (At the outset it was intuitively expected that the alphabet size would be a major influencing factor on the performances of the different algorithms; the smaller the size of the alphabet the higher the probability of matching any two random characters from that alphabet, and thus it was expected that if the pattern size was of a reasonable length the simple brute-force approach would suffice because the computational effort required to produce failure vectors for algorithms 2 and 3 could not be justified against the simple approach. Similarly the size of the pattern being searched for was expected to play a large part).

THE ALGORITHMS USED

All the algorithms under consideration were coded in the C programming language and designed to run under UCB UNIX Version 2.8. For analysis purposes only (and not for efficiency) the algorithms were implemented in such a way that the program tries to match the pattern only up to the first occurrence of the pattern.

All the algorithms used could easily be extended to find all occurrences of the pattern in the input text, since they scan sequentially through the text and can be restarted at the point directly after the beginning of the match to find the next match. They could also be extended to take as input a file of any size and to report each line in the file in which the pattern occurs.

In all cases the C optimizer was used to produce efficient executable code.

The analysis assumes that the string and pattern are entirely in primary memory and that each character can be obtained in one instruction after computing its byte address. However, if the string is actually on secondary storage then the characters must be read in.

Throughout the discussions of the algorithms the following notation is assumed:

pattern — pattern being search for
pattern[j] — jth character of the pattern

string   —   text string being searched
string[k]   —   kth character of the string
patlen, m —   number of characters in pattern

NB. In all descriptions of the algorithms when the pattern is shifted by x places or the text is moved along x places, this actually means that the pointer into the string is incremented by x positions.

Algorithm 1

This is the obvious or brute-force approach to solving the problem of pattern matching and is well documented. The essence of this algorithm is to superimpose the pattern on top of each substring of the text string of patlen proceeding from left to right, and to check the characters of the pattern, character by character against the substring of the text string beneath it. As soon as a mismatch is detected, the pattern is shifted to the right one character. The algorithm tries to search at every starting position of the text, abandoning the search as soon as an incorrect character is found; this occurs if an initial substring of the pattern occurs in the string, and is known as a false start, e.g.

```
string : string

string : A string searching example consisting of
         ↑        ↑                     ↑
```

where ↑ signifies a false start.

The pointer into the pattern is incremented four times on execution of the algorithm, once for each s and twice for the first st; these are the false starts. This then involves the backing up of the pointers into the pattern and string, which could add complications, for instance when a large file is being read in from some external device. The backtracking involved when a partially successful search path fails necessitates a lot of storage and bookkeeping and tends to execute slowly.

The actual implementation of the algorithm checks each possible position in the text at which the pattern could match, to see whether it does in fact match. The program keeps one pointer (k) into the text string and another pointer (j) into the pattern. If j and k point to the same characters, then they are both incremented to point to the next character in both the pattern and the string. If j and k point to mismatching characters then j is reset to correspond to moving the pattern to the right by one position for matching against text. If the end of the text string is reached then there is no match.

Informal outline of the algorithm

```
        j=0; k=0;
        while not at end of pattern or string
            if pattern[j] = string[k]
                then
                        k++; j++;
                else
                        k=k−j+1; j=0;
            endif
        endwhile
```

Obviously this algorithm can be very inefficient; consider trying to match the pattern aaa...ab of length m in a string of n a's:

```
pattern :  aaa...ab
string  :  aaa.........aaaa
```

On trying to match the two character strings, the first $m-1$ letters of the pattern will match the characters in the string, but the final, mth, letter of the pattern will not; a mismatch will occur. Thus the whole pattern will be moved along by one position and the matching will be resumed.

```
pattern :  aaa....ab
string  :  aaa.........aaaa
```

Similarly, the first $m-1$ characters of the pattern will match with the string again until mismatch occurs on the mth character of the pattern. Continuing this process we see there will be $n-m+1$ times that the string and the pattern have $m-1$ as in common. Thus the algorithm will require at least $(n-m+1)(m-1)$ comparison operations, i.e. $O(mn)$, and thus the number of direct character comparisons in the worst case is quadratic.

The quadratic nature of this algorithm, however, appears only when initial substrings of the pattern occur in the text string being searched, which appears to be a fairly rare phenomenon in English text, and so in the majority of cases the running time is expected to be less than this. Thus an optimized version of the brute force approach often provides a good 'standard'. This investigation aimed to show how the algorithm actually behaves under (simulated) realistic conditions.

Summarizing, the theoretical behaviour of this algorithm in the worst case is quadratic, $O(mn)$, whereas the average theoretical behaviour is better than this but is dependent on statistical properties of the pattern and the text string being searched.

Algorithm 2

The basic idea behind algorithm 2 is to take advantage of the fact that when a mismatch occurs the false start consists of characters that are already known since they are already in the pattern. This information can then be used to prevent backing up through the text string over all those known characters. 'Shifts' can be precomputed specifying how much to move the given pattern when a mismatch occurs, by preprocessing the actual pattern (by shifting the pattern against itself) to form a table. To illustrate this approach, consider Knuth, Morris and Pratt's example, searching for the pattern abcabcacab in the text string babcbabcabcaabcabcabcacabc. Initially the pattern is placed at the extreme left and scanning starts at the leftmost character of the input text:

```
pattern :  abcabcacab
string  :  babcbabcabcaabcabcabcacabc
           ↑
```

where ↑ indicates the current text character.

Since the string pointer points to the character b, which does not match the a in the pattern, the pattern is shifted one place to the right and the next string character is inspected:

```
pattern  :   abcabcacab

string   :   babcbabcabcaabcabcabcacabc
             ↑
```

There is a match, so the pattern remains where it is while the next several characters are scanned until we come to a mismatch:

```
pattern  :    abcabcacab

string   :    babcbabcabcaabcabcabcacabc
                 ↑

              mismatch
```

The first three pattern characters are matched, but there is a mismatch on the fourth; thus it is known that the last four characters of the input text string have been abc? where ? is not equal to a. There is no need to remember the previously scanned characters since the position in the pattern yields enough information to recreate them. In this example as long as the ? character is not equal to a the pattern can be immediately shifted four more places to the right, since a shift of one, two or three positions could not possibly lead to a match. Thus the situation appears as

```
pattern  :        abcabcacab

string   :    babcbabcabcaabcabcabcacabc
                 ↑
```

The characters are scanned again and another partial match occurs; a mismatch occurs on the eighth pattern character:

```
pattern  :        abcabcacab

string   :    babcbabcabcaabcabcabcacabc
                       ↑

                   mismatch
```

Similarly we know that the last eight string characters were abcabca? where ? is not equal to c but might be equal to b. Thus the pattern should be shifted three places to the right:

```
pattern  :          abcabcacab

string   :    babcbabcabcaabcabcabcacabc
                       ↑

                   mismatch
```

51

Comparing the two characters we get a mismatch, so we shift the pattern a further four places:

```
pattern  :             abcabcacab

string   :   babcbabcabcaabcabcabcacabc
                              ↑
```

This produces another partial match; scanning is continued until mismatch occurs, again, on the eighth pattern character:

```
pattern  :             abcabcacab

string   :   babcbabcabcaabcabcabcacabc
                                  ↑
                              mismatch
```

The pattern is then shifted a further three places to the right:

```
pattern  :             abcabcacab

string   :   babcababcabcaabcabcabcacabc
                              ↑
```

This time a match is produced and, on scanning, the full pattern is found; the pattern match has succeeded.

This worked example illustrates that, by knowing the characters in the pattern and the position in the pattern where a mismatch occurs with a character in the text string, it can be determined where in the pattern to continue the search for a match without moving backwards in the input text. It also shows that the process of pattern matching will run much more efficiently if we have an auxilliary table which will provide us with the information of how far to slide the pattern when a mismatch has been detected at the jth character of the pattern. Thus the vector NEXT can now be introduced; NEXT[j] is the character position in the pattern which should be checked next after a mismatch has occurred at the jth character of the pattern. Hence the pattern is actually being slid j–NEXT[j] places relative to the text string.

When the pattern pointer (j) and the string pointer (k) point to mismatching characters, then we know that the last j characters of the text string up to and including string[k] were pattern[1] . . pattern[j−1] x where x ≠ pattern[j]. NEXT[j] is the largest i<j such that the last i characters of the text string were pattern[1]. .pattern[i−1] x and pattern[i] ≠ pattern[j]. If no such i exists NEXT[j]=0.

The NEXT vector can easily be calculated by using a secondary vector f. The jth entry f[j], j>1, is defined as the largest i less than j such that pattern[1]. .pattern[i−1] = pattern[j−i+1]. .p[j−1]. This holds for i=1, and f[j] is always greater than or equal to 1 when j>1. f[1] is defined to be 0. Thus the last i−1 (already matched) characters of the pattern preceding the mismatched character match the subpattern pattern[1]. pattern[i−1].

The values of the vector f can be determined by sliding a copy of the first j−1 characters of the pattern over itself; sliding from left to right with the first character of the copy over the second character of the pattern, stopping when either all overlapping characters match or there are none overlapping. If a mismatch is detected at the jth character of the pattern the value of f[j] is exactly the number of overlapping characters plus one.

The values of the vector NEXT can then be calculated using the following relation:

$$NEXT[j] = \begin{cases} f[j] & \text{if } pattern[j] \neq pattern[f[j]] \\ NEXT[f[j]] & \text{if } pattern[j] = pattern[f[j]] \end{cases}$$

The NEXT vector, however, can be calculated in such a way that the values of f[j] need not be stored in memory (see below). The above example has the following values:

j	=	1	2	3	4	5	6	7	8	9	10
pattern[j]	=	a	b	c	a	b	c	a	c	a	b
NEXT[j]	=	0	1	1	0	1	1	0	5	0	1
f[j]	=	0	1	1	1	2	3	4	5	1	2

NEXT[j]=0 means that the pattern is to be slid all the way past the current text character, that is the pointer to the text string should be incremented. By definition NEXT[1]=0.

On mismatch there is no need to back up the string pointer. If NEXT[j]≠0 then we simply leave the string pointer unchanged and set the pattern pointer to NEXT[j]. Thus the vector NEXT provides a way of eliminating the back up of the text string pointer.

The inclusion of the NEXT vector can be seen in the informal outline of algorithm 2 below:

```
j=0; k=0;
while not at end of pattern or string
    if pattern[j] = string [k]
        then
            j++; k++;
        else
            j=NEXT[j];
            if j=0
                k++;
endwhile
```

The initialization of the NEXT vector is similar to the actual algorithm above except that it matches the pattern against itself:

```
x=1; y=0; NEXT[1]=0;
while not at end of pattern
    if pattern [x] ≠ pattern[y]
        then
            y = NEXT[y];
    x++; y++;
    if pattern[x] = pattern[y]
        then
            NEXT[x] = NEXT[y];
        else
            NEXT[x] = y;
endwhile
```

After the NEXT vector has been set up, then at each step of the scanning process either the text string pointer or the pattern pointer is moved. Assuming that the text string is of length n, both the pattern and string pointers can move at most n times, and so at most $2n$ steps are needed to perform the pattern matching operation. It has been shown by Knuth, using the same argument as above, that the NEXT vector can be set up in O(m) steps, where m is the pattern length, since the NEXT vector is found by shifting the pattern against itself. Thus the whole algorithm is of O($m+n$), i.e. linear.

Algorithm 2 is very good if it us used to search for highly self-repetitive patterns in self-repetitive text, but intuitively this does not seem to be a very common phenomenon. Thus this investigation seeks to find if this algorithm is (significantly) faster and/or more efficient in character comparisons than the brute-force method in (simulated) realistic conditions.

The major virtue of this algorithm is that it proceeds sequentially through the input text and never needs to back up. This makes the algorithm convenient for use on a large file being read in from some external device, because it avoids rescanning the input text string and possible complicated buffering operations.

Summarizing, the expected theoretical behaviour of algorithm 2 is linear, O($m+n$), and can therefore be used as a standard to which the other algorithms can be compared.

Algorithm 3

This algorithm was developed in 1974 by R. S. Boyer and J. S. Moore and the description that follows is essentially theirs. The underlying idea behind algorithm 3 is that a faster searching method can be developed by scanning the pattern from right to left when trying to match it against the text. This is only possible if backing up, that is moving backwards as well as forwards through the character array, is not a problem. The algorithm decides which characters to compare next based on the character that caused the mismatch in the text string as well as the pattern. The next characters to compare are found by appealing to a number of observations (see below).

The essence of this algorithm is to superimpose the pattern $p[1]...p[m]$ on the string $s[1]...s[n]$

$$p[1] \qquad p[2] \qquad ... \; p[m]$$
$$s[k-m+1] \quad s[k-m+2] \; ... \; s[k] \; ... \; s[n]$$

and to match the characters of the pattern against those of the underlying segment of the string in right to left order while the pattern is being moved to the right.

Observation 1

If the rightmost character of the pattern $p[m]$ does not match the underlying character $s[k]$ of the string, and it is also the case that the character corresponding to $s[k]$ does not occur anywhere in the pattern, then the pattern can be slid, in its entirety, over to the right all the way past $s[k]$ since no character of the pattern superimposed above $s[k]$ would ever match. Thus the situation, from above, would be:

$$p[1] \qquad p[2] \qquad ... \; p[m]$$
$$s[k] \quad s[k+1] \quad s[k+2] \; ... \; s[k+m] \; ... \; s[n]$$

Matching can then be resumed. Since there was no need to compare any of the $s[k-m+1] \ldots s[k-1]$ with $p[1] \ldots p[m-1]$, then $(m-1)$ character comparisons were omitted.

If however $s[k]$ does match with $p[m]$, then the pattern pointer can be shifted by the minimum amount consistent with a match:

$$p[1] \qquad \ldots p[m-1] \quad p[m]$$
$$s[k-m+1] \ldots s[k-1] \quad s[k] \ldots s[n]$$

$$\uparrow$$
Current text character

Observation 2

Generally, if the rightmost occurrence of the character corresponding to the character $s[k]$ in the pattern is r characters from the right end of the pattern, then we can automatically slide the pattern right r characters without checking for matches, since if the pattern were moved right by any amount less than r positions, then the character $s[k]$ would be aligned with some character that it could not possibly match. Such a match would require an occurrence of the character $s[k]$ in the pattern to the right of the last occurrence. The distance r is a function of the characters in the text string being searched. If the character $s[k]$ does not occur in the pattern, then r is patlen positions, i.e. shift the whole pattern along; this is a direct result ascertainable from observation 1. If the character $s[k]$ does occur in the pattern, then r is defined as the difference between the pattern length and the position of the rightmost occurrence of the character $s[k]$ in the pattern, i.e. simply shift the pattern so that the two known occurrences of the character corresponding to $s[k]$ coincide.

Assuming that the last character of the pattern, $p[m]$, matches the underlying character in the string, $s[k]$ say, it must be determined whether the previous character in the string $s[k-1]$ matches the second to last character in the pattern:

$$p[1] \qquad \ldots p[m-1] \quad p[m]$$
$$s[k-m] \quad s[k-m+1] \ldots \quad s[k-1] \quad s[k]$$

$$\uparrow$$

If the characters match then the process of comparing characters working from right to left through the pattern continues until either all of the pattern has been matched, and therefore the algorithm has succeeded in finding a match, or a mismatch is detected at some character $s[k-h]$ after matching the last h characters of the pattern:

$$p[1] \qquad \ldots p[m-h] \ldots p[m]$$
$$s[k-m+1] \qquad \ldots s[k-h] \ldots s[k] \ldots s[n]$$

$$\uparrow$$
mismatch

In the second case, it is necessary to shift the pattern down, ideally by as much as possible, and to resume matching at the next plausible position for matching.

55

Observation 3

If the character $s[k-h]$, which caused the mismatch, occurs in the pattern, the pattern can now be slid down by, say, g positions so as to align the two known occurrences of the character $s[k-h]$. Then the character in the string which is aligned with the last character in the pattern will be compared:

$$p[m-h-g] \ldots p[m-g] \ldots p[m]$$
$$s[1] \ldots \ldots s[k-h] \quad \ldots s[k] \quad \ldots s[k+g] \ldots \ldots s[n]$$
$$\uparrow$$
$$\text{resume matching}$$

($s[k-h]$ and $p[m-h-g]$ are identical).

Thus our attention is shifted down the string by $g + h$ positions. The distance g by which the pattern can be slid depends on where the character $s[k-h]$ occurs in the pattern. If the rightmost occurrence of the character corresponding to $s[k-h]$ in the pattern is to the right of the mismatched character (e.g. it occurs in that part of the pattern which has already been scanned) then by definition the pattern would have to be moved backwards to align the two known occurrences of the character corresponding to $s[k-h]$. This is obviously to be avoided and thus the pattern is slid down by $g=1$ positions (this is always sound). Thus our attention to the text string is shifted down by $1 + h$ positions. Applying this to the above example ($g=1$):

$$\ldots p[m-1] \quad p[m]$$
$$s[k-h] \ldots s[k] \qquad s[k+1] \ldots s[n]$$
$$\uparrow$$

On the other hand, if the rightmost occurrence of the character equivalent to $s[k-h]$ in the pattern is to the left of the mismatch, then we can slide forward by $g = r - h$ positions, where r comes from observations 1 and 2, to align the two known occurrences of the character causing the mismatch.

Thus observation 3 is concerned with shifting the pattern after mismatch has occurred at a character char, say, to align the two known occurrences of char in the pattern and string and then to resume matching from the rightmost end of the pattern with the corresponding character in the string.

This can be improved upon by considering not only the known (multiple) occurrences of a single character but also known occurrences of substrings of the text string in the pattern:

Observation 4

Having matched the last h characters of the pattern and reached a mismatch:

$$p[1] \qquad \ldots p[m-h] \ldots p[m]$$
$$\ldots s[k-m+1] \ldots s[k-h] \quad \ldots s[k] \ldots s[n]$$
$$\uparrow$$
$$\text{mismatch}$$

Then, by definition it is known that the final h characters of the pattern match with the next h characters of the text string (in left to right reading order). The last h characters of the pattern can be treated as a subpattern,

$$\text{subpatt} = p[m-h+1] \ldots p[m] \text{ , length } h$$

This occurrence of subpatt in the text string is preceded by a character, here $s[k-h]$, which is different from that character preceding the terminal occurrence of subpatt in the pattern, here $p[m-h]$. Then, by using roughly similar reasoning to that used in conjunction with observation 3, the next-to-last (rightmost) occurrence of subpatt can be located, if it exists, in the pattern. The pattern can then be slid down by some amount, g, say, so as to align this rightmost occurrence of the subpattern in the pattern which is not preceded by the character char, which caused the mismatch, with its terminal occurrence in the pattern $s[k-h] \ldots s[k]$. Thus:

$$p[1] \qquad \ldots p[m-h-g] \ldots p[m-g] \ldots p[m]$$
$$s[k+g-m+1] \quad \ldots s[k-h] \qquad \ldots s[k] \qquad \ldots s[k+g] \ldots s[n]$$
$$\uparrow$$
$$\text{resume matching}$$

This reoccurrence of subpatt in the pattern is known as a plausible reoccurrence. Thus now the character pointer to the string can be incremented by an amount $g + h$, so it will align the last character $p[m]$ of the pattern in the new patterns position, ready for the next character comparison.

   More precisely if the last h characters of the pattern have been matched before finding a mismatch, then the pattern can be moved down by g characters, where g is based on the position in the pattern of the rightmost plausible occurrence of the terminal substring of the pattern having h characters. After sliding down by g positions, the characters of the text string aligned with the last character of the pattern are compared. Thus in actuality we are moving down the string by $h + g$ characters, which allows for the h matched characters before the mismatch occurred. This distance is called R, and is defined as a function of the position j in the pattern at which mismatch occurred. g is simply the distance between the terminal occurrence of the subpattern and its rightmost plausible reoccurrence (if it exists) and is always greater than or equal to 1. h is simply the length of the pattern minus the index position at which mismatch occurred, i.e. that number of characters which have been matched before a mismatch occurs.

   Quite simply by observation 4 the pattern is shifted to the right so that the known occurrences of a subpattern occurring both in the string and (at least twice) in the pattern can be aligned. Scanning is then resumed from the far right of the pattern.

   Thus if the final h characters of the pattern have been matched before failing at $p[m-h]$ then we wish to slide the pattern to the right by an appropriate amount, and to increment the string pointer by $1+h$ or $r(\text{string}[k-h])$ or $R(j)$, whichever allows the largest shift (and therefore decreases the number of comparisons required). Matching can then be resumed with the last character of the pattern and the corresponding string character. By definition of $R (= h + g)$ it is obvious that $R(j)$ is always greater than or equal to $1 + h$, $g \geq 1$. Therefore the string pointer can simply be incremented by the maximum of the two shifts r and R.

Worked example

Consider the following example; it is used to illustrate how the preceding observations can be used to decrease (in the general case) the number of direct character comparisons:

```
pattern : AT-THAT

string  : WHICH-FINALLY-HALTS.--AT-THAT-POINT
                ↑

                mismatch
```

When the action of pattern matching is started the seventh character of the string, F, is compared with the last character of the pattern and fails. Since F is known not to appear anywhere in the pattern, by appealing to observation 1 the string pointer can be automatically incremented by 7:

```
pattern :        AT-THAT

string  : WHICH-FINALLY-HALTS.--AT-THAT-POINT
                      ↑

                      mismatch
```

The next comparison is of the hyphen in the string with the T in the pattern. They mismatch and by appealing to observation 2 the pattern can be moved down 4 positions to align the two hyphens. Scanning is then resumed from the right end of the pattern, comparing it directly with the corresponding string character directly below the pattern:

```
pattern :            AT-THAT

string  : WHICH-FINALLY-HALTS.--AT-THAT-POINT
                          ↑
```

The characters match and so the pointer is moved backwards through both the string and pattern character arrays:

```
pattern :            AT-THAT

string  : WHICH-FINALLY-HALTS.--AT-THAT-POINT
                         ↑

                         mismatch
```

A mismatch is detected and by observation 3 the string pointer can be moved to the right by 7 positions, since the character causing the mismatch, L, does not occur anywhere in the pattern:

```
pattern :                AT-THAT

string  : WHICH-FINALLY-HALTS.--AT-THAT-POINT
                             ↑
```

Again the corresponding characters of the string and pattern match, so the string pointer is moved backwards. The previous character in the text string matches with its corresponding character in the pattern and so the pointer is moved back again:

```
pattern :                    AT-THAT

string  : WHICH-FINALLY-HALTS.--AT-THAT-POINT
                                      ↑

                      mismatch
```

A mismatch is detected again and by now appealing to observation 4 the text pointer can be moved to the right by 7 places, so as to align the discovered substring AT with the beginning of the pattern:

```
pattern :                    AT-THAT

string  : WHICH-FINALLY-HALTS.--AT-THAT-POINT
                                 ↑
```

Scanning is now resumed, the characters are successfully compared and both the string and pattern pointers are decremented and the whole pattern is worked through character by character. Here it can be seen that each character in the pattern matches the corresponding character in the string and so the pattern has been found.

It is important to note that only 14 references to the text string were made, and of these 7 were required to confirm the actual match. The other 7 comparisons allowed the movement past the first 22 characters of the string, e.g. those preceding the first occurrence of the pattern.

A brief outline of the algorithm can now be sketched:

```
j = k = patlen;
repeat
    while not end of pattern or string
        if pattern[j] = string[k]
            j--; k--;
        else
            k = k + max(r(string[k]),R(j));
            j = patlen;
        endif
    endwhile
until string found or EOF
```

The implementation of algorithm 3 depends on the existence of two precomputed vectors which determine the values of r and R, the failure jumps. A more rigorous definition of the two string pointer incrementing functions can now be made.

The vector for the r values has an entry for each character in the alphabet being used, its entry is denoted for r(char) where char is some valid character. The precise definition is

$$r(char) = \{s \ (s=patlen) \ or$$
$$(\ 0<=s<patlen \ and \ pattern[patlen-s] = char) \ \}$$

If char does not occur in the pattern than r is the pattern length, otherwise it is the pattern length minus j, where j is the maximum integer such that pattern[j] = char.

This vector is derivable from observations 1 and 2. Assuming that g is the alphabet size the preprocessing for r requires an array of size q. The implementation sets up the vector in a linear scan (right to left) through the pattern. Thus the preprocessing for r is linear in patlen plus the size of the alphabet, $O(q+m)$.

The second vector, for the R values, has as many entries as there are character positions in the pattern.

To define R(j) precisely it is necessary to define the rightmost plausible reoccurrence of a terminal substring of the pattern. The following conventions are used : $ is a character that does not occur in the pattern and if i<0 then pattern[i] is $. Two sequences of characters c[0..n] and d[o..n] 'unify' if for all i from 0 to n either c[i]=d[i] or c[i]=$ or d[i]=$. The position of the rightmost plausible reoccurrence of the terminal substring, rpr(j), which starts at position j+1 is defined to be the greatest k less than or equal to patlen such that (pattern[j+1] .. pattern[patlen]) and (pattern[k]..pattern[k+patlen−j−1]) unify and either k<=0 or pattern[k−1]≠pattern[j], i.e. the position of rpr(j) is the rightmost place where subpatt occurs in the pattern and is not preceded by the character, pattern[j], which precedes its terminal occurrence. This position may be beyond the left end of the pattern, and consequently rpr(j) may be negative.

Thus the distance the pattern must be slid down to align the discovered substring (starting at j+1) with its rightmost plausible reoccurrence is j+1−rpr(j).

The pointer into the string must then be aligned with the last character in the pattern, i.e. moved patlen−j. Thus R(j), which is the sum of these two values, is defined as

$$R(j) = patlen + 1 - rpr(j)$$

In Reference 1 Knuth shows that there is an algorithm for setting up the vector for the R values in time linear in patlen, that is $O(m)$.

Example

pattern :	b	a	d	b	a	c	b	a	c	b	a
r :	1	0	8	1	0	2	1	0	2	1	0
R :	19	18	17	16	15	8	13	12	8	12	1

patlen = 11

In Reference 1 Knuth has also proved that the execution of the Boyer–Moore algorithm in the worst case is linear: $O(n+m)$, assuming the availability of array space linear in patlen plus the size of the alphabet. More specifically he shows that in order to discover that the pattern does not occur in the first p characters of the string a maximum of $6p$ characters from the string are matched with characters in the pattern.

In the average case, however, the algorithm is expected to behave sublinearly, that is the expected value of the number of inspected characters in the string is c*(i+patlen), where i is the index position of the leftmost character in the first occurrence of the pattern in the string, and c<1. By using the two precomputed vectors, which depend on the statistical properties of the characters in the pattern and the string, on average, not all the string characters preceding the first occurrence of the pattern in the string need to be inspected; the earlier worked example illustrates this.

Summarizing, the expected theoretical behaviour of algorithm 3 is sublinear, $<O(n+m)$, whereas the theoretical worst case behaviour is linear, $O(n+m)$. A further modification to this algorithm is described in the paper by Galil.[4]

Algorithm 4

This is an algorithm developed by R. M. Karp and O. M. Rabin. It is a brute-force approach to pattern matching which uses a large memory to advantage by treating each possible m-character section of the text string as a key in a standard hash table. In the actual implementation m is the length of the pattern being searched for. It does not use up as much memory as at first thought because it is not necessary to keep a whole hash table in memory, the problem being set up in such a way that only one key is being sought, that of the pattern. Thus all that is required is that the hash function of each possible m-character section of the text is in turn calculated and this is compared with the hash function of the pattern. This algorithm therefore really only finds the first m-character section in the text which has the same value as that of the pattern, so for preciseness, a direct comparison of that section of text and the pattern has then to be made.

On first thought it seems just as hard to compute the hash function for each m-character section from the text as it does to check to see if each character in the pattern is the same as in the text (algorithm 1). Rabin and Karp solved this problem by taking advantage of a fundamental mathematical property of the mod operation when using the hash function:

$$h(k) = k \bmod q$$

where k is the key to be hashed and q is the table size.

They based their method on computing the hash function for position i in the text string, given its hash value for position $i-1$. To facilitate the application of the hash function on an m-character section of text, each section was transformed into an integer key upon which the hashing function could then be performed. This was achieved by writing the characters as numerals in a base d number system, where d is the number of possible characters. Thus the numeral x corresponding to the m-character section string$[i]$ ... string$[i+m-1]$ is

$$x = \text{string}[i] \times d^{m-1} + \text{string}[i+1] \times d^{m-2} + \ldots + \text{string}[i+m-1]$$

This is derived by using the same method as with any numeric system; consider the representation of the number 345 in base 10. This is equivalent to

$$x = 3 \times 10^2 + 4 \times 10^1 + 5$$

Shifting by one position right in the text string, i.e. taking the section string$[i+1]$ ... string$[i+m]$, the value of x becomes

$$x = \text{string}[i+1] \times d^{m-1} + \text{string}[i+2] \times d^{m-2} + \ldots + \text{string}[i+m]$$

which is equivalent to replacing x by

$$(x - \text{string}[i] \times d^{m-1}) \times d + \text{string}[i+m]$$

Proof

$$((\text{string}[i] \times d^{m-1} + \ldots + \text{string}[i+m-1]) - \text{string}[i] \times d^{m-1}) \times d + \text{string}[i+m]$$

$$= (\text{string}[i+1] \times d^{m-2} + \ldots + \text{string}[i+m-1]) \times d + \text{string}[i+m]$$

$$= \text{string}[i+1] \times d^{m-1} + \ldots + \text{string}[i+m]$$

A fundamental property of the mod operation is that it can be performed at any time during the above operation and the result will still be the same; if we take the remainder when divided by q after each arithmetic operation then we arrive at the same answer that we would get if all the operations were to be performed and then the remainder when divided by q taken. Thus, assuming that the original value of $h(x) = x \bmod q$ is already known, then by shifting one position right in the text the new hashed value can easily be computed using the above property.

Algorithm 4 can now be outlined:

```
dm=1; h1=0; h2=0;
for i=0 .. patlen−2
    dm = (d*dm) mod q
for i=0 .. patlen−1
    h1 = (h1*d + rk(pattern[i])) mod q
for i=0 .. patlen−1
    h2 = (h2*d + rk(string[i])) mod q
i=0;
while not at end of string and h1!=h2
    h2 = (h2+d*q − rk(string[i])*dm) mod q
    h2 = (h2*d + rk(string[i])) mod q
    i++;
endwhile
```

rk(char) is a function which returns a unique integer for each character in the specified alphabet.

The algorithm first computes a hash value, h1, for the pattern and a hash value, h2, for the first m-character section of the text string and also the computed value $d^{m-1} \bmod q$ in the variable dm. Then the hashed value of each m-character section starting a position i for all possible values of i is computed, taking advantage of the associativity of the mod operation. Each new hash value of h2 is in turn compared with h1. If h1 and h2 have the same values, then the characters are directly compared, as a final check.

The table size q is chosen to be a very large prime, so that synonyms, that is keys which hash to the same value, can be avoided, but it is small enough so that overflow does not occur.

Intuitively the major drawback of this algorithm is that the computation of the hashed values of the m-character text string sections is quite expensive in terms of machine cycles—each value requires three multiplications, and so this investigation aims to show how its actual performance compares with the other three algorithms. The major advantage of this method is that it can easily be extended to image processing. It facilitates 'pattern matching' in two-dimensional patterns and text, which the other algorithms do not, and thus can be used in the field of computer graphics and pattern recognition.

In the very worst case, where each m-character section produces the same hash value, the algorithm would take $O(nm)$ steps, but because such a large value of q is used with the mod operations in the hashing functions the likelihood of a collision occurring is expected to be very small. Thus in the majority, if not all, of cases where there are no synonyms for the hashed value of the pattern except an identical m-character section, the number of hashing operations performed is obviously linear, and thus algorithm 4 is $O(m+n)$.

TESTING

The four algorithms were tested on various types of test data, with patterns of length 2 to 14. Each separate experiment consisted of finding the first occurrence of the pattern in the text string. Because it was intuitively thought that the performances of the algorithms depended upon the statistical properties of the pattern and the source string from which the test patterns were obtained, experiments were performed on five different source strings, each of length 32,000.

1. Binary strings

The first source string consisted of a random sequence of 0s and 1s. A program was written to randomly generate sequences of binary digits. As the program is called with an integer argument specifying the number of characters to be produced, this program was used to generate both the source string and the patterns.

2. Technical English

The second source string consisted of a piece of technical English from an on-line manual. The patterns were chosen at random from the manual, not all of them occurring in the test file.

3, 4. Random text

The third and fourth source strings consisted of random text from a given character set. A program was written to produce output text in which each character from a given character set has an equally likely chance of occurring. The program takes two arguments, the first specifies the number of characters to be produced, the second specifies the number of distinct characters allowable, the alphabet size. This program was also used to produce both the patterns and the source string.

For the experiments the third source string consisted of characters from a 15 character alphabet, and the fourth source string from a 35 character alphabet.

The range 0–32,767 (the maximum number of 16 bit integer quantities) was divided into a number of bands equal to the alphabet size; the text was then produced by supplying a unique seed to the system random number generator and the random numbers produced were divided by the number of bands. This was added to a base and, using ASCII codes, a random character was produced.

5. Pseudo-English text

The fifth source string consisted of characters that occur in the same frequency as they do in the English language. A program was written that took as input any specified text file, read it and computed the relative frequencies of each letter occuring in that file. These frequencies were then converted into probabilities, and characters were produced in a similar fashion to the above method. The relative frequencies of punctuation marks as well as letters are taken into account with this method. The limitation of this method to produce text is that the resulting text strings are only as 'English-like' as the input file supplied to the program. This program was used to produce both the source string and the patterns.

Measures of comparison

Each experiment consisted of finding the first occurrence (or non-occurrence) of the pattern in the source string. The pattern lengths were varied from 2 to 14, and five different source files were used. From each experiment the following variables were noted:
  (a) the pattern length
  (b) the number of comparisons made
  (c) the alphabet size from which the strings arose
  (d) the index position of the pattern in the string
  (e) the user time for the execution of each experiment.
Once the above measures had been collected, the problem of how to compare the performances of the algorithms arose. An independent measure was needed so that the performances could be compared fairly.

The first measure of comparison used was one of those suggested by Boyer and Moore,[2] the number of references made to the text string. To ensure that the measure was independent of the particular implementation of the algorithm concerned, the number of references to the string was divided by the number of characters occurring before the pattern (the index position of the pattern minus one) thus obtaining the number of inspected characters in the text string per character passed. These measures were then averaged for each pattern length over all the samples, for each source string in turn. These results are represented graphically (Figures 1–5).

The second measure of comparison was the actual time spent on execution of the algorithm. A system utility was used to measure the real time, the time spent in the system (e.g. executing system calls such as open or close a file etc.) and the time spent in execution of the command (user time). The CPU times are accurate to 1/60th of a second. As the programs were identical except for the actual code used to pattern match and the same set of patterns and source files were used with all the different algorithms it was deemed reasonable to allow a comparison on the user time. As with the first measure each separate experiment was timed and then averaged for each pattern length over each source string. These results are also represented graphically (Figure 6–10).

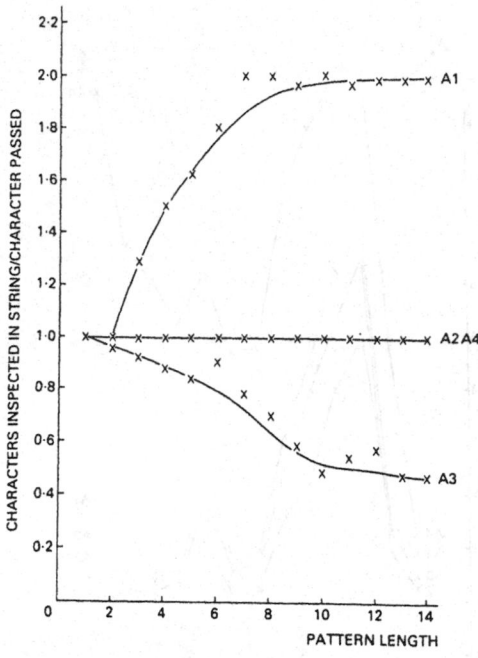

Figure 1. Binary text

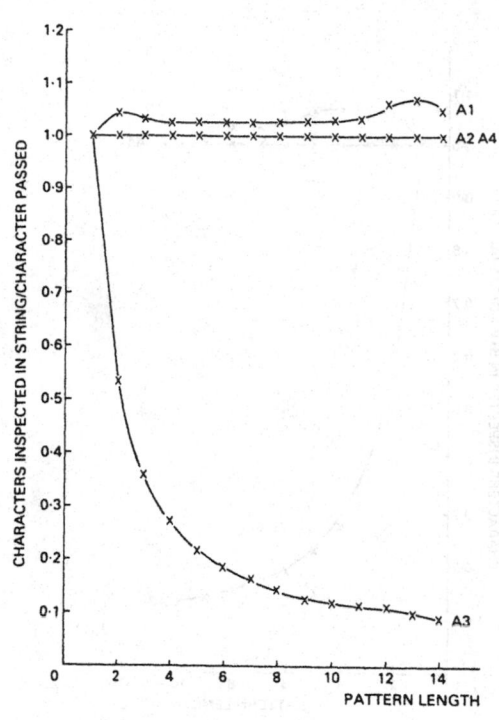

Figure 3. Random (35 character)

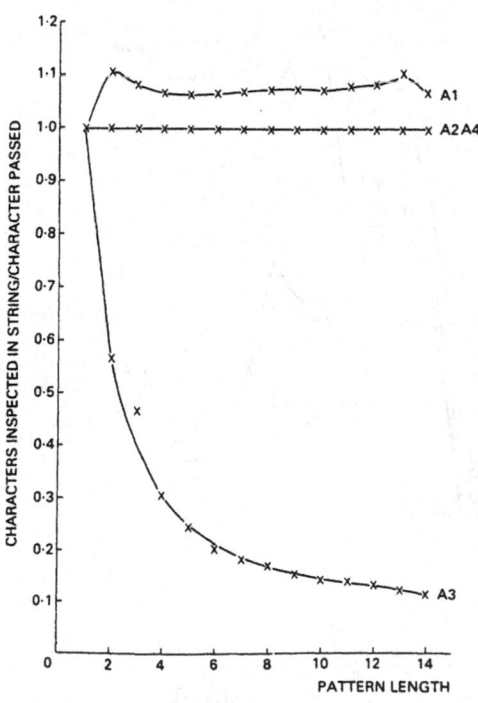

Figure 2. Random (15 character)

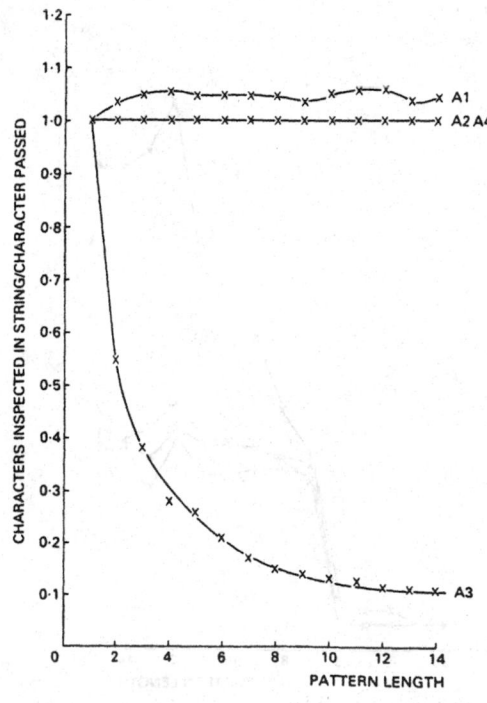

Figure 4. Technical English

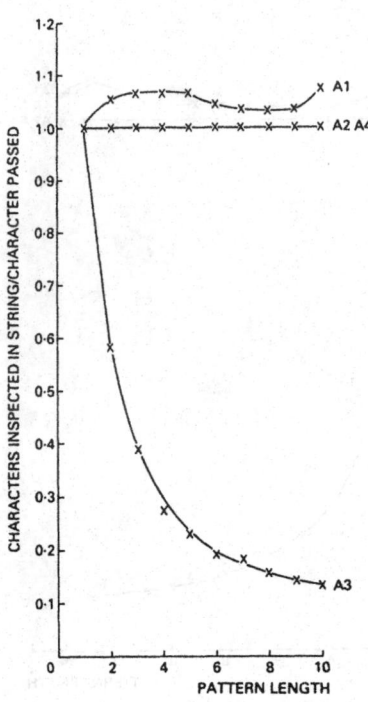

Figure 5. English-like text

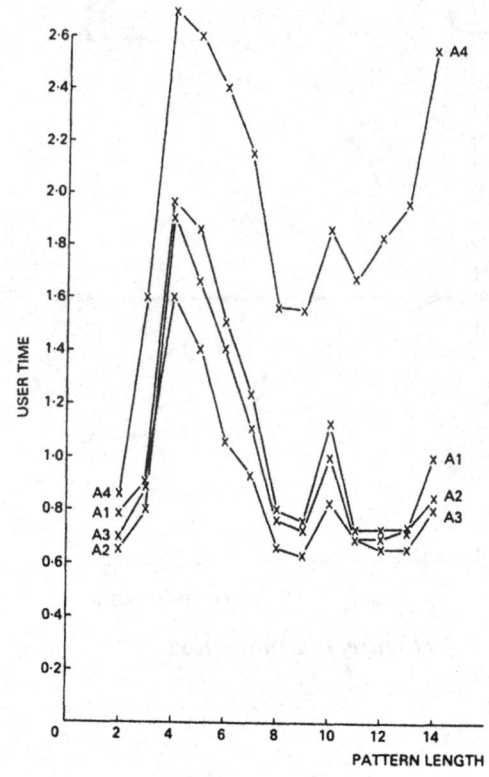

Figure 7. Random (15 character)

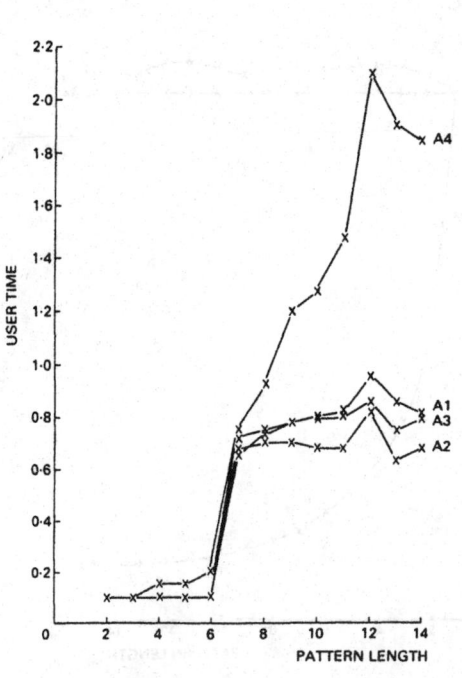

Figure 6. Binary text

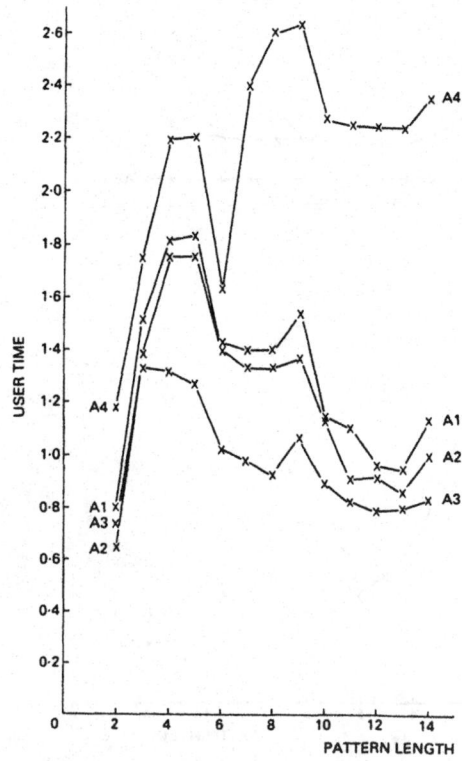

Figure 8. Random (35 character)

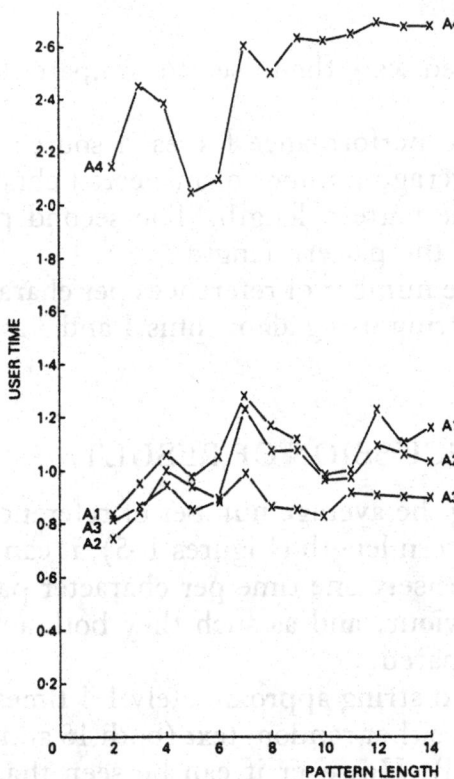

Figure 9. Technical English

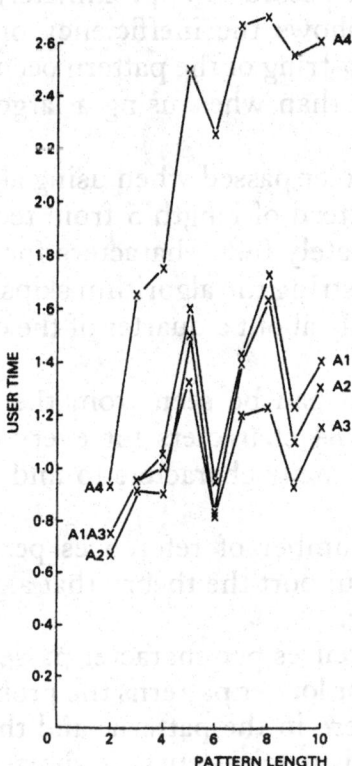

Figure 10. English-like text

Results

The two measures as described were then used to compare the relative performances of the algorithms.

To illustrate the comparative performance for each source string two graphs were drawn. The first plotted the average number of inspected characters in the text string per character passed against the pattern length. The second plotted the average user time for each algorithm against the pattern length.

Additional graphs plotting the number of references per character passed against each pattern length for each source string using algorithms 1 and 3 are also given (Figures 11 and 12).

DISCUSSION OF RESULTS

Referring to the graphs plotting the average number of references to the text string per character passed against the pattern length (Figures 1–5), it can be seen that algorithms 2 and 4 reference the string precisely one time per character passed. This corresponds exactly to their predicted behaviour, and as such they both act as standards to which algorithms 1 and 3 can be compared.

Algorithm 1 references the text string approximately 1·1 times per character passed if the source string is derived from either random text (both 15 and 35 character alphabets) or English (pseudo or technical). However it can be seen that this measure tends to increase if the source string and patterns are obtained from a binary alphabet. For patterns of length greater than six, from the empirical evidence, the average number of references to the string per character passed is approximately 2, double the number made by algorithms 2 and 4. This shows the inefficiency of algorithm 1. It occurs because the probability of an initial substring of the pattern occurring in the text is much greater with a two character alphabet than when using a larger alphabet, and so false starts occur.

The number of references per character passed when using algorithm 3 can be seen to be less than 1. For example, for a pattern of length 5 from technical English text, the algorithm typically inspects approximately 0·26 characters for every character passed. That is, for every reference to the text string the algorithm skips over about 4 characters, or equivalently algorithm 3 inspects only about a quarter of the characters it passes when searching for a pattern of length 5.

If a binary alphabet is used then it can be seen from the empirical evidence that algorithm 3 needs to inspect about 0·84 characters for every character passed, i.e. it needs to inspect three to four times as many characters to find a match as with English text.

It should also be noted that the number of references per character drops as the pattern length increases. The results support the theory that algorithm 3 is sublinear in the number of references to the string.

The reason why the number of references per character passed decreases more slowly as the pattern length increases is that for longer patterns the probability is higher that the character just fetched occurs somewhere in the pattern, and therefore the distance the pattern can be moved forward (if a mismatch occurs) is shortened.

It is also interesting to note that when using algorithm 3 the average number of references per character string passed when a binary alphabet is used is significantly

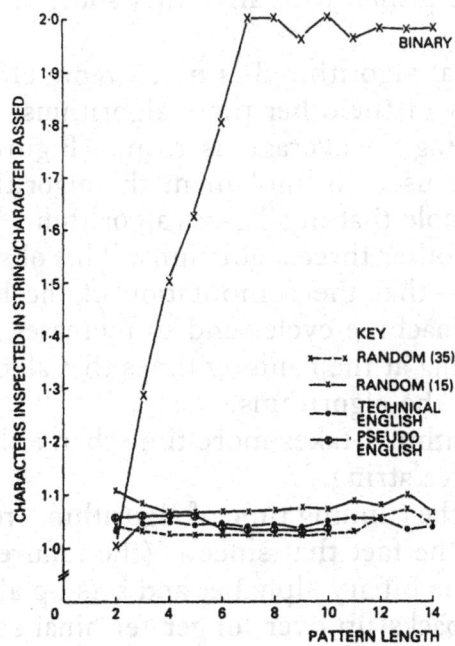

Figure 11. Algorithm 1

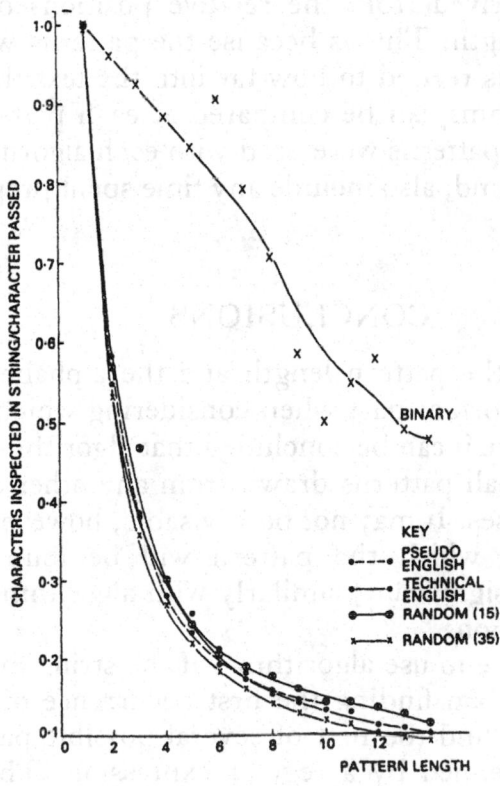

Figure 12. Algorithm 3

higher by a factor of about 4 or 5 than with any other source string for patterns greater than length 5.

In all cases it can be seen that algorithm 3 is much more efficient in terms of direct character comparisons than any of the other three algorithms.

Referring to the graphs plotting the average user time (Figures 6–10), i.e. time spent in execution of the actual code used to implement the algorithm, against the pattern length, it is immediately noticeable that in all cases algorithm 4 takes substantially more time to execute than any of the other three algorithms. This observation agrees with the intuitively expected behaviour—that the computation of the hash values is computationally expensive in terms of machine cycles and so increases the running time of the algorithm. It is clear from looking at the running times that algorithm 4 is not a feasible option if offered a choice of all the algorithms.

It can also be seen that algorithm 1 takes more time than either algorithm 2 or 3, on the whole, for any type of source string.

The comparative increase in the running time of algorithm 3 relative to algorithm 2 on binary strings is explained by the fact that since R (the failure vector concerned with subpatterns) predominates in the binary alphabet and sets up alignments of the pattern and the string, the algorithm backs up over longer terminal substrings of the pattern before finding mismatches. This is because there is a higher probability of subpatterns occurring in the text string.

Thus it can be seen that in the majority of cases, except when using either binary strings or small patterns, algorithm 3 has a faster running time than any of the other three algorithms.

Nothing can be deduced from the absolute shapes of the lines on the user time graph. Information can only be derived from the relative positions of the curves for each algorithm at each pattern length. This is because the patterns were chosen at random and obviously the user time is related to how far into the text the pattern occurs. The times for all the four algorithms can be compared at each pattern length because the same source string and set of patterns were used with each algorithm. The times, which are accurate to 1/60th of a second, also include any time spent preprocessing the pattern, as with algorithms 2 and 3.

CONCLUSIONS

The results show that both the pattern length and the alphabet size from which the strings are taken play an important part when considering which algorithm to use.

From the empirical evidence it can be concluded that algorithm 2 should be used with a binary alphabet or with small patterns drawn from any other alphabet. Algorithm 3 should be used in all other cases. It may not be advisable, however, to use algorithm 3 if the expected penetration at which the pattern will be found is small, since the preprocessing time becomes significant; similarly with algorithm 2, and so algorithm 1 would be better in this situation.

It would also be unadvisable to use algorithm 3 if the string matching problem to be solved is more complicated than finding the first occurrence of a single pattern. For instance if the problem is to find the first of several possible patterns or to identify a location in the text string defined by a regular expression. This is also because the preprocessing time would be significant.

In no case was algorithm 1 more efficient in terms of either character comparisons made or running time compared to algorithms 2 and 3. This shows that the computational effort required by algorithms 2 and 3 to preprocess the pattern is justified by an increase in performance.

Although algorithm 4 is linear in the number of references to the text string per character passed the substantially higher running time of this algorithm does not make it a feasible option when considering pattern matching in strings. The advantage of this algorithm over the other three lies in its extension to two-dimensional pattern matching. It can be used for pattern recognition and image processing and thus in the expanding field of computer graphics.

REFERENCES

1. D. E. Knuth, J. H. Morris and V. R. Pratt, 'Fast pattern matching in strings', *SIAM Journal of Computing,* **6**, (2), 323–350 (1977).
2. R. S. Boyer and J. S. Moore, 'A fast string searching algorithm', *Comm. ACM,* **20**, (10), 762–772 (1977).
3. R. Sedgewick, *Algorithms*, Addison-Wesley, pp. 252–253 (1983).
4. Z. Galil, 'On improving the worst-case running time of the Boyer–Moore string matching algorithm', *Comm. ACM,* **22**, (9), 505–508 (1979).

Chapter 2: Matching Sets of Keywords

Introduction

Some matching algorithms locate all occurrences of any of a finite number of keywords, or multiple patterns, in a string of text. The problems arise in bibliographic search, lexical analysis, code generation, term-rewriting, text retrieval, and natural language processing. For these problems a good survey is [Aho, 90]. Let K be a finite set of keywords and let x be an arbitrary text string. The problem is to locate and identify all substrings of x that are keywords in K and where substrings may overlap with one another. Such matching algorithms have a broader class of application fields than single keyword matching, but they differ from the single keyword matching algorithms in that the construction of matching machines needs more time. The algorithm by Aho and Corasick is a well-known technique for matching sets of keywords. The AC algorithm consists of constructing a finite state pattern matching machine from the keywords and then using the machine to process the text string in a single pass. Construction of the AC machine takes a time proportional to the sum of the lengths of the keywords. The AC algorithm can be applied to a multiple string replacement algorithm that replaces the longest first-found pattern by some word.

There are several improvements of the AC machines involving removal of the redundant operations and combining the shift table of the BM algorithm with the AC algorithm. Storing a transition table compactly and providing a constant-time access to its elements are important problems. Many techniques (such as perfect hashing and sparse table compression) for representing transition tables are introduced together with their references. Since variants of regular expressions are used to describe patterns in many text-processing systems, matching of regular expressions and the corresponding automaton approaches are introduced. In the rest of this chapter, repeated patterns and their related problems are also discussed along with the corresponding references.

A more efficient multiple pattern match algorithm that combines deterministic finite state automata (DFSA) and the BM algorithm is proposed. Actual experiments are held and the results show that in the average case this algorithm is able to perform pattern match operations sublinearly; that is, it does not need to inspect every character of the string to perform pattern match operations.

In this chapter the paper by Aho and Corasick (1975) provides an introduction to matching sets of keywords, and the next paper, by Aoe, Yamamoto, and Shimada (1984), presents one of the improvements. They present a technique for detecting the redundant operations of the AC machine and removing them. The third paper, by Fan and Su (1993), proposes an algorithm that combines deterministic finite state automata and the BM approach.

Aho-Corasick (AC) algorithm

The AC algorithm consists of constructing a finite state pattern matching machine from the keywords and then using the machine to process the text in a single pass. The behavior of the pattern matching machine is indicated by three functions: a goto function, g; a failure function, f; and an output function, *output*. Consider a set of keywords $K=\{hatch, he, heir, that, the, their, them\}$ based on [Aho et al., 75]. Figure 1 shows the functions, for K, used by the AC algorithm.

The goto function, g, maps a state-character pair into a state or message *fail*. The arc labeled a from s to r indicates that $g(s, a)=r$; the absence of an arrow indicates that $g(s, a)=fail$. In Figure 1a the arc labeled t from the initial state 0 is defined and points to state 1, thus confirming $g(0, t)=1$. The arc labeled a from state 0 is not defined, so $g(0, a)=fail$. The failure function, $f(s)$, is a state-to-state mapping. This function is consulted whenever the goto function reports a failure. $f(14)=7$, as in Figure 1b, indicates that matching is restarted from state 11 when matching is failed in state 4. Certain states are designated as output states, which indicate that a set of keywords has been found. The output function formalizes this concept by associating a subset of keywords (possibly empty) with every state.

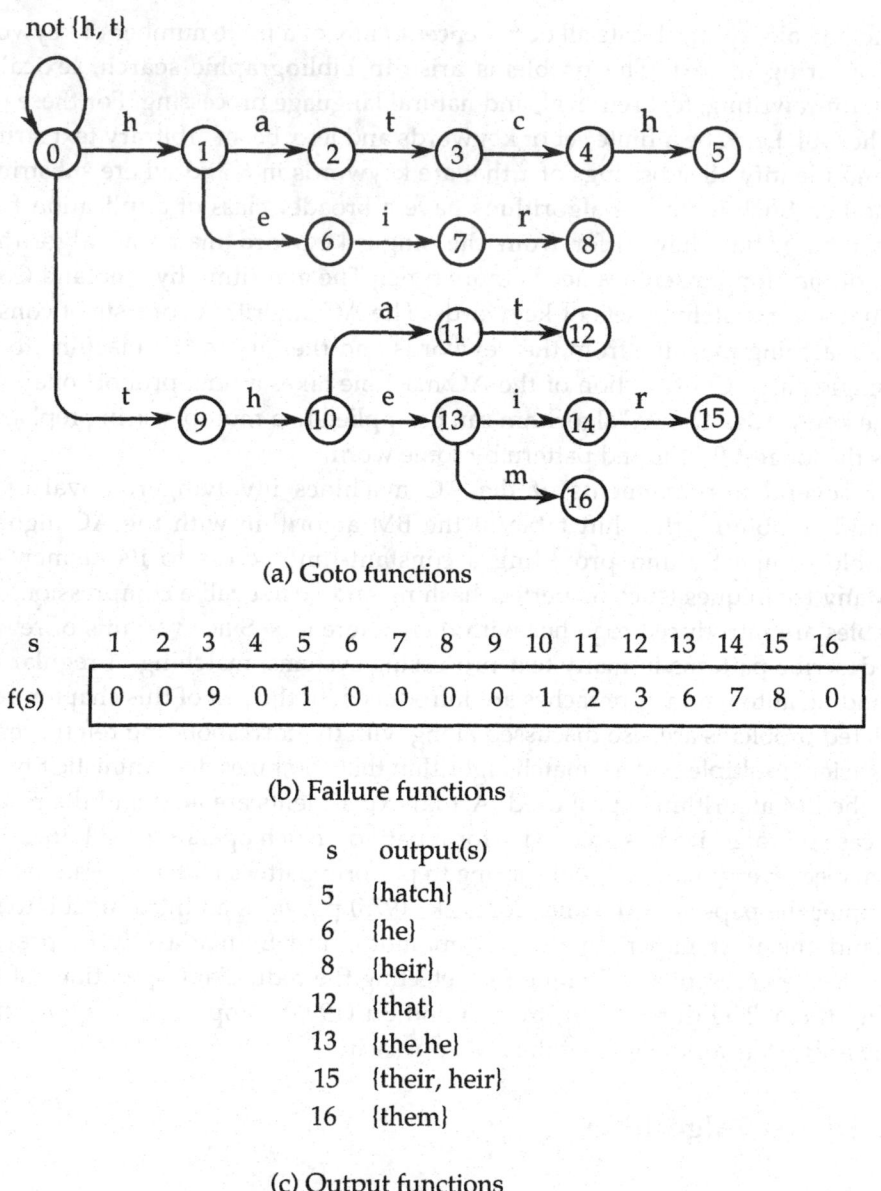

(a) Goto functions

s	1	2	3	4	5	6	7	8	9	10	11	12	13	14	15	16
f(s)	0	0	9	0	1	0	0	0	0	0	1	2	3	6	7	8	0

(b) Failure functions

s	output(s)
5	{hatch}
6	{he}
8	{heir}
12	{that}
13	{the,he}
15	{their, heir}
16	{them}

(c) Output functions

Figure 1. Functions of a pattern matching machine AC

Let s be the current state of the machine and a the current symbol of the input string, x. An operating cycle of the machine is defined as follows.

1. If $g(s, a)=s'$, the machine makes a goto transition. It enters state s', and the next symbol of x becomes the current input symbol. In addition, if $output(s')$ is not empty, the machine emits the set $output(s')$ along with the position of the current input symbol. The operating cycle is now complete.

2. If $g(s, a)=fail$, the machine consults the failure function, f, and is said to make a failure transition. If $f(s)=s'$, the machine repeats the cycle with s' as the current state and a as the current input symbol.

Consider the text string *thatche*. The following is a sequence of state transitions.

$$g(0,t) = 9 \rightarrow g(9,h) = 10 \rightarrow g(10,a) = 11 \rightarrow g(11,t) = 12 \rightarrow$$
$$g(12,c) = \text{fail} \rightarrow f(12) = 3 \rightarrow g(3,c) = 4 \rightarrow g(4,h) = 5 \rightarrow$$
$$g(5,e) = \text{fail} \rightarrow f(5) = 1 \rightarrow g(1,e) = 6.$$

In state 5 the machine emits output(5), indicating that it has found the keywords *hatch* at the end of position seven in the text string.

Construction of the machine by the AC algorithm takes a time proportional to the sum of the lengths of the keywords. The number of state transitions made by the pattern matching machine in processing the text string is independent of the number of keywords.

Bloch ([Bloch, 89]) has determined the relationships among the AC algorithm and its variants and evaluated their performance by theoretical and experimental observations. In the early 1970's the AC algorithm was used to improve the speed of a library bibliographic search program by a factor from 5 to 10 and to implement a keyword-matching program, fgrep, of Unix. The AC algorithm is applied to matching in trees in [Aho et al., 89] and [Hoffman et al., 82]. The usage of the AC algorithm for two-dimensional pattern matching has been described in [Ben-Yehuda et al, 89] and [Zhu et al., 89]. It is very difficult to apply the AC technique to Japanese texts because of the different kinds of characters (including Chinese, Katakana, and Latin). The Arikawa group ([Arikawa et al., 84a], [Arikawa, et al. 88], and [Shinohara et al., 86]) has developed Japanese text database systems by extending the goto graph based on the AC algorithm to Japanese texts.

Arikawa et al. ([Arikawa et al., 84b]) have presented a technique of replacing multiple strings by modifying the AC algorithm and using the idea of patterns with pictures. Takeda ([Takeda, 89]) has proposed a multiple string replacing algorithm that replaces the longest first-found pattern by the corresponding word. Tsuda et al. ([Tsuda et al., 92a] and [Tsuda et al., 92b]) have proposed a nonbacktracking multiple string-replacing algorithm and used it for a proofreading system of Japanese texts.

Improvement of the AC algorithm

Kanbayashi et al. ([Kanbayashi et al., 79]) have accelerated pattern matching by reusing the previous matching results when the test is invariant. Commentz-Walter ([Commentz-Walter, 79]) has combined the shift table of the BM algorithm with the AC algorithm. The CW algorithm first builds a trie[†] structure for the set of keywords reversed and computes the shift tables from the tree. In the case of small numbers of keywords, the CW algorithm becomes faster than the AC algorithm. Aoe et al. ([Aoe et al., 84a] and [Aoe, 91a]) have found out the redundant operations of the AC machine and presented a technique for removing these operations from the machine. The matching algorithm and the data structure of the transition table are partitioned into several cases by combining these characteristics. Consequently, each operation corresponding to the states is able to use the most effective instruction stream and data structure.

[†]The etymology of *"trie"* is the middle part of the word *"retrieval"*, and pronunciation of *"trie"* is the same as the word *"try"*, in order to distinguish it from *"tree."*

A more efficient multiple pattern match algorithm is proposed in [Fan et al., 93] that combines deterministic finite state automata (DFSA) and the BM algorithm. Actual experiments are held, and the result shows that in the average case this algorithm performs pattern match operations sublinearly; that is, it does not need to inspect every character of the string to perform pattern match operations.

Data structure of state transition tables

Pattern matching occupies a reasonable portion of the application systems, since it is the only process that must look at the input one character at a time. How to store a transition table compactly and how to provide constant-time access to its elements are very important problems. The goto function of the AC algorithm can be stored in a two-dimensional array, allowing us to determine the value of $g(s, a)$ in constant time for each s and a. If the size of the input alphabet and the keyword set are large, however, it is far more economical to store the nonfail values in a linear list for each state ([Knuth, 73], [Aho et al., 74]). Aho et al. ([Aho et al., 75]) have suggested storing the most frequently used states (such as state 0) as direct access tables in which the next state can be determined by indexing directly into the table with the current input symbol. Then for the most frequently used states we can determine $g(s, a)$ for each a in constant time. Less frequently used states and states with few nonfail values of the goto function can be encoded as linear lists.

Perfect hashing approaches of [Fredman et al., 84], [Aho et al., 86a], and [Dietzfelbinger et al., 88] are useful for a compact representation of the transition tables. The other way to represent the goto function is to compress a two-dimensional form. Tarjan et al. ([Tarjan et al., 79]) have presented a row displacement approach of reducing sparse tables, and Aoe ([Aoe et al., 84b]) have proposed a reduction algorithm of sparse matrices using consecutive elements. It is easy to apply these algorithms to the reduction of transition tables, but these approaches are more suitable for static tables. On the other hand, Aoe ([Aoe, 91b]) has proposed a dynamic technique of reducing tables using row displacements. The double-array structure, by [Aoe et al., 85], [Aoe, 89a], [Aoe, 89b], and [Aoe et al., 92], is a good representation of static and dynamic sparse transition tables. An alternative to creating a transition table is to generate machine codes directly to simulate the automaton as in [Pennello, 86] and [Thompson, 68].

The incremental construction of the AC machine is in [Meyer, 85], but his approach needs extra space for the strings from the initial state to some specified states. More general dynamic construction of the AC machine, using only reverse failure functions, is in [Tsuda et al., 94].

Related problems

A more efficient technique for finding repeated patterns is to construct a compact index to all the distinct substrings of a set of strings in linear time ([Weiner, 73]). The Karp-Miller-Rosenberg algorithm([Karp et al., 72]) was one of the first efficient (almost linear) sequential algorithms for finding repeated patterns and for string matching. The KMR algorithm must be considered a basic technique in parallel computations. It also gives a general unifying framework for a large variety of problems, such as the longest repeated factor and the maximal symmetric factor. There are many variants of this index, such as position trees ([Aho et al., 74], [Majester et al., 80], and [Kemp et al., 87]), subword trees ([Apostolico, 85], and [Chen et al., 85]), complete inverted files ([Blumer et al., 84a], [Blumer et al., 84b], [Blumer et al., 85], and [Blumer et al., 87]), PATRICIA trees ([Morrison, 68]), suffix trees ([Chrochemore, 86], [McCreight, 76], and [Rodeh et al., 81]), parallel computations ([Cochemore et al., 90]), and minimal suffix automata ([Perrin, 90]). A simple fingerprinting algorithm is given in [Rabin, 85].

Algorithms finding all squares, that is, all substrings of the form xx with x nonempty, are discussed in [Apostolico et al., 83], [Crochemore, 81], [Main et al., 84], and [Main et al., 85]. Palindromes, which are strings of the form xx^Ry with x nonempty, can be recognized by a 2DPDA; algorithms for finding palindromes in strings are described in [Galil, 76], [Galil, 81], [Galil et al., 78], [Galil et al., 80], [Galil et al., 83], [Garey et al., 79], [Manacher, 75], [Seiferas et al., 77] and [Slisenko, 83].

Lee et al. ([Lee et al., 90]) have applied the AC method to an efficient and flexible indexing mechanism for retrieving design objects that possess similar design features as described by the user. Sridhar ([Sridhar, 90]) discusses augmentation of the AC machine with a new pattern string both online and offline.

Theoretical consideration concerning the relative succinctness of different notations for regular sets is discussed in [Hartmanis, 80] and [Meyer et al., 71]. Some variants of the regular expression matching are used by awk ([Aho et al., 88]), egrep ([McIlroy, 86]), and lex ([Lesk, 75]) on Unix. The SNOBOL programming language ([Farber et al., 64]) and Unix commands ed and grep ([McIlroy, 86] and [Hume, 88]) have added back referencing, which specifies repeated string operators as regular expressions. Algorithms for generating deterministic finite automata from regular expressions are discussed in [Aho et al., 86b], [Thompson, 68], and [Berry et al., 86]. Pattern matching in writing tools, term-rewriting systems, and editors is discussed in [Cherry, 82], [Huet et al., 80], and [Julian et al., 82]. Extending the KMP method to efficient pattern matchers for finite trees (Prolog terms with variables), for Boolean algebra, and for finite sets is described in [Smith, 91]. Structured pattern matching by Forth is developed in [Scolnicov, 92].

Programming
Techniques

Glenn Manacher
Editor

Efficient String Matching: An Aid to Bibliographic Search

Alfred V. Aho and Margaret J. Corasick
Bell Laboratories

This paper describes a simple, efficient algorithm to locate all occurrences of any of a finite number of keywords in a string of text. The algorithm consists of constructing a finite state pattern matching machine from the keywords and then using the pattern matching machine to process the text string in a single pass. Construction of the pattern matching machine takes time proportional to the sum of the lengths of the keywords. The number of state transitions made by the pattern matching machine in processing the text string is independent of the number of keywords. The algorithm has been used to improve the speed of a library bibliographic search program by a factor of 5 to 10.

Keywords and Phrases: keywords and phrases, string pattern matching, bibliographic search, information retrieval, text-editing, finite state machines, computational complexity.

CR Categories: 3.74, 3.71, 5.22, 5.25

Reprinted from *Communications of the ACM*, Volume 18, No. 6, June 1975, pp. 333-340. Copyright 1975, Association for Computing Machinery, Inc., reprinted by permission.

Authors' present addresses: A. V. Aho, Bell Laboratories, Murray Hill, N.J. 07974. M. J. Corasick, The MITRE Corporation, Bedford, Mass. 01730.

1. Introduction

In many information retrieval and text-editing applications it is necessary to be able to locate quickly some or all occurrences of user-specified patterns of words and phrases in text. This paper describes a simple, efficient algorithm to locate all occurrences of any of a finite number of keywords and phrases in an arbitrary text string.

The approach should be familiar to those acquainted with finite automata. The algorithm consists of two parts. In the first part we construct from the set of keywords a finite state pattern matching machine; in the second part we apply the text string as input to the pattern matching machine. The machine signals whenever it has found a match for a keyword.

Using finite state machines in pattern matching applications is not new [4, 8, 17], but their use seems to be frequently shunned by programmers. Part of the reason for this reluctance on the part of programmers may be due to the complexity of programming the conventional algorithms for constructing finite automata from regular expressions [3, 10, 15], particularly if state minimization techniques are needed [2, 14]. This paper shows that an efficient finite state pattern matching machine can be constructed quickly and simply from a restricted class of regular expressions, namely those consisting of finite sets of keywords. Our approach combines the ideas in the Knuth-Morris-Pratt algorithm [13] with those of finite state machines.

Perhaps the most interesting aspect of this paper is the amount of improvement the finite state algorithm gives over more conventional approaches. We used the finite state pattern matching algorithm in a library bibliographic search program. The purpose of the program is to allow a bibliographer to find in a citation index all titles satisfying some Boolean function of keywords and phrases. The search program was first implemented with a straightforward string matching algorithm. Replacing this algorithm with the finite state approach resulted in a program whose running time was a fifth to a tenth of the original program on typical inputs.

2. A Pattern Matching Machine

This section describes a finite state string pattern matching machine that locates keywords in a text string. The next section describes the algorithms to construct such a machine from a given finite set of keywords.

In this paper a *string* is simply a finite sequence of symbols. Let $K = \{y_1, y_2, \ldots, y_k\}$ be a finite set of strings which we shall call *keywords* and let x be an arbitrary string which we shall call the *text string*. Our problem is to locate and identify all substrings of x which are keywords in K. Substrings may overlap with one another.

A pattern matching machine for K is a program which takes as input the text string x and produces as output the locations in x at which keywords of K appear as substrings. The pattern matching machine consists of a set of *states*. Each state is represented by a number. The machine processes the text string x by successively reading the symbols in x, making state transitions and occasionally emitting output. The behavior of the pattern matching machine is dictated by three functions: a goto function g, a failure function f, and an output function *output*.

Figure 1 shows the functions used by a pattern matching machine for the set of keywords {he, she, his, hers}.

Fig. 1. Pattern matching machine.

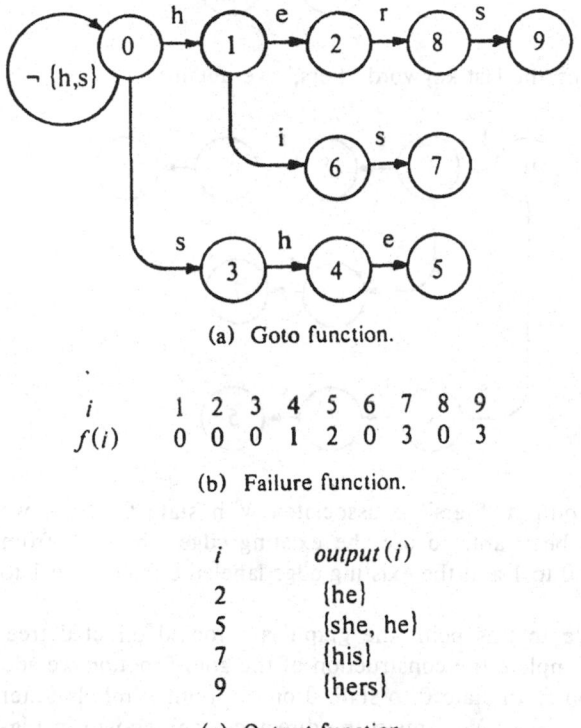

(a) Goto function.

i	1	2	3	4	5	6	7	8	9
$f(i)$	0	0	0	1	2	0	3	0	3

(b) Failure function.

i	$output(i)$
2	{he}
5	{she, he}
7	{his}
9	{hers}

(c) Output function.

One state (usually 0) is designated as a *start* state. In Figure 1 the states are 0, 1, . . . , 9. The goto function g maps a pair consisting of a state and an input symbol into a state or the message *fail*. The directed graph in Figure 1(a) represents the goto function. For example, the edge labeled h from 0 to 1 indicates that $g(0, h) = 1$. The absence of an arrow indicates *fail*. Thus, $g(1, \sigma) = fail$ for all input symbols σ that are not e or i. All our pattern matching machines have the property that $g(0, \sigma) \neq fail$ for all input symbols σ. We shall see that this property of the goto function on state 0 ensures that one input symbol will be processed by the machine in every machine cycle.

The failure function f maps a state into a state. The failure function is consulted whenever the goto function reports *fail*. Certain states are designated as output states which indicate that a set of keywords has been found. The output function formalizes this concept by associating a set of keywords (possibly empty) with every state.

An *operating cycle* of a pattern matching machine is defined as follows. Let s be the current state of the machine and a the current symbol of the input string x.

1. If $g(s, a) = s'$, the machine makes a *goto transition*. It enters state s' and the next symbol of x becomes the current input symbol. In addition, if

output$(s') \neq empty$, then the machine emits the set *output*(s') along with the position of the current input symbol. The operating cycle is now complete.

2. If $g(s, a) = fail$, the machine consults the failure function f and is said to make a *failure transition*. If $f(s) = s'$, the machine repeats the cycle with s' as the current state and a as the current input symbol.

Initially, the current state of the machine is the start state and the first symbol of the text string is the current input symbol. The machine then processes the text string by making one operating cycle on each symbol of the text string.

For example, consider the behavior of the machine M that uses the functions in Figure 1 to process the text string "ushers." Figure 2 indicates the state transitions made by M in processing the text string.

Fig. 2. Sequence of state transitions.

```
u  s  h  e  r  s
0  0  3  4  5  8  9
               2
```

Consider the operating cycle when M is in state 4 and the current input symbol is e. Since $g(4, e) = 5$, the machine enters state 5, advances to the next input symbol and emits *output*(5), indicating that it has found the keywords "she" and "he" at the end of position four in the text string.

In state 5 on input symbol r, the machine makes two state transitions in its operating cycle. Since $g(5, r) = fail$, M enters state 2 = $f(5)$. Then since $g(2, r) = 8$, M enters state 8 and advances to the next input symbol. No output is generated in this operating cycle.

The following algorithm summarizes the behavior of a pattern matching machine.

Algorithm 1. Pattern matching machine.
Input. A text string $x = a_1 a_2 \cdots a_n$ where each a_i is an input symbol and a pattern matching machine M with goto function g, failure function f, and output function *output*, as described above.
Output. Locations at which keywords occur in x.
Method.

```
begin
    state ← 0
    for i ← 1 until n do
        begin
            while g(state, aᵢ) = fail do state ← f(state)
            state ← g(state, aᵢ)
            if output(state) ≠ empty then
                begin
                    print i
                    print output(state)
                end
        end
end
```

Each pass through the **for**-loop represents one operating cycle of the machine.

79

Algorithm 1 is patterned after the Knuth-Morris-Pratt algorithm for finding one keyword in a text string [13] and can be viewed as an extension of the "trie" search discussed in [11]. Hopcroft and Karp (unpublished) have suggested a scheme similar to Algorithm 1 for finding the first occurrence of any of a finite set of keywords in a text string [13]. Section 6 of this paper discusses a deterministic finite automaton version of Algorithm 1 that avoids all failure transitions.

3. Construction of Goto, Failure, and Output Functions

We say that the three functions g, f, and *output* are *valid* for a set of keywords if with these functions Algorithm 1 indicates that keyword y ends at position i of text string x if and only if $x = uyv$ and the length of uy is i.

We shall now show how to construct valid goto, failure and output functions from a set of keywords. There are two parts to the construction. In the first part we determine the states and the goto function. In the second part we compute the failure function. The computation of the output function is begun in the first part of the construction and completed in the second part.

To construct the goto function, we shall construct a *goto graph*. We begin with a graph consisting of one vertex which represents the state 0. We then enter each keyword y into the graph, by adding a directed path to the graph that begins at the start state. New vertices and edges are added to the graph so that there will be, starting at the start state, a path in the graph that spells out the keyword y. The keyword y is added to the output function of the state at which the path terminates. We add new edges to the graph only when necessary.

For example, suppose {he, she, his, hers} is the set of keywords. Adding the first keyword to the graph, we obtain:

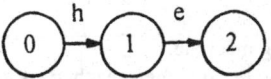

The path from state 0 to state 2 spells out the keyword "he"; we associate the output "he" with state 2. Adding the second keyword "she," we obtain the graph:

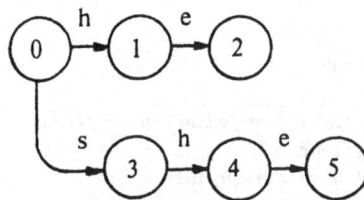

The output "she" is associated with state 5. Adding the keyword "his," we obtain the following graph. Notice that when we add the keyword "his" there is already an edge labeled h from state 0 to state 1, so we do not need to add another edge labeled h from state 0 to state 1. The output "his" is associated with state 7.

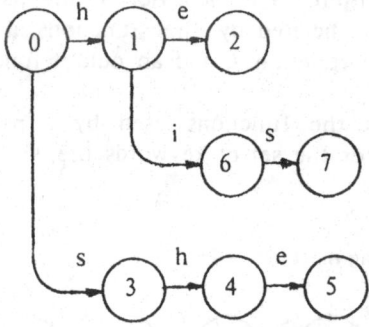

Adding the last keyword "hers," we obtain:

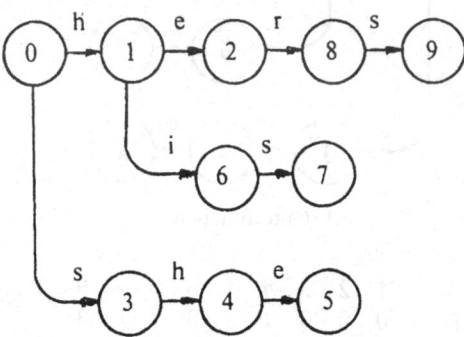

The output "hers" is associated with state 9. Here we have been able to use the existing edge labeled h from state 0 to 1 and the existing edge labeled e from state 1 to 2.

Up to this point the graph is a rooted directed tree. To complete the construction of the goto function we add a loop from state 0 to state 0 on all input symbols other than h or s. We obtain the directed graph shown in Figure 1(a). This graph represents the goto function.

The failure function is constructed from the goto function. Let us define the *depth* of a state s in the goto graph as the length of the shortest path from the start state to s. Thus in Figure 1(a), the start state is of depth 0, states 1 and 3 are of depth 1, states 2, 4, and 6 are of depth 2, and so on.

We shall compute the failure function for all states of depth 1, then for all states of depth 2, and so on, until the failure function has been computed for all states (except state 0 for which the failure function is not defined). The algorithm to compute the failure function f at a state is conceptually quite simple. We make $f(s) = 0$ for all states s of depth 1. Now suppose f has been computed for all states of depth less than d. The failure function for the states of depth d is computed from the failure function for the states of depth less than d. The states of depth d can be determined from the nonfail values of the goto function of the states of depth $d-1$.

Specifically, to compute the failure function for the states of depth d, we consider each state r of depth $d-1$ and perform the following actions.

1. If $g(r, a) = fail$ for all a, do nothing.

2. Otherwise, for each symbol a such that $g(r, a) = s$, do the following:

(a) Set $state = f(r)$.

(b) Execute the statement $state \leftarrow f(state)$ zero or more times, until a value for $state$ is obtained such that $g(state, a) \neq fail$. (Note that since $g(0, a) \neq fail$ for all a, such a state will always be found.)

(c) Set $f(s) = g(state, a)$.

For example, to compute the failure function from Figure 1(a), we would first set $f(1) = f(3) = 0$ since 1 and 3 are the states of depth 1. We then compute the failure function for 2, 6, and 4, the states of depth 2. To compute $f(2)$, we set $state = f(1) = 0$; and since $g(0, e) = 0$, we find that $f(2) = 0$. To compute $f(6)$, we set $state = f(1) = 0$; and since $g(0, i) = 0$, we find that $f(6) = 0$. To compute $f(4)$, we set $state = f(3) = 0$; and since $g(0, h) = 1$, we find that $f(4) = 1$. Continuing in this fashion, we obtain the failure function shown in Figure 1(b).

During the computation of the failure function we also update the output function. When we determine $f(s) = s'$, we merge the outputs of state s with the outputs of state s'.

For example, from Figure 1(a) we determine $f(5) = 2$. At this point we merge the output set of state 2, namely {he}, with the output set of state 5 to derive the new output set {he, she}. The final nonempty output sets are shown in Figure 1(c).

The algorithms to construct the goto, failure and output functions from K are summarized below.

Algorithm 2. Construction of the goto function.
Input. Set of keywords $K = \{y_1, y_2, \ldots, y_k\}$.
Output. Goto function g and a partially computed output function $output$.
Method. We assume $output(s)$ is empty when state s is first created, and $g(s, a) = fail$ if a is undefined or if $g(s, a)$ has not yet been defined. The procedure $enter(y)$ inserts into the goto graph a path that spells out y.

```
begin
    newstate ← 0
    for i ← 1 until k do enter(yᵢ)
    for all a such that g(0, a) = fail do g(0, a) ← 0
end
```

```
procedure enter(a₁ a₂ ··· aₘ):
begin
    state ← 0; j ← 1
    while g(state, aⱼ) ≠ fail do
        begin
            state ← g(state, aⱼ)
            j ← j + 1
        end
    for p ← j until m do
        begin
            newstate ← newstate + 1
            g(state, aₚ) ← newstate
            state ← newstate
        end
    output(state) ← {a₁ a₂ ··· aₘ}
end
```

The following algorithm, whose inner loop is similar to Algorithm 1, computes the failure function.

Algorithm 3. Construction of the failure function.
Input. Goto function g and output function $output$ from Algorithm 2.
Output. Failure function f and output function $output$.
Method.

```
begin
    queue ← empty
    for each a such that g(0, a) = s ≠ 0 do
        begin
            queue ← queue ∪ {s}
            f(s) ← 0
        end
    while queue ≠ empty do
        begin
            let r be the next state in queue
            queue ← queue − {r}
            for each a such that g(r, a) = s ≠ fail do
                begin
                    queue ← queue ∪ {s}
                    state ← f(r)
                    while g(state, a) = fail do state ← f(state)
                    f(s) ← g(state, a)
                    output(s) ← output(s) ∪ output(f(s))
                end
        end
end
```

The first for-loop computes the states of depth 1 and enters them in a first-in first-out list denoted by the variable $queue$. The main while-loop computes the set of states of depth d from the set of states of depth $d-1$.

The failure function produced by Algorithm 3 is not optimal in the following sense. Consider the pattern matching machine M of Figure 1. We see $g(4, e) = 5$. If M is in state 4 and the current input symbol a_i is not an e, then M would enter state $f(4) = 1$. Since M has already determined that $a_i \neq$ e, M does not then need to consider the value of the goto function of state 1 on e. In fact, if the keyword "his" were not present, then M could go directly from state 4 to state 0, skipping an unnecessary intermediate transition to state 1.

To avoid making unnecessary failure transitions we can use f', a generalization of the $next$ function from [13], in place of f in Algorithm 1. Specifically, define $f'(1) = 0$. For $i > 1$, define $f'(i) = f'(f(i))$ if, for all input symbols a, $g(f(i), a) \neq fail$ implies $g(i, a) \neq fail$; define $f'(i) = f(i)$, otherwise. However, to avoid making any failure transitions at all, we can use the deterministic finite automaton version of Algorithm 1 given in Section 6.

4. Properties of Algorithms 1, 2, and 3

This section shows that the goto, failure, and output functions constructed by Algorithms 2 and 3 from a given set of keywords K are indeed valid for K.

We say that u is a *prefix* and v is a *suffix* of the string uv. If u is not the empty string, then u is a *proper* prefix. Likewise, if v is not empty, then v is a *proper* suffix.

We say that string u *represents* state s of a pattern matching machine if the shortest path in the goto graph from the start state to state s spells out u. The start state is represented by the empty string.

Our first lemma characterizes the failure function constructed by Algorithm 3.

LEMMA 1. *Suppose that in the goto graph state s is represented by the string u and state t is represented by the string v. Then, $f(s) = t$ if and only if v is the longest proper suffix of u that is also a prefix of some keyword.*

PROOF. The proof proceeds by induction on the length of u (or equivalently the depth of state s). By Algorithm 3 $f(s) = 0$ for all states s of depth 1. Since each state of depth 1 is represented by a string of length 1, the statement of the lemma is trivially true for all strings of length 1.

For the inductive step, assume the statement of Lemma 1 is true for all strings of length less than j, $j > 1$. Suppose $u = a_1 a_2 \cdots a_j$ for some $j > 1$, and v is the longest proper suffix of u that is a prefix of some keyword. Suppose u represents state s and $a_1 a_2 \cdots a_{j-1}$ represents state r. Let $r_1, r_2, \cdots, r_n$ be the sequence of states such that

1. $r_1 = f(r)$,
2. $r_{i+1} = f(r_i)$ for $1 \leqslant i < n$,
3. $g(r_i, a_j) = fail$ for $1 \leqslant i < n$, and
4. $g(r_n, a_j) = t \neq fail$.

(If $g(r_1, a_j) \neq fail$, then $r_n = r_1$.) The sequence $r_1, r_2, \cdots, r_n$ is the sequence of values assumed by the variable *state* in the inner **while**-loop of Algorithm 3. The statement following that **while**-loop makes $f(s) = t$. We claim that t is represented by the longest proper suffix of u that is a prefix of some keyword.

To prove this, suppose v_i represents state r_i for $1 \leqslant i \leqslant n$. By the inductive hypothesis v_1 is the longest proper suffix of $a_1 a_2 \cdots a_{j-1}$ that is a prefix of some keyword; v_2 is the longest proper suffix of v_1 that is a prefix of some keyword; v_3 is the longest proper suffix of v_2 that is a prefix of some keyword, and so on.

Thus v_n is the longest proper suffix of $a_1 a_2 \cdots a_{j-1}$ such that $v_n a_j$ is a prefix of some keyword. Therefore $v_n a_j$ is the longest proper suffix of u that is a prefix of some keyword. Since Algorithm 3 sets $f(s) = g(r_n, a_j) = t$, the proof is complete. $\square$

The next lemma characterizes the output function constructed by Algorithms 2 and 3.

LEMMA 2. *The set output (s) contains y if and only if y is a keyword that is a suffix of the string representing state s.*

PROOF. In Algorithm 2 whenever we add to the goto graph a state s that is represented by a keyword y we make $output(s) = \{y\}$. Given this initialization, we shall show by induction on the depth of state s that $output(s) = \{y \mid y$ is a keyword that is a suffix of the string representing state $s\}$.

This statement is certainly true for the start state which is of depth 0. Assuming this statement is true for all states of depth less than d, consider a state s of depth

d. Let u be the string that represents state s.

Consider a string y in $output(s)$. If y is added to $output(s)$ by Algorithm 2, then $y = u$ and y is a keyword. If y is added to $output(s)$ by Algorithm 3, then y is in $output(f(s))$. By the inductive hypothesis, y is a keyword that is a suffix of the string representing state $f(s)$. By Lemma 1, any such keyword must be a suffix of u.

Conversely, suppose y is any keyword that is a suffix of u. Since y is a keyword, there is a state t that is represented by y. By Algorithm 2, $output(t)$ contains y. Thus if $y = u$, then $s = t$ and $output(s)$ certainly contains y. If y is a proper suffix of u, then from the inductive hypothesis and Lemma 1 we know $output(f(s))$ contains y. Since Algorithm 3 considers states in order of increasing depth, the last statement of Algorithm 3 adds $output(f(s))$ and hence y to $output(s)$. $\square$

The following lemma characterizes the behavior of Algorithm 1 on a text string $x = a_1 a_2 \cdots a_n$.

LEMMA 3. *After the jth operating cycle, Algorithm 1 will be in state s if and only if s is represented by the longest suffix of $a_1 a_2 \cdots a_j$ that is a prefix of some keyword.*

PROOF. Similar to Lemma 1. $\square$

THEOREM 1. *Algorithms 2 and 3 produce valid goto, failure, and output functions.*

PROOF. By Lemmas 2 and 3. $\square$

5. Time Complexity of Algorithms 1, 2, and 3

We now examine the time complexity of Algorithms 1, 2, and 3. We shall show that using the goto, failure and output functions created by Algorithms 2 and 3, the number of state transitions made by Algorithm 1 in processing a text string is independent of the number of keywords. We shall also show that Algorithms 2 and 3 can be implemented to run in time that is linearly proportional to the sum of the lengths of the keywords in K.

THEOREM 2. *Using the goto, failure and output functions created by Algorithms 2 and 3, Algorithm 1 makes fewer than $2n$ state transitions in processing a text string of length n.*

PROOF. In each operating cycle Algorithm 1 makes zero or more failure transitions followed by exactly one goto transition. From a state s of depth d Algorithm 1 can never make more than d failure transitions in one operating cycle.[1] Thus the total number of failure transitions must be at least one less than the total number of goto transitions. In processing an input of length n Algorithm 1 makes exactly n goto transitions. Therefore the total number of state transitions is less than $2n$. $\square$

The actual time complexity of Algorithm 1 depends on how expensive it is:

1. to determine $g(s, a)$ for each state s and input symbol a,

---

[1] As many as d failure transitions can be made. [13] shows that, if there is only one keyword in K, $O(\log d)$ is the maximum number of failure transitions which can be made in one operating cycle.

2. to determine $f(s)$ for each state s,

3. to determine whether $output(s)$ is empty, and

4. to emit $output(s)$.

We could store the goto function in a two-dimensional array, which would allow us to determine the value of $g(s, a)$ in constant time for each s and a. If the size of the input alphabet and the keyword set are large, however, then it is far more economical to store only the nonfail values in a linear list [1,11] for each state. Such a representation would make the cost of determining $g(s, a)$ proportional to the number of nonfail values of the goto function for state s. A reasonable compromise, and one which we have employed, is to store the most frequently used states (such as state 0) as direct access tables in which the next state can be determined by directly indexing into the table with the current input symbol. Then for the most frequently used states we can determine $g(s, a)$ for each a in constant time. Less frequently used states and states with few nonfail values of the goto function can be encoded as linear lists.

Another approach would be to store the goto values for each state in the form of a binary search tree [1, 12].

The failure function can be stored as a one-dimensional array so that $f(s)$ can be determined in constant time for each s.

Thus, the non-printing portion of Algorithm 1 can be implemented to process a text string of length n in cn steps, where c is a constant that is independent of the number of keywords.

Let us now consider the time required to print the output. A one-dimensional array can be used to determine whether $output(s)$ is empty in constant time for each s. The cost of printing the output in each operating cycle is proportional to the sum of the lengths of the keywords in $output(s)$ where s is the state in which Algorithm 1 is at the end of the operating cycle. In many applications $output(s)$ will usually contain at most one keyword, so the time required to print the output at each input position is constant.

It is possible, however, that a large number of keywords occur at every position of the text string. In this case Algorithm 1 will spend a considerable amount of time printing out the answer. In the worst case we may have to print all keywords in K at virtually every position of the text string. (Consider an extreme case where $K = \{a, a^2, a^3, \ldots, a^k\}$ and the text string is a^n. Here a^i denotes the string of i a's.) Any other pattern matching algorithm, however, would also have to print out the same number of keywords at each position of the text string so it is reasonable to compare pattern matching algorithms on the basis of the time spent in recognizing where the keywords occur.

We should contrast the performance of Algorithm 1 with a more straightforward way of locating all keywords in K that are substrings of a given text string. One such way would be to take in turn each keyword in K and successively match that keyword against all character positions in the text string. The running time of this technique is at best proportional to the product of the number of keywords in K times the length of the text string. If

there are many keywords, the performance of this algorithm will be considerably worse that that of Algorithm 1. In fact it was the time complexity of the straightforward algorithm that prompted the development of Algorithm 1. (The reader may wish to compare the performance of the two algorithms when $K = \{a, a^2, \ldots, a^k\}$ and the text string is a^n.)

Finally let us consider the cost of computing the goto, failure, and output functions using Algorithms 2 and 3.

THEOREM 3. *Algorithm 2 requires time linearly proportional to the sum of the lengths of the keywords.*

PROOF. Straightforward. □

THEOREM 4. *Algorithm 3 can be implemented to run in time proportional to the sum of the lengths of the keywords.*

PROOF. Using an argument similar to that in Theorem 2, we can show that the total number of executions of the statement $state \leftarrow f(state)$ made during the course of Algorithm 3 is bounded by the sum of the lengths of the keywords. Using linked lists to represent the output set of a state, we can execute the statement $output(s) \leftarrow output(s) \cup output(f(s))$ in constant time. Note that $output(s)$ and $output(f(s))$ are disjoint when this statement is executed. Thus the total time needed to implement Algorithm 3 is dominated by the sum of the lengths of the keywords. □

6. Eliminating Failure Transitions

This section shows how to eliminate all failure transitions from Algorithm 1 by using the next move function of a deterministic finite automaton in place of the goto and failure functions.

A deterministic finite automaton [15] consists of a finite set of states S and a next move function δ such that for each state s and input symbol a, $\delta(s, a)$ is a state in S. That is to say, a deterministic finite automaton makes exactly one state transition on each input symbol.

By using the next move function δ of an appropriate deterministic finite automaton in place of the goto function in Algorithm 1, we can dispense with all failure transitions. This can be done by simply replacing the first two statements in the for-loop of Algorithm 1 by the single statement $state \leftarrow \delta(state, a_i)$. Using δ, Algorithm 1 makes exactly one state transition per input character.

We can compute the required next move function δ from the goto and failure functions found by Algorithms 2 and 3 using Algorithm 4. Algorithm 4 just precomputes the result of every sequence of possible failure transitions. The time taken by Algorithm 4 is linearly proportional to the size of the keyword set. In practice, Algorithm 4 would be evaluated in conjunction with Algorithm 3.

The next move function computed by Algorithm 4 from the goto and failure functions shown in Figure 1 is tabulated in Figure 3.

The next move function is encoded in Figure 3 as follows. In state 0, for example, we have a transition on h to state 1, a transition on s to state 3, and a transition on any other symbol to state 0. In each state, the dot stands

Algorithm 4. Construction of a deterministic finite automaton.

Input. Goto function g from Algorithm 2 and failure function f from Algorithm 3.

Output. Next move function δ.

Method.

```
begin
    queue ← empty
    for each symbol a do
        begin
            δ(0, a) ← g(0, a)
            if g(0, a) ≠ 0 then queue ← queue ∪ {g(0, a)}
        end
    while queue ≠ empty do
        begin
            let r be the next state in queue
            queue ← queue − {r}
            for each symbol a do
                if g(r, a) = s ≠ fail do
                    begin
                        queue ← queue ∪ {s}
                        δ(r, a) ← s
                    end
                else δ(r, a) ← δ(f(r), a)
        end
end
```

Fig. 3. Next move function.

	input symbol	next state
state 0:	h	1
	s	3
	.	0
state 1:	e	2
	i	6
	h	1
	s	3
	.	0
state 9: state 7: state 3:	h	4
	s	3
	.	0
state 5: state 2:	r	8
	h	1
	s	3
	.	0
state 6:	s	7
	h	1
	.	0
state 4:	e	5
	i	6
	h	1
	s	3
	.	0
state 8:	s	9
	h	1
	.	0

for any input character other than those above it. This method of encoding the next move function is more economical than storing δ as a two-dimensional array. However, the amount of memory required to store δ in this manner is somewhat larger than the corresponding representation for the goto function from which δ was constructed since many of the states in δ each contain transitions from several states of the goto function.

Using the next move function in Figure 3, Algorithm 1 with input "ushers" would make the sequence of state transitions shown in the first line of states of Figure 2.

Using a deterministic finite automaton in Algorithm 1 can potentially reduce the number of state transitions by 50%. This amount of saving, however, would virtually never be achieved in practice because in typical applications Algorithm 1 will spend most of its time in state 0 from which there are no failure transitions. Calculating the expected saving is difficult, however, because meaningful definitions of "average" set of keywords and "average" text string are not available.

7. An Application to Bibliographic Search

Algorithm 1 is attractive in pattern matching applications involving large numbers of keywords, since all keywords can be simultaneously matched against the text string in just one pass through the text string. One such application in which this algorithm has been successfully used arose in a library bibliographic search program which locates in a cumulative citation index all citations satisfying some Boolean function of keywords.

The data base used for this retrieval system is the cumulated machine-readable data used for *Current Technical Papers*, a fortnightly citation bulletin produced for internal use by the technical libraries of Bell Laboratories. These citations are gathered from journals, covering a broad classification of technical interests. In the summer of 1973 there were three years of cumulated data, representing about 150,000 citations with a total length of about 10^7 characters.

With this search system a bibliographer can retrieve from the data base all titles satisfying some Boolean combination of keywords. For example, the bibliographer can ask for all titles in the data base containing both the keywords "ion" and "bombardment." The bibliographer can also specify whether a keyword is required to be preceded and/or followed by a punctuation character such as space, comma, semicolon, etc. A specification of this nature can explicitly deny matching on keywords embedded in the text. For example, it is often reasonable to accept the word "ions" as a match for the substring "ion." However, it is usually unreasonable to accept a word such as "motion" as a match on that keyword. The implementation permits specification of acceptance with full embedding, left embedding, right embedding, or none at all. This provision creates no difficulty for Algorithm 1 although the use of a class of punctuation characters in the keyword syntax creates some states with a large number of goto transitions. This may make the deterministic finite automaton implementation of Algorithm 1 more space consuming and less attractive for some applications.

An early version of this bibliographic search program

employed a direct pattern matching algorithm in which each keyword in the search prescription was successively matched against each title. A second version of this search program was implemented, also in FORTRAN, in which the only difference was the substitution of Algorithms 1, 2 and 3 for the direct pattern matching scheme. The following table shows two sample runs of the two programs on a Honeywell 6070 computer. The first run involved a search prescription containing 15 keywords, the second a search prescription containing 24 keywords.

	15 keywords	24 keywords
old	.79	1.27
new	.18	.21

CPU Time in Hours

With larger numbers of keywords the improvement in performance became even more pronounced. The figures tend to bear out the fact that with Algorithm 1 the cost of a search is roughly independent of the number of keywords. The time spent in constructing the pattern matching machine and making state transitions was insignificant compared to the time spent reading and unpacking the text string.

8. Concluding Remarks

The pattern matching scheme described in this paper is well suited for applications in which we are looking for occurrences of large numbers of keywords in text strings. Since no additional information needs to be added to the text string, searches can be made over arbitrary files.

Some information retrieval systems compute an index or concordance for a text file to allow searches to be conducted without having to scan all of the text string [7]. In such systems making changes to the text file is expensive because after each change the index to the file must be updated. Consequently, such systems work best with long static text files and short patterns.

An interesting question from finite automata theory is: Given a regular expression R of length r and an input string x of length n, how quickly can one determine whether x is in the language denoted by R? One method for solving this problem is first to construct from R a nondeterministic finite automaton M and then to simulate the behavior of M on the input x. This gives an $O(rn)$ solution [1].

Another approach along these lines is to construct from R a nondeterministic finite automaton M, then to convert M into a deterministic finite automaton M' and then to simulate the behavior of M' on x. The only difficulty with this approach is that M' can have on the order of 2^r states. The simulation of M' on the other hand is linear in n of course. The overall complexity is $O(2^r + n)$.

Using Algorithm 4 we can construct a deterministic finite automaton directly from a regular expression R in time that is linear in the length of R. However, the regular expression is now restricted to be the form $\Sigma^*(y_1 + y_2 + \cdots + y_k)\Sigma^*$ where Σ is the input symbol alphabet. By "concatenating" a series of deterministic finite automata in tandem, we can extend this result to regular expressions of the form $\Sigma^*Y_1\Sigma^*Y_2 \cdots \Sigma^*Y_m\Sigma^*$ where each Y_i is a regular expression of the form $y_{i1} + y_{i2} + \cdots + y_{ik_i}$.

A related open question is what new classes of regular sets can be recognized in less than $O(rn)$ time. Along these lines, in [5] it is shown that regular expressions of the form $\Sigma^*y\Sigma^*$ where y is a keyword with "don't care" symbols can be recognized in $O(n\log r \log\log r)$ time.

Acknowledgements

The authors are grateful to A. F. Ackerman, A. D. Hall, S. C. Johnson, B. W. Kernighan, and M. D. McIlroy for their helpful comments on the manuscript. This paper was produced using the typesetting system developed by Kernighan and Cherry [9]. The assistance of B. W. Kernighan and M. E. Lesk in the preparation of the paper was appreciated.

Received August 1974; revised January 1975

References

1. Aho, A.V., Hopcroft, J.E., and Ullman, J.D. *The Design and Analysis of Computer Algorithms.* Addison-Wesley, Reading, Mass., 1974.
2. Booth, T.L. *Sequential Machines and Automata Theory.* Wiley, New York, 1967.
3. Brzozowski, J.A. Derivatives of regular expressions. *J. ACM* 11:4 (October 1964), 481-494.
4. Bullen, R.H., Jr., and Millen, J.K. Microtext - the design of a microprogrammed finite state search machine for full-text retrieval. *Proc. Fall Joint Computer Conference,* 1972, pp. 479-488.
5. Fischer, M.J., and Paterson, M.S. String matching and other products. Technical Report 41, Project MAC, M.I.T., 1974.
6. Gimpel, J.A. A theory of discrete patterns and their implementation in SNOBOL4. *Comm. ACM* 16:2 (February 1973), 91-100.
7. Harrison, M.C. Implementation of the substring test by hashing. *Comm. ACM* 14:12 (December 1971), 777-779.
8. Johnson, W.L., Porter, J.H., Ackley, S.I., and Ross, D.T. Automatic generation of efficient lexical processors using finite state techniques. *Comm. ACM* 11:12 (December 1968), 805-813.
9. Kernighan, B.W., and Cherry, L.L. A system for typesetting mathematics. *Comm. ACM* 18:3 (March 1975), 151-156.
10. Kleene, S.C. Representation of events in nerve nets. In *Automata Studies,* C.E. Shannon and J. McCarthy (eds.), Princeton University Press, 1956, pp. 3-40.
11. Knuth, D.E. *Fundamental Algorithms,* second edition, The Art of Computer Programming 1, Addison-Wesley, Reading, Mass., 1973.
12. Knuth, D.E. *Sorting and Searching,* The Art of Computer Programing 3, Addison-Wesley, Reading, Mass., 1973.
13. Knuth, D.E., Morris, J.H., Jr., and Pratt, V.R. Fast pattern matching in strings. TR CS-74-440, Stanford University, Stanford, California, 1974.
14. Kohavi, Z. *Switching and Finite Automata Theory.* McGraw-Hill, New York, 1970.
15. McNaughton, R., and Yamada, H. Regular expressions and state graphs for automata. *IRE Trans. Electronic Computers* 9:1 (1960), 39-47.
16. Rabin, M.O., and Scott, D. Finite automata and their decision problems. *IBM J. Research and Development* 3, (1959), 114-125.
17. Thompson, K. Regular search expression algorithm. *Comm. ACM* 11:6 (June 1968), 419-422.

A Method for Improving String Pattern Matching Machines

JUNICHI AOE, YONEO YAMAMOTO, AND RYOSAKU SHIMADA

Abstract—This correspondence describes an efficient string pattern matching machine to locate all occurrences of any of a finite number of keywords and phrases in an arbitrary text string. Some conditions are defined on the states of the machine in order to improve the speed and size of the machine by Aho and Corasick [1]. The pattern matching algorithm is partitioned into various cases by combining these conditions. Finally, the correspondence illustrates the proposed approach by applying it to the analysis of the machines for a simple search.

Index Terms—Data structure, finite state machine, keywords, matching algorithm, storage requirements, string pattern matching machine.

I. INTRODUCTION

A string pattern matching machine has been applied to various fields such as lexical analysis of a compiler, voice recognition, library bibliographic search, spelling check, text editing, and so on. Recently, Aho *et al.* [1] presented an efficient string pattern matching algorithm to locate all occurrences of any of a finite number of keywords in a text string and Knuth *et al.* [2] presented a fast matching algorithm to find all occurrences of one given keyword in a text string. This correspondence presents a technique for improving the speed and size of the machine by Aho *et al.*

Manuscript received April 5, 1982; revised February 28, 1983.

The authors are with the Department of Information Science and Systems Engineering, Faculty of Engineering, Tokushima University, Minami-josanjima-cho, Tokushima-shi 770, Japan.

The applications of a string pattern matching machine can be classified into two scopes by whether a set of keywords is variant or invariant. The first, called "a dynamic machine" permits the information on the keyboards to be modified. The second, a "static machine" does not allow this modification. That is, the former implies that the transition table is variant and the latter is invariant. We must, therefore, consider individually the evaluation criterion to the machines as follows.

1) In the dynamic case it is required that not only the machine but also the machine generator is efficient and compact.

2) In the static case it is only required that the machine is efficient and compact.

We can say that the machine to a bibliographic search belongs to the dynamic case.

The aim of this correspondence is to find out the redundant operations of the machine by Aho *et al.* and to present a technique for removing these operations from the machine. Some conditions are defined on each state of the machine in order to improve the speed and size of the machine. The matching algorithm and the data structure of the transition table are partitioned into several cases by combining these conditions. Consequently, each operation corresponding to the states is able to use the most effective instructions steam and data structure. Although the scheme makes the matching program size increase, our matching program is encoded in a reasonable size by means of jointing to the common statements of the algorithms each other.

Our construction algorithm of the improved machine is also executed in the time proportional to a total length of the keywords as Aho *et al.*, so the presented machine satisfies the evaluation criterion of the dynamic machine.

II. A PATTERN MATCHING MACHINE

This chapter describes a finite state string pattern matching machine that locates keywords in a text string.

0-8186-5460-0/94 $3.00 © 1984 IEEE

In this paper a string is simply a finite sequence of symbols. Let

$$K = \{y_1, y_2, \cdots, y_k\}$$

be a finite set of strings which we shall call keywords and let x be an arbitrary string which we shall call the text string. Our problem is to locate and identify all substrings of x which are keywords in K. Substrings may overlap with one another.

A pattern matching machine for K is a program which takes as input the text string x and produces as output the locations in x at which keywords of K appear as substrings. The pattern matching machine consists of a set of states. Each state is represented by a number. One state (usually 0) is designated as the start state. The pattern matching machine processes the text string x by successively reading the symbols in x, making state transitions and occasionally emitting output. Let S be a set of states and let I be a set of input symbols. The behavior of the pattern matching machine is dictated by three functions:

Goto function $\qquad g: S \times I \to S \cup \{\text{fail}\}$,

Failure function $\qquad f: S \to S$,

Output function $\qquad output: S \to K$.

Fig. 1 shows the functions used by a pattern matching machine for the set of keywords {he, she, his, hers }[1]. Here $\neg$ indicates all input symbols except h and s.

The goto function g maps a pair consisting of a state and an input symbol into a state or the message fail. The directed graph in Fig. 2(a) represents the goto function. For example, the edge labeled h from 0 to 1 indicates that $g(0, h) = 1$. The absence of an arrow indicates fail. Thus, $g(1, \sigma) = $ fail for all input symbols σ that are not e or i. All our pattern matching machines have the property that $g(0, \sigma) \neq$ fail for all input symbols σ.

The failure function f maps a state into a state. The failure function is constructed whenever the goto function reports fail. Certain states are designated as output states which indicate that a set of keywords has been found. The output function formalizes this concept by associating a set of keywords (possibly empty) with every state.

The following algorithm summarizes the behavior of a pattern matching machine (for short, a machine M) by Aho *et al.* [1].

Algorithm 1: Pattern matching machine M.

Input: A text string $x = a_1 a_2 \cdots a_n$ where each a_i is an input symbol and a pattern matching machine M with goto function g, failure function f, and output function *output*, as described above.

Output: Locations at which keywords occur in x.
Method:

begin
    $state \leftarrow 0$;
    for $i \leftarrow 1$ **until** n **do**
        begin
            while $g(state, a_i) = $ fail **do** $state \leftarrow f(state)$;
            $state \leftarrow g(state, a_i)$;
            if $output(state) \neq$ empty **then** **print** i, $output(s)$
        end
end.

III. Improvement of Machine M

The algorithm of a pattern matching machine (for short, a machine SPM) to be introduced here is partitioned into several cases by combining some conditions on the states. Each algorithm consists of a sequence of instructions which has a label

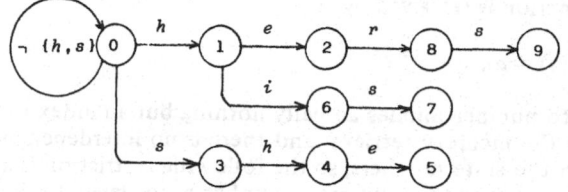

(a)   Goto function.

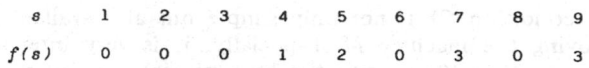

s	1	2	3	4	5	6	7	8	9
$f(s)$	0	0	0	1	2	0	3	0	3

(b)   Failure function.

s	output(s)
2	{he }
5	{she, he }
7	{his }
9	{hers }

(c)   Output function.

Fig. 1.   Example of a pattern matching machine.

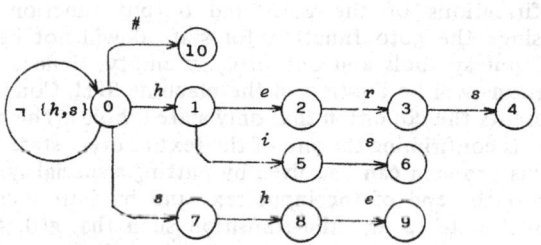

10 represents a state number of state s_F.

Fig. 2.   Goto function with revised state numbers.

in the first instruction. The label associated with state s is represented by the case function *case* and we shall use

sub0, sub1, sub2, $\cdots$

as *case(s)*.

Definition 1: Let *outdegree(s)* be the number of arrows drawing from state s. We define four conditions on the states of the machine M.

1) We say that state s holds condition $C1$ if *outdegree(s)* > 1. We call this state "a multistate" and state s such that *outdegree(s)* $= 1$ is called as "a single state."

2) We say that state s holds condition $C2$ if *outdegree(s)* $= 0$. We call this state s "a terminal state."

3) We say that state s holds condition $C3$ if $f(s) = 0$.

4) We say that state s holds condition $C4$ if *output(s)* $\neq$ empty and state s is not the terminal state.

In our approach, the goto function to the multistate can be stored as a two-dimensional array, called N. We denote the entry in N at the row for state s and the column for a symbol a_i as $N(s, a_i)$. The goto function go single state s such that $g(s, a_i) = s'$ can be stored as a one-dimensional array, called *unit*, which is faster to retrieve a random entry and need less memory space than the two-dimensional array N. Thus the goto function is retrieved by

$$unit(s) = a_i. \tag{1}$$

The state number implies actually nothing but an index to the table at the memory retrieval and there is no interdependence between the state numbers, so the following restriction is used in order to cause the next state number s' to depend on only the current state number s:

$$s' = s + 1. \tag{2}$$

Thus condition $C1$ is not only simple but also available for improving the machine M. Especially, it is very interesting that expression (2) is executed by a typical efficient register increment instruction.

For state s under condition $C2$ the goto function will always fail on any input symbols and $output(s) \neq$ empty, so the machine SPM will be omitted the confirmations of the goto and output functions. Consequently, the goto function for this state s will be unnecessary in the machine SPM.

The machine M confirms again the goto function for state 0 after $g(s, a_i)$ was fail for state s under condition $C3$ and $f(s)$ became state 0. The goto function for state 0, however, will not be always fail on any input symbols, so the machine SPM will omit this confirmation.

Although the machine M always confirms the output function at all state transitions, condition $C4$ enables us to eliminate this confirmation in the machine SPM.

The above explains how to use the conditions on each state in order to improve the machine M. The machine M, however, contains two more redundant operations. One is the confirmations of the goto and output functions for state 0 since the goto function for state 0 will not be fail on any input symbols and $output(0) =$ empty. Hence, these confirmations will be omitted in the machine SPM. Condition CO represents the condition that only state 0 holds. The other operation is confirming the end of the text at every state transition. This problem can be solved by putting a special symbol $\#(\notin I)$ into the end of the input text and by introducing a proper final state s_F and the transition such that $g(0, \#) = s_F$. Condition $C5$ represents the condition that only state s_F holds.

We define the relation between twelve kinds of algorithms to be used in the machine SPM and the conditions as follows:

sub0: $C0$	sub1: $C1, C4$
sub2: $C1$	sub3: $C1, C3, C4$
sub4: $C1, C3$	sub5: $C4$
sub6:	sub7: $C3, C4$
sub8: $C3$	sub9: $C2$
sub10: $C5$	sub11: $C2, C3$.

We consider now the following algorithms with labels sub1 and sub2, but we ignore the confusion of the fail loop in this example:

```
sub1:   i ← i + 1;
fail:   if N(s, a_i) = fail then s ← f(s) goto fail;
        s ← N(s, a_i);
        print i, output(s);
        goto case(s);
sub2:   i ← i + 1;
fail:   if N(s, a_i) = fail then s ← f(s) goto fail;
```

```
        s ← N(s, a_i);
        goto case(s);
```

In the example, both algorithms are the same except a statement **print** i, $output(s)$, but the common statement cannot be merged into one. We show the alternative specification of Algorithm 1 in order to solve the undesirable feature:

```
        begin
            s ← 0; i ← 0.
40:         if output(s) ≠ empty then print i, output(s);
            i ← i + 1;
            if i = n + 1 then goto 50;
30:         if g(s, a_i) = fail then begin s ← f(s); goto 30 end;
            s ← g(s, a_i);
            goto 40
50:     end
```

Starting from the confirmation of the output in this algorithm is based on the idea such that $output(0) =$ empty.

To obtain the proper loop by a label 30 associated with failure function, another case function, denoted by $case'$, is used in the machine SPM as follows:

$$case'(s) = 20 \text{ if } case(s) = \text{sub}1 \text{ or } \text{sub}2,$$
$$case'(s) = 40 \text{ if } case(s) = \text{sub}3 \text{ or } \text{sub}4,$$
$$case'(s) = 60 \text{ if } case(s) = \text{sub}5 \text{ or } \text{sub}6,$$
$$case'(s) = 80 \text{ if } case(s) = \text{sub}7 \text{ or } \text{sub}8.$$

Otherwise, $case'$ function is undefined because every terminal state(sub9, sub11) is not indicated by $f(s)$ and the machine SPM does not confirm the goto function for state 0 even if $f(s)$ indicated state 0(sub0).

Let FAIL be the abbreviation of

$$\textbf{begin } s \leftarrow f(s); \textbf{ goto } case'(s) \textbf{ end}$$

and ADVANCE be

$$\textbf{begin } s \leftarrow N(0, a_i), \textbf{ goto } case(s) \textbf{ end}.$$

The machine SPM is summarized by the following algorithm.
Algorithm 2: Pattern Matching Machine SPM.
Input: A text string $x = a_1 a_2 \cdots a_n \#$ where each a_i is an input symbol and a machine SPM with arrays N and unit, fail function f, case functions $case$ and $case'$, and output function $output$.
Output: Location at which keyboards occur in x.
Method:

```
        begin
            i ← 0;
sub0:       i ← i + 1; ADVANCE;
sub1:       print i, output(s);
sub2:       i ← i + 1;
20:         if N(s, a_i) = fail then FAIL;
            s ← N(s, a_i); goto case(s);
sub3:       print i, output(s);
sub4:       i ← i + 1;
```

```
40:        if N(s, a_i) = fail then ADVANCE;
           s ← N(s, a_i); goto case (s);
sub5:      print i, output (s);
sub6:      i ← i + 1;
60:        if unit (s) ≠ a_i then FAIL;
           s ← s + 1; goto case (s);
sub7:      print i, output (s);
sub8:      i ← i + 1;
80:        if unit (s) ≠ a_i then ADVANCE;
           s ← s + 1; goto case (s);
sub9:      print i, output (s); i ← i + 1; FAIL;
sub10:     goto 50;
sub11:     print i, output (s); i ← i + 1; ADVANCE
50:        end.
```

From Definition 1, the alternative specification of the machine M, and Algorithm 2, it is obvious that the machine M is equivalent to the machine SPM.

The case function in the goto graph in Fig. 1 as follows:

$case(0) = sub0$, $case(1) = sub4$, $case(2) = sub7$,

$case(3) = case(6) = case(4) = sub6$,

$case(5) = case(7) = case(9) = sub9$.

The machine SPM can be constructed by adding the slight modification to the statements of the construction algorithm [1] of the machine M. Specially, we can produce the expected single state number by taking as input the keywords in descending order of length. Fig. 2 shows the goto function computed by this idea in the order hers, his, she, he.

In practical, a two-dimensional array N to the multistate s is stored by row-major as a one-dimensional array (called N'). Let m be the address in N' corresponding to the first datum of the sth row in N. Suppose that we set unit(s) to m-1. Then information on $g(s, a)$ in the multistate is retrieved by

$$N'(unit(s) + a)$$

where character a is treated as an integer.

This manner is interesting in that no unit entries remain unused.

In our actual implementation [7] we store the most frequently used state 0 with many transitions as a direct access table in which the next state can be determined by directly indexing into the linear table with the current input symbol and we store the other states as a linear list. This reason is to make the time which fills up blank elements (undefined parts of the goto function) of the two-dimensional array as short as possible.

IV. EMPIRICAL TIME AND SPACE OBSERVATIONS

We applied the machine SPM to a text string consisting of a bibliography of "Principles of Compiler Design" by Aho *et al.* [3]. The text string has a total length 14 647 characters and a total number of about 2500 words.

Fig. 3 shows the time spent in constructing the pattern matching machines and the time spent in searching the keywords in the text string, where SC(MC) represents the time to construct the machine SPM(M), and SS(MS) the time to search the keywords by the machine SPM(M). The simulation was run on a FACOM 230-38 [4] computer and the machine construc-

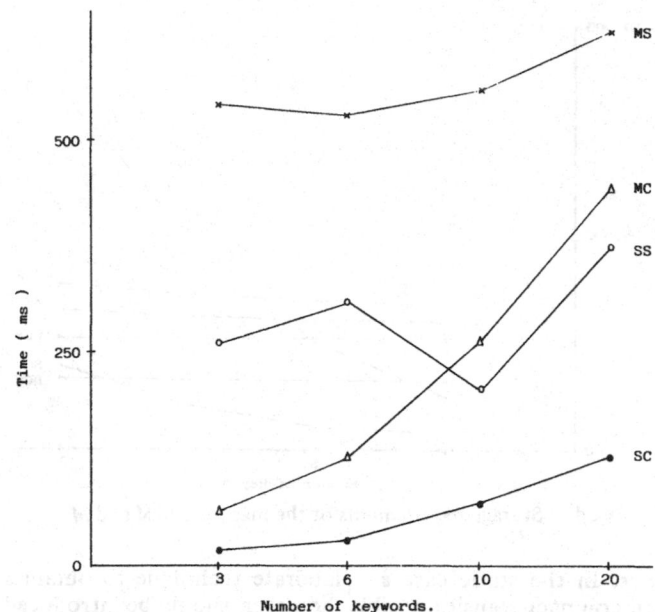

Fig. 3. Run times of the machines SPM and M.

tion program is written in Pascal and the retrieval program in FASP, an assembly language of FACOM 230-38.

It turns out from the results that MC/SC increases with the number of keywords but MS/SS is roughly independent of the number of keywords and it is about 1.5 on the average. The machine SPM becomes more efficient for a application that takes merely information on the output as data to be processed in main memory since the fast retrieval of the machine SPM is spoiled by a considerable amount of the time required to print the output.

Fig. 4 shows the storage requirements associated with the machines SPM and M, where SCP(MCP) represents the memory required in the construction program of the machine SPM(M), SSP(MSP) in the search progam of the machine SPM(M), and SG(MG) in the transition table of the machine SPM(M). Although SCP, SSP, MSP and MCP are constant, SG and MG are dependent on the number of states.

Let $n(m)$ be the total number of states (input symbols) and let n' the number of single states. The asymptotic space complexity of the transition table of the machine SPM is

$$0((n - n') \cdot m) + 0(n')$$

and that of the machine M is

$$0(n \cdot m).$$

In general, n' is much larger than $(n - n')$, so the increase of the table space of the machine SPM by the number of states is much less than that of the machine M. It implies that MC/SC increases with the number of keywords. Hence, the machine SPM is more compact than the machine M for large number of keywords.

V. CONCLUSIONS

We have described a method for improving the pattern matching machine by Aho and Corasick [1]. The pattern matching scheme is well suited not only for application on dynamic machines but also for static machines to look occurrences of large number of keywords in the text string such as lexical analysis since the driver routine is static in the both ma-

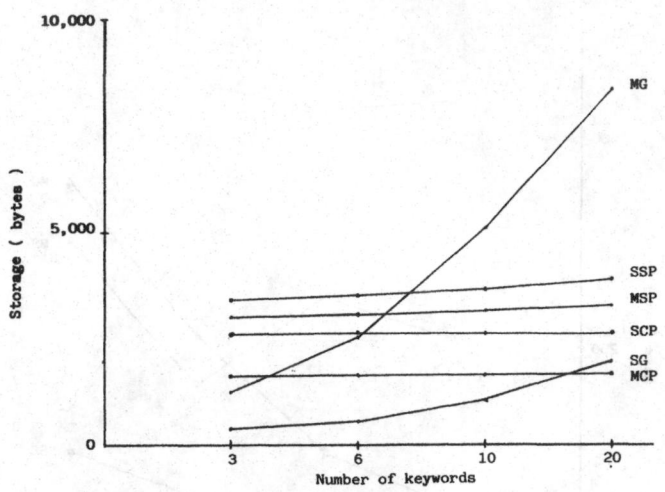

Fig. 4. Storage requirements of the machines SPM and *M*.

chines. In the static case an elaborate technique to obtain a more compact transition table, however, should be introduced in the machine generator.

Although divining the control algorithm of finite state ma-chine into several cases is somewhat expensive in terms of space, the speed is improved by the technique if the division is reasonable. The same approach is used for speeding up and/ or reducing LR(*k*) parsers in [5] and [6]. It is, however, important to find out available conditions of the states of the machine.

REFERENCES

[1] A. V. Aho and M. J. Corasick, "Efficient string matching: An aid to bibliographic search," *Commun. Ass. Comput. Mach.*, vol. 18, pp. 333–340, June 1975.
[2] D. E. Knuth, J. H. Morris, Jr., and V. R. Pratt, "Fast pattern matching in strings," *SIAM J. Comput.*, vol. 6, pp. 323–350, June 1977.
[3] A. V. Aho and J. D. Ullman, *Principles of Compiler Design*. Reading, MA: Addison-Wesley, 1978.
[4] FACOM 230-38 OSII/VS User's Manual, Fujitsu Co., Ltd.
[5] W. R. Lalonde, "The construction of stack-controlling LR parsers for regular right part grammars," *ACM Trans. Program. Lang. Syst.*, vol. 3, pp. 168–206, Apr. 1981.
[6] J. Aoe, Y. Yamamoto, and R. Shimada, "A method for speeding up LR(k) parsers using action patterns" (in Japanese), *Trans. IECE*, vol. J64-D, pp. 940–946, Oct. 1981.
[7] J. Aoe, Y. Yamamoto, R. Shimada, and S. Aso, "Improving string pattern matching machines" (in Japanese), *Trans. IECE*, vol. J65-D, pp. 989–996, Aug. 1982.

An Efficient Algorithm for Matching Multiple Patterns

Jang-Jong Fan and Keh-Yih Su, *Member, IEEE*

Abstract—An efficient algorithm to perform multiple pattern match in a string is described in this paper. The proposed match algorithm combines the concept of deterministic finite state automata (DFSA) and Boyer–Moore's algorithm to achieve better performance. Actual experiments were held and the result shows that in the average case it is able to perform pattern match operations *sublinearly*, i.e., it does not need to inspect every character of the string to perform pattern match operations. The analysis shows that the number of characters to be inspected decreases as the length of patterns increases, and increases slightly as the total number of patterns increases. To match an eight-character pattern in an English string using the proposed algorithm, it inspects only about 17% of all characters of the string, and 33% of all characters of the string when the number of patterns is seven. On the contrary, the DFSA method for matching multiple patterns needs to inspect every character of the string. In an actual testing, this new algorithm running on SUN 3/160 takes only 3.7 s to search seven eight-character patterns in a 1.4 Mbytes English text file.

Index Terms— Multiple pattern match, finite state automata, information retrieval, text editing, computational complexity, linear time bond.

I. INTRODUCTION

SEARCHING a text file for user-specified patterns is a common requirement in information retrieval and text editing applications. Currently, deterministic finite state automata (DFSA) is the most commonly used method in solving pattern match problem. However, DFSA requires inspection of every character in the text file. A more efficient algorithm, which does not need to inspect every character is required to search patterns embedded in a large text.

Based on the number of patterns to be matched at a time, a pattern match problem can be classified into single-pattern and multiple pattern match problems. The difference between them is that the single-pattern match algorithm searches through the text to match only one given pattern at one scan, while the multiple pattern match algorithm searches through the text to match a given set of patterns at one scan. There are three primary single-pattern match algorithms—Knuth–Morris–Pratt's algorithm [1], Boyer–Moore's algorithm [2], and Karp–Rabin's algorithm [3]. In Knuth–Morris–Pratt's algorithm, the pattern is placed over the string and then slides rightward to find

Manuscript received November 20, 1989; revised August 31, 1991. This work was supported by the National Science Council of the Republic of China under Grant NSC 81-0408-E-007-01.

The authors are with the Department of Electrical Engineering, National Tsing Hua University, Hsinchu, Taiwan 300, R.O.C.

IEEE Log Number 9200961.

any possible match in a way that each character in the string is inspected exactly once. Thus its time complexity is $O(n + m)$, where n and m are the string length and the pattern length, respectively. In Boyer–Moore's algorithm, the pattern is matched from its right end rather than the left end. When a mismatch occurs, the pattern slides rightward in a way that some characters in the string are skipped without inspection. In the worst case, its time complexity is $O(n + r * m)$ [1], [4] where n and m are the string length and the pattern length, respectively, and r is the total number of patterns that occur in the string. The advantage of Boyer–Moore's algorithm is that in the average case it does not need to inspect every character in the string, especially for an English string. In Karp–Rabin's algorithm, the string is first transformed into an array of hash values by hashing each possible m-character sequence in the string, where m is the pattern length. Then the values in the array are checked sequentially to match the hash value of the pattern. This algorithm's time complexity is $O(n + m)$, where n and m are the string length and pattern length, respectively.

To solve the multiple pattern match problem, different algorithms based on the finite state automata (FSA), implemented by either software or hardware [5]–[11], were proposed. Both the DFSA and the nondeterministic finite state automata (NFSA) can be used to match multiple patterns. However, as each input character in NFSA initiates state transitions from a set of active states to another set of active states, NFSA cannot operate as fast as DFSA does. However, in some circumstances the size of the transition table required for DFSA is much larger than that required for NFSA [12]. Since the memory is not expensive now, the execution speed rather than the memory is of more concern. The time complexity for matching multiple patterns by DFSA is proportional to the length of the string. That means the number of state transitions during the pattern matching operation is proportional to the number of characters in the string.

Comparing to the DFSA method mentioned previously, Boyer–Moore's algorithm does not require inspection of every character in the string. However, it is only designed for matching a single pattern. In this paper, we propose a more efficient multiple pattern match algorithm, which combines the concept of DFSA and Boyer–Moore's idea to attain efficiency. In the average case, the total number of state transitions performed by the proposed algorithm during a pattern match operation is much less than the length of the string, i.e., inspection of every character in the string is not necessary. The actual number of characters inspected is dependent on the statistical properties of the characters in the patterns and the string. Our theoretical analysis shows that the number of characters inspected decreases as the length of patterns increases, and increases slightly as the number of patterns increases.

In the next section, we will describe the basic idea and the algorithm for matching multiple patterns. The efficient methods to construct the required functions, which determine the distance that we can skip the substring which is not possible for a match, are also described in that section. Then the theoretical discussion and the actual experiments on the multiple pattern match algorithm are given in Section III. Finally, Section IV concludes this paper with some remarks.

II. THE BASIC IDEA AND ALGORITHM FOR MATCHING MULTIPLE PATTERNS

A. The Basic Concept of Boyer–Moore's Algorithm

Since the basic idea of Boyer–Moore's algorithm is adopted to develop the new multiple pattern match algorithm, we briefly describe the algorithm as follows for the reader's convenience.

The basic idea of Boyer–Moore's algorithm is to match the pattern from the right end rather than from the left end. At the beginning, the pattern is placed on the top of the string such that the first characters of the pattern and the string are aligned. The search process is conducted by matching each character of the pattern with each aligned character of the string from the right end to the left end. If a mismatch occurs during the search, the pattern is shifted rightward, and the amount of shifts are determined by two precomputed tables, named $delta_1$ and $delta_2$. The same search process continues until another new mismatch occurs.

The key features of Boyer–Moore's algorithm are to determine the values stored in those precomputed tables $delta_1$ and $delta_2$. Let $pattern[j]$ and $string[i]$ be the jth character of the pattern and the ith character of the string respectively. The table of $delta_1$ is used to shift the pattern rightward such that the rightmost occurrence of $string[i]$ in the pattern can align with $string[i]$. Therefore, for each character $char$ in the alphabetic set, the value of $delta_1$ is defined as follows:

$$delta_1(char) = \begin{cases} m, & \text{if } char \text{ does not occur in the pattern;} \\ m - j, & \text{if } j \text{ is the maximum integer, such that pattern } [j] = char, \\ & \text{where } m \text{ is the pattern length.} \end{cases}$$

The table of $delta_2$ is used to shift the pattern rightward such that one of the following two cases can be satisfied.

Case 1: The rightmost reoccurrence of $pattern[j + 1: m]$ in the pattern (except for $pattern[j + 1: m]$) can align with $string[i + 1 : i + m + j]$, and the character preceding the rightmost reoccurrence of $pattern[j + 1: m]$ must not be equal to $pattern[j]$.

Case 2: The longest prefix of the pattern that is also the suffix of $pattern[j + 1: m]$ can align with the suffix of $string[i + 1 : i + m-j]$.

Note that $pattern[j+1:m] = string[i+1:i+m-j]$ in these two cases. Therefore, the values of $delta_2$ can be determined from the pattern itself. The formal definition of $delta_2$ given by Knuth [1] can be stated as follows:

$$delta_2(j) = \min \{d + m - j | d \geq 1 \text{ and}$$
$$(d \geq j \text{ or } pattern[j - d] \neq pattern[j])$$
$$\text{and } ((d \geq i \text{ or } pattern[i - d] = pattern[i]),$$
$$\text{for } j < i \leq n)\}.$$

Using Boyer–Moore's algorithm, when a mismatch occurs at $pattern[j]$, the shift distance is determined by the largest value of $delta_1(char)$ and $delta_2(j)$, where $char$ denotes the character in the string which causes a mismatch with $pattern[j]$. In fact, we can improve Boyer–Moore's algorithm by shifting the pattern rightward even further. When the pattern is shifted $delta_1(char)$ characters rightward, whether the substring following the rightmost reoccurrence of the $char$ in the pattern can match $pattern[j + 1 : m]$ is not considered. Also, when the pattern is shifted $delta_2(j)$ characters rightward, whether $char$ can match the character preceding the rightmost reoccurrence of $pattern[j + 1 : m]$ is not considered. To overcome this drawback, we can take $char$ and $pattern[j+1 : m]$ simultaneously to determine the distance to shift the pattern as a mismatch occurs. Now $delta'_2$, the modification of $delta_2$, can be specified as follows, suppose that a mismatch occurs between $pattern[j]$ and $string[i]$ (i.e., $char$):

$$delta'_2(j, char) = \min \{d + m - j | d \geq 1 \text{ and}$$
$$(d \geq j \text{ or } patttern[j - d] = char)$$
$$\text{and } ((d \geq i \text{ or } pattern[i - d]$$
$$= pattern[i]), \text{ for } j < i \leq n)\}.$$

The main purpose of $delta'_2$ is to shift the pattern rightward such that one of the following two cases can be satisfied.

Case 1: The rightmost reoccurrence of $pattern[j + 1 : m]$ in the pattern (except for $pattern[j + 1 : m]$) can align with $string[i + 1 : i + m - j]$, and the character preceding the rightmost reoccurrence of $pattern[j + 1 : m]$ is equal to $string[i]$.

Case 2: The longest prefix of the pattern that is also the suffix of $pattern[j + 1 : m]$ can align with the suffix of $string[i + 1 : i + m - j]$.

The concept of $delta'_2$ will be used in the proposed multiple pattern match algorithm.

B. The Basic Concept of the DFSA Method

This section briefly describes the basic concept of the DFSA method for the reader's convenience. As described in [5], three functions — goto, failure, and output are initially constructed from a given set of patterns. The pattern matching process now becomes the state transition process, which begins with the start state. The goto function continues mapping a state and an input character from the string into another state. If a final state is reached, the patterns specified by the *output* function are matched. During the state transition process, the *goto* function outputs the *fail* message, when an input character causes a mismatch. When it occurs, the *failure* function is used to choose a state, and the state transition restarts from that state.

C. The Multiple Pattern Match Algorithm

Now, we have enough background to explain our multiple pattern match algorithm. The behavior of the proposed algorithm is similar to that of the DFSA method. Each input character causes a state transition. If it reaches a final state, then the corresponding patterns are matched. However, there are three differences between the proposed algorithm and the DFSA method.

1) The state transition function, which is referred to as the *goto* function in this paper, is constructed from a set of reversed patterns, for all patterns are matched from their rightmost characters.
2) The sequence of characters retrieved from the string for matching is not the sequence of characters in the string. The first character retrieved from the string is the *minlen*-th character, where *minlen* is defined as the shortest length of all patterns. If this character does not cause a state transition to the *start* state, the (*minlen* − 1)-th character is retrieved next. The process of retrieving characters from the string in the reversed order continues until a character causes a state transition to the *start* state.
3) When a retrieved character causes a state transition from the *start* state to itself, the $skip_1$ table is consulted to determine which character in the string will be retrieved next. However, when a state transition is from a state (other than the *start* state) to the *start* state, the $skip_2$ table is consulted. The $skip_1$ and $skip_2$ are similar to $delta_1$ and $delta'_2$, respectively, and will be discussed in detail later. Usually, the next character retrieved is located several characters to the right of the current character retrieved. The purpose of consulting $skip_1$ or $skip_2$ is to skip the portion of the string which is impossible for a match for gaining execution efficiency.

In the proposed algorithm we use a string pointer i to point to the current character retrieved, and a state variable *state* to indicate the current state in DFSA. The *goto* function maps the pair of the current state and the current character retrieved into the next state. The *output* function maps each final state into a set of patterns that can be matched when we reach that final state. Thus the proposed algorithm can be specified as follows.

Algorithm 1 Matching Multiple patterns.
Input: A text $string[1 : n]$ and *goto*, *output*, $skip_1$ and $skip_2$.
Output: Locations of matched patterns in a given string.
Method:
    $i := min \{$ lengths of all patterns $\}$;
    $state := 0$;
    while $i \leq n$ **do**
        begin

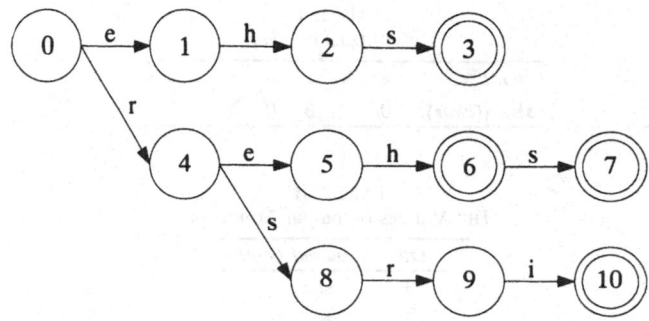

Fig. 1. The *goto* graph constructed from a set of patterns {she, sher, her, irsr }.

```
        if goto(state, string[i]) = 0 then
            begin
                if state = 0 then
                    i := i + skip₁(string[i]);
                else
                    i := i + skip₂(state, string[i]);
                    state := 0;
            end
        else
            begin
                state := goto(state, string[i]);
                if output(state) ≠ NULL then
                    print i;
                i := i - 1;
            end
    end.
```

The following is an example to illustrate the behavior of the proposed multiple pattern match algorithm. Suppose that we want to match patterns { she, sher, her, irsr } in a given string "youandshercometoseeherdog", and the corresponding *goto*, *output*, $skip_1$, and $skip_2$ have been given in Fig. 1 and Tables I to Table III. Note that each numbered double circle denotes a final state. For each state, any alphabetic character other than that indicated in the output arc will cause a state transition from the current state to the *start* state. In order to simplify the *goto* graph, the output transitions from each state to the *start* are not shown in the figure.

In this example, we use the symbol "↑" as the string pointer. Initially, the symbol "↑" is placed below the third character of the string and the value of the state variable *state* is set to 0. The current situation is shown as follows:

    state : 0

    string : *youandshercometoseeherdog*
          ↑

With $goto(0, u) = 0$ (i.e., remains in the *start* state), the string pointer is shifted rightward with $skip_1(u)$ characters, which are equal to 3, and the state variable is unchanged. Therefore, the situation becomes

    state : 0

    string : *youandshercometoseeherdog*
              ↑

TABLE I
The Values of $skip_1$

char:	e	h	i	r	s	others
$skip_1(char)$:	0	1	3	0	1	3

TABLE II
The Values of *output* Function

state	output (state)
3	she
6	her
7	she, sher
10	irsr
others	NULL

TABLE III
The Values of $skip_2$

state	char	$skip_2$ (state, char)
1	$\Sigma - \{h\}$	4
1	h	0
2	$\Sigma - \{s\}$	3
2	s	0
3	Σ	4
4	$\Sigma - \{i,e,s\}$	4
4	i	3
4	e,s	0
5	$\Sigma - \{h\}$	5
5	h	0
6	$\Sigma - \{h\}$	6
6	s	0
7	Σ	7
8	$\Sigma - \{r\}$	5
8	r	0
9	$\Sigma - \{i\}$	6
9	i	0
10	Σ	7

Σ: denotes the whole alphabetic set.

Now with $goto(0, d) = 0$, the string pointer is shifted rightward with $skip_1(u)$ characters, which are equal to 3, and the state variable is set to 0 again. The situation becomes

> state : 0
>
> string : *youandshercometoseeherdog*
>
> $\uparrow$

Next with $goto(0, e) = 1$, the string pointer is shifted leftward one character and the state variable is set to 1. The new situation is

> state : 1
>
> string : *youandshercometoseeherdog*
>
> $\uparrow$

Then with $goto(1, h) = 2$, the string pointer is shifted left-hand one character again and the state variable is set to 2. Now with $goto(2, s) = 3$, the string pointer is shifted left-hand one character and the state variable is set to 3. Because

$output(3) = $ "she," there is a match for pattern "she." After finding "she," the situation becomes

> state : 3
>
> string : *youandshercometoseeherdog*
>
> $\uparrow$

Now with $goto(3, d) = 0$, the value of $skip_2(3, d)$, which is equal to 4, is added to the string pointer and the state variable is set to 0. So the situation changes to

> state : 0
>
> string : *youandshercometoseeherdog*
>
> $\uparrow$

The searching operation continues until the string pointer is shifted over the entire string. All the patterns "she," "her," and "sher" are found, and the total number of characters inspected is 20, which is only 80% of total characters in the string in this example.

D. The Construction of goto, output, and $skip_1$

In this section, we will show how to construct $skip_1$. The *goto* and *output* functions are constructed from a set of reversed patterns. For a detailed description about how to construct the *goto* and *output* functions from a set of patterns, interested readers may refer to Aho's paper [5].

As for the $skip_1$ table, it can be considered as the $delta_1$ table by taking all patterns into account. It is defined as follows:

$$skip_1(char) = \begin{cases} d, & d \leq \text{minlen and } d \text{ is the} \\ & \text{minimum integer such that} \\ & pattern[m_i - d] = char \\ & \text{for some } i, \text{ where } 1 \leq i \leq k \\ \text{minlen,} & \text{otherwise.} \end{cases}$$

where minlen is the minimum length of all patterns, m_i is the length of the ith pattern and k is the total number of patterns. The difference between constructing the $delta_1$ table and the $skip_1$ table is that when computing $delta_1(char)$, we try to find the rightmost reoccurrence of *char* in a pattern for each alphabetic character *char*. However, when computing $skip_1(char)$, we first imagine that all patterns are aligned with their last characters. Then we try to find the rightmost reoccurrence of *char* among all the patterns for each alphabetic character *char*. The $skip_1$ table can be computed by the following two steps.

Step 1: For each alphabetic character *char*, set

$$skip_1(char) = \text{minlen}.$$

Step 2: For the jth character of the ith pattern $pattern_i$, set

$$skip_1(pattern_i[j]) = \min\{skip_1(pattern_i[j]), \\ m_i - j\}$$

where m_i is the length of $pattern_i$.

For example, given patterns { she, hers, his } and character "i", the $skip_1(i)$ is initialized to 3. Then we scan each character of all the patterns once. When we reach the second character "i" of the third pattern "his," the $skip_1(i)$ is set to $\min\{3, 1\} = 1$.

E. The Construction of skip₂

In the single pattern match, if a mismatch occurs between $pattern[j]$ and $string[i]$, the $delta'_2(j, string[i])$ is consulted to shift the pattern rightward. In a similar way, to match multiple patterns, if the character $string[i]$ causes the current state s (not the *start* state) transit to the *start* state, the $skip_2(s, string[i])$ is consulted to determine the shift of the string pointer. In the following paragraphs, the computation of the $skip_2$ table is described.

Before constructing the $skip_2$ table, we first introduce several notions. Since the *goto* graph is constructed from a set of reversed patterns, we say that the string u is matched at state s if the sequence of characters in the shortest path from state s to the *start* state spells out u. It should also be noticed that string u is the suffix of some patterns. Let $depth(s)$ be the number of edges in the shortest path from state s to the *start* state. Then the length of string u is $depth(s)$

Suppose that the character $string[i]$ causes the current state s (not the *start* state) to travel to the *start* state, then the purpose of $skip_2(s, string[i])$ is to shift the string pointer rightward such that one of the following two cases can be satisfied.

Case 1: The rightmost reoccurrence of u in a certain pattern (except for the string u matched at state s) can align with $string[i + 1 : i+depth(s)]$. At the same time, the character preceding the rightmost reoccurrence of u is equal to $string[i]$.

Case 2: The longest prefix of a certain pattern that is also the suffix of u can align with the suffix of $string[i + 1: i+depth(s)]$.

Now we describe how to construct the $skip_2$ table from the *goto* graph. The key point is: for each state s, find the reoccurrence of u in a certain pattern or the longest prefix of a certain pattern that is also the suffix of u. Before explaining this step in detail, we first introduce the property of *failure* function $f(s)$ for each state s in the *goto* graph. Suppose that string u is matched at state s and string v is matched at state t, by the Lemma 1 in [5], $f(t) = s$ if and only if u is the longest prefix of v that is also the suffix of a certain pattern.

To find the reoccurrence of u in a certain pattern for each state s in the *goto* graph, we can use the property of *failure* function f described previously. During the computation of f, if we have computed $f(t) = s$, then a reoccurrence of u can be found in v, and a number of $(depth(t) - depth(s))$ shifts of v on u is required, such that the first characters of these two strings are aligned. If $goto(t, string[i]) \neq 0$, then the value of $skip_2(s, string[i])$ is given by $(depth(t) - depth(s) + depth(s))$.

To find the longest prefix of a certain pattern that is the suffix of u for each state s in the *goto* graph, we start from each final state. Suppose that state t is a final state, $f(t) = r$, and the string matched at state r is w. According to Lemma 1 in [5], the longest prefix of v that is the suffix of all the strings matched at those states, which can be reached from

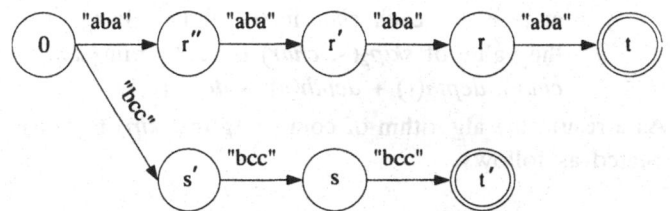

Fig. 2. An example of a *goto* graph.

state r (including state r), is w. For example, assume that state s can be reached from state r, a number of $(depth(t) - depth(r))$ shifts of v on u is required such that the longest prefix of v, which is w, is aligned with the suffix of u. Then the value of $skip_2(s, string[i])$ is given by $(depth(t) + depth(s) - depth(r))$. Suppose that we again have $f(r) = r'$ and the string matched at state r' is w', according to the Lemma 1 in [5], the longest prefix of v that is the suffix of all the strings matched at those states, which can be reached from state r' (including state r') but cannot be reached from state r, is w'. Repeat the above process until $f(r^{(n)}) = r^{(n+1)}$ and $r^{(n+1)} = 0$ (i.e., the *start* state).

The following is an example of the process to find the longest prefix of a certain pattern that is the suffix of u for each state s in the *goto* graph. Consider the *goto* graph shown in Fig. 2. The states t and t' are final states, and $f(t) = r$, $f(r) = r'$, $f(r') = r''$, and $f(r'') = 0$. The strings matched at states t, r, r', and r'' are "abaabaabaaba," "abaabaaba," "abaaba," and "aba," respectively. According to Lemma 1 in [5], we can see that the longest prefix of "abaabaabaaba" that is the suffix of all the strings matched at those states, located between states r and t (including state r and state t), is "abaabaaba." The longest prefix of "abaabaabaaba" that is the suffix of all the strings matched at those states, located between states r' and r (including state r' and excluding state r), is "abaaba." The longest prefix of "abaabaabaaba" that is the suffix of all the strings matched at those states, located between states r'' and r' (including state r'' and excluding state r'), is "aba."

To summarize, the computation of $skip_2$ can be divided into three steps as follows.

Step 1: For each state s in the *goto* graph and each *char* in the alphabetic set, set the values of $skip_2(s, char)$ to $(depth(s) + minlen)$, where minlen is the shortest length of all patterns. The length of skipped string cannot exceed minlen. Otherwise, the pattern with shorter length may be missed. Therefore, this is the maximum distance that the string pointer can be shifted rightward when a transition to the *start* state occurs at state s.

Step 2: Compute the *failure* function $f(s)$ for each state s in the *goto* graph. After computing $f(t) = s$, for each *char* in the alphabetic set such that $goto(t, char) \neq 0$, the value of $skip_2(s, char)$ is set by $\min\{skip_2(s, char), depth(t) - depth(s) + depth(s)\}$.

Step 3: Start from each final state t to find the longest prefix of v such that it is a suffix of u for each state s in the *goto* graph. Suppose that state t is a final state, $f(t) = r$, and state s can be reached from state r, for each *char* in the alphabetic set, then the value of $skip_2(s, char)$ is set by $\min\{skip_2(s, char), depth(t) + depth(s) - depth(r)\}$.

As a result, the algorithm of computing the $skip_2$ table can be stated as follows.

Algorithm 2 Compute the $skip_2$ table.
Input: *goto* graph.
Method

```
queue := empty;
for each char such that goto(0, char) = s ≠ 0 do
    begin
        for each a in the alphabet do skip₂(s, a) =
minlen + depth(s);
        f(s) = 0;
        queue := queue ∪ { s };
    end
while queue ≠ empty do
    begin
        let r be the next state in the queue;
        queue = queue − { r };
        for each a such that goto(r, a) = s ≠ 0 do
            begin
                for each a in the alphabet do skip₂(s, a)
= minlen + depth(s);
                queue := queue ∪ { s };
                state = f(r);
                while goto(state, a) = 0 and state ≠ 0
do
                    begin
                        skip₂(state, a) = min{skip₂(state,
a), depth(r)};

                        state = f(state);
                    end
                f(s) = goto(state, a);
                output(s) = output(s) ∪ output(f(s));
            end
    end


for each final state t do
    begin
        state = f(t);
        while state ≠ 0 do
            begin
                flag(state) = 1;
                queue = queue ∪ { state };
                while queue ≠ empty do
                    begin
                        let r be the next state in the queue;
                        queue = queue − { r };
                        for each a in alphabet do
                            begin
                                if goto(r, a) = s ≠ 0 then
                                    if flag(s) = 1 then
                                        flag(s) = 0;
                                    else
```

```
                                        queue = queue ∪ { s
};
                        skip₂(r, a) = min{skip₂(r,
a), depth(t) + depth(r) − depth(state)};
                    end
            end
        state = f(state);
    end
end.
```

In Algorithm 2, we use an additional function *flag* in Step 3. The function *flag* is used to mark those states r, r', and r'' discussed previously. Initially, $flag(s)$ for each state s in the *goto* graph is set to 0. When we first reach $r = f(t)$ in Step 3 of Algorithm 2, where t is a final state, $flag(r)$ is marked to 1. Next time when we reach state r traveling from state r', $flag(r')$ is marked to 1 and $flag(r)$ is marked to 0. In this way, the function *flag* can be used to identify those states where all the matched strings have the same suffix that is the longest prefix of the string matched at state t, for each final state t in the *goto* graph.

F. The Implementation of the goto Function, and the skip₁ and skip₂ Tables

In the previous sections, we have discussed how to construct the *goto* function and the $skip_1$, $skip_2$ tables. In implementation, the values of the *goto* function and the $skip_1$ and $skip_2$ tables can be stored in a state transition table. The advantage of storing one function and two tables in one state transition table is that no additional time is required to access $skip_1$ or $skip_2$ tables when a mismatch occurs. We know that when the *goto* function is represented by a state transition table, each state corresponds to a row and each character which causes a state transition corresponds to a column in the table. Each entry in the table indexed by state s and character *char* stores the next state that can be reached from state s on *char*.

From Section II-B, we have seen that when the input *char* causes a state transition from the *start* state to itself, the string pointer is shifted rightward with $skip_1(char)$ characters. When the input *char* causes a state transition from state s (which is not the *start* state) to the *start* state, the string pointer is shifted rightward with $skip_2(s,char)$ characters. At this point, each entry for state s and character *char* in the state transition table can be modified as follows.

1) Each entry consists of an indicator and a data field.
2) If the indicator is set to 1, the data field is occupied by the state that can be reached from the state s on input character *char*.
3) If the indicator is set to 0 and state s is the *start* state, the data field is occupied by $skip_1(char)$.
4) If the indicator is set to 0 and state s is not the *start* state, the data field is occupied by $skip_2(s, char)$.

For example, suppose that we have a set of patterns {she, sher, her, irsr}, the values of which *goto*, $skip_1$, and $skip_2$ can be calculated as in Section II-C. Now we can store these values in a modified state transition table as Table IV. In this table, the content of each entry is represented by a pair of indicators and data field.

characters state	e	h	i	r	s	other characters
0	(1,1)	(0,1)	(0,3)	(1,4)	(0,1)	(0,3)
1	(0,4)	(1,2)	(0,4)	(0,4)	(0,4)	(0,4)
2	(0,3)	(0,3)	(0,3)	(0,3)	(1,3)	(0,3)
3	(0,4)	(0,4)	(0,4)	(0,4)	(0,4)	(0,4)
5	(0,5)	(1,6)	(0,5)	(0,5)	(0,5)	(0,5)
6	(0,6)	(0,6)	(0,6)	(0,6)	(1,7)	(0,6)
7	(0,7)	(0,7)	(0,7)	(0,7)	(0,7)	(0,7)
8	(0,5)	(0,5)	(0,5)	(1,9)	(0,5)	(0,5)
9	(0,6)	(0,6)	(1,10)	(0,6)	(0,6)	(0,6)
10	(0,7)	(0,7)	(0,7)	(0,7)	(0,7)	(0,7)

Now the pattern matching operation can proceed as follows. When an entry is indexed by an input character and the current activated state, the next activated state is indicated by the second item of the pair and the string pointer is minus one if the first item of the pair is "1;" otherwise, the next activated state is the *start* state and the string pointer is added by the second item of the pair.

III. TIME COMPLEXITY ANALYSIS

A. Time Analyses for Constructing goto Function, and skip₁, and skip₂ Tables

In this section, we will assess the performance of the proposed multiple pattern match algorithm and estimate the preprocessing time required to construct the *goto* function and the *skip₁* and *skip₂* tables.

According to the algorithm proposed in Aho's paper [5], the time required to construct the *goto* function is linearly bounded by the total length of all the patterns. The construction of the *skip₁* table can be described in the following two steps.

Step 1: For every *char* in the alphabet, set $skip_1(char) =$ minlen.

Step 2: Scan every character in all the patterns once to construct the *skip₁* table according to its definition.

So the time required to construct the *skip₁* table is also linearly bounded by the sum of the size of the alphabetic set and the total length of all the patterns.

As described in Section II-D, the construction of *skip₂* is divided into three steps. In Step 1, each state in the *goto* graph is scanned once. Since the sum of total states in the *goto* graph is less than that of total length of all the patterns, the execution time required in Step 1 is linearly bounded by the size of the alphabetic set times the total length of all the patterns. In Step 2, the total number of state transitions is linearly bounded by the sum of the length of each pattern according to Theorem 4 in [5]. Similarly, the execution time required in Step 2 is also linearly bounded by the size of the alphabetic set times the total length of all patterns. In Step 3, the total number of states scanned is bounded by the total

number of final states times the number of different states in the *goto* graph. Therefore, the execution time required in Step 3 is linearly bounded by the total number of patterns, times the total length of all the patterns, and times the size of the alphabetic set. From the earlier discussion, the time required to construct the *skip₂* table is linearly bounded by the total number of patterns, times the total length of all patterns, and times the size of the alphabetic set.

We have coded Algorithm 2 for computing the *skip₂* table in C language and have executed it on Sun 3/160. The result shows that about 0.4 s is required for seven English patterns with the length of fifteen characters, and 0.07 s is required for seven binary patterns with the length of fifteen characters. Since in real applications only a few patterns are matched at the same time, we did not measure the processing time of computing the *skip₂* table for more than ten patterns. Note that by comparing with the preprocessing time required in the DFSA method, the proposed multiple pattern match algorithm requires additional time to construct the *skip₁* and *skip₂* tables. However, for matching multiple patterns in a large file, this preprocessing time is actually negligible.

B. The Theoretical Analysis of Searching Time

This section discusses the search time of the proposed multiple pattern match algorithm in the best, average, and worst cases. We know that the first character in the string that will be inspected is the *minlenth* character of the string. If this character does not match the last character of every pattern, then the longest distance that we can shift the string pointer rightward is minlen. So, the best-case performance of the proposed multiple pattern match algorithm occurs when the string pointer is always shifted rightward with minlen characters after inspecting one character in the string. Under this circumstance, the ratio of the number of character inspected in the string to the length of the string is given by 1/minlen.

For the worst case, as described in Knuth's paper [1], when matching the pattern a^m (i.e., a string consists of a sequence of *ma*'s) in the text a^n, the Boyer–Moore's algorithm shows quadratic behavior. The running time is essentially proportional to the pattern length times the text length. Similar to Boyer–Moore's algorithm, the worst-case performance of this proposed multiple pattern match algorithm also shows quadratic behavior, when one of the patterns to be matched is a^m in the text a^n. However, it rarely occurs in actual applications.

For investigating the average case performance of the proposed multiple pattern match algorithm, we need a probabilistic model to analyze the average case performance. In Boyer–Moore's paper [2], a probabilistic model has been proposed to analyze their algorithm. The average case performance is measured by the expected value of the ratio between the cost of discovering the mismatch and the distance to slide the pattern rightward upon finding the mismatch. Let the cost of discovering the mismatch be the total number of inspections made to string before discovering the mismatch, then the expected value of the ratio is given by

$$\frac{\sum_{m=0}^{patlen-1} cost(m) * Prob(m)}{\sum_{m=0}^{patlen-1} Prob(m) * \left(\sum_{k=1}^{patlen} k * P_{skip}(m,k)\right)} \quad (1)$$

where $cost(m)$ is the cost of discovering the mismatch that occurs at the last $(m+1)$th character of the pattern, $Prob(m)$ is the probability that the mismatch occurs at the last $(m+1)$th character of the pattern, and $P_{skip}(m, k)$ is the probability that the pattern is slid k characters rightward when the mismatch occurs at the last $(m+1)$th character of the pattern.

To adopt (1) to evaluate the performance of matching multiple patterns, the calculation of $Prob(m)$ and $P_{skip}(m, k)$ must be modified to take multiple patterns into consideration. In addition, (1) only measures the performance of finding the first occurrence of the pattern in a string. However, the performance of finding all possible occurrences of multiple patterns in a string is required in this case. So the expected value of the ratio is modified as

$$\frac{\sum_{m=0}^{maxlen} cost(m) * Prob(m)}{\sum_{m=0}^{maxlen} Prob(m) * \left(\sum_{k=1}^{minlen} k * P_{skip}(m,k)\right)} \quad (2)$$

where maxlen and minlen are the longest and the shortest pattern lengths among all the patterns. Note that in (2), the additional term, $cost(m)$ for m = maxlen, is included as compared to (1). That means the cost of discovering a mismatch after the longest pattern is matched. Moreover, the maximum distance that the patterns can be shifted rightward is limited to minlen. The ways of calculating $Prob(m)$ and $P_{skip}(m, k)$ for multiple patterns are given in Appendix A.

Using the probabilistic model described previously, we can compute the expected ratio between the cost of discovering the mismatch and the distance we can skip in the string upon finding the mismatch. Because the performance of the proposed algorithm is dependent on the statistical characteristics of patterns and strings, three typical source strings are chosen

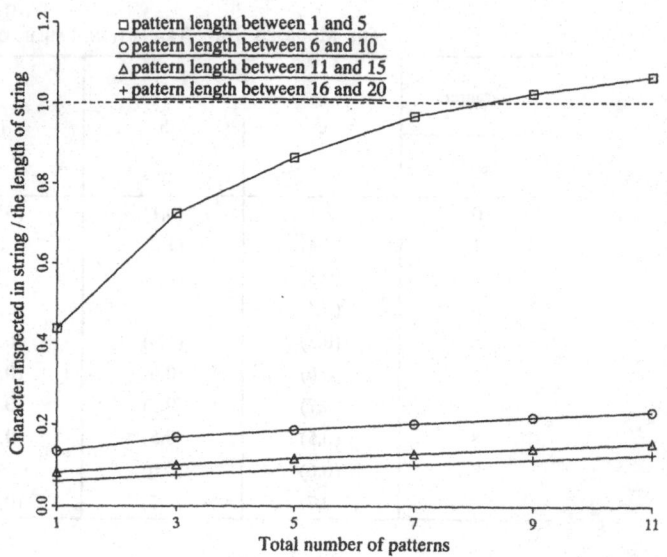

Fig. 3. The performance of finding all possible patterns in a random alphabetic string ($p = 0.01$).

for analysis. As described in Boyer–Moore's paper [2], for a random alphabetic string, p can be set to 0.01; for an English string, p can be set to 0.09; and for a random binary string, p can be set to 0.5. In the following performance analysis, for a given number of patterns, each pattern length is randomly selected from a specific range. For example, the pattern length may be randomly selected between 1 and 5.

Figs. 3–5 show the expected value of ratios for $p = 0.01$, 0.09, and 0.5. The dash line in each figure indicates the performance of the DFSA method. Since the DFSA method requires inspection of each character in the string only once, the expected ratio must be 1. From these figures, we can find that the expected ratio increases as the total number of patterns increases, but it decreases as the pattern length increases. When $p = 0.01$, the expected ratio is less than 0.2 (i.e., only 20% of all characters in the string need to be inspected) for the pattern length greater than 6. When $p = 0.09$, the expected ratio is also less than 0.4 for the pattern length greater than 6. However, when $p = 0.5$, the expected ratio is greater than 1 in most cases.

In actual applications, we found that the total number of patterns is rarely greater than 5 and the pattern length is usually between 5 and 15. As shown in the figures, the proposed algorithm performs much better than the DFSA method for searching a random alphabet string or an English string. For searching a random binary string, the DFSA method is better in most cases. Therefore, we can conclude that the proposed algorithm is suitable for matching random alphabetic or English patterns. However, it is not recommended for matching binary patterns because p is large.

C. Experiments

In order to confirm the performance of the proposed algorithm, we have conducted a series of experiments. We chose three typical source strings, each of 10 000 characters for analysis. The first source string is a random sequence

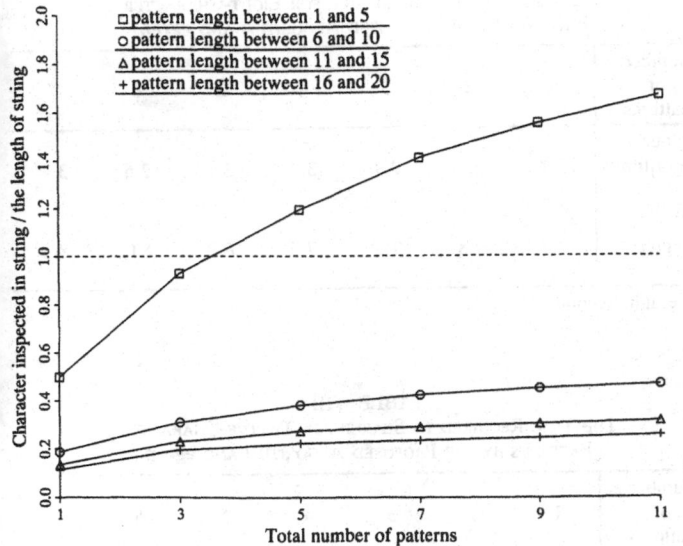

Fig. 4.   The performance of finding all possible patterns in an English string ($p = 0.09$).

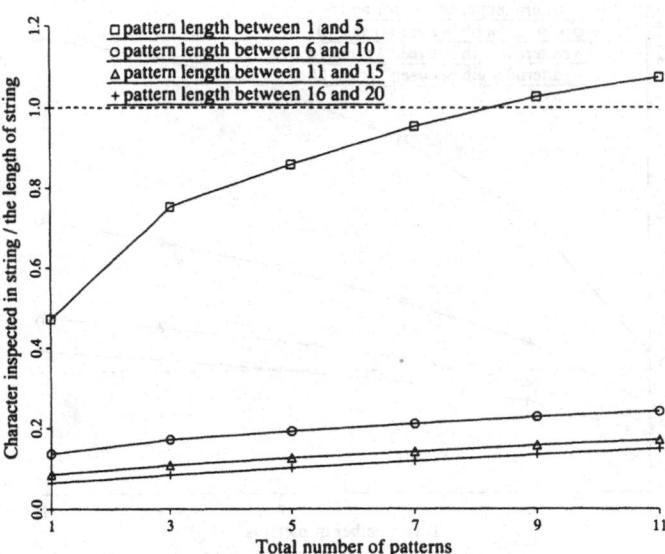

Fig. 6.   The actual performance of finding all possible patterns in a random alphabetic string ($p = 0.01$).

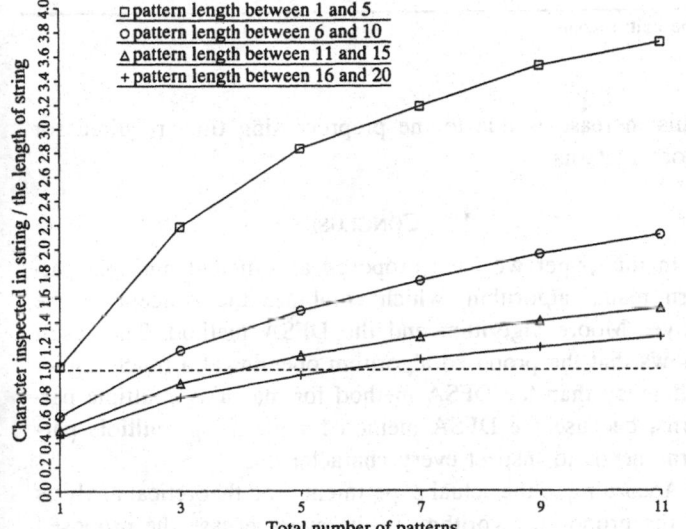

Fig. 5.   The performance of finding all possible patterns in a random binary string ($p = 0.5$).

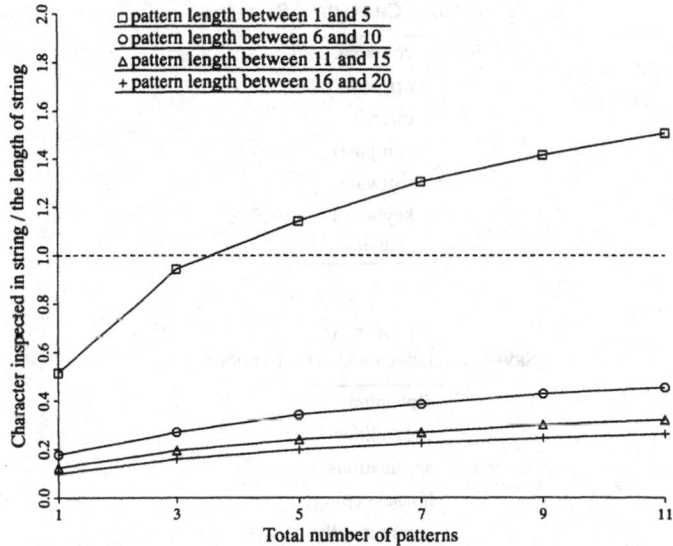

Fig. 7.   The actual performance of finding all possible patterns in an English string ($p = 0.09$).

of characters from a set of 100 alphabetic characters. The second source string is randomly selected from an English textbook. The third source string is composed of a random sequence of 0's and 1's. Then, for each typical source string, we randomly select n substrings from that source string, with each length chosen from a specific range. Afterwards, we searched through the source string with these n substrings by the proposed algorithm. The performance of the proposed algorithm is measured by the ratio of the average number of characters inspected in the source string to the length of the source string.

In order to accurately measure the ratios (i.e., to let the standard deviation of each value be less than the difference between different values), we perform 100 times experiments

for each kind of source string such that the coefficient of variation [13] is less than 0.1. In Figs. 6–8 the ratios are plotted against the various pattern lengths and the number of patterns for each kind of source string, respectively. The result is quite close to that measured by the probabilistic model. That confirms our probabilistic model!

D. The Actual Testing

In this section, we will compare the proposed multiple pattern match algorithm with the **egrep** program, which is a search program provided by the **UNIX** system and which adopts the DFSA method. In the actual testing, the proposed algorithm (coded in C language) and **egrep** are both executed

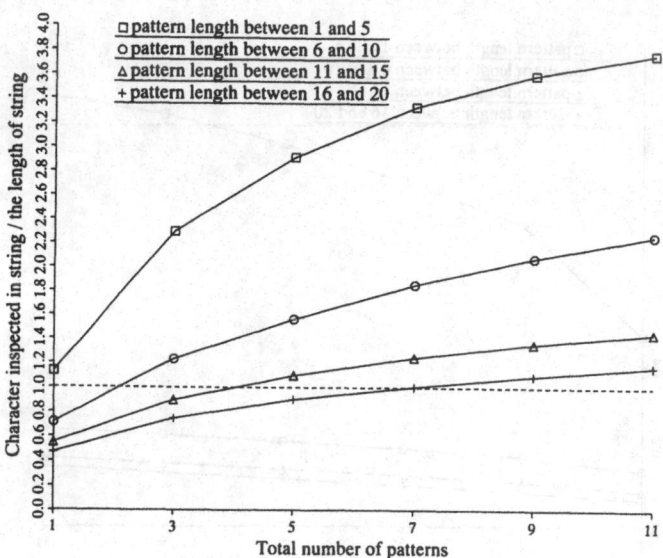

Fig. 8. The actual performance of finding all possible patterns in a random binary string (p = 0.5).

TABLE V
SEVEN EIGHT-CHARACTER PATTERNS

contaons
original
directly
computer
software
keyboard
diskette

TABLE VI
SEVEN TWELVE-CHARACTER PATTERNS

alphanumeric
capabilities
applications
housekeeping
commercially
supplemental
circumstance

on **SUN 3/160**. We randomly select two sets of patterns from a 1.4-Mbytes English text file. The first set consists of seven eight-character patterns and the other set consists of seven twelve-character patterns. The patterns in these two sets are shown in Table V and VI.

For each set of patterns, we search for all the patterns in the English text file. The result is shown in Table VII and VIII. From the above two tables, we can find that the multiple pattern searching time required for the proposed algorithm decreases as the length of the pattern increases and increases slightly as the number of patterns increases. Note that **egrep** must scan every character in the text file once regardless of the number of patterns. Therefore, the searching time required for **egrep** increases slightly as the number of patterns increases.

TABLE VII
THE TIME REQUIRED TO SEARCH FOR EIGHT-CHARACTER PATTERNS BY THE PROPOSED ALGORITHM AND **egrep**

number of patterns	1	2	3	4	5	6	7
our algorithm	2.1	2.3	2.9	3.2	3.5	3.6	3.7
egrep	7.7	7.8	7.9	7.9	8.0	8.0	8.1

Time unit: second

TABLE VIII
THE TIME REQUIRED TO SEARCH FOR TWELVE-CHARACTER PATTERNS BY THE PROPOSED ALGORITHM AND **egrep**

number of patterns	1	2	3	4	5	6	7
our algorithm	1.4	1.9	2.2	2.3	2.6	2.7	2.8
egrep	7.7	7.8	7.9	8.1	8.2	8.3	8.3

Time unit: second

This increase is due to the preprocessing time required for more patterns.

IV. CONCLUSIONS

In this paper we have proposed an efficient multiple pattern match algorithm, which combines the concept of the Boyer–Moore algorithm and the DFSA method. The result shows that the proposed algorithm operates at a much higher efficiency than the DFSA method for matching multiple patterns, because the DFSA method for matching multiple patterns needs to inspect every character once.

According to the actual experiments and theoretical analysis of the proposed algorithm, in the average case the proposed algorithm can perform very efficiently for matching multiple patterns in random alphabetic or English strings. In the case of matching seven eight-character patterns in a random alphabetic string, only about 20% of all characters in the string need to be inspected; when matching seven eight-character patterns in an English string, it is necessary to inspect only about 33% of all characters in the string. However, it is not recommended to use this algorithm to match multiple patterns in random binary strings. Although the proposed algorithm needs to construct the *goto* and *output* functions, and the $skip_1$ and $skip_2$ tables, the preprocessing time for constructing these functions and tables are negligible in our tests.

APPENDIX A

The Generating Functions for Combinations

This section introduces the generating functions for combinations [14] which will be used for theoretical analysis of searching time. Let $(a_0, a_1, a_2, \cdots, a_r, \cdots)$ represent a sequence of events. According to [14], the function

$$F(x) = a_0\mu_0(x) + a_1\mu_1(x) + a_2\mu_2(x) + \cdots + a_r\mu_r(x) + \cdots$$

is called the ordinary generating function of the sequence $(a_0, a_1, a_2, \cdots, a_r \cdots)$, where

$$a_0\mu_0(x), a_1\mu_1(x), a_2\mu_2(x), \cdots, a_r\mu_r(x), \cdots$$

is a sequence of functions of x that are used as indicators. In fact, the most usual and useful form of $\mu_r(x)$ is x^r. In this case, the ordinary generating function for the sequence $(a_0, a_1, a_2, \cdots, a_r \cdots)$ becomes

$$F(x) = a_0 + a_1x^1 + a_2x^2 + \cdots + a_rx^r + \cdots.$$

To find the number of combinations of n distinct objects, we have the ordinary generating function

$$(1+x)^n = 1 + nx + \frac{n(n-1)}{2!}x^2 + \cdots$$
$$+ \frac{n(n-1)\cdots(n-r+1)}{r!}x^r + \cdots + x^n$$
$$= C(n,0) + C(n,1)x + C(n,2)x^2 + \cdots$$
$$+ C(n,r)x^r + \cdots + x^n.$$

In the expansion of $(1+x)^n$, the coefficient of the term x^r is the number of ways to select r distinct objects from n distinct objects.

Suppose that there are n distinct objects $Y_1, Y_2, \cdots, Y_n$, each object Y_i has the probability p_i to be selected and the probability $q_i = 1 - p_i$ not to be selected. To find the probability that r distinct objects are selected from n distinct objects, we have the ordinary generating function

$$F(x) = (q_1 + p_1x)(q_2 + p_2x)\cdots(q_n + p_nx)$$
$$= a_0 + a_1x + \cdots + a_rx^r + \cdots + a_nx^n.$$

In the expansion of the above ordinary generating function, the coefficient of term x^r is the probability to select r distinct objects from n distinct objects.

The Calculation of Prob (m) and $P_{skip}(m, k)$

This section discusses the calculation of $Prob(m)$ and $P_{skip}(m,k)$. Suppose that there are n patterns

$$pat(1), pat(2), \cdots, pat(n)$$

, and each has the length $len(1), len(2), \cdots, len(n)$ respectively. Without loss of generality, we assume that the patterns $pat(1), pat(2), \cdots, pat(n_1)$ have the same pattern length l_1, the patterns $pat(n_1 + 1), pat(n_1 + 2), \cdots, pat(n_1 + n_2)$ have the same pattern length l_2, ..., and the patterns

$$pat\left(\sum_{i=1}^{k-1} n_i + 1\right), pat\left(\sum_{i=1}^{k-1} n_i + 2\right), \cdots, pat\left(\sum_{i=1}^{k-1} n_i + n_k\right)$$

have the same pattern length l_k, where $1 \leq l_1 = $ minlen $< l_2 < \cdots < l_k = $ maxlen and

$$\sum_{i=1}^{k} n_i = n.$$

Let p denote the probability that two characters selected from some patterns or the string are equal. Let A_i be the event that the mismatch occurs at the last $(m+1)$th character of the pattern $pat(i)$. Then the probability that event A_i occurs is given as

$$P(A_i) = \begin{cases} (1-p) * p^m, & 0 \leq m < \text{len}(i) \\ p^{\text{len}(i)}, & m = \text{len}(i). \end{cases}$$

Let A_i' be the event that the mismatch occurs before the last $(m+1)$th character of the pattern $pat(i)$ (i.e., the mismatch occurs at the last character, at the last second character, ..., or at the last mth character of the pattern $pat(i)$). Then the probability that event A_i' occurs is given as

$$P(A_i') = \sum_{j=0}^{m-1} (1-p) * p^j = 1 - p^m, 0 \leq m \leq \text{len}(i).$$

Now the probability $Prob(m)$ is calculated as follows.

1) When $m = 0$, that means the last character of each pattern does not match with the inspected character *char* in the string, $Prob(m) = (1-p)^n$.

2) When $0 < m \leq l_1$, the probability $Prob(m)$ is determined by the probability to select r patterns from n patterns such that the selected patterns have a mismatch that occurs at the last $(m+1)$th character, and the other patterns have a mismatch that occurs before the last $(m+1)$th character. Therefore, the ordinary generating function is given as

$$F(x) = \prod_{i=1}^{n} (P(A_i') + P(A_i)x)$$
$$= a_0 + a_1x + a_2x^2 + \cdots + a_nx^n$$

and

$$Prob(m) = \sum_{i=1}^{n} a_i.$$

3) When $l_1 < m \leq l_2$, the first n_1 patterns $pat(1), pat(2), \cdots, pat(n_1)$ are ignored during the calculation of $Prob(m)$, for these pattern lengths are equal to l_1. In this case, the ordinary generating function is given as

$$F(x) = \prod_{i=n_1+1}^{n} (P(A_i') + P(A_i)x)$$
$$= a_0 + a_1x + a_2x^2 + \cdots + a_{n-n_1}x^{n-n_1}$$

and

$$Prob(m) = \sum_{i=1}^{n-n_1} a_i.$$

4) With the similar argument mentioned previously, the probability $Prob(m)$ is calculated for $l_2 < m \leq l_3, \cdots,$ and $l_{k-1} < m \leq l_k$.

According to the values of m, the calculation of $P_{skip}(m, k)$ needs to consider two distinct cases of $m = 0$ and $m \neq 0$. First consider the case of $m = 0$, which denotes that the last character of each pattern does not match with the inspected character *char* in the string; the *skip₁* function determines the distance to slide all patterns rightward with k characters. Let B_i be the event that *char* matches with the last $(k+1)$th character of pattern *pat(i)*. Then the probability that event B_i occurs is given as

$$P(B_i) = \begin{cases} p * (1 - p)^{k-1}, & 1 \leq k < \text{len}(i); \\ (1 - p)^{k-1}, & k = \text{len}(i). \end{cases}$$

Let B_i' be the event that the character matches with *char* occurring after the last $(k+1)$th character of pattern *pat(i)* (i.e., the last $(k+2)$th character, the last $(k+3)$th character, etc., or no matched character). Then the probability that event B_i' occurs is given as

$$P(B') = 1 - \sum_{j=1}^{k} p * (1 - p)^{j-1} = (1 - p)^k, 1 \leq k < \text{len}(i).$$

Now the probability $P_{skip}(0, k)$ is calculated as follows.

1) When $1 \leq k < l_1 = $ minlen, the probability $P_{skip}(0, k)$ is determined by the probability to select r patterns from n patterns such that in those r selected patterns *char* matches with the last $(k+1)$th character and in other patterns the character matched with *char* occurs after the last $(k+1)$th character. Therefore, the ordinary generating function is given as

$$F(x) = \prod_{i=1}^{n} (P(B_i') + P(B_i)x)$$
$$= a_0 + a_1 x + a_2 x^2 + \cdots + a_n x^n$$

and

$$P_{skip}(0, k) = \sum_{i=1}^{n} a_i, \ 1 \leq k \leq l_1 = \text{minlen}.$$

However, for $1 \leq k < l_1 = $ minlen, we have

$$P(B_1) = P(B_2) = \cdots = P(B_n)$$

and

$$P(B_1') = P(B_2') = \cdots = P(B_n').$$

So $P_{skip}(0, k)$ can be simplified to

$$\sum_{i=1}^{n} C'(n, i) * P(B_1)^i * P(B_1')^{n-i}.$$

2) When $k = l_1 = $ minlen, that means *char* does not occur in the first n_1 patterns $pat(1), pat(2), \cdots, pat(n_1)$ and it occurs after the last l_1th character of the other patterns $pat(n_1 + 1), pat(n_1 + 2), \cdots, pat(n)$. So $P_{skip}(0,$ minlen$)$ is given as

$$\left[(1 - p)^{\text{minlen}-1} \right]^{n_1} * \left[(1 - p)^{\text{minlen}-1} \right]^{n-n_1}$$
$$= (1 - p)^{(\text{minlen}-1)*n}.$$

Next, consider the case of $m \neq 0$, this is the case that a mismatch occurs at the last $(m+1)$th character of some patterns. The *skip₂* function determines the distance to slide all patterns rightward with k characters. For a specific pattern *pat(i)*, the probability $pdelta'_2(m, k, i)$ that the pattern can be slid rightward with k characters according to the *delta'₂* function is given as

$$pdelta'_2(m, k, i) = \begin{cases} p * p^m, & (m + k) < \text{len}(i) \\ p^{\text{len}(i)-k}, & (m + k) \geq \text{len}(i). \end{cases}$$

However, $pdelta'_2(m, k, i)$ is the probability under the condition that the distance to slide the pattern rightward is k characters. So the probability, denoted as $Pdelta'_2(m, k, i)$, that the pattern is slid rightward with exact k characters according to the *delta'₂* function is expressed in the following recursive form:

$$Pdelta'_2(m, k, i) =$$
$$\begin{cases} pdelta'_2(m, k, i) \left(1 - \sum_{j=1}^{k-1} Pdelta'_2(m, j, i) \right), & k < len(i); \\ 1 - \sum_{j=1}^{k-1} Pdelta'_2(m, j, i), & k = len(i). \end{cases}$$

Let D_i be the event that the pattern *pat(i)* slides rightward with the k character according to the *delta'₂* function, then the probability that the event D_i occurs is given as

$$P(D_i) = Pdelta'_2(m, k, i).$$

Let D_i' be the event that the pattern *pat(i)* slides rightward with more than k characters according to the *delta'₂* function, then the probability that the event D_i' occurs is given as

$$P(D_i') = 1 - \sum_{j=1}^{k} Pdelta'_2(m, j, i).$$

Now the probability $P_{skip}(m, k)$, for $m > 1$, is calculated as follows.

1) When $1 \leq m \leq l_1$, the probability $P_{skip}(m, k)$ is determined by the probability to select r patterns from n patterns such that those selected r patterns will slide rightward with k characters and other patterns will slide rightward with more than k characters. Therefore, the ordinary generating function is given as

$$F(x) = \prod_{i=1}^{n} (P(D_i') + P(D_i)x)$$
$$= a_0 + a_1 x + a_2 x^2 + \cdots + a_n x^n$$

and

$$P_{skip}(m, k) = \sum_{i=1}^{n} a_i, \ 1 \leq k \leq l_1 = \text{minlen}.$$

2) When $l_1 < m \leq l_2$, the first n_1 patterns $pat(1), pat(2), \cdots, pat(n_1)$ are ignored during the calculation of $P_{skip}(m, k)$, because these pattern lengths

are equal to l_1. In this case, the ordinary generating function is given as

$$F(x) = \prod_{i=n_1+1}^{n} (P(D_i') + P(D_i)x)$$
$$= a_0 + a_1 x + a_2 x^2 + \cdots + a_{n-n_1} x^{n-n_1}$$

and let

$$X(k) = \sum_{i=1}^{n-n_1} a_i, \quad 1 \le k \le l_2$$

then

$$P_{skip}(m, k) = \begin{cases} X(k), & 1 \le k < \text{minlen} \\ \sum_{i=minlen}^{l_2} X(i), & k = \text{minlen}. \end{cases}$$

For those patterns with pattern lengths greater than minlen, they have the probability to slide rightward with more than minlen characters. However, as discussed in Section II-D, the maximum distance that all patterns can slide rightward is limited to minlen characters. Therefore, $P_{skip}(m, \text{minlen})$ must include the probability to slide patterns rightward with more than minlen characters.

3) With the similar argument mentioned previously, the probability $P_{skip}(m, k)$ is calculated for $l_2 < m \le l_3, \cdots,$ and $l_{k-1} < m \le l_k$.

REFERENCES

[1] D. E. Knuth, J. H. Morris, and V. R. Pratt, "Fast pattern in strings, " *SIAM J. Comput.*, vol. 6, pp. 323–350, June 1977.
[2] R. S. Boyer and J. S. Moore, " A fast string searching algorithm,"*Commun. ACM*, vol. 20, pp. 762–772, Oct. 1977.
[3] R. Sedgewick, *Algorithms.* Reading, MA: Addison-Wesley, 1983.
[4] L. J. Guibas and A. M. Odlyzko, "A new proof of the linearity of the Boyer–Moore string searching algorithm," *Found. Comput. Sci.*, pp. 189–195, 1977.
[5] A. V. Aho and M. J. Corasick, "Efficient string matching: An aid to bibliographic search," *Commun. ACM*, vol. 18, pp. 333–340, June 1979.
[6] F. Bancilhon, F. S. Gamerman, J. M. Laubin, L. P. Richard, M. Scholl, D. Tusera, and A. Verroust, "Verson: A relational database machine," in *Advance Database Machine Architecture*, D. K. Hsiao, ed. Englewood Cliffs, NJ: Prentice-Hall, 1983.
[7] R. L. Haskin and L. A. Hollaar, "Operational characteristics of a hardware-based pattern matcher," *ACM Trans. Database Syst.*, vol. 8, pp. 15–40, Jan. 1983.
[8] R. Gonzalez-Rubio, J. Rohmer, and D. Terral, "The Schuss filter: A processor for non-numerical data processing," in *Proc. 11th Ann. Int. Symp. on Computer Architecture*, June 5–7, 1984, pp. 64–73.
[9] S. Pramanik, " Database filters," in *Proc. 9th Ann. Symp. Computer Architecture*, Apr. 26–29, 1982, pp. 201–210.
[10] K. Takahashi, H. Yamada, H. Nagai, and K. Matsumi, "A new string search hardware architecture for VLSI," in *Proc. 13th Ann. Int. Symp. on Computer Architecture*, June 2–5, 1986, pp. 20–27.
[11] S. L. Ou and K. Y. Su, "A new pattern matcher used in the data filter of mrdbm," in *Proc. IEEE TENCON*, 1987, pp. 307–312.
[12] A. V. Aho, R. Sethi, and J. D. Ullman, *Compilers, Principles, Techniques, and Tools.* Reading, MA: Addison-Wesley, 1985.
[13] P. J. Bickel and K. A. Doksum, *Mathematical Statistics: Basic Ideas and Selected Topics.* San Francisco, CA: Holden-Day, 1977.
[14] C. L. Liu, *Introduction to Combinatorial Mathematics.* Englewood Cliffs, NJ: Prentice-Hall, 1977.

Jang-Jong Fan received the B.S. degree in electronic engineering from Fun Cha University, Taiwan, in 1984 and the M.S. degree in electrical engineering from the National Tsing Hua University, in 1986, where he is also currently pursuing the Ph.D. degree in electrical engineering.

His research interests include computer algorithms, parallel computer architecture, file structure, and performance evaluation.

Keh-Yih Su (S'80–M'85) received the B.S. degree in nuclear engineering from National Tsing Hua University, Taiwan, in 1976, and the M.S. and Ph.D. degrees in electrical engineering from the University of Washington, Seattle, in 1980 and 1984, respectively.

From 1989 to 1990, he was with the Speech Research Department, AT&T Bell Laboratories, Murray Hill, NJ, as a Visiting Scientist, where he conducted research in the areas of discrimination and robustness oriented recognition. Currently, he is an Associate Professor with the Department of Electrical Engineering, National Tsing Hua University. He has been involved in a number of research projects, including Database Machine, English-to-Chinese Translation, and Chinese Phonetic Typewriter. Since 1985, he has been the Director of the ARCHTRAN Machine Translation Machine Development Project, which is currently being used to translate technical manuals by a number of computer companies in Taiwan. His current research interests include the area of natural language processing and speech understanding.

Dr. Su is a member of Tau Beta Pi and Phi Tau Phi.

Chapter 3: Approximate String Matching

Introduction

The matching techniques discussed in the previous chapters are concerned with exact string pattern matching problems. The approximate matching of strings is suitable for finding an item in a database when there may be a spelling mistake or some error in the keyword. It arises in areas such as file comparison, molecular biology, error correction, spelling correction, and speech recognition. This chapter discusses typical problems of approximate string matching such as edit distance, longest common subsequence, k-mismatches, k-differences, spelling correction, and related problems.

The edit distance between two files is the smallest number of editing transformations required to change one of the files into the other. A simple dynamic programming algorithm for computing this edit distance has been discovered independently by many researchers. The running time of this algorithm is proportional to $m \times n$, the product of the sizes of the two files. Another approach extracts a longest common subsequence from the two strings and produces the editing changes from the subsequence. Assuming that $n \geq m$, the time required is O($n \log n$). The *Hamming distance*, in the k-mismatches problem between two strings of equal length, is the number of positions with mismatching characters. The *Levenshtein distance*, in the k-differences problem between two strings of not necessarily equal lengths, is the minimum number of character changes, insertions, and deletions required to transform the one string into the other. For the k-mismatch problem the algorithm takes O$[k(n+m\log m)]$ time and O$[k(n+m)]$ space, and the algorithm for the k-difference problem runs in O(kn) sequential time and O($k+\log m$) parallel time, where k is the maximum sum of the error weights. In the rest of this chapter, spelling correction, don't-care symbol matches, and related problems are discussed along with corresponding references.

The paper by Hall and Dowling (1980) is a good survey, so it has been selected as an introduction to approximate string matching. The problem of substring matching, when the strings are from a finite alphabet, is investigated thoroughly in the next selected paper, that by Wang and Pavlidis (1990). They present definitions of string distances, an effective way of computing them, and matching algorithms minimizing them. The paper by Kashyap and Oommen (1983) discusses the noisy string matching problem.

The approximate string matching problem is to find all substrings in a text that are close to a pattern according to some measure of closeness. Good surveys on this problem are [Sankoff et al., 83], [Aho, 90], and [Hall et al., 80]. Approximate matching of strings is suitable for finding an item in a database when there may be a spelling mistake or other errors in the keyword. The problems are classified as either equivalence or similarity problems. Equivalence problems are readily solved using canonical forms. For similarity problems different measures are defined, with a full description of the well-established dynamic programming method relating this to the approach using probabilities and likelihoods. Other applications arise in areas such as file comparison, molecular biology, and speech recognition.

Edit distance

Perhaps the simplest problem is the file difference problem: given two files x and y, determine how "close" x is to y. A usual way to compute the closeness of the two files is to determine the shortest sequence of editing changes that will convert the first file into the second. The *edit distance* between two strings is the smallest number of editing transformations required to change one string into the other. For example, if the first string is *cabbaab* and the second by *bcbaba*, the edit distance is 6. A simple dynamic programming algorithm that computes the edit distance has been discovered independently by many researchers; see [Aho, 90], [Nemhauser, 66], and [Sankoff et al., 83]. The following are based on Aho's description.

Let $d(i,j)$ be the edit distance between the prefix, of length i, of the first string and the prefix, of length j, of the second string. Let $d(0,0)$ be 0, $d(i,0)$ be i for $1 \leq m$, and $d(0,j)$ be j for $1 \leq j \leq n$. Then, for $1 \leq i \leq m$ and $1 \leq j \leq n$, compute $d(i,j)$ by taking the minimum of the three quantities:

(1) $d(i-1, j)+1$,   (2) $d(i, j-1)+1$,   (3) $d(i-1, j-1)$ if $a_i = b_j$

The first quantity represents the deletion of the *j*th character from the first string, and the third says that $d(i,j) \leq d(i-1, j-1)$ if the *i*th character in the first string agrees with the *j*th character in the second string. After completing this computation, we can easily show that $d(m,n)$ gives the minimum number of edit changes required to transform the first file into the second.

From these distance calculations we can construct the corresponding sequence of editing transformations. Figure 1 shows the matrix of edit distances for the strings *cabbaab* and *bcbababa*.

```
a  8 | 8   7   6   7   7   6   6
b  7 | 7   6   5   6   6   6   6   5
a  6 | 6   5   4   6   6   5   5   6
b  5 | 5   4   3   5   5   5   6   6
a  4 | 4   3   2   5   5   4   5   6
b  3 | 3   2   3   4   4   5   6   6
c  2 | 2   1   2   4   4   5   6   7
b  1 | 1   2   3   3   3   4   5   6
   0 | 0   1   2   3   4   5   6   7
       ----------------------------
         0   1   2   3   4   5   6   7
         c   a   b   b   a   a   b
```

Figure 1. The matrix of edit distances for the strings *cabbaab* and *bcbababa*

The worst-case time complexity of this algorithm is O(nm), as shown in [Aho et al., 76]. For short strings the implementation of [Hunt et al., 77] demonstrates that the linear space version ([Hirschberg, 75], [Hirschberg, 77], and [Hirschberg, 78]) works very well but is slow for long strings. Minimum edit distance is discussed in [Megson, 90].

Longest common subsequence

Another approach to the string difference problem is to find a longest common subsequence of the two strings and produce the editing changes from the remaining subsequence ([Hunt et al., 77]). A subsequence of a string x is a sequence of characters obtained by deleting zero or more characters from x. A common subsequence of two strings x and y is a string that is a subsequence of both x and y, and a longest common subsequence is a common subsequence that is of greatest length. For example, *baba* and *cbba* are both longest common subsequences of *abcabba* and *cbabac*. Ukkonen ([Ukkonen, 92]) has studied approximate string matching in connection with two string distance functions that can find the locally best approximate occurrences of pattern and maximal common substrings in time $O(n)$. Kuo et al. ([Kuo et al., 91]) describe an improvement to the algorithm in [Wagner et al., 74] for finding the longest common subsequence that runs in linear space and quadratic time.

In the file difference problem the time complexity of their algorithm is $O(n\log n)$, significantly faster than the dynamic programming solution. By treating the program as one of constructing a least-cost path in a graph, a third solution for this problem is proposed in [Myers, 86] and [Ukkonen, 85a]. The time complexity of Myers's approach using suffix trees is $O(n\log n + d^2)$ for edit distance d, and Masek et al. ([Masek et al., 80]) have proposed an $O(n^2/\log n)$-time algorithm using the "four Russians" trick. The algorithm of [Kim et al., 92] involves building a trie from the text string, which takes time $O(n\log n)$ for a text. Once this data structure has been built, any number of approximate searches can be made for a pattern. The expected look up time for each pattern is $O(m\log n)$. Other algorithms are discussed in [Allison et al., 86], [Apostolico, 86], [Apostolico, 87], [Apostolico et al., 87], [Chvatal et al., 75], [Fredman, 75], [Miller et al., 85], [Nakatsu et al., 82], [Tichy, 84], and [Wong et al., 76]. In partial matching, an approach of omitting strings common to the patterns and the text is introduced in [Landau et al., 85].

The optimal correspondent subsequence (OCS) problem is derived from the longest common subsequence (LCS) problem and arises in data processing applications such as the comparison of two files and in genetic applications such as the study of molecular evolution. In the paper [Wang et al., 90] the definition of OCS, which extends the finite-alphabet editing error minimization matching to the infinite-alphabet penalty minimization matching, is given. The paper discusses the application of the string-to-string OCS to the stereo epipolar line-matching problem and the feasibility of applying OCS to UPC bar code recognition.

Edit distance measures

Under the condition that the distance between the pattern and the substring is at most k, there are two very common edit-distance measures. One of them is the Hamming distance between two strings of equal length, which is the number of positions with mismatching characters. For example, the Hamming distance between *abcabb* and *cbacba* is four. This is called the k-mismatches problem. Another distance measure is the Levenshtein distance between two strings of not necessarily equal length, which is the minimum number of character changes, insertions, and deletions required to transform one string into the other. For example, the Levenshtein distance between *abcabba* and *cbabac* is four. This is called the k-differences problem.

For the k-mismatch problem the algorithm of [Landau et al., 86b] takes $O[k(n+m\log m)]$ time and $O[k(n+m)]$ space. Although it is fast, the space required is unacceptable for practical purposes. The method of [Galil et al., 86] uses $O(kn+m\log m)$ time and $O(m)$ space, but it is slower than the algorithm of [Landau et al., 86b] in practice because the constant in the linear term is large. Quong ([Quong, 92]) has proposed the technique of multiplexing sparse tables for the k-mismatches problem. Other algorithms for the k-mismatches problem are presented in [Galil et al., 88] and [Ivanov, 85]. The papers [Majster et al., 80], [Ukkonen, 85a], and [Wong et al., 76] present algorithms for computing the Levenshtein distance between a pair of strings, and algorithms for the k-differences problem are described in [Landau et al., 86b], [Landau et al., 88], [Ukkonen, 85b], and [Wagner et al., 74]. A generalized version of [Wagner, 74] is discussed in [Bunke et al., 92].

The BM algorithm is generalized in [Tarhio et al., 90] to these distance measures. The expected time for the k-mismatches problem is $O[kn(1/(m-k)+k/c)]$, where c is the size of the alphabet, and a related algorithm is developed for the k-differences problem. Various $O(kn)$ algorithms based on dynamic programming are carefully implemented and analyzed in [Chang et al., 92]. An algorithm in sublinear expected time is discussed in [Chang et al., 90] for restricted k-differences problems, such as when the text string is random and errors are not too frequent. Jong et al. ([Jong et al., 92]) have proposed a modified WLD (weighted Levenshtein distance) algorithm for the design of a code string matching processor and have quite accurately approximated the deformation of cursive Chinese characters. The paper [Bradford, 90] introduces an algorithm that encodes pairs of strings as binary numbers such that the Hamming distance between binary code words is equal to the Levenshtein distance between the original strings.

More general distance measures are considered in [Abrahamson, 87], [Lowrance et al., 75], and [Miller, 87]. Wen-Tsuen et al. ([Wen-Tsuen et al., 92]) have introduced a robust distance measure between patterns, and have obtained a quite accurate approximation to the deformation of cursive Chinese characters with much lower cost. Efficient data structures for approximate matching are presented in [Galil et al., 88]. The approximate string matching algorithm for regular expressions is considered in [Myers et al., 89], [Wagner, 74], and [Wagner et al., 78]. Jokinen et al. ([Jokinen et al., 91]) have proposed approximate string matching algorithms for a static text that use two preprocessing methods based on suffix automata and n-gram lists. Bertossi et al. consider weighted differences (errors) between a pattern and a text and develop fast sequential and parallel algorithms. In particular, they allow the following types of errors: mismatch whose weight depends on the mismatching characters, extra character with constant weight, missing character with constant weight, and transposition of two consecutive characters with constant weight. It runs in $O(kn)$ sequential time and $O(k+\log m)$ parallel time with $\max(n+k+1, m^2)$ processors, where k is the maximum sum of the error weight. Distance computation in pattern recognition is discussed in [Sellers, 80], and similarities in the amino acid sequence of two proteins is proposed in [Needleman et al., 70].

Spelling correction

Approximate string matching algorithms are useful for correcting words automatically in text. The paper [Kukich, 92b] is a good survey of this field. The minimum edit distance spelling correction algorithm is implemented in [Damerau, 64]. Levenshtein's algorithm is generalized to cover multierror misspellings in [Wagner et al., 74]. Some metrics of [Kashyap et al., 81], [Lowrance et al., 75], [Okuda et al., 76], and [Wong et al., 76] are tested in the spelling corrector for the Unix command language interface by Hawley ([Hawley, 82]).

The weighting of graphemic edit distances, in [Veronis, 88], based on phonemic similarity is necesary because phonetic misspellings frequently result in greater deviation from the correct orthographic spelling. A reverse minimum edit distance technique is used by Gorin ([Gorin, 71]) in the DEC 10 spelling corrector and by Durham et al. ([Durham et al., 83]) in their command language corrector. The techniques are also used to generate candidates for the probabilistic spelling corrector ([Kernighan et al., 90], [Church et al., 91a], and [Church et al., 91b]). The combination of key search techniques and minimum-distance algorithms are introduced in [Boivie, 81], [Dunlavey, 81], [Muth et al., 77], and [Taylor, 81].

The notion behind similarity key techniques is to map every string into a key such that similarly spelled strings have identical or similar keys. The techniques are used in [Pollock et al., 84] and [Tenczar et al., 72]. A fuzzy similarity measure has been patented by Bocast ([Bocast, 91]). Letter n-grams, including trigrams, bigrams, and unigrams, have been used in a variety of ways in text recognition and spelling correction techniques ([Angell et al., 83], [Deheer, 82], [Kohonen, 80], [Mor, 82], [Riseman et al., 74], [Ullman, 77] and [Zamora, 81]).

Techniques utilizing vector distance metrics and correlation matrix memory are discussed in [Cherkassky et al., 92], [Dahl et al., 90], [Deloche et al., 90], and [Kukich, 92a]. Methods using the generalized inverse (GI) matrix and singular value decomposition (SVD) are described in [Cherkassky et al., 90], [Cherkassy et al., 91], [Deerwester et al., 90], and [Kukich, 90]. Bickel ([Bickel, 87]) has devised a hybrid unigram and a heuristically based vector distance correction technique for a database retrieval application that uses employee names as access keys. Other techniques of spelling correction are surveyed in [Kukich, 92b].

Let $T(U)$ be the set of words in the dictionary H that contains U as a substring. The problem considered in [Kashyap et al., 83] is the estimation of the set $T(U)$ when U is not known, but Y, a noisy version of U, is available. The suggested set estimate, $S*(Y)$, of $T(U)$ is a proper subset of H such that its every element contains at least one substring that resembles Y most according to the Levenshtein metric. The proposed algorithm for the computation of $S*(Y)$ requires cubic time. Berghel et al. ([Berghel et al., 90]) have shown how approximate string matching can be involved in the automation of various aspects of word game construction or solution.

Related problems

Suppose that the don't-care symbol matches any single character, including a don't-care symbol. String matching with don't-care symbols has been investigated by Fischer et al., ([Fischer et al., 74]), who have achieved $O[n (\log m) (\log \log m) (\log c)]$ asymptotic search time, where c is the number of symbols. Pinter ([Pinter, 85]) also gives an $O(mn)$ algorithm that is faster than a naive algorithm. For small patterns, the algorithm of [Abrahamson, 87] runs in $O[n+m\sqrt{n} (\log n)(\log \log n)]$ time. An algorithm in [Manber et al., 91] searches for a pattern with don't-care symbols in a preprocessed text. The number of occurrences of the pattern can be found in $O(\log n)$ time, and a list of all occurrences can be found in time $O(n^{1/4}+R)$, where R is the number of occurrences, but it takes $O[n(k+m)]$ space, where k is an upper bound on the number of don't-care symbols.

Shift and string matching approaches are presented in [Baeza-Yates et al., 92]. The approaches allow don't-care symbols, the complement of a symbol, and any finite class of symbols, and they solve this problem for one or more patterns, with or without mismatches. For small patterns the worst-case time is linear in the size of the text (the authors state that a pattern is small if m is bounded by a constant). The main idea is to represent the state of the search as a number and for each search step to do a small number of arithmetic and logical operations, provided that the numbers are large enough to represent all possible states of the search. Hence, for $m \leq w$, w being the word size in bits of the computer used, the algorithm runs in $O(n)$ time using $O(c)$ extra space and $O(m+c)$ preprocessing time, where c denotes the number of symbols. The algorithm serves as a basis for the software package for Unix called agrep ([Wu et al., 92a] and [Wu et al., 92b]), which has been in use since June 1991. The agrep package is available by anonymous ftp from cs.arizona.edu. The string matching heuristics in [Gonzalez et al., 91] return a numerical measure of the similarity between the unknown description and the various candidate identifications in the external databases.

Parallel processing of approximate string matching is discussed in [Landau et al., 86a]. A simple hardware algorithm based on VLSI is proposed in [Grossi, 91] for the approximate string matching problem. Ibarra et al. ([Ibarra et al., 92]) present an efficient parallel algorithm for the string edit problem. The model of computation is a one-way linear array of identical finite state machines (nodes). Takahashi et al. ([Takahashi et al., 90]) describe a new string search processor hardware architecture, an LSI chip, and applications. That chip can store variable-length pattern strings, search for text data at 10 million characters per second, and provide flexible matching functions such as nonanchor functions for don't-care, wildcard, and approximate matching.

Approximate String Matching

PATRICK A. V. HALL

SCICON Consultancy International Limited, Sanderson House, 49 Berners Street, London W1P 4AQ, England

GEOFF R. DOWLING

Department of Computer Science, The City University, Northampton Square, London EC1V OHB, England

Approximate matching of strings is reviewed with the aim of surveying techniques suitable for finding an item in a database when there may be a spelling mistake or other error in the keyword. The methods found are classified as either equivalence or similarity problems. Equivalence problems are seen to be readily solved using canonical forms. For similarity problems difference measures are surveyed, with a full description of the well-established dynamic programming method relating this to the approach using probabilities and likelihoods. Searches for approximate matches in large sets using a difference function are seen to be an open problem still, though several promising ideas have been suggested. Approximate matching (error correction) during parsing is briefly reviewed.

Keywords and Phrases: approximate matching, spelling correction, string matching, error correction, misspelling, string correction, string editing, errors, best match, syntax errors, equivalence, similarity, longest common subsequence, searching, file organization, information retrieval

CR Categories: 1.3, 3.63, 3.7, 3.73, 3.74, 4.12, 5.42

Reprinted from *ACM Computing Surveys*, Volume 12, No. 4, December 1980, pp. 381-402. Copyright 1980, Association for Computing Machinery, Inc., reprinted by permission.

INTRODUCTION

Looking up a person's name in a directory or index is an exceedingly common operation in information systems. When the name is known in exactly the form in which it is recorded in the directory, then looking it up is easy. But what if there is a difference? There may be a legitimate spelling variation, or the name may be misspelled. In either situation the lookup procedure will fail unless some special search is undertaken. Yet this requirement of searching when the string is almost right is very common in information systems.

This paper shows builders of information systems what is possible in finding approximate matches for arbitrary strings. Exist-

ing methods are placed within a general framework, and some new techniques are added.

Behind this string matching problem is a yet more general problem of approximately matching arbitrary information items or groups of items. This survey avoids this very general problem, although many of the methods surveyed are applicable. We concentrate instead on the matching of a single string within a set of strings. Strings have special properties, and string matching has many important applications.

Many investigations of string matching have concentrated on searching for a particular string embedded as a substring of another, to satisfy retrieval problems such

CONTENTS

---

as finding a document whose title mentions some particular word. Methods for finding a substring within another string have culminated in the elegant method of Boyer and Moore [BOYE77, GALI79] where by preprocessing the substring it is possible to make large steps through the string to find a match in sublinear time on average. Rivest [RIVE77] has shown that the worst case behavior must take linear time.

Instead of searching for a single substring one could search for a "pattern." This facility is common in string processing languages (it is illustrated by the language SNOBOL, which is documented in GIMP76) and has been developed by Aho and Corasick [AHO75] and Knuth, Morris, and Pratt [KNUT77]. However, general pattern matching is equivalent to asking whether the string conforms to a grammar, and thus the algorithms involved are parsing algorithms (see, for example, HOPC69).

The basic problem we examine is different. It is as follows.

Problem: Approximate String Matching

Given a string s drawn from some set S of possible strings (the set of all strings composed of symbols drawn from some alphabet A), find a string t which approximately matches this string, where t is in a subset T of S.

The task is either to find all those strings in T that are "sufficiently like" s, or the N strings in T that are "most like" s. The intuitive concepts "approximate," "sufficiently like," and "most like" need elucidation. We shall see two broad categories of the problem in Sections 2 and 3, where the idea of "like" is regarded as "equivalent," or as "different but similar."

A secondary factor in our problem is the representation of the set of strings T. This set can either be represented extensionally as an enumeration of the strings in the set (that is, all the strings are explicitly stored), or intensionally as a set of rules such as a grammar. Most of the discussions in this paper are in terms of extensional sets. Discussion of intensional sets is delayed until Section 4.

1. REASONS FOR APPROXIMATE MATCHING

Before describing the various approaches to approximate matching in Sections 2, 3, and 4, it is worth examining further the reasons for approximate matching. There are two very different viewpoints: "error correction" and "information retrieval."

We can suppose that what should be provided as a search string corresponds precisely to what has been stored in some record or records. The search string does not match because of some corruption process which has changed it. The corruption process has a magnitude associated with it, and we can talk of large corruptions and small corruptions. Furthermore we can imagine that the string gets so badly corrupted that it becomes similar or identical to some other stored string. Thus if the corruptions are larger than the differences between correct strings, we must expect to retrieve falsely, and only if we were to weaken our retrieval criterion, would we expect to be able to retrieve the correct string as an outlying match.

We can think of ourselves as trying to correct the errors introduced by the corruption, with the retrieval process being the attempt to correct the error, and with retrieval of a string which is not relevant being an error. This corruption-correction point of view is adopted in communication theory [PETE61] and pattern recognition [RISE74].

Alternatively, we can take the viewpoint of information retrieval: our search string indicates, as best we can, the information required. We could be unsuccessful in two ways. There is the risk that unwanted records will be retrieved, while required records are missed. In conventional information retrieval these two phenomena are captured by the notion of precision and recall [SALT68, PAIC77]:

- *precision*—proportion of retrieved records that are relevant;
- *recall*—proportion of relevant records actually retrieved.

It is assumed that the relevance of records is known from other sources. These measures are not fully satisfactory, and Paice [PAIC77] suggests refinements. Recently alternative information-theoretic measures were proposed [RADE76]. Nevertheless, precision and recall remain useful conceptually; we see that in general we can trade one against the other. By being less exacting in what is retrieved, recall can be made to approach 100 percent at the expense of precision approaching zero, and vice versa. With retrieval based upon a similarity or difference measure and a threshold, the trade-off can be controlled by varying the threshold; this is covered in Section 3.1. In the information retrieval literature the imagery of precision and recall appears to encourage ad hoc approaches, possibly because a correct analysis is very difficult and something is better than nothing.

Before we move to consider these ideas in further detail, we hope that two facts have been seen emerging. First, we must understand the sources of the corruptions or variability that are requiring us to make approximate matchings, and we must compensate for them accurately. Second, we must know something about the size of the corruptions and adjust our retrieval criterion accordingly, and expect that for large corruptions we will get a degraded performance however we choose to measure it.

2. EQUIVALENCE

2.1 The Equivalence Problem

One notion of "approximate" and "like" is *equivalence*. If two strings which are super-ficially different can be substituted for each other in all contexts without making any difference in meaning, then they are equivalent.

Common examples of equivalence are alternate spellings of the same word, the use of spaces as formatting characters, optional use of upper- or lowercase letters, and alternative scripts. For example, all the following strings might be considered as equivalent.

Data Base   data-base   data base   database

data base   d a t a b a s e   Database.

In Arabic and other languages using the Arabic script, there is considerable discretion in how words are typed, associated with the art of calligraphy [HALL78].

Another very different example of equivalence occurs in arithmetic expressions. The same basic calculation can be expressed in many ways by using different orders, bracketing, and repeating arguments in order to give an infinite variety of expressions, all of which are equivalent (see, for example, JENK76).

A very important example in keyword searching in information retrieval [PAIC77] is the treatment of all grammatical variants of a word as equivalent as far as retrieval is concerned. Normally, mechanisms here attempt to reduce words to their stem or root, and then to treat all words that can be reduced to the same stem as equivalent.

In some interpretations [UNES76] synonyms can be viewed as equivalents, but synonyms are more properly considered as similarities and are discussed in Section 3.1.

It is possible that some abbreviations can be viewed as alternative spellings and thus as equivalences—for example, LTD. for LIMITED. In general this is not possible, since several words may have the same abbreviation—for example, ST. for both SAINT and STREET.

The idea of equivalence is well understood in mathematics [BIRK70]. One can talk of an equivalence relation "$\approx$" on the set S of all possible strings, such that for strings r, s, t in S

(i) $s \approx s$ reflexivity
(ii) $s \approx t \Rightarrow t \approx s$ symmetry
(iii) $r \approx s$ and $s \approx t \Rightarrow r \approx t$

                           transitivity

The first two properties are obvious. It is the third property that is important, the property that if r is equivalent to s, and s is equivalent to t, then r is equivalent to t.

We can now reformulate our matching problem for equivalences.

Equivalence Problem

Given s in S, find all t in T such that $s \approx t$.

The equivalence relation divides the set S of all strings into subsets $S_1, S_2, S_3, \ldots$, such that all strings in a subset are equivalent to each other and not equivalent to any string in any other subset. These subsets are called "equivalence classes." We can paraphrase our problem as finding all the elements of T which are in the same equivalence class as the search string s.

Equivalence classes can be characterized by some typical or exemplary member of the class. This exemplary member is frequently known as the *canonical form* for the class [BIRK70], and usually there are rules for transforming any element into its canonical form (that is, the canonical form of its equivalence class). Since there is a one-to-one correspondence between canonical forms and equivalence classes, it gives another formulation of our problem, to find all the elements t in T with the same canonical form as the search string s.

2.2 Storing and Retrieving Equivalent Strings

All methods rely upon the well-established technology of storing and retrieving *exact* matches using a retrieval key, as exemplified by Knuth [KNUT73] or Martin [MART75].

To solve the equivalence problem directly, all strings are separately indexed, and all members of an equivalence class are linked together in some manner. Thus any string indexes into its equivalence class, and all equivalent strings can be retrieved. This method can be used for alternative spellings and for thesauri where synonyms are treated as equivalences [UNES76]. For symbol tables in interpreters and compilers where alternative keywords which are not systematic abbreviations are used (as, for example, in PL/1), these indexes would be predetermined and would be hand opti-

(1) Change internal z's to s's when preceded and followed by a vowel or y.

Examples: razor, analyze, realize
Counterexamples: hazard, squeeze

(2) Replace all internal occurrences of 'ph' by 'f'.

Examples: sulphur, peripheral, symphony
Counterexamples: uphill, haphazard

(3) For words of at least six letters, replace a word ending 'our' by 'or'.

Examples: flavour, humour
Counterexample: devour

(4) After removing endings such as 'e', 'ate', and 'ation', replace the endings 'tr' by 'ter'.

Examples: centr(e), filtr(ate)

FIGURE 1. Rules for producing a canonical form for English and American spellings. (From PAIC77.)

mized in their design. However equivalences sometimes are only obtained as part of the acquisition of data and would be generated dynamically, as happens with EQUIVALENCE statements in programming languages [GRIE71, TARJ75].

The equivalence problem based on canonical forms is much the more common form of the problem encountered, so we first consider methods for reducing a string to a canonical form. Often the transformation is trivial, involving the removal of some extraneous characters and/or the replacement of optional characters by some standard choice [SLIN79]. But in the cases of alternative spellings and the roots of words, the methods are more elaborate. The differences between English and American spelling can mostly be defined by rules which convert words to some standard spelling. Figure 1, taken from Paice [PAIC77], gives a set of possible rules.

The extraction of true roots of words is seldom attempted, but the removal of alternative word endings is common. Truncation is not adequate, and more elaborate methods known as "conflation" are used. Table 1, from Paice, gives a set of "simple" rules; understanding the precise effect of these is helped by the example. Rules like these could be applied to most languages. They will usually be incomplete in that there will be many variants that are not accounted for, and they will also treat as

TABLE 1. PAICE'S CONFLATION RULES FOR REDUCING A FAMILY OF WORDS TO A COMMON ROOT—THE RULES ARE INCOMPLETE, BUT ARE CLAIMED TO BE SATISFACTORY [PAIC77]

Label	Ending	Replacement	Transfer
	—ably	—	goto IS
	—ibly	—	finish
	—ily	—	goto SS
SS	—ss	—ss	finish
	—ous	—	finish
	—ies	—y	goto ARY
	—s	—	goto E
	—ied	—y	goto ARY
	—ed	—	goto ABL
	—ing	—	goto ABL
E	—e	—	goto ABL
	—al	—	goto ION
ION	—ion	—	goto AT
	—	—	finish
ARY	—ary	—	finish
	—ability	—	goto IS
	—ibility	—	finish
	—ity	—	goto IV
	—ify	—	finish
	—	—	finish
ABL	—abl	—	goto IS
	—ibl	—	finish
IV	—iv	—	goto AT
AT	—at	—	goto IS
IS	—is	—	finish
	—ific	—	finish
	—olv	—olut	finish
	—	—	finish

equivalent words that are not equivalent. This leads to degraded performance as measured by precision and recall.

For example, consider the reduction of the word "conducts" to its root "conduct." Starting at the top of Table 1 we compare word endings until the ending "–s" is found. The replacement rule indicates no replacement, so the "s" is deleted. The transfer column indicates that we should continue searching from the label "E." So, starting from label "E," searching continues, matching word endings until the null ending is reached which does match, leading to no replacement and "finish." The root "conduct" has been found.

Having defined the canonical forms for the equivalence classes and rules for transforming arbitrary strings to their canonical forms, these are two ways in which the canonical form can be used.

First, the canonical form can be produced immediately on input, so that the canonical form is the only form that is manipulated

in the computer, being stored, used for indexes, and so on. This means that the original string as input is lost, and therefore that strings which are retrieved will in general be different from those which were input. Indeed, they may be unreadable unless some compensating transformation is undertaken to render them readable. This method is invariably used in programming languages for strings representing numerical data—these strings are reduced to a canonical binary form—but it is otherwise of limited applicability. It is used for identifiers in some compilers, for example in FORTRAN where spaces are removed, and in some Arabic systems where the reduction to canonical form is made in the peripherals themselves [HALL78].

Second, the canonical form need only be used where it matters, and the string as input is stored and retrieved. The canonical form is used whenever two strings are compared. If a string item in a record is indexed, the string is reduced to canonical form before searching the index or adding a new entry to the index. When strings are sorted, a sort key consisting of the canonical form is extracted, and this sort key is used in sorting. An example of such a use is given in the system reported by Slinn [SLIN79].

Of course it is possible to store a string as received and on retrieval test all stored strings for equivalence. This is very time consuming for large sets and underutilizes the structure present in the problem. Because the methods of this section use standard searching technology, they are effective for large sets. As will be seen in the next section, searching a database with a keyword similar to the one stored is difficult to do efficiently.

3. SIMILARITY

3.1 The Similarity Problem

By far the most usual understanding of "approximate" or "like" is that of *similarity* between two strings. By some inspection process, two strings can be determined to be similar or not. The important property of similarity which makes it very different from equivalence is that similarity is not necessarily transitive; that is, if *r* is similar to s and s is similar to t, then it does not necessarily follow that r is similar to t.

In computer-based information systems, errors of typing and spelling constitute a very common source of variation between strings. These errors have been widely investigated. Shaffer and Hardwich [SHAF68] found in typing that substitution of one letter for another was the most common error, followed by the omission of a letter and then the insertion of a letter. Bourne [BOUR77] has investigated typing errors in a number of bibliographic databases, finding as many as 22.8 percent of its index terms to be misspellings in one database and as low as 0.4 percent in another, with an average of 10.8 percent over all the databases sampled. Litecky and Davis [LITE76] have investigated errors in COBOL programs and found that approximately 20 percent of all errors were due to misspellings and mistypings. All investigations agree that the most common typing mistakes found are single character omissions and insertions, substitutions, and the reversal of adjacent characters. Damerau [DAME64] has reported that over 80 percent of all typing errors are of this type. This has been confirmed by Morgan [MORG70]. Spelling errors, by contrast, may be phonetic in origin. In a study by Masters reported by Alberga [ALBE67], it was found that 65 percent of dictation errors were phonetically correct, and a further 14 percent almost phonetically correct. Phonetic variations are particularly common in transliterations, as in the example "Tchebysheff" and "Chebyshev." Investigations of errors vary in motivation. Bourne [BOUR77] was concerned with the quality of information retrieval and advised better controls to reduce the proportion of these errors. Litecky and Davis [LITE76] and others [JAME73, LYON74, MORG70] have been interested in error recovery and error correction in compilers. Bell [BELL76] was interested in errors as an indicator of programming competence.

Optical character recognizers and other automatic reading devices introduce similar errors of substitutions, deletions, and insertions, but not reversal. The frequency and type of errors are characteristics of the particular device. Pattern recognition re-searchers seek to "correct" these errors using "context" [RISE74], either by finding the best match among a repertoire of possible inputs (the problem considered in this section) or by using general linguistic structure.

Many approaches to speech recognition deal with strings of phonemes or symbols representing sounds, and attempt to match a spoken utterance with a directory of known utterances [SAKO79, WHIT76, ERMA80]. Variations in strings here can be due to "noise" where one phoneme is substituted for another similar to it, or phonemes are omitted or inserted, but again not transposed. Note that phonemes vary in their similarity to each other, which, for example, makes it more likely that a "d" sound will be misheard as a "t" sound rather than as an "m" or "f" sound [NEWE73, POTT66]. Another source of variation in phoneme strings is the duration of the spoken word. While words and phrases can be spoken at various speeds, speech to phoneme transducers often work at fixed time intervals, and thus slow speakers produce longer sequences of the same or similar phonemes [VELI70].

Synonyms constitute a very different source of variations. In all languages there are many words which mean more or less the same things. If we consider the following example taken from Roget's thesaurus [ROGE61]:

GUN   RIFLE   CANNON
         REVOLVER

we might be tempted to think of synonyms as equivalences, but if we look at the example

HOT   WARM   COOL   COLD

we see that synonymity is not transitive; HOT is not synonymous with COLD. However, when synonyms are controlled by a thesaurus, they are often treated as equivalent (see for example the SPINES thesaurus [UNES76]), often referring to the various alternative words as denoting a particular "concept." Thesauri and synonyms are discussed in most books on information retrieval [SALT68, PAIC77].

A problematic example is abbreviations, especially when used in names. Note that this has the flavor of a similarity relationship, not an equivalence one. For example, "P." might be an abbreviation for both "PATRICK" and "PETER," but Patrick and Peter are certainly not equivalent! A survey of methods for systematically generating abbreviations while retaining discrimination ability has been given by Bourne and Ford [BOUR61]. Although a full treatment of the handling of abbreviations is beyond the scope of this paper, we suggest that an abbreviation denotes a set of strings and thus denotes partial knowledge about the actual string intended. The partial knowledge problem is very close to the problem we are studying here, and the recent pioneering paper by Lipski [LIPS79] is highly recommended.

In all these examples we have been hypothesizing some mechanism for testing whether two strings are similar to each other. Analogous to an equivalence relation, we can define a similarity relation "~" on the set S, such that for r, s, and t in S

  (i) $s \sim s$ reflexivity,
  (ii) $s \sim t \Rightarrow t \sim s$ symmetry,

but

  (iii) $r \sim s$ and $s \sim t \not\Rightarrow r \sim t$
                      not necessarily
                      transitive.

Our problem now becomes

Similarity Problem

Given s in S, find all t in T such that $s \sim t$.

Now in most examples there is some idea of degree of similarity. There can be one or many typing mistakes; a spelling mistake can be almost right or completely wrong; two spoken utterances can sound very similar or completely different; and even synonyms can have degrees of similarity. Thus we can postulate a similarity function

$$\sigma : S \times S \to R$$

which for a pair of strings s and t produces a real number $\sigma(s, t)$. This similarity is usually taken to have a value $+1.0$ for identical objects, and ranges down to 0.0 (or sometimes -1.0) for very different objects. Thus we could solve the similarity problem by finding all strings t such that $\sigma(s, t)$ is greater than some threshold of acceptability, or we could find the N strings, t_1, t_2, ..., t_N such that their $\sigma(s, t_i)$ have the N largest values.

Similarity functions in this form were favored by Alberga [ALBE67] and are very popular in information retrieval [SALT68, PAIC77] and in classification and clustering [CORM71]. The value of $+1.0$ for an exact match seems to have strong intuitive appeal, and the range of values from -1.0 to $+1.0$ appears to gain respectability from correlation coefficients and normalized inner products [RAHM68]. For example, Salton gives a similarity function

$$\sum_i \min(v_i, w_i) / \sum_i v_i$$

for the property vectors v and w of two terms. It has the range $[0.0, +1.0]$.

To begin with, we use a difference function

$$d : S \times S \to R$$

with properties

  (i) $d(s, t) \geq 0$
  (ii) $d(s, t) = 0$ if and only if $s = t$
  (iii) $d(s, t) = d(t, s)$
  (iv) $d(s, t) + d(t, r) \geq d(s, r)$
                  triangular inequality.

It is this triangular inequality which is useful, as seen in Section 3.3. When a difference function satisfies all these properties, we say it is a *metric* [BIRK70]. Thus by using a difference function, we could formulate our problem as finding all the strings t in T which are closer to the search string s than some threshold δ. Alternatively, we could find the N strings t which are closest to s, that is, for which $d(s, t)$ is smallest.

Most string matching problems will of course involve both equivalence and similarity. That is, there is both an equivalence relation on the set of strings, which groups them into equivalence classes, and a similarity function or difference function between strings. Misspellings and mistypings of natural language are of a combined kind. There is an optional variation which is unimportant, for example, the use of spaces for formatting and (perhaps) uppercase letters; and there is variation which must be classed as error. With this hybrid problem, the similarity must be taken between equivalence classes. Where the similarity function or difference function is between strings, then it should be between canonical forms; this could influence the choice of canonical form.

3.2 Measures of Similarity

How do we assess whether two strings are similar to each other? How do we quantify this similarity or difference?

A very early method for assessing similarity is the Soundex system of Odell and Russell [ODEL18], which reduces all strings to a "Soundex code" of one letter and three digits, declaring as similar all those with the same code. However, the relationship of having the same code is an equivalence relation, but the string matching problem this proposes to solve is a similarity problem. Not suprisingly, the Soundex method and other methods like it can sometimes go very wrong. Yet these approaches can provide significant extra flexibility to systems that use them. The application of the Soundex method in a hospital patient index was recently reported [BRYA76], and a related method has been used successfully in airline reservations [DAVI62].

Let us examine the Soundex method and its shortcomings. The idea is to transform the name into a Soundex code of four characters in such a way that like-sounding names end up as the same four characters. The first character is the first letter of the name. Thereafter numbers are assigned to the letters as follows:

```
0   A E I O U H W Y      1   B F P V
2   C G J K Q S X Z      3   D T
4   L                    5   M N
6   R
```

Zeros are removed, then runs of the same digit are reduced to a single digit, and finally the code is truncated to one letter followed by three digits. Note that while DICKSON and DIXON are assigned the same code of D25, RODGERS and ROGERS are not assigned the same code. And what of like-sounding names HODGSON and DODGSON?

Related approaches have been taken by Blair [BLAI60] and Davidson [DAVI62]. Both defined rules for reducing a word to a four-letter abbreviation. Davidson, whose application was airline reservations, then appended to the abbreviation of the family name, the letter of the first name. So far these methods are very similar to the Soundex method, but they go further and introduce aspects of similarity. Blair did not allow multiple matches, and if they occurred, used longer abbreviations to resolve the ambiguity. He thus found the best match, provided that it was close enough. Davidson, by contrast, allowed multiple matches but insisted on finding at least one match by approximately matching the abbreviations looking for the longest subsequences of characters in common.

3.2.1 The Damerau–Levenshtein Metric

Damerau [DAME64] tackled the problem of misspellings directly, concentrating on the most common errors—namely, single omissions, insertions, substitutions, and reversals. He used a special routine for checking to see if the two given strings differed in these respects. This work stands out as an excellent early work: the author has analyzed the problem clearly, and made his solution fit the problem. Damerau's algorithm has since been used by Morgan [MORG70].

Damerau had only considered strings in which a single change had occurred. The idea can be extended to consider a sequence of changes of substitutions, deletions, insertions, and possibly reversals. By using sequences of such operations any string can be transformed into any other string. We can take the smallest number of operations required to change one string into another as the measure of the difference between them. Given two arbitrary strings, how do we find this difference measure?

Once the problem has been formulated as an optimization problem, standard optimization techniques can be applied. In 1974 Wagner and Fischer [WAGN74a] published a dynamic programming method. To motivate this method, consider the example of ROGERS and HODGE. Assume that somehow you have found the best matches for all the substrings ROGER and HODG (with difference 4), ROGER and HODGE (with difference 3), and ROGERS and HODG (with difference 5), and you are about to consider the best match for ROGERS and HODGE. If the last two characters are to be matched, then the score will be 5, 4 from the ROGER/HODG match and 1 for the mismatch of S and E. If the S will be unmatched at the end of ROGERS and treated as an insertion/omission, then the score will be 4, 3 from the ROGER/HODGE match and again 1 from the insertion/omission. If the E at the end of HODGE is treated as an insertion/omission then the score will be 6. Thus the best match of ROGERS and HODGE is 4, the smallest of these three alternatives.

Generalizing the idea of this example leads to the dynamic programming method. A function $f(i, j)$ is calculated iteratively using the recurrence relations below: $f(i, j)$ is the string difference for the best match of substrings $s_1 s_2 s_3 \cdots s_i$ and $t_1 t_2 t_3 \cdots t_j$.

$$f(0, 0) = 0$$

$$f(i, j) = \min[f(i - 1, j) + 1,$$
$$f(i, j - 1) + 1,$$
$$f(i - 1, j - 1) + d(s_i, t_j)]$$

where

$$d(s_i, t_j) = 0 \quad \text{if} \quad s_i = t_j$$
$$= 1 \quad \text{otherwise}.$$

Here we assume insertion, omission, and substitution are each assessed a "penalty" of 1. This method can be represented as a problem of finding the shortest path in a graph, as is shown in the example of Figure 2. It does not, however, take into account reversals of adjacent characters.

This basic method can be extended in several directions, Lowrance and Wagner [LOWR75] have given an extension to allow general reversals of order. Transposition of adjacent characters is a special case, and the recurrence relation above is quite easily extended to cope with this, by adding to the minimization the term

$$f(i - 2, j - 2) + d(s_{i-1}, t_j) + d(s_i, t_{j-1}),$$

which allows for the transposed neighbors that do not match exactly. It is clearly also

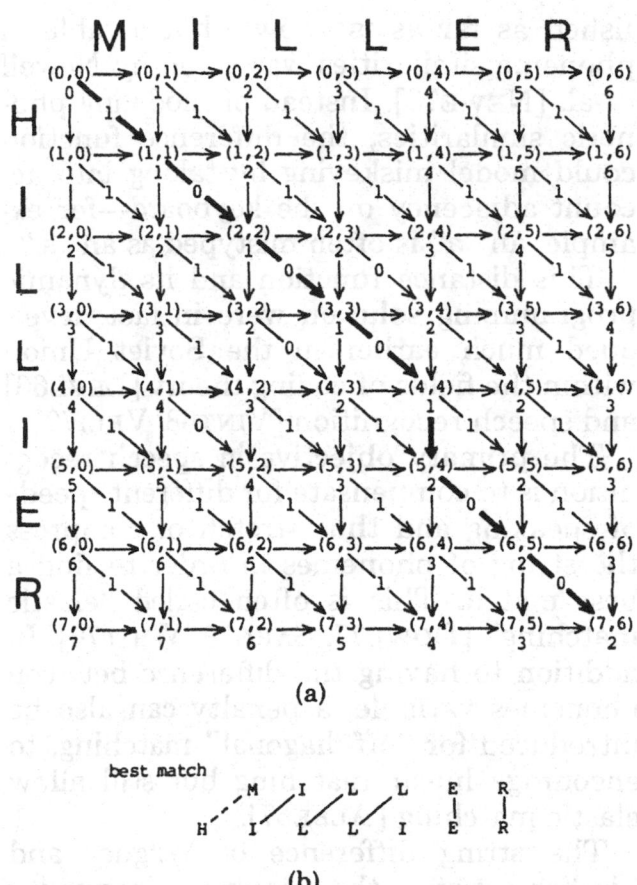

(a)

(b)

FIGURE 2. (a) Example of the comparison of two strings. The two strings are shown along the top and down the side. Each node of the graph is labeled, (i, j) as appropriate, and below the label is shown the value of $f(i, j)$ for that node. The weights along the diagonal edges are the $d(s_i, t_j)$ values, and along the horizontal and vertical edges they are the penalty values, here set to 1. (b) The best match occurs with a difference of 2, the value of $f(7, 6)$, and the manner of this best match can be deduced from the shortest path, which is drawn in heavy lines.

possible to allow multiple character matches, for example CKS and X, but no work known to us makes this extension. Such an extension would be very necessary for comparisons of transliterations, where multiple characters in one language frequently represent one sound or letter in another language.

Another direction of generalization is to allow for substitutions and even insertions and deletions to have different weights, as a function of the character or characters concerned. Thus, for example, $d(i, y)$ could be small while $d(i, f)$ could be large. No table of letter similarities has been published as far as is known, but a table of phoneme similarities was given by Newell et al. [NEWE73]. Instead of modeling phonetic similarities, the difference function could model miskeying by taking into account adjacency on the keyboard—for example, an "a" is often mistyped as an "s."

This distance function and its dynamic programming solution were in fact developed much earlier in the Soviet Union within the fields of coding theory [LEVE66] and speech recognition [VINT68, VELI70].

The primary objective in speech recognition is to compensate for different speeds of speaking and thus stretch or compress the string of phonemes in order to find a best match. This is often called "elastic matching" [DOWL77, SAKO79, WHIT76]. In addition to having the difference between phonemes variable, a penalty can also be introduced for "off-diagonal" matching, to encourage linear matching but still allow elastic matching [ALBE67].

The string difference of Wagner and Fischer satisfies the triangular inequality and thus is a metric. The definition of the difference as the minimum number of changes required to convert one string into the other establishes the triangular inequality. All the variations discussed above also form metrics, although it is important that when nonequal character differences are used, these character differences themselves form a metric. We refer to all distance functions in this general class as Damerau–Levenshtein metrics, after the two pioneering authors in the field [DAME64, LEVE66].

The dynamic programming method takes on the order of n^2 operations to produce its best match where n is the length of the strings being matched. Wong and Chandra [WONG76] have analyzed this in detail, showing that it is the best possible unless special operations are used. As seen below, methods can be derived which are faster in some cases, but these use special methods. The order n^2 processing time is not unduly prohibitive, and one of the authors has used the method in near-real-time speech recognition [DOWL77]. The Damerau algorithm [DAME64, MORG70], which checks just for single errors, is of order n.

One of the by-products of finding the best match between two strings by the Wagner and Fischer method is that it also yields the longest common subsequence. We could also work in the opposite direction: find the longest common subsequence first and then from this compute the difference. A number of techniques other than the dynamic programming method have been published [HUNT77]. These methods have best cases with better than n^2 complexity. Aho, Hirschberg, and Ullman [AHO76] have derived complexity bounds for the longest common subsequence problem and have shown that alphabet size is important. For finite alphabets (as in our problem) an improvement on the n^2 limit should be possible. Heckel [HECK78] has given a method for comparing files which is similar to the methods based on longest common subsequences, but highlights subsequences which have been moved as a body. In some applications, particularly file comparisons, this may be thought to model the real differences and similarities between the two strings more closely.

3.2.2 Similarity as Probability

Another approach to string matching and similarity is through probabilities and likelihoods. This approach has been taken by Fu for error-correcting syntax analysis [FU76]. He follows the conventions of communications theory using conditional probabilities [BACO73, PETE61] to model the production of errors, but there are problems with this approach. We present an alternative formulation.

Let us investigate the joint event {s and t} that string t is "correct" while string s is the observed string. We compute the probability of this event $P\{s \text{ and } t\}$. To do this, let us imagine a generation process which jointly produces s and t from left to right. After this process has created the first i characters of s and the first j characters of t, we can postulate the generation of the next character of s or t or both, with the possible events being (where e is the empty string)

{x and e} = the next character of s is x, and no character of t is generated;

{e and y} = no character of s is generated, and the next character of t is y;

{x and y} = the next character of s is x, and the next character of t is y.

These events exhaust the possibilities, and thus

$$\sum_x \sum_y P\{x \text{ and } y\} = 1$$

where we sum over the alphabet including the possibility that x or y is the empty symbol e. Notice that in this generation model we have avoided cause and effect as embodied in conditional probabilities, because of the difficulty of postulating a cause for inserted characters.

With this model of the joint generation of s and t, we can compute a probability for any matching of s and t as the product of the probabilities of the individual generating events. We can compute the best match as the most probable (most likely) matching using our dynamic programming algorithm, recasting the recurrence relations as

$$q(0, 0) = 1$$

$$q(i, j) = \max[q(i-1, j)P\{s_i \text{ and } e\}$$
$$q(i, j-1)P\{e \text{ and } t_j\},$$
$$q(i-1, j-1)P\{s_i \text{ and } t_j\}].$$

Note that it is the most probable matching that we are finding, so $q(n, m)$ is not $P\{s$ and $t\}$ but $P\{s$ and t and $M\}$ where M is the best match between s and t. If we take logarithms of these recurrence relations and suitably adjust signs, setting

$$f = -\log q,$$

$$D = -\log P\{x \text{ and } e\}$$
$$= -\log P\{e \text{ and } y\},$$

$$d(x, y) = -\log P\{x \text{ and } y\},$$

we obtain the earlier recurrence relations for differences. However, now the weights, the logarithms of the probabilities, must satisfy certain constraints.

To find $P\{s$ and $t\}$, we must sum over all possible matchings. This can be done iteratively by computing the function

$$Q(0, 0) = 1,$$

$$Q(i, j) = Q(i-1, j)P\{s_i \text{ and } e\}$$
$$+ Q(i, j-1)P\{e \text{ and } t_j\}$$
$$+ Q(i-1, j-1)P\{s_i \text{ and } t_j\},$$

$$P\{s \text{ and } t\} = Q(n, m).$$

The similarity to the earlier dynamic programming recurrences is remarkable, although this computation has nothing to do with dynamic programming. To choose the best matching string t, we simply choose the t such that $P\{s$ and $t\}$ is largest. $P\{s$ and $t\}$ is a true similarity function, satisfying the property

$$0 \leq P\{s \text{ and } t\} \leq 1,$$

and generally being close to zero.

In this model the various $P\{x$ and $y\}$ can be estimated experimentally by observing errors. Such observations have been made for phonemes [NEWE73] but not for keying errors, and thus there is a need for studies in this area. The model is very appealing but is open to objections because the generation process could generate any pair of strings (unless some of the $P\{x$ and $y\}$ are zero), and in real applications the set T is a comparatively small subset of S. However this case can be modeled using regular grammars, and methods for these are surveyed in Section 4.

3.3 Storing and Retrieving Similar Strings

Our problem is to find approximate matches for a given search string s within a set T of strings which are stored explicitly. We must be able to retrieve a record associated with these approximate matching strings and extract associated information.

The primary consideration is the size of the set to be searched. If the set is very small, then all the strings in the set can be tested in turn to see if they satisfy the search criterion (within a threshold δ, or one of the closest N). Often the set is large, perhaps containing millions of entries, and then something must be done to avoid exhaustive searches.

A secondary consideration is the relative importance of the approximate matching necessary. Suppose the problem requires an exact match if one exists, and otherwise a best match. If exact matches are common, then it could be that the primary requirement is that exact matches be quick to find, while finding approximate matches need not be that efficient. In many applications we can expect 80 percent or more success for exact matches, following the figures of Bourne [BOUR77] and Litecky and Davis [LITE76]. However, in other applications, such as speech recognition, exact matches are most unlikely, and all storage should be structured for approximate matching.

In his review Alberga [ALBE67] made no mention of these search considerations, but three years later Morgan [MORG70] gave a sound discussion of these issues. Morgan's application was searching symbol tables, so he did not consider the extremely large sets that could be encountered in information systems.

There are two basic approaches to searching large sets for approximate matches. The first is to structure the storage of the set T for efficient exact matching, and then when looking for a near match to generate all the strings similar to the search string and test whether these are in the set. The second approach is to structure the storage of the set T with approximate matching in mind using a partitioning strategy. First we look at exhaustive serial searches in order to establish some basis upon which to judge other methods.

3.3.1 Serial Searches

Let us examine simple serial searches and obtain preliminary quantitative figures. We are going to compare and contrast methods by estimating the number of disk accesses required, using a very naive analysis.

Let $|T|$ be the number of strings that are stored, and let m be the (average) number of strings retrieved per disk access. Then a simple serial scan of the set T requires

$$Q_1 = \frac{|T|}{m} \text{ disk accesses.}$$

For example, if we take $|T| = 2,000,000$ and strings have an average length of 10 bytes and are stored on disk pages of 2K bytes, then $m = 200$ and $Q_1 = 10,000$. These example figures are used again in later comparisons.

3.3.2 Generating Alternatives

Given a search string s, we can start by testing to see if s itself is in T and an exact match is possible. If this fails, then we can look for a member or members of T close to s by generating all the elements of S in the neighborhood of s and testing each of these in turn to see if it is in T.

The elements of T need to be stored so that searching for an exact match is fast. The technology of exact matching is highly developed [KNUT73, MART75]. Thus testing for membership of T is easy, and can be coupled with the retrieval of the associated record. Suppose we use B-trees for our indexing [COME79]; following KNUT73 (page 476) there will be approximately

$$1 + \log_{\lceil m/2 \rceil} \frac{|T| + 1}{2}$$

disk accesses per index probe, that is, per member of the neighborhood being tested. This is approximately four disk accesses for $|T| = 2,000,000$ and $m = 200$.

Now if the alternatives to be tested consist only of a few synonyms, then the neighborhood is small, and this method would be very effective. A more common requirement is the correction of misspellings or mistypings involving insertions, deletions, substitutions, and reversals, as discussed in Section 3.2. The members of the neighborhood could be generated, but the neighborhood is now large. A systematic method for generating all the members of the neighborhood needs to be constructed. Riseman and associates [RISE74] have produced such an algorithm, though no details are known. The algorithm would be worth publishing because the generation of the neighborhoods is a nontrivial combinatorial problem.

These neighborhoods are very large. Consider a string s of length n with symbols drawn from an alphabet A of size k. Allowing for insertions, deletions, substitutions, and reversals of adjacent characters, we find the size of the neighborhood of strings with difference 1 from s is

$$\begin{aligned} N(n, 1) &\leq (n + 1)k + n \\ &\quad + n(k - 1) + (n - 1) \\ &= k(2n + 1) + n - 1. \end{aligned}$$

Equality holds provided no two adjacent characters are the same. The size of the neighborhood of distance 2 from s is

$$N(n, 2) \approx N(n, 1)^2.$$

If we consider testing all strings differing by only one error from a string of length 10, with a 26-letter alphabet, the neighborhood size is 565. If we have to use our index and access a disk page for each of these, we then require four disk accesses per string, or a total of

$$Q_2 = 2260 \text{ disk accesses}$$

which is about 4.5 times better than the exhaustive search case. However, to test for up to two errors, we find that

$$Q_2 \approx 1 \text{ million,}$$

which is disastrous.

So, at first assessment, the idea of generating all the strings in the neighborhood seems worthless. But suppose we had some simple test which could be used to eliminate most of the members of the neighborhood before accessing the disk to look for the strings in T. All we need is a test for membership of some set X which covers T.

The only published test known to us is that of Riseman and Hanson [RISE74] and Ullman [ULLM77] discussed below. Their approach is ad hoc, but clearly some idea of well-structured strings for English (say) could be derived, since some combinations of letters simply do not occur in English. Any structural test derived from the words or phrases involved would suffice. Structural tests in the form of grammars would provide a very convenient method [GRIE71, HOPC66]. It has been claimed that over 40 percent of possible consecutive letter pairs do not occur in English (Sitar, quoted in RISE74), which suggests that a sensitive test should be possible. Riseman and Hanson review a number of structural tests which are not based on grammars but on checking for the occurrence of sequences of letters within a word or the occurrence of particular letters at particular positions in the words. Their best test can detect simple errors with approximately 99 percent accuracy, but this is only on small vocabularies and is expensive in storage. While Riseman's methods, and those derived from him

[ULLM77], may not be ideal for the large sets of strings that concern us here, they do indicate what should be possible. A quick test should at least be able to reduce by an order of magnitude the number of disk accesses required and thus make matching to within a single error by generating alternatives a viable method.

3.3.3 Set Partitioning and Cluster Hierarchies

In the section on exhaustive serial searches, the critical factor was the size of the set T. If we could partition T into subsets T_1, T_2, ..., and select only a few of these subsets for exhaustive searching, we should be able to reduce our number of disk accesses considerably.

Morgan [MORG70] and Szanzer [SZAN69] have suggested partitioning by string length. Assuming that we are only looking for strings differing by only one error, then we need only search strings differing from the length of the search string by 1. This idea will not have a very significant impact but may improve the search cost two- to fivefold. This is because strings in applications, such as name indexes, do not vary much in length and have a very nonuniform distribution in length.

Another idea would be to partition the set on the first letter. There may be no attempt made to compensate for errors in the initial letter, for example, Muth and Tharp [MUTH77]; or the errors in the first letter may be searched for in some separate operation, as proposed by Szanzer [SZAN73].

Ideally any partitioning strategy should produce sets of the same size, and the search efficiency is sensitive to departures from a uniform distribution. The average number of disk accesses for exact matching, assuming each stored string is equally likely, is given by

$$Q_3 = \sum_i \left(\begin{array}{l} \text{Number of disk} * \text{Probability of} \\ \text{accesses to} \qquad \text{search string} \\ \text{search } T_i \qquad \text{being in } T_i \end{array} \right)$$

$$= \sum_i \frac{|T_i|}{m} * \frac{|T_i|}{|T|}$$

$$= \sum_i \frac{|T_i|^2}{m|T|}.$$

If we use some simple rule based on string length or leading letters, we inevitably come up against the uneven distribution of real data. Moreover, the use of data is very uneven. Knuth [KNUT73, pp. 396–398] has a stimulating discussion of this; a useful rule for us here is the 80–20 law, that 80 percent of the activity appears in 20 percent of the file.

Morgan [MORG70] also suggested a technique for partitioning the set based on the first two letters

$$T_{XY} = \{t \text{ in } T \text{ such that } t \text{ begins XY}\}.$$

For the usual 26-letter alphabet, this gives 676 subsets. Of course, following our earlier remarks that 40 percent of pairs do not occur, many of these subsets will be empty. When searching for a string beginning PQ, for example, we would only need to search the 77 subsets where at least one of the defining letters was a P or a Q (that is, subset PQ for an exact match on the first two letters, P? for substitution or deletion of Q or a reversal of the second and third letters, ?Q for substitution of P, QP for reversal of PQ, and Q? for deletion of P). Making the most favorable uniformity assumptions, this means at most a ninefold speedup. Extending the idea to the first three letters, we can hope for as much as a 200-fold speedup on single errors, but the number of partitions is beginning to get out of hand. We could do some hashing however, to randomize and superimpose subsets as Morgan suggested.

So far these methods have not appeared very effective. Though the exact search behavior is not known, they appear to have a search time proportional to $|T|$, since the partitioning strategy is fixed and independent of $|T|$. What we would like ideally is a search behavior of order $\log|T|$, as is found for exact matches.

An interesting search method has been suggested by Shapiro [SHAP77] in the context of general pattern recognition. The method consists of imposing a linear ordering on all the elements of the set of patterns to be searched, finding a most likely match by using binary searching to find a candidate match, and then searching in that neighborhood for a best match. The linear ordering is determined by the difference from some reference point, and it is this difference which gives the means for computing bounds that keeps the search to the neighborhood of the first candidate match. Because the string difference metric does not provide fine discrimination, the method is unlikely to work well for strings.

Knuth [KNUT73] has suggested a method based on the observation that strings differing by a single error must match exactly in either the first or the second half. He does no more than hint at a method of exploiting this observation, but one method might be the following. Index the set using both the first and last halves—the first and last $\lceil n/2 \rceil - 1$ characters—so that the central two characters are omitted from an even-length string to allow for central reversals. For retrieval try the first and last halves, both the $\lfloor n/2 \rfloor$ and the $\lfloor n/2 \rfloor - 1$ first or last characters, so as to allow for insertions and deletions. Thus we retrieve two sets of strings which must be serially searched to find any actual matches to within a single error. (Notation: $\lfloor x \rfloor$ is the greatest integer less than or equal to x, and $\lceil y \rceil$ is the smallest integer greater than or equal to y.) This method will be sensitive to the actual distribution of the strings but does seem very promising. No theoretical or empirical results concerning its effectiveness are known.

$\log|T|$ search behavior is obtained in tree-structured searches. Muth and Tharp's method [MUTH77] forms a character tree, but since they then backtrack up the tree on encountering an error, much of the advantage of the tree is lost. The only substantive gain they do get is by partitioning on the first character, but they do not attempt to correct errors in that first character place.

A general tree-structured approach has been suggested by Salton and his associates for use in information retrieval [SALT68, SALT78]. The method uses the similarity distance function as its basis for partitioning, dividing the set into "clusters" of strings which are similar to one another. That is, strings within the same subset T_i have $d(s, t)$ small, and strings in different subsets have $d(s, t)$ large. The automatic formation of subsets with these characteristics is known variously as clustering or

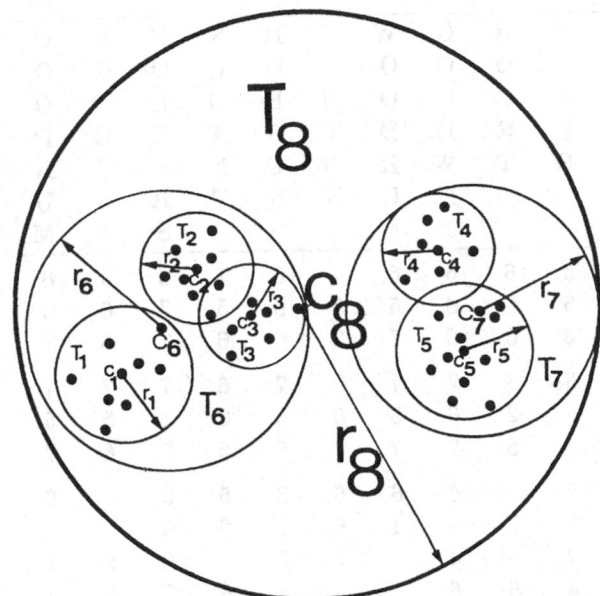

FIGURE 3. A hierarchy of clusters, with T_1, T_2, and T_3 contained in T_6, T_4 and T_5 contained in T_7, and T_6 and T_7 contained in T_8, the whole of T.

classification (see, for example, the review by Cormack [CORM71]). This method shows promise of approaching the $\log|T|$ goal and is described in some detail.

A hierarchy of clusters is formed, and each cluster T_i is described by a center c_i and a radius r_i:

$$T_i = \{t : d(t, c_i) \leq r_i \text{ and } t \text{ in } T\}.$$

Clusters at higher levels contain clusters below them, and clusters at a particular level could overlap. Figure 3 illustrates this.

To search for all the strings within δ of the search string s, we start at the highest level and search within a cluster $T_i(c_i, r_i)$ if and only if $d(s, c_i) \leq r_i + \delta$. This guarantees finding *all* t in T with $d(s, t) \leq \delta$, provided that the difference function satisfies the triangular inequality.

To search for the best match (or N best matches), we use what is basically a branch-and-bound technique [HALL71]. For any subset $T_i(c_i, r_i)$ we have the bounds

$$d(c_i, s) - r_i \leq d(s, t) \leq d(c_i, s) + r_i$$

for all t in T; this follows from the triangular inequality. We search in the most promising subset (the one with the minimum value of $d(c_i, s) - r_i$) to find the best candidate match t^* and then search in the next best remaining subset provided that it could

possibly yield an improvement, that is, provided that $d(c_i, s) - r_i \leq d(s, t^*)$. Thus successively better matches t^* are found until it is evident that no further searching is necessary. Both variations of the search use the triangular inequality to guarantee the search algorithms.

Alternatively, the decisions to stop searching can be based upon empirically determined parameters, which is the approach taken by Salton.

Let us illustrate the search process with a small string searching example. Figure 4 shows the differences for a set of 15 names, while Figure 5 shows the set divided into five clusters, including one miscellaneous cluster to accommodate the two strings which did not happily fit into any other cluster. Figure 6 then shows two searches for all matches within a given tolerance. Figure 7 shows a search for a best match. Note that the miscellaneous set is always searched.

It is necessary to define insertion and deletion strategies, as well as the search strategy. Salton and Wong describe an insertion method which they claim provides a good basic clustering method, but they do not describe a deletion method. They liken their approach, quite correctly, to B-trees [KNUT73, COME79] without pursuing the analogy.

Assuming a balanced tree, or reasonably uniform tree, the average depth of the tree will be of order $\log|T|$. But the search methods reported above do not only search a single path from root to leaf, they also try other branches if these are found to be necessary. These other paths could completely destroy the potential $\log|T|$ behavior, and in the worst case lead to an exhaustive search. Salton and Wong suggest limiting the extra searching at each level in the hierarchy to some small number of branches p. Suppose that the tree branches k ways at each level, and at each level we search p of these branches. Clearly p is less than k. We must search p branches at each of the $\log_k|T|$ levels in the tree, and thus must search

$$p^{\log_k|T|} = |T|^{\log_k p}$$

strings at the lowest level. If, for example, $p = \sqrt{k}$, then $\log_k p = \frac{1}{2}$, and we must search

	J O H N S O N	A L W O O D	F E N L O N	B U B E N K O	R O G E R S	S E N K O	R O G E T	G O O D W I N	W O O D R U M	H I N T O N	H O D G E S	S L O A N E	R O D G E R S	D O D G S O N	G O O D R U M
JOHNSON	–	6	4	6	6	5	6	5	6	4	6	7	6	3	6
ALWOOD	6	–	5	7	6	5	6	6	5	5	6	5	7	6	6
FENLON	4	5	–	5	6	3	6	6	7	3	6	6	7	5	7
BUBENKO	6	7	5	–	6	3	6	7	7	6	7	6	7	7	7
ROGERS	6	6	6	6	–	5	2	6	5'	6	3	6	1	5	5
SENKO	5	5	3	3	5	–	5	7	7	4	6	5	7	6	7
ROGET	6	6	6	6	2	5	–	6	6	6	3	5	3	5	6
GOODWIN	5	6	6	7	6	7	6	–	4	6	5	6	6	6	3
WOODRUM	6	5	7	7	5	7	6	4	–	7	5	6	6	6	1
HINTON	4	5	3	6	6	4	6	6	7	–	5	6	7	5	7
HODGES	6	6	6	7	3	6	3	5	5	5	–	5	2	4	5
SLOANE	7	5	6	6	6	5	5	6	6	6	5	–	6	7	6
RODGERS	6	7	7	7	1	7	3	6	6	7	2	6	–	4	6
DODGSON	3	6	5	7	5	6	5	6	6	5	4	7	4	–	6
GOODRUM	6	6	7	7	5	7	6	3	1	7	5	6	6	6	–

FIGURE 4. Difference matrix for a set of 15 names. The differences shown are the best match differences, which have been found using the simple dynamic programming approach.

Cluster	Center c_i, Radius r_i	Members
T_1	GOODRUM, 3	WOODRUM, GOODRUM, GOODWIN
T_2	RODGERS, 3	ROGERS, RODGERS, ROGET, HODGES
T_3	SENKO, 4	FENLON, HINTON, SENKO, BUBENKO
T_4	JOHNSON, 3	JOHNSON, DODGSON
T_5	MISCELLANEOUS	ALLWOOD, SLOANE

FIGURE 5. Clusters formed from the names of Figure 4.

$\sqrt{|T|}$ strings. While we do not have a $\log|T|$ law, we have certainly done better than a linear search.

Consider our example where $|T| = 2,000,000$. Suppose our index branches 100 ways at each level, and the index is arranged with the specification that all 100 ways stored are on one disk page, as in B-trees. Suppose further that we only search at most ten branches at any level. Then our law above says we must search some 1400 strings, or seven pages at 200 strings per page. Including the index, this requires around ten disk accesses in total.

This approach will only be good if the clustering is good and ensures that only a few of the branches need searching. And this clustering must be preserved under insertion and deletion. There is a real need for some research here to determine what clustering property is necessary to ensure a good search behavior, and what insertion and deletion algorithms will guarantee preservation of this property.

At the moment too little is known about this cluster hierarchy method for the use of it to be anything better than a gamble. But if somebody did gamble and validate the method empirically, that would be worth reporting.

4. ERROR CORRECTION USING SYNTACTIC STRUCTURE

Instead of the set of strings being stored explicitly, as has been assumed up to this point, the set could be defined by a collection of structural rules such as a grammar.

		Search 1	Search 2
Search string s		GOODGE	FENKON
Tolerance δ		1	2
Distance of search string from center of cluster	T_1	3	7
	T_2	4	7
	T_3	6	2
	T_4	6	4
Clusters requiring further searching		T_1, T_2 T_5	T_3, T_4 T_5
Strings found		None	FENLON SENKO

FIGURE 6. Two searches of the cluster hierarchy of Figure 5.

If a string fails to conform to the rules, it is in "error." By suitable use of the rules, the error can be "corrected" and the string identified.

Riseman and Hanson [RISE74] describe a set of rules based upon the occurrence or nonoccurrence of particular sequences of letters. The sequences can be either adjacent letters occurring at any point in the string or they can be letters occurring at fixed points in the string. The application is error correction following optical character recognition. Riseman and Hanson acquire their rules directly from the set of strings that are permitted. From the particular rules that are violated, they deduce a correction which when applied will make the string conform to the rules. However a proportion of the strings in error (as high as 30 percent) are "uncorrectable" because no correction can be readily deduced from the violated rules.

All other methods of structural error correction are based upon a grammar. Following Hopcroft and Ullman, we use the notation $G = (V_N, V_T, P, S)$ for a grammar, where V_N are the nonterminals, V_T are the terminals, P the productions, and S the start symbol in V_N [HOPC69]. In error-correcting parsing, instead of rejecting a string found to be in error during parsing, the string is corrected to that member of $L(G)$, the language generated by the grammar G, which is closest to the given string.

A halfway stage to full error correction is

HOODGUS

(a)

Cluster	$d(s, c_i)$	$d(s, c_i) - \delta_i$
T_1	3	0
T_2	4	1
T_3	7	3
T_4	5	2

(b)

Step	Search	Strings found	Differences
1	T_5	SLOANE	6
2	T_1	GOODRUM WOODRUM	3
3	T_2	HODGES	2
4	T_4	Know that we cannot find a closer match, but could find an equal match. Continue only if all best matches required, then STOP.	

(c)

HODGES, difference 2.

(d)

FIGURE 7. Finding a best matching string: (a) search string; (b) results of comparisons with cluster centers; (c) steps in search for the closest match; (d) result.

error detection and error recovery [EGGE72, GRAH75, GRIE71, LITE76, MICK78, SMIT70, WILC76]. In compilers an error should be detected as early as possible, and a meaningful error message output which will help the user to correct the error himself. Then the compiler should recover and keep on parsing so as to subject the complete program to syntax checking. In order to recover, the compiler must compensate for the error and thus make some "correction," but it does not necessarily produce an alternative complete program which is correct and which could be executed.

Error-correction parsing goes the whole way and produces a program string which is valid and can be executed. An illustration at this point may help. Morgan reported an error-correcting system used with the CUPL compiler at Cornell University [MORG70]. The card deck

```
/JOB 2065 MORGAN, H 10S 30P
/CUP6
  READ ROWSUB, COLSUB, NOCOLS
  MATSUB =
    ROWSUB + COLSUB * NOCOLS
  WRITE MATSBU
  STPO
*DATA
  3.0 4, 5
/ENDJOB
```

contains a keypunching error in one job control card and two errors in the program. Their system would have corrected these errors without requiring a rerun. Of course, such corrections may be wrong, and in fact dangerous in that they do not agree with the programmer's original intention, but Morgan's system was used favorably.

Error correction during language analysis has been widely reported, starting with some very early ideas by Irons [IRON63] and Freeman [FREE63]. There was then a lapse of several years before Morgan's work and an ad hoc approach by James and Partridge [JAME73], and then error correction in languages was put on a sound theoretical footing. A theoretical analysis had been given by Hopcroft and Ullman [HOPC66] in 1966, and this was followed by full error-correction techniques for most classes of languages being reported in the literature during the early 1970s.

Regular languages were treated by Wagner in 1974 [WAGN74b] using a dynamic programming approach similar to the one developed with Fischer for simple string matching [WAGN74a]. A function $f(A, i)$ is defined. This measures the best match between the first i symbols of the input string and the strings generated by starting with the start symbol S and ending with the nonterminal A. The recurrence formulas for computing $f(A, i)$ follow directly from the grammar. Terminal productions $A \rightarrow a$ are rewritten as $A \rightarrow a\#$, where $\# \notin V_N \cup V_T$. The recurrence relations are

$$f(S, 0) = 0,$$

$$f(A, i) = \min\{ \min_{\text{all } B:B \rightarrow aA} [f(B, j - 1) + d(s_i, a)], \\ f(A, i - 1) + 1, \\ \min_{\text{all } B:B \rightarrow aA} [f(B, i) + 1]\}$$

$$f(\#, n) = \text{difference of the best match},$$

where again following the notation of Section 3.2

$$d(s_i, a) = 0 \quad \text{if} \quad s_i = a$$
$$= 1 \quad \text{otherwise},$$

and the insertion/omission penalty is 1.

This algorithm for regular grammars has complexity which is linear in the length of the input string, but of course depends upon some function of the size of the grammar. Independently, and at about the same time, Hall and Dowling discovered the same algorithm and applied it to speech recognition [DOWL74]. Figure 8 gives a matching graph for regular grammars; there is an obvious similarity here with Figure 2.

Context-free languages, because of their importance for programming, have received considerable attention [AHO72, FU76, FUNG75, LEVY75, LYON74, TANA78, WAGN72]. Aho and Peterson [AHO72] add error productions to their grammar, and select derivations with fewest error productions using an Earley parser [EARL70]. Lyons [LYON74] by contrast tackles errors directly using dynamic programming principles, without the need to resort to error productions. He also uses the Earley parser. Levy concentrates on local corrections to gain parsing speed, while Tanaka and Fu use a Cocke–Younger–Kasami parser and Chomsky normal form. Teitlebaum, by contrast, takes an algebraic approach to language analysis, modeling the error-production process by a weighted sequential transducer, to produce an elegant method for error correction. While recognition of a context-free language theoretically can be done as fast as matrix multiplication ($O(n^{2.61})$ [PAN79]), normal parsing methods are of n^3 complexity [HOPC69, EARL70], and by suitable and careful choice of method, the error-correction parsers can also have complexity n^3 [LYON74, TEIT76, WAGN72]. Fung and Fu [FUNG75] consider only substitution errors, allowing for different probabilities for different substitutions of characters, and thus obtain probabilities for transformations from one string into another. They give an error-correcting parser which returns the string with highest probability.

Using probabilities, one can take into account the frequency with which particular linguistic constructs are used. This is done by Fu, who adds probabilities of use to each production (a stochastic grammar) and adopts the Aho and Peterson algorithm to handle these probabilities, selecting the most likely derivation for a given string. Clearly Fu's method can easily be applied to regular grammars. A regular grammar could be arranged to generate a particular set of strings and thus overcome the objections to probabilistic string similarity at the end of Section 3.2.

Best-match recognition in context-free languages has also been studied in speech recognition. A number of systems are surveyed by Erman et al. [ERMA80]. The process of recognizing connected speech is represented as problem solving using a sequence of "knowledge systems," where the selection of a best match is heuristic. This process is clearly equivalent to a bottom-up parse, and the discussion of the speech recognition methods surveyed could be complemented with a comparison based on language analysis.

Correction for context-sensitive languages has been investigated by Tanaka and Fu [TANA78]. They use the Cocke–Younger–Kasami parser, and although they

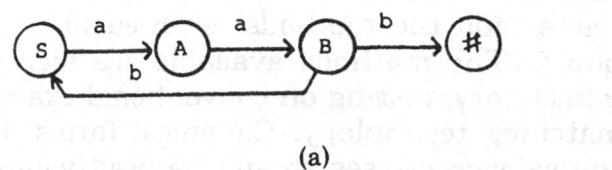

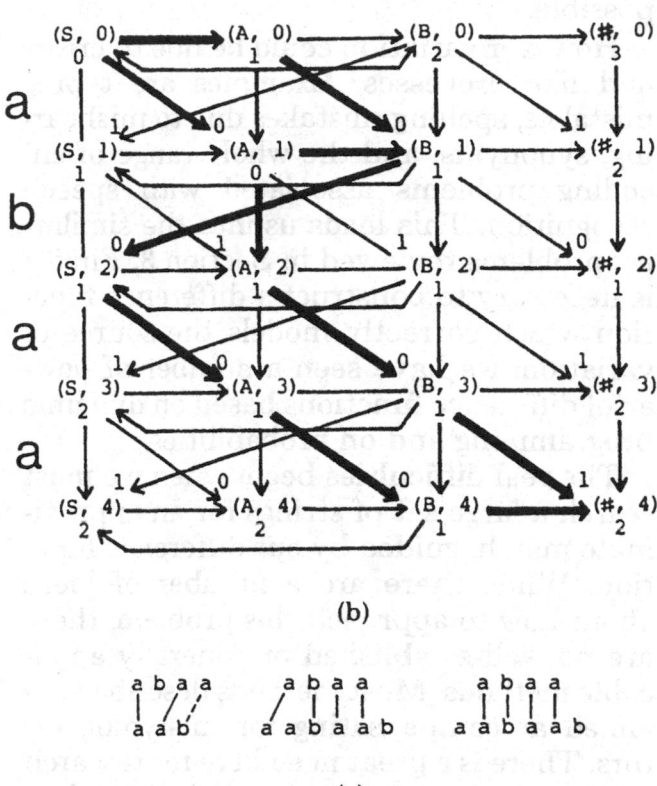

FIGURE 8. Example of error correction in a regular grammar. A graphical representation is used; the regular language is represented by a state-transition graph in (a) and this is combined with the matching string "abaa" in (b) to give a graph in which the best match problem has again become a shortest path problem. The edge weights are the mismatch penalties, and all horizontal and vertical paths have a weight of 1. The diagonal edges have $d(s_i, a) = 0$ if $s_i = a$, and 1 otherwise. Each node is labeled with its "coordinates," and the smallest mismatch from $(S, 0)$ to that node. The manner of the three best matches, shown by the heavy lines, is given in (c).

do not actually use dynamic programming, they formulate their solution in an equivalent way.

5. SUMMARY

When tackling a string matching problem where retrieval is to be achieved even with nonexact matches, it is important to ascertain the source of the variation leading to the need for nonexact matching.

Variations could be legitimate, as in the use of alternative spellings or formatting characters. This leads to equivalence classes and the methods reviewed in Section 2. The methods available are highly satisfactory, resting on conventional exact-matching technology. Canonical forms of equivalence classes should be used where possible.

However variation could be due to errors and like processes. Examples are typing mistakes, spelling mistakes due to mishearing, synonyms, and the whole range of encoding problems associated with speech recognition. This leads us into the similarity problems reviewed in Section 3. First it is necessary to construct a difference function which correctly models the source of variation; we have seen a number of powerful difference functions based on dynamic programming and on probabilities.

The real difficulties begin when we must search a large set of strings for an approximate match, guided by our difference function. While there are a number of ideas about how to approach this problem, there are no well-established or generally applicable methods. Most methods described are aimed at compensating for mistyping errors. There is a great need here for research to give the currently proposed methods a firm theoretical foundation and to generate alternative methods.

One class of string matching problems is concerned with finding the best match in a set of strings defined by a grammar. This error-correcting problem is briefly reviewed in Section 4.

Finally, it is interesting to note that during the preparation of this review, a spelling correction program for microcomputer systems was announced in the popular computer press [COMP80]. The program can correct some spelling mistakes it finds in its input text using a 25,000-word list supplied by Oxford University Press and draws attention to those it can recognize but not rectify. After the complete text has been scanned, an operation which processes about 60 words per minute, a list of alterations with references is given. With this facility now available on microcomputer systems, it should not be too long before some of the techniques outlined in this paper do find their way into large commercial information retrieval systems.

ACKNOWLEDGMENTS

The authors would like to thank their employers for providing facilities for this paper. It is a pleasure, too, to thank the Associate Editor, Bruce Weide, and the referees for their help in preparing this manuscript, and in (dare we say) spotting numerous spelling mistakes.

REFERENCES

AHO72   AHO, A. V., AND PETERSON, T. G. "A minimum distance error-correcting parser for context-free languages." *SIAM J. Comput.* 1 (Dec. 1972), 305–312.

AHO75   AHO, A. V., AND CORASICK, M. J. "Fast pattern matching: An aid to bibliographic search," *Commun. ACM* 18, 6 (June 1975), 333–340.

AHO76   AHO, A. V., HIRSCHBERG, D. S., AND ULLMAN, J. D. "Bounds on the complexity of the longest common subsequence problem, *J. ACM* 23, 1 (Jan. 1976), 1–12.

ALBE67   ALBERGA, C. N. "String similarity and misspellings," *Commun. ACM* 10, 5 (May 1967), 302–313.

BACO73   BACON, M. D., AND BULL, G. M. *Data transmission*, Macdonald and Jane's, London, 1973.

BELL76   BELL, D. "Programmer selection and programming errors," *Comput. J.* 19, 3 (1976), 202–206.

BIRK70   BIRKOFF, G., AND MACLEAN, S. *A survey of modern algebra*, Macmillan, New York, 1970.

BLAI60   BLAIR, C. R. "A program for correcting spelling errors," *Inf. Control* 3 (1960), 60–67.

BOUR61   BOURNE, C. P., AND FORD, D. J. "A study of methods for systemtically abbreviating English words and names," *J. ACM* 8, 4 (Oct. 1961), 538–552.

BOUR77   BOURNE, C. P. "Frequency and impact of spelling errors in bibiographic data bases," *Inf. Process. Manage.* 13, 1 (1977), 1–12.

BOYE77   BOYER, R. S., AND MOORE, J. S. "A fast string searching algorithm." *Commun. ACM* 20, 10 (Oct. 1977), 762–772.

BRYA76   BRYANT, J. R., AND FENLON, S. M. "The design and implementation of an on-line index," *Database Technol.* (ON-LINE, 1976).

COME79   COMER, D. "The ubiquitous B-tree," *Comput. Surv.* 11, 1 (June 1979), 121–138.

COMP80   "Spelling correction program for micros," *Comput. Weekly* (July 3, 1980), 7.

CORM71   CORMACK, R. M. "A review of classification," *Royal Statistical Soc. J.* 134 (Series A, 1971), 321–367.

DAME64   DAMERAU, F. J. "A technique for computer detection and correction of spelling errors," *Commun. ACM* 7, 3 (March 1964), 171–176.

DAVI62   DAVIDSON, L. "Retrieval of misspelled

names in an airline's passenger record system," *Commun. ACM* **5,** 3 (March 1962), 169–171.

Dowl74 DOWLING, G. R., AND HALL, P. A. V. "Elastic template matching in speech recognition, using linguistic information," in *2nd Int. Joint Conf. Pattern Recognition*, Copenhagen, Aug. 1974, pp. 249–250 (available from IEEE.).

Dowl77 DOWLING, G. R. "Automatic segmentation of continuous speech," Ph.D. Dissertation, The City University, London, 1977.

Earl70 EARLEY, J. "An efficient context-free parsing algorithm," *Commun. ACM* **13,** 2 (Feb. 1970), 94–102.

Egge72 EGGERS, B. "Error reporting, error treatment and error correction in ALGOL translation, part II," in *2nd Annual Meeting, G.I.*, Karlsruhe, Oct. 1972.

Erma80 ERMAN, L. D., HAYES-ROTH, F., LESSER, V. R., AND REDDY, D. R. "The HEARSAY-II speech understanding system: Integrating knowledge to resolve uncertainty," *Comput. Surv.* **12,** 2 (June 1980), 213–253.

Free63 FREEMAN, D. "Error correction in CORC: The Cornell computing language," Ph.D. Dissertation, Cornell University, Ithaca, N.Y., 1963.

Fu76 FU, K. S. "Error-correcting parsing for syntactic pattern recognition," in *Data-structures, computer graphics and pattern recognition*, Klinger et al. (Eds.) Academic Press, New York, 1976.

Fung75 FUNG, L. W., AND FU, K. S. "Maximum-likelihood syntactic decoding," *IEEE Trans. Inform. Theory* **IT-21** (July 1975), 423–430.

Gali79 GALIL, Z. "On improving the worst case running time of the Boyer–Moore string matching algorithms," *Commun. ACM* **22,** 9 (Sept. 1979), 505–508.

Gimp76 GIMPEL, J. F. *Algorithms in SNOBOL 4*, Wiley-Interscience, New York, 1976.

Grah75 GRAHAM, S. L., AND RHODES, S. P. "Practical syntactic error recovery," *Commun. ACM* **18,** 11 (Nov. 1975), 639–650.

Grie71 GRIES, D. *Compiler construction for digital computers*, Wiley, New York, 1971.

Hall71 HALL, P. A. V. "Branch and bound and beyond," in *Int. Joint Conf. Artificial Intelligence*, Imperial College, London, Sept. 1971, pp. 641–650 (available from British Computer Society).

Hall78 HALL, P. A. V., AND HUSSEIN, I. "Design of information systems for Arabic," in *Information systems methodology*, ECI 78 Conference, Venice, Springer-Verlag, New York, 1978, pp. 643–663.

Heck78 HECKEL, P. "A technique for isolating differences between files," *Commun. ACM* **21,** 4 (April 1978), 264–268.

Hopc66 HOPCROFT, J. E., AND ULLMAN, J. D. "Error correction for formal languages," Tech. Rep. 52, Princeton Univ., Princeton, N.J., Nov. 1966.

Hopc69 HOPCROFT, J. E., AND ULLMAN, J. D. *Formal languages and their relation to automata*, Addison-Wesley, Reading, Mass., 1969.

Hunt77 HUNT, J. W., AND SZYMANSKI, T. G. "A fast algorithm for computing longest common subsequences," *Commun. ACM* **20,** 5 (May 1977), 350–353.

Iron63 IRONS, E. T. "An error-correcting parser algorithm," *Commun. ACM* **6,** 11 (Nov. 1963), 669–673.

Jame73 JAMES, E. B., AND PARTRIDGE, D. P. "Adaptive correction of program statements," *Commun. ACM* **16,** 1 (Jan. 1973), 27–37.

Jenk76 JENKS, R. D. *1976 ACM Conf. Symbolic and Algebraic Computation* (ACM), 1976.

Knut73 KNUTH, D. E. *Sorting and searching*, Addison-Wesley, Reading, Mass., 1973.

Knut77 KNUTH, D. E., MORRIS, J. H., AND PRATT, V. R. "Fast pattern matching in strings," *SIAM J. Comput.* **6** (1977), 323–350.

Leve66 LEVENSHTEIN, V. I. "Binary codes capable of correcting deletions, insertions, and reversals," *Sov. Phys. Dokl.* **10** (Feb. 1966), 707–710.

Levy75 LEVY, J. P. "Automatic correction of syntax errors in programming languages," *Acta Inf.* **4** (1975), 271–292.

Lips79 LIPSKI, W., JR. "On semantic issues connected with incomplete information databases" *ACM Trans. Database Syst.* **4,** 3 (Sept. 1979), 262–296.

Lite76 LITECKY, C. R., AND DAVIS, G. B. "A study of errors, error-proneness, and error diagnosis in COBOL," *Commun. ACM* **19,** 1 (Jan. 1976), 33–37.

Lowr75 LOWRANCE, R., AND WAGNER, R. A. "An extension of the string-to-string correction problem," *J. ACM* **22,** 2 (April 1975), 177–183.

Lyon74 LYON, G. "Syntax-directed least-errors analysis for context-free languages: A practical approach," *Commun. ACM* **17,** 1 (Jan. 1974), 3–14.

Mart75 MARTIN, J. *Computer data base organization*, Prentice-Hall, Englewood Cliffs, N.J., 1975.

Mick78 MICKUNAS, M. D., AND MODRY, J. A. "Automatic error recovery for LR parsers," *Commun. ACM* **21,** 6 (June 1978), 459–465.

Morg70 MORGAN, H. L. "Spelling correction in systems programs," *Commun. ACM* **13,** 2 (Feb. 1970), 90–94.

Muth77 MUTH, F. E., JR., AND THARP, A. L. "Correcting human error in alphanumeric terminal input," *Inf. Process. Manage.* **13,** 6 (1977), 329–337.

Newe73 NEWELL, A., BARNETT, J., FORGIE, J. W., GREEN, C., KLATT, D., LICKLIDER, J. C. R., MUNSON, J., REDDY, D. R., AND WOODS, W. A. "Speech understanding systems. Final report of a study group," in *Artificial intelligence*, North-Holland Elsevier, New York, 1973.

ODEL18 ODELL, M. K., AND RUSSELL, R. C. U.S. Patent nos. 1,261,167 (1918) and 1,435,663 (1922).

PAIC77 PAICE, C. D. *Information retrieval and the computer*, MacDonald and Jane's Computer Monographs, London, 1977.

PAN79 PAN, V. YA. "Field extension and trilinear aggregating, uniting, and canceling for the acceleration of matrix multiplications," in *Proc. 20th Annual Symp. Foundations of Computer Science*, Oct. 1979, pp. 28–38.

PETE61 PETERSON, W. W. *Error-correcting codes*, Wiley, New York, 1961.

POTT66 POTTER, R. K., KOPP, G. A., AND KOPP, H. G. *Visible speech*, Dover, New York, 1966.

RADE76 RADECKI, T. "New approach to the problem of information system effectiveness evaluation," *Inf. Process. Manage.* **12**, 5 (1976), 319–326.

RAHM68 RAHMAN, N. A. *A course in theoretical statistics*, Griffin, London, 1968.

RISE74 RISEMAN, E. M., AND HANSON, A. R. "A contextual post-processing system for error-correction using binary n-grams," *IEEE Trans. Comput.* **C-23**, 5 (1974), 480–493.

RIVE77 RIVEST, R. L. "On the worst-cast behavior of string-searching algorithms," *SIAM J. Comput.* **6**, 4 (Dec. 1977), 669–673.

ROGE61 ROGET *The new Roget's thesaurus*, N. Lewis (Ed.), Putnam, 1961.

SAKO79 SAKOE, H. "Two level DP-matching—A dynamic programming based pattern matching algorithm for connected word recognition," *IEEE Trans. Acoust., Speech, Signal Proc.* **ASSP-27**, 6 (Dec. 1979), 588–595.

SALT68 SALTON, G. *Automatic information organization and retrieval*, McGraw-Hill, New York, 1968.

SALT78 SALTON, G., AND WONG, A. "Generation and search of clustered files," *ACM Trans. Database Syst.* **3**, 4 (Dec. 1978), 321–346.

SHAF68 SHAFFER, L. H., AND HARDWICH, J. "Typing performance as a function of text," *Qt. J. Exper. Psychol.* **20**, 4 (1968), 360–369.

SHAP77 SHAPIRO, M. "The choice of reference points in best match file searching," *Commun. ACM* **20**, 5 (May 1977), 339–343.

SMIT70 SMITH, W. B. "Error detection in formal languages," *J. Comput. Syst. Sci,* 4 (1970), 385–405.

SLIN79 SLINN, C. "Retrieval mechanisms and Arabic strings," in *5th Saudi Arabian Computer Conf.*, Dhahran, Saudi Arabia, March 1979.

SZAN69 SZANZER, A. J. "Error-correcting methods in natural language processing," in *Information processing 68*, IFIP 1969, pp. 1412–1416.

SZAN73 SZANZER, A. J. "Bracketing technique in elastic matching," *Comput. J.* **16**, 2 (1973), 132–134.

TANA78 TANAKA, E., AND FU, K. S. "Error-correcting parsers for formal languages," *IEEE. Trans. Comput.* **C-27**, 7 (July 1978), 605–616.

TARJ75 TARJAN, R. E. "Efficiency of a good but not linear set union algorithm," *J. ACM* **22**, 2 (April 1975), 215–225.

TEIT76 TEITELBAUM, R. "Minimal distance analysis of syntax errors in computer programs," Ph.D. Dissertation, Carnegie-Mellon Univ., Pittsburgh, Pa., 1976.

ULLM77 ULLMAN, J. R. "A binary n-gram technique for automatic correction of substitution, deletion, insertion and reversal errors in words," *Comput. J.* **20**, 2 (1977), 141–147.

UNES76 UNESCO *SPINES thesaurus*, The UNESCO Press, Paris, 1976.

VELI70 VELICHKO, V. M., AND ZAGARUIKO, N. G. "Automatic recognition of 200 words," *Int. J. Man-Mach. Stud.* **2** (1970), 223–234.

VINT68 VINTSYUK, T. K. "Speech discrimination by dynamic programming," *Kibernetika* **4**, 1 (1968), 81–88 (in Russian); translated in *Cybernetics* **4**, 1, 52–58.

WAGN72 WAGNER, R. A. "An n^3 minimum edit-distance correction algorithm for context-free languages," Tech. Rep., Systems and Information Sci. Dept., Vanderbilt Univ., Nashville, Tenn., 1972.

WAGN74a WAGNER, R. A., AND FISCHER, M. J. "The string-to-string correction problem," *J. ACM* **21**, 1 (Jan 1974), 168–178.

WAGN74b WAGNER, R. A. "Order-n correction for regular languages," *Commun. ACM* **17**, 5 (May 1974), 265–268.

WHIT76 WHITE, G. M., AND NEELY, R. B. "Speech recognition experiments with linear prediction, bandpass filtering, and dynamic programming," *IEEE Trans. Acoust., Speech, Signal Proc.* **ASSP-24**, 2 (April 1976), 183–188.

WILC76 WILCOX, T. R., DAVIS, A. M., AND TINDALL, M. H. "The design and implementation of a table-driven interactive diagnostic programming system," *Commun. ACM* **19**, 11 (Nov. 1976), 609–616.

WONG76 WONG, C. K., AND CHANDRA, A. K. "Bounds for the string editing problem," *J. ACM* **23**, 1 (Jan. 1976), 13–16.

Optimal Correspondence of String Subsequences

Ynjiun P. Wang, *Member, IEEE*, and Theo Pavlidis, *Fellow, IEEE*

Abstract—The problem of substring matching when the strings are from a finite alphabet has been investigated thoroughly in the literature. The corresponding problem when the alphabet is infinite (for example strings of numbers) has received less attention. We present definitions of string distance, an effective way of computing them, and matching algorithms minimizing such distances. Our analysis also includes the matching of strings to regular expressions. We include two diverse applications: the stereo epipolar line matching and the bar code recognition.

Index Terms—Matching algorithms, pattern recognition, stereo vision.

I. INTRODUCTION

THE *partial matching* (or segment-matching [9]) problem arises in many fields of image analysis and speech recognition: for example, the correspondence problem in stereo [6], [25], the contour matching problem [28], the occluding object matching (recognition) problem [30], and syllable recognition in speech [10], etc. The general techniques for such matching task include *correlation* [5], *relaxation* [9], *time-warping* [22], and *elastic matching* [7]. However, in many one dimensional applications the cumbersome computations of relaxation and elastic matching seem unnecessary. For example, in stereo the epipolar lines correspondence problem is one-dimensional, and the contour matching problem can also be considered as a string matching (or feature vector matching) problem. It is hard to apply syntactic information to the relaxation and elastic matching techniques to do incremental matching. And the correlation technique has limitations when applied to partial matching [9]. Furthermore, we also would like the matching cost defined by the matching procedure to be a metric in pattern classification applications. The time-warping technique is not a metric [1]. These considerations motivate the development of the *optimal correspondent subsequence* problem.

The optimal correspondent subsequence (OCS) problem is derived from the classical longest common subsequence (LCS) and approximate string matching [4], [3], [15], [14], [32] problem which arises in data processing applications such as comparing two files and in genetic applications such as studying molecular evolution. The matching is defined as a notion of *exact* match or of *compatible* relation [2] on a finite alphabet. Only recently has the nonexact string matching in infinite alphabet domain received attention in the literature [12], [21]. Although in a noisy system the sampling data can always be digitized into numbers with quantization unit above the inherent noise level and represented by a finite alphabet, to handle the uncertainty of the size of finite alphabet due to the change of quantization unit conceptually is equivalent to handle an infinite alphabet. Moreover, if the size of an alphabet is too large, to maintain a huge lookup table to keep track of the interpretation of each symbol is infeasible. In this paper, the definition of optimal correspondent subsequence (OCS), which extends the finite alphabet editing error minimization matching to the infinite alphabet penalty minimization matching, is given. We also prove that the string distance derived from OCS is a metric.

An algorithm to compute the string-to-string OCS is given. The computation complexity of OCS[1] is analyzed, which is more efficient than relaxation and elastic matching for one-dimensional problems. Furthermore, an algorithm combining syntactic information in template matching is also given to show how easy it is to integrate the regular grammar into the OCS technique.

Since in different applications different penalty functions may be required, we discuss two of them: one pointwise and the other piecewise.

Finally, we discuss the application on the stereo epipolar line matching problem by using string-to-string OCS in Application A. The feasibility of applying OCS to an application, called UPC bar code [18] recognition, is investigated in Application B, and this will show the elegance of string-to-regular-expression OCS, compared to the relaxation and elastic matching techniques, on dealing with this problem.

II. OPTIMAL CORRESPONDENT SUBSEQUENCE (OCS) PROBLEM

We define the optimal correspondent subsequence (OCS) problem as an infinite alphabet penalty minimization problem using the following entities.

Definition 1: Alphabet. The alphabet is an infinite set N which contains all characters, and lifted N, denoted as $N_\perp$, is $N \cup \{\epsilon\}$, where ϵ is a null character. By $\perp$ itself, we mean a null character or number. In many applications the reasonable choice of N is an interval of real numbers R.

Definition 2: Penalty. We say $p(x, y)$ is a penalty function, if $p : N_\perp \times N_\perp \to R$, $\forall x, y, z \in N$ such that

- $p(x, y) \geq 0$,
- $p(x, x) = 0$,
- $p(x, y) = p(y, x)$,
- $p(x, y) + p(y, z) \geq p(x, z)$.

In addition,

- $p(x, \epsilon) = p(\epsilon, x) = \tau$, where τ is a constant in R.

Notice that $p(x, y)$ is a metric over N but not over $N_\perp$.

Lemma 1: If τ is maximum (or upper bound) of R, then $p(x, y)$ is a metric over $N_\perp$.

Manuscript received May 19, 1989; revised January 23, 1990. Recommended for acceptance by R. De Mori. This work was supported by the National Science Foundation under Grant IRI-8702168 and Equipment Grant DMC-8705290, and by Symbol Technologies, Inc., Bohemia, NY.

Y. P. Wang was with the Department of Computer Science, State University of New York at Stony Brook, Stony Brook, NY 11794. He is now with Symbol Technologies, Inc., Bohemia, NY 11716.

T. Pavlidis is with the Department of Computer Science, State University of New York at Stony Brook, Stony Brook, NY 11794.

IEEE Log Number 9038390.

---

[1] In general, the complexity of longest common subsequence (LCS) algorithm is quadratic in time and space [32]. Hirschberg [15] gives an algorithm with linear space and quadratic time complexity. Aho, Hirschberg, and Ullman [4] have derived complexity bounds for the LCS problem and have shown that alphabet size is important. For finite alphabets an improvement on the quadratic limit should be possible. A survey of approximate string matching [14], [3] gives additional references.

0-8186-5460-0/94 $3.00 © 1990 IEEE

Proof: We only need to verify that $p(x,y) + p(y,z) \geq p(x,z)$ for $y = \epsilon$. Since τ is the maximum, $p(x,\epsilon) + p(\epsilon,z) = 2\tau \geq p(x,z)$.　　　　　　　　Q.E.D.

Definition 3: Association function. F is an association function of string $A = a_1 a_2 \cdots a_n$ and $B = b_1 b_2 \cdots b_m$ if and only if there is a mapping $F : \{1, 2, \cdots, n\} \rightarrow \{1, 2, \cdots, m, \perp\}$ such that $F(i) = \perp$ or $(F(i) \neq \perp \wedge F(j) \neq \perp \wedge i < j) \Rightarrow (F(i) < F(j))$. The number of nontrivial correspondences of A and B, denoted as $\#|F|$, is the number of $F(i)$ which $F(i) \neq \perp$ and $1 \leq i \leq n$.

Now we can express the optimal correspondent subsequence problem as follows: given strings $A = a_1 a_2 \cdots a_n$ and $B = b_1 b_2 \cdots b_m$ (over alphabet N), find an association function F of A and B such that the total penalty

$$S_F(A,B) = (m + n - 2q)\tau + \sum_{\forall i F(i) \neq \perp} p(a_i, b_{F(i)}) \quad (1)$$

where $q = \#|F|$, is minimized.

The LCS problem is a special case of OCS. If we set $0 \leq \tau < \epsilon$, where $\epsilon = \frac{1}{2} \min_{a_i \neq b_j}(|a_i - b_j|)$ then the F satisfying OCS will be $\forall i F(i) \neq \perp \Rightarrow a_i = b_{F(i)}$.

Roughly speaking: if τ increases, then the number of correspondences of OCS would increase. When we set $\tau \geq \sup R$ then the number of correspondences is equal to $\min(n, m)$.

Example: Given two real number strings $A = 1.3\ 0.5\ 1.8\ 11.3$, $B = 1.2\ 1.9\ 11.9\ 9.0\ 5.0$ and an absolute difference of two real numbers as a penalty function. If $\tau < 0.05$, the number of correspondences is zero, i.e., $\#|F| = 0$, with minimum $S_F(A,B) = 9\tau$. If $\tau = 0.5$, we have $F : \{1,2,3,4\} = \{1, \perp, 2, 3\}$ satisfying OCS, i.e., $\#|F| = 3$, with minimum $S_F(A,B) = 2.3$. If $\tau = 300$, we have $F : \{1,2,3,4\} = \{1,2,3,4\}$ satisfying OCS, i.e., $\#|F| = 4 = \min(4,5)$, with minimum $S_F(A,B) = 313.9$.

III. String Distance

Now, let us define the distance of two strings A, B as follows:

$$D(A,B) = \min_{\forall F} S_F(A,B). \quad (2)$$

Theorem 1: The distance defined by (2) is a metric.

Proof: For strings A, B, the first two properties, $D(A,B) \geq 0$ and $D(A,A) = 0$, are obviously true.

To prove the symmetric property, we show that S_F is symmetric. From (1), the first term of the right-hand side is commutative for m and n, i.e., the order of m and n cannot effect the evaluation value, and the second term is also symmetric by the definition of the penalty function. Furthermore, the min operator is a symmetric operator, too. Therefore the symmetric property holds.

The triangular inequality can be proved by contradiction. Let us assume that F_{AB}, F_{BC}, and F_{AC} are optimal association functions corresponding to $D(A,B)$, $D(B,C)$ and $D(A,C)$, respectively, and $D(A,B) + D(B,C) < D(A,C)$. Then we can establish a new association function $F'_{AC} = F_{AB} \circ F_{BC}$ and show that $S_{F'_{AC}}(A,C) \leq D(A,B) + D(B,C) < D(A,C)$, i.e., F_{AC} is not optimal, it is a contradiction.

In detail, let $n = |A|$, $m = |B|$, and $r = |C|$; then

$$D(A,B) = (n + m - 2q_{AB})\tau + \sum_{\forall i F_{AB}(i) \neq \perp} p(a_i, b_{F_{AB}(i)}) \quad (3)$$

$$D(B,C) = (m + r - 2q_{BC})\tau + \sum_{\forall i F_{BC}(i) \neq \perp} p(b_i, c_{F_{BC}(i)}) \quad (4)$$

$$S_{F'_{AC}}(A,C) = (n + r - 2q'_{AC})\tau + \sum_{\forall i F'_{AC}(i) \neq \perp} p(a_i, c_{F'_{AC}(i)}). \quad (5)$$

Since $\forall x, y, z \in N$, $p(x,y) + p(y,z) \geq p(x,z)$, $\sum_{\forall i F_{AB}(i) \neq \perp} p(a_i, b_{F_{AB}(i)}) + \sum_{\forall i F_{BC}(i) \neq \perp} p(b_i, c_{F_{BC}(i)}) \geq \sum_{\forall i F'_{AC}(i) \neq \perp} p(a_i, c_{F'_{AC}(i)})$. And $m = q_{AB} + q_{BC} - q'_{AC} + m'$, where, $m' \geq 0$, therefore $(n + m - 2q_{AB})\tau + (m + r - 2q_{BC})\tau \geq (n + r - 2q'_{AC})\tau$.　　Q.E.D.

The concept of string distance is not new. See [1] and [13] for examples. However, most of the previous work has concentrated on the finite alphabet domain. We will emphasize here the development of the penalty function in an infinite alphabet domain and elaborate the relationship between the penalty function and string distance definition.

IV. Algorithm

Suppose that we are given two strings A and B with length n and m, respectively. In order to find out the required association function F of A and B, we use a dynamic programming technique to build a minimum penalty table which accumulates the information of correspondence, and from the table we can trace back the correspondence and construct the desired F.

First, let us postulate the function $K(i,j)$ which is the minimum penalty of the match of $a_1 \cdots a_i$ against $b_1 \cdots b_j$. We could find the recurrence relation

$$K(i,j) = \min\{[K(i-1,j-1) + p(a_i,b_j)], [K(i-1,j) + \tau], [K(i,j-1) + \tau]\} \quad (6)$$

with $K(0,0) = 0$, and $p(a_i, b_j)$ giving the penalty of the difference between characters a_i and b_j. The three terms of this recurrence relation can be understood as: the first term a_i matches b_j, the second term leaves the a_i unmatched, and the third term allows to skip b_j without matching any character from A. The algorithm is depicted in Fig. 1. This algorithm is the extension of the Wagner and Fischer result (Algorithm X) [32]. The differences between Algorithm A and Algorithm X are: 1) the alphabet size of Algorithm A is infinite but that of Algorithm X is finite, 2) Algorithm A tries to minimize the penalty, while Algorithm X tries to construct a sequence of least editing operations to correct the Morgan editing error [26].

Computing the required $K(n,m)$ necessitates iterating over i and j, therefore it is easy to see that the complexity of Algorithm A is $O(nm)$ in time and space.

The following theorem shows that $K(n,m)$ is optimal.

Theorem 2: Given A and B strings with length n and m, respectively, and F is the association function of A and B, then

$$\forall F, K(n,m) \leq (m + n - 2q)\tau + \sum_{\forall i F(i) \neq \perp} p(a_i, b_{F(i)}), \quad (7)$$

where $q = \#|F|$, i.e., $K(n,m)$ is optimal [w.r.t. all possible $F()$].

Proof: We shall prove it by double induction over i and j, which $0 \leq i \leq n$, $0 \leq j \leq m$.

Basis: $K(0,0) = 0$ is obviously optimal, and for all $i, j, K(i,0) = i\tau$, $K(0,j) = j\tau$ are optimal by the definition of OCS.

Induction Step: We assume that for all $0 \leq i \leq n-1$ and $0 \leq j \leq m-1$, $K(i,j)$ are optimal, then by definition of $K()$, we can prove by induction that $K(n-1,m)$ is optimal from the basis $K(0,j) = j\tau$. That is, it follows the basis that $K(0,m)$ is optimal and if we assume that $K(n-2,m)$ is optimal, then

134

```
Algorithm A(n,m,A,B,K)

1.  Initialization: K(0,0) := 0;
                     K(i,0) := i*t [i=1..n];
                     K(0,j) := j*t [j=1..m];
2.  for i:=1 to n do
    begin
3.  for j:=1 to m do
        K(i,j) := min{K(i-1,j-1)+p(A[i],B[j]),
                      K(i-1,j)+t,
                      K(i,j-1)+t}
    end
4.  return(K(n,m));
```

Fig. 1. Algorithm A (t stands for τ).

```
Algorithm B(n,m,K,Fset)

1.  Initialization: i:= n
                     j:= m
2.  while(i != 0 && j != 0) do
    begin
3.    if K(i,j) == K(i-1,j) + t then i:= i-1
      else if K(i,j) == K(i,j-1) + t then j:= j-1
      else begin
        add (i,j) to Fset
        i:= i-1
        j:= j-1
      end
    end
```

Fig. 2. Algorithm B (t stands for τ).

by the above assumption on $K(i,j)$ for $0 \le i \le n-1$ and $0 \le j \le m-1$ and by definition

$$K(n-1,m) = \min\{[K(n-2,m-1)+p(a_n,b_m)],$$
$$[K(n-2,m)+\tau], [K(n-1,m-1)+\tau]\}$$

is optimal. Similarly we can prove that $K(n,m-1)$ is also optimal. Therefore, the $K(n,m)$, which by definition

$$K(n,m) = \min\{[K(n-1,m-1)+p(a_n,b_m)],$$
$$[K(n-1,m)+\tau], [K(n,m-1)+\tau]\},$$

is optimal.   Q.E.D.

Next we shall make use of the minimum penalty table, $K(i,j)$, to construct the association function F. The algorithm is similar to Algorithm Y in Wagner's paper [32] (see Fig. 2—Algorithm B).

We define the *Fset* as the set of all (i,j) such that $F(i) = j$, and for those $(i,j) \notin Fset$, $F(i) = \perp$. The proof of the correctness of this algorithm is also by induction; interested readers are referred to [32].

V. TEMPLATE MATCHING: INTEGRATING REGULAR GRAMMARS INTO OCS

Usually in a recognition system a matching technique incorporates a set of templates which are used to recognize objects. Templates could be explicitly stored as a list or could be implicitly defined by rules. It turns out that it is easy to integrate a grammar into OCS and do the computation incrementally. Here we use a regular grammar to represent a set of templates (more specifically "strings"). We are going to show how to combine the regular grammar and the matching technique [11], [31] in the following paragraphs.

Suppose that we are given a regular grammar $G = (V,T,P,S)$ [16], where V is the set of variables, T is the set of terminals, P is the set of productions of the form $A \rightarrow aB$ or $A \rightarrow a(A, B$ in V, a in $T)$, and S is the start symbol. The OCS problem then becomes that of finding the sentence y in the language which is closest to the input string x. For description purposes, we will write $A \rightarrow a$ as $A \rightarrow a\#$. Using a technique similar to that introduced in the previous section, we also define a function $k(i,A)$, which is the minimum penalty of the match of $x_1 \cdots x_i$ against all strings y in the language which can be generated by starting with S and substituting using the productions until a sentential form yA is obtained. We could find the recurrence relation which is similar to (6)

$$k(i,A) = \min\Big\{ \min_{\forall B: B \rightarrow aA} [k(i-1,B)+p(x_i,a)],$$

$$k(i-1,A)+\tau, \min_{\forall B: B \rightarrow aA} [k(i,B)+\tau] \Big\} \quad (8)$$

with $k(0,S) = 0$, and $p(x_i,a)$ giving the penalty of the difference between the terminals x_i and a. The three terms of this recurrence relation can be understood as follows: the first term expresses the optimal matching of a single generated symbol in the language with an input symbol, the second term generates no symbols and leaves the input symbol unmatched, and the third term expresses the generation of language symbols which cannot match an input symbol. This recurrence equation is the extension of Dowling's result [11]. Although about the same time (1974) Wagner [31] also came out with a similar result, his algorithm cannot be extended to our purpose since it tightly depends on a finite alphabet lookup table.

Computing the optimal $k(n,\#)$ necessitates iterating over the i, starting from $k(0,S)$, and for each successive i finding $\Gamma(i)$ from the preceding $\Gamma(i-1)$, where $\Gamma(i)$ is the set of $k(i,A)$ for all variables A in V.

It is natural to implement the minimization recursive function in two stages:

1) From the first and second terms of (8), let us calculate the tentative value, $k^1(i,A)$, of $k(i,A)$.

$$k^1(i,A) = \min\Big\{ \min_{\forall B: B \rightarrow aA} [k(i-1,B)+p(x_i,a)],$$

$$k(i-1,A)+\tau \Big\} \quad (9)$$

2) From the third term of (8), following (9) we iterate through variables of the grammar to let values propagate until no more changes occur.

$$k^{l+1}(i,A) = \min\Big\{ k^l(i,A), \min_{\forall B: B \rightarrow aA} [k^l(i,B)+\tau] \Big\} \quad (10)$$

For each i this iteration continues for at most $|V|$ cycles, leading eventually to the values $k(i,A)$ for $\Gamma(i)$.

Lemma 2: The iteration of (10) will converge within $|V|$ cycles.

Proof: Convergence Property: $\Gamma^l(i)$ is the set of $k^l(i,A)$ for all variables A in V. First we prove that if $\Gamma^{N+1}(i) = \Gamma^N(i)$ then $\forall l > N$, $\Gamma^{l+1}(i) = \Gamma^l(i)$. The definition of the iteration process, denoted as $\Psi(\Gamma^l(i))$,, is according to (10) through variables in V over the index l, i.e., $\Gamma^{l+1}(i) = \Psi(\Gamma^l(i))$. Since $\Gamma^{N+1}(i) = \Psi(\Gamma^N(i)) = \Gamma^N(i)$, we have $\Gamma^{N+2}(i) = \Psi(\Gamma^{N+1}(i)) = \Psi(\Psi(\Gamma^N(i))) = \Psi(\Gamma^N(i)) = \Gamma^N(i)$. By induction, we prove that $\forall l > N$, $\Gamma^{l+1}(i) = \Gamma^l(i) = \Gamma^N(i)$. In this case we say that $\Gamma^N(i)$ achieves a stable state.

Bounded Property: The definition of the minset of $\Gamma^l(i)$ denoted as $\overline{\min}(\Gamma^l(i))$, is the set of elements which do not change value any more through the iteration over l, i.e., $\forall l' \; \forall k^l(i,A), k^l(i,A) \in \overline{\min}(\Gamma^l(i)) \wedge l' > l \Rightarrow k^{l'}(i,A) = k^l(i,A)$.

Now we claim that $\overline{\min}(\Gamma^1(i))$ is not empty. Since the $\Gamma^1(i)$ is a finite set, there must be a lower bound, say $k^1(i,A')$, in $\Gamma^1(i)$. Furthermore, according to (10) $k^1(i,A')$ is fixed w.r.t. Ψ operation, i.e., $\forall l \geq 1, k^{l+1}(i,A') = k^l(i,A')$.

Next we claim that $\overline{\min}(\Psi(\Gamma^l(i)))$ increases at least one more element than $\overline{\min}(\Gamma^l(i))$ until $\Psi(\Gamma^l(i)) = \Gamma^l(i) \Rightarrow \overline{\min}(\Psi(\Gamma^l(i))) = \overline{\min}(\Gamma^l(i))$ which means that $\Gamma^l(i)$ achieves the stable state because of the convergence property.

To prove this, we can construct a loopless precedence graph $H(E,N)$. The elements, $k(i,B)$, in $\overline{\min}(\Gamma^1(i))$ are root nodes in N without predecessors. For each root, we create a set Q_B and put $k(i,B)$ in it. Then let all $k(i,A)$, such that $B \rightarrow aA$ and $k(i,A)$ is not in Q_B, be the descendants of $k(i,B)$ and put these elements in Q_B. Follow the above step to build the descendants of descendants of each root $k(i,B)$ until no elements can be added on.

Since there is no loop in the graph H and the longest path cannot be greater than $|V|$, it takes at most $|V|$ iterations to achieve the stable state. Q.E.D.

Example: Given a regular grammar $G = (V,T,P,S)$ where $V = \{A,B\}$, $T = \{1,2,3\}$ and $P = \{S \rightarrow 1A, A \rightarrow 2B, S \rightarrow 3B, B \rightarrow 1\#, B \rightarrow 1S\}$. An input string is 1.9 0.8 3 1. If τ is equal to 0.5, and initialize $k(0,S) = 0$, $k(0,A) = \tau$, $K(0,B) = \tau$ and $k(0,\#) = 2\tau$. Then the set $k^1(1,\{V\}) = \{k^1(1,S), k^1(1,A), k^1(1,B)\} = \{0.5, 0.9, 0.6\}$ and it is easy to verify that $k^2(1,\{V\}) = k^1(1,\{V\})$, thus $\overline{\min}(\Gamma^1(i)) = k^1(1,\{V\})$. The result $k(4,\#)$ is equal to 0.8 and the OCS is $(1,2,1,3,1) \rightarrow (\bot, 1.9, 0.8, 3, 1)$.

The following theorem gives the complexity of (8).

Theorem 3: Given an input string x with length n and $|V|$ is the number of variables of given grammar. The complexity of (8) is $O(n|V|^3)$.

Proof: To compute the second term of (10), we need to iterate at most $|V|$ times in the innermost loop. Similarly, to compute $\Gamma^l(i)$, we need to update $k^l(i,A)$ for each variable A in V which contributes to the intermediate loop of $|V|$ iterations. By Lemma 2, the outermost loop iterates over the index l at most $|V|$ times. The iteration over the index i which is the input string pointer is at most n times. Q.E.D.

Similarly, the closest sentence y can be constructed by tracing back the modified minimum penalty table entry $(k^l(i,A))$ which is defined as a record: $k'(i,A) \rightarrow c$ stores the character a generated by grammar during computing the $k(i,A)$ if the first item or the third item of (8) is the min, stores ϵ otherwise, and $k'(i,A) \rightarrow v$ stores the value of $k(i,A)$ The algorithm is shown in Fig. 3.

The boolean function $exist(A,B,t)$ is defined as: it returns *TRUE* if there is a B in V such that $k'(i,A) \rightarrow v = k'(i,B) \rightarrow v + t$ and $B \rightarrow aA$ in P where a is the character stored in record $k'(i,A) \rightarrow c$; *FALSE* otherwise.

VI. PENALTY FUNCTIONS

A. Pointwise Penalty Function

For real numbers the simplest pointwise penalty function is the Euclidean distance, $p(x,y) = |x-y|$. It is easy to check that this definition satisfies the definition of penalty (cf. Section II).

```
Algorithm D(n,k',y)

1.  Initialization: i:= n
                     A:= #
                     y:= NULL
2.  while(i != 0 && A != S) do
    begin
3.    if k'(i,A)->v == k'(i-1,A)->v + t then i:= i-1
      else if exist(A,B,t)
          then begin
              y:=k'(i,A)->c @ y
              A:=B
          end
      else begin
          y:=k'(i,A)->c @ y
          i:= i-1
          A:= B
      end
    end
```

Fig. 3.   Algorithm D (t stands for τ, @ means concatenation).

B. Piecewise Penalty Function

In some applications, the local structure matching is more important than the pointwise matching. For these cases, the piecewise penalty function is introduced.

The basic idea for the piecewise penalty function (*ppf*) is using the neighborhood information. There are many functions satisfying the definition of piecewise penalty. The following are two examples together with proofs that are well defined *ppf*.

Let us define the *ppf* $p_b(x_i, y_j)$ as follows:

$$p_b(x_i, y_j) = \sum_{k=-b}^{b-1} |(x_{i+k+1} - x_{i+k}) - (y_{j+k+1} - y_{j+k})|. \quad (11)$$

In the domain of real numbers, $p_b(x_i, y_j)$ is a metric. The first three metric properties, $p_b(x_i, y_j) \geq 0$, $p_b(x_i, x_i) = 0$, and $p_b(x_i, y_j) = p_b(y_j, x_i)$ are easy to check. Furthermore, the above definition is a discrete version of Euclidean distance of the first derivatives of each correspondent neighbor points. Therefore, the triangular inequality holds.

Another example, if we consider these two patches around x_i and y_j as two strings. Then we can define *ppf* as an OCS with pointwise penalty function. We already proved that string distance measured by (2) is a metric. Therefore this definition meets the definition of penalty. This example gives an important view of the OCS problem, i.e., the OCS algorithm is a recursively applicable algorithm. We will find its importance in the stereo epipolar line matching later.

The definition of (11) is a two-sided piecewise penalty function. In order to take advantage of the incremental matching property of the recurrence equation (8), we would like the penalty function to be one-sided piecewised.[2] The one-sided version of above *ppf* is defined

$$p_b^-(x_i, y_j) = \sum_{k=-b}^{-1} |(x_{i+k+1} - x_{i+k}) - (y_{j+k+1} - y_{j+k})|. \quad (12)$$

It is easy to check that the above one-sided *ppf* is a metric.

[2] In the terminology of digital signal processing, this corresponds to a causal system which can filter input signal out in real time response.

136

VII. Revised OCS Algorithm for the One-Sided Piecewise Penalty Function

Algorithm A can be adapted to the *ppf* easily with an independent penalty function module to compute the penalty, since both string values are accessible during the run time. But the recurrence equation (8) is not obviously adapted to the one-sided *ppf*. The reason is that there is no accessible string generated by the grammar before finishing the matching. Therefore, a modification of memorizing the partial string being generated in the state variable $k(i, A)$ is needed. The revised recurrence equation (8) is as below:

$$k_\beta(i, A) = \min\left\{\min_{\forall B: B \to aA}[k_{\gamma c}(i-1, B) + p_b^-(x_i, a)],\right.$$
$$\left. k_{\gamma c}(i-1, A) + \tau, \min_{\forall B: B \to aA}[k_{\gamma c}(i, B) + \tau]\right\} \quad (13)$$

where $\beta = a\gamma$ when the minimum occurs at the first or the third term of the right-hand side of (13), $\beta = \gamma c$ when the minimum occurs at the second term, and $|\beta| = |\gamma| + 1 = b$.

The complexity of revised OCS algorithm is increased by a constant factor, b, i.e., the order of the complexity remains the same.

VIII. Application A: The Epipolar Lines Correspondence Problem

Finding the conjugate points of two images on epipolar lines is intrinsically an OCS problem [17], [25], [6]. Several matching schemes for stereo matching have been proposed, e.g., a cooperative algorithm [24] is a neural net-like implementation. Kim and Aggarwal [20] used a relaxation method. Ohta and Kanade [27] and Lloyd [23] used dynamic programming.

Dan and Dubuisson [8] is probably the first paper applying string matching scheme to the stereo matching problem. But they used a finite alphabet, called edges-based coding, to do string matching. In our approach, we directly use the raw images (could be gray level images, or raw zero-crossing images) to do the matching without any precoding process. The use of an infinite alphabet avoids the quantization errors. In the raw images a lot of details (e.g., amplitudes around zero-crossings) are required for correct matching. These details will not be preserved by some feature coding processes, like edge-based coding. Furthermore, since the OCS algorithm is a general matching scheme, we can choose any kind of primitive, e.g., gray level, edgelet, as a matching entity.

A. Algorithm

The algorithm (see Fig. 4) for finding the conjugate points of left and right images can be described in two stages.

1) Epipolar Line Registration: For each scan line *left*$_i$ of the left image, search the correspondent scan line of the right image *right*$_j$ such that the penalty of OCS (*left*$_i$, *right*$_j$) is minimum for j in the range of ($i - maxshift, i + maxshift$).

2) Finding Conjugate Points: For two registered scan lines (i.e., on the same epipolar line), for each segment, $leftseg_i = x_{i-r}x_{i-r+1} \cdots x_{i+r}$ (which can be considered as a string consisting of a sequence of real-valued pixels centered by pixel x_i with radius r), of the left eye scan line, search the correspondent segment of the right eye scan line, $rightseg_j = y_{j-r}y_{j-r+1} \cdots y_{j+r}$, such that the penalty of OCS ($leftseg_i, rightseg_{j'}$) is minimum for j in the range of ($i - maxdisparity, i + maxdisparity$).

In Fig. 4, the Algorithm Registration (n, L, R) registers the right scan line $R[$register$]$ to the left scan line $L[n]$ in two given M

```
Algorithm Registration(n,L,R)
    /*Epipolar line registration*/
    min := A(M,M,L[n],R[n-maxshift]);
    register := n-maxshift;
    for i:=n-maxshift+1 to n+maxshift do
        if min > A(M,M,L[n],R[i]) then
            min := A(M,M,L[n],R[i]);
            register := i;
    return(register);

Algorithm Correspondence(p,r,L[n],R[m])
    /*Finding conjugate points*/
    l:=2*r+1;
    min := A(l,l,&L[n][p-maxdisparity-r],
             &R[m][p-maxdisparity-r]);
    disparity := -maxdisparity;
    for i:=p-maxdisparity+1 to p+maxdisparity do
        if min > A(l,l,&L[n][i-r],&R[m][i-r]) then
            min := A(l,l,&L[n][i-r],&R[m][i-r]);
            disparity := i-p;
    return(disparity);
```

Fig. 4. OCS stereo algorithm.

by M images $L[ ] [ ]$ and $R[ ] [ ]$. The Algorithm Correspondence $(p, r, L[n], R[m])$ computes the disparity of the point $L[n][p]$ with respect to the scan line $R[m]$. The r is the matching patch radius. Both algorithms use Algorithm A to compute the matching cost.

B. Experiment

The algorithm was tested by Dr. William Sakoda on a pair of *SPOT* images at Grumman Data Systems. The goal was to construct the depth map of two 512 by 512 aerial images (see Fig. 5). The inputs were $\nabla^2 G$ filtered images with $\sigma = 2.0$. The output was a 128 by 128 depth map. The OCS algorithm replaced an earlier matching procedure which used a correlation matching algorithm.

Figs. 6 and 7 are the depth maps by using correlation method and OCS algorithm, respectively. The gray level in Figs. 6 and 7 represents the relative height, the brighter the lower and the darker the higher. Those yellow and green areas are unmatching and mismatching areas, respectively. Compared to Fig. 6's large unmatching and mismatching areas, Fig. 7's unmatching and mismatching areas have been reduced significantly.

The images (Fig. 5) can be displayed by using different color maps, and a human observer with color glasses can fuse the images to verify the depth map [19]. An interesting case is presented at the right-upper corner where there is a big unmatched area in Fig. 6. The OCS algorithm gives the correct solution in that area; see Fig. 7.

As we mentioned in Section VI-B, it is possible to apply OCS recursively (or in other sense *hierarchically*). In the aerial imagery, we can also apply *ordering constraints* [8] in the global matching (i.e., consider the epipolar lines as strings). Therefore, in phase two of Fig. 4 instead of finding a local minimum in the range of ($i - maxdisparity, i + maxdisparity$), we can take that as a piecewise penalty function and apply Algorithm A once more on the whole scan lines to find out the OCS and to compute the disparities accordingly. This deserves further investigation.

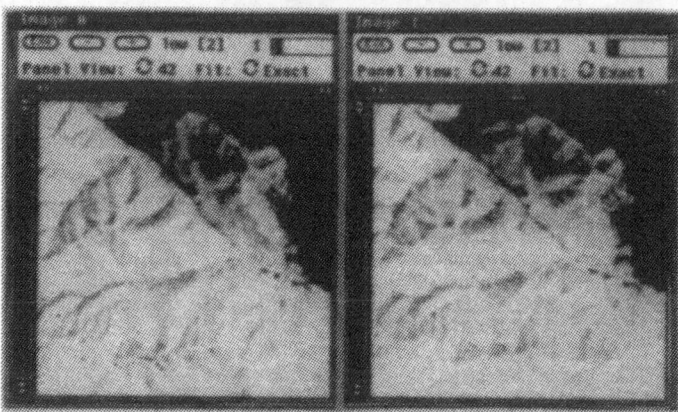

Fig. 5. Pair of aerial images.

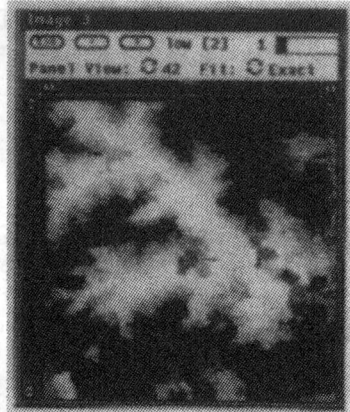

Fig. 6. Depth map by correlation method.

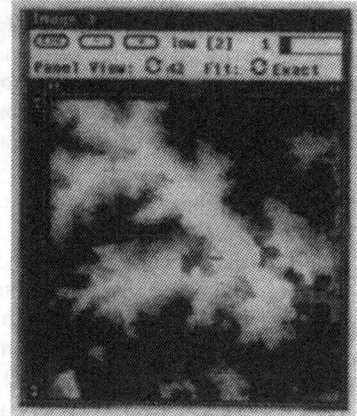

Fig. 7. Depth map by OCS algorithm.

IX. APPLICATION B: AN INVESTIGATION OF THE APPLICABILITY OF OCS TO A UPC DECODING SCHEME

Another application of OCS matching is to UPC bar code recognition. The information in bar codes is conveyed by the arrangement of bars and spaces (elements) of different widths. The elements are translated by a scanner from their printed form to an analog electrical signal that represents the relative widths of the elements in the symbol.

The UPC (Universal Product Code) symbol [29], [18] is usually printed on the products for identification purposes. The symbol consists of 59 elements. Every element width ranges from 1 to 4 modules. The first (last) three consecutive one module elements are leading (trailing) guard elements. There are five consecutive one module central guard elements in the center of the symbol which divide the symbol into two even blocks. Each block contains 24 elements representing 6 digits. Every four consecutive elements with fixed length of seven modules represent a digit.

We can use a regular grammar (see Fig. 8) to describe the legal UPC codes on the level of element width string input. In Fig. 8 the grammar has 288 states with sentence length of 59. The numbers 1, 2, 3, 4 represent the module numbers. After three consecutive one module transitions, the grammar describes the first digit by 22 states. The following five rectangular boxes represent the same structure as the first digit. Then following by five consecutive central guard elements the long rectangular box represents the same grammar structure as the left-hand side 6 digit block. The symbol ends with three consecutive one module trailing guard elements.

The output of the optoelectric circuit of the bar code scanner is a sequence of numbers representing interleaving bar and space width. Since there is a noise in the scanning process, the raw data could be any occurrence of number, it is not an ideal target for decoding. In order to reduce the effects of noise, searching the best matching sentence generated by the presetting grammar is necessary. The use of an infinite alphabet in matching phase can avoid quantization errors. After the matching process, we use the matching result, i.e., the sentence closest to the input string, to decode.

Example: Data in the second column of Fig. 9 are collected from a hand-held laser scanner on scanning a UPC label forward. Because of limited space we only illustrate up to data no. 35, which is the left-side block of the UPC label including the leading guard elements, the first six digits, and the central guard elements. Let us set the module equal to 24^3 and use the grammar depicted in Fig. 8 to parse the data, and we obtain a sentence as in the third column of Fig. 9, which is the sentence closest to the data collected from the scanner. In this example, the original data is undecodable because of an error on data no. 17 into which three elements are merged. But the resulting sentence is decodable and the decoding result is in the fourth column of Fig. 9.

X. CONCLUSIONS

The classical LCS problem is well understood [4]. It seems that the OCS problem has not been explored as much as LCS. This paper gives the definition of the optimal correspondent subsequence (OCS) problem and the algorithms. The complexity of OCS is quadratic. It is superior to relaxation and elastic matching of which complexity are cubic. In comparison to relaxation and elastic matching techniques, the OCS also shows its elegance in combining syntactic information and doing matching incrementally. The diversity of the OCS algorithm is shown in the last two applications. It can tackle either the string-to-string or string-to-regular-grammar approximate matching problem in the infinite alphabet domain.

ACKNOWLEDGMENT

The authors would like to thank Dr. W. Sakoda and K. Huang for their help in using their systems and for discussions on this paper. We thank Grumman Data Systems for the testing of our algorithm in their Laboratory.

---

[3] This number is from finding the minimum module by histogramming method. Since it is out of the scope of this paper, we omit the discussion of this step here. Interested readers are referred to [33].

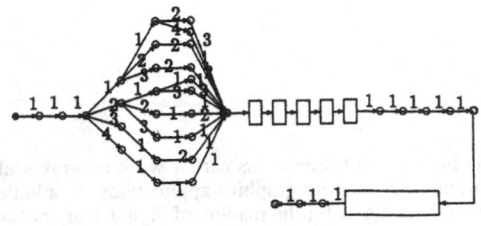

Total states = 288

Final state ○
State ○
Starting state ●

Fig. 8.   Regular grammar used in UPC recognition.

MODULE = 24

No.	DATA	SENTENCE	DECODE	No.	DATA	SENTENCE	DECODE
1	255			19	23	1	4
2	255			20	26	1	
3	255			21	71	3	
4	255			22	51	2	
5	255			23	70	3	0
6	24	1	leading	24	49	2	
7	24	1	guard	25	22	1	
8	28	1	elements	26	27	1	
9	71	3	0	27	71	3	0
10	48	2		28	47	2	
11	23	1		29	23	1	
12	23	1		30	23	1	
13	25	1	4	31	25	1	central
14	26	1		32	23	1	guard
15	71	3		33	24	1	elements
16	46	2		34	24	1	
17	72	-- 1 a 6		35	25	1	
		\ 1 merge			:		
		\ 1 error			:		
18	96	4			:		

Fig. 9. An example of parsing UPC.

REFERENCES

[1] K. Abe and N. Sugita, "Distances between strings of symbols, review and remarks," in *Proc. 6th Int. Conf. Pattern Recognition*, Oct. 1982, pp. 172–174.

[2] K. Abrahamson, "Generalized string matching," *SIAM J. Comput.*, vol. 16, no. 6, pp. 1039–1051, Dec. 1987.

[3] A. V. Aho, "Algorithms for finding pattern in strings," in *The Handbook of Theoretical Computer Science*. Amsterdam, The Netherlands: North-Holland, 1989.

[4] A. V. Aho, D. S. Hirschberg, and J. D. Ullman, "Bounds on the complexity of the longest common subsequence problem," *J. ACM*, vol. 32, no. 1, pp. 1–12, Jan. 1976.

[5] D. H. Ballard and C. M. Brown, *Computer Vision*. Englewood Cliffs, NJ: Prentice-Hall, 1982.

[6] S. T. Barnard and M. A. Fischler, "Computational stereo," *Comput. Surveys*, vol. 14, no. 4, pp. 553–572, Dec. 1982.

[7] D. J. Burr, "Elastic matching of line drawings," *IEEE. Int. Joint Conf. Pattern Recognition*, 1980, pp. 223–228.

[8] H. Z. Dan and B. Dubuisson, "String matching for stereo vision," *Pattern Recognition Lett.*, vol. 9, pp. 117–126, Feb. 1989.

[9] L. S. Davis, "Shape matching using relaxation techniques," *IEEE Trans. Pattern Anal. Machine Intell.*, vol. PAMI-1, no. 1, pp. 60–72, Jan. 1979.

[10] R. de Mori, P. Laface, and Y. Mong, "Parallel algorithms for syllable recognition in continuous speech," *IEEE Trans. Pattern Anal. Machine Intell.*, vol. PAMI-7, no. 1, pp. 56–69, Jan. 1985.

[11] G. R. Dowling and P. A. V. Hall, "Elastic template matching in speech recognition, using linguistic information," in *Proc. 2nd Int. Joint Conf. Pattern Recognition*, Aug. 1974, pp. 249–250.

[12] T. Eilam-Tzoreff and U. Vishkin, "Matching patterns in strings subject to multi-linear transformations," *Theoretical Comput. Sci.*, vol. 60, pp. 231–254, 1988.

[13] K. S. Fu, *Syntactic Pattern Recognition and Applications*. Englewood Cliffs, NJ: Prentice-Hall, 1982.

[14] P. A. V. Hall and G. R. Dowling, "Approximate string matching," *Comput. Surveys*, vol. 12, no. 4, pp. 381–402, Dec. 1980.

[15] D. S. Hirschberg, "A linear space algorithm for computing maximal common subsequences," *Commun. ACM*, vol. 18, no. 6, pp. 341–343, June 1975.

[16] J. E. Hopcroft and J. D. Ullman, *Formal Languages and Their Relation to Automata*. Reading, MA: Addison-Wesley, 1969.

[17] B. K. P. Horn, *Robot Vision*. Cambridge, MA: MIT Press, 1986.

[18] *UPC Symbol Specification*, Uniform Product Code Council, Inc., May 1982.

[19] B. Julesz, *Foundations of Cyclopean Perception*. Chicago, IL: University of Chicago Press, 1971.

[20] Y. C. Kim and J. K. Aggarwal, "Finding range from stereo images," *Comput. Vision Pattern Recognition*, pp. 289–294, 1985.

[21] D. Sankoff and J. B. Kruskal, Eds., *Time Warps, String Edits, and Macromolecules: The Theory and Practice of Sequence Comparison*. Reading, MA: Addison-Wesley, 1983.

[22] J. B. Kruskal and M. Liberman, "The symmetric time-warping problem: From continuous to discrete," in *Time Warps, String Edits, and Macromolecules: The Theory and Practice of Sequence Comparison*, D. Sankoff and J. B. Kruskal, Eds. Reading, MA: Addison-Wesley, 1983, ch. 4.

[23] S. A. Lloyd, "Stereo matching using intra- and inter-row dynamic programming," *Pattern Recognition Lett.*, vol. 4, pp. 273–277, Sept. 1986.

[24] D. Marr and T. Poggio, "Cooperative computation of stereo disparity," *Science*, vol. 194, pp. 283–287, 1976.

[25] D. Marr, *Vision*. San Francisco, CA: Freeman, 1982.

[26] H. L. Morgan, "Spelling correction in systems programs," *Commun. ACM*, vol. 13, no. 2, pp. 90–94, Feb. 1970.

[27] Y. Ohta and T. Kanade, "Stereo by intra- and inter-scanline search using dynamic programming," *IEEE Trans. Pattern Anal. Machine Intell.*, vol. 7, no. 2, pp. 139–154, 1985.

[28] T. Pavlidis, "The use of a syntactic shape analyzer for contour matching," *IEEE Trans. Pattern Anal. Machine Intell.*, vol. PAMI-1, no. 3, pp. 307–310, July 1979.

[29] D. Savir and G. J. Laurer, "The characteristics and decodability of the universal product code symbol," *IBM Syst. J.*, vol. 1, pp. 16–33, 1975.

[30] J. T. Schwartz and M. Sharir, "Identification of partially obscured objects in two and three dimensions by matching of noisy 'characteristic curves'," *Int. J. Robotics Res.*, vol. 6, no. 2, pp. 29–44, 1987.

[31] R. A. Wagner, "Order-*n* correction for regular languages," *Commun. ACM*, vol. 17, no. 5, pp. 265–268, May 1974.

[32] R. A. Wagner and M. J. Fischer, "The string to string correction problem," *J. ACM*, vol. 21, no. 1, pp. 168–173, Jan. 1974.

[33] Y. P. Wang and T. Pavlidis, "Bar code recognition," Dep. Comput. Sci., SUNY at Stony Brook, Stony Brook, NY, Tech. Rep., Feb. 19, 1988.

Ynjiun P. Wang (S'88–M'89) received the B.S. degree from National Chiao Tung University, Taiwan, in 1984, and the M.S. and Ph.D. degrees from the State University of New York at Stony Brook in 1987 and 1989, respectively, all in computer science.

Since 1988, he has been an R&D Scientist at Symbol Technologies, Inc., Bohemia, NY, and is responsible for the development of a new two-dimensional bar code symbology. This involves research in optical scanning, signal processing, information theory, coding theory, and algorithms. His current research interests besides bar code symbology include spatial information theory, coding theory, image processing and analysis, and string matching algorithms.

Theo Pavlidis (S'62–M'64–SM'77–F'79) received the Diploma in mechanical and electrical engineering from the National Technical University of Athens, Greece, in 1957, and the M.S. and Ph.D. degrees in electrical engineering from the University of California at Berkeley in 1962 and 1964, respectively.

He is a leading Professor with the Department of Computer Science of SUNY at Stony Brook where he has been since 1986. He is also a scientific advisor to Symbol Technologies and a consultant to AT&T Bell Laboratories. From 1980 to 1986 he was with the Computer Science Research Center of AT&T Bell Laboratories, Murray Hill, NJ. Between 1964 and 1980 he was on the faculty of the Department of Electrical Engineering and Computer Science at Princeton University. During the 1978–1979 academic year he was a Visiting Professor of Electrical Engineering and Computer Science at the University of California at Berkeley. His industrial experience includes also consulting with RCA, various U.S. Army Laboratories, Datacopy, and other companies. His research interests are in the areas of image analysis, pattern recognition, and computer graphics. His research during 1980–1986 centered on the recognition of text and graphics together and the development of a graphics editor using image analysis techniques. More recently he has also resumed his earlier work on gray scale image analysis with emphasis on cartographics applications. In addition, he is investigating methodologies for the reading of high density bar codes. He is the author of three books, *Biological Oscillators: Their Mathematical Analysis* (New York: Academic, 1973), *Structural Pattern Recognition* (New York: Springer-Verlag, 1977), (translated into Chinese, 1981), and *Algorithms for Graphics and Image Processing* (Rockville, MD: Computer Science Press, 1982), (translated into Russian, 1986, Polish, 1987, and Chinese, 1988) and over 100 technical papers.

Dr. Pavlidis was the Editor-in-Chief of the IEEE TRANSACTIONS ON PATTERN ANALYSIS AND MACHINE INTELLIGENCE (PAMI) from 1982 to 1986, and has been a member of the editorial board of the *Proceedings of IEEE* (since 1988) and three other journals. His conference-related activities include: Chairman of the Dahlem Workshop on Biomedical Pattern Recognition and Image Processing (Berlin 1979), General Chairman of the Fifth International Conference on Pattern Recognition (December 1980, Miami Beach), Scientific Chairman of the NATO Workshop on Syntactic Pattern Recognition (October 1986, Barcelona), and General Chairman of the IEEE Robotics and Automation Conference (Philadelphia, 1988). He has been a member of various advisory councils of the National Science Foundation and he is a member of the Universities Space Research Association Science Council for Computer Science. He is a member of the Association for Computing Machinery and Sigma-Xi.

The Noisy Substring Matching Problem

R. L. KASHYAP, FELLOW, IEEE, AND B. JOHN OOMMEN

Abstract—Let $T(U)$ be the set of words in the dictionary H which contains U as a substring. The problem considered here is the estimation of the set $T(U)$ when U is not known, but Y, a noisy version of U is available. The suggested set estimate $S^*(Y)$ of $T(U)$ is a proper subset of H such that its every element contains at least one substring which resembles Y most according to the Levenshtein metric. The proposed algorithm for the computation of $S^*(Y)$ requires cubic time. The algorithm uses the recursively computable dissimilarity measure $D^k(X, Y)$, termed as the kth distance between two strings X and Y which is a dissimilarity measure between Y and a certain subset of the set of contiguous substrings of X. Another estimate of $T(U)$, namely $S^M(Y)$ is also suggested. The accuracy of $S^M(Y)$ is only slightly less than that of $S^*(Y)$, but the computation time of $S^M(Y)$ is substantially less than that of $S^*(Y)$. Experimental results involving 1900 noisy substrings and dictionaries which are subsets of 1023 most common English words [11] indicate that the accuracy of the estimate $S^*(Y)$ is around 99 percent and that of $S^M(Y)$ is about 98 percent.

Index Terms—Error correction in strings, Levenshtein metric, noisy substring matching, string dissimilarity in terms of the dissimilarity of their substrings, string set estimation, text editing.

I. INTRODUCTION

A COMMON problem in text editing is that of finding the occurrence of a given substring in a file. This is usually done to locate one's bearings in the file or to replace the occurence of one substring by another. This problem is termed as the exact substring matching problem.

With no loss of generality, the file can be considered as a sequence of words from a finite dictionary. If the occurrence of a certain substring U is sought for, the exact substring matching problem aims to obtain the *set* of all the words in the dictionary which contains U as a contiguous substring. Many algorithms [1], [2] have been proposed to solve this problem, the best of which have sublinear time complexities.

One mishap that often occurs is that the substring sought for, U, is noisily represented, either due to mistyping or ignorance of spelling. Let the noisy version of U be Y. If Y is a contiguous substring of some words in the dictionary, the output of an exact substring matching algorithm will be the set of those particular words. On the other hand, if Y is not a contiguous substring of any word in the dictionary, any

substring matching algorithm will give the user no information about the occurrence of the substring sought for [3].

Let $T(U)$ be the *set* of words in the dictionary which contains U. In this paper, we consider the problem of estimating the *set* $T(U)$ when U is not known, but Y, the noisy version of U, is available. Substitution, insertion, and deletion errors transform U into Y.

Besides having applications in file editing, the noisy substring matching problem has also potential applications in the area of information retrieval. Consider a database which consists of many records each identified by a distinct keyword. Let us suppose that the system managing the database permits the user to access a record by merely referring to a contiguous substring of the keyword. In such a case the program that solves the noisy substring matching problem can be used to process a noisy (incorrectly spelled) version of a *fragment* of a keyword, and locate a record characterized by the entire keyword.

Ideally, the set estimate $S(Y)$ should include the set $T(U)$. In that case, given additional information in the form of (noisy) prefixes or suffixes of U, we can identify the correct word in the dictionary, by searching the relatively small set $S(Y)$. Hence, we measure the quality of the estimate $S(Y)$ by the frequency of $S(Y)$ containing $T(U)$. Our goal is to obtain a set estimate $S(Y)$ which has a high value of that frequency, but is not a very large subset of the dictionary. The solution $S(Y)$ which equals the entire dictionary is trivial and useless.

The proposed estimate $S^*(Y)$ is computed by comparing the noisy string Y with all the contiguous substrings of the words in the dictionary using an appropriate measure of dissimilarity between two strings. Many measures can be used for this purpose such as the generalized Levenshtein distance (GLD) between them, the length of their shortest common supersequence, and a monotonically decreasing function of the length of their longest common subsequence [4]–[7]. Throughout this paper the generalized Levenshtein distance (GLD) $D(V, Y)$ is used as the measure to quantify the measure the dissimilarity between the strings V and Y. The results obtained here can easily be extended for any of the other dissimilarity measures referred to above [6].

Let H^* be the set of all the substrings of the words in the dictionary. Let R be a subset of H^* whose members are most similar to the given string Y according to the GLD. The required set estimate $S^*(Y)$ is the subset of the dictionary, each member containing at least one member of R.

To compute the set $S^*(Y)$, we define a dissimilarity measure $D^k(X, Y)$ between the strings X and Y as the minimum value of the GLD between Y and the individual elements of a cer-

Manuscript received August 18, 1981; revised September 8, 1982. This work was supported in part by the National Science Foundation under Grant ECS-80-09041.

R. L. Kashyap is with the School of Electrical Engineering, Purdue University, West Lafayette, IN 47907.

B. J. Oommen was with the School of Electrical Engineering, Purdue University, West Lafayette, IN 47907. He is now with the Department of Computer Science, Carleton University, Ottawa, Ont., Canada K1S 5B6.

0-8186-5460-0/94 $3.00 © 1983 IEEE

tain subset of the contiguous substrings of X. The measure $D^k(X, Y)$ has the property that it can be recursively computed. The solution to the noisy substring matching problem is exactly the set of words in the dictionary which minimizes $D^{|X|}(X, Y)$, where X is any arbitrary word in the dictionary. The measure $D^{|X|}(X, Y)$, can be computed in time proportional to $|Y| \cdot |X|^2$. Hence the set estimate $S^*(Y)$ can be computed in cubic time.

In Section II we formulate the problem explicitly, and present $S^*(Y)$, the proposed solution. Its computation is discussed in Section III. In this section, we also suggest an approximation of $S^*(Y)$ as an alternative solution to the problem. This approximation, $S^M(Y)$, is almost as accurate as $S^*(Y)$ but is more easily computable. We conclude the paper with some experimental results obtained using dictionaries which are subsets of the 1023 most common English words [11].

A. Notation

Uppercase symbols from the latter part of the English alphabet such as $U, V, \cdots, Z$, will always refer to strings. Lowercase symbols, subscripted or otherwise, are used to represent letters of the alphabet under consideration. Upper- and lowercase letters of the English alphabet from I to N will be used as integers. We reserve the symbols $A, B, H, Q, R, S,$ and T to represent sets of strings. Otherwise, the symbols used in the paper are self-explanatory.

II. FORMULATION OF THE PROBLEM AND PROPOSED SOLUTION

Let A be any finite alphabet, and H a finite dictionary which is a subset of A^*, the set of strings over A. Let H^* be the set of all the nonnull contiguous substrings of the words in H. Let U be any nonnull string in A^*. We seek the words in H which contain U. The solution to the exact substring matching problem is the *set* $T(U)$ defined by (2.1):

$$T(U) = \{X | X \in H, U \text{ is a substring of } X\}, \quad \text{if } U \in H^*$$

$$= \phi, \text{ the null set, } \quad \text{otherwise.} \quad (2.1)$$

If Y is a noisy version of U, the aim of the noisy substring matching problem is to obtain a nontrivial estimate of the *set* $T(U)$ by processing only Y.

Before giving the solution we need the concept of the generalized Levenshtein distance (GLD) $D(Z, Y)$ between two strings Z and Y of arbitrary lengths [4], [5], [9]. The GLD measures the dissimilarity between Z and Y in terms of the edit operations on the individual symbols of Y needed to transform it into Z. The edit operations are substitution, deletion and insertion. Let $d(b, c)$ be the weight associated with replacing the letter "b" in Y by the letter "c." Similarly $d(b, \lambda), d(\lambda, b)$ are the weights associated with the erasure of "b" in Y and insertion of "b" into Y, respectively:

$$d(c, c) = 0, 0 < d(b, c) < \infty, \quad \forall c \neq b;$$

$$0 < d(\lambda, b), d(b, \lambda) < \infty, \quad \forall b.$$

Then the GLD $D(Z, Y)$ is the minimum of the sum of the weights associated with the various edit operations on Y to

transform it into Z. Typically, $d(c, b)$ is chosen to reflect the frequency of the noisy mechanism to convert "b" into "c" [5], [10]. The simplest choice of the weights is: $d(b, c) = 1$ only if $c \neq b, d(\lambda, b) = d(b, \lambda) = 1$. This choice will be termed as the zero–one Levenshtein distance.

The solution to the problem posed earlier is obtained by comparing Y with all the elements of H^*, the set of all the contiguous substrings of H. A subset of the latter, $R(Y)$, can be extracted which is the set of contiguous substrings most similar to Y according to the generalized Levenshtein distance. The estimate $S^*(Y)$ of $T(U)$ is obtained as a union of the words in H which have at least one of the substrings most resembling Y. Explicitly,

$$R(Y) = \{Z | Z \in H^*, D(Z, Y) \leqslant D(Z', Y) \quad \forall Z' \in H^*\}$$

$$(2.2)$$

$$S^*(Y) = \bigcup_{V \in R(Y)} T(V). \quad (2.3)$$

The example below will help clarify these sets.

Example 1: Let $H = \{$construction, attention, attending, opinion$\}$ and $Y =$ sion. The dissimilarity measure is the Levenshtein metric with zero–one weights. Then,

$$R(Y) = \{\text{tion, nion}\}$$

$$S(Y) = \{\text{construction, attention, opinion}\}.$$

***

Theorem 1: Let Y be any noisy version of a string $U \in H^*$. The set estimate of $T(U)$ given by $S^*(Y)$ has the following properties.

i) If $Y = U, S^*(Y) = T(U)$.

ii) $T(U)$ is a subset of $S^*(Y)$ if U or any one of its contiguous substrings is in $R(Y)$. ***

The proof of the theorem follows directly from the properties of the GLD between two strings [4]–[8], and the definition of $S^*(Y)$.

Remarks:

1) From (2.2) it can be seen that if $Y = U$ or $Y \in H^*, S^*(Y)$, the solution to the noisy substring matching problem, is identically equal to the solution to the exact substring matching problem.

2) In some applications, it may be desirable to have $S^*(Y)$ identical to the set $T(U)$ as frequently as possible. This is equivalent to maximizing the frequency of obtaining $R(Y)$ as the *singleton set* $\{U\}$. The latter can be achieved by defining the GLD in terms of intersymbol edit distances which are *real* nonnegative numbers, and which are functions of the probabilities of the mechanism which noisily transforms U into Y [4]–[6], [10].

3) As mentioned earlier, the quality of the estimate $S(Y)$ can be measured by the frequency of $T(U)$ being a subset of $S(Y)$, given that Y was generated from U. An analytical expression for this frequency is very difficult to obtain, even after making appropriate assumptions regarding the noisy mechanism which generates Y from U. The experimental results of Section IV indicate that for $S^*(Y)$, this frequency is relatively high.

III. Computation of $S^*(Y)$ and its Approximation

The computation of $S^*(Y)$ from its definition is far too cumbersome, since the set H^* is usually *many orders* larger than the set H. We propose a computational scheme which computes $S^*(Y)$ by sequentially comparing Y with the *individual elements of H*. We first introduce the concept of the kth distance between two strings, $D^k(X, Y)$. This quantity is defined in terms of the GLD between Y and V, where V is an element of a subset of the contiguous substrings of X. The kth distance between X and Y can be recursively computed, and further if $|X| = N$, the Nth distance is exactly the minimum value of GLD between Y and all the contiguous substrings of X. By computing $D^{|X|}(X, Y)$ for every $X \in H$, the set $S^*(Y)$ can be obtained.

A. The kth Distance $D^k(X, Y)$

Let $X = x_1 \cdots x_N$ be any string of length N, where each $x_i \in A$. We define $Q^k(X)$ as the set of all the prefixes of every suffix of X which is of length greater than or equal to $N - k + 1$. The kth distance $D^k(X, Y)$ is defined as the minimum of the GLD between V and Y for all $V \in Q^k(X)$.

$$Q^k(X) = \bigcup_{i=1}^{k} \bigcup_{j=i}^{|X|} \{X_{i,j}\} \qquad (3.1)$$

where $X_{i,j} = x_i x_{i+1} \cdots x_j$, $1 \leq i \leq j \leq |X|$.

$$D^k(X, Y) = \min_{V \in Q^k(X)} [D(V, Y)]. \qquad (3.2)$$

The following example illustrates these quantities.

Example 2: Let $X = $ nion and $Y = $ son,

$Q^1(X) = \{\text{n, ni, nio, nion}\}$, $Q^2(X) = Q^1(X) \cup \{\text{i, io, ion}\}$

$Q^4(X) = Q^3(X) = \{\text{n, ni, nio, nion, i, io, ion, o, on}\}$.

The intersymbol edit distances in the GLD are only zero or one.

$D^1(X, Y) = 2$ and $D^i(X, Y) = 1$ for $i = 2, 3, 4$. *******

We now demonstrate that $D^k(X, Y)$ is recursively computable.

Theorem 2: Let $D^k(X, Y)$ be the kth distance between X and Y, defined as in (3.2). Then $D^k(X, Y)$ can be evaluated using $D^{k-1}(X, Y)$ and the distances obtained in the process of computing $D(X_{k,N}, Y)$ where $|X| = N$.

Proof: Let

$B_k(X) = \{V | V \text{ is a prefix of } X_{k,N}; |X| = N\}$.

By definition,

$Q^k(X) = Q^{k-1}(X) \cup B_k(X)$.

Hence,

$D^k(X, Y) = \min [D^{k-1}(X, Y), \min_{V \in B_k(X)} \{D(V, Y)\}]$.

The computation of $D(X_{k,N}, Y)$ by the Wagner–Fischer algorithm [7] yields all the distances $D(V, Y)$, $V \in B_k(X)$. *******

We now present an algorithm to compute $D^k(X, Y)$, which is essentially an application of the above theorem. The heart of the algorithm is the Wagner–Fischer algorithm [7]. We

have utilized the fact that in the computation of any GLD, $D(Z, W)$, the latter algorithm automatically computes the GLD between the individual prefixes of both Z and W.

Algorithm D^k:

Input: $X = x_1 x_2 \cdots x_N$, $Y = y_1 y_2 \cdots y_M$ and any k, $1 \leq k \leq N$. The intersymbol edit distances are also prespecified for all $a, b \in A$ as below:

$d(a, b)$: the distance associated with substituting "a" with "b"

$d(a, \lambda)$: the distance associated with deleting "a"

$d(\lambda, b)$: the distance associated with inserting "b."

Output: The quantity $D^k(X, Y)$ defined by (3.2).

Method:

$D^k(X, Y) = \infty$
for $q = N - k + 1$ to N do
  $V = X_{N-q+1, N}$
  $P(0, 0) = 0$
  for $i = 1$ to q do
    $P(i, 0) = P(i - 1, 0) + d(v_i, \lambda)$
  end
  for $j = 1$ to M do
    $P(0, j) = P(0, j - 1) + d(\lambda, y_j)$
  end
  for $i = 1$ to q do
    for $j = 1$ to M do
      $r1 = P(i - 1, j - 1) + d(v_i, y_j)$
      $r2 = P(i, j - 1) + d(\lambda, y_j)$
      $r3 = P(i - 1, j) + d(v_i, \lambda)$
      $P(i, j) = \min [r1, r2, r3]$
    end
    $D^k(X, Y) = \min [D^k(X, Y), P(i, M)]$
  end
end
END Algorithm D^k.

Remarks:

1) The string V sequentially assumes the value of the suffixes of X. The array element $P(i, j)$ is the GLD between the prefix of V of length i and the prefix of Y of length j. Thus, $P(i, M)$ will be the GLD between $V_{1,i}$ and Y. As each $P(i, M)$ is computed, the value of $D^k(X, Y)$ is updated.

2) If $|V| = q$ and $|Y| = M$, the quantity $D(V, Y)$ can be computed using exactly qM symbol comparisons. Hence, the number of symbol comparisons required to compute $D^k(X, Y)$ is

$$\sum_{q=N-k+1}^{N} qM = M \left[\frac{N \cdot (N+1)}{2} - \frac{(N-k) \cdot (N-k+1)}{2} \right]$$

$$= M \left[N \cdot k - \frac{k \cdot (k-1)}{2} \right]. \qquad (3.3)$$

From (3.3) we see that the number of symbol comparisons required to compute $D^k(X, Y)$ is cubic in M, N, and k, the terms in k being *monotonically decreasing*.

3) Since $Q^{|X|}(X)$ is exactly the set of all the contiguous substrings of X, the quantity $D^{|X|}(X, Y)$ is the minimum GLD between any substring of X, and Y. This quantity can be computed in $O(M|X|^2)$ time.

B. Procedure for Obtaining $S^*(Y)$

We now present an algorithm to compute $S^*(Y)$ by redefining it in terms of the distances $D^{|X|}(X, Y)$, $X \in H$.

Theorem 3: $S^*(Y)$ defined by (2.3) has the following expression:

$$S^*(Y) = \{X | X \in H, D^{|X|}(X, Y) \leqslant D^{|X'|}(X', Y) \; \forall X' \in H\}. \tag{3.4}$$

Proof: From (3.1) we see that $Q^{|X|}(X)$ is the set of all the contiguous substrings of X. Hence,

$$\bigcup_{X \in H} Q^{|X|}(X) = H^*. \tag{3.5}$$

By definition,

$$D^{|X|}(X, Y) = \min_{V} D(V, Y), \qquad V \text{ is a substring of } X.$$

Minimizing both sides over X, $X \in H$, and using (3.5), we get

$$\min_{X \in H} D^{|X|}(X, Y) = \min_{V \in H^*} D(V, Y). \tag{3.6}$$

Thus, if $V \in H^*$ minimizes $D(V, Y)$ and X contains the substring V, then X will definitely minimize $D^{|X|}(X, Y)$. Conversely, if any $X \in H$ minimizes $D^{|X|}(X, Y)$, then X will contain at least one substring V, which minimizes $D(V, Y)$. Hence the definition of $S^*(Y)$ given by (3.4) is equivalent to the one given by (2.2). ***

Using this definition, $S^*(Y)$ can be computed as below.

Algorithm S^*:
Input: The dictionary H and the noisy string Y.
Output: The set $S^*(Y)$ defined by (2.2).
Method:

$S^*(Y) = \phi$
for every $X \in H$
　　compute $D^{|X|}(X, Y)$ using Algorithm D^k
end
$A = \min\limits_{X \in H} [D^{|X|}(X, Y)]$
for every $X \in H$
　　if $D^{|X|}(X, Y) = A$
　　　　$S^*(Y) = S^*(Y) \cup \{X\}$
end
END Algorithm S^*.

Since any one $D^{|X|}(X, Y)$ can be computed in time proportional to $|X|^2|Y|$, the set $S^*(Y)$ can be computed in cubic time. We now propose an approximation of $S^*(Y)$ which is more easily computable.

C. An Approximation to $S^*(Y)$

By definition, Y is a substring of an unknown string U, containing substitution, insertion and deletion errors. Since U can be any element of H^*, $S^*(Y)$ was defined in terms of the GLD between Y and any arbitrary element of H^*. To compute $S^*(Y)$, the measure $D^{|X|}(X, Y)$ was computed for every $X \in H$.

An approximation to $S^*(Y)$ can be obtained by terminating the recursive computation of $D^k(X, Y)$ at some i, $1 \leqslant i \leqslant |X|$. This would be equivalent to comparing Y with only those substrings of X which are in the set $Q^i(X)$. If the string Y is of length M, and if $M \leqslant |X|$, then we can be sure that every suffix of X of length greater than or equal to M will be in the set $Q^{|X|-M+1}(X)$. Further, the latter set will contain *all the prefixes* of every one of these suffixes. Hence a good approximation to $D^{|X|}(X, Y)$ is the quantity $D^{|X|-M+1}(X, Y)$, if $M \leqslant |X|$.

To generalize this for all M, we approximate $D^{|X|}(X, Y)$ by the quantity $D^K(X, Y)$, where K is given by (3.7):

$$K = \max [|X| - M + 1, 1]. \tag{3.7}$$

The estimate $S^M(Y)$ which approximates $S^*(Y)$ is obtained by comparing Y with only those prefixes of X of length greater than or equal to K, defined above. We define $S^M(Y)$ as the set of all the words in H which minimizes $D^K(X, Y)$. Explicitly,

$$S^M(Y) = \{X | X \in H; D^K(X, Y) \leqslant D^K(X', Y), \quad \forall X' \in H,$$
$$\text{where } K = \max [|X| - M + 1, 1]\}.$$

An algorithm similar to Algorithm S^* can be given to compute this set.

In practice, it is observed that the frequency of $S^M(Y)$ containing $T(U)$ is only slightly less than the frequency of $S^*(Y)$ containing $T(U)$. However, it is definitely less expensive to compute. Consider the computation of $D^K(X, Y)$, where K is given by (3.7) for any X. Using Algorithm D^k, this can be compute using $\tau_{X, M}$ symbol comparisons, where

$$\tau_{X, M} = M \left[|A| \cdot K - \frac{K \cdot (K - 1)}{2} \right] \quad \text{if } K > 1$$
$$= M|X| \quad \text{if } K = 1.$$

The latter expression simplifies to (3.8) using (3.7):

$$\tau_{X, M} = \frac{M}{2} [|X| (|X| + 1) - M(M - 1)] \quad \text{if } M < |X|$$
$$= M|X| \quad \text{if } M \geqslant |X|. \tag{3.8}$$

Just as $D^{|X|}(X, Y)$ requires cubic computation time, we see from (3.8) that $D^K(X, Y)$ also requires cubic time. However, due to the negative quadratic terms in M in $\tau_{X, M}$ the value of the latter *decreases* as M increases. The fractional decreases in computation is the ratio of $M(M - 1)$ to $|X|(|X| + 1)$ which is of the order of $(M/|X|)^2$. Further, in the limit, the expression for $\tau_{X, M}$ is quadratic. This renders $S^M(Y)$ to be, in the limit, one order computationally less expensive than $S^*(Y)$.

IV. Experimental Results and Discussion

The noisy substring matching problem was studied in five experiments involving 1900 noisy strings and two dictionaries which are subsets of the 1023 most common English words [11]. In the first two experiments the 292 most common English words of length greater than or equal to seven, constituted the dictionary. In the last three experiments, the

TABLE I
RESULTS OF THE FIVE EXPERIMENTS

Exp.	Nstr.	Dict.	Min $|U|$	Av. Noise	Estimate	Acc.	Av. Size
I	200	H1	5	1.38	$S^*(Y)$	0.990	3.38
I	200	H1	5	1.38	$S^M(Y)$	0.970	2.89
II	200	H1	6	1.36	$S^*(Y)$	0.980	1.89
II	200	H1	6	1.36	$S^M(Y)$	0.970	1.81
III	500	H2	5	1.36	$S^*(Y)$	0.980	2.39
III	500	H2	5	1.36	$S^M(Y)$	0.964	2.35
IV	500	H2	6	1.40	$S^*(Y)$	0.992	1.48
IV	500	H2	6	1.40	$S^M(Y)$	0.990	1.47
V	500	H2	7	1.43	$S^*(Y)$	0.991	1.30
V	500	H2	7	1.43	$S^M(Y)$	0.992	1.23

Nstr : No. of noisy strings used in the experiment.
H1 : Dictionary consisting of 292 words of length ≥ 7.
H2 : Dictionary consisting of 166 words of length ≥ 8.
Acc. : Frequency of the estimate S^* or S^M containing $T(U)$.
Av. Noise : Average no. of errors in a single string Y.
Av. Size : Average size of the estimate set.

TABLE II
SOME RESULTS OBTAINED IN EXPERIMENT 3. IN ALL THE CASES $S^*(Y)$ CONTAINS $T(U)$.

U	Y	An element of $S^*(Y)$	Size of $S^*(Y)$
dditio	ditxo	addition	3
administ	ndmibist	administration	1
advanta	advuantpa	advantage	1
altoget	altkget	altogether	1
nything	nthing	anything	3
ently	etly	apparently	5
artill	vrtfill	artillery	1
lable	lablr	available	1
ginnin	ginin	beginning	2
ombardm	imbardmr	bombardment	1
uildi	uslsi	building	7
siness	sinejss	business	1
paign	paiyb	campaign	1
ittee	ittzee	committee	1
communi	vomuni	community	1
conditio	donditio	condition	2
idenc	idenx	confidence	2
nside	nsde	consider	7
erable	ezrable	considerable	1
idere	ivdere	considered	2
ntinue	sntinue	continue	1
ontract	ohtraget	contract	1
onden	onlcen	correspondent	1
clared	ckared	declared	1
defende	defepde	defender	1
ivere	ivee	delivered	4
evelop	eelop	developed	1
enclos	enclod	enclosed	1
nforced	nfkrcec	enforced	1
uipment	uuipment	equipment	1
blishe	bpishe	established	1
verythi	veeythi	everything	1
verywher	veryahef	everywhere	1
utive	ucive	executive	1
istence	iztence	existence	1
xistin	xistiny	existing	1
expect	expecti	expected	1
press	eess	expressed	7
llowed	lliwec	followed	1
enera	eeray	generally	9

dictionary was the 166 most common words of length greater than or equal to eight.

Noisy strings were generated as follows. A substring U was randomly chosen from a string $X \in H$. The number of insertions in Y was randomly obtained from a geometric distribu-

TABLE III
COMPARISON OF THE NUMBER OF SYMBOL COMPARISONS REQUIRED TO COMPUTE $S^*(Y)$ WITH THE NUMBER OF SYMBOL COMPARISONS REQUIRED TO COMPUTE $S^M(Y)$

M	r^*	r^M
5	55,565	40,965
6	66,678	40,398
7	77,791	34,867
8	88,904	30,552
9	100,017	27,891
10	111,130	27,480
11	122,243	28,138
12	133,356	29,376
13	144,469	31,200
14	155,582	33,236

M : Length of the string Y. r^* : No. of symbol comparisons required to compute $S^*(Y)$.
r^M : No. of symbol comparisons required to compute $S^M(Y)$.

tion, and the positions of these insertions and the symbols inserted were assumed to be equally likely. Subsequently, the individual symbols of U were either deleted or substituted by a predefined probability distribution. This distribution was symbol dependent and was related to the relative proximity of the individual letters of the alphabet on a typewriter keyboard. The noisy strings used in the study contained at least one error, but not more than two. The average number of errors per noisy string was approximately 1.4. Variations in the experiments were achieved by varying the minimum length of U.

For purposes of standardization, the elementary edit distances used in the Levenshtein metric were zero or one. The performance index used to evaluate the estimates was the frequency of the estimates $S^*(Y)$ and $S^M(Y)$ containing $T(U)$. Details of the experiments are given in Tables I and II. From the tables, we see that the estimate $S^*(Y)$ is very accurate. $S^*(Y)$ was least accurate in Experiment 3, in which, it contained $T(U)$ in 490 out of the 500 cases studied. This corresponds to an accuracy of 98.0 percent. The average size of the set $S^*(Y)$ in this experiment was 2.39. From Table II, we also see that the estimate $S^M(Y)$ is almost as accurate as $S^*(Y)$. In the same experiment, $S^M(Y)$ contained $T(U)$ in 482 out of the 500 cases studied corresponding to an accuracy of 96.4 percent. The average size of $S^M(Y)$ in this experiment was 2.35.

To compare the computations required to compute $S^*(Y)$ and $S^M(Y)$, the number of symbol comparisons required in the first two experiments, was evaluated for various values of M, the length of Y. The results are tabulated in Table III and graphically presented in Fig. 1. From both these, we see that the number of symbol comparisons required to compute $S^*(Y)$ is much greater than the number of symbol comparisons required to compute $S^M(Y)$. For example, if $M = 9$, $S^*(Y)$ and $S^M(Y)$ required 100 017 and 27 891 symbol comparisons, respectively. The decrease in the computation required for $S^M(Y)$ with increasing values of M is also obvious from Fig. 1. In our judgment, the marginal loss in the accuracy of $S^M(Y)$ is more than compensated by its computational advantage.

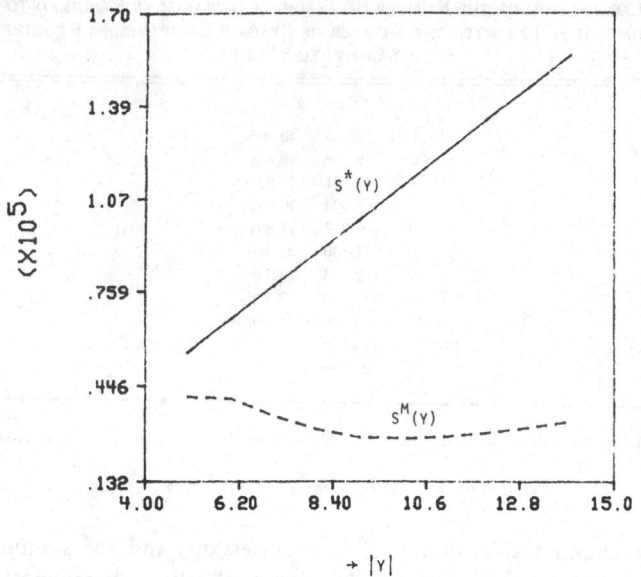

Fig. 1. Graphs of the number of symbol comparisons required to compute $S^*(Y)$ and $S^M(Y)$ versus $|Y| = M$ in Experiments 1 and 2.

V. CONCLUSIONS

We considered the problem of estimating the set $T(U)$, the subset of words in the dictionary H which contains U as a substring, using only Y, a noisy version of U. The suggested set estimate $S^*(Y)$ which needs cubic time for computation has relatively high accuracy as verified by experiments. Another estimate $S^M(Y)$ was also proposed which is only slightly less accurate than $S^*(Y)$ but requires substantially less computation. The estimate, $S^*(Y)$ is the proper subset of H, every element of which contains a substring which resembles Y the most according to the generalized Levenshtein metric. The algorithms for the computation of $S^*(Y)$ or $S^M(Y)$ are easily extendible to other measures of dissimilarity between strings such as the length of their shortest common supersequence, and the length of their longest common subsequence.

REFERENCES

[1] D. E. Knuth, J. H. Morris, Jr., and V. R. Pratt, "Fast pattern matching in strings," *SIAM J. Comput.*, vol. 6, no. 2, pp. 323–350, 1977.
[2] R. S. Boyer and J. S. Moore, "A fast string searching algorithm," *Commun. Ass. Comput. Mach.*, vol. 20, no. 10, pp. 762–772, 1977.
[3] The UNIX text editor.
[4] R. L. Kashyap and B. J. Oommen, "An effective algorithm for string correction using a generalized edit distance–I. Description of the algorithm and its optimality," *Inform. Sci.*, vol. 23, no. 2, pp. 123–142, 1981.
[5] ——, "An effective algorithm for string correction using a generalized edit distance–II. Computational complexity of the algorithm and some applications," *Inform. Sci.*, vol. 23, no. 3, pp. 201–217, 1981.
[6] ——, "A unifying theory for order preserving properties involving two strings," in *Proc. Princeton Conf. on Inform. Sci. Syst.*, 1980, pp. 193–198.
[7] R. A. Wagner and M. J. Fischer, "The string to string correction problem," *J. Ass. Comput. Mach.*, vol. 21, pp. 168–173, 1974.
[8] D. S. Hirschberg, "Algorithms for the longest common subsequence problem," *J. Ass. Comput. Mach.*, vol. 24, pp. 664–675, 1977.
[9] T. Okuda, E. Tanaka, and T. Kasai, "A method of correction of garbled words based on the Levenshtein metric," *IEEE Trans. Comput.*, vol. C-25, pp. 172–177, Feb. 1976.
[10] R. L. Kashyap, "Syntactic dec. rules for the recognition of spoken words and phrases using a stochastic automaton," *IEEE Trans. Pattern Anal. Machine Intell.*, vol. PAMI-1, pp. 154–163, 1979.
[11] G. Dewey, *Relative Frequency of English Speech Sounds*. Cambridge, MA: Harvard Univ. Press, 1923.

R. L. Kashyap (M'70–SM'77–F'79) received the D.I.I.Sc. and M.E. degrees from the Indian Institute of Science, Bangalore, India, in 1960 and 1962, respectively, and the Ph.D. degree in engineering from Harvard University, Cambridge, MA, in 1965.

During 1965 and 1966 he was a Postdoctoral Fellow in Applied Mathematics at Harvard University, where he conducted research in stochastic automata. In 1966 he joined the faculty of Purdue University, West Lafayette, IN, where he currently holds the rank of Professor of Electrical Engineering. During spring semester of 1974, he was a Visiting Research Associate at the University of California, Berkeley, in the Department of Electrical Engineering and Computer Science, engaged in research in data management systems and time series analysis. In the fall semester of 1974, he was a Visiting Professor at the Division of Engineering and Applied Physics, Harvard University. He was an Associate Editor of the IEEE TRANSACTIONS ON AUTOMATIC CONTROL. He is the coauthor of the book *Stochastic Dynamic Models from Empirical Data* (New York: Academic, 1976).

Dr. Kashyap is a member of Sigma Xi and the Associatiation for Computing Machinery. In 1966 he won the National Electronics Conference Annual Best Research Paper Award for his paper "Optimization of stochastic finite-state machines." He was the Coprogram Chairman of the 1978 IEEE Computer Society Conference on Pattern Recognition and Image Processing.

B. John Oommen was born in Coonoor, India, on September 9, 1953. He received the B.Tech. degree from I.I.T., Madras, India, in 1975, the M.E. degree from the Indian Institute of Science, Bangalore, India, specializing in learning systems, and the M.S. and Ph.D. degrees in electrical engineering from Purdue University, West Lafayette, IN.

His major area was pattern recognition. He is currently on the Faculty in the School of Computer Science, Carleton University, Ottawa, Ont., Canada. His research interests include statistical and syntactic pattern recognition, learning systems, formal languages, and the theory of algorithms.

Chapter 4: Multi-Dimensional Matching

Introduction

If multidimensional matching problems are reduced to the string matching problems discussed in the previous sections, efficient string matching algorithms can be applied to broader fields. This section describes how to apply string pattern matching algorithms to multidimensional matching problems, such as trees, graphs, pictures, protein sequences, nucleic acids, and molecular phylogeny.

Tree pattern matching is an interesting special problem, which occurs as a crucial step in a number of programming tasks. Among them are design of interpreters for nonprocedural programming languages, automatic implementations of abstract data types, code optimization in compilers, symbolic computation, context searching in structure editors, and automatic theorem proving. A classic open problem on tree pattern matching is whether the naive, $O(mn)$-step algorithm for finding all the occurrences of a pattern tree of size m in a text tree of size n can be improved. There are two general techniques, called bottom-up and top-down, for patterns assumed to be linear. Although the bottom-up approach needs precomputation, the matching time is clearly $O(n)$ for computing the codes of all the nodes in the subject tree. The main drawback is the size of the tables and the preprocessing time required to create these tables. In contrast to the bottom-up algorithm, the top-down algorithm requires only $O(m)$ time to preprocess the pattern. Its matching time can range anywhere between that of the bottom-up algorithm and that of the naive algorithm, depending on the structure of the pattern. Tree pattern matching algorithms for code generation applications have been presented in a tree-manipulation language called *twig*. The tree-to-tree correction problem is to determine, for two labeled ordered trees T and T', the distance from T to T' as measured by the minimum-cost sequence of edit operations needed to transform T into T'. Tree pattern matching can be applied to measurement of the similarity between trees, automatic error recovery and correction for programming languages, and determination of the largest common substructure of two trees.

Two-dimensional matching is used for pattern recognition and image processing in the expanding field of computer graphics. Suppose that the size of the pattern is $m_1 \times m_2$ and that the size of the text is $n_1 \times n_2$. By using both the KMP and KR algorithms, the two-dimensional matching algorithm takes time $O(n_1 n_2 + m_1 m_2)$. An extension of the AC algorithm to two-dimensional pattern matching is also discussed.

The rest of this chapter discusses string pattern matching problems applied to the recognition of patterns, such as shapes, pictures, scenes, molecular sequence homologies, and protein structures, and to related problems, including parallel approaches.

For pattern matching in trees, the paper of Hoffmann and O'Donnell (1982) has been selected. It reviews the relationships among the typical string and tree matching techniques, and provides the bottom-up and top-down techniques for patterns assumed to be linear. Space and time complexitiesfor preprocessing and eight tree matching techniques are evaluated in the paper. The next paper, that of Aho, Ganapathi, and Tjiang (1989) discusses bottom-up tree matching problems using the AC algorithm through code generation application. The paper by Tai (1979), selected for tree-to-tree correction problems, defines the distance between two labeled ordered trees and presents an algorithm that computes the distance in time $O(hh'd^2d'^2)$, where h and h' are the numbers of nodes of the two trees and d and d' are the maximum depths of the two trees. The set of allowable edit operations includes (1) changing one node into another node (changing the label of the node), (2) deleting one node from a tree, and (3) inserting a node into a tree. For two-dimensional matching the paper written by Zhu and Takaoka (1989) has been selected. It describes an efficient combination of the KR algorithm and the KMP (or BM) algorithm. From the simulation results for 11 pattern sizes, they show that the average cost by their approach is significantly lower.

Tree matching algorithms

Tree pattern matching is an interesting special problem, which occurs as a crucial step in a number of programming tasks, for instance, design of interpreters for nonprocedural programming languages, automatic implementations of abstract data types, code optimization in compilers, symbolic computation, context searching in structure editors, and automatic theorem proving ([Hoffman et al., 82], [Karp et al., 72], [Ramesh et al., 92] and [Salomaa, 88]).

Term-rewriting systems have been used extensively as a basis of programming languages ([Futatsugi et al., 85] and [O'Donnell, 85]), completion procedures ([Knuth et al., 70]), data-type specification and verification ([Guttag et al., 76]), theorem proving, and so on. The term system R [Ramesh et al., 92] is a finite set of *rewrite* rules, each of the form $h \rightarrow r$, where h and r are terms built from *function* symbols in a set F and (universally quantified) *variables* in a set F. A rule $h \rightarrow r$ can be applied to a term s if a subterm u of s matches h with some substitutions w for variables appearing in h (that is, $u=hw$). The rule is applied by replacing the subterm u in s with the corresponding right-hand side rw of the rule, within which the same substitution w for variables has been made. This process is called reduction. A term s can be reduced repeatedly until an irreducible term, called its *normal* form, is obtained. In the normalization process the term to be reduced (such as s above) is called the subject and the left-hand sides of the rules (such as h above) are called patterns. If every variable in a pattern occurs only once, it is a linear pattern; otherwise, it is said to be *nonlinear*. Many important problems in computer science can be viewed as applications of normalization. Normalization can be regarded as a process of tree replacement wherein terms are represented as trees and the subject tree is simplified by repeatedly replacing its subtrees according to rewrite rules. A reduction step now involves the following two operations [Ramesh et al., 92]:

1. Identification of subtrees that can be replaced
2. Selection of one or more of these trees for replacement

The first operation is referred to as *tree pattern matching*, and the second one is referred to as the *reduction strategy*.

Consider trees, t, p and q in Figure 1 based on [Ramesh et al, 92], where t is called a subject tree, p and q are called pattern trees. *Pattern matching in trees* is to identify nodes in t such that the subtrees rooted at these nodes are identical to p following the replacement of nodes labeled with variables X and Y in p by appropriate subtree of t. If every variable in a pattern occurs only once, then it is called a *linear* pattern; otherwise, it is said to be *nonlinear*. As shown in Figure 1, the pattern tree p represents the linear term $f(Y, f(X, a))$ and the subject tree t represents the term $f(f(a, f(a, a)), f(b, a))$. Then, the pattern tree p matched the subject tree t at node 1 since $f(a, f(a, a))$ and b can be determined as substitutions for the variables Y and X respectively. The pattern tree q represents the nonlinear term $f(X, f(a, X))$. Although pattern q matches t only at node 2, it does not match at node 1 because the substitutions for different occurences of X are not identical. This step of verifying that the substitutions computed for multiple occurrences of a variable are identical, is known as *consistency checking*.

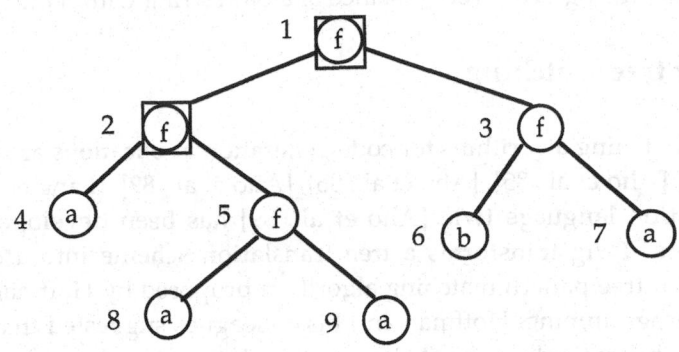

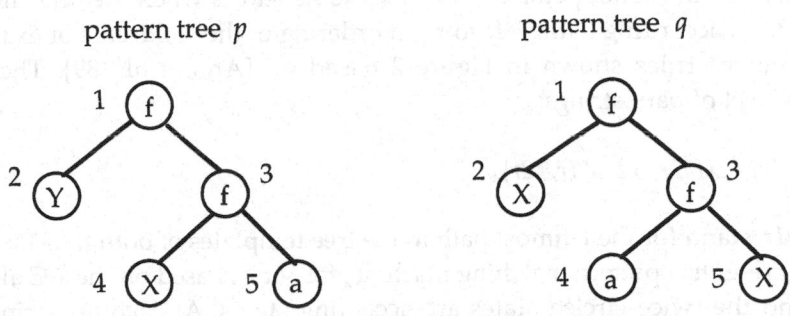

Figure 1. Examples of subject and pattern trees

It is easy to conceive a naive tree pattern matching algorithm. Such an algorithm operates by traversing a tree in preorder and, at each node visited, calling a recursive comparison procedure to check for possible occurrence of p at that node. The comparison procedure is terminated as soon as a mismatch is detected. In the worst case this naive algorithm requires $O(nm)$ time for matching all the occurrences of a pattern tree of size m in a text tree of size n. Steyaert et al. ([Steyaert et al., 83]) have shown that the expected time complexity of this approach is linear in the sizes of the two trees. The problem of linear string matching with don't-care symbols and linear string max-min convolution are treated in [Kosaraju, 89].

Hoffman et al. ([Hoffmann et al., 82]) have developed two general techniques, called bottom-up and top-down, for patterns assumed to be linear. The key idea of the bottom-up matching algorithm is to find, at each point in the subject tree, all patterns and all parts of patterns that match at this point. This algorithm needs to build the tables, which determine the code of the matching set assigned to the node having the function symbol on the basis of the codes of the matching sets assigned to its children. Once these tables have been precomputed, the matching time is clearly $O(n)$ for computing the codes of all the nodes in the subject tree. The main drawback of the bottom-up method is the size of the tables and therefore the preprocessing time required to create them. Certain optimizations aimed at decreasing the table size are reported in [Chase, 87].

In contrast to the bottom-up method, the top-down algorithm requires only $O(m)$ time to pre-process the pattern. Its matching time can range anywhere between that of the bottom-up algorithm and that of the naive algorithm, depending on the structure of the pattern. In this algorithm, each root-leaf path is regarded as a string. These strings are then preprocessed using the AC approach to produce an automaton that recognizes every instance of a path string within the subject tree.

Code generation by tree matching

Several tree pattern matching algorithms for code generation applications are presented in [Aho et al., 76b], [Aho et al., 77], [Aho et al., 85], [Aho et al., 86], [Aho et al., 89], [Lang et al., 80], and [Snyder, 82]. The tree manipulation language twig [Aho et al., 89] has been developed to help construct efficient code generators. Twig transforms a tree translation scheme into a code generator that combines a fast top-down tree pattern matching algorithm proposed by Hoffman et al. ([Hoffman et al., 82]) with dynamic programming. Hoffman and his colleagues suggested that template matching can be done efficiently by extending the AC algorithm into a top-down tree pattern matching algorithm. This algorithm can be directly generalized into a tree matching algorithm by noting that a tree is characterized by the set of paths from its root to its leaves when the branches from each node are numbered 1, 2, . . . according to the left-to-right ordering of the children. For example, consider the three tree-replacement rules shown in Figure 2 based on [Aho et al., 89]. These trees have the following keyword set of path strings:

$$K = \{+1r, +2i1*1c, +2i1*2r, +2r, *1r, *2r\}$$

The first string, +1r, stand for the leftmost path in the tree templates of both tree-1 and tree-2. Figure 3 [Aho et al., 89] represents a pattern matching machine, for set K, based on the AC algorithm. State 0 is the start state, and the twice-circled states are accepting states. At each accepting state, we know which partial string of which tree templates has been recognized. For example, at state 3, the recognized string +1r matches the leftmost path in the tree templates of tree-1 and tree-2.

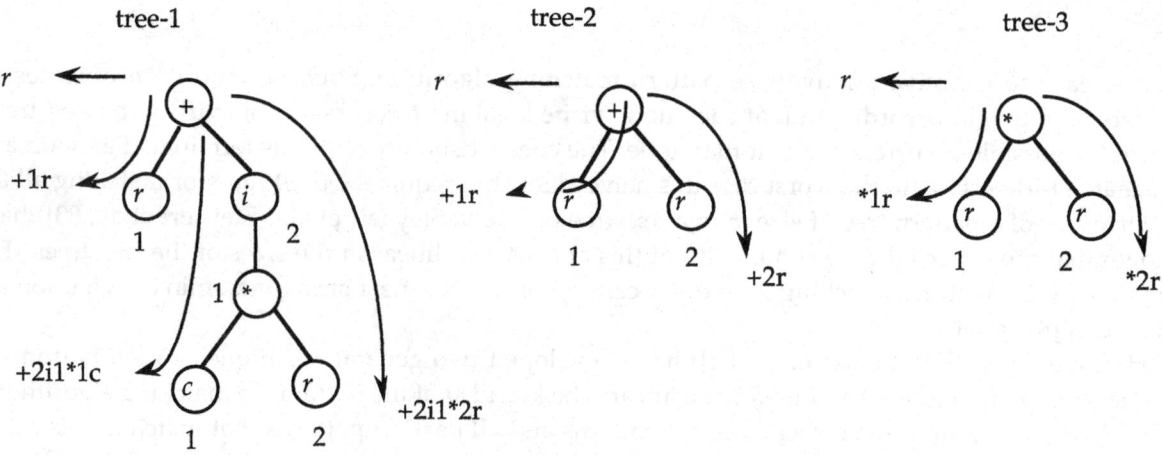

Figure 2. Three tree-replacement rules

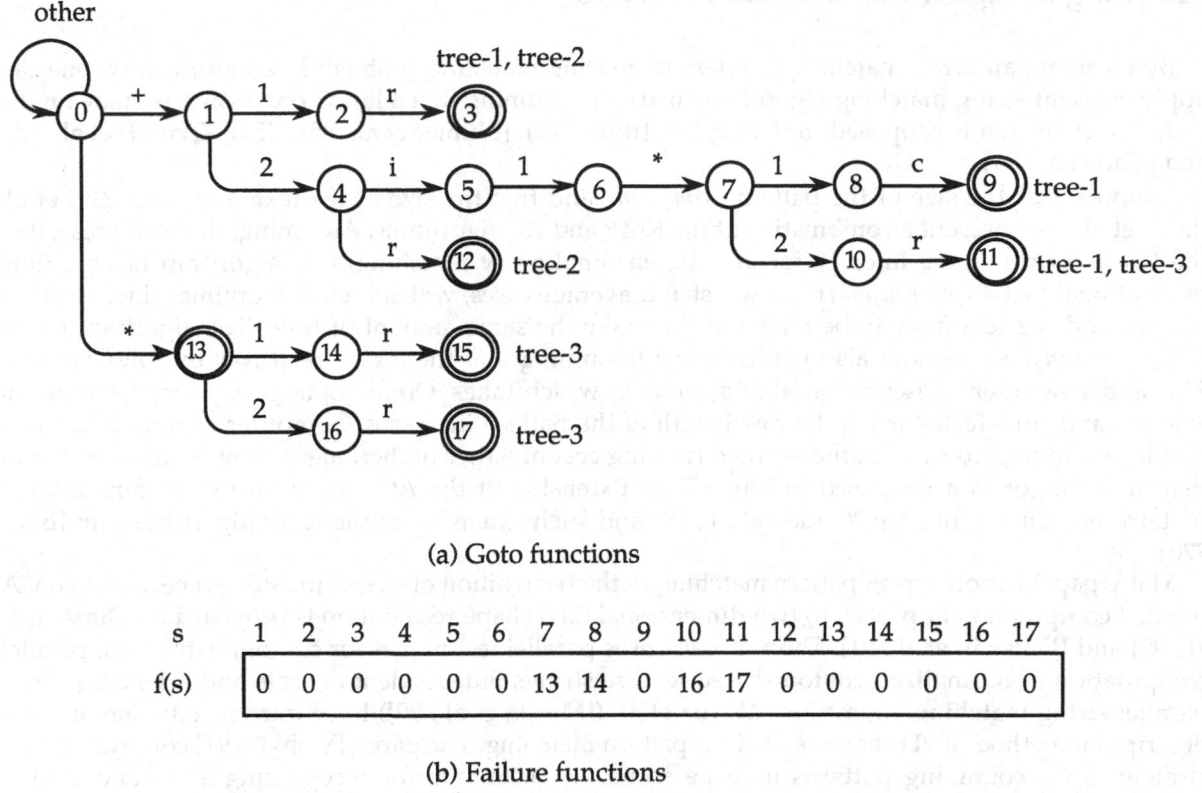

(a) Goto functions

s	1	2	3	4	5	6	7	8	9	10	11	12	13	14	15	16	17
f(s)	0	0	0	0	0	0	13	14	0	16	17	0	0	0	0	0	0

(b) Failure functions

Figure 3. Path-string-matching machine for K

Tree-to-tree correction problems

Trees are considered the most important nonlinear structures arising in computer algorithms ([Knuth, 73]). Tree automata, tree grammars, and their applications for syntactic pattern recognition are studied in [Fu et al., 73]. The tree-to-tree correction problem is to determine, for two labeled, ordered trees T and T', the distance from T to T' as measured by the minimum-cost sequence of edit operations needed to transform T into T'. Possible applications are measurement of the similarity between trees, automatic error recovery and correction for programming languages, and determination of the largest common substructure of two trees. In [Aho et al., 76b], it is suggested that for the selection of an error recovery or correction, the similarity between a corrected string and its replacement should be based on the two strings as well as their associated parse trees.

The paper by Tai reprinted here defines the distance between two labeled ordered trees and presents an algorithm that computes the distance in time $O(hh'd^2d'^2)$, where h and h' are the numbers of nodes of the two trees and d and d' are the maximum depths of the two trees. The set of allowable edit operations includes (1) changing one node into another node (changing the label of the node), (2) deleting one node from a tree, and (3) inserting a node into a tree. For the simpler problem in which the deletion and insertion operations can be applied only to the leaves of trees, Selkow ([Selkow, 77]) has proposed a simple algorithm that computes the distance in time $O(tt')$, where t and t' are the number of nodes in T and T', respectively.

Matching in higher dimensional structures

By reducing an array matching problem to a string matching problem in a natural way, one can apply efficient string matching algorithms to arrays assuming that a linear processing is made on the text. The extension is proposed in [Baker, 78], [Bird, 77a], [Blumer et al., 85], [Eilan-Tzoreff et al., 88], and [Zhu et al., 89].

Suppose that the size of the pattern is $m_1 \times m_2$ and that the size of the text is $n_1 \times n_2$. Zhu et al. ([Zhu et al., 89]) present a combination of the KMP and KR algorithms. Assuming, the worst case, that the KR algorithm runs linearly for one-dimensional array matching, this algorithm takes a time proportional to $O(n_1 n_2 + m_1 m_2)$n the worst and average cases, which is clearly optimal since both the pattern and the text have to be read and they take the same amount of time. The algorithm needs $O(n_1 n_2 + m_1 m_2)$ space, and also works online (assuming that the text is read row by row). Second, Zhu and coworkers describe another approach, which takes $O(n_1 n_2 \log(m_2) / m_2 + m_1 m_2)$ time on average and runs faster when the row length of the pattern increases. Computer experiments show that for various pattern sizes the average running cost of either of theri algorithms is much less than that of the algorithm proposed in [Bird, 77a]. Extension of the AC algorithm to two-dimensional pattern matching is in [Ben-Yehuda et al., 89] and such extension of the KMP algorithm is in [Bird, 77b].

Many papers apply string pattern matching to the recognition of shape, picture, scene, and so on. A parallel computation approach to two-dimensional (2D) shape recognition is proposed in [Dinstein et al., 90] and [Dinstein et al., 91]. The approach uses parallel techniques for contour extraction, parallel computation of normalized contour-based feature strings independent of scale and orientation, and parallel string matching algorithms. Morita et al. ([Morita et al., 90]) have introduced a hierarchical description method of 2D shapes suited for pattern matching. The paper [Vishkin, 91] considers three-strategy for recognizing patterns in large scene. A technique for recognizing a 2D unoccluded polygonal object by combining the alignment method with efficient string matching algorithms is presented in [Schreiber et al., 90] and [Maes, 91]. Hashiguchi et al. ([Hashiguchi et al., 92]) have studied the two string matching problems over free partially commutative monoids. As a compact representation of a real image, the 2D string is also suitable for formulating picture queries, thus transforming image retrieval into a 2D string matching problem ([Tucci et al., 91]). Techniques of matching geometric figures are discussed in [Cortelazzo et al., 92] and [Flammia, 92]. A machine vision algorithm for finding the longest common subcurve of two 3D curves is presented in [Eyal et al., 91]. The shape signature strings (discussed in Section 5) are matched using an efficient hashing technique that finds the longest matching strings. Two algorithms for finding the longest common subcurve of two 2D curves are presented in [Wolfson, 90]. These algorithms are based on conversion of the curves into shape signature strings and application of string matching techniques to find long matching substrings, followed by direct curve matching of the corresponding candidate subcurves to find the longest matching subcurve.

Related problems

Database search for molecular sequence homologies is the most direct computational approach to decipher gene sequences for determining protein structure and function. The domain database would be embedded in a neural network so that the search problem is replaced by a pattern recognition problem ([Wu et al, 90]). The paper by Fischer et al. ([Fischer at al., 92]) presents an application of pattern recognition techniques, in particular matching algorithms, to structural comparison of proteins, and that by Fischetti et al. ([Fischetti et al., 92]) considers a string matching problem where the pattern is a template that matches many different strings with various degrees of perfection.

A new algorithm for searching a two dimensional $m \times m$ pattern in a two dimensional $n \times n$ text is presented in [Baeza-Yates, 90]. It performs fewer comparisons on the average than the size of the text: n^2/m time using m^2 extra space. The author also presents a new multiple-string searching algorithm based in the BM method. The average number of comparisons is proved to be an^2/m, $a < 1$. The paper by Amir ([Amir, 92]) presents an algorithm for two-dimensional dictionary problems. This involves finding each occurrence of a set of two-dimensional patterns in a text. Two-dimensional similarity problems are discussed in [Powell, 90], and parallel matching techniques on string and longest common subarray are described in [Crochmore et al., 90]. An O(1)-time parallel algorithm for string pattern matching is designed on a two-dimensional $(n-m+1) \times n$ processor array with a reconfigurable bus system ([Gen-Huey, 92]). The paper [Kedem et al., 89] describes a parallel algorithm for suffix-prefix matching, which runs in time O($\log n$) using $n/\log n$ processors. This algorithm can be used for multipattern, multidimensional, and incremental string matching problems. For given a text of length n, an algorithm in [Kuo-Liang, 92] can run in O($\log n$) time on the hypercube network with O($n/\log n$) processors.

There are some discussions about a dynamic time-warping (DWP) algorithm for matching two arbitrary utterances in [Zhu et al., 92]. An online system for recognizing handwritten Chinese characters is described in [Lin et al., 90]. A sampling technique for fast pattern matching is discussed in [Vishkin, 90].

Pattern Matching in Trees

CHRISTOPH M. HOFFMANN AND MICHAEL J. O'DONNELL

Purdue University, West Lafayette, Indiana

ABSTRACT. Tree pattern matching is an interesting special problem which occurs as a crucial step in a number of programming tasks, for instance, design of interpreters for nonprocedural programming languages, automatic implementations of abstract data types, code optimization in compilers, symbolic computation, context searching in structure editors, and automatic theorem proving. As with the sorting problem, the variations in requirements and resources for each application seem to preclude a uniform, universal solution to the tree-pattern-matching problem. Instead, a collection of well-analyzed techniques, from which specific applications may be selected and adapted, should be sought. Five new techniques for tree pattern matching are presented, analyzed for time and space complexity, and compared with previously known methods. Particularly important are applications where the same patterns are matched against many subjects and where a subject may be modified incrementally. Therefore, methods which spend some time preprocessing patterns in order to improve the actual matching time are included.

Categories and Subject Descriptors: F.2.2 [**Analysis of Algorithms and Problem Complexity**]: Nonnumerical Algorithms and Problems—*pattern matching*; G.2.2 [**Discrete Mathematics**]: Graph Theory—*trees*

General Terms: Algorithms, Theory

Additional Key Words and Phrases: incremental pattern matching, bottom-up matching, top-down matching, subtree replacement systems, interpreter generation, theorem proving

1. Introduction

Many computing techniques involve simplifying expressions (trees) by repeatedly replacing special types of subexpressions (subtrees) according to a set of replacement rules. For example,

(1) Hoffmann and O'Donnell [14] show how tree replacements may be used in automatically generated interpreters for nonprocedural programming languages. The defining equations for the programming language are taken as the replacement rules. An interpreter may then process an input expression by replacing subexpressions according to the given rules until no more replacements are possible. Interpreters may be generated which are absolutely faithful to the semantics of the language as given by the defining equations. The tree-replacement approach is very convenient for producing interpreters for existing languages such as LISP and LUCID or for implementing experimental languages. Elsewhere, the merits of the language of equations as a programming language in its own right are examined [15].

(2) Guttag et al. [12] and Wand [34] suggest that defining equations may be treated as tree replacement rules to yield direct implementations of abstract data types. Guttag et al. [13] describe a working system based on this idea, as does Goguen [11].

This work was supported in part by the National Science Foundation under Grant MCS 78-01812.

Authors' address: Department of Computer Science, Purdue University, West Lafayette, IN 47907.

Reprinted from *Journal of the ACM*, Volume 29, No. 1, January 1982, pp. 68-95. Copyright 1982, Association for Computing Machinery, Inc., reprinted by permission.

Such a system does not differ in essence from the interpreters or equational programs in (1) but in this case would be embedded into a procedural language as subroutine.

(3) Intermediate code produced by a compiler may be represented by trees. Certain types of code optimizations, for example, the elimination of redundant operations and constant propagation, may be viewed as replacement rules [10, 16, 33].

(4) In [7] Collins represents algebraic terms as trees and formulates symbolic computation as tree replacements. The replacement rules formalize operations such as differentiation and certain algebraic simplifications.

(5) One approach to the automatic proving of equational theorems is to treat a set of equational axioms as replacement rules and transform one side of the equation to be proved into the other by a sequence of tree replacements. Knuth and Bendix [20] discuss some of the cases in which tree replacements yield efficient theorem provers. Most studies of equational theorem proving, such as [9, 22, 25, 31], have not used the replacement system approach. Chew [6] has recently developed an algorithm combining replacement systems with the methods of Nelson and Oppen [25].

Many of the theoretical properties of tree replacement systems have been studied in [3a, 11, 23, 26, 30]. In this paper we develop theoretically and practically efficient algorithms for one of the key technical issues in implementing replacement systems.

An implementation of a tree replacement system requires practical solutions for the following:

(a) a method for finding subtrees which may be replaced;
(b) a way of choosing the next replacement to be performed;
(c) a way of actually replacing the subtree.

Part (c) is an easy programming problem; (b) is a question which is quite complicated in its theoretical effects. It has been treated abstractly in [26] and algorithmically in [14]. Part (a) is the subject of this paper.

A large part of the overhead in implementing tree replacements comes from the repeated searching for the next subtree to be replaced. This is essentially a tree-pattern-matching problem. We believe that good solutions to the problem of tree pattern matching are a prerequisite for making implementations based on tree replacements competitive in efficiency with ad hoc methods, especially in the realm of interpreters for nonprocedural languages.

Tree pattern matching is analogous to the problem of pattern matching in strings studied in [1, 4, 21]. We consider two essentially different ways of extending the Knuth–Morris–Pratt string-matching algorithm to tree patterns, each with several variations.

One may view first-order unification as a tree-pattern-matching problem [3, 28, 29]. However, first-order unification differs from the tree pattern matching considered here in that a pattern is matched against the entire subject tree and not against proper subtrees as well. Pattern matching in our sense has been studied in [18, 23, 24, 27]. With the exception of [23], these papers examine the problem without considering the specific requirements of subtree replacement systems. Karp et al. [18] give an algorithm which finds all matches of a pattern tree to subtrees of a subject. By preprocessing the pattern(s) involved we get more efficient methods. Recently, Overmars and van Leeuwen [27] have studied tree pattern matching, but with a different class of trees. They discovered independently many of the techniques we develop in Section 8, and their fastest algorithm has a performance equal to our

Algorithm D. We discuss their results and the relationship to our work in Section 9. Kron's work [23] is related to the bottom-up techniques of Sections 3 and 4. We discuss the details at the end of Section 4.

In applications of tree replacements the same set of rules is typically used many times. Preprocessing of the rules is advantageous if it speeds up their application. Each replacement causes a local change in the subject tree. So our pattern-matching techniques should be able to respond incrementally to local changes in the subject to avoid repeated rescanning of the entire tree. For the sake of a simple presentation we discuss each algorithm in terms of a static subject first and then introduce adaptations to handle changing subjects.

In Section 2 we precisely define the matching problem and our criteria for a good solution. The remainder of the paper divides into two parts, corresponding to the two basic approaches we give. Sections 3–7 develop the bottom-up approach to pattern matching. Here we match in a subject tree by traversing it from the leaves to the root. This method is a significant generalization of the Knuth–Morris–Pratt string-matching algorithm. In Sections 8 and 9 we give our second approach, matching top down by traversing the subject root to leaves. While the bottom-up method generalizes string matching, the top-down method reduces tree matching to a string-matching problem.

The bottom-up method is characterized by more expensive preprocessing but faster matching and a better response to local changes. It is developed from the notion of *match sets*—sets of subpatterns which match at a particular tree node. The basic matching algorithm is introduced in Section 3. Properties of match sets are studied in Section 4. Since it turns out that certain tree patterns have exponentially many different match sets, which would lead to an exponential preprocessing algorithm, we introduce in Section 5 a restriction on tree patterns which allows efficient preprocessing algorithms. Section 6 gives the preprocessing algorithm and discusses its relationship with the preprocessing algorithms in [1, 21]. In Section 7 we sketch a better preprocessing algorithm for binary tree patterns.

Sections 8 and 9 give our top-down algorithm and discuss possible improvements. These algorithms have better preprocessing times than the bottom-up method, but the matching times and update behavior are inferior to the bottom-up method. Tree patterns are reduced to strings which are matched along paths in the subject, as in [18]. The preprocessing for this technique is little more than the preprocessing algorithm for string matching [1]. The basic idea of the top-down method lies in the use of counters for coordinating the matches of different path strings. This counting also turns out to be the limiting factor of the algorithm and is responsible for the worst-case bound. We can improve this bound on machines with bit-string operations, as indicated in Section 9.

For the restricted class of tree patterns introduced in Section 5 we have preprocessing algorithms which require

$$O(patsize^2 + patsize^{rank} \times ht)$$

steps. Here *patsize* is the sum of the pattern sizes, *ht* the height of a specific tree which has to be constructed as part of preprocessing, and *rank* the highest rank in the alphabet. In the worst case *ht* may be as big as *patsize*. The actual match, bottom up, requires $O(subsize + match)$ time, where *subsize* is the size of the subject tree and *match* is the number of matches found. For binary alphabets we have a preprocessing algorithm which requires only $O(patsize \times ht^2)$ steps when coupled with a modified bottom up matching algorithm requiring

$$O(subsize \times ht + match).$$

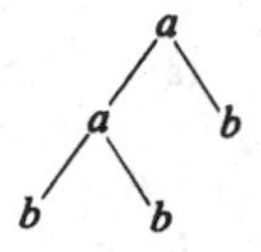

Figure 1

For top-down matching we have an $O(patsize)$ preprocessing algorithm. Here we need no restrictions on the tree patterns. The matching requires

$$O(subsize \times suf \times patno)$$

steps, where suf is a quantity depending on the structure of the pattern suffixes (at most equal to the maximum height of a pattern) and $patno$ is the number of tree patterns to be matched. For machines with bit-string operations we can, within the same time bound for preprocessing, match using a different technique in only $O(subsize \times patno)$ steps. If each pattern has a height not exceeding the number of bits in a machine word, then this algorithm is of practical importance.

In Section 10 we discuss other possibilities of bottom-up tree pattern matching on machines with bit-string operations, and a trade-off principle for matching time versus preprocessing time and space.

2. The Tree-Matching Problem

We are given a finite ranked alphabet Σ of function symbols, including constants as nullary functions. S denotes the set of Σ-terms, formally defined as follows.

Definition 2.1

(i) For all b in Σ of rank 0, b is a Σ-term.

(ii) If a is a symbol of rank q in Σ, then $a(t_1, \ldots, t_q)$ is a Σ-term provided each of the t_i is.

(iii) Nothing else is a Σ-term.

We view Σ-terms as labeled ordered trees. Thus the term $a(a(b, b), b)$ is the tree of Figure 1. Note that the trees $a(a(b, b), b)$ and $a(b, a(b, b))$ are considered to be different. In the following we use "Σ-tree" and "Σ-term" interchangeably.

We are also given a special nullary symbol v, not in Σ, to serve as placeholder for any Σ-tree. We define the set of $\Sigma \cup \{v\}$-terms just as Σ-terms but add to (i) that v is a $\Sigma \cup \{v\}$-term. S_v denotes the set of $\Sigma \cup \{v\}$-terms.

Definition 2.2. A *tree pattern* is any term in S_v. If $b(t_1, \ldots, t_q)$ is a term, then define $\text{son}_i(b(t_1, \ldots, t_q))$ to be t_i for $1 \leq i \leq q$.

We now explain how tree patterns are to be matched in Σ-trees.

Definition 2.3. A pattern p in S_v with k occurrences of the symbol v *matches* a subject tree t in S at node n if there exist Σ-trees $t_1, \ldots, t_k$ in S (not necessarily the same) such that the Σ-tree p', obtained from p by substituting t_i for the ith occurrence of v in p, is equal to the subtree of t rooted at n.

Example 2.1. Consider the pattern $p = a(a(b, v), v)$, with two occurrences of the symbol v, and the Σ-tree $t = a(a(b, c), a(a(b, b), b))$. Then p matches t at the two nodes marked in Figure 2. For the match at the root, the trees t_1 and t_2 to be substituted in p are $t_1 = c$ and $t_2 = a(a(b, b), b)$. For the match at the marked interior node we have $t_1 = b$ and $t_2 = b$. □

We wish to solve a matching problem in which we are given a finite set of patterns $p_1, \ldots, p_k$ from S_v and a subject tree t from S and are asked to identify in t every node at which any of the p_i match.

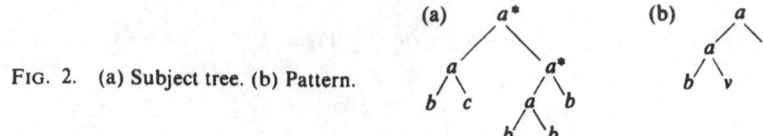

FIG. 2. (a) Subject tree. (b) Pattern.

Definition 2.4 (The Matching Problem). A *matching problem* consists of a finite set of patterns $p_1, \ldots, p_k$ in S_v and a subject tree t in S. A *solution* to a matching problem is a list of all the pairs (n, i), where n is a node in t and p_i matches at n.

Our definition is motivated principally by algorithmic problems arising in the implementation of subtree replacement systems. Allowing different substitutions for different occurrences of v is equivalent to using a different variable symbol at each occurrence. This restriction is motivated by theoretical problems which arise when repeated variables are permitted in the specification of the replacement axioms [26, Sec. VII].

Note that S_v contains S as subset. Thus every Σ-tree is also a pattern. We develop our results assuming patterns contain at least one occurrence of v, since patterns without variable occurrences are uninteresting from a practical viewpoint. This assumption does not limit our results.

Our matching problem is in some ways more specific, and in some ways more general, than first-order unification. Our use of v corresponds to allowing terms with nonrepeated variables as patterns, while in first-order unification repeated variables are allowed and variables may also appear in the subject. On the other hand, in unification only two trees are matched against each other, and only at the root, whereas we match any number of patterns anywhere in the subject tree.

Definition 2.5. The *size* of a *tree* is the total number of subtrees (equivalently, nodes) in it. The *size* of a *forest* is the sum of the sizes of all trees in it. The *height* of a tree is the number of edges in a longest path from the root to a leaf of the tree.

We are especially interested in applications in which the set of patterns remains fixed and is to be matched against a sequence of subject trees. We therefore consider preprocessing the tree patterns and distinguish *preprocessing time*, involving operations on the patterns independent of any subject tree, and *matching time*, involving all subject dependent operations. Minimizing matching time is the first priority. Preprocessing time is then minimized with respect to a fixed process for matching. Trade-offs between preprocessing time and matching time are considered if the improvement in preprocessing is dramatic and the degradation in matching is small. We also consider the space requirements in preprocessing and matching.

We are especially interested in algorithms which may clearly be adapted to assimilate local changes to the subject without rescanning the entire tree. For bottom-up matching we achieve linear matching times, but preprocessing time may be exponential. To keep bottom-up preprocessing time polynomial, we need some additional constraints on patterns. For top-down matching we lower the preprocessing time to linear, with no restrictions on patterns, at the cost of a slight increase in matching time. The bottom-up method adapts more easily to changes in the subject.

For the remainder of this paper, complexities will be expressed in terms of

patno: the number of different patterns involved
patsize: the size of the pattern forest
subsize: the size of the subject tree
sym: the number of symbols in the alphabet Σ

rank: the highest rank (arity) of any symbol in Σ
match: the number of matches which are found

All suggested methods for tree matching should be compared to the naive algorithm (based on a simple form of unification), which merely tries every pattern at every position in the subject tree. The naive algorithm does no preprocessing but takes $O(patsize \times subsize)$ matching time.

3. The Bottom-Up Matching Algorithm

The key idea of the bottom-up matching algorithm is to find, at each point in the subject tree, all patterns and all parts of patterns which match at this point. Let n be a node in the subject labeled with the q-ary symbol b, and suppose we wish to compute the set M of all those pattern subtrees other than v which match at n in the sense of Definition 2.3. (Since v matches anywhere, we always have a match of v.) Suppose we have already computed such sets for each of the sons of n, and call these sets, from left to right, $M_1, \ldots, M_q$. Then M contains v plus exactly those pattern subtrees $b(t_1, \ldots, t_q)$ such that t_i is in M_i, for $1 \leq i \leq q$. Therefore we could compute M by forming trees $b(t_1, \ldots, t_q)$ for all combinations $(t_1, \ldots, t_q)$, where the t_i are chosen from M_i, and then asking whether each candidate for membership in M is a subpattern. Once we have assigned these sets to each node in the subject tree, we have essentially solved the matching problem, since each match is signaled by the presence of a complete pattern in some set.

Note that there can be only finitely many such sets M, because both Σ and the set of subpatterns are finite. Thus we could *precompute* these sets, code them by some enumeration, and then construct tables. Given a node symbol b and the codes of the M_i, these tables give the code for M. In the case of a q-ary symbol b, we would have a q-dimensional matrix for that symbol.

Given such tables, the matching algorithm becomes trivial: Traverse the subject tree in postorder and assign to each node n the code c representing the set of partial matches at n as discussed. The tables consist of arrays, one for each alphabet symbol. If node n is labeled with the q-ary symbol b, then the q-dimensional array for b is used. The code c at n is the value indexed by the tuple $(c_1, \ldots, c_q)$ where c_i is the code assigned to the ith son of n (from the left). If the set represented by c contains the pattern p_i, then the pair (n, i) is added to the solution.

The matching time of this algorithm is clearly $O(subsize)$ for computing all codes plus $O(match)$ for listing the solution. The constant of linearity involves one array reference for computing the codes, a single test to determine whether a complete pattern match is present, plus the overhead for the postorder traversal. Note that the codes may be assigned so that all codes indicating matches are contiguous. The space requirements depend on the table size and are discussed in Section 4.

Example 3.1.   Consider a matching problem in which the patterns

$$p_1 = a(a(v, v), b) \qquad \text{and} \qquad p_2 = a(b, v)$$

are to be matched. Assume the alphabet Σ is $\{a, b, c\}$, where a is binary and b and c are nullary symbols. For reasons to be explained later, of the thirty-two possible sets of pattern subtrees only the following five can arise as result of matching:

$$\text{Set } 1 = \{v\},$$
$$\text{Set } 2 = \{b, v\},$$
$$\text{Set } 3 = \{a(v, v), v\},$$
$$\text{Set } 4 = \{a(b, v), a(v, v), v\},$$
$$\text{Set } 5 = \{a(a(v, v), b), a(v, v), v\}.$$

Table for node label a:

Left son	Right son				
	1	2	3	4	5
1	3	3	3	3	3
2	4	4	4	4	4
3	3	5	3	3	3
4	3	5	3	3	3
5	3	5	3	3	3

Figure 3

Table for node label b: 2
Table for node label c: 1

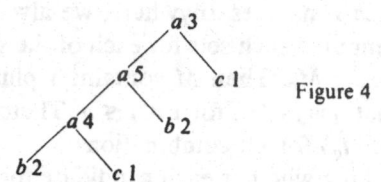

Figure 4

Thus, assigning a 4 to some node n of a subject would indicate that each of the members of Set 4 matches at n. In particular, p_2 matches. Assigning 5 implies a match of p_1.

Figure 3 shows the tables for a, b, and c. For instance, the entry at (3, 2) in the table for a is 5, because at the left son we have a match of both $a(v, v)$ and v, and at the right son of b and of v. For the nullary symbols b and c the tables are 0-dimensional, consisting of one entry each.

Figure 4 shows the complete assignment of codes when using the bottom-up algorithm with these tables. Note that p_1 matches at the node with code 5 and p_2 at the node with code 4. □

There is some similarity between bottom-up matching and formal parsing methods such as LR(k) parsing. In both cases a finite number of possible configurations are precomputed, and tables are formed to drive the parsing/matching process. As with LR(k) parsing, our tables will sometimes be very large, but we isolate a significant class of problems in which the table size is kept small.

When a local change is made to a subject tree, matching codes must be recomputed for the changed portion and some ancestors of the changed portion. In Section 4 we see that the number of ancestors whose codes must be recomputed is bounded by the largest height of a pattern. Note that in these ancestors new matches could appear or old matches disappear. Thus it seems intuitively unlikely that any method could update with less recomputation.

4. Pattern Relations and Match Sets

We now turn to studying the sets of partial matches used in the bottom-up matching algorithm of Section 3. We begin by precisely defining these sets and deriving properties which we will later exploit in designing good preprocessing algorithms.

Definition 4.1.   Let $F = \{p_1, \ldots, p_k\}$ be a set of patterns in S_v and PF the set of all subtrees of the p_i. A subset M of PF is a *match set* for F if there exists a tree t in S such that every pattern in M matches t at the root and every pattern in PF $- M$ does not match t at the root.

160

Note that if v is in PF, then v is in every match set. Observe also that the concept of match sets depends on the pattern forest F.

Example 4.1.   Consider the pattern forest $F = \{p_1, p_2\}$, where p_1 and p_2 are as in Example 3.1. Then the set $M = \{a(b, v), a(v, v), v\}$ is a match set because of the tree $a(b, c)$. However, $M' = \{a(b, v), v\}$ is not a match set, because a match of $a(b, v)$ implies a match of $a(v, v)$ at the same node.   □

Observe that the set of all possible match sets contains all sets which the bottom-up matching algorithm could assign (in encoded form) in any subject tree, given the pattern forest F.

Given F, let Match(t) denote the match set which must be assigned at the root of the subject tree t. PF is the set of all pattern subtrees from F. We can now formally state the two properties on which the bottom-up matching algorithm is based.

Definition 4.2

(1) If a is a nullary symbol, then

$$\text{Match}(a) = \begin{cases} \{a, v\} & \text{if } a \text{ is in PF,} \\ \{v\} & \text{otherwise.} \end{cases}$$

(2) If a is q-ary, $a > 0$, then

$$\text{Match}(a(t_1, \ldots, t_q)) = \{v\} \cup \{p' \mid p' \text{ has root } a \text{ and is in PF, and for } 1 \le j \le q, \text{son}_j(p) \text{ is in Match}(t_j)\}.$$

Note that because of (2), Match(t) does not depend on any node in t whose distance from the root exceeds the maximum height of a pattern. Because of this and the manner in which codes are assigned, the bottom-up matching algorithm responds well to local changes in a subject tree. See [15] for details.

In principle, the required enumeration of sets and tables may be generated by a simple closure strategy which starts with Match(a) for all nullary symbols a and repeatedly closes under the operation (2) of Definition 4.2. Such an algorithm would require

$$O(set^{(rank+1)} \times sym \times patsize)$$

time, where *set* is the number of distinct match sets generated. The table size would be $O(set^{rank} \times sym)$. In order to improve this time limit and to bound the size of *set*, which could be as bad as $O(2^{patsize})$, we need to understand certain relations between patterns and members of match sets. We define the following relations on tree patterns.

Definition 4.3.   Let p and p' be patterns in S_v. Then p is *inconsistent* with p' (written $p \| p'$) if there is no subject tree t in S with both p and p' in Match(t). p and p' are *independent* (written $p \sim p$) if there are trees t_1, t_2, t_3 in S such that p is in Match(t_1), p' is not in Match(t_1), p is not in Match(t_2), p' is in Match(t_2), and p and p' are in Match(t_3). p *subsumes* p' ($p \ge p'$) if, for all t in S, p in Match(t) implies that p' is in Match(t). p strictly subsumes p' ($p > p'$) if $p \ge p'$ and $p \ne p'$. $p < p'$ iff $p' > p$.

Example 4.2. $a(b, v) \| a(c, v)$, since b and c cannot both be matched in the same position. $a(b, v) \sim a(v, c)$, since $a(b, v)$ in Match($a(b, b)$), $a(v, c)$ not in Match($a(b, b)$); $a(b, v)$ not in Match($a(c, c)$), $a(v, c)$ in Match($a(c, c)$); $a(b, v)$ in Match($a(b, c)$), $a(v, c)$ in Match($a(b, c)$). Finally, $a(b, v) > a(v, v)$.   □

Figure 5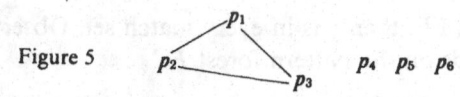

Given distinct patterns p and p', exactly one of the relations $\parallel$, $\sim$, $>$, and $<$ must hold between p and p'. The elementary properties of the three relations are summarized below. Note that in the absence of variables distinct patterns must be inconsistent.

PROPOSITION 4.1. *For trees p_1, p_2, p_3 in S_v:*

(a) $p_1 > p_2$ and $p_2 > p_3$ implies $p_1 > p_3$;
(b) $p_1 \parallel p_2$ iff $p_2 \parallel p_1$;
(c) $p_1 \sim p_2$ iff $p_2 \sim p_1$;
(d) $p_1 \parallel p_2$ and $p_3 > p_2$ implies $p_1 \parallel p_3$;
(e) $p_1 \sim p_2$ and $p_2 > p_3$ implies $p_1 \sim p_3$ or $p_1 > p_3$.

Recall that M' of Example 4.1 is not a match set because $a(b, v)$ subsumes $a(v, v)$. The inclusion of one pattern (e.g., $a(v, v)$) in M may be the consequence of the presence of another pattern which subsumes it (e.g., $a(b, v)$). Therefore, there may be a subset of patterns in M which completely determines M. We partition each match set M into a set M_0 of pairwise independent trees and a set M_1 of trees subsumed by some tree in M_0. M_0 is called the *base* of M.

PROPOSITION 4.2. *Given a pattern forest F and match set M for F, there is a unique partition of M into sets M_0 and M_1 such that for distinct p_1, p_2 in M_0, $p_1 \sim p_2$ holds, and for each p' in M_1 there is a p in M_0 such that $p > p'$.*

Observe that different match sets must have different base sets, owing to Proposition 4.1a. Thus we may represent match sets by their base sets.

Definition 4.4. Given a pattern forest F, the *independence graph* G_I of F is as follows: The vertices of G_I are distinct trees in PF. There is an undirected edge between p and p' iff $p \sim p'$.

Example 4.3. Consider the pattern forest $F = \{p_1, p_2, p_3\}$, where $p_1 = a(b(b(v)), v)$, $p_2 = a(b(v), b(v))$, and $p_3 = a(v, b(b(v)))$. There are three additional trees in PF: $p_4 = b(b(v))$, $p_5 = b(v)$, and $p_6 = v$. Since the trees p_1, p_2, p_3 are pairwise independent, whereas no other tree pairs are, the independence graph G_I of F is as shown in Figure 5, with a connected component p_1, p_2, p_3 and three isolated points. $\square$

From the independence graph we can derive an upper bound on the number of possible match sets of a given pattern forest.

THEOREM 4.3. *The number of possible match sets of a pattern forest F is at most the number of cliques in the independence graph G_I of F, counting all subcliques, including the trivial ones.*

This theorem follows easily from Proposition 4.2. To illustrate it, consider F of Example 4.3. The theorem would limit the number of match sets of F to ten, for G_I has six trivial cliques, three cliques of size 2, and one clique of size 3. We would thus expect six match sets with a base set of a singleton, three match sets with base sets consisting of two trees each, and one match set with a base set of three elements. However, in this example there is no match set with the base $\{p_1, p_3\}$, since matching both p_1 and p_3 at the root implies that p_2 matches at the root as well. Thus Theorem 4.3 gives an upper bound only. For deriving exact limits we would need to introduce other structural properties and analyze relations between more than two patterns.

For certain pattern forests the graphs G_1 could be such that the number of cliques grows exponentially with the number of subtrees in F and hence exponentially with the size of F. In such cases the number of distinct match sets may also grow exponentially.

THEOREM 4.4. *There are classes of pattern forests for which the number of distinct match sets grows exponentially with the size of the forest.*

PROOF. We define a class of balanced binary trees p_j^i, $0 \leq i$, $0 \leq j \leq 2^i$, of height i, with all interior nodes labeled a. In p_j^i, all leaves are labeled v except the jth leaf from the left, which is labeled b. For $j = 0$, all leaves are labeled v.

$$p_0^0 = v,$$
$$p_1^0 = b,$$
$$p_j^{i+1} = a(p_j^i, p_0^i), \qquad 0 \leq j \leq 2^i,$$
$$p_j^{i+1} = a(p_0^i, p_{j-2^i}^i), \qquad 2^i < j \leq 2^{i+1}.$$

Define the pattern forest $F_n = \{ p_i^n \mid 1 \leq i \leq 2^n \}$. The *size* of F_n is $O(2^n)$. Furthermore, $p_i^n \sim p_j^n$ for distinct nonzero values of i and j. Now consider sets Q of integers between 1 and 2^n, and define for each such set Q a balanced binary tree P_Q of height n with all interior nodes labeled a and such that the ith leaf from the left is labeled b if i is in Q, c otherwise. Then p_i^n matches P_Q at the root iff i is in Q. There are 2^{2^n} such sets Q; thus there must be at least as many different match sets. $\square$

As a consequence of Theorem 4.4, a preprocessing algorithm based on computing tables indexed by match sets to drive the bottom-up matching algorithm must be impractical in certain cases. Since independence among subpatterns in a forest is responsible for a possible exponential growth of the number of match sets, we conclude the section with a necessary condition for independence based on the structure of patterns.

PROPOSITION 4.5. *Let p, p' be independent patterns. Then p contains disjoint subtrees t_1 and t_2 and p' contains disjoint subtrees t_1' and t_2', in corresponding positions, such that $t_1 > t_1'$ and $t_2' < t_2$.*

PROOF. Since v and nullary symbols in corresponding positions cannot be independent of other patterns, we may assume that

$$p = a(p_1, \ldots, p_q),$$
$$p' = a(p_1', \ldots, p_q').$$

The proof is by induction on the height of p.

Basis. If p has height 1, then the p_i have height 0, thus are nullary symbols or v, and thus, for $1 \leq i \leq q$, $p_i \geq p_i'$ or $p_i' \geq p_i$. If, for all i, $p_i \geq p_i'$ ($p_i' \geq p_i$), then $p \geq p'$ ($p' \geq p$). But $p \sim p'$ by assumption, and thus we can find the required trees among p_i and p_i'.

Induction Steps. Assume that the proposition holds for all p of height less than h, and assume that p has height h. Surely $p_i \| p_i'$ cannot hold; otherwise p and p' would be inconsistent. If there is some i such that $p_i \sim p_i'$, then apply the induction hypothesis to p_i and p_i'. Otherwise, for all i, $p_i \geq p_i'$ or $p_i' \geq p_i$, and the argument of the induction basis completes the proof. $\square$

Note that mutual subsumption, in opposite directions, of disjoint subtrees is necessary but not sufficient for independence, since it does not rule out the possibility that other subtrees are inconsistent. For example, $a(b, v, c)$ and $a(v, b, d)$ are inconsistent, yet there are disjoint subtree pairs satisfying the "only if" condition of Proposition 4.5.

Proposition 4.5 is used when testing the restrictions imposed on tree patterns in the next section.

We have recently learned that the idea of bottom-up tree pattern matching was discovered independently by Kron [23]. He calls match sets "batches" and defines the relations $>$, $\|$, $\sim$ (which he calls "more specific than," "not overlapping," and "intersecting," respectively) equivalently by containment and intersection properties of the sets of Σ-terms which two patterns match at the root.

He matches patterns in a subject tree using an automaton as well. Instead of using matrices as tables, however, he computes the match set to be assigned to node n with q sons by a subautomaton which, in q transition steps reading the match set codes of the sons, determines the code for the new match set. There is one subautomaton per alphabet symbol. As a result, his match time is $O(subsize)$. One can visualize each subautomaton as a trie encoding of one of our matrices. Depending on the pattern structure, this leads to smaller space requirements in certain cases.

The preprocessing of Kron is essentially the method sketched in the paragraphs following Definition 4.2. Because of Theorem 4.4, this preprocessing takes time exponential in the pattern size in the worst case. As Kron tells us, he was aware of this, but it was not a concern of his research in [23]. We are going further and analyzing match sets seeking a definition of a subclass of tree patterns with polynomial preprocessing time. We give such a definition in the following section.

Preprocessing in Kron's sense has been used in practical situations by Wilhelm [10]. Since this work seems to accomplish practically viable preprocessing times, we conclude that the exponential worst case of bottom-up matching does not arise frequently in these applications.

5. *Simple Pattern Forests*

Because of the exponential growth of the number of match sets for certain pattern forests (Theorem 4.4), we wish to restrict patterns when generating tables to drive the bottom-up matching algorithm of Section 3. Theorem 4.3 suggests disallowing independence among pattern subtrees. This restriction is not as drastic as it might seem and has not seriously hindered us when generating interpreters for LISP, LUCID, and the Combinator Calculus using these techniques [14].

Definition 5.1.   A pattern forest F is *simple* if it contains no independent subtrees.

For simple forests, the independence graph has no edges; hence, by Theorem 4.3, the number of distinct match sets is at most the size of the forest. Furthermore, simple forests have a number of useful properties which can be exploited in the design of efficient matching algorithms.

Definition 5.2.   If F is a pattern forest, and p, p' are subpatterns in PF, then p *immediately* subsumes p', $p >_i p'$, iff $p > p'$ and there is no other subpattern p'' in PF such that $p > p''$ and $p'' > p'$. Immediate subsumption is the transitive reduction of subsumption on the set of all subpatterns of F.

Definition 5.3.   The *immediate subsumption graph* G_S of the forest F has as vertices all distinct subpatterns in F. There is a directed edge from p to p' iff $p >_i p'$. In general, G_S is a directed acyclic graph with v as the only leaf.

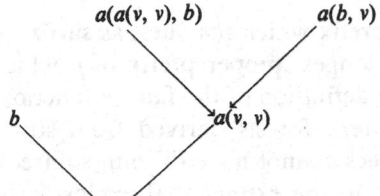

$$a(a(v, v), b) \qquad a(b, v)$$

$$b \qquad\qquad a(v, v)$$

$$v$$

FIG. 6. The immediate subsumption graph of F.

LEMMA 5.1. *The immediate subsumption graph G_S of a simple forest F is an inverted tree with v as root.*

PROOF. Let p, p', and p'' be distinct subtrees in F, and assume that p subsumes both p' and p'', but neither $p > p''$ nor $p'' > p'$. Since p subsumes both trees, $p' \| p''$ is impossible (Proposition 4.1d); hence p' and p'' must be independent. But then F cannot be simple. Hence either $p' > p''$ or $p'' > p'$. □

Observe that for simple forests, the base set M_0 of any match set must be a singleton. Using Lemma 5.1 and Proposition 4.2, we thus easily obtain

THEOREM 5.2. *Let F be a simple forest and M any match set for F with base set $\{p\}$. Then M consists precisely of the trees encountered on the path from p to v in G_S.*

This theorem is the central result for simple forests. It frees us from having to construct explicitly the individual match sets, for G_S provides them at once along with their structure and interrelation. We conclude the section with an example illustrating Theorem 5.2, and a discussion of the relationship between G_S and the failure function f constructed in the algorithm for string pattern matching in [1, 21].

Example 5.1. The pattern forest $F = \{a(a(v, v), b), a(b, v)\}$ is simple, since there are no independent trees or subtrees. Its immediate subsumption relation is

$$b >_i v, \qquad\qquad a(v, v) >_i v,$$
$$a(b, v) >_i a(v, v), \qquad a(a(v, v), b) >_i a(v, v),$$

which has the graph G_S shown in Figure 6. From this graph we then obtain as possible match sets the five sets of Example 3.1:

$$\{v\},$$
$$\{b, v\},$$
$$\{a(v, v), v\},$$
$$\{a(b, v), a(v, v), v\},$$
$$\{a(a(v, v), b), a(v, v), v\}.$$

Note the correspondence of these sets to the paths in G_S. □

There is a connection between the immediate subsumption graph G_S and the failure function f used in string-pattern-matching algorithms in [1, 21]. This connection is observed by visualizing a string pattern $a_1 a_2 \cdots a_m$ as the nonbranching tree $a_m(\ldots a_2(a_1(v))\ldots)$. Note the reversal of the character sequence. The addition of v as a leaf permits us to conceptualize the a_i as symbols of arity 1 and permits sliding the nonbranching tree in the subject. Matching this pattern in the subject $b_1 b_2 \cdots b_n$ is now equivalent to matching the nonbranching tree pattern in the tree $b_n(\ldots b_2(b_1(c))\ldots)$, where c is a new nullary symbol. Having translated the string-matching problem into a tree-matching problem in this way, we now observe that G_S is just the graph of the failure function f constructed for the original string problem by the algorithms in [1, 21]. To observe this, note that a subtree corresponds to a pattern prefix, and that $p > p'$ iff p' is a pattern prefix which matches, as suffix, in the pattern prefix p. Hence $p >_i p'$ iff p' is the longest proper prefix of p which matches, as suffix, in the prefix p, which is just the definition of the failure function.

Note also that because of Proposition 4.5, pattern forests derived from string patterns must be simple, because nonbranching trees cannot have disjoint subtrees. Hence there is no counterpart in string matching to the exponential explosion of match sets, which can occur for nonsimple forests in tree matching.

6. Table Construction for Simple Forests

For a simple pattern forest F, the tables to drive the bottom-up algorithm of Section 3 may be constructed in two steps. First, construct the subsumption graph $\bar{G}_S$ whose vertices are the trees in PF. $\bar{G}_S$ has a directed edge from p to p' iff $p \geq p'$. Observe that this is equivalent to finding all match sets which can occur when matching in any subject. Then, for each alphabet symbol a of arity m, we use $\bar{G}_S$ to construct a table T_a such that $T_a[p_1, \ldots, p_m]$ is the match-set code which should be assigned to any node labeled a at whose sons we have assigned the match-set codes p_1 to p_m from left to right, respectively.

We find it convenient to represent a match set M by its base set tree, that is, by the largest (in the sense of $>$) tree in M. This is a reasonable choice since, by Proposition 4.2 and Theorem 5.2, the largest tree in M completely determines M. The advantages of this coding is that we can now define the entry $T_a[p_1, \ldots, p_m]$ as the largest tree in PF subsumed by $a(p_1, \ldots, p_m)$, because of observation (2) below. Note that the tree $a(p_1, \ldots, p_m)$ need not occur in PF.

To construct $\bar{G}_S$, observe that for distinct patterns p, p',

(1) If $p > p'$, then height(p) $\geq$ height(p').
(2) Let $p = a(p_1, \ldots, p_m)$. Then $p > p'$ iff either $p' = v$ or $p' = a(p'_1, \ldots, p'_m)$, where $p_j \geq p'_j$ for $1 \leq j \leq m$.

So we may process patterns in order of increasing height and compare each pattern to all patterns of no greater height using observation (2). Since the subpatterns p_i and p'_i in (2) above are of strictly smaller height than p and p', respectively, $p_j \geq p'_j$ has already been checked by the time p is compared to p'.

Algorithm A

Input: Simple pattern forest F.

Output: Subsumption graph $\bar{G}_S$ for F.

Method:

1. List the trees in PF by increasing height.
2. Initialize $\bar{G}_S$ to the graph with vertices PF and no edges.
3. **For each** $p = a(p_1, \ldots, p_m)$, $m \geq 0$, of height h, by increasing order of height, **do**
4.   for each p' in PF of height $\leq h$ do
5.   If $p' = v$ or
           $p' = a(p'_1, \ldots, p'_m)$ where, for $1 \leq i \leq m$, $p_i \rightarrow p'_i$ is in $\bar{G}_S$,
        then
6.   Add $p \rightarrow p'$ to $\bar{G}_S$.

For the analysis of Algorithm A, observe that step 1 requires $O(patsize)$ time using bucketsort. Steps 3–6 require $O(patsize^2 \times rank)$ steps, assuming that $\bar{G}_S$ is stored as an adjacency matrix, so that checking whether $p_j \rightarrow p'_j$ requires constant time. The space complexity is dominated by the $O(patsize^2)$ adjacency matrix. Thus Algorithm A requires $O(patsize^2 \times rank)$ steps and $O(patsize^2)$ space.

To generate the table T_a, recall that for the m-ary symbol a and trees $p_1, \ldots, p_m$ in PF, $T_a[p_1, \ldots, p_m] = p$, where p is the largest (in the sense of $>$) tree in PF such that $a(p_1, \ldots, p_m) \geq p$. This can be seen as follows. If $a(p_1, \ldots, p_m) \geq t$, then either $t = v$ or $t = a(p_1', \ldots, p_m')$ and, for $1 \leq i \leq m$, $p_i \geq p_i'$. Then the set

$$M = \{t \text{ in PF} \mid a(p_1, \ldots, p_m) \geq t\}$$

is precisely the match set which should be coded by the entry $T_a[p_1, \ldots, p_m]$, assuming p_i codes the match set with base set tree p_i. Recall that by Lemma 5.1 subsumption induces a total order on the elements of M; hence the largest tree p in PF subsumed by $a(p_1, \ldots, p_m)$ is precisely the base set tree of M and thus the code which should be assigned to $T_a[p_1, \ldots, p_m]$.

Now observe that by (2), $a(p_1, \ldots, p_m) > p$ is easily testable from $\bar{G}_S$. Furthermore, if we process the patterns in PF in increasing order of subsumption and for each p in PF assign p to all of the entries $T_a[p_1, \ldots, p_m]$ such that $a(p_1, \ldots, p_m) \geq p$, then the last assignment made to the entry will be the maximal subsumed p in PF. Thus, if we write each p into the appropriate table positions when p is processed, the final values in the table are the correct ones.

Algorithm B

Input: $\bar{G}_S$ for a simple pattern forest F.

Output: Tables to drive the bottom-up matching algorithm. $T_a[p_1, \ldots, p_m]$ will contain the largest (under subsumption) tree in PF which is subsumed by $a(p_1, \ldots, p_m)$.

Method:

1. List PF in increasing order of subsumption by performing a topological sort on G_S.
2. Initialize all entries in all tables T_a to v.
3. **For each** pattern $p = a(p_1, \ldots, p_m)$ by increasing order of subsumption **do**
4.   **For each** m-tuple $\langle p_1', \ldots, p_m' \rangle$ such that, for $1 \leq j \leq m$, $p_j' \geq p_j$ **do**
5. $T_a[p_1', \ldots, p_m'] := p$.

The table for the symbol a of arity q has $patsize^q$ entries. Thus Algorithm B constructs no more than $patsize^{rank} \times sym$ entries. When a tree p is assigned to an entry in T_a, then p belongs to the match set which should be coded by this entry. Thus the number of repeated assignments to each entry cannot exceed the size of the largest match set, that is, the height of $\bar{G}_S$. Thus at most $patsize^{rank} \times sym \times ht$ assignments are done in step 5.

Note that p_i' ranges over those trees in PF such that $p_i' \to p_i$. Hence we can find the necessary tuples easily from the adjacency matrix of $\bar{G}_S$. In an implementation of this algorithm the patterns in PF are numbered, and the tables T_a are indexed by these numbers. We summarize the complexity of preprocessing patterns in simple forests by the following.

THEOREM 6.1. *We can construct tables to drive the bottom-up matching algorithm in the case of simple pattern forest in*

$$O(patsize^2 \times rank + patsize^{rank} \times ht \times sym)$$

time and

$$O(patsize^2 + sym + patsize^{rank})$$

space.

Note that it is easy to test whether a pattern forest is simple. Using Proposition 4.6, it suffices to test, in step 5 of Algorithm A, whether p and p' contain two (immediate)

TABLE 1. TABLE T_a GENERATED FOR THE SYMBOL a

Left subtree match	Right subtree match				
	v	b	$a(v, v)$	$a(b, v)$	$a(a(v, v), b)$
v	$a(v, v)$	$a(v, v)$	$a(v, v)$	$a(v, v)$	$a(v, v)$
b	$a(b, v)$	$a(b, v)$	$a(b, v)$	$a(b, v)$	$a(b, v)$
$a(v, v)$	$a(v, v)$	$a(a(v, v), b)$	$a(v, v)$	$a(v, v)$	$a(v, v)$
$a(b, v)$	$a(v, v)$	$a(a(v, v), b)$	$a(v, v)$	$a(v, v)$	$a(v, v)$
$a(a(v, v), b)$	$a(v, v)$	$a(a(v, v), b)$	$a(v, v)$	$a(v, v)$	$a(v, v)$

subtrees in corresponding positions which subsume each other in opposite directions. If such a pair exists, then the pattern forest is not simple.

Example 6.1. We illustrate Algorithm B with the table T_a generated for the symbol a, given the pattern forest of Example 5.1. The table is essentially that of Example 3.1; however, for readability we represent entries and index values by trees, rather than enumerating them.

In this example, all table entries are assigned by step 5, so none of them is v. Consider $p = a(a(v, v), b)$ in the traversal of step 3. The m-tuples of steps 4 and 5 now range over the sets p'_1 in $\{a(v, v), a(a(v, v), b), a(b, v)\}$, since $a(a(v, v), b)$ and $a(b, v)$ are the two trees subsuming $a(v, v)$, and p'_2 in $\{b\}$, since there is no other tree subsuming b. So $a(a(v, v), b)$ is entered in $T_a[a(v, v), b]$, $T_a[a(a(v, v), b), b]$, and $T_a[a(b, v), b]$. The entry $T_a[a(v, v), b]$ had already been assigned the smaller pattern $a(v, v)$, since $a(v, v) > v$ and $b > v$, but this entry is wiped out by $a(a(v, v), b)$ at this time. Table I shows the table T_a. □

Clearly Algorithm B constitutes the bottleneck of preprocessing, both in space and in time requirements. Often the situation can be improved by introducing one or more pairing functions, thereby reducing *rank* to 2. Although pairing is always possible, it need not preserve simplicity of the forest and is thus of limited value.

Example 6.2. Consider the pattern forest $\{a(b, v, c), a(v, b, d), a(e, c, v)\}$. All subtrees other than v are pairwise inconsistent, and thus the forest is simple. Introducing a pairing function, no matter which subtrees are paired, will introduce independence. For example, pairing the first and second subtree results in a new forest $\{a'(\text{pair}(b, v), c), a'(\text{pair}(v, b), d), a'(\text{pair}(e, c), v)\}$ in which pair(b, v) and pair(v, b) are independent subtrees. □

There is a different approach to speeding up preprocessing. Recall that G_S generalizes the failure function of string matching. We suspect that there is an efficient bottom-up matching algorithm using G_S directly, without any tables. So far we have only achieved a running time of

$$O(\textit{subsize} \times \textit{patsize} \times \textit{ht})$$

by this approach, which is inferior to the naive method.

7. *Faster Preprocessing for Binary Simple Forests*

Algorithm A is quadratic in *patsize* since it constructs $\bar{G}_S$, the transitive closure of G_S, rather than G_S. It seems there should be an algorithm for computing G_S for simple pattern forests which requires $O(\textit{patsize})$ steps only. So far, we have not found an algorithm this efficient, but in the special case of binary simple pattern forests we can construct G_S in $O(\textit{patsize} \times \textit{ht}^2)$ steps. Here *ht* may be as large as *patsize*, but it is usually much smaller. Given the algorithm for computing G_S, it is then possible to

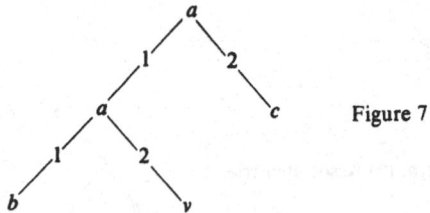

Figure 7

adapt it to do the pattern matching as well, bypassing the expensive step of table generation. We sketch the idea of this algorithm next.

Recall that in a simple forest F, for each subpattern p in PF there is exactly one largest subsumed subpattern p' in PF, except when $p = v$. Let $f(p)$ denote this tree p', that is, the tree immediately subsumed by p. Denote the *ith iterate* of f by $f^i(p)$, $0 \leq i$, where

$$f^0(p) = p,$$
$$f^{i+1}(p) = f(f^i(p)).$$

Note that G_S is the graph of the function f.

Consider computing $f(p)$, where the root of p is a binary symbol, that is, $p = a(p_1, p_2)$. We should examine trees of the form $a(f^i(p_1), f^j(p_2))$, $i + j > 0$, as possible candidates for $f(p)$. For this purpose we will maintain sets $S(a, p_1)$, where a is in Σ and p_1 is a pattern subtree. Each set contains pairs $\langle p_2, p \rangle$ of subpatterns. The pair $\langle p_2, p \rangle$ is in $S(a, p_1)$ iff $p = a(p_1, p_2)$ is in PF. In computing $f(p)$ we now probe in the sets $S(a, p_1)$, $S(a, f(p_1))$, $S(a, f^2(p_1))$, ... for pairs whose first component is p_2, $f(p_2)$, etc. The first such pair found (other than the pair $\langle p_2, p \rangle$ in $S(a, p_1)$) must be $f(p)$, since F is a simple forest. We make at most $O(ht^2)$ probes, since $f^{ht}(t) = v$, for any subpattern.

We can make a single probe efficiently by representing the set $S(a, p_1)$ by an array in which the second component of a pair is stored as the element indexed by the first component. In order to avoid an $O(patsize^2)$ overhead for initializing all vectors, we use the constant time array initialization of [2, Ex. 2.12]. The running time of the algorithm is thus $O(patsize \times ht^2)$.

Observe that the algorithm can be adapted to do the matching using the sets $S(a, p_1)$ without using the table generation (Algorithm B). This leads to a matching algorithm which requires at most $O(subsize \times ht^2)$ steps.

8. *Top-Down Matching Algorithm*

Like the bottom-up matching algorithm, our top-down matching algorithm is related to the Knuth–Morris–Pratt string-matching algorithm. Instead of generalizing string matching, however, the top-down approach reduces tree matching to string matching. The top-down method has slower matching time than the bottom-up, but better preprocessing time.

The key idea of reducing tree pattern matching to string matching is to regard each path from root to leaf in a tree as a string in which symbols in the alphabet are interleaved with numbers indicating which branch from father to son has been followed. Since variables always match, we do not include them in these strings.

Example 8.1.   The tree pattern $a(a(b, v), c)$ is associated with the set of strings $\{a1a1b, a1a2, a2c\}$. Note that we have omitted the symbol v from the end of the second string. Figure 7 shows how the set of strings appears in the given tree.   □

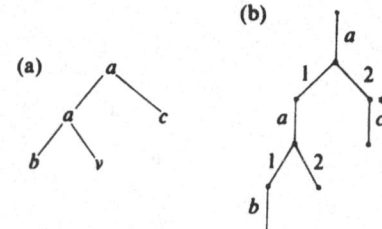

FIG. 8. (a) Tree pattern. (b) Associated trie.

This idea was first noticed by Karp et al. [18] and used in a tree-matching algorithm with no preprocessing. Their algorithm achieved a matching time of

$$O((\mathit{patsize} + \mathit{subsize}) \times \log(\mathit{patsize}))$$

for one pattern, which must be a full binary tree. For several patterns their algorithm would require

$$O((\mathit{patsize} + \mathit{subsize}) \times \log(\mathit{patsize}) \times \mathit{patno}).$$

Our contribution is to show how, using the Knuth–Morris–Pratt algorithm for string matching, we can improve the bounds to $O(\mathit{patsize})$ preprocessing, plus $O(\mathit{subsize} \times \mathit{patno})$ for matching, in the case of patterns which are full trees. If the patterns are not full trees, more time for matching is needed. We thus improve the bound of Karp et al. by a factor of $\log(\mathit{patsize})$.

For simplicity of presentation we develop our results for the case of a single tree pattern first. Given the pattern p, it is easy to generate all path strings for the root-to-leaf paths. We could then use the algorithm of Aho and Corasick [1] to produce an automaton which recognizes every instance of a path string within a subject tree. Since the combined length of all strings could be $O(\mathit{patsize}^2)$, we need to modify this construction so as to avoid generating the strings explicitly. In this way we can lower the preprocessing to $O(\mathit{patsize})$.

The first step in the Aho–Corasick algorithm is to build a trie for the path strings of the tree pattern p. This trie is called the "goto function" in [1]. A trie is a tree whose nodes represent the distinct prefixes of the path strings. If node n represents x and n' represents xa, a in $\Sigma \cup N$, then n is father of n', and the edge from n to n' is labeled a. We illustrate the construction with an example. Since it amounts to a simple tree transformation, we do not formally give an algorithm.

Example 8.2.   The pattern tree $a(a(b, v), c)$ has the associated trie shown in Figure 8. For example, the marked node represents the prefix $a2$. $\square$

Informally, the trie is constructed by first enumerating the outedges of every pattern node and then splitting every node labeled with a symbol other than v into two nodes connected by an edge which is labeled with the original node label.

The subsequent steps in constructing a matching automaton are exactly as in [1], for we are now dealing with a string problem. Thus the entire construction requires $O(\mathit{patsize})$ steps if we use a failure-function representation of the automaton and $O(\mathit{patsize} \times \mathit{sym})$ if we use a transition-matrix representation.

We need to include in this construction a simple modification which records, with each accepting state of the automaton, the length(s) of the accepted string(s). The length of a path string is the number of alphabet symbols in it (numbers are ignored). Thus the length for $a2c$ and $a1a2$ is 2 in both cases.

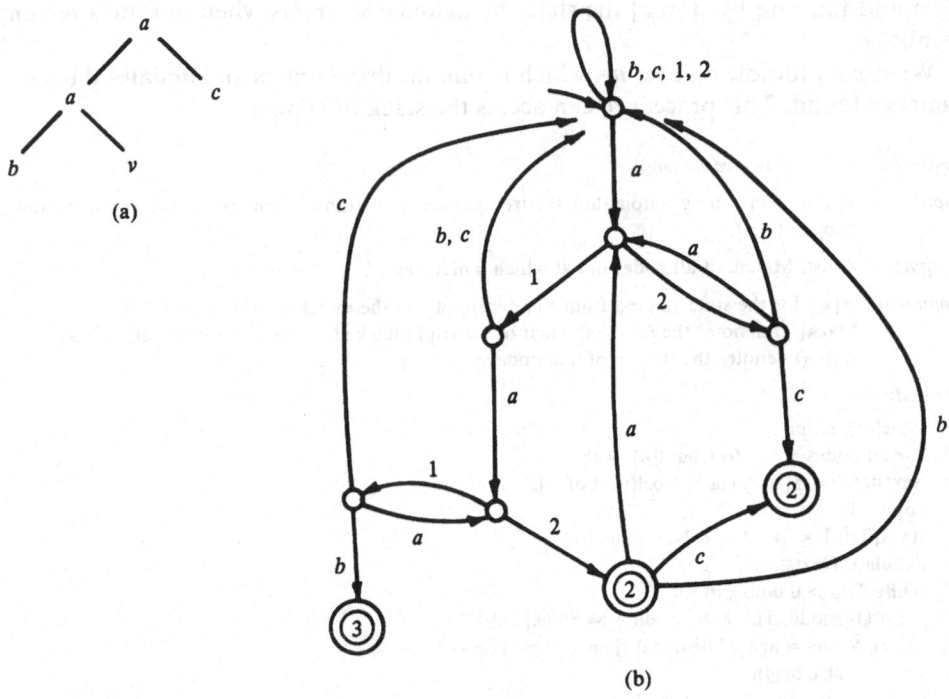

FIG. 9. (a) Pattern. (b) Matching automaton.

Example 8.3.   In Figure 9 we give the automaton associated with the pattern of the previous example. Accepting states are circled twice and are labeled with the length of the accepted path string.   □

We now have to solve the problem of how the matching algorithm can decide whether two different path strings begin at the same node and thus contribute to a pattern match at that node. For this purpose we associate with each node a counter, initialized to zero. Each counter will record the number of distinct root-to-leaf paths which match beginning at that node.

Let us traverse the subject tree t in preorder, computing the automaton states as we visit nodes and traverse edges. For recovering former states when returning from a completely traversed subtree we can use the traversal stack. Every time the matching automaton enters a final state, we have matched one or more path strings, and we should indicate this fact at the points at which the matched paths begin. So we increment the counters of those nodes by 1. The traversal stack for the preorder traversal is kept in an array. Thus we can find the beginning node of a matched path string in the traversal stack and can access it in constant time once we know the length of the matched string.

At the end of the traversal the pattern matches at each node whose counter equals the number of leaves in the pattern (i.e., the number of path strings). We can now give the matching algorithm.

We will use an array of triples $\langle n, s, j \rangle$ as traversal stack, where n is a node in the subject tree, s the state the automaton has entered when the traversal visits n, and j a number indicating how many sons of n have been visited. Additionally, we have an array *Count*, indexed by nodes n of the subject tree, which contains the associated counters.

We assume that the algorithm uses a transition-table representation of the automaton and indicate by $A[s, c]$ the state the automaton enters when in state s reading symbol c.

We use a procedure *Tabulate*, which maintains the counters and updates the list of matches found. This procedure can access the stack of triples.

Algorithm D (*Top Down Matching*)

Input: A string matching automaton for tree pattern p in transition matrix representation, and a subject tree t.

Output: A list, Match, of all nodes in t at which p matches.

Comment: $A[s, c]$ is the state entered from s under input c in the matching automaton.
Stack$[t].i$ denotes the ith component of the triple stacked at position t in the array Stack.
son$_i(n)$ denotes the ith son of tree node n.

Method:

```
 1.  Match := empty;
 2.  For all nodes n in t do Count[n] := 0;
 3.  Nextstate := A[start state, label(root of t)];
 4.  Top := 1;
 5.  Stack[Top] := ⟨root of t, Nextstate, 0⟩;
 6.  Tabulate(Nextstate);
 7.  While Top > 0 do begin
 8.      ⟨Thisnode, Thisstate, Nsons⟩ := Stack[Top];
 9.      If Nsons = arity(Thisnode) then Top := Top − 1;
10.          else begin
11.              Nsons := Nsons + 1;
12.              Stack[Top].3 := Nsons;
13.              Intstate := A[Thisstate, Nsons];
14.              Tabulate(Intstate);
15.              Nextnode := son_Nsons(Thisnode);
16.              Nextstate := A[Intstate, label(Nextnode)];
17.              Top := Top + 1;
18.              Stack[Top] := ⟨Nextnode, Nextstate, 0⟩;
19.              Tabulate(Nextstate);
20.          end (if)
21.      end (while)
```

Procedure Tabulate (State)

```
1.  For all s such that State has a match of length s
2.      do begin
3.          n := Stack[Top − s + 1].1;
3.          Count[n] := Count[n] + 1;
4.          If Count[n] = number of leaves in pattern then
5.              Add n to Match;
6.      end (for)
```

Except for the work of procedure Tabulate, the complexity of Algorithm D is $O(subsize)$, since each edge is traversed at most twice. This is also true for the failure-function representation of the matching automaton (see [1]). The total work of procedure Tabulate is proportional to the number of times any counter has been incremented, or equivalently, to the sum of all counter values upon completion of the traversal. We can estimate this sum by deriving a bound on the number of different counters which can be incremented in an accepting state, for this will also bound the work done for each call of the procedure.

Definition 8.1. Given a tree pattern p and a path string s of p, the *suffix number* of s is the number of path strings s of p which are suffixes of s, including p itself. The *suffix index* of p is the maximum suffix number of the path strings of p.

Equivalently, the suffix index is the largest number of counters which could be incremented in any accept state of the automaton.

Example 8.4. For the pattern $p = a(a(a(v, b), c), b)$ we have the path strings $a1a1a1$, $a1a1a2b$, $a1a2c$, $a2b$. The suffix number of $a1a1a1$ is 1, whereas the suffix number of $a1a1a2b$ is 2, since $a2b$ is a suffix which occurs as root to leaf path in p. The suffix index of p is also 2. □

THEOREM 8.1. *Algorithm D requires* $O(subsize \times suf)$ *steps, where suf is the suffix index of the pattern to be matched.*

For patterns which are full trees, that is, all path strings are of equal length, *suf* must be 1, since a distinct path string s_1 can be a proper suffix of a distinct path string s_2 only if s_1 is shorter than s_2. This gives us

COROLLARY 8.2. *If Algorithm D matches a pattern which is a full tree, then only* $O(subsize)$ *steps are needed.*

In the worst case, *suf* could be $O(patsize)$.

Example 8.5. Consider the pattern,

$$p_k = a(a(\dots a(v, b) \dots b), b).$$
$$\underbrace{\qquad\qquad\qquad}_{k \text{ times}}$$

Its suffix index is k, owing to the path string $(a1)^{k-1}a2b$, which has every shorter path string as suffix. Note that *patsize* is $2k + 1$. □

COROLLARY 8.3. *The bound of* $O(subsize \times patsize)$ *for Algorithm D is attained for certain patterns.*

PROOF. Consider matching the pattern p_k of Example 8.5 in the subject,

$$t_n = a(a(\dots a(c, b) \dots b), b),$$
$$\underbrace{\qquad\qquad\qquad}_{n \text{ times}}$$

where $n = k + m$. Then the sum of the counter values in t_n after Algorithm D has finished exceeds $m \times k$. Note that *patsize* is $2k + 1$ and *subsize* is $2n + 1$. □

We thus have in Algorithm D a performance range anywhere between that of the bottom-up algorithm and that of the naive matching algorithm, depending on the structure of the pattern.

Without going into details we note that Algorithm D may be adapted to assimilate local changes in the subject tree. As in the case of the bottom-up algorithm, we need to reprocess only a small area surrounding the part which has changed. However, the algorithmic details are far more complicated than in the case of the bottom-up algorithm, although in principle quite straightforward.

We conclude this section with a brief discussion of how to match more than one tree pattern, using the approach of Algorithm D.

Recall that we represent a tree pattern by its root-to-leaf path strings. We can do this for several patterns as well, but we should keep track of which pattern(s) each path string comes from. The preprocessing algorithm can be adapted to process several patterns by building separately for each pattern the associated trie and then merging these tries, keeping track of which pattern(s) each path string at a leaf of the trie belongs to. This can be done in $O(patsize)$ steps resulting in a trie of $O(patsize)$ nodes. Now apply the methods of [1] to complete the trie to a matching automaton.

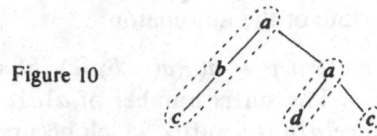

Figure 10

In the case of a single pattern we associated with each of the final states a list of the lengths of the matched path strings. For multiple patterns we now associate with final states lists of pairs. Each pair gives the length of the matched path string and the pattern to which it belongs.

It remains to explain how we can correlate matches of individual path strings. We do this simply by associating *patno* counters with each node in the subject tree and dedicating the ith counter to counting how many path strings of the ith pattern have been matched, beginning at that node. If the ith counter reaches a value equal to the number of leaves of the ith pattern, then we have just matched the ith pattern.

As before, the work is proportional to the subject size plus the sum of all counter values and can be estimated as

$$O(subsize \times \max(suf) \times patno),$$

where the maximum is taken over all tree patterns in the forest. This bound is easily shown to be the best possible, generalizing Corollary 8.2. Furthermore, if no path string is a suffix of another, then we have only $O(subsize)$ steps for matching such a pattern forest.

9. *Improvements to Top-Down Matching and Related Work*

Recently, Lang et al. [24] improved Algorithm D by basing the matching of path strings on the Boyer–Moore algorithm [4]. Since the Boyer–Moore algorithm requires the ability to skip portions of the subject string, a different representation of trees is used: Trees are represented by ordered lists of *left paths*.

Example 9.1.   For the tree $t = a(b(c), a(d, c))$ the list of left paths is $\langle abc, ad, c \rangle$, as shown in Figure 10.   □

We can obtain left paths by first deleting from each path string the longest prefix ending with a branch number greater than 1 and then deleting the remaining branch numbers. Thus, from *a2a1d* we obtain *ad*, and from *a2a2c* we get *c*. The list of these left paths uniquely determines a binary tree. For alphabet symbols of arity higher than 2, additional information has to be given for each left path string.

The algorithm first preprocesses the list of left paths of the pattern, constructing a Boyer–Moore-type automaton for recognizing the first left path, combined with an Aho–Corasick-type automaton for recognizing the remaining left paths. A match of the remaining left paths is attempted only at places at which the first left path has been completely matched. Note that the advantages of the Boyer–Moore machine diminish as the number of different strings to be matched increases. See [8] for a discussion of this phenomenon. The subject tree is also represented as an ordered list of (linked) left paths, so that we can skip ahead for the Boyer–Moore matching technique.

A subtlety of the algorithm, when it is applied to trees of arity exceeding 2, arises from the fact that a match of the jth left path implies an update of the appropriate counter only if the counter has a specific value, because the left path may be descending from a node with more than two sons. For details see [24].

Lang et al. [24] implemented both their algorithm and our Algorithm D. First experiments seem to indicate a sublinear average matching time for their algorithm. The worst-case performance of their algorithm is the same as that of Algorithm D.

Overmars and van Leeuwen [27] have given algorithms to match *lexicographic* trees, that is, trees in which the branches rather than the nodes are labeled with symbols from an alphabet. They assume that the branches emanating from each node are ordered left to right by their labels and that no label occurs more than once. Lexicographic trees arise as tries.

Overmars and van Leeuwen consider matching a given lexicographic tree (the pattern) in a larger lexicographic tree (the subject). A match is an alignment of the pattern nodes with certain subject nodes. The alignment must respect the father–son relation in such a way that the branches emanating from a subject node are labeled with the same symbol as the corresponding pattern branches. Note that not all branches of a subject node need to be covered by corresponding pattern branches.

Their algorithms were discovered independently from our work. Their technique, like our Algorithm D, is based on Karp et al.'s idea of matching path strings. In the case of lexicographic trees, however, no branch numbers need to be interleaved in path strings. Overmars and van Leeuwen also use counters to coordinate the matches of path strings.

Their best algorithm does preprocessing of the pattern similar to ours, identifying for each path string the suffixes which are also path strings. They give the preprocessing in their own terminology, but it amounts essentially to the algorithms of [1]. Their best matching algorithm has the same worst-case time bound as our Algorithm D. Other algorithms given in [27] do little or no preprocessing of the pattern and have inferior bounds on the matching time.

We wish to stress that the approaches of Algorithm D, Overmars and van Leeuwen, and Lang et al. are inherently limited by using counters for deciding whether there is a match. As long as counters are used and incremented in steps of one up to the number of leaves of a pattern, a simple counting argument shows that the bound of Theorem 8.1 cannot be improved except by a constant factor. We see only two ways for improving this situation. Either means are found to increment counters in larger steps (or, equivalently, to smaller values) or a new method for coordinating path strings is used. The former would imply that recording of matches is delayed in some way. For the latter approach we can offer a solution which reduces the worst case bound to $O(subsize + match)$.

Assuming a machine model in which, in constant time, we can perform bit-string operations of union, intersection, and right shift by one position, we can improve Algorithm D as follows. We associate with each node n of the subject tree a bit string b_n in which the ith bit (from the right) is 1 iff every path from the ancestor of n at distance i, through n, to every descendant of n, has a prefix which is a path string of the pattern we wish to match. Note that we do not need to use bit strings longer than the height of the pattern. There is a match of the pattern at node n iff b_n has a 1 in the rightmost position.

Example 9.2. Consider the tree pattern $a(a(b(v), c), a(v, v))$. Assume we wish to match it in the subject fragment shown in Figure 11. We should assign the bit string 100 to node 3, since we have a match of the path string $a1a1b1$, and also to node 4, because of the path string $a1a2c$. Note that both path strings are of length 3. To node 5 the bit string 010 is assigned, because the two path strings a2a1 and $a2a2$ match, both of length 2. To node 2 we assign the bit string 010, since every path originating

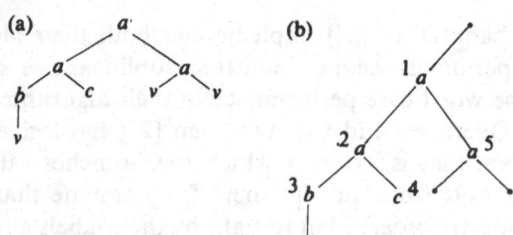

(a) **(b)**

FIG. 11. (a) Pattern. (b) Subject.

at node 1, the ancestor of node 2 at distance 1, and going through node 2 has a prefix which is a path string in the pattern. Note that 010 can be obtained as the right shift by one of $(100 \cap 100)$, the intersection of the two bitstrings assigned to the two sons of node 2. Node 1 will be assigned the bitstring 001. The 1 at the extreme right signals the presence of a pattern match. □

Note that in this example bit strings of length 3 are used, since the length of the longest path string in the pattern is 3. We need to explain how these bit strings can be computed. During preprocessing we associate with each accepting state s a bit string b_s in which the ith bit is 1 iff a path string of length i is accepted. By carefully considering the techniques of [1] we can design this preprocessing step to require $O(patsize)$ time at most.

Traverse the subject tree in preorder as before. When reaching a node for the first time in the traversal, initialize b_n to b_s, where s is the corresponding state in the matching automaton. Then, when coming to n for the last time, that is, after all subtrees have been visited, update b_n by

$$b_n := b_n \cup \bigcap_j \text{rightshift}(b_{\text{son}_j(n)}),$$

where rightshift means a shift by one bit position to the right, introducing 0 on the left. This method then has, as worst case, $O(subsize + match)$ time requirement for matching, since we eliminated the work of procedure Tabulate.

Note that we need not associate bit strings with nodes permanently: Upon completing the traversal of a subtree rooted in n, the bit strings associated with the sons of n are no longer needed. Thus we may keep all bit strings in the traversal stack (plus *rank* additional cells). Similarly, we could have reduced the space requirements for Algorithm D by keeping the counters on the traversal stack.

10. *Bottom-Up Matching with Bit-String Operations*

Since most computers allow unions, intersections, and complements of sets represented as bit strings to be performed in a small fixed number of instructions, we explore the possibility of representing match sets by bit strings and computing them directly at match time, thus avoiding the costly table generation of Section 6.

Let F be a pattern forest and PF the set of all subpatterns in F.

Definition 10.1.   Define the sets U_a for each a in the alphabet as follows;

$$U_a = \begin{cases} \{v\} & \text{if } a \text{ is nullary and not in } \text{PF}, \\ \{a, v\} & \text{if } a \text{ is nullary and in } \text{PF}, \\ \{t \text{ in PF} \mid t = a(t_1, \ldots, t_q)\} \cup \{v\} & \text{if } a \text{ is } q\text{-ary}, \quad q > 0. \end{cases}$$

Furthermore, define a set valued function on pattern sets by

$$\text{Father}_i(M) = \{t' \text{ in PF} \mid \text{son}_i(t') \text{ in } M\}.$$

176

We now recast Definition 4.2 as

Definition 10.2
(1) Match(a) $= U_a$ if a is nullary.
(2) Match $(a(t_1, \ldots, t_q)) = (U_a \cap \text{Father}_1(\text{Match}(t_1)) \cap \cdots \cap \text{Father}_q(\text{Match}(t_q)))$
     $\cup \{v\}$.

Part (2) says that the subpatterns which match at $a(t_1, \ldots, t_q)$ are exactly v plus those trees within U_a whose sons match the $t_1, \ldots, t_q$. A table for the sets U_a is easily precomputed in a single pass over the patterns in F in $O(patsize)$ time and $O(sym)$ additional space. Now, if we can find a simple way to compute $\text{Father}_i(M)$, we may assign match sets in bit-string form to each node of the subject in a simple postorder traversal of the subject tree.

A direct computation of $\text{Father}_i(M)$ seems to require a loop through all subpatterns. We suggest therefore a hashing approach. We precompute a hash table for all match sets and store $\text{Father}_i(M)$ for $1 \le i \le rank$ at the table entry for M. Such a table consumes $O((set/load) \times rank)$, where *load* is the loading factor of the hash table, compared to $O(set^{rank} \times sym)$ for the tables described in Section 4.

Given a hashing function for the M, the precomputation of $\text{Father}_i(M)$ in the most straightforward way takes time

$$O(set \times rank \times patsize).$$

In time $O(set \times patno)$ we can add to each entry M a list of indices i such that the entire pattern p_i is in M. This list allows us to detect matches immediately from the match sets. The only additional problem is how to choose a suitable hashing function. Since we deal with a fixed forest of tree patterns, we would like to derive "perfect" hashing functions [32], that is, hashing functions which have no collisions on the set of keys. For this, we offer two alternatives.

In the case of simple pattern forests, we take advantage of the results of Section 5, which showed that all match sets have singleton base sets. We enumerate the patterns in PF in increasing order of subsumption, for example, a depth-first numbering of G_S. In this way the base-set subpattern is always represented by the leftmost nonzero bit in the string representation of the set. Since different match sets have different base sets, they must have different numbers of leading zeros. Our hashing function now simply counts the leading bits, thereby achieving a perfect minimal hashing function. Note that a practical implementation of this is possible, since on most computers there is an instruction to normalize floating-point numbers, which involves counting leading zero bits.

For nonsimple forests the work of Sprugnoli can be used [32]. His algorithms derive a perfect hashing function using multiplication, addition, and division, but the function does not guarantee a high loading factor. Unfortunately, there is no analysis of his algorithms, so the exact space and time bounds are not known. Further research is needed to investigate whether there are special properties of match sets which lead to minimal perfect hashing functions which can be derived in a reasonable amount of time.

Bit-string representation of match sets offers another advantage. Recall that the number of match sets may be exponential in the pattern size. Therefore we should control the table size in those cases. This is possible with the following observation about the Father function:

$$\text{Father}_i(M_1 \cup M_2) = \text{Father}_i(M_1) \cup \text{Father}_i(M_2).$$

TABLE II. SPACE AND TIME COMPLEXITIES FOR PREPROCESSING AND MATCHING TECHNIQUES

Method	Restrictions	Preprocessing time	Matching time	Preprocessing space	Matching space excluding space occupied by output
Naive algorithm	None	None	$O(subsize \times patsize)$	None	$O(subsize + patsize)$
Bottom up with naive preprocessing	None	$O(set^{rank+1} \times sym \times patsize)$	$O(subsize + match)$	$O(set^{rank} \times sym)$	$O(subsize + set^{rank} \times sym)$
Bottom up with Algorithms A and B	Simple pattern forest	$O(patsize^2 \times rank + ht \times sym \times patsize^{rank})$	$O(subsize + match)$	$O(patsize^{rank} \times sym)$	$O(subsize + patsize^{rank} \times sym)$
Bottom up with Algorithm C	Simple binary forest	$O(patsize \times ht^2)$	$O(subsize \times ht^2 + match)$	$O(patsize^2)$	$O(subsize + patsize^2)$
Top down with *Algorithm D*	Patterns are full trees	$O(patsize)$	$O(subsize \times patno)$	$O(patsize)$	$O(subsize \times patno + patsize)$
	None	$O(patsize)$	$O(subsize \times suf)$	$O(patsize)$	$O(subsize \times patno + patsize)$
	Uniform cost for bit-string operations	$O(patsize)$	$O(subsize + match)$	$O(patsize^2)$	$O(subsize \times patsize + patsize^2)$
Bottom up, fixed hashing	Uniform cost for bit-string operations	$O(set \times (rank \times patsize + patno))$	$O(subsize + match)$ (average) $O(subsize \times set)$ (worst case)	$O((set/load) \times (rank + patno) + sym)$	$O(subsize + (set/load) \times (rank + patno) + sym)$
Bottom up, perfect hashing	Uniform cost for bit-string operations	Simple forest: $O(set \times (rank \times patsize + patno))$ General case: ?	$O(subsize + match)$	Simple forest: $O(set \times (rank + patno) + sym)$	$O(subsize + (set/load) \times (rank + patno) + sym)$
Bottom up with partitioned bit strings where $set \approx 2^{patsize}$	Uniform cost for bit-string operations	$O(part \times 2^{patsize/part} \times (rank \times patsize + patno))$	$O(subsize \times part + match)$ (average) $O(subsize \times part \times 2^{patsize/part})$ (worst case)	$O(part \times 2^{patsize/part}/load \times (rank + patno) + sym)$	$O(subsize + part \times 2^{patsize/part}/load \times (rank + patno) + sym)$

Thus we may partition the set PF into a fixed, chosen number *part* of blocks $P_1, \ldots, P_{part}$ and represent each match set M by the tuple,

$$\langle M \cap P_1, M \cap P_2, \ldots, M \cap P_{part} \rangle.$$

Then (1) and (2) of Definition 10.2 become

(1') $\mathrm{Match}(a) \cap P_j = U_a \cap P_j$.

(2') $\mathrm{Match}(a(t_1, \ldots, t_q)) \cap P_j = (U_a \cap \{\bigcup_{k=1}^{part} \mathrm{Father}_1(\mathrm{Match}(t_1)) \cap P_k\} \cap \cdots \cap \{\bigcup_{k=1}^{part} \mathrm{Father}_q(\mathrm{Match}(t_q)) \cap P_k\} \cup \{v\}) \cap P_j$.

For the analysis, let set_i be the number of match set segments in the ith partition block P_i:

$$set_i = |\{\mathrm{Match}(t) \cap P_i \,|\, t \text{ in } S\}|.$$

We can then express the table size as

$$O\left(\frac{set_1 + \cdots + set_{part}}{load \times (rank + part)} \right),$$

and the matching time as $O(subsize \times part + match)$.

For the case where *set* is nearly $2^{patsize}$ and the partition sizes $|P_i|$ are each approximately equal, that is, *patsize/part*, the table size may be expressed as

$$O\left(\frac{part}{load} \times 2^{patsize/part} \times (rank + patno) \right).$$

This formula gives a good idea of the space–time trade-off involved. Given a set of patterns, the problem of choosing a good partition is as yet unexplored. Since it may lead to a clique problem (Theorem 4.3), it can perhaps only be approximated.

11. *Conclusions*

Table II summarizes the time and space complexities for the preprocessing and matching techniques we have discussed. The trade-offs are so complex that we cannot choose an all-round best method. Each of the techniques offers some strengths and has certain weaknesses.

As in the case of sorting, users of tree-matching algorithms must choose a strategy carefully, on the basis of special properties of the patterns and subjects involved, the number of different subjects expected (and their relationship, if any) for the same set of patterns, and the available time and space resources.

We note that our top-down algorithm is always better than the one of Karp et al. [18] and as good as the one of Overmars and van Leeuwen [27], although they have a different notion of matching in mind. It is only in especially space-limited situations that the naive matching algorithm should be chosen. The version of Lang et al. [24] might be an interesting alternative, but further experimentation seems necessary to understand better what practical advantages it has to offer.

For the quickest matching time, the bottom-up algorithm, driven by tables, is best. We have used it in our interpreter generator and feel that for this application, the additional matching speed justifies the added preprocessing time, as long as the table size stays reasonable. Our experience with the algorithm is confirmed by the work in [10]. When too many match sets are expected, we suggest the bit-string and hash-table methods which trade off space and time very flexibly.

(Note. References [5, 19] are not cited in the text.)

1. AHO, A.V., AND CORASICK, M.J. Efficient string matching: An aid to bibliographic search. *Commun. ACM 18*, 6 (June 1975), 333–340.
2. AHO, A.V., HOPCROFT, J.E., AND ULLMAN, J.D. *The Design and Analysis of Computer Algorithms.* Addison-Wesley, Reading, Mass., 1974.
3. BAXTER, L.D. The complexity of unification. Ph.D. Dissertation, Dep. of Computer Science, Univ. of Waterloo, Waterloo, Ontario, Canada, 1976.
3a. BERRY, G., AND LÉVY, J.-J. Minimal and optimal computations of recursive programs. 4th ACM Symp. on Principles of Programming Languages, Los Angeles, Calif., 1977, pp. 215–226.
4. BOYER, R.S., AND MOORE, J.S. A fast string searching algorithm. *Commun. ACM 20*, 10 (Oct. 1977), 762–772.
5. CARTER, J.L., AND WEGMAN, M.N. Universal classes of hashing functions. Proc. 9th Ann. Symp. on Theory of Computing, Boulder, Colo., 1977, pp. 106–112.
6. CHEW, P. An improved algorithm for computing with equations. Proc. 21st IEEE Symp. on Foundations of Computer Science, Syracuse, N.Y., 1980, pp. 108–117.
7. COLLINS, G. The SAC-1 system: An introduction and survey. Proc. 2nd ACM Conf on Symbolic and Algebraic Manipulation, Los Angeles, Calif., 1971, pp. 144–152.
8. COMMENTZ-WALTER, B. A string matching algorithm fast on the average. In *Automata, Languages and Programming*, Lecture Notes in Computer Science 71, H. A. Maurer, Ed., Springer-Verlag, Berlin, Heidelberg, New York, 1979, pp. 118–132.
9. DOWNEY, P.J., SAMET, H., AND SETHI, R. Off-line and on-line algorithms for deducing equalities. Proc. 5th Ann. ACM Symp. on Principles of Programming Languages, Tucson, Ariz., 1978, pp. 158–170.
10. GLASNER, I., MONCKE, U., AND WILHELM, R. OPTRAN, a language for the specification of program transformations. 6th G.I. Fachtagung uber Programmiersprachen, Darmstadt, W. Germany, 1980; to appear in Lecture Notes in Computer Science.
11. GOGUEN, J.A. Some design principles and theory for Obj-0. Proc Int. Conf. on Mathematical Studies of Information Processing, Kyoto, Japan, 1978, pp. 429–475.
12. GUTTAG, J., HOROWITZ, E., AND MUSSER, D. Abstract data types and software validation. ISI Rep. 76-48, Univ. of Southern California, Los Angeles, Calif., 1976.
13. GUTTAG, J.V., HOROWITZ, E., AND MUSSER, D.R. Abstract data types and software validation. *Commun. ACM 21*, 12 (Dec. 1978), 1048–1064.
14. HOFFMANN, C.M., AND O'DONNELL, M.J. An interpreter generator using tree pattern matching. Proc. 6th Ann. ACM Symp. on Principles of Programming Languages, San Antonio, Texas, 1979, pp. 169–179.
15. HOFFMANN, C.M., AND O'DONNELL, M.J. Programming with equations. *ACM Trans. Prog. Lang. Syst. 4*, 1 (Jan. 1982).
16. HUET, G., AND LANG, B. Proving and applying program transformations expressed with second order patterns. Tech. Rep. 266, IRIA Laboria, LeChesnay, France, 1977.
17. HUET, G., AND LEVY, J.-J. Call by need computations in nonambiguous linear term rewriting systems. Tech. Rep. 359, IRIA Laboria, LeChesnay, France, 1979.
18. KARP, R., MILLER, R.E., AND ROSENBERG, A. Rapid identification of repeated patterns in strings, trees and arrays. Proc 4th Ann. ACM Symp. on Theory of Computing, Denver, Colo., 1972, pp. 125–136.
19. KNUTH, D. *The Art of Computer Programming, Vol. 3: Sorting and Searching.* Addison-Wesley, Reading, Mass., 1973.
20. KNUTH, D., AND BENDIX, P. Simple word problems in universal algebras. In *Computational Problems in Abstract Algebra*, J. Leech, Ed., Pergamon Press, Elmsford, N.Y., 1970, pp. 263–297.
21. KNUTH, D., MORRIS, J., AND PRATT, V. Fast pattern matching in strings. *SIAM J. Comput. 6*, 2 (1977), 323–350.
22. KOZEN, D. Complexity of finitely presented algebras. Proc 9th Ann. ACM Symp. on Theory of Computing, Boulder, Colo., 1977, pp. 164–177.
23. KRON, H. Tree templates and subtree transformational grammars. Ph.D. Dissertation, Univ. of California, Santa Cruz, Calif., 1975.
24. LANG, H.-W., SCHIMMLER, M., AND SCHMECK, H. Matching tree patterns sublinear on the average. Tech. Rep., Dep. of Informatik, Univ. Kiel, Kiel, W. Germany, 1980.
25. NELSON, G., AND OPPEN, D. Fast decision procedures based on congruence closure. *J. ACM 27*, 2 (April 1980), 356–364.
26. O'DONNELL, M.J. Computing in systems described by equations. In *Computing and Systems De-*

180

scribed by Equations, Lecture Notes in Computer Science 58, G. Goos and J. Hartmanis, Eds., Springer–Verlag, 1977.

27. OVERMARS, M.H., AND VAN LEEUWEN, J.   Rapid subtree identification revisited. Tech. Rep. CS-79-3, Univ. of Utrecht, Utrecht, Netherlands, 1979.

28. PATERSON, M.S., AND WEGMAN, M.   Linear unification. Proc. 8th ACM Symp. on Theory of Computing, Hershey, Pa., 1976, pp. 181–186.

29. ROBINSON, J.A.   A machine-oriented logic based on the resolution principle. *J. ACM 12*, 1 (Jan. 1965), 23–41.

30. ROSEN, B.   Tree-manipulating systems and Church–Rosser theorems. *J. ACM 20*, 1 (Jan. 1973), 160–187.

31. SHOSTAK, R.E.   An algorithm for reasoning about equality. *Commun. ACM 21*, 7 (July 1978), 583–585.

32. SPRUGNOLI, R.   Perfect hashing functions: A single probe retrieving method for static sets. *Commun. ACM 20*, 11 (Nov. 1977), 841–850.

33. STAFFORD, G.   Structure of the Eh compiler. Master's Thesis, Dep. of Computer Science, Univ. of Waterloo, Waterloo, Ontario, Canada, 1977.

34. WAND, M.   Algebraic theories and tree rewriting systems. Tech. Rep. 66, Dep. of Computer Science, Indiana Univ., Bloomington, Ind., 1977.

RECEIVED MARCH 1979; REVISED NOVEMBER 1980; ACCEPTED DECEMBER 1980

Code Generation Using Tree Matching and Dynamic Programming

ALFRED V. AHO
AT&T Bell Laboratories
MAHADEVAN GANAPATHI
Stanford University
and
STEVEN W. K. TJIANG
AT&T Bell Laboratories

Reprinted from *ACM Transactions on Programming Languages and Systems*, Volume 11, No. 4, October 1989, pp. 491-516. Copyright 1989, Association for Computing Machinery, Inc., reprinted by permission.

Compiler–component generators, such as lexical analyzer generators and parser generators, have long been used to facilitate the construction of compilers. A tree-manipulation language called *twig* has been developed to help construct efficient code generators. *Twig* transforms a tree-translation scheme into a code generator that combines a fast top-down tree-pattern matching algorithm with dynamic programming. *Twig* has been used to specify and construct code generators for several experimental compilers targeted for different machines.

Categories and Subject Descriptors: D.3.4 [**Programming Languages**]: Processors—*code generation, compilers, optimization compiler generators*; F.2.2 [**Analysis of Algorithms and Problem Complexity**]: Nonnumerical Algorithms and Problems—*pattern matching*; F.4.2 [**Mathematical Logic and Formal Languages**]: Grammars and Other Rewriting Systems—*parallel rewriting systems*

General Terms: Algorithms

Additional Key Words and Phrases: Code generation, code generator-generator, code optimization, dynamic programming, pattern matching

---

1. INTRODUCTION

Research in code generation has yielded theoretical insights and practical techniques [7, 21, 37]. On the theoretical front, efficient algorithms for generating provably optimal code on broad classes of uniform-register machines have been developed for expressions with no common subexpressions [3, 40]. However, once common subexpressions are encountered or optimal code needs to be generated for machines with irregular architectures, the problem of optimal code generation

---

Authors' current addresses: A. V. Aho, AT&T Bell Laboratories, 600 Mountain Avenue, Murray Hill, N.J. 07974; M. Ganapathi and S. W. K. Tjiang, Stanford University, Department of Computer Science, Stanford, CA 94305.

has been proven to be combinatorially difficult [4, 10], and heuristic techniques for generating good code have been proposed and theoretically analyzed [4, 5].

On the experimental front, several innovative approaches to retargetable code generation have been pursued. These approaches have focused on the use of table-driven techniques to separate the machine description from the code-generation algorithm. Compilers based on some of these techniques have been easily retargeted [11, 13, 17, 25, 32, 46].

This paper presents a new language called *twig* that encapsulates some of these theoretical and experimental advances into a tree-based notation for describing and implementing code generators. The language builds on the experience of grammar-based descriptions of code generators. A compiler for *twig* has been constructed that combines an efficient tree-pattern matching algorithm along with a dynamic programming algorithm for optimal code selection. *Twig* has been used by the authors to construct several code generators, including one for the VAX that has been incorporated into the `pcc2` compiler [32] and one for the MIPS-X project [12]. *Twig* has also been used by A. W. Appel to construct code generators for the VAX and the Motorola 68020 [9]. In addition to producing traditional code generators for compilers, *twig* can be used as a tool for creating tree-rewriting and tree-manipulation programs. In this vein, K. Keutzer and W. Wolf have used *twig* to construct a standard-cell synthesizer for VLSI circuits [33, 34].

2. CODE GENERATION BY TREE REWRITING

Simply speaking, a compiler consists of a front end that analyzes the source program and transforms it into an intermediate representation (IR), and a back end that transforms the IR into the target program [7]. Many factors are involved in choosing an appropriate IR, but in most cases the IR is some encoding of a graphical representation of the source program. In this paper, it is sufficient to assume the IR is a sequence of trees at the semantic level of the target machine as in [18, 23, 29].

Figure 1 shows an IR tree for an assignment statement a [i] := b in which a and i are locals, stored on the stack, whose run-time addresses are given as offsets, $const_a$ and $const_i$, from a stack pointer stored in register SP. The leaves in the tree are type attributes with subscripts; the subscript indicates the value of the attribute.

The assignment to a [i] is an indirect assignment in which the contents of the location for a [i] are set to the *r*-value of the global b. The address of the first element of the array a is found by adding the value $const_a$ to the contents of register SP; the value of i is in the location obtained by adding the value $const_i$ to the contents of register SP.

In the tree, the ind operator makes its argument a memory address. As the left child of an assignment operator, the ind node gives the location into which the *r*-value on the right side of the assignment operator is to be stored. If an argument of a + or ind operator is a memory location or a register, then the contents of that memory location or register are taken as the value.

For code generation, the target-machine instructions can be represented by tree-rewriting rules, consisting of a replacement node, a tree template, a cost,

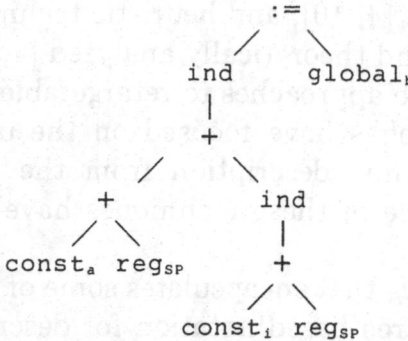

Fig. 1. Intermediate-code tree for a [i] := b.

and an action. The target code is generated by a process in which each IR tree is reduced into a single node by repeatedly finding subtrees in the IR tree that match templates and rewriting the matched subtrees by the corresponding replacement nodes. The sequence of subtrees rewritten in this process is called a *cover* of the IR tree. The target code is emitted by the actions associated with the rules used in the cover, and the total cost is the sum of the costs of the covering rules.

To be more precise, a tree-rewriting rule is a statement of the form

$$replacement \leftarrow template\ \{cost\} = \{action\}$$

where

(1) *replacement* is a single node,
(2) *template* is a tree,
(3) *cost* is a code fragment that computes the cost associated with this template, and
(4) *action* is a code fragment.

A set of tree-rewriting rules is called a *tree-translation scheme*.

A tree-translation scheme is a convenient way to represent the instruction-selection phase of code generation. Each tree template represents a computation performed by one or more target machine instructions. The leaves of a template are attributes with subscripts, as in the IR tree. Often, certain restrictions apply to the values of the subscripts in the templates. For example, a constant may be required to fall in a certain range. These restrictions can be specified as semantic predicates in the cost function or the action, and these predicates must be satisfied before a template can match a subtree of the IR tree. Register allocation is done by the user-specified actions.

As an example of a tree-rewriting rule, consider the rule for a register-to-register add instruction, ADD Rj, Ri:

$$reg_i \leftarrow \overset{+}{\diagup\diagdown}_{reg_i\quad reg_j}$$

If the IR tree contains a subtree that matches this tree template, that is, a subtree whose root is labeled by the operator + and whose left and right children are quantities in registers i and j, then we might replace that subtree by a single node

184

Table I. Tree-Rewriting Rules for Some Target-Machine Instructions

	Rewrite rule	Cost	Instruction
(1)	$\text{reg}_i \leftarrow \text{const}_c$	2	MOV #c, Ri
(2)	$\text{reg}_i \leftarrow \text{mem}_a$	2	MOV a, Ri
(3)	$\lambda \leftarrow$:= (mem_a, reg_i)	$2 + \text{cost.reg}_i$	MOV Ri, a
(4)	$\lambda \leftarrow$:= (ind (reg_i), global_b)	$2 + \text{cost.reg}_i$	MOV b, * Ri
(5)	$\text{reg}_i \leftarrow$ ind (+ (const_c, reg_j))	$2 + \text{cost.reg}_j$	MOV c(Rj), Ri
(6)	$\text{reg}_i \leftarrow$ + (reg_i, ind (+ (const_c, reg_j)))	$2 + \text{cost.reg}_i + \text{cost.reg}_j$	ADD c(Rj), Ri
(7)	$\text{reg}_i \leftarrow$ + (reg_i, reg_j)	$1 + \text{cost.reg}_i + \text{cost.reg}_j$	ADD Rj, Ri
(8)	$\text{reg}_i \leftarrow$ + (reg_i, const_1)	$1 + \text{cost.reg}_i$	INC Ri

labeled reg_i simulating the execution of the instruction ADD Rj, Ri. If more than one template can match a subtree or a portion thereof, then dynamic programming is used to determine a minimum-cost cover.

Table I contains tree-rewriting rules for a few instructions for a VAX-like target machine. Instead of showing the code for the actions, we have shown the machine instruction that is generated by each rule. The first two rules correspond to load instructions, the next two to store instructions, and the remainder to indexed loads and additions. Note that rule (8) requires the value of the constant to be 1. This condition can be enforced by a semantic predicate in the cost.

A tree-translation scheme generates code from an IR tree in the following way. All templates in the tree-rewriting rules are matched against the subtrees of the IR tree during a depth-first traversal of the tree. At each node, the costs are used to determine the best match, and the selected subtree is replaced in the IR tree by the associated replacement node. Sometimes the replacement is delayed until the cost of another larger including match can be evaluated. By this process a minimum-cost cover for the IR tree is found.

Then a second depth-first traversal of the original IR tree is made and the actions associated with the rules used in the cover are executed. If an action emits a sequence of target-machine instructions, the instructions become part of the output. The sequence of machine instructions thus generated constitutes the output of the tree-translation scheme.

To illustrate, let us use the tree-translation scheme in Table I to process the IR tree in Figure 1. The template of the first rule

$$reg_0 \leftarrow const_a$$

matches the leftmost leaf of the IR tree with $i = 0$ and $c = a$. If we use this rule, the label of the left-most leaf is changed from $const_a$ to reg_0, and during the second traversal the instruction MOV #a, R0 will be generated to load the constant a into register R0. The template of the seventh rule with $i = 0$ and $j = SP$

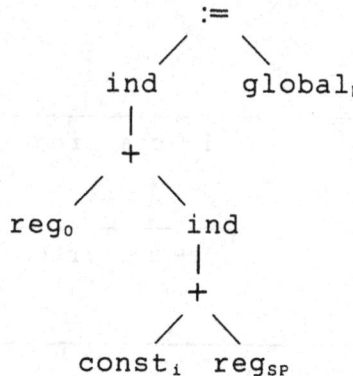

now matches the leftmost subtree with root labeled +. Using this rule, we would rewrite this subtree into a single node labeled reg_0 and later generate the instruction ADD SP, R0. Now the tree looks like

```
                    :=
                  /    \
               ind      global_b
                |
                +
              /   \
          reg_0    ind
                    |
                    +
                  /   \
             const_i  reg_SP
```

At this point, we could apply rule (5) to reduce the subtree

```
         ind
          |
          +
        /   \
   const_i   reg_SP
```

to a single node labeled reg_1. However, we can also use rule (6) to reduce the larger subtree

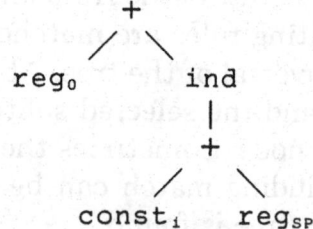

into a single node labeled reg_0 and later generate the instruction ADD i(SP), R0. Assuming it is more efficient to use a single instruction to compute the larger subtree rather than the smaller one, we choose the latter reduction to get

```
              :=
            /    \
        ind      global_b
         |
       reg_0
```

This remaining tree is matched by rule (4), which reduces the tree to a single node and later generates the instruction MOV b, * R0.

This sequence of tree reductions defines a covering that generates the following code sequence during the second traversal:

```
MOV #a, R0
ADD SP, R0
ADD i (SP), R0
MOV b, * R0
```

With a tree-translation scheme, specifying a code generator is similar to writing a syntax-directed specification for a translator. The tree-rewriting rules that describe the instruction set of a target machine are analogous to the productions of a context-free grammar, and the output code is generated as part of a tree-pruning process that is reminiscent of parsing. However, there are also several major differences. First, tree-pattern matching is used instead of parsing and there is no left-to-right bias in the matching algorithm as there is with some parsing algorithms. Second, a dynamic programming algorithm that runs concurrently with the tree-matching process selects an optimal covering for the IR tree using the costs associated with the tree-rewriting rules. Finally, the actions are executed after an optimal covering of the IR tree has been found.

3. PATTERN-DIRECTED CODE GENERATION

Wasilew [43] and Weingart [44] were among the first to treat code generation as a tree-rewriting process. These early approaches employed direct tree-pattern matching techniques. Fraser [15] and Cattell [11] emphasized the use of heuristic search; Fraser relied on knowledge-based rules that direct the pattern matching, whereas Cattell advocated a goal-directed heuristic search. In Cattell's approach, subgoals are created as the search continues and heuristics are used, both to order subgoal selection and to order patterns when trying to match.

Graham and Glanville pioneered the use of LR parsing techniques for code generation [22, 23]. A code generator can be constructed as syntax-directed translator in which a linearized prefix form of the IR trees is parsed by an LR parse built from a context-free grammar that describes the target machine. In this approach, the instructions of the target machine are described by a set of grammar rules. A parse of the prefix form of an IR tree corresponds to a covering of the tree with instruction templates. The target-machine instructions are generated during the reductions of the parsing process.

With the LR-parsing approach there are several practical difficulties that need to be overcome. First, an LR grammar describing a target machine such as a VAX can have over 1000 productions [26]. Machine-description grammars can produce large parser tables that may require specialized table-compression techniques [14]. Second, an LR parser does the pattern matching in a left-operand biased fashion. That is, the code for the left operand of an operator must be selected without considering the right operand. In a number of cases, the resulting code is suboptimal.

For example, consider the expression *op A B* that might appear in the prefix representation of an IR tree. Usually, machine architectures allow only certain combinations of addressing modes for the subexpressions *A* and *B*. Examples of these addressing-mode restrictions on op-code use are common in microprocessor architectures such as the iAPX-86, Z-8000, and MC-68000. If the addressing mode for *A* is selected without considering *B*, then the code generator may have to undo this selection when the time comes to select the machine instruction for *op*. Consequently, extra machine code would be needed to move *A* to an acceptable addressing mode.

Another problem in a purely syntactic approach is the difficulty of specifying target-machine architectural constraints such as register restrictions on addressing modes, of tracking expressions with results in multiple locations, and of modeling condition codes. A purely syntactic treatment requires this semantic information to be encoded syntactically as much as possible. Several tools and techniques have been developed to help cope with some of these difficulties [8, 26–29, 38].

Ganapathi and Fischer [17–20] extended the grammatical approach to code generation by using an attribute grammar to describe the instruction set of the target machine. Grammar productions specify the general form of the machine instructions, and semantic attributes and predicates specify architectural restrictions. Attributes are also used to track multiple instruction results and instruction selection is done by attributed parsing. Addressing modes are described by separate individual productions and so are operation codes. Addressing-mode selection is still left biased in the true tree-pattern matching sense, but the selection of operation codes is not biased toward any operand. Productions corresponding to operation codes usually have symmetric operand patterns. This symmetry enables the code generator to delay decisions regarding destination requirements. In effect, this decision is made on seeing the entire subtree for the operator. Thus, efficient code is produced in cases when either of the operands can be used to store the result of evaluation. Only in cases where their original results need be preserved is a call made to a register/temporary allocator.

Ganapathi and Fischer emphasize the incremental development of a code generator. Initially, productions describing the most general form of a target-language construct are listed. Later, special-case productions can be added to improve the performance of the target code [20]. To the scheme in Table I, for example, we could add rules to generate three-address instructions if desired. These special-case productions make the underlying grammar ambiguous. With ambiguous grammars, subsequent modifications can be made to a code generator with reduced effort. It is for this reason that ambiguous grammars are particularly useful in the design and specification of code generators. Deterministic parsers can be mechanically constructed from ambiguous specifications provided rules are provided to disambiguate the resulting parsing-action conflicts [6].

Attributes and semantic predicates can also be used to reduce the size of the specification of the addressing modes of the target machine. In an attribute grammar the number of grammar productions is usually smaller (a hundred or two productions instead of a thousand) than in a purely grammatical approach. Extensive grammar factoring is therefore not needed to implement a code generator based on semantic attributes and predicates, but care must now be given to the design of the attributes and predicates.

4. CODE GENERATION BY TREE MATCHING AND DYNAMIC PROGRAMMING

In this paper, we introduce a new language called *twig* for constructing code generators. A target machine is specified as a tree-translation scheme. *Twig* converts this specification into a code generator that combines a fast tree-pattern matching algorithm with an efficient dynamic programming algorithm for generating high-quality output code.

The underlying tree-matching algorithm is a generalization of Aho and Corasick's linear-time keyword-matching algorithm as suggested by Hoffman and O'Donnell [30]. The dynamic programming algorithm is a simplification of Aho and Johnson's optimal code-generation algorithm [3] that has been used in several compilers [32, 39]. This style of code generation can be readily integrated with the tree-matching process.

This approach seems to have several advantages. A *twig* machine specification is concise. With a tree-translation scheme, similar machine instructions can be factored into a common pattern, so that one syntactic match can correspond to several instructions. Rules that have the same templates but differing costs and actions can be factored into a single rule with multiple cost-action pairs. Similar factoring can be performed on rules in which only the operators differ. For example, a generic binary operator can often be defined to derive both the addition and subtraction instructions of a target machine. Since fewer patterns are needed, the description of the code generator is significantly simplified.

The dynamic programming algorithm allows the rules to be written in any order and obviates the need to deal with pattern-matching conflicts. In a parser-based approach the order of the productions is important, and parsing-action conflicts have to be carefully resolved. The dynamic programming algorithm produces code that is optimal with respect to the costs provided and eliminates the need for explicitly breaking cycles to prevent the code generator from looping, as may be necessary in a parser-based approach.

Finally, *twig* produces code generators quickly, and their size is small. For example, our *twig* specification of a VAX has 115 rules. It takes *twig* 5 seconds on a VAX 11/780 to produce the code generator from this specification, and the total size of the resulting code generator is under 50K bytes.

5. THE AHO–JOHNSON DYNAMIC PROGRAMMING ALGORITHM

Aho and Johnson [3] presented an algorithm based on the principle of dynamic programming to generate code for expressions on register machines. Their algorithm generates optimal code for a uniform-register machine that has r

interchangeable registers R0, R1, ..., Rr − 1 and instructions of the form
Ri := E, where E is any expression containing operators, registers, and memory
locations. The cost of a program is the sum of the costs of the instructions in the
program.

The dynamic programming algorithm partitions the problem of generating
optimal code for an expression E into subproblems of generating optimal code
for the subexpressions of E. An optimal program for an expression of the form
$E_1 + E_2$ is formed by combining optimal programs for the subexpressions E_1 and
E_2, in one or the other order, followed by code to evaluate the operator +. The
subproblems of generating optimal code for E_1 and E_2 are solved recursively. A
program produced by the dynamic programming algorithm has an important
property: It evaluates an expression "contiguously."

Consider the syntax tree T for the expression $E = E_1 \ op \ E_2$

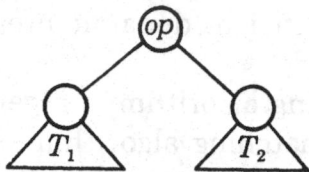

where T_1 and T_2 are trees for E_1 and E_2, respectively. We say a machine-language
program P evaluates T *contiguously* if it first evaluates those subtrees of T that
need to be computed into memory and then evaluates the remainder of T, either
in the order T_1, T_2, and then the root, or in the order T_2, T_1, and then the root,
in either case using the previously computed values from memory whenever
necessary. As an example of noncontiguous evaluation, P might first evaluate
part of T_1, leaving the value in a register (instead of memory), next evaluate T_2,
and then return to evaluate the rest of T_1.

For the uniform-register machine, Aho and Johnson proved that given any
machine-language program P to evaluate an expression tree T, there is a program
P' that computes the same expression such that

(1) P' is of no higher cost than P,

(2) P' uses no more registers than P, and

(3) P' evaluates the tree in a contiguous fashion.

This result implies that every expression tree can be evaluated optimally by a
contiguous program on a uniform-register machine [3].

Some real machines have architectural features that do not always allow
optimal contiguous evaluations. For example, for machines with even–odd register
pairs such as the IBM System/370 machines there are examples of expression
trees in which an optimal machine-language program must first evaluate into a
register a portion of the left subtree of the root, then a portion of the right
subtree, then another part of the left subtree, then another part of the right, and
so on. This type of unbounded oscillation is unnecessary for an optimal evaluation
of any expression tree using the uniform-register machine.

The contiguous evaluation property defined above says that for any expression
tree T there always exists an optimal program that consists of optimal programs
for subtrees of the root, followed by an instruction to evaluate the root. This

property allows us to use dynamic programming to generate an optimal program for T.

The dynamic programming algorithm as presented in [3] proceeds in three phases. In the first phase, it computes bottom-up for each node n of the expression tree T an array C of costs, in which the ith component $C[i]$ is the optimal cost of computing the subtree S rooted at n into a register, assuming i registers are available for the computation, for $1 \leq i \leq r$. The cost includes whatever loads and stores are necessary to evaluate S in the given number of registers. It also includes the cost of computing the operator at the root of S. The zeroth component of the cost vector is the optimal cost of computing the subtree S into memory. The contiguous evaluation property ensures that an optimal program for S can be generated by considering combinations of optimal programs only for the subtrees of the root of S. This restriction sharply reduces the number of cases that need to be considered.

To compute $C[i]$ at node n, the algorithm considers each machine instruction R $:= E$ whose expression E matches the subexpression rooted at node n. By examining the cost vectors at the corresponding descendants of n, it determines the costs of evaluating the operands of E. For those operands of E that are registers, it considers all possible orders in which the corresponding subtrees of T can be evaluated into registers. In each ordering, the first subtree corresponding to a register operand can be evaluated using i available registers, the second using $i - 1$ registers, and so on. To account for node n, it adds in the cost of the instruction R $:= E$ that was used to match node n. The value $C[i]$ is then the minimum cost over all possible orders.

The cost vectors for the entire tree T can be computed bottom-up in time linearly proportional to the number of nodes in T. The smallest cost in the vector for the root of T gives the minimum cost of evaluating T.

In the second phase, the algorithm traverses T, using the cost vectors to determine which subtrees of T must be computed into memory. In the third phase, the algorithm traverses each tree using the cost vectors and associated instructions to generate the final target code. The code for the subtrees computed into memory locations is generated first. These two phases can also be implemented to run in time linearly proportional to the size of the expression tree. See Aho and Johnson [3] and Aho et al. [7] for more details.

Twig uses a simplified form of this algorithm. In the compilers so far implemented with *twig*, the IR trees have been sufficiently simple that it was possible to separate register management from instruction selection. Consequently, *twig* uses an algorithm in which each subtree of the IR tree is characterized by a single scalar cost, rather than a cost vector. These scalar costs are computed using the cost expressions in the tree-translation scheme. Register assignment is done separately by a user-provided routine. These modifications have increased the speed and flexibility of *twig* without noticeably degrading the quality of the code generated for the VAX. More research is needed to determine how generally these observations apply to other machines.

6. TREE-PATTERN MATCHING

Several tree-pattern matching algorithms have been presented [30, 31, 35, 36, 41]. For code generation applications, a scheme proposed by Hoffman and

O'Donnell [30] appears promising. They suggested that template matching can be done efficiently by extending the Aho–Corasick multiple-keyword pattern-matching algorithm [1] into a top-down tree-pattern matching algorithm.

First consider the problem of finding all substrings of an input string that are contained in a given set of keywords. The essence of the Aho–Corasick algorithm is to construct a trie from the set of keywords, convert the trie into a pattern-matching automaton, and then use the pattern-matching automaton to perform a parallel search for the keywords in the input string.

Let K be the set of keywords. The trie is built by first making a root node and then, for each keyword in K, creating a path from the root to a node whose branch labels spell out the keyword. Each node of the trie is thus uniquely characterized by the sequence of symbols on the branch labels of the path from the root to that node.

The pattern-matching automaton is constructed from the trie. The states of the automaton are the nodes of the trie; the start state is the root and the accepting states are those corresponding to complete keywords. There is a transition from state s to state t on input character c if there is a branch in the trie labeled c from node s to node t. In addition, we add a transition from the start state to itself on every input character that is not the first character of a keyword.

The pattern-matching automaton has a failure function for every state other than the start state. The failure function for a state characterized by a string u is a pointer to the state characterized by the longest prefix of some keyword in K that is also a proper suffix of u.

Both the trie and the pattern-matching automaton can be constructed in time linearly proportional to the sum of the lengths of the keywords in K. The resulting pattern-matching automaton can be run on an input string x in time linearly proportional to the length of x, independent of the size of K. Thus the entire problem of finding all substrings of x that are contained in K can be done in time $O(|K| + |x|)$ [1].

This algorithm can be directly generalized into a tree-matching algorithm by noting that a tree is characterized by the set of paths from its root to its leaves when the branches from each node are numbered $1, 2, \ldots$, according to the left-to-right ordering of the children [30]. For example, consider the following three tree-replacement rules

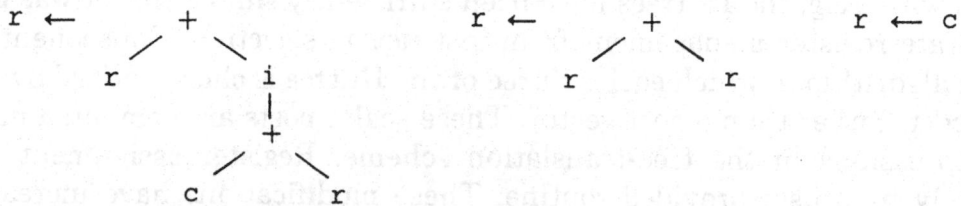

which we will refer to as t_1, t_2, and t_3, respectively. They have the following set of path strings:

```
+1r
+2i1+1c
+2i1+2r
+2r
c
```

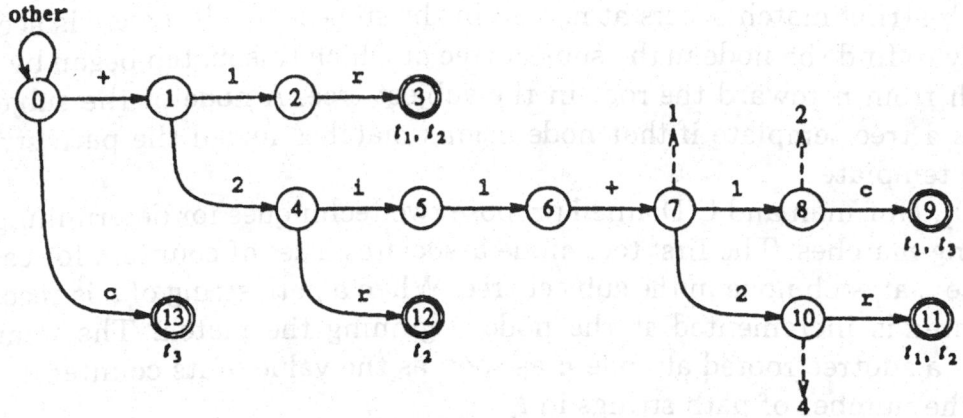

Fig. 2. Path-string-matching automaton.

The first string $+1r$ represents the leftmost path in the tree templates of both t_1 and t_2. Note that a path of length j in t_i is represented by a path string of length $2j + 1$. From the set of path strings, using the methods in Aho and Corasick [1], we can construct a pattern-matching automaton to match the path strings in parallel.

From the trees above, we would construct the pattern-matching automaton shown in Figure 2. State 0 is the start state and the doubly circled states are accepting. In this automaton the failure function for state 7 points to state 1, for state 8 to state 2, for state 10 to state 4, and for all the other states to state 0; the failure functions that do not point to state 0 are shown as dashed lines. At each accepting state, we also know which path string of which tree templates has been recognized. For example, at state 3, the recognized string $+1r$ matches the leftmost path in the tree templates of t_1 and t_2.

Let T be a set of tree-replacement rules of the form $l_i \leftarrow t_i$, where l_i is a label and t_i a tree template. We can build an automaton similar to the one above to recognize the tree templates in T in parallel in a subject tree. Let $succ(\sigma, a)$ denote the state reached from state σ on input symbol a by the automaton. The automaton creates a record of information at each node n of the subject tree: $n.parent$ is the parent of n, $n.symbol$ is a path-string symbol associated with n, and $n.state$ is the state of the automaton after it visits n. We assume that nodes in the subject tree and the tree templates labeled by the same symbol have the same arity. The following routine, $visit(n)$, will traverse the subject tree in depth-first order starting at node n, assign a state to each node, and call $post\_process$ to determine the matching tree templates.

```
visit(n)
{
   if n is the root then
      n.state ← succ(0, n.symbol)
         where 0 is the start state of the automaton
   else
      n.state ← succ(succ(n.parent.state, k), n.symbol)
         where n is the kth child of n.parent
   for every child c of n do
      visit(c)
   post_process(n)
}
```

193

A path-string match occurs at node n in the subject tree if $n.state$ is accepting. It is easy to find the node in the subject tree at which this match began by tracing the path from n toward the root in the subject tree. A node of the subject tree matches a tree template if that node begins matches for all the path strings in the tree template.

In [30], Hoffman and O'Donnell propose two techniques for determining nodes beginning matches. The first technique associates a set of counters for each tree template t_i at each node in the subject tree. When a path string of t_i is recognized, its counter is incremented at the node beginning the match. The template t_i matches a subtree rooted at node n as soon as the value of its counter at node n equals the number of path strings in t_i.

Twig uses the second technique of maintaining bit strings rather than counters to keep track of partial matches. With each node n in the subject tree *twig* associates a bit string $n.b_i$ for each tree template t_i. The number of bits in b_i is equal to one plus the length of the longest path in t_i; the bits of b_i are indexed consecutively from the right starting with 0. When a path string in t_i of length $2j + 1$ is recognized at node n in the subject tree, bit j of $n.b_i$ is set. Intuitively, if bit j of $n.b_i$ is set, then node n in the subject tree matches a node at depth j in tree template t_i. (The root of a tree is at depth 0.) Bit strings allow overlapping matches to the same tree template to be recorded.

Tree recognition occurs in the call of *post_process* after all the children of a node have been visited (see the function *visit* above). At each node n, the new bit string $n.b_i$ is computed by shifting the bit strings for t_i at the children of n right 1 bit (this is equivalent to dividing by 2) and bitwise or'ing their logical product with the current bit string $n.b_i$. The intuition is that node n of the subject tree matches a node of t_i at depth j if the label of n matches the node of t_i and all of n's children match the nodes of t_i at depth $j + 1$. Under the assumption of matching arities of similarly labeled nodes, this method provides a necessary and sufficient condition for tree matching. The following routine gives the details of the tree-matching process.

```
post_process(n)
{
    n.b_i ← 0
    if n.state is accepting then
        set_partial(n, n.state)
    for every t_i do
        n.b_i ← n.b_i or ∏_{c∈C(n)} c.b_i/2
            where C(n) is the set of all children of node n
    do_reduce(n)
}

set_partial(n, σ)
{
    for each path string of t_i of length 2j + 1 recognized at σ do
        n.b_i ← n.b_i or 2^j
}
```

The routine *do_reduce* keeps track of reductions, which are discussed in the following paragraphs. The routine *set_partial* sets the jth bit of b_i for each recognized path string of t_i of length $2j + 1$; *set_partial* requires the length of the recognized path strings to be available at the accepting states. After *post_process*,

t_i matches the subtree rooted at node r if and only if $r.b_i$ is odd, that is, its rightmost bit is set to 1.

To find a cover, it is necessary to consider reductions. That is, once the tree part of t_i is recognized, the possible reduction of the tree part to the label of t_i must be considered in order to find covers containing this match of t_i. Since *twig* is considering many matches in parallel, the process of reduction should not change the shape of the subject tree; only some node fields are updated to reflect the reduction. The routine *do_reduce* performs the updates and implements dynamic programming.

The function $cost(t_i, n)$ determines the cost of a rule t_i matching at node n. In general, the cost of a match will also depend on the costs of matches at leaves of t_i that are label symbols. The dynamic programming costs are kept in an array $n.cost$. Each element $n.cost[l]$ is the cost of the cheapest match of some rule $l \leftarrow tree$. The index of the rule that achieves $n.cost[l]$ is stored in $n.match[l]$; that is, if $n.match[l] = j$, then $cost(t_j, n) = n.cost[l]$ and $l = l_j$. Initially, before the first call of *visit*, $n.cost[l] = \infty$ and $n.match[l] = 0$ for all nodes n.

```
do_reduce(n)
{
    for every t_i such that the zeroth bit of n.b_i is 1 do
        if cost(t_i, n) < n.cost[l_i] then
        {
            n.cost[l_i] ← cost(t_i, n)
            n.match[l_i] ← i
            if n is the root then
                σ ← succ(0, l_i)
            else
                σ ← succ(succ(n.parent.state, k), l_i)
                    where n is the kth child of n.parent
            if σ is an accept state then
                set_partial(n, σ)
        }
}
```

For example, consider the rule set $T = \{t_1, t_2, t_3\}$ as given at the beginning of this section. At each node n, let the cost function be

$cost(t_1, n) = 3 +$ cost of matches at leaves labeled r
$cost(t_2, n) = 1 +$ cost of matches at leaves labeled r
$cost(t_3, n) = 1.$

Consider the subject tree S:

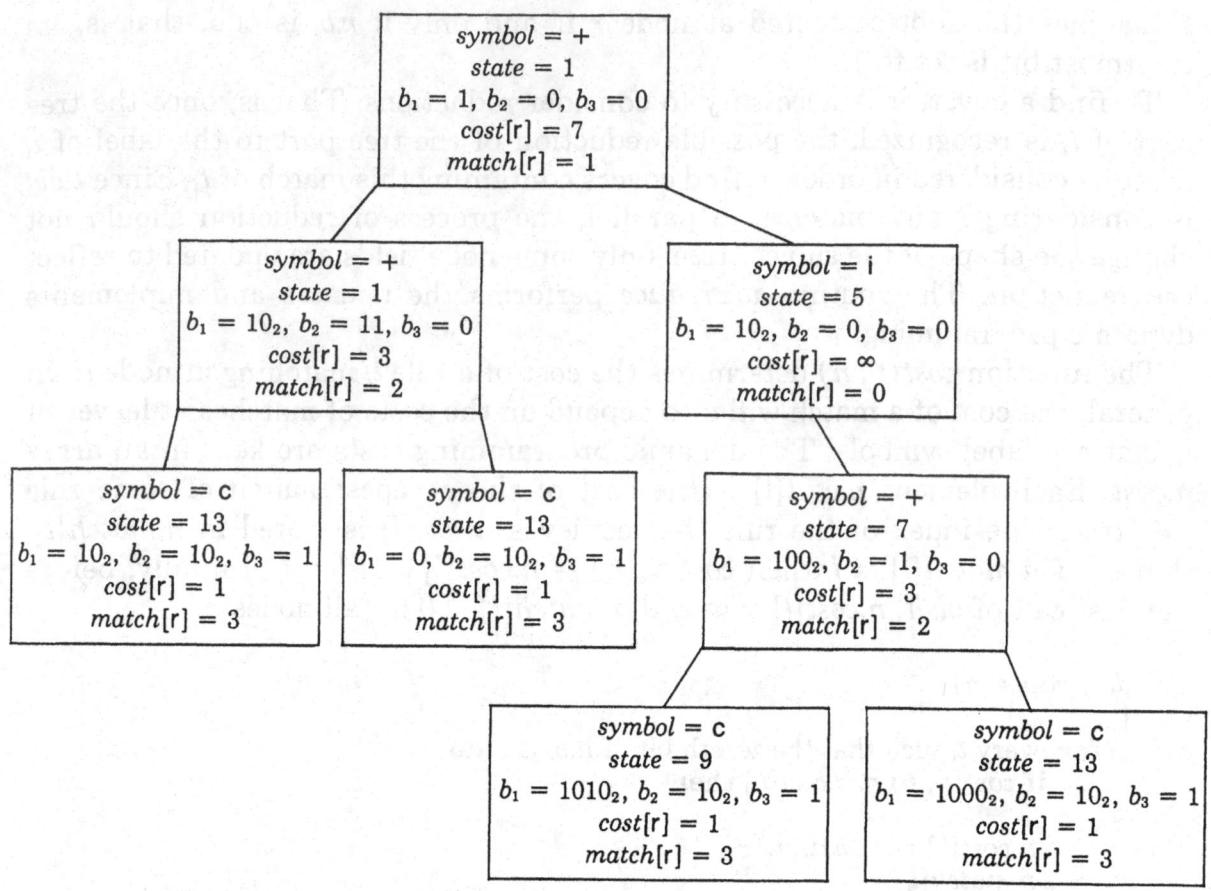

Fig. 3.   An algorithm that finds matches not included in any cover.

Applying *visit* to the root of S yields the values at each node shown in Figure 3. The subscript 2 on the values of the b_i denotes "binary string."

In Figure 3, we see that the only cover starts with rule t_1 at the root and has cost seven.

The algorithm finds matches that are not included in any cover. For example, at the node with symbol + on the right branch of the root, the tree pattern t_2 matches with cost three. The cover is shown below in a form reminiscent of a parse tree with arrows indicating reductions.

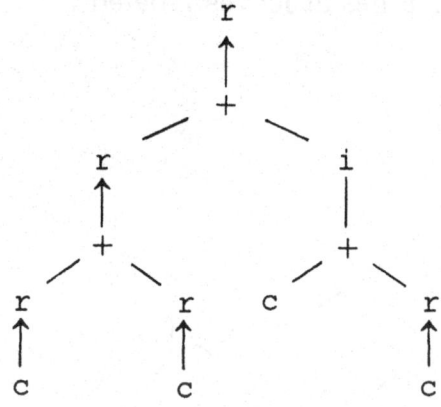

7. TWIG—A LANGUAGE FOR MANIPULATING TREES

Twig is a language for processing trees that incorporates the algorithms described above. Although *twig* can be used in other tree-manipulation contexts, this section only presents its use in code generation. For other applications of *twig*, see Keutzer [33] and Keutzer and Wolf [34].

A *twig* program, hereafter called a *twig* specification, is a set of pattern-action rules together with ancillary declarative statements. To construct the *twig* portion of a code generator, we compile the *twig* specification with the *twig* compiler to create a C source file. This file will contain a subroutine that performs the matching operation. Once it has been compiled, the subroutine can be linked with the *twig* runtime library and the other parts of the code generator. To invoke the pattern matcher, we call the generated subroutine on the root of the tree to be matched. In the following sections, this tree is referred to as the subject tree.

Pattern-Action Rules

The syntax of a rule in *twig* is

$$label\_id : pattern [\{cost\}] [= \{action\}]$$

(1) The *label_id* is an identifier that is analogous to the left-hand nonterminal symbol of a production in a context-free grammar.

(2) The *pattern* is a parenthesized prefix expression representing a tree. The pattern matcher will find all subtrees of the subject tree matching this tree pattern. When a subtree matches the pattern and the cost part does not abort, we say that the rule *matches*. Abortion is explained later.

(3) The *cost* is C source code executed by the pattern matcher when it finds a subtree matching the tree pattern. This code should return a cost to the matcher for purposes of dynamic programming. The code also determines when the action part should be called by the pattern matcher if this rule is in the minimal cost cover of the subject tree.

The cost part is optional. When omitted, the *twig* compiler and pattern matcher assume the default cost is returned. The default cost is specified elsewhere in the *twig* specification.

(4) Like the cost part, the *action* is also C source code. The code is called by the matcher once it has been determined that this rule is part of the minimal cost cover. The code may return a tree to replace the subtree matching this rule. If no return value is given, then the subtree is left unchanged. The action part may also perform other functions, such as emitting code and updating code generator data structures.

The action part is also optional. If the action is missing, the default action is to leave the subtree unchanged.

Tree Patterns

Tree patterns are written in parenthesized prefix form and can be described by the following BNF:

```
pattern ← node_id
pattern ← label_id
pattern ← node_id(subtree_list)
subtree_list ← pattern
subtree_list ← pattern, subtree_list
```

That is to say, a tree pattern is written with its root identifier, followed by an optional parenthesized list representing the subtrees of the root in order from left to right. For example,

```
identifier
op(left, right)
plus(expr, times(constant, expr))
```

are all tree patterns.

As the BNF above suggests, there are two types of identifiers in *twig*, *node_ids* and *label_ids*, corresponding to the terminals and nonterminals of tree patterns. A *node_id* denotes an internal node or leaf while a *label_id* forms the label part of a rule. Each of the *node_ids* and *label_ids* is assigned a unique integer by *twig*. The identifier-to-integer mapping is provided in a generated source file. During pattern matching, *twig* will call a user-supplied function `mtValue(n)` that returns the integer corresponding to the symbol of node n.

Leaves of a pattern with *label_ids* are called labeled leaves. The textually leftmost labeled leaf is first, the next second, and so on. Labeled leaves play a special role as they represent rules matching subtrees rooted at their position just as nonterminals stand for reductions of substrings in context-free grammars. For example, the subject tree given in the example at the end of Section 6 can be written as

```
plus(plus(c, c), i(plus(c, c)))
```

and the rules t_1, t_2, and t_3 are written as

```
r: plus(r, i(plus(c, r)));
r: plus(r, r);
r: c;
```

respectively. The symbol `plus` is used instead of + because the latter would be syntactically incorrect in *twig*. In the cover shown at the end of Section 6, the first labeled leaf r of t_1 represents a match of t_2 in the subject tree; the second labeled leaf is a match of t_3.

Trees, Costs, and Actions

The *twig* pattern matcher treats trees and costs as an abstract data type, so as to minimize the constraints placed on their representation. All manipulations and accesses to tree and cost values are done via a well-defined procedural interface. The details of the interface are given in [42].

All legal C constructs are permitted in the C source code of the cost and action part of a rule. In addition, the following notations are provided for access to the subject tree and internal data structures of the pattern matcher.

(1) $\%n\$ denotes a pointer to the matcher data structure for the nth labeled leaf. The next section will discuss this data structure in more detail. To access the cost value associated with that leaf, the notation $\%n\$ → `cost` may be used.

(2) \$\$ denotes a point to the root of the subject tree.

(3) $n_1.n_2.n_3 \ldots n_{k-1}.n_k\$ denotes a pointer to child n_k of child n_{k-1} of child $n_{k-2} \ldots$ of child n_1 of the root of the subject tree. Each n_i is a positive integer.

(4) Cost values can be returned to the matcher by assigning to the variable cost in the cost part of a rule.

Refinements on Pattern Matching

The pattern matcher used in *twig* is similar to that described in Section 6 with a few additional modifications for improved efficiency.

The function $cost(t_i, n)$ used in the function *do_reduce* of Section 6 is implemented by calling the cost code associated with rule t_i. A match is aborted if, during the execution of the cost code, the ABORT statement is encountered; this is identical to returning an infinite cost value. The cost code also determines the mode of a match, which is described below.

Once a cover has been found, the reductions are performed during which time the action parts of the tree rules forming the cover are executed. Traditionally, one thinks of a reduction as consuming a subtree and replacing it with the label or nonterminal symbol of the rule. In *twig*, it is the execution of the action part of the rule during reduction that is important. Although the action part may modify the subject tree, *twig* does not require this to happen.

In the following, the word *reduction* will be used to mean the execution of the action part of a matching rule. The standard course of action is for *twig* to reduce matches in depth-first order. For the example of Section 6, the order of reductions is given by the numbers on the arrows in the following tree:

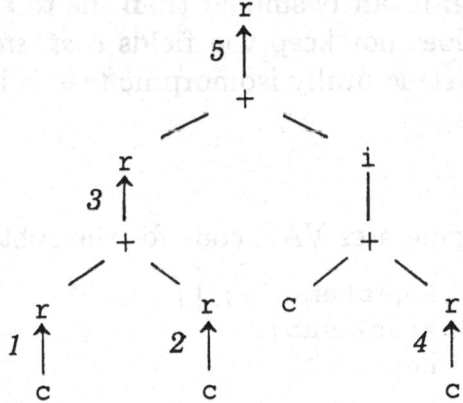

However, this standard order is changed if there are *top-down* mode matches. For example, if reduction 3 is from a top-down match, then it will be invoked before reductions 1 and 2. In fact, the latter two reductions will only be invoked if the built-in functions tDO($%1$) and tDO($%2$) are encountered while executing the action part of the rule causing reduction 3. In general, the function tDO($%n$) initiates reduction at the nth labeled leaf (and not at the nth reduction.) Explicit invocation allows the user to customize the exact ordering of execution in the cover.

A match can also be of *rewrite* mode. In that case the action code of the matching rule is executed immediately during the pattern-matching operation before any covers are computed. Matches below the rewrite-match in the tree are not reduced. To add this feature, the function *visit* is modified to call, just before returning, the routine *do_rewrite* given below.

```
do_rewrite(n)
{
    if min{n.cost} = n.cost[l] for some l and n.match[l] = m
       and t_m matches with mode rewrite then
          execute the action associated with t_m
    visit(n)
}
```

Executing the action part of the tree-rewriting rule t_m may modify n and its
subtree. Pattern matching continues after rewriting by calling $visit(n)$ to recon-
sider the new subtree rooted at n. This can be done without modifying other
parts of the tree because the bit-string technique of tracking partial matches will
not propagate pattern-matching information of the replaced subtree past n
toward the root. Rewrite-matches transform the subject tree during pattern
matching. They are useful for canonizing subtrees for commutative operators
and for performing constant folding.

Modes are determined by the cost code of a rule. While executing the cost
code, if the built-in TOPDOWN is encountered, the match will be of top-down
mode; if REWRITE is encountered, the mode will be rewrite; and if neither is
encountered, the match is executed in the standard fashion.

Twig uses some additional techniques to improve its efficiency. If there are
many tree rules, keeping a bit string for each rule at each node would consume
large amounts of memory. In *twig* only the nonzero bit strings of each node are
recorded. This saves memory because, on average, the number of rules that have
nonzero bit strings is significantly smaller than the total number of rules.

Our version of *twig* does not keep the fields *cost*, *state*, and b_i in the actual
subject tree. A separate structurally isomorphic tree is built by *twig* to hold this
information.

Example 1

This *twig* specification generates VAX code for the subtract instruction:

```
prologue  { NODEPTR gettemp( ); };
node      long constant sub;
label     operand temp;

operand: long;                                    /* rule 1 */
operand: constant;                                /* rule 2 */
operand: temp;                                    /* rule 3 */
temp:    operand;                                 /* rule 4 */
         {  cost = TEMP_COST+$%1$→cost; }
         ={ NODEPTR t = gettemp( );
            emit (''MOV'', $$, t, 0);
            return(t);
         };
operand: sub(operand, operand)                    /* rule 5 */
         {  cost = SUB_COST+$%1−→cost+$%2$→cost; }
         ={ NODEPTR t = gettemp( );
            emit(''SUB'', $1$, $2$, t, 0);
            return(t);
         };
```

```
temp:      sub(temp, constant)                        /* rule 6 */
           { if(value($2$) ==1)
               cost = DEC_COST+$%1$→cost;
             else ABORT;
           }
         ={ emit(''DEC'', $1$, 0);
             return($1$);
           };
```

Notes

(1) The `prologue` statement provides C source code that can be referenced by the action and cost code in the rules.

(2) The `node` and `label` declarations indicate the node and label identifiers.

(3) `SUB_COST` and `DEC_COST` are the cost values for a subtract and decrement instruction, respectively. They should be provided by the user in a separate source file.

(4) Rules 3 and 4 form a potential loop, `temp`→`operand`→`temp`→`operand` $\cdots$, which is broken by the matcher recognizing that the cost of the second match of `temp` is less than that of the first match of `temp`.

(5) In Rule 5, the cost is the sum of the cost of the leaves plus the cost of the subtract instruction. The action clause emits code to subtract the two operands and to leave the result in a temporary location. The temporary is returned as a substitution for the subject tree.

(6) Rule 6 handles a special case where the left operand is already in a temporary and the constant is 1. In this case, the temporary is directly decremented and returned as the new tree.

(7) The routine `emit` takes a variable number of arguments, and value 0 marks the end of the argument list. The first argument is the opcode and subsequent arguments are operands of the instruction. Each operand node is converted to a representation dependent on the target machine.

Example 2

The following is a *twig* specification for the tree-rewriting rules in Figure 2:

```
node const mem assign plus ind;
label reg no_value;

reg : const                                           /* rule 1 */
   { cost = 2; }
  ={ NODEPTR regnode = getreg();
     emit('MOV', $1$, regnode, 0);
     return(regnode);
   };
reg : mem                                             /* rule 2 */
   { cost = 2; }
  ={ NODEPTR regnode = getreg();
     emit('MOV', $1$, regnode, 0);
     return(regnode);
   };
```

```
  no_value: assign(mem, reg)                      /* rule 3 */
     {   cost = 2+$%1$→cost; }
   = { emit(''MOV'', $2$, $1$, 0);
       return(NULL);
     };

  no_value: assign(ind(reg), mem)                 /* rule 4 */
     {   cost = 2+$%1$→cost; }
   ={  emit(''MOV'', $2$, $1$, 0);
       return(NULL);
     };

  reg: ind(plus(const, reg))                      /* rule 5 */
     {   cost = 2+$%1$→cost; }
   ={  NODEPTR regnode = getreg( );
       emit(''MOV'', $$, regnode, 0);
       return(regnode);
     };

  reg: plus(reg, ind(plus(const, reg)))           /* rule 6 */
     {   cost = 2+$%1$→cost+$%1$→cost; }
   ={  emit(''ADD'', $2$, $1$, 0);
       return($1$);
     };

  reg: plus(reg, reg)                             /* rule 7 */
     {   cost = 1+$%1$→cost+$%2$→cost; }
   ={  emit(''ADD'', $2$, $1$, 0);
       return($1$);
     };

  reg: plus(reg, constant)                        /* rule 8 */
     {   if(value($2$) ==1)
           cost = 1+$%1$→cost
         else ABORT;
     }
   ={  emitop(''INC'', $1$, 0);
       return($1$);
     };
```

Notes

(1) In rules 4 and 6, we assume that the emit routine will convert the tree ind(reg) and ind(plus(const, reg)) into the correct target-machine addressing modes.

Additional details and applications of the *twig* language can be found in [42]. Appel [9] discusses *twig* specifications for the VAX and Motorola 68020 in detail.

8. EXPERIMENTAL RESULTS

To test these ideas, an experimental code generator for a VAX computer was built using *twig* and incorporated into the pcc2 C compiler [32]. The modular design of the pcc2 compiler made it easy to conduct this experiment. The compiler with the *twig* code generator is abbreviated tcc. Table II summarizes the overall compile times for tcc and the original pcc2 compiler on 13 C programs. The first column gives the lines of code in each of these benchmark

Table II. Comparison of tcc and pcc2 Compile Times

Program	Lines	tcc	pcc2	Percentage improvement
test1.c[a]	47	1.2 (0.6)	1.6 (0.6)	25.0
nm.c[b]	391	10.0 (1.3)	12.3 (1.2)	18.7
test3.c[c]	442	29.4 (2.8)	45.0 (2.8)	34.7
grep.c	458	12.1 (1.7)	15.2 (1.5)	20.4
local2.c[c]	530	8.9 (1.0)	12.3 (1.5)	27.6
local.c[c]	553	10.6 (1.3)	12.8 (1.3)	17.2
pmach.c	610	17.4 (2.3)	20.4 (2.5)	14.7
yacc	792	34.0 (3.0)	49.0 (2.9)	30.6
reader.c	1005	29.2 (2.6)	40.0 (2.4)	27.0
gencode.c[c]	1017	41.1 (4.6)	52.8 (4.2)	22.2
vmmem.c[d]	1041	19.3 (1.9)	24.4 (2.3)	20.9
cgram.c[c]	1181	30.4 (2.8)	38.6 (2.6)	21.2
ed.c	1729	42.5 (3.9)	47.0 (3.4)	9.6

[a] Tests arithmetic operators.
[b] Prints symbols from object module.
[c] Part of pcc2.
[d] part of Unix kernel.

programs. The second and third columns give the compile times in seconds on a VAX-11/780. The first number in these columns is the time spent in the compiler, the second parenthesized number is the time spent in the operating system.

As the table indicates, tcc is faster than pcc2 (the average improvement was 23 percent). However, the system times for tcc are higher; these higher system times are caused by calls to the runtime system for dynamic storage. For a tree node, the average storage requirement is about 200 bytes; this storage is reclaimed and reused for every new IR tree. The faster compile times of tcc are due to the efficient tree-matching algorithm.

Creating the *twig* specification for tcc was straightforward. The *twig* specification for the VAX without the indexed-addressing modes was done in two weeks (while concurrently debugging the tree walker). The indexed-addressing modes were then added in a few hours once we were confident that the initial *twig* specification was correct. The final *twig* specification for the VAX code generator had 115 rules. Of these, 17 described addressing modes, another 17 were chain or transfer productions, 3 described labels, 1 reversed evaluation order, and the rest described single instructions or sequences of instructions. The specification file contained 853 lines of *twig* (about 14 pages). The figures are comparable to those of Appel's *twig* VAX specification [9].

The *twig* specification was also easy to modify. One reason is that new rules can be added to a *twig* specification independently of the other rules. The dynamic programming algorithm eliminates the possibility of looping and assures that an optimal covering of templates will always be chosen. Another reason is speed of the *twig* compiler. The *twig* compiler produced the code-generation tables from this specification very quickly, in 5.2 seconds to be precise. Thus, creating and testing the code generator could be done quickly. The code-generation tables were also very small—7.5K bytes. The entire *twig*-generated code generator for the VAX was 47.5K bytes in size.

Since pcc2 also uses dynamic programming, it was not surprising to note that the code generated by pcc2 for the sample programs was of the same quality as code generated by tcc. Only a few minor differences were noticeable because of different targeting and register-allocation strategies used by the two compilers. Occasionally tcc did better targeting. For example, tcc would generate

```
addl3  -4(fp), -8(fp), -12(fp)
```

where pcc2 would generate

```
addl3  -4(fp), -8(fp), r0
movl   r0, -12(fp)
```

However, it should be pointed out that the peephole optimizer usually used with pcc2 will perform this retargeting.

Occasionally pcc2 handled temporary registers better. For example, tcc would generate

```
cvtbl  (r0), r1
```

using two registers, where pcc2 would only use one:

```
cvtbl  (r0), r0
```

This aspect of code generation is a symptom of how temporary registers were allocated in tcc. Registers were allocated before code was emitted, and thus any registers freed during code emissions were not reused until they were explicitly freed by the action rule.

The MIPS-X Compiler

For the MIPS-X project [12], a new compiler was generated using *twig* and compared with a previously hand-generated compiler written in Pascal. The *twig*-generated code generator compiled significantly faster (about 40 percent) than the hand-generated compiler and generated slightly faster code (a few percent) even though the hand-generated compiler did some peephole optimizations. However, precise numerical comparisons are not meaningful here because the hand-generated MIPS-X compiler worked by generating MIPS code that a cross assembler transformed into MIPS-X code.

9. CONCLUSIONS

We believe the main advantages of *twig*'s approach to code generation are specification ease, compact tables, and fast generation times. We have found the *twig*-style tree-specification scheme well suited for describing the instruction-selection phase of code generation. Since *twig* automatically finds a minimum-cost covering using dynamic programming, the user does not need to worry about the order of the patterns in the tree-specification scheme. Moreover, additional patterns can be easily added subsequently to take advantage of machine idioms and peephole optimizations. As a consequence, we feel that a strong point of *twig* is its concise and expressive notation for describing efficient code generators. The fast compilation time of *twig* due to the efficient algorithm for constructing tree-pattern matchers also facilitates the incremental design of a code generator.

Another advantage of *twig* is the quality of the output code. The dynamic programming algorithm guarantees a minimum cost cover for each target tree. If the intermediate representation has been generated with care and if the costs of the target machine instructions have been faithfully represented in the *twig* rules, then our experience has shown that the output code is at least as good as can be generated by a hand-crafted code generator. However, *twig* does not do common subexpression elimination, algebraic simplification, or any other high-level optimizations, so further code improvement is still possible.

The speed of a *twig*-generated code generator is still slow compared with that of hand-crafted code generator for a specific machine, but, as we have seen, the speed of a *twig*-generated code generator is comparable to that of a retargetable compiler like `pcc2`. Of the total compile time, 60 percent was spent in code generation. However, we believe the speed of a *twig*-generated code generator can be further improved in several ways.

(1) About 80 percent of the time in a *twig*-generated code generator goes into the pattern matcher; of this, 20 percent is in simulating the automaton, 35 percent is in bookkeeping for the dynamic programming, and 6 percent is in computing costs. The current compact representation of the tree-pattern matching automaton uses a linear list to represent the transitions at each state except at the start state where an array representation is used. More efficient representations of the other states would speed up the tree-pattern matching. For example, storing the transitions of all states of the pattern-matching automaton for the *twig*-generated VAX code generator as arrays would use about 50K bytes but would provide a significant performance improvement.

(2) For every transition of the pattern-matching automaton a *twig*-generated code generator performs at least one procedure call to access a tree node. These procedure calls can be replaced by in-line macros.

(3) A *twig* specification may contain many chain rewrite rules such as

```
operand: temp
```

These rules increase the running time of *twig* since the effect of each of these rewrite rules is computed at run time. In many cases, it is possible to precompute the effect of these chain rewrite rules.

In summary, we feel *twig* is a promising tool for helping automate the construction of code generators. Integrating peephole optimization into code generation gives significant advantages [16, 20], and it would be interesting to evaluate adding peephole optimization into framework of *twig*.

ACKNOWLEDGMENTS

The authors are indebted to Charles Fischer, Steve Johnson, and Peter Weinberger for many valuable comments and stimulating discussions. The test programs in Table II were provided by Peter Weinberger.

REFERENCES

1. AHO, A. V., AND CORASICK, M. J.   Efficient string matching: An aid to bibliographic search. *Commun. ACM 18*, 6 (June 1975), 333–340.

2. AHO, A. V., AND GANAPATHI, M.   Efficient tree pattern matching: An aid to code generation. In *Proceedings of the 12th ACM Symposium on Principles of Programming Languages.* ACM, New York, 1985, pp. 334–340.

3. AHO, A. V., AND JOHNSON, S. C.   Optimal code generation for expression trees, *J. ACM 23*, 3 (1976), 488–501.

4. AHO, A. V., JOHNSON, S. C., AND ULLMAN, J. D.   Code generation for expressions with common subexpressions. *J. ACM 24*, 1 (1977), 146–160.

5. AHO, A. V., JOHNSON, S. C., AND ULLMAN, J. D.   Code generation for machines with multi-register operations. In *Proceedings of the 4th ACM Symposium on Principles of Programming Languages.* ACM, New York, 1977, pp. 21–28.

6. AHO, A. V., JOHNSON, S. C., AND ULLMAN, J. D.   Deterministic parsing of ambiguous grammars. *Commun. ACM 18*, 8 (Aug. 1975), 441–452.

7. AHO, A. V., SETHI, R., AND ULLMAN, J. D.   *Compilers: Principles, Techniques, and Tools.* Addison-Wesley, Reading, Mass., 1986.

8. AIGRAIN, P., GRAHAM, S., HENRY, R., McKUSICK, M., AND PELEGRI-LLOPART, E.   Experience with a Graham-Glanville style code generator. In *Proceedings of the ACM SIGPLAN Symposium on Compiler Construction, ACM SIGPLAN Notices 19*, 6 (June 1984), 13–24.

9. APPEL, A. W.   Concise specifications of locally optimal code generators. Tech. Rep. CS-TR-080-87, Dept. of Computer Science, Princeton University, Princeton, N.J., Feb. 1987.

10. BRUNO, J., AND SETHI, R.   Code generation for a one-register machine. *J. ACM 23*, 3 (1976), 502–510.

11. CATTELL, R. G. G.   Automatic derivation of code generators from machine descriptions. *ACM Trans. Program. Lang. Syst. 2*, 2 (April 1980), 173–190.

12. CHOW, P., AND HOROWITZ, M.   The MIPS-X microprocessor. In *Proceedings of Wescon 1985* (San Francisco, Nov. 19–21, 1985). IEEE, New York, sec. 6-1, pp. 1–6.

13. DAVIDSON, J. W., AND FRASER, C. W.   Code selection through object code optimization. *ACM Trans. Program. Lang. Syst. 6*, 4 (Oct. 1984), 505–526.

14. DENCKER, P., DURRE, K., AND HEUFT, J.   Optimization of parser tables for portable compilers. *ACM Trans. Program. Lang. Syst. 6*, 4 (Oct. 1984), 546–572.

15. FRASER, C. W.   Automatic generation of code generators. Ph.D. dissertation, Yale University, New Haven, Conn., 1977.

16. FRASER, C. W., AND WENDT, A.   Integrating code generation and optimization. In *Proceedings of ACM SIGPLAN Symposium on Compiler Construction, ACM SIGPLAN Notices 21*, 6 (June 1986), 242–248.

17. GANAPATHI, M., AND FISCHER, C. N.   Affix grammar driven code generation. *ACM Trans. Program. Lang. Syst. 7*, 4 (Oct. 1985), 560–599.

18. GANAPATHI, M., AND FISCHER, C. N.   Attributed linear intermediate representations for retargetable code generators. *Softw. Pract. Exper. 14* (April 1984), 347–364.

19. GANAPATHI, M., AND FISCHER, C. N.   Description-driven code generation using attribute grammars. In *Proceedings of the 9th Annual ACM Symposium on Principles of Programming Languages.* ACM, New York, 1982, pp. 108–119.

20. GANAPATHI, M., AND FISCHER, C. N.,   Integrating code generation and peephole optimization. *Acta Inf. 25* (Jan. 1988), 85–109.

21. GANAPATHI, M., FISCHER, C. N., AND HENNESSY, J. L.   Retargetable compiler code generation. *ACM Comput. Surv. 14*, 4 (Dec. 1982), 573–592.

22. GLANVILLE, R. S.   A machine independent algorithm for code generation and its use in retargetable compilers. Ph.D. dissertation, University of California, Berkeley, Dec. 1977.

23. GLANVILLE, R. S., AND GRAHAM, S. L.   A new method for compiler code generation. In *Proceedings of the 5th Annual ACM Symposium on Principles of Programming Languages.* ACM, New York, 1978, pp. 231–240.

24. GLASNER, I., MONCKE, U., AND WILHELM, R.   OPTRAN, a language for the specification of program transformations. *Inf. Fach.*, 1980, 125–142.

25. GRAHAM, S. L.   Table-driven code generation. *IEEE Comput. 13*, 8 (Aug. 1980), 25–34.

26. GRAHAM, S. L., HENRY, R. R., AND SCHULMAN, R. A.   An experiment in table driven code generation. In *Proceedings of the ACM SIGPLAN Symposium on Compiler Construction, ACM SIGPLAN Notices 17*, 6 (June 1982), 32–43.

27. HATCHER, P. J., AND CHRISTOPHER, T. W. High-quality code generation via bottom-up tree pattern matching. In *Proceedings of the 11th Annual ACM Symposium on Principles of Programming Languages*. ACM, New York, 1986, pp. 119–130.

28. HATCHER, P. J., KUKUCK, R. C., AND CHRISTOPHER, T. W. Using dynamic programming to generate optimized code in a Graham–Glanville style code generator. In *Proceedings of the ACM SIGPLAN Symposium on Compiler Construction, ACM SIGPLAN Notices 19*, 6 (June 1984), 25–36.

29. HENRY, R. R. Graham–Glanville code generators. Ph.D. dissertation, Computer Science Division, Electrical Engineering and Computer Science, University of California, Berkeley, 1984.

30. HOFFMAN, C. W., AND O'DONNELL, M. J. Pattern matching in trees. *J. ACM 29*, 1 (1982), 68–95.

31. HUET, G., AND LEVY, J.-J. Call by need computations in non-ambiguous linear term rewriting systems. Tech. Rep. 359, IRIA Laboria, LeChesnay, France, 1979.

32. JOHNSON, S. C. A portable compiler: Theory and practice. In *Proceedings of the 5th ACM Symposium on Principles of Programming Languages*. ACM, New York, 1978, pp. 97–104.

33. KEUTZER, K. Dagon: Technology binding and local optimization by dag matching. In *Proceedings of the 24th Design Automation Conference*. ACM/IEEE, New York, 1987, pp. 341–347.

34. KEUTZER, K., AND WOLF, W. Anatomy of a hardware compiler. In *Proceedings of the ACM SIGPLAN '88 Conference on Programming Language Design and Implementation, ACM SIGPLAN Notices 23*, 7 (July 1988), 95–104.

35. KRON, H. Tree templates and subtree transformational grammars. Ph.D. dissertation, University of California, Santa Cruz, 1975.

36. LANG, H.-W., SCHIMMLER, M., AND SCHMECK, H. Matching tree patterns sublinear on the average. Tech. Rep. Dept. of Informatik, University of Kiel, Kiel, West Germany, 1980.

37. LUNELL, H. Code Generator Writing Systems. Software Systems Research Center, S-58183, Linkoping, Sweden, 1983.

38. PELEGRI-LLOPART, E., AND GRAHAM, S. L. Optimal code generation for expression trees: An application of BURS theory. In *Proceedings of the 15th Annual ACM Symposium on Principles of Programming Languages*. ACM, New York, 1988, pp. 294–308.

39. RIPKEN, K. Formale Beschreibun von Maschinen, Implementierungen und Optimierender Maschinen-codeerzeugung aus Attributierten Programmgraphe. Tech. Rep. TUM-INFO-7731, Institut fur Informatik, Technische Universitat Munchen, Munich, West Germany, July 1977.

40. SETHI, R. AND ULLMAN, J. D. The generation of optimal code for arithmetic expressions. *J. ACM 17*, 4 (1970), 715–728.

41. SNYDER, L. Recognition and selection of idioms for code optimization. *Acta Inf. 17* (1982), 327–348.

42. TJIANG, S. W. K. Twig reference manual. Computing Science Tech. Rep. 120, AT&T Bell Laboratories, Murray Hill, N.J., 1985.

43. WASILEW, S. G. A compiler writing system with optimization capabilities for complex order structures. Ph.D. dissertation, Northwestern University, Evanston, Ill., 1972.

44. WEINGART, S. W. An efficient and systématic method of compiler code generation. Ph.D. dissertation, Computer Sciences Dept., Yale University, New Haven, Com., 1973.

45. WULF, W. A. PQCC: A machine-relative compiler technology. In *Proceedings of the IEEE 4th International COMPSAC Conference*. IEEE, New York, 1980, pp. 24–36.

46. WULF, W., LEVERETT, B., CATTELL, R., HOBBS, S., NEWCOMER, J., REINER, A., AND SCHATZ, B. An overview of the production quality compiler-compiler project. *IEEE Comput. 13*, 8 (Aug. 1980), 38–49.

Received January 1986; revised February 1987, August 1988, and May 1989; accepted May 1989

The Tree-to-Tree Correction Problem

KUO-CHUNG TAI

North Carolina State University, Raleigh, North Carolina

ABSTRACT.   The tree-to-tree correction problem is to determine, for two labeled ordered trees T and T', the distance from T to T' as measured by the minimum cost sequence of *edit* operations needed to transform T into T'. The edit operations investigated allow changing one node of a tree into another node, deleting one node from a tree, or inserting a node into a tree. An algorithm is presented which solves this problem in time $O(V * V' * L^2 * L'^2)$, where V and V' are the numbers of nodes respectively of T and T', and L and L' are the maximum depths respectively of T and T'. Possible applications are to the problems of measuring the similarity between trees, automatic error recovery and correction for programming languages, and determining the largest common substructure of two trees.

KEY WORDS AND PHRASES: tree correction, tree modification, tree similarity

CR CATEGORIES: 3.79, 4.12, 4.22, 5.23, 5.25

1. *Introduction*

The string-to-string correction problem, which is to determine the *distance* between two strings as measured by the minimum cost sequence of *edit* operations needed to transform one string into the other, was investigated in [7, 8, 10, 12, 13, 14]. In [13] Wagner and Fischer considered the following three edit operations: changing a character into another character, deleting a character, and inserting a character; and they presented an algorithm that computes the distance between two strings in time $O(m * n)$, where m and n are the lengths of the two given strings.

The various attempts to achieve high-dimensional generalizations of strings include trees, graphs, webs, and plex structures. Trees are considered the most important nonlinear structures arising in computer algorithms [6]. Tree automata, tree grammars, and their applications for syntactic pattern recognition have been studied (e.g. [2]).

In this paper we define the notion of distance between two labeled ordered trees and present an algorithm that computes the distance in time $O(V * V' * L^2 * L'^2)$, where V and V' are the numbers of nodes of the two trees and L and L' are the maximum depths of the two trees. The set of allowable edit operations includes: (1) changing one node into another node (changing the label of the node); (2) deleting one node from a tree; and (3) inserting a node into a tree.

Since each string can be considered a tree of depth two (with a virtual root added), the string-to-string correction problem is just a special case of the tree-to-tree correction problem with $L = L' = 2$. Possible applications of the notion of distance between two trees are discussed at the end of this paper.

2. *Edit Operations on Trees*

In this paper all trees we discuss are rooted, ordered, and labeled. Let T be a tree. $|T|$

Author's address: Department of Computer Science, North Carolina State University, P.O. Box 5972, Raleigh, NC 27607.

denotes the number of nodes of T. $T[i]$ denotes the node of T whose position in the preorder for nodes of T is i. The preorder traversal on T is to first visit the root of T and then traverse the subtrees of T from left to right, each subtree traversed in preorder. The following diagram illustrates how nodes of a tree T are denoted:

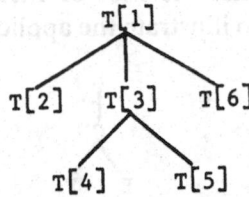

LEMMA 2.1. *Assume that $T[i_1]$ and $T[i_2]$ are nodes of T with $T[i_1]$ being an ancestor of $T[i_2]$. Then*

(1) $i_1 < i_2$;

(2) *For any i such that $i_1 < i \leq i_2$, $T[i]$ is a descendant of $T[i_1]$;*

(3) *For the father $T[i_3]$ of $T[i_2]$, $T[i_3]$ is $T[i_2 - 1]$ or an ancestor of $T[i_2 - 1]$, and $T[i_3]$ is on the path from $T[i_1]$ to $T[i_2 - 1]$.*

PROOF. The proof follows from the definition of preorder traversal. Q.E.D.

Let Λ denote the null node. An edit operation is written $b \rightarrow c$, where each of b and c is either a node or Λ. $b \rightarrow c$ is a *change* operation if $b \neq \Lambda$ and $c \neq \Lambda$, a *delete* operation if $b \neq \Lambda = c$, and an *insert* operation if $b = \Lambda \neq c$. Let T' be the tree that results from the application of an edit operation $b \rightarrow c$ to tree T; this is written $T \Rightarrow T'$ via $b \rightarrow c$. The relations between T and T' are described as follows:

(1) If $b \rightarrow c$ is a change operation, then node b is replaced by node c, i.e.,

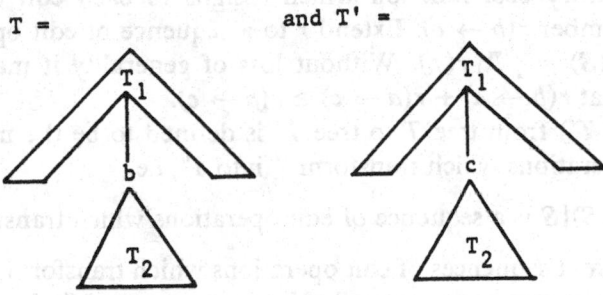

for some trees T_1 and T_2.

(2) If $b \rightarrow c$ is a delete operation, then node b is deleted, i.e.,

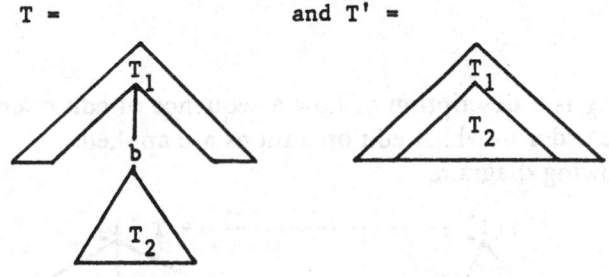

for some trees T_1 and T_2.

(3) If $b \rightarrow c$ is an insert operation, then node c is inserted, i.e.,

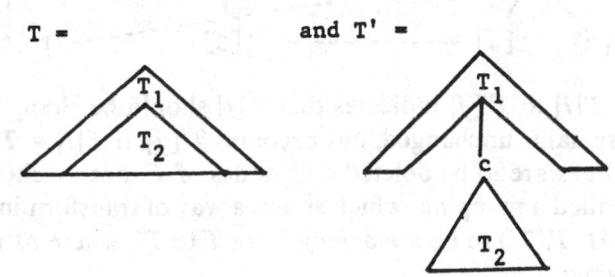

for some trees T_1 and T_2.

Each node of a tree except the root is associated with a unique edge connecting the node and its father. For the deletion or insertion of a node, both the node and its associated edge are included. Without loss of generality it may be assumed that the roots of all trees have the same unique label and that the root of each tree remains unchanged during editing. Examples are given below to illustrate the applications of the three edit operations.

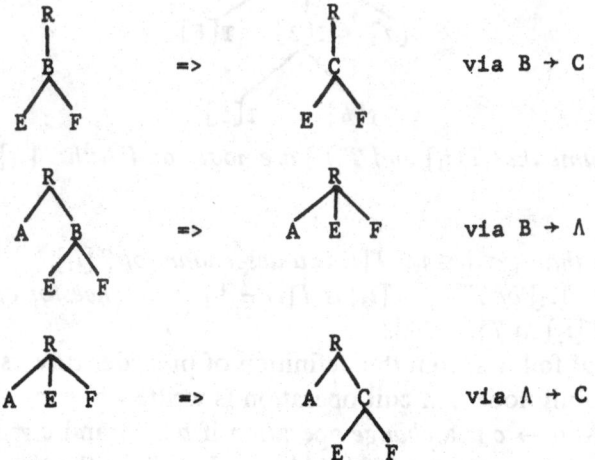

Let S be a sequence $s_1, s_2, \ldots, s_m$ of edit operations. S transforms tree T to tree T' if there is a sequence of trees $T_0, T_1, \ldots, T_m$ such that $T = T_0, T' = T_m$ and $T_{i-1} => T_i$ via s_i for $1 \leq i \leq m$.

Let r be an arbitrary cost function which assigns to each edit operation $b \to c$ a nonnegative real number $r(b \to c)$. Extend r to a sequence of edit operations $S = s_1, s_2, \ldots, s_m$ by letting $r(S) = \sum_{i=1}^{m} r(s_i)$. Without loss of generality it may be assumed that $r(b \to b) = 0$ and that $r(b \to a) + r(a \to c) \geq r(b \to c)$.

The *distance* $d(T, T')$ from tree T to tree T' is defined to be the minimum cost of all sequences of edit operations which transform T into T', i.e.,

$$d(T, T') = \min\{r(S) | S \text{ is a sequence of edit operations which transforms } T \text{ into } T'\}.$$

The number of different sequences of edit operations which transform T into T' is infinite. Therefore, it is impossible to enumerate all valid sequences and find the minimum cost. In the next section, structures called mappings are defined so that $d(T, T')$ can be computed in polynomial time.

3. Mappings

Intuitively, a *mapping* is a description of how a sequence of edit operations transforms T into T', ignoring the order in which edit operations are applied.

Consider the following diagram:

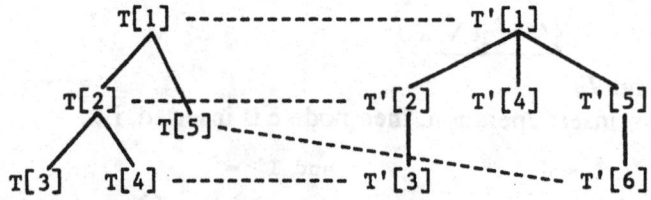

A dotted line from $T[i]$ to $T'[j]$ indicates that $T[i]$ should be changed to $T'[j]$ if $T[i] \neq T'[j]$, or that $T[i]$ remains unchanged, but becomes $T'[j]$, if $T[i] = T'[j]$. Nodes of T not touched by dotted lines are to be deleted and nodes of T' not touched are to be inserted. Such a diagram is called a mapping, which shows a way of transforming T to T'. Formally, we define a triple (M, T, T') to be a *mapping* from T to T', where M is any set of pairs of integers (i, j) satisfying:

(1) $1 \leq i \leq |T|$, $1 \leq j \leq |T'|$;

(2) For any two pairs (i_1, j_1) and (i_2, j_2) in M,

    (a) $i_1 = i_2$ iff $j_1 = j_2$;

    (b) $i_1 < i_2$ iff $j_1 < j_2$;

    (c) $T[i_1]$ is an ancestor (descendant) of $T[i_2]$ iff
$T'[j_1]$ is an ancestor (descendant) of $T'[j_2]$.

Where there is no resulting confusion, we do not distinguish between the triple (M, T, T') and the set M.

Each pair (i, j) in M is interpreted to be a line segment joining $T[i]$ and $T'[j]$. Condition (2a) ensures that each node of both T and T' is touched by at most one line. Conditions (2b) and (2c) ensure that after untouched nodes of both T and T' are deleted, T and T' become similar (i.e., they have the same structure), and the one-to-one correspondence between nodes of T and T' which preserves the structure is indicated exactly by the lines of M. By deleting untouched nodes, the preceding diagram becomes:

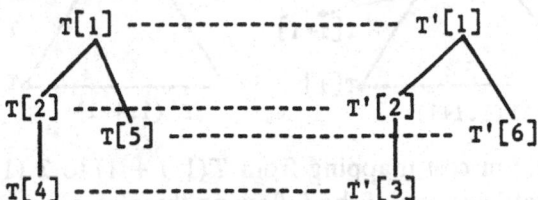

Let M be a mapping from T to T' and let I and J be the sets of untouched nodes of T and T' respectively. We define the *cost* of M:

$$cost(M) = \sum_{(i, j) \in M} r(T[i] \rightarrow T'[j]) + \sum_{i \in I} r(T[i] \rightarrow \Lambda) + \sum_{j \in J} r(\Lambda \rightarrow T'[j]).$$

Thus, the cost of M is just the cost of the sequence of edit operations which consists of a change operation $T[i] \rightarrow T'[j]$ for each line (i, j) of M, a delete operation $T[i] \rightarrow \Lambda$ for each node $T[i]$ not touched by a line of M, and an insert operation $\Lambda \rightarrow T'[j]$ for each node $T'[j]$ not touched by a line of M.

In order to show that $d(T, T')$ can be determined by a minimum cost mapping from T to T', the following two lemmas need to be verified:

LEMMA 3.1. *Let M_1 be a mapping from T_1 to T_2 and let M_2 be a mapping from T_2 to T_3. Then:*

(1) $M_1 \circ M_2 = \{(i, k) | (i, j) \in M_1 \text{ and } (j, k) \in M_2 \text{ for some } j\}$ *is a mapping from T_1 to T_3;*

(2) $cost(M_1 \circ M_2) \leq cost(M_1) + cost(M_2)$.

PROOF.

(1) Let (i_1, k_1) and (i_2, k_2) be two lines of $M_1 \circ M_2$. Then there exist j_1 and j_2 such that (i_1, j_1), $(i_2, j_2) \in M_1$ and (j_1, k_1), $(j_2, k_2) \in M_2$. By the definition of a mapping:

    (a) $(i_1 = i_2$ iff $j_1 = j_2)$ and $(j_1 = j_2$ iff $k_1 = k_2)$;

    (b) $(i_1 < i_2$ iff $j_1 < j_2)$ and $(j_1 < j_2$ iff $k_1 < k_2)$;

    (c) $(T_1[i_1]$ is an ancestor (descendant) of $T_1[i_2]$ iff
$T_2[j_1]$ is an ancestor (descendant) of $T_2[j_2])$, and
$(T_2[j_1]$ is an ancestor (descendant) of $T_2[j_2]$ iff
$T_3[k_1]$ is an ancestor (descendant) of $T_3[k_2])$.

Therefore, $M_1 \circ M_2$ is a mapping from T_1 to T_3.

(2) The proof that $cost(M_1 \circ M_2) \leq cost(M_1) + cost(M_2)$ follows closely the proof of Lemma 1 in [13] and is omitted. This proof relies on the assumption that $r(b \rightarrow c) \leq r(b \rightarrow a) + r(a \rightarrow c)$.   Q.E.D.

LEMMA 3.2. *For any sequence S of edit operations which transforms T into T', there exists a mapping M from T to T' such that $cost(M) \leq r(S)$.*

PROOF.   It can be shown by induction on m that if $S = s_1, s_2, \ldots, s_m$ is a sequence of edit operations and $T_0, T_1, \ldots, T_m$ is the sequence of trees from T_0 to T_m via S, then there exists a mapping M from T_0 to T_m such that $cost(M) \le r(S)$. This proof is similar to the proof of Theorem 1 in [13] and is omitted. Q.E.D.

Since $d(T, T') = \min\{cost(S) \,|\, S$ is a sequence of edit operations which transforms T into $T'\}$, we have:

THEOREM 3.1 $d(T, T') = \min\{cost(M) \,|\, M$ is a mapping from T to $T'\}$.

Hence the search for a minimal cost sequence of edit operations has been reduced to a search for a minimal cost mapping.

Let $T(i_1: i_2)$ denote the portion of T which consists of nodes $T[i_1]$, $T[i_1 + 1]$, ... , $T[i_2]$, and their associated edges, where i_1 is an ancestor of i_2; and similarly define $T'[j_1: j_2]$. Let $D(i + 1, j + 1)$ be the distance from tree $T(1: i + 1)$ to tree $T'(1: j + 1)$, i.e., $D(i + 1, j + 1) = d(T(1: i + 1), T'(1: j + 1))$. Consider the following diagram:

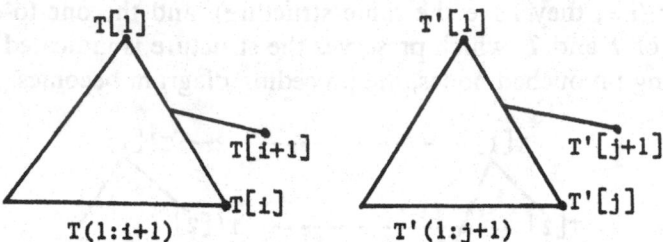

Suppose M is a minimum cost mapping from $T(1: i + 1)$ to $T'(1: j + 1)$, i.e., $cost(M) = D(i + 1, j + 1)$. Then at least one of the following three cases must hold:

Case 1: $T[i + 1]$ is not touched by a line of M. Then $cost(M) = D(i, j + 1) + r(T[i + 1] \to \Lambda)$, corresponding to the cost of transforming $T(1: i)$ to $T'(1: j + 1)$ plus the cost of deleting $T[i + 1]$.

Case 2: $T'[j + 1]$ is not touched by a line of M. Then $cost(M) = D(i + 1, j) + r(\Lambda \to T'[j + 1])$, corresponding to the cost of transforming $T(1: i + 1)$ to $T'(1: j)$ plus the cost of inserting $T'[j + 1]$.

Case 3: $T[i + 1]$ and $T'[j + 1]$ are touched by lines $(i + 1, q)$ and $(p, j + 1)$ of M. By the definition of a mapping, $(i + 1 = p$ iff $q = j + 1)$ and $(i + 1 > p$ iff $q > j + 1)$. Since $i + 1 \ge p$ and $j + 1 \ge q$, $i + 1 = p$ and $j + 1 = q$. Thus, $T[i + 1]$ and $T'[j + 1]$ are both touched by the same line $(i + 1, j + 1)$. Note that if $M' = M - \{(i + 1, j + 1)\}$ is not a minimum cost mapping from $T(1: i)$ to $T'(1: j)$, then

$$cost(M) = cost(M') + r(T[i + 1] \to T'[j + 1]) > D(i, j) + r(T[i + 1] \to T'[j + 1]).$$

Thus, it may be true that $D(i + 1, j + 1) > D(i, j) + r(T[i + 1] \to T'[j + 1])$, for a minimum cost mapping from $T(1: i)$ to $T'(1: j)$ may not be extendable to a mapping by adding $(i + 1, j + 1)$. For example, consider the following trees T_1 and T_2:

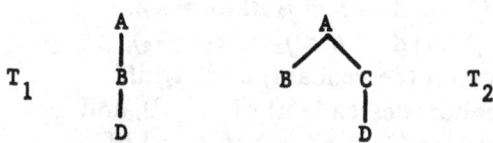

Assume that the cost of each change, delete, or insert operation is 1 for all nodes. $\{(1, 1), (2, 2)\}$ is a minimum cost mapping from $T_1(1: 2)$ to $T_2(1: 3)$. However, $\{(1, 1), (2, 2), (3, 4)\}$ is not a mapping from $T_1(1: 3)$ to $T_2(1: 4)$ because $T_1[2]$ is an ancestor of $T_1[3]$ but $T_2[2]$ is not an ancestor of $T_2[4]$.

Define

$MIN\_M(i + 1, j + 1) = \min\{cost(M) \,|\, M$ is a mapping from
$\qquad\qquad\qquad T(1: i + 1)$ to $T'(1:\!\cdot j + 1)$ such that $(i + 1, j + 1) \in M\}$.

From the above argument we have the following theorem:

THEOREM 3.2.

$$D(i + 1, j + 1) = min\{D(i, j + 1) + r(T[i + 1] \rightarrow \Lambda),$$
$$D(i + 1, j) + r(\Lambda \rightarrow T'[j + 1]),$$
$$MIN\_M(i + 1, j + 1)\}$$

for all i, j, $1 \leq i < |T|$, $1 \leq j < |T'|$.

For the special case that $MIN\_M(i + 1, j + 1) = D(i, j) + r(T[i + 1] \rightarrow T'[j + 1])$ for all i, j, $1 \leq i \leq |T|$, and $1 \leq j \leq |T'|$, $D(|T|, |T'|)$ can be computed in time $O(|T| * |T'|)$ (see [13]).

The computation of $MIN\_M(i + 1, j + 1)$ is not trivial. In the next section we explore some properties of mappings and then show that $MIN\_M(i + 1, j + 1)$ can be computed in polynomial time. With the assumption that the root of any tree remains unchanged during editing, every mapping from $T(1: i + 1)$ to $T'(1: j + 1)$ contains $(1, 1)$ and $D(1, 1) = 0$.

LEMMA 3.3.

$$D(1, 1) = 0,$$

$$D(i, 1) = \sum_{k=2}^{i} r(T[k] \rightarrow \Lambda), \quad 1 < i \leq |T|, \quad and$$

$$D(1, j) = \sum_{k=2}^{j} r(\Lambda \rightarrow T'[k]), \quad 1 < j \leq |T'|.$$

4. *Computation of MIN_M(i + 1, j + 1)*

We first show that a mapping from $T(1: i + 1)$ to $T'(1: j + 1)$ may be decomposed into submappings such that each submapping is a mapping from one portion of $T(1: i + 1)$ to one portion of $T'(1: j + 1)$. Consequently, for a minimum cost mapping, each of its submappings is also a minimum cost mapping.

LEMMA 4.1. *Assume that $T[p]$ and $T'[q]$ are ancestors of $T[i + 1]$ and $T'[j + 1]$, respectively, and that M is a mapping from $T(1: i + 1)$ to $T'(1: j + 1)$ such that (p, q) and $(i + 1, j + 1)$ are in M. Let M_1 and M_2 be the subsets of M defined by*

$$M_1 = \{(m, n)|(m, n) \in M, 1 \leq m \leq p \text{ and } 1 \leq n \leq q\}$$

and

$$M_2 = \{(m, n)|(m, n) \in M, p \leq m \leq i \text{ and } q \leq n \leq j\}.$$

Then

(1) *M_1 is a mapping from $T(1: p)$ to $T'(1: q)$;*
    M_2 is a mapping from $T(p: i)$ to $T'(q: j)$;
    $M = M_1 \cup M_2 \cup \{(i + 1, j + 1)\}$; and
    $cost(M) = cost(M_1) + cost(M_2) - r(T[p] \rightarrow T'[q]) + r(T[i + 1] \rightarrow T'[j + 1])$.

(2) *$cost(M) = min\{cost(M')|M' \text{ is a mapping from } T(1: i + 1) \text{ to } T'(1: j + 1)$*
       such that (p, q) and $(i + 1, j + 1)$ are in $M'\}$ iff
    $cost(M_1) = min\{cost(M_1')|M_1' \text{ is a mapping from } T(1: p) \text{ to } T'(1: q)$
       such that $(p, q) \in M_1'\}$ and
    $cost(M_2) = min\{cost(M_2')|M_2' \text{ is a mapping from } T(p: i) \text{ to } T'(q: j)$
       such that $(p, q) \in M_2' \text{ and } M_2' \cup \{(i + 1, j + 1)\} \text{ is a mapping}\}$.

PROOF. Consider the following diagram:

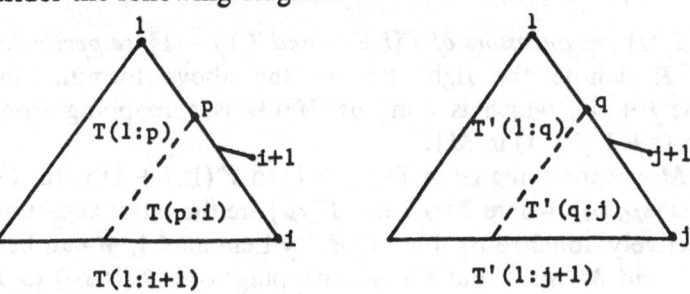

(1) For each (m, n) in M, $m \geq p$ if and only if $n \geq q$. Therefore, $M = M_1 \cup M_2 \cup \{(i + 1, j + 1)\}$ and M_1 and M_2 have exactly one common line, (p, q).

(2) *Only if*: Assume that

$$cost(M_1) > \min\{cost(M_1') | M_1' \text{ is a mapping from}$$
$$T(1: p) \text{ to } T'(1: q) \text{ with } (p, q) \text{ in } M_1'\} = cost(M_1''),$$

where M_1'' is a mapping from $T(1: p)$ to $T'(1: q)$ with (p, q) in M_1''. Then $M'' = M_1'' \cup M_2 \cup \{(i + 1, j + 1)\}$ is a mapping from $T(1: i + 1)$ to $T'(1: j + 1)$ with (p, q) and $(i + 1, j + 1)$ in M'', and $cost(M'') < cost(M)$. Thus

$$cost(M) > \min\{cost(M') | M' \text{ is a mapping from } T(1: i + 1) \text{ to}$$
$$T'(1: j + 1) \text{ with } (p, q) \text{ and } (i + 1, j + 1) \text{ in } M'\}.$$

The same conclusion holds if

$$cost(M_2) > \min\{cost(M_2') | M_2' \text{ is a mapping from } T(p: i) \text{ to } T'(q: j)$$
$$\text{with } (p, q) \text{ in } M_2' \text{ and } M_2' \cup \{(i + 1, j + 1)\} \text{ is a mapping}\}.$$

If: The proof is similar to the "only if" proof.   Q.E.D.

Assume that M is a mapping from $T(1: i + 1)$ to $T'(1: j + 1)$ with $(i + 1, j + 1)$ in M. Let $T[s_M]$ and $T'[t_M]$ be the latest ancestors of $T[i + 1]$ and $T'[j + 1]$, respectively, touched by lines of M. (It has been assumed that every mapping from $T(1: i + 1)$ to $T'(1: j + 1)$ contains the line $(1, 1)$, and therefore $T[s_M]$ and $T'[t_M]$ must exist.) Since $(i + 1, j + 1)$ is in M, (s_M, t_M) is in M. The following diagram illustrates the meaning of nodes $T[s_M]$ and $T'[t_M]$:

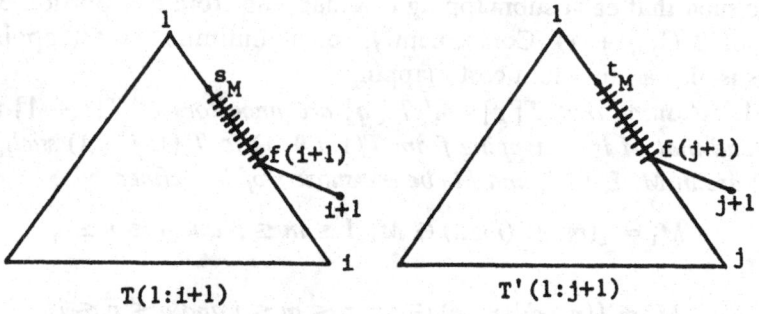

In the above diagram, $f(x)$ denotes the father of node x. By Lemma 2.1, $T[f(i + 1)]$ $(T'[f(j + 1)])$ is on the path from $T[s_M]$ $(T'[t_M])$ to $T[i]$ $(T'[j])$. Slashes crossing the line from s_M to $f(i + 1)$ (not including s_M) indicate that any descendant of $T[s_M]$ on the path from $T[s_M]$ to $T[f(i + 1)]$ is not touched by any line of M. Slashes in $T'(1: j + 1)$ are defined similarly.

LEMMA 4.2.

$$MIN\_M(i + 1, j + 1) = \quad r(T[i + 1] \rightarrow T'[j + 1])$$
$$+ \min_{s,t} \{\min\{cost(M_1) | M_1 \text{ is a mapping from } T(1: s) \text{ to } T'(1: t) \text{ with } (s, t) \text{ in } M_1\}$$
$$+ \min\{cost(M_2) | M_2 \text{ is a mapping from } T(s: i) \text{ to } T'(t: j) \text{ such that } (s, t) \text{ is in}$$
$$M \text{ and any descendant of } T[s] \ (T'[t]) \text{ on the path from } T[s] \ (T'[t])$$
$$\text{to } T[f(i + 1)] \ (T'[f(j + 1)]) \text{ is not touched by any line of } M_2\} -$$
$$r(T[s] \rightarrow T'[t])\}$$

where $T[s]$ and $T'[t]$ are ancestors of $T[i + 1]$ and $T'[j + 1]$, respectively.

PROOF. Let R denote the right side of the above formula and let L denote $MIN\_M(i + 1, j + 1)$, which is $\min\{cost(M) | M \text{ is a mapping from } T(1: i + 1) \text{ to } T'(1: j + 1) \text{ with } (i + 1, j + 1) \text{ in } M\}$.

Assume that M is a mapping from $T(1: i + 1)$ to $T'(1: j + 1)$ with $(i + 1, j + 1)$ in M. Then M contains (s_M, t_M), where $T[s_M]$ and $T'[t_M]$ are the latest ancestors of $T[i + 1]$ and $T'[j + 1]$, respectively, touched by lines of M. By Lemma 4.1, M can be decomposed into submappings M_1 and M_2 such that M_1 is a mapping from $T(1: s_M)$ to $T'(1: t_M)$, M_2 is a mapping from $T(s_M: i)$ to $T'(t_M: j)$, and $M = M_1 \cup M_2 \cup \{(i + 1, j + 1)\}$. It follows that $L \geq R$.

Assume that $T[s]$ and $T'[t]$ are ancestors of $T[i + 1]$ and $T'[j + 1]$, respectively. Let M_1 be a mapping from $T(1: s)$ to $T'(1: t)$ with (s, t) in M_1 and let M_2 be a mapping from $T(s: i)$ to $T'(t: j)$ such that (s, t) is in M_2 and any descendant of $T[s]$ $(T'[t])$ on the path from $T[s]$ $(T'[t])$ to $T[f(i + 1)]$ $(T'[f(j + 1)])$ is not touched by any line of M_2. Then $M = M_1 \cup M_2 \cup \{(i + 1, j + 1)\}$ is a mapping from $T(1: i + 1)$ to $T'(j + 1)$. Therefore $L \leq R$. From $L \geq R$ and $L \leq R$, it follows that $L = R$.   Q.E.D.

Assume that $s \leq u \leq i$, $t \leq v \leq j$, $T[u]$ is on the path from $T[s]$ to $T[i]$, and $T'[v]$ is on the path from $T'[t]$ to $T'[j]$. Define $E[s: u: i, t: v: j]$ to be $\min\{cost(M)|M$ is a mapping from $T(s: i)$ to $T'(t: j)$ such that (s, t) is in M and no descendant of $T[s]$ $(T'[t])$ on the path from $T[s]$ $(T'[t])$ to $T[u]$ $(T'[v])$ is touched by a line of $M\}$. Then we have the following theorem from Lemma 4.2:

THEOREM 4.1.

$$MIN\_M(i + 1, j + 1) = r(T[i + 1] \rightarrow T'[j + 1])$$
$$+ \min_{s,t} \{MIN\_M(s, t) + E[s: f(i + 1): i, t: f(j + 1): j] - r(T[s] \rightarrow T'[t])\}$$

where $T[s]$ and $T'[t]$ are ancestors of $T[i + 1]$ and $T'[j + 1]$, respectively.

Now the remaining problem is how to compute $E[s: u: i, t: v: j]$, where $s \leq u \leq i$, $t \leq v \leq j$, and $T[u]$ $(T'[v])$ is on the path from $T[s]$ $(T'[t])$ to $T[i]$ $(T'[j])$. First, assume that $s \leq u < i$ and $t \leq v < j$. Then $T[u]$ $(T'[v])$ has a son on the path from $T[u]$ $(T'[v])$ to $T[i]$ $(T'[j])$. Consider the following diagram:

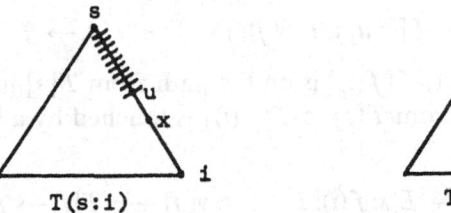

where $T[x]$ $(T'[y])$ is the son of $T[u]$ $(T'[v])$ on the path from $T[u]$ $(T'[v])$ to $T[i]$ $(T'[j])$.

LEMMA 4.3.   *Assume that $s \leq u < i$ and $t \leq v < j$. Then*

$$E[s: u: i, t: v: j] = \min\{E[s: x: i, t: v: j],$$

$$E[s: u: i, t: y: j],$$

$$E[s: u: x - 1, t: v: y - 1] + E[x: x: i, y: y: j]\}.$$

PROOF.   Let M be a mapping from $T(s: i)$ to $T'(t: j)$ such that $cost(M) = E[s: u: i, t: v: j]$, (s, t) is in M, and no descendant of $T[s]$ $(T'[t])$ on the path from $T[s]$ $(T'[t])$ to $T[u]$ $(T'[v])$ is touched by a line of M. Then at least one of the following three cases must hold:

Case 1: $T[x]$ is not touched by a line of M. Then $E[s: u: i, t: v: j] = E[s: x: i, t: v: j]$.

Case 2: $T'[y]$ is not touched by a line of M. Then $E[s: u: i, t: v: j] = E[s: u: i, t: y: j]$.

Case 3: $T[x]$ and $T'[y]$ are touched by lines (x, q) and (p, y) of M. Assume that $p > x$. Since $T[i]$ is a descendant of $T[x]$ and $i \geq p > x$, by Lemma 2.1 $T[p]$ is a descendant of $T[x]$. By the definition of a mapping, $y > q$ and $T'[y]$ is a descendant of $T'[q]$. Thus, $T'[q]$ is a descendant of $T'[t]$ on the path from $T'[t]$ to $T'[v]$. However, this contradicts the assumption that no descendant of $T'[t]$ on the path from $T'[t]$ to $T'[v]$ is touched by a line of M. Also, $p < x$ will cause a similar contradiction. Therefore, $p = x$ and $q = y$. Let M_1 and M_2 be defined by

$$M_1 = \{(m, n)|(m, n) \text{ is in } M, m < x \text{ and } n < y\},$$

and

$$M_2 = \{(m, n)|(m, n) \text{ is in } M, m \geq x \text{ and } n \geq y\}.$$

Then M_1 is a mapping from $T(s: x - 1)$ to $T'(t: y - 1)$, M_2 is a mapping from $T(x: i)$ to $T'(y: j)$, and $cost(M) = cost(M_1) + cost(M_2)$. Since $cost(M) = E[s: u: i, t: v: j]$, it follows that $cost(M_1) = E[s: u: x - 1, t: v: y - 1]$ and $cost(M_2) = E[x: x: i, y: y: j]$. (Since $T[u]$ is the father of $T[x]$, by Lemma 2.1 $T[u]$ is on the path from $T[s]$ to $T[x - 1]$ and likewise for $T'[v]$.) Therefore,

$$E[s: u: i, t: v: j] = E[s: u: x - 1, t: v: y - 1] + E[x: x: i, y: y: j]. \qquad \text{Q.E.D.}$$

To compute $E[s: u: i, t: v: j]$, we now consider the cases in which one or both of $T[x]$ and $T[y]$ do not exist, i.e., $u = i$ or $v = j$. Let M be a mapping from $T(s: i)$ to $T'(t: j)$ such that $cost(M) = E[s: u: i, t: v: j]$, (s, t) is in M, and no descendant of $T[s]$ $(T'[t])$ on the path from $T[s]$ $(T'[t])$ to $T[u]$ $(T'[v])$ is touched by a line of M.

Case 1: $u = i$ and $v < j$. There are two subcases to be considered:

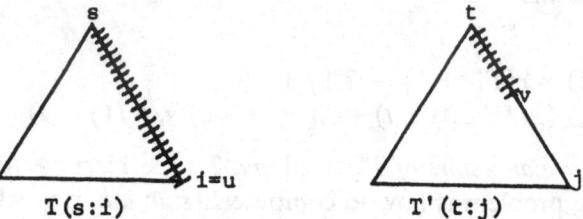

$$T(s:i) \qquad\qquad T'(t:j)$$

(a) $s = u = i$. Then $T(s: i)$ contains exactly one node, $T[s]$, and no descendant of $T'[t]$ is touched by a line of M. By Lemma 2.1, $T'[f(j)]$ is on the path from $T'[t]$ to $T'[j - 1]$. Therefore,

$$E[s: u: i, t: v: j] = E[s: u: i, t: f(j): j - 1] + r(\Lambda \to T'[j]).$$

(b) $s < u = i$. By Lemma 2.1, $T[f(i)]$ is on the path from $T[s]$ to $T[i - 1]$. Since no descendant of $T[s]$ on the path from $T[s]$ to $T[f(i)]$ is touched by a line of M, it follows that

$$E[s: u: i, t: v: j] = E[s: f(i): i - 1, t: v: j] + r(T[i] \to \Lambda).$$

Case 2: $u < i$ and $v = j$. This case is similar to case 1.

(a) $t = v = j$. Then

$$E[s: u: i, t: v: j] = E[s: f(i): i - 1, t: v: j] + r(T[i] \to \Lambda).$$

(b) $t < v = j$. Then

$$E[s: u: i, t: v: j] = E[s: u: i, t: f(j): j - 1] + r(\Lambda \to T'[j]).$$

Case 3: There are four subcases to be considered:

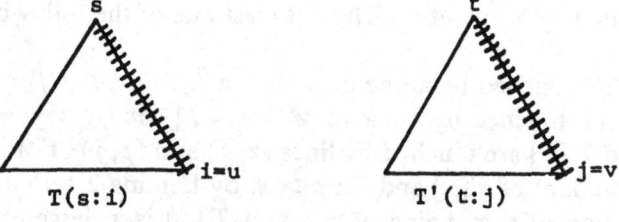

$$T(s:i) \qquad\qquad T'(t:j)$$

(a) $s = u = i$ and $t = v = j$. Then

$$E[s: u: i, t: v: j] = r(T[i] \to T'[j]).$$

(b) $s = u = i$ and $t < v = j$. Then

$$E[s: u: i, t: v: j] = E[s: u: i, t: f(j): j - 1] + r(\Lambda \to T'[j]).$$

(c) $s < u = i$ and $t = v = j$. Then

$$E[s: u: i, t: v: j] = E[s: f(i): i - 1, t: v: j] + r(T[i] \to \Lambda).$$

(d) $s < u = i$ and $t < v = j$. Then neither $T[i]$ nor $T'[j]$ is touched by a line of M. Therefore,

$$E[s\colon u\colon i, t\colon v\colon j] = E[s\colon f(i)\colon i - 1, t\colon v\colon j] + r(T[i] \to \Lambda), \quad \text{or}$$

$$E[s\colon u\colon i, t\colon f(j)\colon j - 1] + r(\Lambda \to T'[j]), \quad \text{or}$$

$$E[s\colon f(i)\colon i - 1, t\colon f(j)\colon j - 1] + r(T[i] \to \Lambda) + r(\Lambda \to T'[j]).$$

Although eight subcases are considered in Cases 1, 2, and 3, only four different formulas are used.

5. An Algorithm for the Tree-to-Tree Correction Problem

Based on the results shown in Sections 3 and 4, an algorithm is presented which computes the distance from tree T to tree T' in polynomial time. This algorithm consists of the following three steps:

(1) Compute $E[s\colon u\colon i, t\colon v\colon j]$ for all s, u, i, t, v, j, where

$$1 \le i \le |T|, \ 1 \le j \le |T'|,$$

$T[u]$ ($T'[v]$) is on the path from $T[1]$ ($T'[1]$) to $T[i]$ ($T'[j]$),

$T[s]$ ($T'[t]$) is on the path from $T[1]$ ($T'[1]$) to $T[u]$ ($T'[v]$);

(2) Compute $MIN\_M(i, j)$ for all i, j, where $1 \le i \le |T|$ and $1 \le j \le |T'|$;

(3) Compute $D(i, j)$ for all i, j, where $1 \le i \le |T|$ and $1 \le j \le |T'|$.

Define $f^n(x) = f(f^{n-1}(x))$ for $n \ge 1$ and $x > 1$, where $f(x)$ is the father of node x, and $f^0(x) = x$. The following is an algorithm for step (1):

```
for i = 1, 2, ... , |T| do
for j = 1, 2, ... , |T'| do
for u = i, f(i), f²(i), ... , 1 do
for s = u, f(u), f²(u), ... , 1 do
for v = j, f(j), f²(j), ... , 1 do
for t = v, f(v), f²(v), ... , 1 do
if s = u = i ∧ t = v = j then E[s: u: i, t: v: j] = r(T[i] → T'[j])
else if s = u = i ∨ t < v = j then E[s: u: i, t: v: j] = E[s: u: i, t: f(j): j − 1] + r(Λ → T'[j])
else if s < u = i ∨ t = v = j then E[s: u: i, t: v: j] = E[s: f(i): i − 1, t: v: j] + r(T[i] → Λ)
else E[s: u: i, t: v: j] = min{E[s: x: i, t: v: j], E[s: u: i, t: y: j], E[s: u: x − 1, t: v: y − 1] + E[x: x: i, y: y: j]}.
```

($T[x]$ is the son of $T[u]$ on the path from $T[u]$ to $T[i]$, and $T'[y]$ is the son of $T'[v]$ on the path from $T'[v]$ to $T'[j]$.)

The following is an algorithm for step (2):

```
MIN_M(1, 1) = 0;
for i = 2, 3, ... , |T| do
  for j = 2, 3, ... , |T'| do
  begin
    MIN_M(i, j) ← INFINITE;
    for s = f(i), f²(i), ... , 1 do
      for t = f(j), f²(j), ... , 1 do
      begin
        temp ← MIN_M(s, t) + E[s: f(i): i − 1, t: f(j): j − 1] − r(T[s] → T'[t]);
        MIN_M(i, j) ← min(temp, MIN_M(i, j))
      end;
    MIN_M(i, j) ← MIN_M(i, j) + r(T[i] → T'[j])
  end;
```

Finally, an algorithm for step (3) is given below:

```
D(1, 1) ← 0;
D(i, 1) ← D(i − 1, 1) + r(T[i] → Λ)   for   i = 2, 3, ... , |T|;
D(1, j) ← D(1, j − 1) + r(Λ → T'[j])   for   j = 2, 3, ... , |T'|;
for i = 2, 3, ... , |T| do
  for j = 2, 3, ... , |T'| do
    D(i, j) ← min(D(i, j − 1) + r(Λ → T'[j]), D(i − 1, j) + r(T[i] → Λ), MIN_M(i, j));
```

Now the tree-to-tree correction problem has been completely solved. The following theorem shows the time complexity of the proposed algorithm for computing the distance from one tree to another.

THEOREM 5.1 *Given two trees T and T', the proposed algorithm computes the distance from T to T' in time $O(V * V' * L^2 * L'^2)$, where V and V' are the numbers of nodes respectively of T and T', and L and L' are the maximum depths respectively of T and T'.*

PROOF. Step (1) computes $E[s: u: i, t: v: j]$ for all s, u, i, t, v, j, where

$$1 \leq i \leq V, \ 1 \leq j \leq V',$$

$T[u] \ (T'[v])$ is on the path from $T[1] \ (T'[1])$ to $T[i] \ (T'[j])$,

$T[s] \ (T'[t])$ is on the path from $T[1] \ (T'[1])$ to $T[u] \ (T'[v])$.

Thus, step (1) takes $O(V * V' * L^2 * L'^2)$ time.

Step (2) computes $MIN\_M(i, j)$ for all i, j, where $1 \leq i \leq V$ and $1 \leq j \leq V'$. Thus, step (2) takes $O(V * V' * L * L')$ time.

Step (3) computes $D(i, j)$ for all i, j, where $1 \leq i \leq V$ and $1 \leq j \leq V'$. Thus, step (3) takes $O(V * V')$ time.

From steps (1), (2), and (3), the distance $D(V, V')$ from T to T' can be computed in time $O(V * V' * L^2 * L'^2)$.   Q.E.D.

6. Conclusion

The notion of *distance* between two trees can be applied to measuring the *similarity* between two trees. Since trees have been used for different applications, the similarity between trees can have different interpretations. One possible application is to the problem of syntactic error recovery and correction for programming languages. In [11] it was suggested that for the selection of an error recovery or correction, the similarity between a corrected string and its replacement should be based on the two strings as well as their associated parse trees.

The *longest common subsequence* problem, which is a special case of the string-to-string correction problem, has received much attention [1, 3, 4, 5, 13]. The notion of longest common subsequence between two strings can be extended for trees as well. Tree T'' is a *substructure* of tree T if there exists a mapping M from T'' to T such that every node of T'' is touched by a line of M and for every $(p, q) \in M$, $T[p] = T'[q]$. Tree T'' is a *common substructure* of trees T and T' if T'' is a substructure of both T and T'. Tree T'' is a *largest common substructure* of T and T' if there is no common substructure of T and T' that has more nodes than T''. With constant cost W_C, W_D, W_I for changing, deleting, and inserting any node, and with $W_C = W_I + W_D$, the tree resulting from T by deleting nodes of T that are changed or deleted during a minimum cost transformation from T to T' is a largest common substructure of T and T'.

In [7, 12] the string-to-string correction problem was extended by allowing the operation of interchanging two adjacent characters. Wagner [12] showed that under certain restrictions the extended string-to-string correction problem can be solved in deterministic polynomial time, but the general problem is NP-complete. How to extend the tree-to-tree correction problem by allowing the operation of interchanging two adjacent nodes is currently being investigated.

The tree-to-tree correction problem may also be extendable by modifying the definitions of change, delete, and insert operations. One example is to add the restriction that the delete and insert operations can only be applied to the leaves of trees. For this restricted problem, one more condition should be added to the definition of a mapping M:

$$\text{For every } (i, j) \in M, \quad \text{if} \quad i \neq 1 \neq j, \quad \text{then} \quad (f(i), f(j)) \in M.$$

This condition implies that if $T[i]$ and $T'[j]$ are touched by the same line, then they have the same level number. The algorithm presented in Section 5 can be simplified to solve the restricted problem, but the simplification process is not trivial. In [9] Selkow proposed a simple algorithm which solves this restricted problem in time $O(|T| * |T'|)$.

ACKNOWLEDGMENTS. I would like to thank the referees for their helpful suggestions for improving the readability of this paper. The notion of $E[s: u: i, t: v: j]$ was motivated by a suggestion given by one referee. Using this notation, the computation of MIN__$M(i, j)$ has been substantially simplified.

REFERENCES

1. Aho, A.V., Hirschberg, D.S., and Ullman, J.D. Bounds on the complexity of the longest common subsequence problem. *J. ACM 23*, 1 (Jan. 1976), 1–12.
2. Fu, K.S., and Bhargava, B.K. Tree systems for syntactic pattern recognition. *IEEE Trans. Comptrs. C-22*, 12 (Dec. 1973), 1087–1099.
3. Hirschberg, D.S. A linear space algorithm for computing maximal common subsequences. *Comm. ACM 18*, 6 (June 1975), 341–343.
4. Hirschberg, D.S. Algorithms for the longest common subsequence problem. *J. ACM 24*, 4 (Oct. 1977), 664–675.
5. Hunt, J.W., and Szymanski, T.G. A fast algorithm for computing longest common subsequences. *Comm. ACM 20*, 5 (May 1977), 350–353.
6. Knuth, D.E. *The Art of Computer Programming, Vol. 1: Fundamental Algorithms.* Addison-Wesley, Reading, Mass., sec. ed., 1973.
7. Lowrance, R., and Wagner, R.A. An extension of the string-to-string correction problem. *J. ACM 22*, 2 (April 1975), 177–183.
8. Sankoff, D. Matching sequences under deletion/insertion constraints. *Proc. Nat. Acad. Sci. USA 69*, 1 (Jan. 1974), 4–6.
9. Selkow, S.M. The tree-to-tree editing problem. *Inform. Processing Letters 6*, 6 (Dec. 1977), 184–186.
10. Sellers, P.H. An algorithm for the distance between two finite sequences. *J. Combin. Theory, Ser. A*, 16 (1974), 253–258.
11. Tai, K.C. Syntactic error correction in programming languages. Ph.D. Th., Dept. Comptr. Sci., Cornell U., Ithaca, N.Y., 1977.
12. Wagner, R.A. On the complexity of the extended string-to-string correction problem. Proc. Seventh Annual ACM Symp. on Theory of Comptng., Albuquerque, New Mex., 1975, pp. 218–223.
13. Wagner, R.A., and Fischer, M.J. The string-to-string correction problem. *J. ACM 21*, 1 (Jan. 1974), 168–173.
14. Wong, C.K., and Chandra, A.K. Bounds for the string editing problem. *J. ACM 23*, 1 (Jan. 1976), 13–16.

RECEIVED MARCH 1977; REVISED JANUARY 1979

Edgar H. Sibley
Panel Editor

By reducing an array matching problem to a string matching problem in a natural way, it is shown that efficient string matching algorithms can be applied to arrays, assuming that a linear preprocessing is made on the text.

A Technique for Two-Dimensional Pattern Matching

Rui Feng Zhu and Tadao Takaoka

Three major efficient pattern matching algorithms were proposed in the past decade, one by Knuth, Morris, and Pratt (KMP algorithm) [8], one by Boyer and Moore (BM algorithm) [5], and one by Rabin and Karp (RK algorithm) [6].

A natural generalization of the pattern matching problem is the two-dimensional pattern matching problem where the pattern is a two-dimensional array of characters PATTERN [1 .. P1, 1 .. P2] and the text is a second array TEXT [1 .. N1, 1 .. N2]. In this case the problem is to determine where, if anywhere, the pattern occurs as a subarray of the text.

In this article we first present an efficient pattern matching algorithm for the two-dimensional case, one which is a combination of the KMP and RK algorithms. Assuming, in the worst case, that the RK algorithm runs linearly for one-dimensional array matching, this algorithm takes time proportional to $O(N1 * N2 + P1 * P2)$ in the worst and average cases, which is clearly optimal since both the pattern and the text have to be read and this takes $O(N1 * N2 + P1 * P2)$ time. The algorithm needs $O(N1 * N2 + P1 * P2)$ space, and also works on-line (assuming the text is read row by row). Second, we describe another approach, which takes $O(N1 * N2 * \log(P2)/P2 + P1 * P2)$ time on average and also runs faster when the row length of the pattern increases.

Computer experiments show that for various pattern sizes the average cost for either of our algorithms is much less than that of the algorithm proposed by Bird (B algorithm) [4].

Reprinted from **Communications of the ACM**, Volume 32, No. 9, September 1989, pp. 1110-1120. Copyright 1989, Association for Computing Machinery, Inc., reprinted by permission.

THE KMP ALGORITHM

The KMP algorithm [8] solves the problem by comparing the characters of the pattern with those of the text from the left end of the pattern. To illustrate this approach, consider an example, searching for pattern = 'ababb' in text = 'babbababacababb'.

```
pattern:  ababb
text:     babbababacababb
```

Since the text pointer points to the character b, which does not match 'a' in the pattern, the pattern is shifted one place to the right and the next text character is inspected.

```
pattern:   ababb
text:      babbababacababb
```

There is a match, so the pattern remains where it is while the next several characters are scanned until we come to a mismatch.

```
pattern:   ababb
text:      babbababacababb
```

The first two pattern characters are matched, but there is a mismatch on the third. Thus it is known that the last three characters of the text have been ab?, where '?' is not equal to 'a'. Next the pattern can be shifted three more places to the right, since '?' is not equal to 'a' and a shift of one or two positions could not lead to a match. Thus the situation appears as:

```
pattern:       ababb
text:      babbababacababb
```

The characters are scanned again and another partial match occurs. A mismatch occurs on the fifth pattern character.

```
pattern:      ababb
text:     babbababacababb
```

Similarly we know that the last five text characters were abab?, where ? is not equal to 'b' but might be equal to 'a'. Thus the pattern should be shifted two places to the right.

```
pattern:        ababb
text:     babbababacababb
```

Comparing the two characters we get a mismatch, so we shift the pattern further four places.

```
pattern:            ababb
text:     babbababacababb
```

Scanning the following characters, the full pattern is found. The pattern match has succeeded.

```
pattern:            ababb
text:     babbababacababb
```

This example shows that by knowing the characters in the pattern and the position where a mismatch occurs, it can be determined where in the pattern to continue to search for a match without moving backward in the text. It also tells us that the process of pattern matching will run much more efficiently if we have an auxiliary table which will provide us with the information of how far to slide the pattern when a mismatch has been detected at a certain position in the pattern. The following algorithm summarizes the behavior of the KMP algorithm.

ALGORITHM 1: KMP Algorithm.
INPUT.

```
    The text(pattern) is stored in the
    array TEXT[1 .. N] (PT[1 .. M]), h is
    the auxiliary function, p and q are
    pointers of pattern and text,
    respectively.
OUTPUT.
    Location at which the pattern is
    found.
METHOD.
    begin
      compute-h;
      p := 1; q := 1;
      while (p ≤ M) and (q ≤ N) do
      begin
        while (p > 0) and (PT[p]
        ≠ TEXT[q]) do p := h[p];
          p := p + 1; q := q + 1
      end;
      if p ≤ M then writeln('not found')
          else writeln
              ('The left end of the pattern
               is found at', q - p + 1)
```

```
    end.
procedure compute-h;
begin
    t := 0; h[1] := 0;
    for p := 2 to M do
      begin
      while (t > 0) and (PT[p - 1]
      ≠ PT[t]) do t := h[t];
      t := t + 1;
      if PT[p] ≠ PT[t] then h[p] := t
      else h[p] := h[t]
    end
end.
Note:
    The definition of the h function is:
      h[p] = max{s | (s = 0)
      or ((PT[1 .. s - 1] = PT[p - s
        + 1 .. p - 1]
      and PT[s] ≠ PT[p] and (1 ≤ s < p))},
      h[1] = 0.
```

The value of $h[p]$ gives the position at which matching starts again after a mismatch occurs. The detailed reasoning of this computation of h is given in [8]. For our example of PT = 'ababb' h is computed as (0, 1, 0, 1, 3).

THE RK ALGORITHM

The RK algorithm [6] solves the problem by treating each possible M-character section (where M is the pattern length) of the text as a key in a hash table, then computing the hash function of it and checking to see if it is equal to the hash function of the pattern. Here the hash function is defined as follows: $h(k) = k \bmod q$, where q is a large prime. The use of such a large value of q makes it extremely unlikely that a collision will occur. We translate the M-character to numbers by packing them together in a computer word, which we then treat as an integer—k in the above. This corresponds to writing the characters as numbers in a radix-d number system, where d is the number of possible characters. The number k corresponding to the M-character section TEXT[i] ... TEXT[i + M - 1] is:

$$k = \text{ord}(\text{TEXT}[i]) * d^{M-1} + \text{ord}(\text{TEXT}[i + 1]) * d^{M-2} + \ldots + \text{ord}(\text{TEXT}[i + M - 1])$$

where ord(x) is the order of character x. Shifting one position to the right in the text simply corresponds to replacing k by

$$(k - \text{ord}(\text{TEXT}[i]) * d^{M-1}) * d + \text{ord}(\text{TEXT}[i + M]).$$

This leads to the very simple pattern matching algorithm implemented below.

ALGORITHM 2: RK Algorithm.
INPUT:

```
    The text(pattern) is stored in the
    array TEXT[1 .. N] (PT[1 .. M]); dm is
    used as a constant equal to d^{M-1}.
```

```
   Location in the text which has the
   same hash value as the pattern.
METHOD:
   begin
      dm := 1; for i := 1 to M - 1
        do dm := (d * dm) mod q;
      h1 := 0; for i := 1 to M
        do h1 := (h1 * d + ord(PT[i]))
              mod q;
      h2 := 0; for i := 1 to M
        do h2 := (h2 * d + ord(TEXT[i]))
              mod q;
      i := 1;
      while (h1 ≠ h2) and (i ≤ N - M) do
        begin
           h2 := (h2 + d * q - ord(TEXT[i])
              * dm) mod q;
           h2 := (h2 * d + ord(TEXT[i + M]))
              mod q;
           i := i + 1;
        end;
      if h1 = h2 then writeln('found at',
        i)
              else writeln ('not
              found')
   end.
```

The algorithm only finds a position in the text which has the same hash value as the pattern. To be sure, we should do a direct comparison of characters in the text with those in the pattern. Obviously, this algorithm takes time proportional to $M + N$, assuming that we can ignore the probability of collision, that is, the case where two different strings have the same hash values.

THE ALGORITHM

The general scheme of our algorithm is to use the hash function method proposed in the RK algorithm vertically. We first translate the two-dimensional arrays of characters of TEXT and PATTERN to one-dimensional numbers of TEXT' and PATTERN', respectively; we then search TEXT' for the occurrences of the PATTERN' using the KMP technique row by row. The algorithm is as follows:

```
ALGORITHM 3.
INPUT:
   The text and pattern are stored in
   the TEXT[1 .. N1, 1 .. N2] and PATTERN
   [1 .. P1, 1 .. P2], respectively.
OUTPUT:
   Location at which pattern occurs.
METHOD:
   1. begin
   2.    texthash; row := P1;
   3.    dm := 1; for j := 1 to P1 - 1
           do dm := (d * dm) mod q;
   4.    read(PATTERN);
   5.    pathash;
```

```
   6.    repeat KMP' (PATTERN',
           TEXT', found, column);
   7.       if (found = false) and (row
             < N1) then change(row);
   8.    row := row + 1;
   9.    until (found = true) or (row
           > N1);
   10.   if found = true
   11.      then writeln
              ('The beginning of the
              pattern is found at', row -
              P1 + 1, column - P2 + 1)
   12.      else writeln
              ('not found')
   13. end.
```

```
procedure pathash;
begin
for j := 1 to P2 do
   begin
      PATTERN'[j] := 0;
      for i := 1 to P1 do
      PATTERN'[j] := (PATTERN' [j] * d
        + ord(PATTERN[i, j])) mod q
   end
end;

procedure texthash;
begin
for j := 1 to N2 do
   begin
      TEXT'[j] := 0;
      for i := 1 to P1 do
      TEXT'[j] := (TEXT'[j] * d + ord
      (TEXT[i, j])) mod q
   end
end;
```

In algorithm 3 we first compute two vectors of PATTERN' and TEXT' from PATTERN and TEXT. For example, suppose PATTERN is:

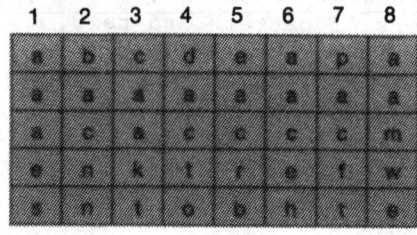

FIGURE 1.   An Example of *PATTERN*

Assume that ord('a') = 0, d = 32, q = 33,554,393, and the distance between two adjacent alphabeti~ characters is 1, so PATTERN' is:

FIGURE 2.   An Example of *PATTERN'*

And the TEXT' can then also be computed in the same way.

Second, the KMP' procedure is used to match PAT-TERN' with TEXT'. If the matching process fails at "row-th" row, that is, found = false, another procedure change(row) is used to change the value of TEXT' from row to row + 1. The change(row) procedure is obviously optimal since shifting one row down in the TEXT simply corresponds to replacing TEXT'[j] by:

$$\text{TEXT'}[j] - \text{ord}(\text{TEXT}[row - P1 + 1, j]) \\ * dm)) * d \\ + \text{ord}(\text{TEXT}[row + 1, j]).$$

Such operations are executed repeatedly, until found = true or row > N1. Procedure change(row) is as follows:

```
procedure change(row);
begin
for j := 1 to N2 do
TEXT'[j]
   := (TEXT'[j] + d * q - ord(TEXT[row
   - P1 + 1, j]) * dm) * d
   + ord(TEXT[row + 1, j]) mod q
end;
```

The KMP' procedure is the same as the KMP algorithm except that it returns the truth value and position in "found" and "column" if the pattern is found and Procedure directcompare(found, row, column) is inserted at the end of the KMP algorithm.

```
procedure directcompare(found, row,
column);
begin
   found := true; i := 1; j := 1;
   while (i ≤ P1) and (found = true) do
     begin
       while (j ≤ P2) and (found = true)
       do
         begin
         if PATTERN[i, j]
           ≠ TEXT[row - P1 + i,
                 column - P2 + j]
           then found := false;
         j := j + 1;
         end;
         i := i + 1
     end
end;
```

Notice that procedure KMP' only works because the KMP algorithm is independent of the size of the character alphabet, which can consequently be arbitrarily large.

The pattern matching algorithms are mainly used for text editing. From the user's point of view, the response time is from the time the pattern is input to the time the pattern is found. To do the job of change(row) in advance, we can modify our algorithm in the following way.

First, we expand TEXT' to an array [P1 .. N1, 1 .. N2] and replace procedure texthash with the following code:

```
procedure texthash';
begin
  for j := 1 to N2 do
  begin
    TEXT'[P1, j] := 0;
    for i := 1 to P1 do
    TEXT'[P1, j] := (TEXT'[P1, j] * d
      + ord(TEXT[i, j])) mod q;
  end;
  for i := P1 + 1 to N1 do
  for j := 1 to N2 do
  TEXT'[i, j] := (TEXT'[i - 1, j] + d * q
    - ord(TEXT[i - P1]) * dm) * d
    + ord(TEXT[i, j]) mod q
end;
```

Then the seventh line and procedure change(row) of algorithm 3 are deleted. We measure the running time after the pattern is read, that is, from the fifth line of algorithm 3, and the B algorithm [4] is also measured in the same way. (The computation of TEXT' is considered to be preprocessing.) The results are shown in the first and second columns of Table I and indicate that for various sizes of patterns the average cost of our algorithm is about one-seventh of that of the B algorithm. The summary of algorithm B is listed in Appendix A. The advantages of this algorithm are:

1. Time complexity is $O(N1 * N2 + P1 * P2)$ for either of the worst case and average case since the number of multiplications during the preprocessing stage for the hash function calculation is $O(N1 * N2 + P1 * P2)$ and the largest number of comparisons made in KMP' procedure is $O((N1 - P1) * N2)$.
2. The actual running time is much less than the B algorithm. We measure running time after the pattern is read.
3. Space complexity is $O(N1 * N2 + P1 * P2)$, including the auxiliary array TEXT'.
4. The algorithm is simpler than other algorithms proposed in the past [2, 3].
5. Its on-line nature, that is, the input is scanned only once, and after scanning the character at any position of the input, before scanning further, it is possible to answer YES or NO to whether the pattern matches at that position.

Another Approach

In this approach, as the strategy proposed in the BM algorithm [5] is used, we first present the BM algorithm in the following section.

TABLE I. Average Costs of the Three Algorithms

Pattern size	Average Cost		
	B Algorithm	Algorithm 3	Algorithm 4
[1 .. 5, 1 .. 5]	41774	4755	14860
[1 .. 10, 1 .. 10]	32910	6730	9060
[1 .. 20, 1 .. 20]	38020	6390	6460
[1 .. 30, 1 .. 30]	38490	6157	5460
[1 .. 40, 1 .. 40]	40730	6140	4750
[1 .. 50, 1 .. 50]	39952	5670	4390
[1 .. 60, 1 .. 60]	41260	5280	3810
[1 .. 70, 1 .. 70]	41910	5360	3810
[1 .. 80, 1 .. 80]	43520	5120	3430
[1 .. 90, 1 .. 90]	43650	4780	3380
[1 .. 100, 1 .. 100]	42910	4500	3310

The size of text is [1 .. 1000, 1 .. 1000]. Text and pattern are derived from random text composed of 24 characters. Costs are measured by computing time in milliseconds.

The BM Algorithm

Unlike the KMP algorithm and the straightforward algorithm, the BM algorithm compares the pattern with the text from the right end of the pattern. The performance of this algorithm is quite good in the average case, where it performs in $O(N/M)$ time. Here N is the length of text, while M is the length of pattern. Several variations were proposed to improve the number of character comparisons in the worst case of the BM algorithm. They are: Knuth [8] which achieved linear time in the worst case but lost the linear time in the preprocessing; Galil [7] which made the worst cost bounded by $14n$; and recently published by Apostolico and Giancarlo [2] which had the worst case bounded by $2n$. The authors have presented a method [9] to improve the average performance of the BM algorithm.

The BM algorithm solves the pattern matching problem by repeatedly positioning the pattern over the text and attempting to match it. For each positioning that occurs, the algorithm starts matching the pattern against the text from the right end of the pattern. If no mismatch occurs, then the pattern has been found, otherwise the algorithm takes a shift that is an amount by which the pattern will be moved to the right before a new matching attempt is undertaken.

```
ALGORITHM 4: BM Algorithm.
INPUT:
  The text(pattern) is stored in the
  array TEXT[1 .. N] (PATTERN[1 .. M]);
  p(q) points to the current characters
  of the PATTERN(TEXT); D[ch] and DD[i]
  are the auxiliary shift functions.
OUTPUT:
  Location at which the pattern is
  found.
METHOD:
```

```
begin
  q := M;
  repeat p := M;
    while (p > 0) and (PATTERN[p]
      = TEXT[q] do
      begin p := p - 1; q := q - 1 end;
    if p ≠ 0 then q := q
      + max(D[TEXT[q]], DD[p])
  until (p = 0) or (q > N)
end.
Note:
  The definitions of the D shift
  function and the DD shift function
  are:
  D[ch] = min{s | s = M
    or (0 < s < M and PATTERN[M - s]
      = ch)};
  DD[p] = min{s + M - p | (s ≥ 1) and
  (s ≥ p
    or PATTERN[p - s] ≠ PATTERN[p]
    and (s ≥ i or PATTERN[i - s]
  = PATTERN[i], p < i ≤ M)}.
```

Here D and DD are often referred to as `shift` functions. The DD `shift` function is based on the idea that when the pattern is moved right, it has to (1) match over all the characters previously matched, and (2) bring a different character over the character of the text that caused the mismatch. Figure 3 illustrates the definition of the DD `shift` function. The D `shift` function uses the fact that we must bring over ch = `text[q]` (the character that caused mismatch), the first occurrence of 'ch' in the pattern viewed from the right end. The definition of the D `shift` function is shown in Figure 4. Both shift functions can be obtained from precomputed tables based solely on the pattern and the alphabet used. The DD `shift` function requires a table of length equal to the pattern, while the D `shift` function requires a table of size equal to the alphabet size. Given the two values of the two shift functions, the BM algorithm chooses the larger one. For reasons of space the details regarding computations of the D `shift` function and the DD `shift` functions are omitted. (Details are given in [5] and [8].)

The Algorithm

Examining the example in Figure 2, we find that the values of PATTERN' and TEXT' vary over a great range. This means that for most cases the comparisons between PATTERN' and TEXT' are mismatches. Based on this observation, we modify our algorithm in the following way. First, using any efficient sorting method, we sort PATTERN' and store the sorted PATTERN' and its indices value into PH1[1 .. 2, 1 .. P2]. The PH1 values of the example in Figure 2 are given in Figure 5.

Second, incorporating the DD `shift` function of the BM algorithm into our situation, we replace procedure KMP' of algorithm 3 by procedure SEARCH in which

224

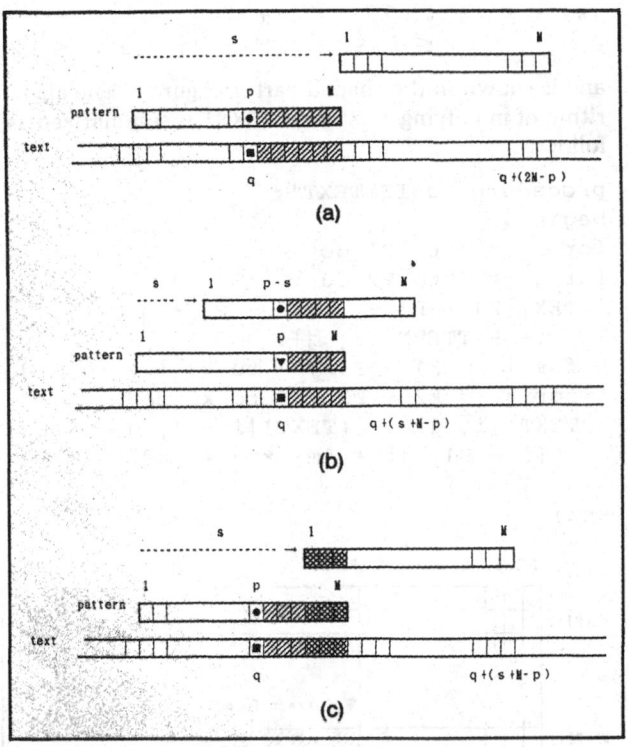

FIGURE 3. The Definition of *DD Shift* Function. (a) $s = M$, (b) $s < p$, (c) $s \geq p$

we begin comparison at the end of PATTERN'. The algorithm is summarized as follows.

ALGORITHM 5.
INPUT:
```
  The text and pattern are stored in
  the TEXT[1 .. N1, 1 .. N2] and
  PATTERN[1 .. P1, 1 .. P2],
  respectively.
```
OUTPUT:
```
  Location at which pattern occurs.
```
METHOD:
```
  1. begin
  2.    texthash;
  3.    for row := P1 to (N1 - 1)
           do change(row);
  4.    row := P1;
  5.    dm := 1; for j := 1 to P1 - 1
           do dm := (d * dm) mod q;
  6.    read(PATTERN);
  7.    pathash;
  8.    repeat SEARCH(PATTERN',
           TEXT', found);
  9.      row := row + 1;
 10.    until (found = true)or
              (row > N1);
 12.    if found = true
 13.      then writeln
              ('The beginning of the
              pattern is found at',
              row - P1 + 1, column + 1)
 14.      else writeln ('not found')
```

```
 15. end.
procedure search (PATTERN', TEXT'
     found);
begin
  j := P2;
  repeat
    i := P2;
  while TEXT'[row, j] = PATTERN'[i]
       do
    begin j := j - 1; i := i - 1 end;
  if i := 0
  then
  begin directcompare
          (found, row, j + P2);
    column := j; end
    else
    begin
      y := binarysearch(TEXT'[row, j]);
      if y = P2 + 1 then j := j + P2
        else
        begin
          k := P2 - PH1[2, y];
          if DD[i] > k
            then j := j + DD[i]
            else j := j + k
        end
    end
  until (j > N2) or (found = true)
end;

function binarysearch(v: integer):
integer;
begin
  l := 1; r := P2;
  repeat
      x := (l + r) div 2;
      if v < PH1[1, x]
        then r := x - 1
        else l := x + 1
  until (v = PH1[1, x]) or (l > r);
  if v = PH1[1, x] then binarysearch := x
  else binarysearch := P2 + 1
end;
```

Notice that the mismatch occurs at the right end of PATTERN' on almost every occasion when PATTERN' is positioned over TEXT', and this will make the BM

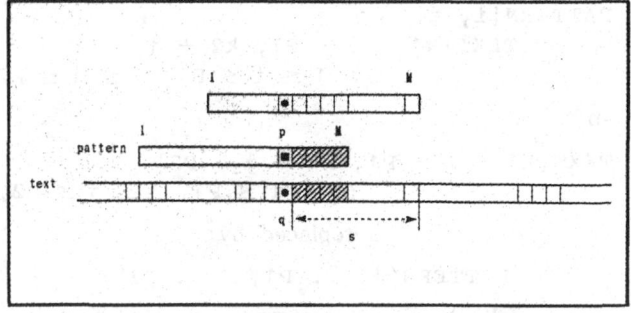

FIGURE 4. The Definition of the *D Shift* Function

	1	2	3	4	5	6	7	8
1	146	2183	12996	105086	196897	2097491	3148398	15730867
2	1	6	8	2	5	3	4	7

FIGURE 5.   An Example of _PH1_

strategy work efficiently.

As the elements of TEXT' are large numbers bounded by q, the size of the character alphabet is equal to q, and also the definition of the D shift function in the BM algorithm is based on the size of the character alphabet; use of the D shift function is not appropriate in this context. Instead, we use function binarysearch to examine whether the value of TEXT' at position j is the same as any of PH1[1, k], $1 \leq k \leq P2$ and give the position in PH1 if the same value exists. As discussed above, in most cases the answer is NO, which means that j is increased by $P2$, that is, PATTERN' is slid to the right $P2$ places. On the other hand, occasionally the answer may be YES. In this case, comparing the two amounts of shifts made by the DD shift function and binarysearch, we choose the larger one. The amount k of shift made by binarysearch is the distance from the position kk where PATTERN'[kk] = TEXT'[row, j] to $P2$. As for the DD shift function, refer to [8].

For each binarysearch, $\log(P2)$ steps are needed; so the average time of this approach is $O(N1 * N2 * \log(P2)/P2 + P1 * P2)$. Obviously, it takes less time when $P2$ increases, that is, the row length of the pattern gets longer. Refer to the third column of Table I. We can find that this approach works best as $P1$ and $P2$ are larger than 30. The advantages of this approach are similar to those listed in the previous section dealing with algorithm 3.

TWO-DIMENSIONAL TEXT MODIFICATION
The main aim of pattern matching is to modify a portion of the TEXT at positions where the pattern is found. In the one-dimensional case, the portion is often lengthened or shortened after modification. But, in the two-dimensional case, the modified portion generally does not change in size. This can be defined formally as follows. Assuming the pattern is found at TEXT[k1, k2], that is:

$$PATTERN[i, j]$$
$$= TEXT[k1 + i - P1, k2 + j - P2]$$
$$1 \leq i \leq P1, 1 \leq j \leq P2$$

and

$$TEXT[k1 + i - P1, k2 + j - P2]$$
$$(1 \leq i \leq P1, 1 \leq j \leq P2)$$

is replaced by

$$PATTERN'[1 .. P1, 1 .. P2];$$

correspondingly, a portion of TEXT' should be substituted. The range of such substitution in TEXT' is

$$[k1 - P1 + i, k2 - P2 + j]$$
$$(1 \leq i \leq 2 * P1 - 1, 1 \leq j \leq P2)$$

and is shown in the shaded part in Figure 6. The algorithm of modifying TEXT and TEXT' is summarized as follows:

```
procedure MODIFYTEXT';
begin
for i := 1 to P1 do
for j := 1 to P2 do
  TEXT[k1 - P1 + i, k2 - P2 + j]
    := PATTERN'[i, j];
  for i := k1 - P1 + 1 to k1 + P1 - 1 do
  for j := k2 - P2 + 1 to k2 do
  TEXT'[i, j] := (TEXT'[i - 1, j] - TEXT
    [i - P1, j] * dm) * d + ord(TEXT
    [1, j])
end;
```

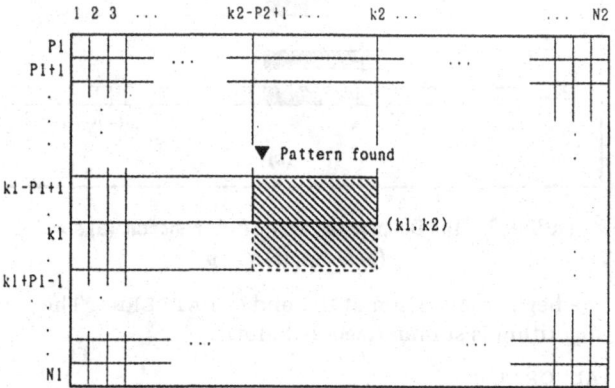

FIGURE 6.   The Range of Substitution in TEXT'

Procedure MODIFYTEXT' takes $O(P1 * P2)$ time. This means that we can use TEXT' many times without spending much time to modify TEXT' when a portion of TEXT is replaced.

APPENDIX A

THE B ALGORITHM

The B algorithm invented by Bird [4] is briefly described as follows. The text[1 .. N, 1 .. N] is read from the upper left corner to the bottom right corner in the order of text[1, 1];...,text[1, N],text[2, 1],...,text[2, N],..., text[N, 1],...,text[N, N]. The pattern pat[1 .. M, 1 .. M] is divided into M rows of $R_1 = pat[1, 1 .. M],...,R_M = pat[M, 1 .. M]$. Note that some of $R_1,...,R_M$ may be equal with each other. Each time text[i, j] is read, it is determined whether the portion text[i, j - M + 1 .. j] = R matches any of $R_1, ..., R_M$ (horizontal matching). See Figure 1 and Figure 2.

We use a one-dimensional array a[1 .. N] such

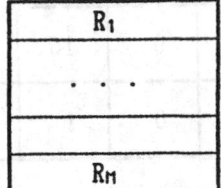

FIGURE 1. An Example of Pattern

that $a[j] = k$ means that $k - 1$ rows R_1, ..., R_{k-1} match the portion $\texttt{text}[i - k + 1 .. i - 1, j - M + 1 .. j]$. If $R = R_k$, $a[j]$ is increased by one. If not, we find maximum s such that:

$$R = R_s, \quad R_1 = R_{k-s+1}, \quad ..., \quad R_{s-1} = R_{k-1} \qquad (1)$$

using the KMP method vertically, and set $a[j]$ to $s + 1$. If there is no such s, $a[j]$ is set to 0. If $a[j] = M + 1$, we can say that the pattern has been found.

This vertical use of the KMP method is done by regarding the sequences of rows R_1, ..., R_M as a linear pattern $r[1 .. M]$. The elements of $r[1 .. M]$ can be up to M different symbols or integers for row patterns. The condition (1) above is illustrated by Figure 3.

An example of $\texttt{pat}[1 .. 5, 1 .. 5]$ and $r[1 .. 5]$ is given in Figure 4; we do not distinguish between rows and their corresponding integer values. While $R \neq r[k]$, we perform $k \leftarrow h[k]$ where h is the h function used in the KMP method. We repeat this until condition (1) is true. For the above r, we have the following h function:

	1	2	3	4	5
r	1	2	3	1	3
h	0	1	1	0	2

Now we go back to the problem of the horizontal matching. The solution is well explained by using the above example. We construct a finite automaton for

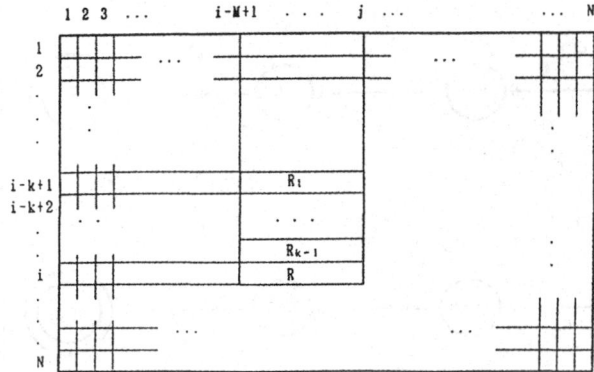

FIGURE 2. An Example of Text

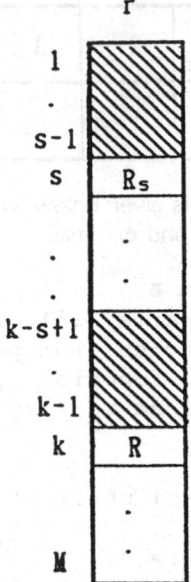

FIGURE 3. Illustration of Condition (1)

multiple pattern matching invented by Aho and Corasick [1] as shown in Figure 5.

In this machine, 0 is the initial state and 5, 8, and 12 are final states shown by double circles. The final states output integer values for corresponding rows. Using the output function $\texttt{out}$, these are specified as:

$$\texttt{out}(5) = 1 = r[1] = r[4],$$

$$\texttt{out}(8) = 2 = r[2],$$

$$\texttt{out}(12) = 3 = r[3] = r[5].$$

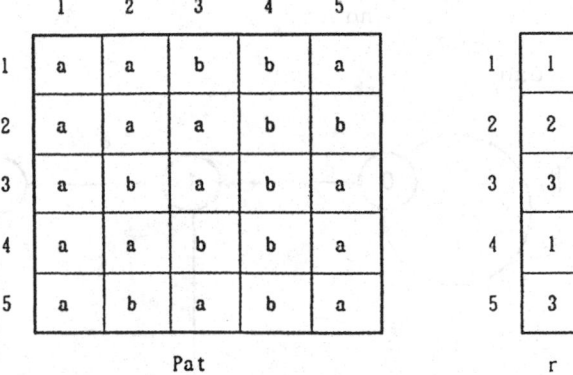

	1	2	3	4	5
1	a	a	b	b	a
2	a	a	a	b	b
3	a	b	a	b	a
4	a	a	b	b	a
5	a	b	a	b	a

1	1
2	2
3	3
4	1
5	3

Pat   r

FIGURE 4. An Example of Pat [1 .. 5, 1 .. 5] and Its Corresponding r [1 .. 5]

The **goto** function g is shown in Figure 5, for example, $g(2, \texttt{b}) = 3, g(2, \texttt{a}) = 6$ and so on. If there is no definition of g in the machine, we set the value of g to "fail," for example, $g(6, \texttt{a}) = \texttt{fail}$. If the value of g is fail, the failure function f is consulted, which tells us from which state the processing should resume. For the above example, f becomes as follows:

j	1	2	3	4	5	6	7	8	9	10	11	12
f(j)	0	1	9	0	1	2	3	4	0	1	9	10

The B algorithm is given below, where i and j are
expressed by row and column.

(a). Algorithm B.
Input: A text array T[1 .. N1, 1 .. N2] of string and a pattern matching machine
        constructed from pattern PT[1 .. P1, 1 .. P2]. The machine is composed
        of **goto** function g, failure function f, and output function out.
Output: locations in T at which PT occurs.
Method:

```
begin
   for row := 1 until N1 do
     begin
       state := 0;
         for column := 1 until N2 do
           begin
             while g(state, T[row, column]) = fail do
               state := f(state);
             state := g(state, T[row, column]);
             if out(state) ≠ 0
               then
                 begin
                   k := a[column];
                   while (k > 0) and (PT[k, 1 .. P2] ≠ out(state)) do
                     k := h(k);
                   a[column] := k + 1;
                   if k = P1
                     then print('PT is found at (row − P1, column − P2)')
                 end
               else a[column] := 0
           end
     end
end.
```

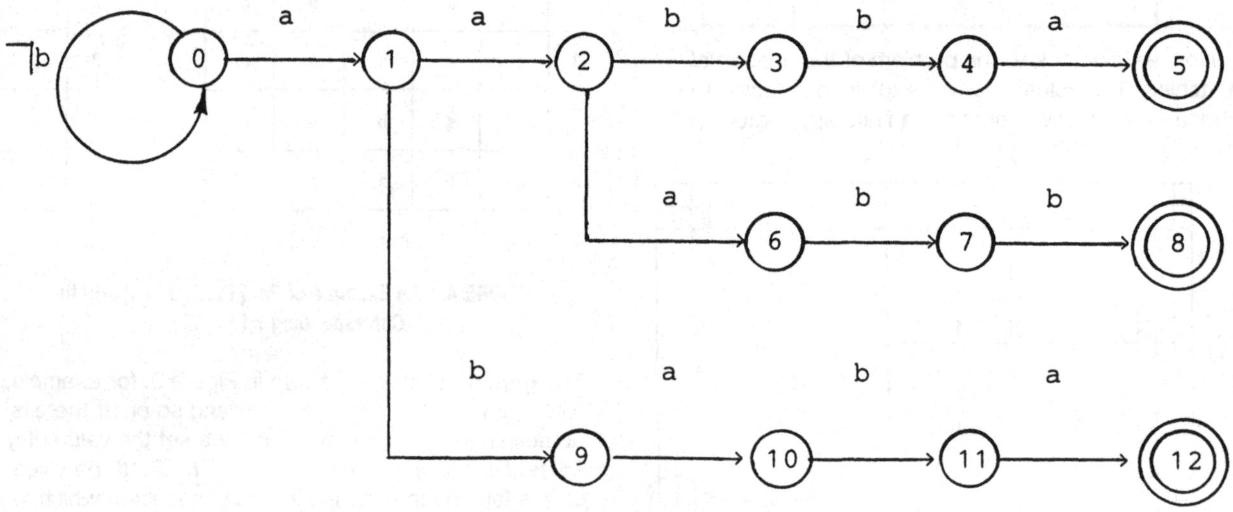

FIGURE 5. Multiple Pattern Matching Machine

(b). Construction of the goto function.

Input: Pattern PT[1 .. P1, 1 .. P2].

Output: Goto function g and output function out.

Method: We assume out(s) = 0 when state s is first created, and g(s, a) =
fail if 'a' is undefined or if g(s, a) has not yet been defined. The
procedure enter(PT) inserts into the **goto** graph a path that spells
out PT. The elements of r[1 .. P1] represent each unique row of PT.

```
  begin
    newstate := 0; out(0) := 0;
    for i := 1 until P1 do
      enter(r[i], PT[i, 1 .. P2]);
    for all 'a' such that g(0, a) = fail do g(0, a) := 0
  end.

procedure enter(i1, A₁ A₂ ... Aₘ);
  begin
    state := 0; j := 1;
    while g(state, Aⱼ) ≠ fail do
      begin
        state := g(state, Aⱼ);
        j := j + 1
      end;
    for p := j until m do
      begin
        newstate := newstate + 1;
        g(state, Aₚ) := newstate;
        state := newstate;
        out(state) := 0
      end;
    out(state) := i1
  end.
```

(c). Construction of the failure function.

Input: Goto function g and output function out.

Output: Failure function f.

Other variables: queue is a first-in-first-out data structure.

Method:

```
  begin
    queue := empty;
    for each 'a' such that g(0, a) = s ≠ 0 do
      begin
        queue := queue.s; {add s to the end of queue}
        f(s) := 0
      end;
    while queue ≠ empty do
      begin
        let r be the head of queue, that is, queue = r.tail;
        queue := tail;
        for each 'a' such that g(r, a) = s ≠ fail do
          begin
            queue := queue.s;
            state := f(r);
            while g(state, a) = fail do state := f(state);
            f(s) := g(state, a);
          end
      end
  end.
```

(d). Computation of h function.

Input: Pattern PT[1 .. P1, 1 .. P2].

```
Output: Shift function h.
Method:
  begin
    t := 0; h[1] := 0;
    for p := 2 to P1 do
      begin
        while (t > 0) and (PT[p - 1, 1 .. P2] ≠ PT[t, 1 .. P2]) do t := h[t];
        t := t + 1;
        if PT[p, 1 .. P2] ≠ PT[t, 1 .. P2] then h[p] := t else h[p] := h[t]
      end
  end.
```

Acknowledgments. The authors would like to thank Mr. Mark F. Villa of the University of Alabama at Birmingham for correcting the English of the first manuscript.

REFERENCES

1. Aho, A.V., and Corasick, M.J. Efficient string matching: An aid to bibliographic search. *Commun. ACM 18,* 6 (June 1975), 333–340.
2. Apostolico, A., and Giancarlo, R. The Boyer–Moore–Galli string searching strategies revisited. *SIAM J. Comput. 15,* 1 (Feb. 1986), 98–105.
3. Baker, T.P. A technique for extending rapid exact-match string matching to arrays of more than one dimension. *SIAM J. Comput. 7,* 4 (Nov. 1978), 533–541.
4. Bird, R.S. Two dimensional pattern matching. *Info. Process. Lett. 6,* 5 (Oct. 1977), 168–170.
5. Boyer, R.S., and Moore, J.S. A fast matching algorithm. *Commun. ACM 20,* 10 (Oct. 1977), 762–772.
6. Davies, G., and Bowsher, S. Algorithms for pattern matching. *Softw. Pract. Exper. 16,* 6 (June 1986), 575–601.
7. Galil, Z. On improving the worst case running time of the Boyer–Moore string matching algorithm. *Commun. ACM 22,* 9 (Sept. 1979), 505–508.
8. Knuth, D.E., Morris, J.H., and Pratt, V.R. Fast pattern matching in strings. *SIAM J. Comput. 6,* 2 (June 1977), 323–350.
9. Zhu, R. F., and Takaoka, T. On improving the average case of the Boyer–Moore string matching algorithm. *J. Inf. Process. 10,* 3 (Mar. 1987), 173–177.

CR Categories and Subject Descriptors: F.2.2 [**Analysis of Algorithms and Problem Complexity**]: Nonnumerical Algorithms and Problems—*pattern matching;* I.5.4 [**Pattern Recognition**]: Applications—*text processing*
General Terms: Algorithms, Performance
Additional Key Words and Phrases: Analysis of algorithms, information retrieval, pattern matching, pattern recognition, string searching, text editing

ABOUT THE AUTHORS:

RUI FENG ZHU is a graduate student of computer science at the University of Ibaraki, Japan.

TADAO TAKAOKA is a professor of computer science at the University of Ibaraki, Japan. His research interests include analysis of algorithms and program verification, and he is co-author of *Fundamental Algorithms.* Authors' Present Address: Department of Computer Science, University of Ibaraki, Hitachi, Japan 316.

Chapter 5: Hardware Matching

Introduction

String pattern matching occupies a substantial portion of the running time of application systems, since it is the only process that must look at one input character at a time. In order to improve the efficiency of processing, numerous hardware-based solutions to pattern matching have been investigated. The basic matching techniques on a hardware matcher are classified into two classes. One is based on the finite state automata (FSA) of some variant of the KMP algorithm, and the other is based on a signature technique introduced in the rest of this chapter. Good surveys of string searching hardware can be found in [Faloutsos, 85] and [Hollaar, 79].

The goal of the FSA approach is to handle every input character in one cycle. The design divides the states of a deterministic FSA into *sequential* states (which have only one nondefault transition) and *index* states (which have more than one). The sequential states are stored consecutively, so there is no need for a next address, and the default address is stored in a globally accessible location. An index state contains a vector of nodes. This approach is presented by Bird, Tu, and Worthy (1977). By improving Bird's approach, Isenman and Shasha (1990) show that the hardware approach can provide a 25-fold to 500-fold performance improvement depending on the complexity of the query, and they show that it is fast enough even in the presence of variable-length don't-cares (VLDCs) to keep up with a 20-million character/second disk. In this section numerous hardware-based solutions to pattern matching are investigated and the corresponding references discussed.

Full text scanning and inverted file approaches represent the two extremes of the spectrum. Full text scanning, although it eliminates processing and storage overhead of access structures, performs rather poorly for large databases if not facilitated by parallel processing techniques. On the other hand, inverted files are fast for locating words that have been indexed, but the storage overhead and thus the maintenance costs can be tremendous. The signature file approach attempts to strike a balance between these two extremes. It requires scanning of the text, but uses a low-overhead access structure to reduce the amount of the text that needs to be scanned. Signatures have been used many times in the past in a variety of applications: for example, to speed up substring testing for text editors, to support differential files in database applications, to compress a dictionary for spelling programs, to accomplish partial match retrieval on a computer file, and to build filtering modules for database update and natural language dictionaries. In the rest of this section hardware approaches for full text search are discussed along with the corresponding references.

The paper by Isenman and Shasha (1990) reviews related works and introduces special heuristics to the KMP algorithm to reduce the time and space required to perform string matching. For signature hardware matcher, the paper of Lee and Lochovsky (1990) has been selected. It describes the introduction of signature file approaches and the design of a text-retrieval machine, called HYTREM (hybrid text-retrieval machine), for the support of large unformatted text databases.

Finite state automata matcher

Bird's goal ([Bird et al., 77]) was to handle every input character in one cycle. His design divides the states of a deterministic finite state automaton into "sequential" states (which have only one nondefault transition) and "index" states (which have more than one). The sequential states are stored consecutively, so there is no need for a next address and the default address is stored in a globally accessible location. Index states contain a vector of nodes. For example, if there is a nondefault transition on A, W, or Z, the bit vector looks like 1000 . . . 01011 and is followed by the first state address of the next state. If the input character is Y, the next state is in two locations above the first state address. Apparently this takes a lot of bits (256 bits) according to [Haskin et al., 83]. A typical large query having 23 patterns with 165 characters without VLDCs requires 800,000 bits in the scheme of [Bird et al., 77].

Isenman et al. ([Isenman et al., 90]) have used Bird's approach for states with one nondefault transition, but not for the others. For states with few nondefault transitions they use explicit comparators and next state addresses for each such transition, using less memory than Bird's approach. Bird's approach has one FSA sensing term without variable length don't-cares (VLDCs) and terms with trailing VLDCs, another for word-initial VLDCs, another for embedded VLDCs, and another for contiguous word phrases. Isenman et al. have found that this organization is not always the fastest and concentrate on hardware that can handle VLDCs. This requirement renders the BM approach inapplicable. From the simulation results Isenman et al. show that the hardware approach can provide a 25-fold to 500-fold performance improvement depending on the complexity of the query, and they show that this is fast enough even in the presence of VLDCs to keep up with a 20 million characters/second disk.

An alternative to the deterministic finite state automaton approach is the nondeterministic finite state automaton. Such an automaton can be in several states at once and can follow a transition from one state to several states. A variant of this approach, called the partitioned finite state automaton (PFSA), has been proposed (and patented) by Haskin et al. ([Haskin et al., 83]).

Signature files matcher

Full text scanning and inverted file approaches represent the two extremes of the spectrum. Although it eliminates processing and storage overhead of access structures, full text scanning performs extremely poorly for large databases if not facilitated by parallel processing techniques. On the other hand, inverted files are fast for locating words that have been indexed, but the storage overhead and thus the maintenance costs may be tremendous. The signature file approach ([Thap et al., 82]) attempts to strike a balance between these two extremes. It requires scanning of the text, but uses a low-overhead access structure to reduce the amount of text that needs to be scanned. Signatures have been used many times in the past in a variety of applications: to speed up the substring testing for text editors ([Harrison, 71]), to support differential files in database applications ([Severance et al., 76]), to compress a dictionary for spelling programs ([McIlroy, 82]), to accomplish partial match retrieval on a computer file ([Roberts, 79]), to build filtering modules for a database update and natural language dictionaries ([Lee, 82], [Mullin, 87], and [Pramanik, 86]), and so on.

The documents are stored sequentially in the text file. Their abstractions are stored sequentially in the signature file. When a query arrives, the signature file is scanned sequentially and a large number of nonqualifying documents are discarded. The rest are either checked (so that the false drop are discarded) or they are returned to the user as they are (a document is a false drop if it does not qualify in a query, even though its signature indicates that it does). The method is faster than full text scanning but is expected to be slower than inversion ([Christodoulakis et al., 84] and [Faloutsos et al., 84]). It requires much smaller space overhead than inversion (about 10 percent), and it can easily handle insertion.

In the superimposed coding method ([Christodoulakis et al., 84] and [Mooers, 49]), the database is divided into a number of blocks of fixed length. Each text block B_i is associated with a signature S_i, which is a fixed-length bit vector S_{i1} S_{i2} . . . S_{im}, where m is the length of the signature. The signature is abstracted from the text block by means of hashing and can be considered a condensed representation of the text block.

Figure 1 is an example illustrating the process of generating a block signature from a text block. Each nontrivial word in the text block is hashed into a bit vector, called a *word signature* ([Larson, 83] and [Tsichritzis et al., 83]). For simplicity, the number of 1's in a word signature is assumed fixed (in the example, four bits are set). The block signature is generated by superimposing the word signatures. When a word is searched for, a query signature, S_Q, of the word is generated from the query, Q, in the same way as described above. S_Q is then matched with every text block signature. A text block signature S_i is qualified if and only if for all bit positions in S_Q that are set to 1, the corresponding bit positions in S_i are also set to 1 (known as the inclusion condition). Formally, the set of qualified signatures is defined by

$$\{S_i \mid S_i \text{ AND } S_Q = S_Q\}$$

A disqualified signature indicates that the associated text block is guaranteed not to contain the word specified in the query. However, a qualified signature only means that the corresponding text block is very likely to satisfy the query. That is, there is a small chance that the text block does not contain the word being searched for (that is, it is a false drop). Therefore, the text block has to be searched to eliminate false drops.

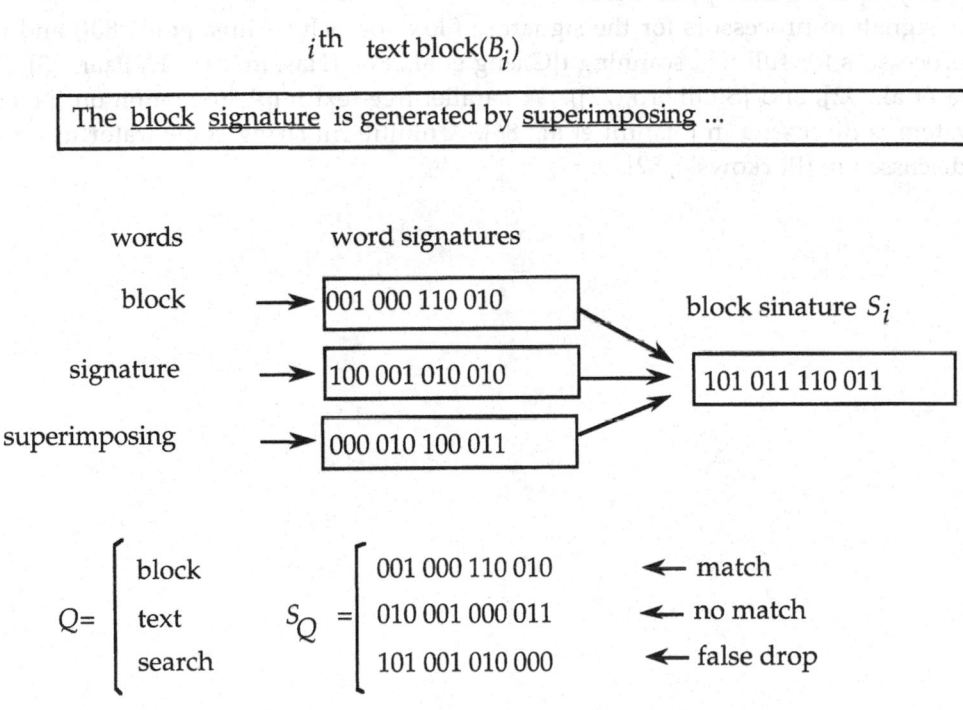

Figure 1. Generating signatures from a text block

Related problems

Numerous hardware-based solutions to pattern matching have been investigated, and some are actually implemented in [Curry et al., 83], [Burkowski, 82], [Foster et al., 80], [Halaas, 83], [Lee 86a], [Lee 86b], [Mead et al., 76], [Schefter, 87], [Takahashi, et al., 87], and [Wakabayashi, et. al., 85]. Mak et al. ([Mak et al., 91]) have proposed a new parallel VLSI pattern matching algorithm, called the date parallel pattern matching (DPPM) algorithm, which serially broadcasts and compares the pattern to a block of data in parallel.

More recently, researches reported in [Ciaccia et al., 93], [Faloutsos et al., 87], [Grandi et al., 92], [Lee et al., 89], and [Zezula et al., 91] have been directed toward efficient strategies for the partitioning of superimposed signature files in order to speed up the retrieval of relevant signatures. Amir et al. ([Amir et al., 92]) present a signature and parallel approach for finger prints and randomized dictionary matching. Optimal signature extraction is discussed in [Faloutsos et al., 87]. Compressed file approaches similar to signature files are discussed in [Sato, 90].

Harrison ([Harrison, 71]) presents a technique for implementing the test that determines whether one string is a substring of another. When there is low probability that the test will be satisfied, the operation can be speeded up considerably if it is preceded by a test on appropriately chosen hash codes of the strings. This uses a hashing function that is assumed to give an integer result in the range from 1 to m. The resulting binary string, which contains 1 only in positions that correspond to certain substrings of length k, is called the *hashed k-signature* of the string S. It is clear that for any particular hashing function a necessary condition that string S_1 be a substring of string S_2 is that the hashed k-signature of S_2 have 1 wherever the hashed k-signature of S_1 has 1. By storing with each line its hashed 2-signature for a conversational editor, the search procedure can be speeded up considerably. There are clearly many other similar applications.

There are signature processors for the signature file approach ([Ahuja et al., 80]) and numerous hardware processors for full text scanning ([Cheng et al., 87], [Haskin, 81], [Hollaar, 83], [Lee et al., 85], [Ogawa et al., 92], and [Stellhorn, 77]). A parallel free-text implementation on the connection machine system is discussed in [Stanfill et al., 86]. A multiterm string comparator using hardware hashing is discussed in [Burkowski, 82].

Performance and Architectural Issues for String Matching

MERRILL E. ISENMAN AND DENNIS E. SHASHA, MEMBER, IEEE

Abstract—String matching is the problem of finding all occurrences of a character pattern in a text. A general query entails finding the locations of multiple terms with "DON'T CARE" symbols in a text. Such queries are in common use in libraries, medical, and legal information services.

We introduce special heuristics to the Knuth-Morris-Pratt algorithm to reduce the time and space required to perform the string matching. We compare our hardware-based approach to the software approaches embodied in the UNIX[1] System grep and fgrep commands. Our simulation results show that the hardware approach can provide a 25-500 fold performance improvement depending on the complexity of the query and that it is fast enough even in the presence of variable length DON'T CARES to keep up with a 20 million character/second disk. Our approach compares favorably to other hardware designs in speed and space. The proposed hardware implementation requires 10 kbytes of one cycle static memory, 28 single character comparators, four 16 bit adders, and control logic for four finite state machines and a term matcher controller. After that, additional hardware produces negligible performance improvements for queries with up to 80 terms, about half of which have variable length DON'T CARES.

I. APPROACH AND MOTIVATION

A. Scope of Present Work

WE propose a hardware architecture to achieve high-speed serial pattern matching on large bodies of text. A pattern is a set of terms, where the terms are alphanumeric strings plus fixed and variable length DON'T CARES. We compile this pattern into a deterministic finite state automaton using standard techniques [16].

A direct realization of the deterministic finite state automaton produced by an input pattern on a simple finite state machine is too slow and memory-consumptive to be practical for complex patterns. Therefore, we incorporated heuristics that have enabled our chip to achieve speeds approaching 1.26 machine cycles per text character even in the presence of patterns with 80 terms, 36 of which have variable length DON'T CARES.

A large part of our work consisted of testing the effectiveness of the heuristics and setting parameters. The two important parameters were

Manuscript received May 1, 1987; revised February 18, 1988 and October 14, 1988.

M. E. Isenman is with AT&T Bell Laboratories, Holmdel, NJ 07733.

D. E. Shasha is with the Courant Institute of Mathematical Sciences, New York University, New York, NY 10012.

IEEE Log Number 8932024.

[1] UNIX is a trademark of Bell Laboratories.

1) the number of finite state automata to implement (they work in parallel on the query)

2) the number of comparators to implement per finite state automaton (most transitions in the finite state automaton require a comparator).

For very complex patterns, increasing the settings of these parameters to four finite state automata, each with seven comparators (six variable comparators plus one fixed delimiter comparator) led to steadily higher performance results. After that point, we show that additional hardware produces negligible performance improvements. This work required simulation[2] of a range of patterns, from very simple ones to very complex ones.

B. String Matching Applications

The largest users of information retrieval systems have exacting requirements. For example, the Patent Office must handle documents with a total of 65 billion characters. Its information retrieval system receives 3.75 million queries per year, with an interarrival time of 2.4 s. A medium size query has between 15 and 20 patterns (or terms) while a large query has up to 80 patterns [1]. Special hardware is vital to this type of application.

Other users of string matching are library systems (ORBIT, DIALOG), lawyers (LEXIS), doctors (MEDLINE), journalists, and news addicts searching through New York Times data (NEXIS, JURIS).

Reuters will soon provide string matching services to stock brokers who will use it for news associated with specific stocks, industries, and so on. Because speed is of the essence in this application, they will also need special hardware.

As offices become more automated, there will be an increasing demand by people to look through office documents [2]. Already, large law offices maintain internal documents containing 350 000 pages of text or about 100 million characters [3], [4].

II. RELATED WORK

In our work, we concentrate on hardware that can handle variable length DON'T CARES (hereafter VLDC's). (This requirement renders the Boyer-Moore approach [5] inapplicable.) A VLDC in a query term is often represented by an

[2] We used an empirical approach, because there is no analytical relationship between gross properties of patterns such as the number of characters per term or the number of DON'T CARES per term and the number of states or the number of transitions per state. See Secton VII-E.

asterisk (e.g., com*s). The asterisk stands for any string of nondelimiter characters. Thus "communes" and "computers" both match "com*s." Systems that do not handle VLDC's, such as [2], [6]–[9], [23], are still useful though they lie outside our purview. A good general survey of early string searching hardware can be found in either [10] or [24].

Parallel approaches to string searching have also been proposed. We reviewed the approach for the Connection Machine described in [11]. It proposes a single-instruction multiple data (SIMD) parallel approach. It replicates a given query (which plays the role of the instruction in the SIMD model) across many nodes of a parallel machine and partitions the data to be searched across those nodes. As it happens, this approach was only applied to text without VLDC's, but that is incidental. This parallel approach could also be used with our hardware, only instead of requiring a 16 000 processor Connection Machine to search through 18 Mbytes of text in 0.004 s, it would require about 250 of our processors, assuming a 25 MHz clock, to achieve the same search speed. The Connection Machine approach ignores the problem of synchronizing the search with the text input.

The work directly relevant to ours handles VLDC's in a disk-synchronous fashion. This work uses finite state automata of some form and some variant of the Knuth–Morris–Pratt algorithm [12]. One innovative approach from which we drew much inspiration was the work of Bird [13].

The goal of Bird's approach was to handle every input character in one cycle. This design divides states of a deterministic finite state automaton into "sequential" states (which have only one nondefault transition) and "index" states (which have more than one). The sequential states are stored consecutively, so there is no need for a next address and the default address is stored in a globally accessible location. Index states contain a vector of ones. For example, if there is a nondefault transition on either A, W, Y, or Z, then the bit vector looks like

$$1\ 0\ 0\ 0\ \cdots\ 0\ 1\ 0\ 1\ 1$$

and is followed by the first state address of the next state. If the input character is Y, then the next state is two locations above the first state address. Apparently this takes a lot of bits (267 bits) according to [14]. A typical large query having 23 patterns with 165 characters without VLDC's requires 800k bits in the Bird scheme according to [15].

We have used Bird's approach for states with one nondefault transition, but not for the others. For states with few nondefault transitions, we use explicit comparators and next state addresses for each such transition. This uses less memory than Bird's approach.

For states with many nondefault transitions, we use an address table that we refer to as an index. We observed that the states having by far the most nondefault transitions in practice follow a terminating delimiter transition. ("Terminating" here either means that recognizing a delimiter causes a transition to a final state or to a nonaccepting state preceding a term's first character. A nonterminating delimiter transition would be caused by a blank within a term, e.g., by the blank encountered while processing "von Neumann.") We represent the transitions from terminating delimiter states by a 256 element array of next state pointers. Using this approach, our design uses approximately 10 kbytes for 80 patterns.

Bird proposed having one FSA sensing term without variable length DON'T CARES (VLDC's) and terms with trailing VLDC's, another for word-initial VLDC's, another for embedded VLDC's, and another for contiguous word phrases. We have found that this organization is not always the best in terms of speed as we explain in Section VII-F. Logicon, Inc., has built hardware based on Bird's ideas.

An alternative to the deterministic finite state automaton approach is the nondeterministic finite state automaton. Such an automaton can be in several states at once and may follow a transition from one state to several states. A variant of this approach, called the partitioned finite state automaton (PFSA), has been proposed (and patented) [14].

A PFSA consists of a set of character matchers (CM's). Each CM is in one state in any time period, can match one input character, and occupies one chip. At each time period, the PFSA is in as many states as there are possible input characters, provided there are enough CM's [18]. By using special heuristics for the first character of words (our index table design is quite similar) terms with different initial characters, e.g., "cat" and "dog," can be put in the same CM. In [14], the authors give an experimentally derived formula for the number of CM's needed as a function of the number of VLDC-free terms: 5 + (terms/16). However, even relatively small pathological examples violate this equation. For example, a PFSA with 16 CM's (a relatively large one) would not be able to handle a set of 17 terms whose first two letters are: sa, sc, se, sh, si, sk, sl, sm, sn, so, sp, sq, sr, st, su, sw, sy.

Haskin and Hollaar say that PFSA's are particularly good at handling VLDC's. The number of CM's will never be more than the number of states in a nondeterministic finite state automaton and will usually be less. In contrast, a deterministic finite state automaton may require an exponential number of states with respect to the number of states in a nondeterministic finite state automaton. On the other hand, each CM contains up to 800 bytes for an eight bit representation of characters, whereas each of our states contains under 30 bytes also assuming an eight bit representation. Moreover, we have found (see Section VII-E) that although pathological examples can produce an exponential blowup, it does not occur for practical queries of substantial complexity. In fact, state table size grows sublinearly with respect to the number of VLDC's per term.

Haskin and Hollaar observe that most queries have fewer than 64 distinct characters. (Bird made a similar observation.) They therefore propose encoding the query and text input characters into 6 bit representations. Using their encoding idea, we could reduce our space and data path requirements by a factor of 3/4.

General Electric [21] and TRW [19] have produced string matchers commercially. The TRW design, called the Fast Data Finder (FDF), is quite novel. First, it is a systolic array. Second, their chip can perform proximity searches (e.g., "computer" within five words of "von Neumann"), a function normally left to postprocessing. Third, it can detect matches within an error tolerance (e.g., "breach" is within a tolerance of 1 of "broach"). Fourth, it can detect numeric ranges (e.g., a number between 1.9 and 10.3). Several of these chips can be used in parallel to keep up with a 4 million character/second text input rate, independent of query complexity. Whereas our chip can process up to 25 million characters per second, it degrades to about 20 million for 80 term queries with 36 VLDC's, although our chips can work in parallel as well. Also, our comparators are simple equality comparators, so they cannot perform range comparisons. However, a system using our chip can simulate the FDF, although features such as proximity searches must be done after term-matching.

From this discussion, the reader may observe that different designers have different ideas about what makes a good string matcher. In most cases, the goal remains the same: to keep up with disk bandwidths of 4–20 million characters per second or perhaps even random access memory speeds. Every design can be made to look bad on pathological examples: multiple VLDC's for the deterministic finite state approaches, and large fan-outs without VLDC's for the nondeterministic finite state automata approach. We believe that our design performs well on most queries of interest: those for which a minority of terms have VLDC's. Its single chip architecture permits us to achieve clock rates high enough for random access memory.

III. HARDWARE VERSUS SOFTWARE

Current state-of-the-art information retrieval systems use indexes. Indexes in this context are structures for mapping words to locations in text (documents or parts of documents). Most such systems are built on large mainframe computers. Indexes will remain necessary for many applications (with the possible exception of some news service and similar applications where timeliness is critical and the time required to construct indexes is unacceptable) because it will always be necessary to avoid searching the entire text database. Searching a moderately sized text database of 100 million characters at one microsecond per character would take 100 s.

The following three problems are associated with indexes.

Size: An index can easily exceed the size of the text data, sometimes by as much as a factor of 3 since each word of the index can require many pointers to different parts of a document [1].

Maintainability: An index must be maintained when text data are modified. This is very difficult in the office environment and in the news wire application.

Merging: Large indexes imply that long lists of pointers must be merged.

The result of using indexes is that complex queries are expensive. With an IBM 370-155 processor, a complex query might cost up to $100 [1]. Searching for a term with VLDC's requires a sequential scan of the index in any case.

IV. ARCHITECTURAL APPROACH

Since our chip is fast enough to handle random access memory inputs, one approach is to put a string matcher unit on the bus with the disk, main memory, and main processor and

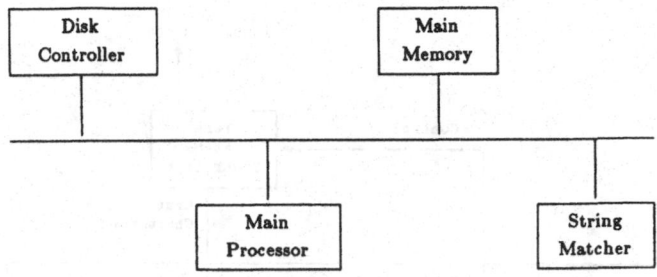

Fig. 1.   System block diagram.

to support two modes of operation (Fig. 1):

$$\text{disk} \rightarrow \text{string matcher unit} \rightarrow \text{memory}$$

and

$$\text{memory} \rightarrow \text{string matcher unit} \rightarrow \text{memory}.$$

If disks are the primary storage devices for text (as is now the case), another approach is to attach the disk itself directly to the string matcher. That would eliminate putting text on the main processor bus, permitting the CPU to access memory for other purposes.

A. Why a Special Purpose Architecture?

One conceivable method is to use a standard CPU chip as the string matcher unit to offload work from the main processor. To evaluate this possibility, we experimented with the UNIX System fgrep (the fastest grep) command. We compiled it from the C language [22] to the object code for an AT&T 32100 microprocessor (comparable to a Motorola 68020) using an optimizing compiler. We further improved fgrep by removing a flag test. We ran a few queries which were set up so that no matches occurred, which eliminated I/O and gave the most optimistic results. In addition, the queries did not include DON'T CARE conditions, which would have forced us to use a slower member of the grep family. We obtained the following results.

- Very simple query ("cat") takes 26 cycles/character. (Unimproved: 117 cycles/character.)
- Medium complex query (19 terms) takes 541 cycles/character.
- Complex query (80 terms) takes 813 cycles/character.

To keep up with a disk transfer rate of 1 Mbyte/s would require a CPU clock frequency of 813 MHz. This is a factor of 30 from today's technology of 25 MHz microprocessors.

The special purpose approach to the design of the string matching unit (described below) can handle up to 80 terms with DON'T CARES in less than 1.26 cycles per character. The performance improvement is thus a factor of up to 500 (assuming an equal cycle time).

V. TECHNICAL DESCRIPTION OF THE STRING MATCHER

A. String Matcher Overview

We began with an architecture consisting of a term matcher controller and from 1 to 6 finite state automata. Each finite state automaton had from 1 to 6 comparators, where each comparator does a bitwise Exclusive OR. Each FSA also had a

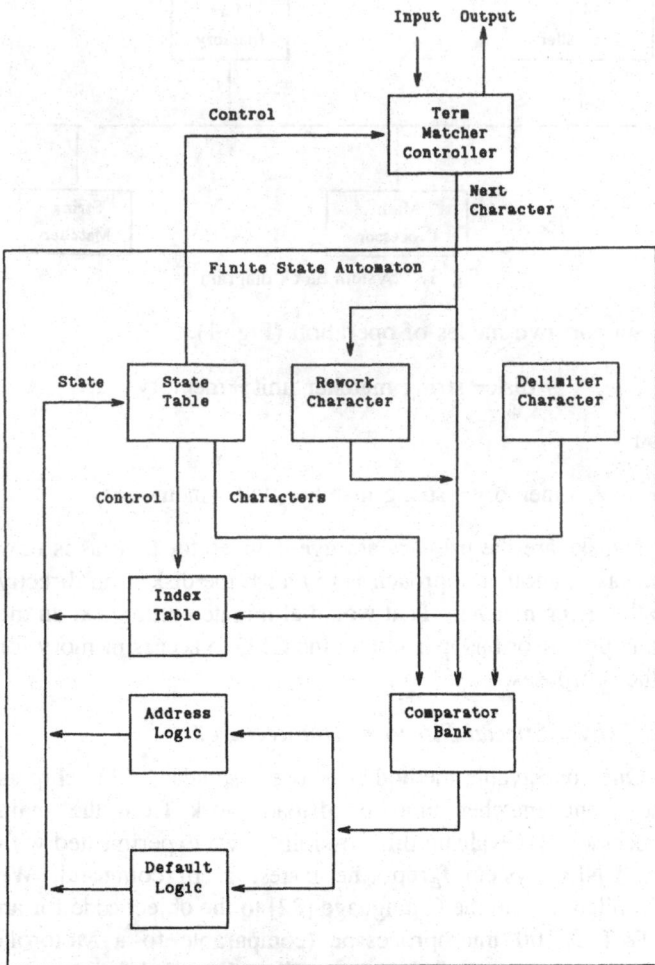

Fig. 2.   String matcher block diagram—one FSA.

fixed delimiter comparator (which compares the input symbol against a special delimiter symbol) and a variable amount of static memory for tables. Fig. 2 shows a block diagram of a single finite state automaton.

Initially, the main processor compiles the query into the proper table format and loads it into the state tables of the string matcher's FSA's. The main processor then either sets up the disk to transfer data to the string matcher or tells the string matcher the text's starting memory address.

The term matcher controller's responsibilities are to buffer character data from the disk or from main memory and broadcast it to the finite state automata. The term matcher controller also reports matches back to the central processor for further processing.

An input character (i.e., from the text) enters all the finite state automata from the term matcher controller. The automata (FSA's) work in parallel. Each one matches the input character against characters from its state table or uses its index table. If the match is successful, the next state of that FSA is known. If all matches are unsuccessful and there are no more characters in the state table for the current FSA state, then a special default transition is taken. Otherwise, the FSA cannot determine the next state (because it has an insufficient number of comparators). So, it "reworks" the character in the next cycle. When using the index table, the next state is the

address held in the location equal to the character's value. This makes it unnecessary to rework the character.

Thus, a cycle involving the comparators entails

1) a parallel readout of the comparison characters and next state addresses from the state table into the comparator bank and address logic, respectively

2) a selection of the next state based on a character match between the comparison characters and the input character (possibly including a signal to the term matcher controller that a final state has been reached); or an indication that more comparisons are needed (the input character is then stored in the rework character register).

In a design with six nondelimiter comparators, this implies a state table bandwidth within each FSA of 21 bytes per cycle (Fig. 3). Therefore, the state table must be on-chip. Using current technology, each cycle should take no more than 40 ns.

B. String Matcher Internals

The state table for each finite state automaton consists of an array of bytes. Each state is represented by a control byte followed by a collection of characters and addresses. The address associated with a character c points to the table location of the next state to use when the input character is c. The control byte consists of the following fields:

count	Is a three bit field. Normally, (for values 0 to 6), it indicates the number of characters to match for the current state. However, if the count is 7, then the number of characters to match is 6. If the count is 7 and none of the characters match, work is continued at the following state using the same input character.
match	Is a one bit field. If reset and the last character matches, go to the following state. If set and the last character matches, use the address associated with the last character.
default	Is a one bit field. If reset and there is no match, go to address 0. If set and there is no match, use the last address for this state. The last address will be different from any character address.
index	Is a one bit field. To indicate that a state should use the index table, the count field is set to 0 and the index field is set.
delimiter	Is a one bit field. If set and the character is a delimiter, go to the address in the delimiter register.
final	Is a one bit field. If set, this is a final state and the term matcher controller reports that a query term has found a match in a string.

Fig. 3 shows the state table for a state with six characters to match, while Fig. 12 shows the state table for processing "cat|d*og."

Note that the address associated with the last character is present only when the match field is set and a default address is present only when the default field is set. Therefore, if the starting address of state s is i and the count field is zero, the

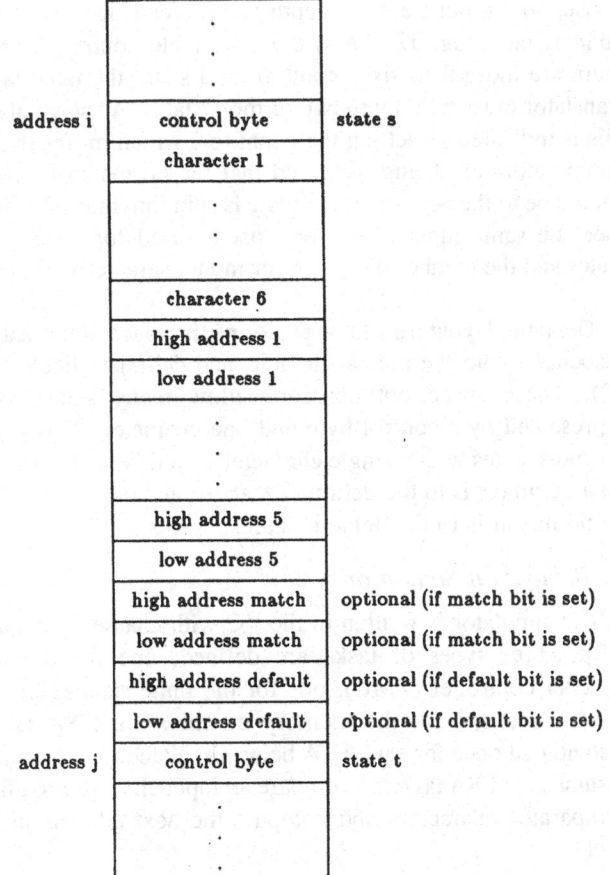

Fig. 3. FSA state table organization.

address of the next state t is

$i + 1$ if the default field is reset

$i + 3$ if the default field is set.

If the count k is between 1 and 6, the address of the next state t is

$i + 3k - 1$ if the default field is reset and the match field is reset.

$i + 3k + 1$ if the default field is reset and the match field is set or the default field is set and the match field is reset.

$i + 3k + 3$ if the default field is set and the match field is set.

Aside from the count and the final state fields, the fields in the control byte are used to save state table space or speed up processing. There are three situations where this is possible: when there is a transition to the following state, a transition to the default state, or a transition to the delimiter state. For example, on a transition from a state to the following state, the address of the following state does not need to be explicitly stored. Instead, the match bit is reset and the character with a transition to the following state is put last. To ensure that there are as many transitions from states to following states as possible, the states are placed in depth first order.

Similarly, a transition from a state to state 0 (the default state) on a failure to match occurs so often that if the default bit is reset, there is no need to explicitly represent address 0. As noted above, states that have more than six nondefault transitions must rework a character, in which case the count field has a count set to 7. This means that the FSA should perform six comparisons and if there is no match, then it should rework the character in the next cycle.

Because of the number of transitions associated with the first character of a word, we implemented an index table for that state. For a large query, it is quite common for there to be 16 or more transitions from this state, each corresponding to a distinct word-initial character. Processed normally, this would require three states and therefore up to three cycles following each delimiter. The index table can do the same processing in a single cycle. Since delimiters occur every six characters or so, this is a valuable improvement. The index table has an entry (2 bytes) for each of the possible 256 characters. When the index table is used (index field set), the incoming text character is used as an address into the table, from which it reads the address of the next state. For example, in the running example of Fig. 7, transitions from state 1 are determined from the index table.

VI. SIMULATION SYSTEM

With the architecture in place, the next step was to determine the necessary size of the state table, how many finite state automata were necessary, and how many comparators each FSA should have. This required a simulation system able to accept text and patterns for the purpose of measurement and correctness testing.

The software components of our simulation system consist of

• the front end of a compiler which produces a logical finite state automaton from a regular expression input language
• the back end of a compiler which produces the physical finite state automaton from the logical finite state automaton using the space compression fields of the control byte of the state table
• a behavioral simulator of the string matcher hardware.

A. Input Language

The input language consists of regular expressions with the following grammar (terms that begin with capital letters are nonterminals):

Exp : = Word
Exp : = Word '|' Exp
Word : = ''String''
String : = Symbol
String : = Symbol String
Symbol : = alphanumeric character
Symbol : = '*'
Symbol : = '?'

where

The * symbol represents a variable length alphanumeric DON'T CARE.

The ? symbol represents a single alphanumeric DON'T CARE.

The | symbol represents the separator between patterns.

For example, the query

*puter|sc?ence|telephone

would match supercomputer, transputer, computer, sczence, science, or telephone. It would not match sczience or putercom.

B. Compiler

The compiler consists of a regular expression parser, a nondeterministic FSA (NFSA) translator, a deterministic FSA (DFSA) translator, and a table layout translator. The compiler has execution time parameters to indicate whether the index table should be used and to specify the number of comparators to use (between 1 and 6).

The parser accepts expressions for up to six FSA's. Expressions are separated by a carriage return. The input therefore specifies the number of FSA's to use. Ultimately the compiler would decide how to assign expressions to each of the available FSA's.

The words are recognized by the parser and given to the NFSA translator which builds entries in an NFSA table. Fig. 7 shows the NFSA table for the following regular expression:

cat|d*og.

Fig. 8 represents the data in the traditional nondeterministic state diagram format. In the state tables and diagrams the following symbols have special meaning:

def refers to any of the unspecified input characters (the "defaults") for this state.

⟨ ⟩ refers to the delimiter input character.

- refers to the empty string, epsilon.

The DFSA translator uses the NFSA table as input and produces the DFSA table by using the epsilon closure algorithm described in [16]. The idea of the algorithm is to view an NFSA as being in a set of states after consuming some input. The states in the set are all the states that can be reached from the initial state by means of that input. For example, the NFSA in Fig. 8, upon receiving ⟨ ⟩, can either be in states 1, 2, or 7 (note that the transition from 1 to 2 or from 1 to 7 requires no input). Therefore, the set of states is $\{1, 2, 7\}$. When it then receives a d, the FSA can either take the transition from state 2 to state 0 or state 7 to state 8. The NFSA could then be in the set $\{0, 8\}$. Upon receiving an o, it can take two transitions from 8, namely back to 8 or to 9, so it can be in set $\{0, 8, 9\}$. Fig. 9 shows these sets. The "group numbers" in the left-hand column then become the states of the DFSA. For example, observe that group 3 corresponds to the set $\{0, 8\}$ and group 5 corresponds to $\{0, 8, 9\}$. Fig. 10 shows the DFSA state diagram. One can see for example from it, that DFSA state 3 takes a transition to state 5 on input o.

Because an NFSA with n states has 2^n subsets with respect to n, there is the theoretical possibility that the DFSA will require an exponential number of states. This does not seem to occur in practice, as we see in Section VII.

The table layout translator uses the symbolic DFSA table representation to build the physical contents of the state table.

It tries to lay out states in depth first order (Fig. 11) to save address bits. Fig. 12 shows the state table control fields. If there are more than six outputs from a state, the table layout translator must split it into two or more states. As noted above, this is indicated by setting the count to 7 which means that six comparators are being used and that the no match transition should be to the next state. If a state is split into multiple states, then the same input character must be used for all of these states and the number of cycles per input character will exceed 1.

The table layout translator performs the space optimizations associated with the match, default, and delimiter fields (Fig. 13). These space optimizations allow many states to be represented by a control byte and one character. This is true for most states with a single character match, whose transition on a delimiter is to the delimiter state d, and whose transition on no match is to the default state.

C. Behavioral Simulator

The simulator is written in the "C with Classes" language [17]. Three types of tasks are defined, one for the term matcher controller (TMC), one for the finite state automaton (FSA), and one for the memory module. The FSA task is instantiated once for each FSA being simulated. The simulator assumes the FSA task can compare an input character to all the comparator characters and compute the next address in one cycle.

VII. Simulation Results

We had three simulation goals.

• to quantify the space and time savings attributed to the use of an index table by each FSA

• to determine the number of finite state automata and the number of comparators for each FSA that would provide a good tradeoff between space and time

• to see if by using different heuristics to assign the terms to the FSA's, the space and/or speed requirements could be improved.

The required state table space can be viewed as either the sum of the size of each of the individual FSA state tables or as the maximum state table size multiplied by the number of FSA's. The first view implies one large memory which is dynamically apportioned to each FSA by the compiler. The second view assumes each FSA has its own state table and the state tables are all of equal size. We take the second view (i.e., the total state table size is computed to be the product of the number of FSA's and the maximum table size) because we assume that each state table can be accessed from only one FSA. Our data in the following graphs reflect this conservative view.

A. Tests

We used 80 patterns with variable length DON'T CARES added to represent four types of queries. The test names are in the left column and have the following interpretation:

None   80 terms with no variable length DON'T
              CARES.

TABLE I
EFFECT OF INDEX TABLE ON SPACE

Total State Table Size in Bytes vs. Use of Index Table		
Test	With Index	Without Index
None	1041	7458
Word-Initial	8601	15627
Initial-Middle	15057	22257
Init-Middle-Final	21663	35301

TABLE II
EFFECT OF INDEX TABLE ON SPEED

Speed in Cycles Per Character vs. Use of Index Table		
Test	With Index	Without Index
None	1.26	1.54
Word-Initial	1.42	1.69
Initial-Middle	1.42	1.69
Init-Middle-Final	1.46	1.73

Word-Initial   12 of the 80 terms with variable length DON'T CARES at the beginning.

Initial-Middle   12 of the 80 terms with variable length DON'T CARES at the beginning and 12 other terms with variable length DON'T CARES in the middle.

Init-Middle-Final   12 of the 80 terms with variable length DON'T CARES at the beginning, 12 other terms with variable length DON'T CARES in the middle, and still 12 other terms with variable length DON'T CARES at the end.

B. Index Table Benefits

To determine the benefits of the index table, the four queries were run with and without index tables while keeping the number of FSA's fixed at three and the number of comparators fixed at six.

Table I illustrates the total space benefit achieved by the index table.

When the size of the three index tables, 1536 bytes, is added to the total state table size in the "With Index" column, the space savings computes to

None	4881 bytes or 65 percent
Word-Initial	5490 bytes or 35 percent
Initial-Middle	5664 bytes or 25 percent
Init-Middle-Final	12102 bytes or 34 percent

Table II[3] illustrates the speed benefit provided by the index table.

The cycles per character vary between 1.26 and 1.46 when the index table is used, compared to 1.54 and 1.73 when the index table is not used. This is a speedup of between 16 and 18 percent.

As shown above, the use of the index table provides

significant space savings and improved speed performance and is included in the final design.

C. Number of Finite State Automata

To determine the benefits of additional FSA's, the four queries were run with index tables while keeping the number of comparators fixed at six and varying the number of FSA's from one to six.

Fig. 4 illustrates the tradeoff between total state table size and the number of FSA's. The size of the index table, 512 bytes, for each FSA included must be added to the total state table size. As the queries become more complex, additional FSA's continue to reduce the amount of space required. For the last test case (VLDC's in 36 of the 80 terms), the fourth FSA reduces the space requirement by 12915 bytes ((21663 + 1536) − (8236 + 2048)) or 56 percent compared to three FSA's. However, for the last test case, adding a fifth and sixth FSA actually increases the space requirements.

Table III illustrates the tradeoff between speed and the number of FSA's. Once again, the four-FSA design significantly benefits the last test case. It reduces the cycles per character from 1.47 to 1.26 or 14 percent. Increasing the number of FSA's beyond four does not further reduce the cycles per character.

The data above show that there is a substantial benefit in using four FSA's, while additional FSA's provide marginal if any benefit.

D. Number of Comparators

Each FSA has a special comparator that looks for delimiter characters, e.g., blanks, periods, commas, and so on. This comparator is always required and was not counted in the following measurements. The following test results reflect using four FSA's with index tables and varying the number of comparators per FSA from one to six. As before, the space for the index tables (2048 bytes) has to be added to the total state table size.

Fig. 5 illustrates the total space benefit provided by adding comparators. The above data show that most of the space benefits are achieved by using four comparators. Table IV illustrates the speed benefit provided by adding comparators. Even though the above data show that the sixth comparator provides only marginal benefits, six comparators incur only a minimal cost in circuitry. In addition, the bit representation of the count field of the control byte in the state table suggests that if more than two comparators are needed, the next choice is six comparators. Going beyond six comparators, however, offers little benefit.

E. Sensitivity to VLDC's

One criticism of the deterministic finite state automaton approach is that its memory requirements may increase exponentially in the presence of VLDC's. This subsection addresses that question directly. We constructed queries consisting of one, two, and ten terms, each term consisting of 12 characters. From each query, we constructed five derivative test queries: one test query whose term(s) contained no VLDC's, a second whose term(s) contained one VLDC, a

---

[3] Please note that the space and speed figures related to the index table differ from our final results of 1.26 cycles per character and 10 kbytes of memory because we are using three rather than four FSA's.

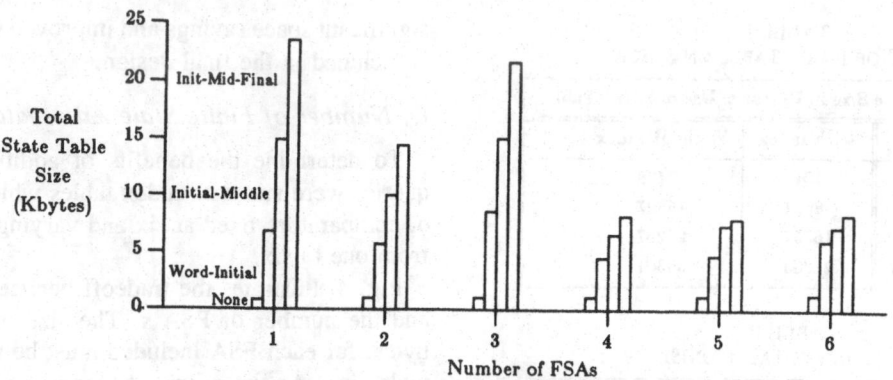

Fig. 4. Effect of FSA's on space.

TABLE III
EFFECT OF FSA's ON SPEED

Speed in Cycles Per Character vs. Number of FSAs						
Test	One	Two	Three	Four	Five	Six
None	1.26	1.26	1.26	1.26	1.26	1.26
Word-Initial	1.46	1.42	1.42	1.26	1.26	1.26
Initial-Middle	1.47	1.42	1.42	1.26	1.26	1.26
Init-Middle-Final	1.46	1.47	1.46	1.26	1.26	1.26

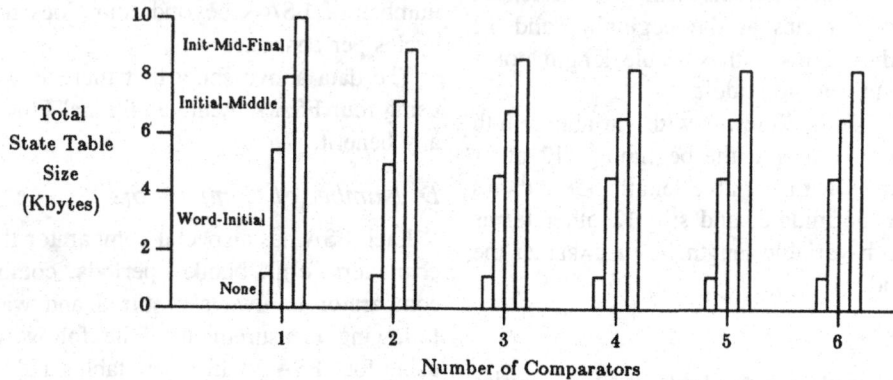

Fig. 5. Effect of comparators on space.

TABLE IV
EFFECT OF COMPARATORS ON SPEED

Speed in Cycles Per Character vs. Number of Comparators						
Test	One	Two	Three	Four	Five	Six
None	1.37	1.29	1.26	1.26	1.26	1.26
Word-Initial	2.87	1.98	1.47	1.31	1.26	1.26
Initial-Middle	2.89	1.98	1.49	1.31	1.26	1.26
Init-Middle-Final	2.96	1.99	1.54	1.32	1.26	1.26

third with two VLDC's, a fourth with three, and a fifth with four VLDC's. Each VLDC replaced an interior character of a term and no two VLDC's were adjacent. The test results in Fig. 6 reflect using one FSA and six comparators. Fig. 6 also shows that the growth in state table size is sublinear with respect to the number of VLDC's.

F. Assignment of Terms

In Section II, we noted that Bird advocated the strategy of dedicating one FSA to terms with no VLDC's or trailing VLDC's, another FSA for word-initial VLDC's, still another FSA for embedded VLDC's, and the final FSA for contiguous word phrases. We refer to this strategy as dedicated assignment. In previous sections, we have used a strategy we call uniform assignment.

In uniform assignment, the terms with each kind of VLDC are distributed evenly among the various FSA's. Thus, these two assignment schemes represent distribution decisions at two extremes. The following data show that dedicated assignment uses less state table space at least for queries where the non-VLDC terms outnumber terms with VLDC's. We measure the performance difference below.

The four queries used in the previous sections were uniformly assigned to the four FSA's as follows:

None	20 terms to each FSA.
Word-Initial	three initial VLDC and 17 non-VLDC terms to each FSA.
Initial-Middle	three initial VLDC, three middle VLDC, and 14 non-VLDC terms to each FSA.
Init-Middle-Final	three initial VLDC, three middle VLDC, three final VLDC, and 11 non-VLDC terms to each FSA.

The dedicated assignment approach produced the following

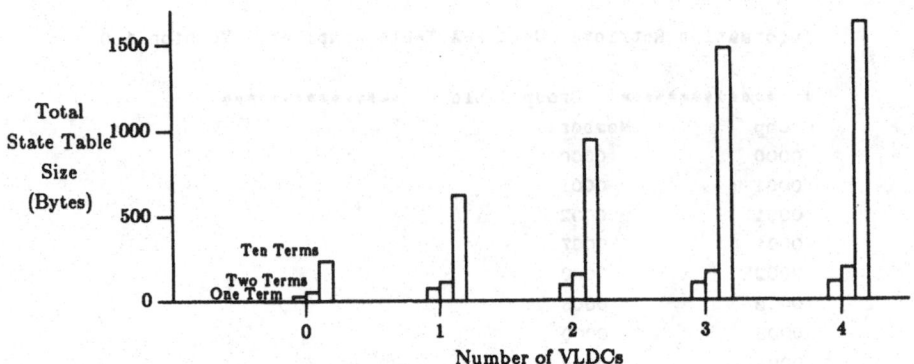

Fig. 6. Effect of VLDC's on size.

```
Information Retrieval Unit FSA Table Compiler - Version 1.0
**************** Nondeterministic FSA Table ****************
Current State      Input         Next State      Output        Asterisk
   0000            < >             0001             0               0
   0000            def             0000             0               0
   0001             -              0002             0               0
   0002             c              0003             0               0
   0002            < >             0001             0               0
   0002            def             0000             0               0
   0003             a              0004             0               0
   0003            < >             0001             0               0
   0003            def             0000             0               0
   0004             t              0005             0               0
   0004            < >             0001             0               0
   0004            def             0000             0               0
   0005            < >             0006             1               0
   0005            def             0000             0               0
   0006             -              0001             0               0
   0001             -              0007             0               0
   0007             d              0008             0               0
   0007            < >             0001             0               0
   0007            def             0000             0               0
   0008             *              0008             0               1
   0008             o              0009             0               1
   0008            < >             0001             0               1
   0009             g              0010             0               0
   0009            < >             0001             0               0
   0009            def             0000             0               0
   0010            < >             0011             1               0
   0010            def             0000             0               0
   0011             -              0001             0               0
```

Fig. 7. NFSA state table for string "cat|d*og."

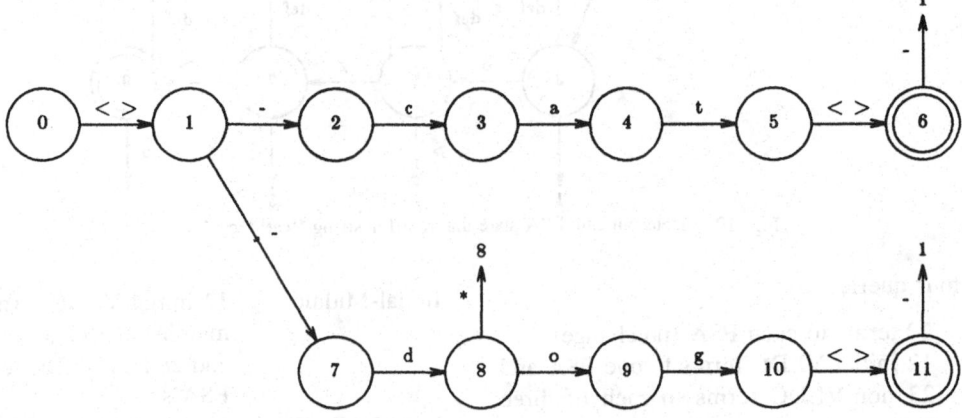

Fig. 8. NFSA state diagram for string "cat|d*og."

243

```
***************     Group Table     ***************
Group                Member
0000                 0000
0001                 0001
0001                 0002
0001                 0007
0002                 0000
0002                 0003
0003                 0000
0003                 0008
0004                 0000
0004                 0004
0005                 0000
0005                 0008
0005                 0009
0006                 0000
0006                 0005
0007                 0000
0007                 0008
0007                 0010
0008                 0001
0008                 0002
0008                 0006
0008                 0007
0009                 0001
0009                 0002
0009                 0007
0009                 0011
```

Fig. 9.   Group table for string "cat|d*og."

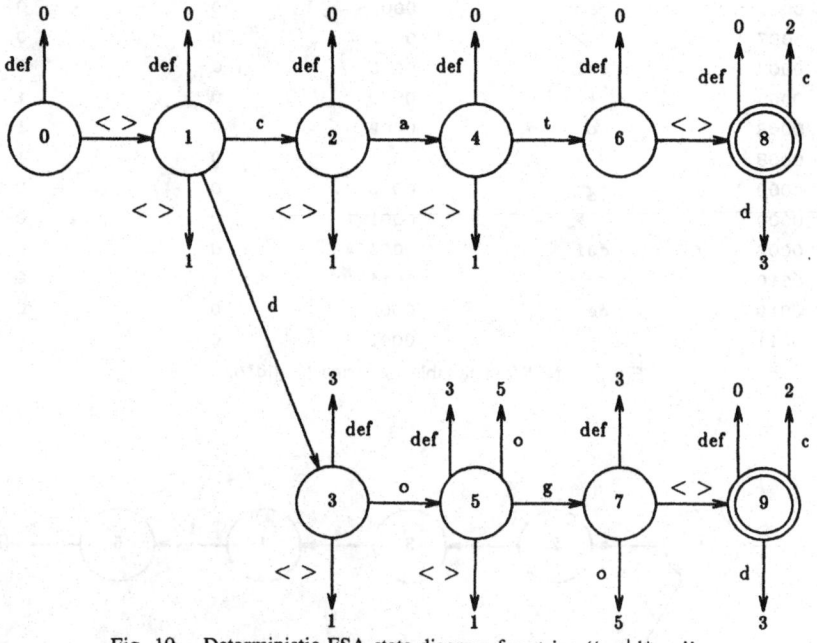

Fig. 10.   Deterministic FSA state diagram for string "cat|d*og."

assignment for the four queries:

None	20 terms to each FSA (no change).
Word-Initial	12 initial VLDC terms to one FSA and 23 non-VLDC terms to each of three FSA's.
Initial-Middle	12 initial VLDC terms to one FSA, 12 middle VLDC terms to another FSA, and 28 non-VLDC terms to each of two FSA's.
Init-Middle-Final	12 initial VLDC terms to one FSA, 12

DFSA State Number	Depth First Search Number
0	0
1	1
2	2
3	6
4	3
5	7
6	4
7	8
8	5
9	9

Fig. 11. Depth first search ordering for string "cat|d*og."

```
Information Retrieval Unit FSA Table Compiler - Version 1.0


**************** State Information Table - Control ****************
State  Final   Delim   Index   Deflt   Match   Count
0000    0       1       0       0       1       0
0001    0       1       1       0       1       0
0002    0       1       0       0       0       1
0003    0       1       0       1       0       1
0004    0       1       0       0       0       1
0005    0       1       0       1       0       2
0006    0       0       0       0       0       1
0007    0       0       0       1       0       2
0008    1       1       1       0       1       0
0009    1       1       1       0       1       0
```

Fig. 12. State table control fields for string "cat|d*og."

Location	Contents
27	state 9 control
26	'< >'
25	'o'
23, 24	address in case 'o' encountered = 13
21, 22	address on default = 9
20	state 7 control
19	'g'
18	'o'
16, 17	address in case 'o' encountered = 13
14, 15	address on default = 9
13	state 5 control
12	'o'
10, 11	address on default = 9
9	state 3 control
8	state 8 control
7	'< >'
6	state 6 control
5	't'
4	state 4 control
3	'a'
2	state 2 control
1	state 1 control
0	state 0 control

Fig. 13. Symbolic representation of the state table for string "cat|d*og."

TABLE V
EFFECT OF TERM ASSIGNMENT ON SPACE

Total State Table Size in Bytes vs. Term Assignment		
Test	Uniform	Dedicated
Word-Initial	4520	3572
Initial-Middle	6556	3572
Init-Middle-Final	8236	3572

TABLE VI
EFFECT OF TERM ASSIGNMENT ON SPEED

Speed in Cycles Per Character vs. Term Assignment		
Test	Uniform	Dedicated
None	1.26	1.26
Word-Initial	1.26	1.39
Initial-Middle	1.26	1.39
Init-Middle-Final	1.26	1.39

middle VLDC terms to another FSA, 12 final VLDC terms to still another FSA, and 44 non-VLDC terms to the remaining FSA.

Table V illustrates the total space savings due to the dedicated assignment heuristic (ignoring the None case where the two approaches agree). This approach reduces the total state table space requirement to 3.5 kbytes.

The total space requirement using dedicated assignment is therefore 5620 bytes ((893 + 512) × 4). For the last test case, dedicated assignment produces a savings of 4664 bytes or 45 percent compared to the uniform assignment approach.

On the other hand, uniform assignment is better for speed as Table VI shows. The data show that a dedicated assignment heuristic is somewhat slower than a uniform assignment heuristic, 1.39 versus 1.26 cycles per character.

We also tested 160 terms without VLDC's on the 4 FSA/6

comparator configuration using uniform assignment. The test results showed that 451 bytes were required for the largest state table and that the speed was 1.26 cycles per character. This indicates that the proposed design performs very well on very large queries.

In summary, given a set of terms T, uniform assignment is the best heuristic to use (because it gives better performance). However, if compiling T using uniform assignment exceeds the state table space available, then recompile T using a dedicated assignment approach. That is, put each different kind of VLDC term in a separate FSA with the remaining terms uniformly distributed over the remaining FSA's. If the total space is within the total available state table space, but the state table of one FSA has insufficient room, then assign some of the terms of the offending FSA to others. Otherwise, save some terms for a second pass (and put in an order to get a second chip that could work in parallel with the first one). This heuristic strategy can be summarized as follows.

1) Try uniform assignment. Exit if success.

2) Try dedicated assignment. Exit if success.

3) If there is sufficient space overall, then try reassigning some terms. Exit if success.

4) Use multiple passes.[4]

A worthwhile orthogonal heuristic is to have terms with as many different first characters as possible in each FSA. The time for first characters is always one because of the index table. Also, the fan-out for the second character will tend to be smaller than if there are many terms beginning with the same character.

VIII. Conclusions

From the above experiments, we conclude that four deterministic finite state automata each having six comparators (plus a dedicated delimiter comparator), approximately 2 kbytes of state table space, and 512 bytes of index table space (a total of 10 kbytes) are sufficient for queries of substantial complexity (80 terms with 36 VLDC's). The compiler takes a set of terms partitioned into four groups (according to the uniform or dedicated assignment rules) and compiles each group into the state table and index table of one FSA. Comparisons can be performed at a rate of 1.26 cycles/ character, even for complicated queries. Assuming (conservatively) a 40 ns cycle time, this comes to about 20 million characters per second. This is fast enough for any disk and approaches random access memory speeds.

This work holds two important lessons. First, an architectural simulator is worth a thousand hunches. The simulator enabled us to fix memory size, the number of comparators, and the number of automata for the class of queries we were interested in. It also told us how to choose among term

assignment rules. It also taught us that variable length DON'T CARES are less frightening in practice than they are in theory.

Second, memory can displace active circuitry. For example, the index table improved performance and decreased the required number of comparators. We have been able to construct queries where several index tables might be useful. Trading memory for circuitry is a good strategy, since increasing the size of memory is the easiest hardware change to make as technology improves.

Acknowledgment

Many thanks to H. Jacobs, P. Lu, and to the referees for their useful suggestions.

References

[1] D. Hsiao, Ed. *Advanced Database Machine Architecture*. Englewood Cliffs, NJ: Prentice-Hall, pp. 130–167.

[2] D. Tsichritzis, Ed., *Office Automation*. New York: Springer-Verlag, 1985, pp. 315–338.

[3] T. A. Welch, *IEEE Comput. Mag.*, vol. 16, no. 6, pp. 8–19, June 1984.

[4] D. C. Blair and M. E. Maron, "An evaluation of retrieval effectiveness for a full-text document-retrieval system," *Commun. ACM*, pp. 289–299, Mar. 1985.

[5] R. S. Boyer and J. S. Moore, "A fast string searching algorithm," *Commun. ACM*, vol. 20, pp. 762–772, no. 10, 1977.

[6] C. Faloutsos and S. Christodoulakis, "Signature files: An access method for documents and its analytical performance evaluation," *ACM Trans. Office Inform. Syst.*, vol. 2, no. 4, Oct. 1984.

[7] M. C. Harrison, "Implementation of the substring test by hashing," *Commun. ACM*, vol. 14, no. 12, pp. 777–779, Dec. 1971.

[8] S. R. Ahuja and C. S. Roberts, "An associative/parallel processor for partial match retrieval using superimposed codes," in *Proc. Seventh Annu. Symp. Comput. Architecture*, May 1980, pp. 218–227.

[9] G. H. Gonnet, "Unstructured databases or very efficient text searching," *SIGMOD*, pp. 117–124, 1983.

[10] L. A. Hollaar, "Text retrieval computers," *IEEE Comput. Mag.*, vol. 12, no. 3, pp. 40–50, 1979.

[11] C. Stanfill and B. Kahle, "Parallel-free text search on the connection machine," *Commun. ACM*, vol. 29, no. 12, pp. 1229–1239, Dec. 1986.

[12] D. E. Knuth, J. H. Morris, and V. R. Pratt, "Fast pattern matching in strings," *Siam J. Comput.*, vol. 6, no. 6, pp. 323–350.

[13] R. M. Bird, J. C. Tu, and R. M. Worthy, "Associative/parallel processors for searching very large textual data bases," in *Proc. Third ACM Workshop Comput. Architecture Nonnumeric Processing*, May 1977, pp. 8–16.

[14] R. L. Haskin and L. A. Hollaar, "Operational characteristics of a hardware-based pattern matcher," *ACM Trans. Database Syst.*, vol. 8, no. 1, Mar. 1983.

[15] R. L. Haskin, "Hardware for searching very large text databases," Ph.D. dissertation, Univ. of Illinois, Aug. 1980.

[16] A. V. Aho and J. D. Ullman, *Principles of Compiler Design*. Reading, MA: Addison-Wesley, pp. 91–94.

[17] B. Stroustrup, *The C++ Programming Language*. Reading, MA: Addison-Wesley.

[18] L. Hollaar, "The Utah Text Search Engine: Implementation experiences and future plans," in *Proc. Fourth Int. Workshop Database Machines*, Mar. 1985.

[19] K. Su, S. Hsu, and P. Otsubo, "The fast data finder—An architecture for very high speed data search and dissemination," in *Proc. IEEE Int. Conf. Data Eng.*, Los Angeles, CA, Apr. 1984, pp. 167–174.

[20] Mayper, Michels, and Nagy, "A practical text search system for unindexed data," in *Proc. COMPSAC, IEEE Comput. Software Appl. Conf.*, Chicago, IL, Nov. 13–16, 1978.

[21] D. A. Morris, "Processor matches text at high speeds," *Mini-micro Syst.*, pp. 227–235, June 1983.

[22] B. W. Kernighan and D. M. Ritchie, *The C Programming Languge*. Englewood Cliffs, NJ: Prentice-Hall.

[23] F. J. Burkowski, "A hardware hashing scheme in the design of a multiterm string comparator," *IEEE Trans. Comput.*, vol. C-31, no. 9, pp. 825–834, Sept. 1982.

[4] As an example of using multiple passes, we modified the Init-Middle-Final test so that the 12 middle VLDC terms each contained two VLDC's. When the terms were assigned uniformly (three initial VLDC terms, three final VLDC terms, three double VLDC terms, and 11 non-VLDC terms to each FSA) the largest state table required 6487 bytes and the cycles per character were 1.32. Dedicating one FSA to the double VLDC terms, required a state table larger than 58 kbytes. By placing the double VLDC terms in a separate second pass the maximum state table space was reduced to 1 kbyte.

[24] C. Faloutsos, "Access methods for text," *ACM Comput. Surveys*, vol. 17, no. 1, pp. 49–74, Mar. 1985.

Merrill E. Isenman received the M.S. degree in electrical engineering from Cornell University, Ithaca, NY, in 1966.

He is a Distinguished Member of Technical Staff at AT&T Bell Telephone Laboratories, Holmdel, NJ. He is currently performing systems integration work in the Offer Integration Laboratory. He previously worked on the architecture and performance analysis of the WE 32100/200 microprocessor chipset. His current interests are in the area of processor-based performance analysis and he has written a number of technical papers on simulation.

Dennis E. Shasha (S'81–M'84) received the Ph.D. degree in applied mathematics from Harvard University, Cambridge, MA, in 1984.

He is an Assistant Professor of Computer Science at the Courant Institute of Mathematical Sciences, New York University, New York, NY. Before obtaining the Ph.D., he worked for IBM, designing circuits and microcode for the IBM 3090 (Sierra) central processor. His research interests are in concurrent and parallel algorithms, especially for data structures, and in databases. He has written a puzzle book based on the adventures of a mathematical detective. The book is titled *The Puzzling Adventures of Dr. Ecco* (San Francisco, CA: Freeman, published in October 1988).

Dr. Shasha is a member of the Association for Computing Machinery.

HYTREM—A Hybrid Text-Retrieval Machine for Large Databases

DIK LUN LEE AND FREDERICK H. LOCHOVSKY

Abstract—This paper describes the design of a text-retrieval machine, called HYTREM (hybrid text-retrieval machine), for the support of large unformatted text databases. A signature file is used as an access method to reduce the amount of data that need to be searched directly. Therefore, *HYTREM* consists of two major subsystems: a signature processor and a text processor. The signature processor is based on a word-parallel, bit-serial (WPBS) organization which is faster, more efficient, and more flexible than a word-serial, bit-parallel (WSBP) organization proposed in the literature. The text processor, called ALTEP (associative linear text processor), is a linear array of logic cells capable of matching regular expressions at a much higher speed than that of previous designs.

Since both the signature processor and ALTEP are highly parallel processors, a high-speed multiple-response resolver (MRR) is provided to facilitate data transfer between the processors and the controllers over a single common bus. Issues about the design of a cost-effective mass-storage system (MSS) are also discussed. Finally, the performance and implementation issues of HYTREM are discussed.

Index Terms— Associative processing, mass-storage system, multiple-response resolution, pattern matching, performance evaluation, text retrieval, text-retrieval machine

I. INTRODUCTION

RETRIEVAL in large text databases requires a tremendous amount of processing time because of the size of the database and the complexity of the retrieval operations. Therefore, many search strategies have been developed and employed by different text-retrieval systems (TRS's) to try to address these problems. These strategies vary in their performance, cost, and complexity. Full text scanning and inverted file approaches represent the two extremes of the spectrum. Full text scanning, while it eliminates processing and storage overhead of access structures, performs extremely poorly for large databases if not facilitated by parallel processing techniques. On the other hand, inverted files are fast for locating words which have been indexed, but the storage overhead and thus the maintenance costs may be tremendous [2].

The signature file approach attempts to strike a balance be-

tween these two extremes. It requires scanning of the text, but uses a low-overhead access structure to reduce the amount of text that needs to be scanned.

As a text database grows in size and its access frequency steadily increases, these traditional software approaches to text searching often fail to provide satisfactory performance because of the inadequacy of von Neumann architectures for nonnumeric processing. With the advent of VLSI technology, it is more and more attractive to exploit special purpose processors to provide high-speed retrieval and complex querying capability. For instance, inverted file processors have been proposed to support the inverted file approach [27], signature processors for the signature file approach [1], and numerous hardware processors for full text scanning [24], [11].

Apart from an improvement in processing speed, a hardware design inherits most of the characteristics from the software approach on which it is based. For example, inverted file processors still face the problem of growing index size and, as such, escalating hardware costs; selecting a set of indexes that suits a variety of query mixes remains difficult; substantial overheads are incurred for frequency insertion and deletion, etc. Full text scanning processors are inefficient in disk bandwidth utilization since most of the data scanned do not satisfy the user query. When the database is large, they either fail to provide adequate speed, or require an unrealistic number of processors, or both.

Signature processors, on the other hand, retain the advantages of the signature file approach. Since the signature file is small and has a simple organization, the signature processor requires only a moderate amount of hardware and is simple and regular in structure. A number of hardware and software techniques have been developed to support efficiently the signature file approach [20].

This paper presents the design of a text-retrieval machine called HYTREM (hybrid text-retrieval machine) [21]. It is a "hybrid" machine since both access method and text search techniques are utilized. A signature file is used as an access method to reduce the amount of data that need to be searched directly. As such, HYTREM consists of two major subsystems: a signature processor for searching the signature file and a pattern matcher for eliminating false drops and performing complex pattern-matching operations which cannot be handled directly by the signature processor.

Inherent to the signature processor and the text processor is a multiple-response resolver (MRR). The purpose of an MRR is to serialize (or prioritize) the output of responses from an associative memory or associative processor. Since a

Manuscript received April 18, 1987; revised June 12, 1988. This work was supported in part by OSU Seed Grant 221835, and NSF IRI-8810564. Any opinions, findings, and conclusions or recommendations expressed in this paper are those of the authors and do not necessarily reflect the views of the National Science Foundation.

D. L. Lee is with the Department of Computer and Information Science, The Ohio State University, Columbus, OH 43210.

F. H. Lochovsky is with the Computer Systems Research Institute, University of Toronto, Toronto, Ont., Canada M5S 1A4.

IEEE Log Number 8931164.

0-8186-5460-0/94 $3.00 © 1990 IEEE

search operation may yield more than one response and there is usually only one common bus connecting the memory cells or processors, a high-speed MRR is necessary to retrieve the responses if the gain in speed by the associative search is not to be overshadowed by this serial retrieve operation.

Following an overview of the signature file method in Section II, each component in HYTREM is described and evaluated individually. A word-parallel, bit-serial (WPBS) signature processor is presented in Section III. A pattern matcher, called ALTEP, capable of recognizing regular expressions at high speed, is then discussed in Section IV. Section V describes a distributed multiple-response resolver (MRR) which has adequate speed for HYTREM. Issues about the design of a cost-effective mass-storage system (MSS) are outlined in Section VI. In the last section, the operations of the integrated HYTREM are described, its performance evaluated, and implementation discussed.

II. SIGNATURE FILES FOR DOCUMENT RETRIEVAL

A signature file is basically a compressed version of the database, typically 10–20 percent the size of the database. Text blocks which are sure not to match the query can be identified by examining the signature file alone, without accessing the text blocks. Since the signature file is much smaller than the database, the amount of data that need to be searched can be substantially reduced. Furthermore, the small storage overhead and the simplicity of the file structure reduce the maintenance costs and facilitate the exploitation of parallel processing techniques. Since a signature file may produce false drops, it can only be viewed as a filtering mechanism which must be followed by a precise match to eliminate the false drops. Implementations of the signature file approach have a number of variants [8], [9]. Our description of the signature file approach will be based on superimposed coding.

In the superimposed coding method, the database is divided into a number of fixed length blocks. Each text block B_i is associated with a signature S_i which is a fixed length bit vector $S_i^1 S_i^2 \cdots S_i^m$, where m is the length of the signature. The signature is abstracted from its associated text block by means of hashing and can be considered as a condensed representation of the text block.

Fig. 1 is an example illustrating the process of generating a block signature from a text block. Each nontrivial word in the text block is hashed into a bit vector, called a *word signature*. For simplicity, the number of one's in a word signature is assumed fixed (in the example, four bits are set). The *block signature* is generated by superimposing the word signatures.

When a word is searched for, a *query signature S_Q* of the word is generated from the query Q in the same way as described above. S_Q is then matched with every text block signature. A text block signature S_i is *qualified*, if and only if for all bit positions in S_Q which are set to 1, the corresponding bit positions in S_i are also set to 1 (known as the *inclusion* condition). Formally, the set of qualified signatures is defined by

$$\{S_i | S_i \wedge S_Q - S_Q\}.$$

A disqualified signature indicates that the associated text block

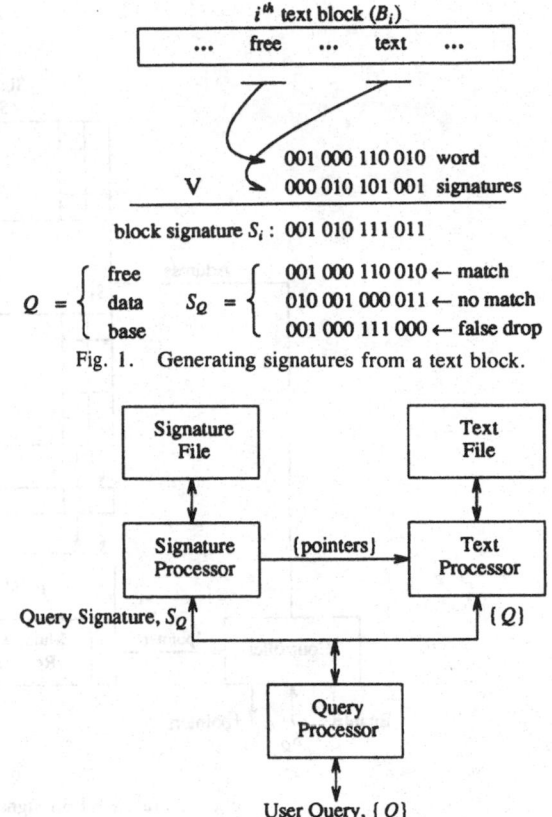

block signature S_i: 001 010 111 011

$$Q = \left\{ \begin{array}{l} \text{free} \\ \text{data} \\ \text{base} \end{array} \right. \quad S_Q = \left\{ \begin{array}{ll} 001\ 000\ 110\ 010 & \leftarrow \text{match} \\ 010\ 001\ 000\ 011 & \leftarrow \text{no match} \\ 001\ 000\ 111\ 000 & \leftarrow \text{false drop} \end{array} \right.$$

Fig. 1. Generating signatures from a text block.

Fig. 2. Block diagram for a TRS based on signature files.

is guaranteed not to contain the word specified in the query. However, a qualified signature only means that the corresponding text block is very likely to satisfy the query. That is, there is a small chance that the text block may not contain the word being searched for (i.e., it is a false drop). Therefore, the text block has to be searched to eliminate false drops.

Fig. 2 illustrates the block diagram of a TRS based on signature files. The query processor generates S_Q from Q and passes S_Q and Q, respectively, to the signature processor and the text processor. The signature processor searches the signature file and obtains a (possibly null) set of pointers for the text processor which compares the corresponding blocks to Q. Matched blocks (or documents containing the matched blocks) are returned to the user.

The signature processor is important since the size of the signature file grows linearly with the database and, as such, the response time deteriorates as the database grows. The text processor not only serves to eliminate false drops but handles complex queries which cannot be dealt with directly by the signature processor. These functions, if performed by software, usually require a large amount of processing time.

III. THE WORD-PARALLEL, BIT-SERIAL SIGNATURE PROCESSOR

The simplest approach to search a signature file is to store the signature file sequentially on disks and scan it bit-serially. Obviously, it takes $n \times m$ time units to search n signatures of m bits each. However, as can be observed from the description in the last section, only those bit positions in a signature specified in S_Q need to be examined. As such, only $(n \times w_{S_Q})$

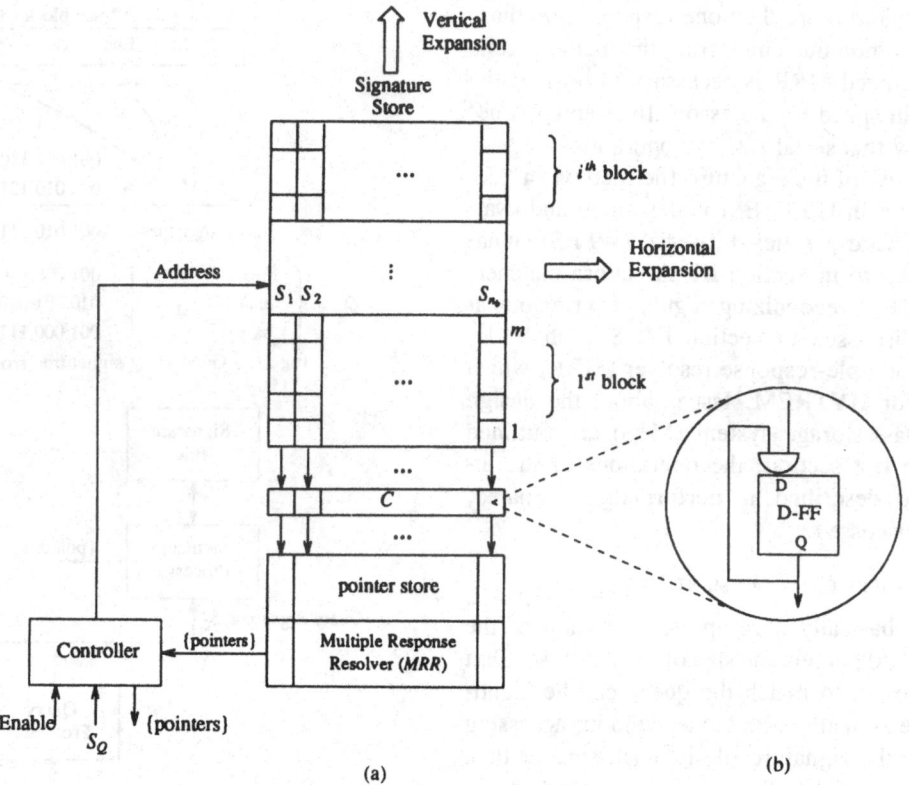

Fig. 3. (a) A WPBS signature processor, and (b) its serial comparator.

of the $n \times m$ bits read are really needed, where w_{S_Q} is the number of one's specified in S_Q. Storing the signatures in a transposed file organization reduces the amount of data to be read from the signature file to $n \times w_{S_Q}$ bits. This approach is optimal in the sense that the smallest possible amount of data are read but is slow for inserting new signatures. These software approaches are in general seriously limited by the disk bandwidth available.

A hardware solution was first proposed by Ahuja and Roberts [1]. Their signature processor was based on a word-serial, bit-parallel (WSBP) architecture in which the signatures were stored in CCD modules and retrieved sequentially for comparison to the query signature. Since the CCD modules have higher access speed than disks and are capable of accessing one signature in one clock cycle, a significant gain in speed can be achieved. This method is a straightforward application of parallelism. However, it is not optimal in the sense that the whole signature file (i.e., $n \times m$ bits), rather than $n \times w_{S_Q}$ bits, is read. Consequently, only w_{S_Q}/m of the total I/O bandwidth and the associated hardware (e.g., the query mask for discarding unwanted bits) of the signature store are utilized. When w_{S_Q} is much less than m, as is usually the case, this approach is inefficient in the use of hardware and, more importantly, I/O bandwidth, resulting in a longer processing time than what is otherwise achievable if the full bandwidth were utilized.

A natural way to make full use of the I/O bandwidth of the signature store is to store the signatures in a transposed file organization [17]. Fig. 3 illustrates the organization of the WPBS signature processor. It consists of a signature store, a comparator C, and a pointer store. In addition, a multiple

response resolver (MRR), to be explained later, is required to retrieve qualified pointers sequentially from the pointer store.

The signatures are transposed and stored in the signature store as shown in the figure (i.e., a word in the signature store holds the same bit from every signature). The signature store is partitioned into a number of *signature blocks*. Each block B_i has a capacity of n_b signatures of the same length m_i. Initially, the first block occupies addresses from 1 to m_1, the second block from $m_1 + 1$ to $m_1 + m_2$, and so on (for convenience, memory locations start from 1).

Signatures within a block are searched in parallel while signature blocks are processed one after another. S_Q is sent to the controller which then addresses the signature store according to the bits set in S_Q. That is, if the ith bit of S_Q is set, the ith word which contains the ith bit from every signature is read. The output words are ANDed together by the comparator C. At the end of the operation, the ith bit of C will be set to one if and only if S_i includes S_Q (i.e., if and only if S_i is qualified). The bit vector from C is used to retrieve the qualified text pointers from the pointer store. After a signature block is searched, C is reset to one. The next block can be processed in the same manner except that the addresses are offset by the signature length m_1. In other words, if the ith bit of S_Q is set, the signature store will be addressed at locations i, $m_1 + i$, $m_1 + m_2 + i$, and so on, when the signature blocks are processed.

As in the transposed file approach, only w_{S_Q} bits from every signature are examined, since the signature store can be directly addressable according to the bits set in S_Q. Thus, the search of a signature block takes only w_{S_Q} steps and is independent of n_b. When the number of signatures n is greater than n_b, $\lceil n/n_b \rceil$ signature blocks are required. Therefore, the total search time is $\lceil n/n_b \rceil \times w_{S_Q}$ steps and depends on n_b (when n_b is large, a smaller number of signature blocks are required).

If more than one pointer has to be sent to the controller, the output of pointers must be serialized by the *multiple response resolver* (MRR). In the WPBS processor, a high-speed MRR is important since signatures in the same block are searched and finished at the same time, whereas, in the WSBP approach, signatures within a module are searched sequentially and thus no MRR is required. A high-speed MRR will be presented later in this paper.

The size of a module can be expanded both horizontally and vertically as shown by the arrows in Fig. 3. *Horizontal* expansion increases the word width of the store so that more signatures can be stored in a signature block (i.e., increases n_b). It does not affect the time for searching a signature block but consumes a larger amount of hardware for the comparators and MRR. *Vertical* expansion increases the number of words ("height") of a module. It serves two purposes. First, the number of signatures per module can be increased by allowing more signature blocks. This method requires little extra hardware, but it slows down searching since the signature blocks are searched one after another. Second, and more importantly, it enables the number of bits per signature to change after initial installation. In general, a module would contain more than one signature block for reducing the hardware costs as well as providing more flexibility. The choice is determined by the available size, configuration, and technology of the memory employed.

It can be observed that both the WPBS and WSBP signature processors require about the same amount of storage. However, the WPBS approach is approximately n_b/w_{S_Q} times faster. For a fair comparison, n_b can be set to m so that both approaches use an equal number of processors and the same total memory bandwidth (i.e., I/O lines of the signature store). In general, w_{S_Q} is much less than m (e.g., one-tenth). Therefore, a substantial gain in speed is achieved in the WPBS approach.

In addition to the gain performance, the WPBS organization offers unique flexibility in managing the signature store. Signatures of different lengths can be easily accommodated in the same signature store. This flexibility is important in efficiently utilizing the signature store, since the access frequency of documents tends to decrease exponentially with their age [10], and, as such, the signatures of old documents can be truncated to save space (i.e., the less they are accessed, the more they are truncated) [6]. The search procedure for such an environment remains more or less the same. S_Q is generated to its original length, but when a truncated signature is encountered, the excess bits in S_Q are ignored (the length of a signature is always less than or equal to the length of S_Q). This procedure can be easily implemented in the WPBS organization but is rather difficult to perform in a WSBP architecture. More details on signature store management may be found in [17].

It may be observed that when signature blocks are stored consecutively, the signature store is accessed with addresses

in ascending order. This property makes it very suitable to implement with sequential memory such as magnetic bubbles without the usual performance penalty of sequential memory.

The structure of the signature store can be mapped into the major–minor loop organization of a magnetic bubble memory easily. That is, a minor loop corresponds to a bit slice in the signature store. In addition to acting as a memory device, magnetic bubbles can be manipulated and perform logic functions [5]. This feature allows the comparator to be implemented on the same memory chip. Putting the logic devices close to the store can greatly reduce the amount of off-chip data movement [29]. The design of the bubble memory can be found in [17] and [19].

IV. Associative Linear Text Processor (ALTEP)

The next component in HYTREM is a text processor to supplement the rudimentary filtering mechanism of the signature processor with more complex pattern matching capability. The text processor, called associative linear text processor (ALTEP) [18], belongs to the logic-with-text category [20]. ALTEP is a linear cellular array which has the full pattern-matching capability of a regular expression. To the best knowledge of the authors, it is the only linear cellular array that can recognize regular expressions without reprogramming the interconnection between the cells for each regular expression.

ALTEP is intended for systems which use signature files as an access method. With signature files, the text is divided into fixed length blocks, and only a small number of the blocks need to be examined. As a result, a logic array of predetermined length can be used within ALTEP, and a text block can be loaded into the cells on demand. Once the text is in the cells, the array functions as a truly associative processor.

A. Organization of ALTEP

ALTEP is a linear array of identical logic cells connected to two common buses. A unidirectional chaining channel connects all cells serially for intercell communication [see Fig. 4(a)]. The *instruction* bus is used to broadcast instructions to the cells. Every cell executes concurrently the instruction it receives and acknowledges to the controller through the *acknowledgment* bus if the operation is successful. The acknowledgment bus is asserted if one of the cells acknowledges positively. The controller may take different actions depending on whether or not an acknowledgment is received. Every cell contains exactly one text character which is loaded into the cell before pattern matching starts. The mechanism for loading the text characters is not shown in the figure for clarity.

A simplified organization of an ALTEP cell is depicted in Fig. 4(b). Each cell has a status bit, **pm** (partial match); two 1-bit wide stacks, A and S; and an 8-bit data register T for holding a text character. We note that each cell may be considered as consisting of a standard iterative comparator (to the left of the dotted line) and a temporary storage area (to the right of the dotted line) provided by A and S for saving and restoring the status of the cell.

The text string is stored in cell 1 to cell n, one character in each cell. The major operation of a cell is to compare the text character with the pattern character broadcast to it. Cell 0 is

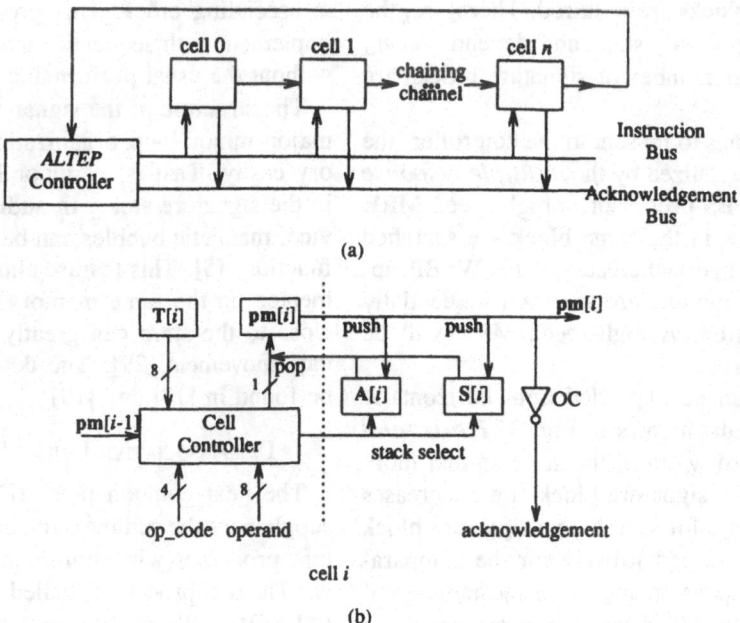

(a)

(b)

Fig. 4. (a) Organization of ALTEP. (b) Organization of an ALTEP cell.

a pseudocell. Its *only* purpose is to initialize the **pm** signal input to the first cell. As such, the cell can be much simpler than the other cells (e.g., A and S stacks can be omitted). However, it is conceptually simpler to regard it as identical to the other cells, except that it does not match with *any* pattern character. Thus, every cell in ALTEP is identical and responds to an instruction in the same way.

B. Instruction Set and Pattern Matching Algorithms

The format and a brief description of the instruction set are illustrated in Fig. 5. The first six instructions are absolutely required for recognizing regular expressions. The remaining four are enhancements which improve the speed and functionality of ALTEP [18].

Regular expressions can be constructed with three basic operators: concatenation, alternation, and closure [12]. When the pattern is a simple sequence of characters (called *simple patterns* for short), the algorithm resembles a conventional iterative cellular comparator. The **pm** bit in every cell is initialized to one and pattern characters are compared in sequence to the text with the **match** operation. It is easy to observe that exactly p steps are required to recognize a simple pattern of p characters in length.

The novel aspect of the algorithm is the way that alternation and closure are handled. Fig. 6 illustrates an example for recognizing a typical regular expression containing concatenation, alternation, and closure. The main idea is that the **pm** bits can be saved in a stack at any point when a pattern is compared. Restoring the **pm** bits will have the same effect as repeating a match of the prefix of the pattern that produced the restored partial match results.

When an alternation is encountered, the current status of the cells is pushed into the A stack (step 3). Each alternation is explored by first restoring the status from the A stack, then processing the alternation and accumulating the result **pm** bits in the S stack. After all alternations are attempted, the

accumulated status is restored (step 9). Since each alternation is explored once, the number of steps required for alternation is $O(p)$ steps.

A closure is in effect a repeating pattern. Therefore, the closure can be compared to the text repetitively until no match is reported on the acknowledgment bus. The result at the end of each repetition is accumulated in the S stack (steps 14 and 17). Since the loop stops when no match can be found, the number of steps required in this case is on the order of the length of the longest substring in the text that matches the closure, denoted by $O(len(max(T(P))))$.

At the end of the comparison, three matches are found. The first match results from steps 10 and 11, the second from steps 13 and 14, and the third steps 16 and 17. A complete recursive algorithm and more complex examples can be found in [18].

The average speed of the algorithms is much better than the worst case speed, since a mismatch may occur before the end of the pattern is reached, which can be detected from the acknowledgment bus. Furthermore, the worst case speed is bounded by $O(t)$ where t is the length of a text block (i.e., the algorithm terminates in $O(t)$ steps, no matter how long the pattern is). This can be shown by observing the fact that a **pm** bit either stays stationary when the stacks are being manipulated (e.g., **accS**, etc.), propagates to its immediate right neighbor in case of a match, or vanishes in case of a mismatch. Since every stack manipulation instruction is accompanied with a **match** instruction, we can observe that a **pm** bit eventually vanishes at the right end of the array, even when the pattern is very long. Therefore, the worst case speed is bounded by $O(t)$.

V. THE DISTRIBUTED MULTIPLE-RESPONSE RESOLVER

We concentrated on the processing aspect when we described the signature processor and ALTEP. However, if the full potential of the processors is to be realized, the I/O aspect

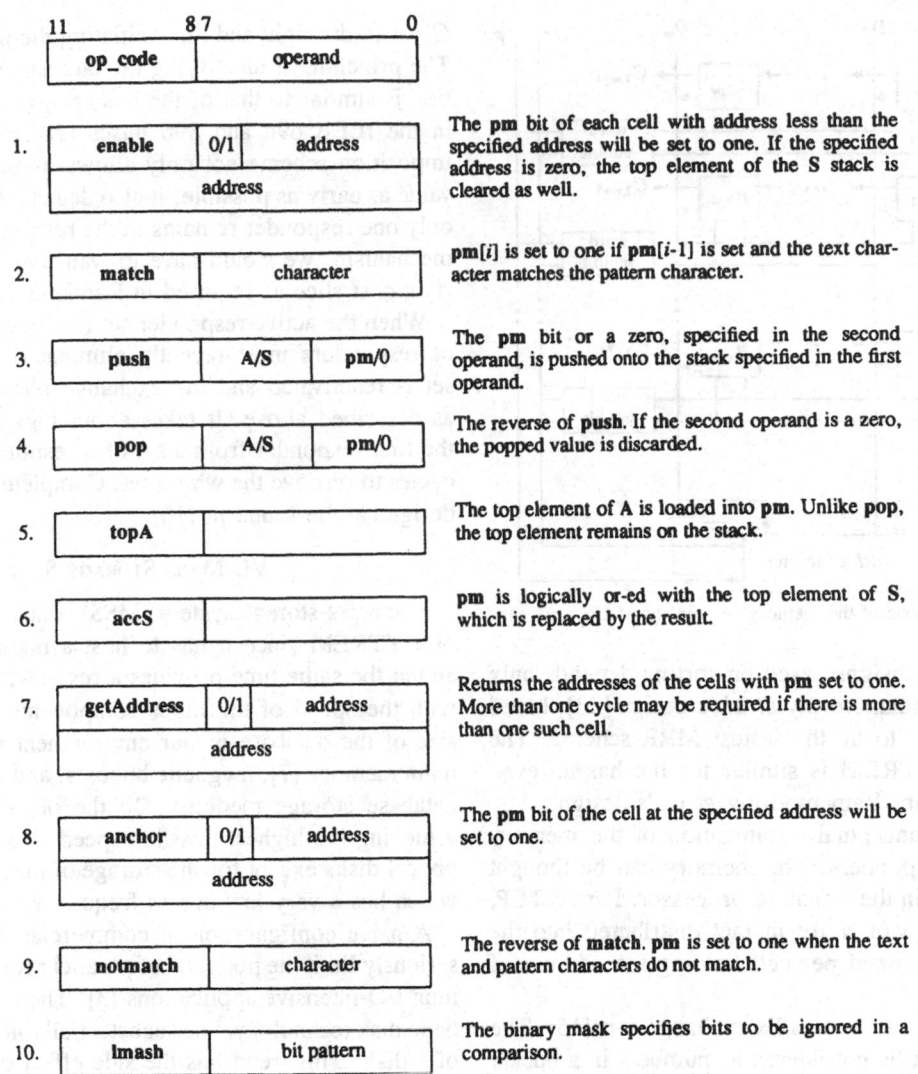

	op_code (11 · 87)	operand (7 · 0)	
1.	enable	0/1 · address / address	The pm bit of each cell with address less than the specified address will be set to one. If the specified address is zero, the top element of the S stack is cleared as well.
2.	match	character	pm[i] is set to one if pm[i-1] is set and the text character matches the pattern character.
3.	push	A/S · pm/0	The pm bit or a zero, specified in the second operand, is pushed onto the stack specified in the first operand.
4.	pop	A/S · pm/0	The reverse of push. If the second operand is a zero, the popped value is discarded.
5.	topA		The top element of A is loaded into pm. Unlike pop, the top element remains on the stack.
6.	accS		pm is logically or-ed with the top element of S, which is replaced by the result.
7.	getAddress	0/1 · address / address	Returns the addresses of the cells with pm set to one. More than one cycle may be required if there is more than one such cell.
8.	anchor	0/1 · address / address	The pm bit of the cell at the specified address will be set to one.
9.	notmatch	character	The reverse of match. pm is set to one when the text and pattern characters do not match.
10.	lmash	bit pattern	The binary mask specifies bits to be ignored in a comparison.

Fig. 5. Instruction set and format.

pattern: a(b|c)d(ef)*
text: a c d e f e f

```
                        _ a c d e f e f
1.  enable(0)           1 1 1 1 1 1 1 1   initialize all pm bits to one
2.  match(a)            0 1 0 0 0 0 0 0
    /* begin alternate */
3.  push(A, pm)         0 1 0 0 0 0 0 0   ←top element of A
4.  match(b)            0 0 0 0 0 0 0 0
5.  accS                0 0 0 0 0 0 0 0   ←top element of S
6.  topA                0 1 0 0 0 0 0 0   pm reinitialized to step 3
7.  match(c)            0 0 1 0 0 0 0 0
8.  accS                0 0 1 0 0 0 0 0   ←top element of S
    /* end alternate */
9.  pop(S, pm)          0 0 1 0 0 0 0 0   both 'b' and 'c' tried
10. match(d)            0 0 0 1 0 0 0 0
    /* begin closure */
11. push(S, pm)         0 0 0 1 0 0 0 0
12. match(e)            0 0 0 0 1 0 0 0
13. match(f)            0 0 0 0 0 1 0 0
14. accS                0 0 0 0 0 1 0 0   accumulate pm after 1st iteration
15. match(e)            0 0 0 0 0 0 1 0
16. match(f)            0 0 0 0 0 0 0 1
17. accS                0 0 0 0 0 0 0 1   accumulate pm after 2nd iteration
18. match(e)            0 0 0 0 0 0 0 0   no match found, stop
    /* end closure */
19. pop(S, pm)          0 0 0 1 0 1 0 1
                              ↑   ↑   ↑   ←hit
```

Fig. 6. Example for matching a general regular expression.

is just as important as the processing aspect. As described, the signature processor may be required to transfer more than one simultaneously available pointer from the pointer store to the controller. There is the same need in ALTEP to send the addresses of the cells at which a match is found to the controller, if we want to know the positions of the matches in the text blocks. Therefore, there must be a fast mechanism with which the transfer can be serialized over a common bus. This is the well-known problem of multiple-response resolution (MRR) in associative memory [20].

A simple priority line will serve the purpose but it is too slow for a large number of processors or memory cells. In this section, we present a distributed MRR scheme which retrieves responders[1] in a sorted order according to their values [16]. When the memory is large, it is surprising that retrieving responders in sorted order is much faster than retrieving responders according to their relative positions in the memory as in the case of a priority line. This is because the speed of a priority line depends on the number of words in memory,

[1] We use the generic term responder to stand for the addresses that need to be sent from the ALTEP cells and the pointers that need to be sent from the pointer store.

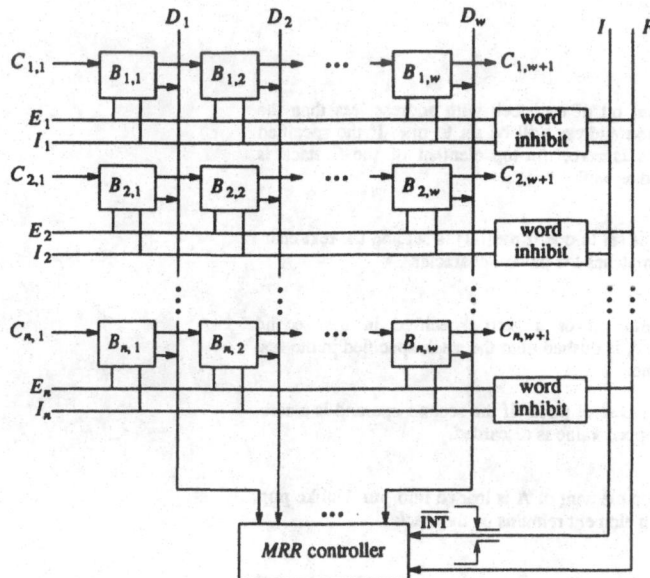

Fig. 7. Organization of the memory cells in the MRR.

but the speed of most designs based on sorting depends only on the word length. Ramamoorthy *et al.*'s design [23], based on sorting, was known to be the fastest MRR scheme. The design adopted in HYTREM is similar to, but has an even better performance than, Ramamoorthy *et al.*'s design.

Fig. 7 shows the conceptual organization of the memory which contains the responders. The memory can be thought of as the pointer store in the signature processor. For ALTEP, however, the memory words are in fact distributed into the ALTEP cells with one word per cell holding the address of the cell.

The MRR scheme is based on radix exchange sort [15]. The values to be output can be considered as numbers in a bucket to be sorted. The numbers are examined by bit slices in each stage (the *exchange* phase) starting from the most significant bit slice. When a bit slice contains both zero's and one's, numbers with zero's in that bit position are removed from the bucket; otherwise, all numbers are retained. This process is repeated until only one number remains in the bucket.

By making use of the capability of performing logical OR on an open-collector bus, our design has one significant improvement over a pure radix exchange sort. Prior to each exchange phase, we may check if any of the values are identical to the logical OR of all the values in the bucket. If there is one such value, that value must be the largest value currently in the bucket. If none exists, we may proceed with the exchange phase. This procedure is repeated until the largest value is identified.

Bit slices can be examined, as in the exchange phase, in turn by propagating the enable signal $C_{i,j}$'s from the first slice towards the right. In the attempt to identify the largest value prior to the start of the exchange phase, the memory words write their values onto the default detection bus D_i's and the values are superimposed (wired-OR). After the bus settles down, the memory words compare the bus value to their own values. The matched responder, if any, identifies itself as the largest responder by interrupting the memory controller. If no match is found, the selection process continues by passing

$C_{i,j}$'s to the right and thus initiating the next exchange phase. The principle of identifying the largest value by superimposition is similar to that of the bus arbitration scheme employed in the IEEE 696 and 896 buses [28]. Note that the superimposition scheme not only allows us to identify the largest value as early as possible, it also detects the situation in which only one responder remains in the responder set. Without this mechanism, we would have to wait until the $C_{i,j}$'s reach the rightmost slice as required in Ramamoorthy *et al.*'s design.

When the active responder set (the bucket) is empty, the set of responders most recently eliminated from the responder set is reactivated and the exchange phase commences again as described above. It takes about $\log_2 n$ cycles to retrieve the first responder from a set of n responders and about $2.5n$ cycles to retrieve the whole set. Complete details of our MRR design can be found in [16].

VI. MASS-STORAGE SYSTEM

The mass-storage system (MSS) is an important component of HYTREM since it has to host a massive amount of data and at the same time provides a response time commensurate with the speed of the other components of the system. The size of the database in our environment rules out the use of main memory [7], magnetic bubbles, and CCD as the primary database storage medium. On the other hand, our goal of achieving the highest possible speed also excludes the use of optical disks except for the storage of that part of the database which has a very low access frequency.

A naive configuration of commercial disks, however, will seriously limit the potential of parallel processing systems running I/O-intensive applications [3]. The advancement of magnetic disk technology,[2] has substantially increased the capacity of a disk. This trend has the side effect of reducing the total number of disks required for a database of a given size, and, as a result, reducing the total bandwidth and the degree of parallelism available in the system.

Fortunately, low-performance and physically small disks have also exhibited remarkable advancement in the past few years. This is analogous to the development of processor technology in which the gap between micro and mainframe computers is narrowing. The introduction of hard disks that fit into one PC slot has demonstrated a significant reduction in price as well as footprint. Thus, a system employing a large number of small disks may become economically and physically feasible.

This configuration increases the degree of parallelism in disk access and data transfer, and thus increases the performance of the overall system despite the fact that each individual disk may have inferior performance to a large disk. When adequately designed, a system will have a higher data availability due to the distribution of the database across a large number of disks, as the failure of one disk only affects a small portion of the database. This is especially true in a TRS in which the availability of a document is in general independent of the availability of other documents. The expandability and flexibility of the system are also improved, since the storage

---

[2] Optical disk may be viewed as an extreme case.

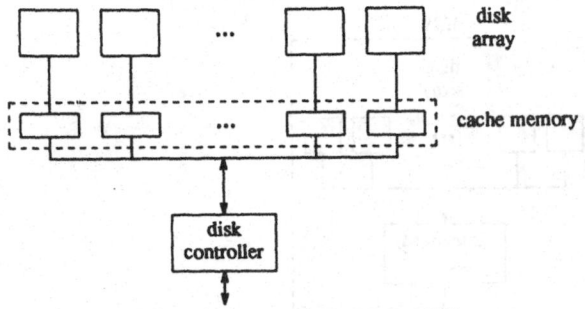

Fig. 8. The configuration of the MSS.

capacity can be increased in small increments and a small number of the disks (instead of the whole system) can be replaced as higher performance disks become available.

For the reasons discussed above, we envisage our MSS to consist of an array of small, low capacity, inexpensive disks (e.g., 100–200 5.25 in. Winchester disks with capacity 100–200 Mbytes each). We argue that such a configuration is not only feasible but competitive with the use of large-capacity, expensive disks (e.g., IBM 3380) in terms of system cost and performance.

Fig. 8 illustrates the organization of the MSS. The MSS consists of an array of (small) disks, each of which is associated with a cache and a small amount of logic to load a specified disk block into the cache. Dedicating a cache to each disk allows more than one disk to transfer data in parallel without contention. Maintaining a 1:1 mapping eliminates the use of an expensive interconnection network between the disks and the buffers [22]. A simple bus connects the caches to the controller which views the caches as a large disk cache and accesses them through direct memory access (DMA). A complex interconnection network [4] does not seem to be necessary for several reasons. Since the number of disk accesses is substantially reduced by the signature processor, the sole function of the MSS is to retrieve data according to the locations given by the signature processor. There are no complex search or comparison functions involved. Furthermore, the disk controller operates at a much higher speed than the disks (microsecond versus milliseconds) it can be regarded as the only master on the bus without much interference from the disks. In the physical implementation, the bus may be partitioned and driven individually.

Since documents are stored consecutively and in most cases the whole document (or a large portion of it) is retrieved, most disk accesses are sequential and thus prefetching can be used to decrease the average access time. For a high-traffic, sequential access environment, it has been shown that the miss ratio in the cache can be as low as 4 percent for a buffer size of 40 tracks per disk [26]. For a typical 5.25 in. disk, the buffer size is about 1 Mbyte/disk (track capacity is 25 kbytes). The average access time of the disk is reduced to 1.2 ms (i.e., 0.04×30 ms). Suppose we replace a 2.5 Gbyte IBM 3380 with 18 143-Mbyte disks, the average access time under heavy load and with uniformly distributed requests would be $1.2/18$ ms = 66 μs. This figure is, of course, optimistic, since it is not always true in a real TRS that all disks have the same utilization and that the access pattern is purely sequential. Nevertheless, this figure indicates that the effect of a cache of appropriate size

on reducing the effective disk access time is very important in an environment consisting of a large number of sequential accesses. Note that the number of disks required in the system, thus the overall performance of the system, depends on the size of the database.

VII. System Integration, Performance, and Cost Evaluation

Having discussed the design of the individual subsystems, namely, the signature processor, text processor AL-TEP, multiple-response resolver, and mass-storage system, we now discuss details concerning the integration of these various subsystems and estimate the performance and cost of the integrated machine.

A. Configuration of the Integrated Machine

Fig. 9 is the detailed configuration of the text-retrieval machine. The signature processor consists of a number of modules connected to a bus. Each module holds a partition of the signature file. The signatures within a module are organized into blocks. The signature-processor controller (SPC) receives query signatures from the query processor and translates them into addresses of the signature store. After the first signature block in each module is searched, the qualified pointers are loaded into the MRR bit serially and retrieved by the text processor controller (TPC) through the common bus, which serves as a data bus as well as an arbitration bus on which multiple-response resolution is performed.[3] The next signature block is processed in the same manner.

The TPC receives pointers from the SPC and passes them to the disk controller which then retrieves the addressed text blocks from the disk array or from the cache (in case of a hit) and loads the requested blocks into the ALTEP. The TPC is informed of the block number loaded (since text blocks may be loaded in an order different from that of the requests). Upon a match in the ALTEP, the TPC issues another request to the mass-storage system (MSS) to retrieve the portion of the (or the whole) qualified document specified in the user query. The query processor is responsible for generating the query signatures, and interfacing with and handling the traffic to and from the host(s).

The data/arbitration bus connecting the signature modules must have a low signal delay so that arbitration using our MRR scheme can be done on it rapidly. The link between SPC and TPC may have a lower bandwidth, since the pointer set is usually small and each pointer has a rather short length. The traffic between the MSS and the text processor could be very high because of long text block lengths. Therefore, a high-speed, parallel transfer bus must be used.[4]

B. Performance Evaluation

The whole process described above is essentially sequential and can be divided into different nonoverlapping phases.

---

[3] If the pointer store has a built-in MRR facility, the loading phase can be eliminated and the following performance analysis should be modified accordingly. We assume the MRR to be shared between the signature blocks within a module in order to lower the cost.

[4] To achieve a high bandwidth, a larger word length (e.g., 16–32 bits) may be used.

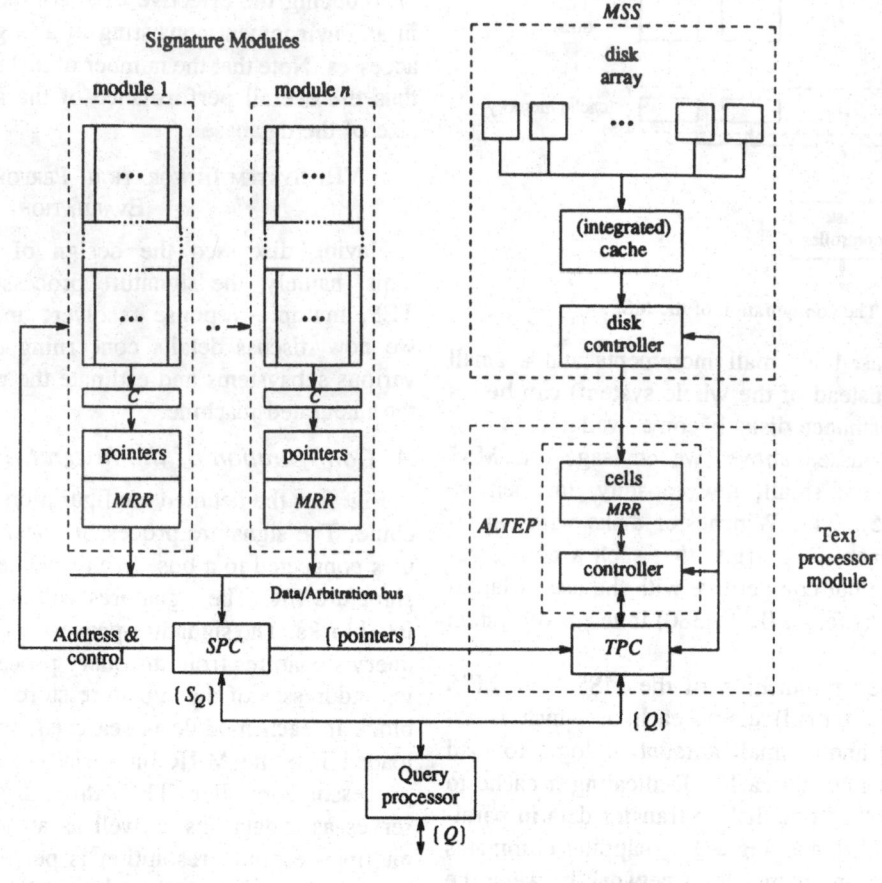

Signature Modules

module 1   module n

C C

pointers   pointers

MRR MRR

Data/Arbitration bus

Address & control

SPC { pointers }

$\{S_Q\}$

Query processor

$\{Q\}$

MSS

disk array

(integrated) cache

disk controller

cells

MRR

$ALTEP$ controller   Text processor module

TPC

$\{Q\}$

Q : user query TPC : text processor controller
S_Q : query signature MSS : mass storage system
SPC : signature processor controller

Fig. 9.   Configuration of HYTREM.

Thus, a query can be processed in a pipelined manner with suitable buffering (i.e., phase i of query j is serviced concurrently with phase $i - 1$ of query $j + 1$) to enhance the system throughput. Fig. 10 illustrates the different phases associated with the search of a signature block and how they are pipelined. Note that all signature blocks have to be searched for a query.

The time spent on each phase depends on the parameters of a particular implementation. Table I defines the parameters we are interested in. Given S_{TF}, BF, SL, N_{MD}, $N_{SG/BK}$, and $\bar{w}_{S_Q}$, we can derive the following expressions:

$$N_{SG} = \left\lceil \frac{S_{TF}}{BF} \right\rceil$$

$$= \frac{S_{TF}}{BF} \text{ (for simplicity, we drop all ceiling functions)}$$

$$N_{SG/MD} = \frac{N_{SG}}{N_{MD}} = \frac{S_{TF}}{BF \cdot N_{MD}}$$

$$N_{BK/MD} = \left\lceil \frac{N_{SG/MD}}{N_{SG/BK}} \right\rceil = \frac{S_{TF}}{BF \cdot N_{MD} \cdot N_{SG/BK}}$$

$$T_{SSB} = \bar{w}_{S_Q}.$$

Since pointers are loaded into the MRR in a bit serial, word

parallel manner,

$$T_{LPTR} = \text{number of bits/pointers}.$$

Since the speed of our MRR is 2.5 cycles/retrieval,

$$T_{RPTR} = 2.5$$

$$\cdot \text{(number of qualified pointers per signature block)}$$

$$\cdot \text{(number of modules)}$$

$$= 2.5 \cdot \text{SL} \cdot N_{SG/BK} \cdot N_{MD}$$

$$T_{RTBK} = \text{(number of text blocks accessed)}$$

$$\cdot \text{(access time per text block)}$$

$$T_{PTBK} = \text{(number of text blocks accessed)}$$

$$\begin{cases} O(p) & \text{patterns without closures} \\ O(len(max(T(P)))) & \text{patterns with closures} \end{cases}$$

where $O(len(max(T(P))))$ stands for the length of the longest substring in a text block which matches the closure.

$$T_{RRES} = O(\text{size of the returned documents}).$$

Ideally, the time spent on each phase should be the same in order to maximize the efficiency of the pipeline. However,

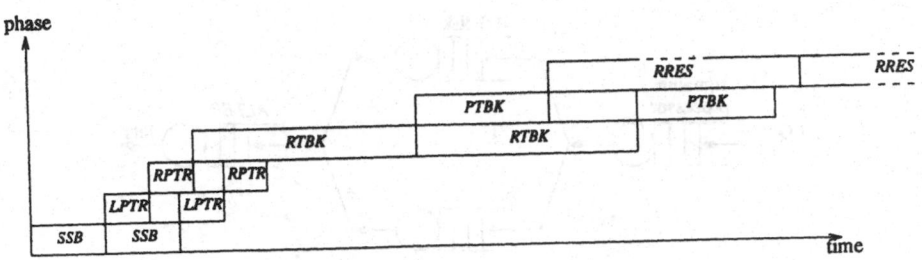

phase

| | | | | | RRES | | RRES |
(Figure showing pipelined processing stages: SSB, LPTR, RPTR, RTBK, PTBK, RRES arranged in a pipeline along time axis)

→ time

SSB : search a signature block
LPTR : load pointers into *MRR*
RPTR : retrieve pointers from *MRR* and send them to *TPC*

RTBK : retrieve text blocks from *MSS*
PTBK : process text blocks in *ALTEP*'s
RRES : return results to user

Fig. 10. Pipelined processing of queries.

TABLE I
DEFINITION OF SYMBOLS

S_{TF} : size of the text file

BF : blocking factor (number of bytes per text block)

N_{SG} : number of signatures in the signature file

N_{MD} : number of modules employed

$N_{SG/MD}$: number of signatures per module

$N_{SG/BK}$: number of signatures per signature block (i.e., number of processors per module)

$N_{BK/MD}$: number of signature blocks per module

$\overline{w}_{S_q}$: average weight of a query signature

SL : percentage of pointers satisfying a query ($\approx$ selectivity)

T_X : time to perform X where X is one of the phases listed in Figure 11

this is impossible to achieve in practice because the duration of each phase depends on the system parameters. In the following example, we consider a bibliographic database (containing abstracts of articles) 10 Gbytes in size with 2000 bytes in each bibliographic record. The database therefore contains 5 million entries. A natural block size to use is 2000 bytes. As such, each record constitutes one physical block and is therefore associated with one signature. The characteristics of the database are summarized below:

$$S_{TF} = 10^{10} \text{ bytes}$$

$$BF = 2000 \text{ bytes/block}$$

$$N_{SG} = 10^{10}/2000 = 5 \times 10^6 \text{ signatures.}$$

The performance of the system also depends on the amount of resources allocated to each subsystem and the characteristics of the query mix. We consider three sets of parameters in our analysis:

Case 1: low selectivity and high parallelism. 100 signature processor modules are used, and within each of the modules 1000 signatures are allocated to one block (the "width" of the module is 1000). The average selectivity of the queries is 10^{-4}.

Case 2: high selectivity and high parallelism. The same

number and configuration of signature processor modules are used, but the average selectivity of the queries is 10^{-5}.

Case 3: high selectivity and low parallelism. The number of signature processor modules is reduced to 50, with average selectivity equal to 10^{-5}.

The following table summarizes the system parameters:

	CASE 1	CASE 2	CASE 3
N_{MD}	100	100	50
SL	10^{-4}	10^{-5}	10^{-5}
$N_{SG/MD}$	5×10^4	5×10^4	10^5
$N_{SG/BK}$	1,000	1,000	1,000
$N_{BK/MD}$	50	50	100

The time to service a query depends not only on the above parameters but also on the details of the pipeline strategy and the disk scheduling policy. To simplify our analysis, we assume that enough buffers are provided to the MSS and ALTEP so that the speeds of the signature processor, the MSS, and the ALTEP do not depend on one another. In other words, the signature processor can continuously deliver pointers to the MSS which is assumed to be either fast enough to consume the pointers or capable of buffering them; the same applies to the MSS and ALTEP. Since the time consumed by the controllers is negligible, the system can be considered as consisting of three major types of servers, namely, the signature processor, the MSS, and ALTEP (see Fig. 11).

Next, we compute the time spent on searching the signature file, which is dependent on the weight of the query signature ($\overline{w}_{S_Q}$). In general, queries with higher selectivity generate query signatures with higher weights. Therefore, we assume $\overline{w}_{S_Q}$ in the three test cases to be 50, 100, and 100, respectively. The total time spent on the signature processor is summarized below:

	CASE 1	CASE 2	CASE 3
$\overline{w}_{S_q}$	50	100	100
T_{SSB} (cycles)	50	100	100
T_{LPTR} (cycles)	30	30	30
T_{RPTR} (cycles)	25	2.5	1.25
Service time at sig. proc. $= T_{SSB} \times N_{BK/MD}$ (cycles)	2,500	5,000	10,000

In the above table, a pointer length of 30 bits is used. Therefore, T_{LPTR} is 30. Since T_{LPTR} and T_{RPTR} are smaller than T_{SSB}, the service time of the signature processor is determined by T_{SSB}.

The time to perform pattern matching on a text block, T_{PTBK}, depends on the pattern length, the frequency with

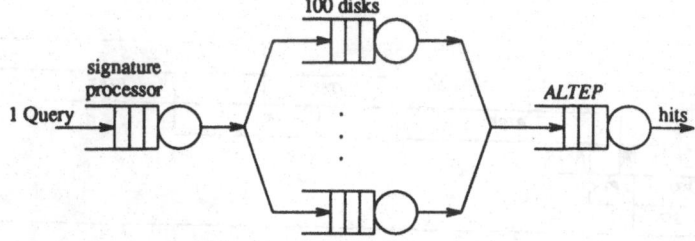

Fig. 11. Performance model.

which a closure appears in the pattern, and the time to match the closure. p is usually short (e.g., 20–40 characters), but closure would make the processing time longer. We expect the pattern to be more complex for queries with higher selectivity (e.g., conjunctive queries of many keywords). Therefore, we assume T_{PTBK} to be 100, 200, and 200 for the three test cases, respectively. The selectivity also determines the number of text blocks to process, which is 500, 50, and 50, respectively. The service time at ALTEP is summarized as follows.

	CASE 1	CASE 2	CASE 3
T_{PTBK}	100	200	200
Service time at *ALTEP* (cycles)	50,000	10,000	10,000

The last component to consider is the time to retrieve a record from MSS into ALTEP. For a database of 10 Gbytes, we assume the MSS to consist of 100 100-Mbyte disks with the following characteristics:[5]

$$\text{average seek time} = 30 \text{ ms}$$

$$\text{average latency time} = 8 \text{ ms}$$

$$\text{transfer rate} = 1.5 \text{ Mbytes/s}.$$

Assuming the text blocks to be retrieved are uniformly distributed across the disks, the service time at the MSS is

	CASE 1	CASE 2	CASE 3
Service time at *MSS*	5×(30+8+1.3) = 196 ms	30+8+1.3 = 39 ms	30+8+1.3 = 39 ms

Note that the given seek time of 30 ms is for unordered disk accesses. If the requests are sorted according to track numbers, as is possible in our system, the actual seek time in the first case is smaller. Furthermore, although there are 100 disks and only 50 records are retrieved in the last two cases, the service time is still bound by the time to retrieve one record.

Since the whole bibliographic record is fetched into ALTEP for comparison, the record can be returned directly to the user upon a successful match. Therefore, T_{RRES} is zero in our example.

Assuming that the system is running at a 1 MHz clock rate, the cycle time is 1 μs. The service time of the whole system can be summarized in the following table:

	CASE 1 (ms)	CASE 2 (ms)	CASE 3 (ms)
Service time at signature processor	2.5	5	10
Service time at *ALTEP*	50	10	10
Service time at *MSS*	196	39	39
Total service time	248.5	54	59

[5] The parameters are typical for advanced 5-1/4 and 3-1/2 in. disk drives.

The performance figures shown in the table, though inevitably optimistic, are encouraging. However, the performance relative to other designs is difficult to evaluate objectively because of the diversity in hardware requirements and functionality. For example, inverted files may have comparable performance but they require substantial storage and processing overhead and in many cases have a limited vocabulary. It is not difficult to see that full text scanning can hardly achieve this level of performance because of the lack of any kind of filtering or indexing. Furthermore, the superiority of HYTREM can be seen from the performance of its individual components, which have been shown to be better than other designs in the same category.

As in other disk-based database systems, the MSS is very likely to become a bottleneck. From the figures, we observe that this problem occurs only in the first case in which queries have low selectivity. For the other two cases, the system is very close to balance. These figures also lead to a number of implications concerning the design of the system. First, to improve the utilization of the system, a high-performance MSS is essential (e.g., by employing a larger disk cache or faster disks). This issue has drawn more and more attention. The general trend seems to be along the same approach taken in HYTREM [14]. That is, to exploit a large number of small, inexpensive disks to achieve parallelism in access and data transfer. Second, more processing can be performed on the access structures without degrading the system throughput, as long as the processing time is hidden by the disk access time. For instance, the signature method can be extended to support attribute data (e.g., DATE) and limited range query to reduce the number of disk accesses [25]. Finally, a slower clock rate could be used for the signature processor to accommodate slower but inexpensive memories (e.g., CCD and bubble memory), while the ALTEP and the disk cache could operate at a higher clock rate. For instance, if the signature processor is implemented in magnetic bubbles as described in [17], the corresponding service time of the signature processor in the three test cases would become 50, 50, and 100 ms, when an average signature length of 300, a clock rate of 300 kHz, and $T_{SSB} > T_{LPTR}$ and T_{RPTR} are assumed. Nevertheless, a well-balanced system can be achieved with an appropriate set of system parameters, and, ideally, an MSS with performance commensurate with the rest of the system must be available.

C. Implementation Issues

The cost of the machine depends on the size of the database as well as the technology available. The designs of the components conform with VLSI design principles. That is, they are simple and regular in structure and have a reasonably small number of I/O pins.

For our example database, there are 5 million signatures. With a 1000-bit signature length and 30-bit pointer length, the signature file takes 625 Mbytes of storage, and the pointer store about 20 Mbytes. This storage requirement is absolutely feasible with the state-of-the-art semiconductor memory technology. The processor array C in the signature processor is very simple, consisting of one latch and one AND gate per element. The signature processor can be implemented with standard RAM chips, with special purpose controller and processor array. To implement the whole processor with commercially available chips, the controller and processor array can be replaced with general ALU's [13]. Since the signature processor has an extremely simple interconnection pattern, we expect it to take no more than 20–40 circuit boards.

The MSS for our example database takes 100 100-Mbyte disks. Although there are no existing systems that we know of that make use of this large number of disks, we anticipate the cost of this configuration to be feasible with the current and near-future hard-disk technology, although issues concerning the interconnection network for the disks, reliability, etc., must be addressed [14].

We are currently working on the VLSI layout of the MRR and ALTEP. The MRR is being laid out on separate chips (instead of integrated with the signature processor and ALTEP). With 1 μm feature size, 2K by 16 bits can be put on one chip. Our next step is to investigate the cost of integrating the MRR into the signature processor and ALTEP and to evaluate the performance gain compared to the costs.

Some architectural optimization has been made on ALTEP. The cell controller has been moved out of each cell and combined into one controller. Therefore, instead of having one cell controller per cell, we have one controller per chip. This results in a smaller cell size. Furthermore, the (chip) controller acts as a driver to the cells. Instead of driving thousands of cells directly, the ALTEP controller now drives a small number of chip controllers which in turn drive the cells. Without the MRR built in, we can put 128 cells on a chip; a 2048-cell array would take 16 chips.

VIII. CONCLUSION

In this paper, we discussed various aspects of the design of a text-retrieval machine called HYTREM (hybrid text-retrieval machine) which was designed for large text databases. It employs conventional moving head disks as the secondary storage medium due to their cost effectiveness. In order to compensate for the relatively slow access time of the disks, a signature file is used as a filtering mechanism to reduce the amount of data accessed from the secondary storage. This design principle indicates that there are two major subsystems in HYTREM: a WPBS signature processor for supporting signature file searching and a text processor called ALTEP for eliminating false drops and handling complex queries. In addition to describing the processing aspects of these processors, we also presented the design of a high-speed distributed MRR to handle the I/O requirements from these processors.

Issues about the design of a cost-effective mass-storage system were also discussed. Finally, we described the operations of the integrated HYTREM, evaluated its performance, and discussed some implementation details. The performance evaluation showed that the performance of the integrated system depends on many system parameters which must be determined at the design phase. Three different sets of parameters were used to demonstrate their impacts on the system performance.

REFERENCES

[1] S. R. Ahuja and C. S. Roberts, "An associative/parallel processor for partial match retrieval using superimposed codes," in *Proc. 7th Annu. Symp. Comput. Architecture*, France, May 1980, pp. 218–227.

[2] R. M. Bird, J. B. Newsbaum, and J. L. Trefftzs, "Text file inversion: An evaluation," in *Proc. 4th Workshop Comput. Architecture Non-Numeric Processing*, Syracuse, NY, Aug. 1978, pp. 42–50.

[3] H. Boral and D. J. DeWitt, "Database machines: An idea whose time has passed? A critique of the future of database machines," in *Database Machines*, M. Missikoff, Ed. Berlin, Germany: Springer-Verlag, 1983, pp. 166–187.

[4] J. C. Browne, A. G. Dale, C. Leung, and R. Jenevein, "A parallel multi-stage I/O architecture with self-managing disk cache for database management applications," in *Database Machines Fourth Int. Workshop*, H. Boral, Ed. Berlin, Germany: Springer-Verlag, 1985, pp. 331–346.

[5] T. C. Chen and H. Chang, "Magnetic bubble memory and logic," in *Advances in Computers, Vol. 17*, M. C. Yovits, Ed. New York: Academic, 1978, pp. 223–282.

[6] S. Christodoulakis and C. Faloutsos, "Design considerations for a message file server," *IEEE Trans. Software Eng.*, vol. SE-10, no. 2, pp. 201–210, Mar. 1984.

[7] D. J. DeWitt, R. H. Katz, F. Olken, and L. D. Shapiro, "Implementation techniques for main memory database systems," in *Proc. Int. Conf. Management Data (SIGMOD 84)*, Boston, MA, June 1984, pp. 1–8.

[8] C. Faloutsos, "Access methods for text," *ACM Comput., Surveys*, vol. 17, pp. 49–74, Mar. 1985.

[9] C. Faloutsos and S. Christodoulakis, "Signature files: An access method for documents and its analytical performance evaluation," *ACM Trans. Office Info. Syst.*, vol. 2, pp. 267–288, Oct. 1984.

[10] C. M. Gravina, "National Westminster Bank mass storage archiving," *IBM Syst. J.*, vol. 17, no. 4, pp. 344–358, 1978.

[11] L. A. Hollaar *et al.*, "Architecture and operation of a large, full-text information-retrieval system," in *Advanced Database Machine Architecture*, D. K. Hsiao, Ed. Englewood Cliffs, NJ: Prentice-Hall, 1983, pp. 256–299.

[12] J. E. Hopcroft and J. D. Ullman, *Introduction to Automata Theory, Languages, and Computation*. Reading, MA: Addison-Wesley, 1979.

[13] M. Jayasooriah and R. M. Colomb, "Attached index machine: A new form of processor and its application to partial match data retrieval," in *Proc. 9th Australian Comput. Sci. Conf.*, Sydney, Jan. 1986, pp. 347–355.

[14] R. Katz, J. Ousterhout, D. Patterson, and M. Stonebraker, "A project on high performance I/O subsystems," *Database Eng.*, vol. 11, no. 1, pp. 40–47, Mar. 1988.

[15] D. E. Knuth, *The Art of Computer Programming, Vol. 3*. Reading, MA: Addison-Wesley, 1973.

[16] D. L. Lee, "A distributed multiple-response resolver for value-ordered retrieval," in *Proc. 12th Int. Symp. Comput. Architecture*, Boston, MA, June 1985, pp. 258–265.

[17] ——, "A word-parallel, bit-serial signature processor for superimposed coding," in *Proc. 2nd Int. Conf. Data Eng.*, Los Angeles, CA, Feb. 1986, pp. 352–359.

[18] ——, "ALTEP—A cellular processor for high-speed pattern matching," *New Generation Comput.*, vol. 4, pp. 255–244, Sept. 1986.

[19] ——, "A word-parallel, bit-serial signature processor and its implementation with magnetic bubbles," OSU-CISRC-5/87-TR14, Dep. Comput. Inform. Sci., Ohio State Univ., Columbus, OH, June 1987.

[20] D. L. Lee and F. H. Lochovsky, "Text retrieval machines," in *Office Automation*, D. C. Tsichritzis. New York: Springer-Verlag, 1985, pp. 339–375.

[21] D. L. Lee, "The design and evaluation of a text retrieval machine for large databases," Ph.D. dissertation, Dep. Comput. Sci., Univ. of Toronto, Toronto, Ont., Canada, Sept. 1985 (also published as Tech. Rep. CSRI-172, Comput. Syst. Res. Instit., Univ. of Toronto).

[22] G. Z. Qadah and K. B. Irani, "A database machine for very large relational databases," in *Proc. Int. Conf. Parallel Processing*, Bellaire, MI, Aug. 1983, pp. 307-314.

[23] C. V. Ramamoorthy, J. C. Turner, and B. W. Wah, "A design of a cellular associative memory for ordered retrieval," *IEEE Trans. Comput.*, vol. C-27, no. 9, pp. 800-815, Sept. 1978.

[24] D. C. Roberts, "A specialized computer architecture for text retrieval," in *Proc. 4th Workshop Comput. Architecture Non-Numeric Processing*, Syracuse, NY, Aug. 1978, pp. 51-59.

[25] R. Sacks-Davis and K. Ramamohanarao, "A two level superimposed coding scheme for partial match retrieval," *Inform. Syst.*, vol. 8, no. 4, pp. 273-280, 1983.

[26] A. J. Smith, "On the effectiveness of buffered and multiple arm disks," in *Proc. 5th Annual Symp. Comput. Architecture*, Palo Alto, CA, Apr. 1978, pp. 242-248.

[27] W. H. Stellhorn, "An inverted file processor for information retrieval," *IEEE Trans. Comput.*, vol. C-26, pp. 1258-1267, Dec. 1977.

[28] D. M. Taub, "Arbitration and control acquisition in the proposed IEEE 896 Futurebus," *IEEE Micro*, vol. 4, no. 4, pp. 28-41, Aug. 1984.

[29] J. C. Wu and F. B. Humphrey, "Computer simulation of magnetic bubble logic devices," *J. Appl. Phys.*, vol. 55, no. 6, pp. 2581-2583, Mar. 1984.

Dik Lun Lee received the B.S. degree in electronics with first honours from the Chinese University of Hong Kong in 1979, and the M.S. and Ph.D. degrees in computer science from the University of Toronto, Toronto, Ont., Canada, in 1982 and 1985, respectively.

He is an Assistant Professor in the Department of Computer and Information Science at The Ohio State University, Columbus. His research interests include special purpose computer architecture, database and text-retrieval machines, knowledge base machines, expert database systems, and document retrieval.

Dr. Lee is a member of the IEEE Computer Society and the Association for Computing Machinery.

Frederick H. Lochovsky received the B.A.Sc., M.Sc., and Ph.D. degrees all from the University of Toronto, Toronto, Ont., Canada.

He is a Professor in the Department of Computer Science and the Faculty of Management at the University of Toronto. He is also a member of the Computer Systems Research Institute. His current research interests are in database design, human-computer interaction, and office information systems.

References

General

[Aho et al., 74]
> Aho, A.V., Hopcroft, J.E., and Ullman, J. D., *The Design and Analysis of Computer Algorithms*, Addison-Wesley, Reading, Mass. (1974).

[Aho, 80]
> Aho, A.V., Pattern matching in strings, in Book, R., ed., *Formal Language Theory, Perspectives and Open Problems*, Academic Press, New York, pp. 325–347 (1980).

[Aho, 90]
> Aho, A.V., Algorithms for finding patterns in strings, in Leeuwen, J., ed., *Handbook of Theoretical Computer Science*, Elsevier, New York, pp. 257–300, (1990).

[Apostolico et al., 85]
> Apostolico, A., and Galil, Z., *Combinatorial Algorithms on Words*, Springer, Berlin (1985).

[Frakes et al., 92]
> Frakes, W. and Baeza-Yates, R., *Information Retrieval: Data Structures and Algorithms*, Prentice Hall, Englewood Cliffs, N. J. (1992).

[Gonnet et al., 85]
> Gonnet, G.H., and Baeza-Yates, R., *Handbook of Algorithms and Data Structures*, Addison-Wesley, Reading, Mass., pp. 251–288 (1985).

[Knuth, 73]
> Knuth, D.E., *The Art of Computer Programming, Vol. 3: Sorting and Searching*, Addison-Wesley, Reading, Mass. (1973).

[Mehlhorn, 84]
> Mehlhorn, K., *Data Structures and Algorithms 1: Sorting and Searching*, Springer, Berlin (1984).

[Sankoff et al., 83]
> Sankoff, D., and Kruskal, J.B., *Time Warps, String Edits, and Macro-Molecules: The Theory and Practice of Sequence Comparison*, Addison-Wesley, Reading, Mass. (1983).

[Sedgewick, 86]
> Sedgewick, R., *Algorithms*, 2d ed., Addison-Wesley, Reading, Mass., pp. 277–346 (1986).

[Standish, 80]
> Standish, T.A., *Data Structure Techniques*, Addison-Wesley, Reading, Mass., pp. 287–346 (1980).

Chapter 1: Single keyword matching

[Aho, 90]
> Aho, A.V., Algorithms for finding patterns in strings, in Leeuwen, J., ed., *Handbook of Theoretical Computer Science*, Elsevier, New York, pp. 257–300, (1990).

[Apostolico et al., 84]
> Apostolico, A., and Giancarlo, R., Pattern matching machine implementation of a fast test for unique decipherability, *Inf. Proc. Lett.*, 18, pp. 155–158 (1984).

[Apostolico et al., 85]
> Apostolico, A., and Galil, Z., eds., *Combinatorial Algorithms on Words*, Springer, Berlin (1985).

[Apostolico et al., 86]
> Apostolico, A., and Giancarlo, R., The Boyer-Moore-Galil string searching strategies revisited, *SIAM J. Comput.*, 15, 1, pp. 98–105 (1986).

[Arikawa, 81]
> Arikawa, S., One-way sequential search systems and their powers, *Bull. Math. Stat.*, 19, 3–4, pp. 69–85 (1981).

[Baeza-Yates, 89a]
> Baeza-Yates, R., Algorithms for string searching: Survey, *ACM SIGIR*, 23, 3–4, pp. 34–57 (1989).

[Baeza-Yates, 89b]

Baeza-Yates, R.A., Improved string searching, *Softw. Pract. & Exper.*, 19, 3, pp. 257–271 (1989).

[Baeza-Yates, 92]

Baeza-Yates, R. A., String searching algorithms, in Frakes, W., and Baeza-Yates, R.A., eds., *Information Retrieval: Algorithms and Data Structures*, Prentice Hall, Englewood Cliffs, N.J., pp. 219–240 (1992).

[Bailey et al., 80]

Bailey, T.A., and Dromey, R.G., Fast string searching by finding subkeys in subtext, *Inf. Proc. Lett.*, 11, pp. 130–133 (1980).

[Barkman et al., 89]

Barkman, O., Breslauer, D., Galil, Z., Schieber, B., and Vishkin, B., Highly parallelizable problems, *20th ACM Symp. Theory of Computing*, pp. 309–319 (1989).

[Barth, 81]

Barth, G., An alternative for the implementation of Knuth-Morris-Pratt algorithm, *Inf. Proc. Lett.*, 13, pp. 134–137 (1981).

[Barth, 84]

Barth, G., An analytical comparison of two string searching algorithms, *Inf. Proc. Lett.*, 18, pp. 249–256 (1984).

[Barth, 85]

Barth, G., Relating the average-case costs of the brute-force and the Knuth-Morris-Pratt string matching algorithm, in Apostolico, A. and Galil, Z., eds., *Combinatorial Algorithms on Words*, Springer, Berlin (1985).

[Bean et al., 85]

Bean, D.R., Ehrenfeucht, A., and McNulty, G.F., Avoidable patterns in strings of symbols, *Pacific J. Math.*, pp. 31–56 (1985).

[Boyer et al., 77]

Boyer, R.S., and Moore, J.S., A fast string searching algorithm, *C. ACM*, 20, 10, pp. 762–772 (1977).

[Breslauer et al., 90]

Breslauer, D., and Galil, Z., An optimal o(log log n) time parallel string matching algorithm, *SIAM J. Comput.*, 19, 6, pp. 1051–1058 (1990).

[Breslauer et al., 92]

Breslauer, D., and Galil, Z., A lower bound for parallel string matching, *SIAM J. Comput.*, 21, 5, pp. 856–862 (1992).

[Chrobak et al., 87]

Chrobak, M., and Rytter, W., Remarks on string-matching and one-way multihead automata, *Inf. Proc. Lett.*, 24, pp. 325–329 (1987).

[Collussi et al., 90]

Collussi, L., Galil, Z., and Giancarlo, R., On the exact complexity of string matching, *31st Symp. Foundations of Comput. Sci.*, pp. 135–144 (1990).

[Cook, 71]

Cook, S.A., Linear time simulation of deterministic two-way pushdown automata, *IFIP Congress*, 71, TA-2, pp. 172–179 (1971).

[Cormen et al, 90]

Cormen, T. H., Leiserson, C. E., and Rivest, R., *Introduction to Algorithms*, The MIT Press, Cambridge, Mass., pp. 853–876 (1990).

[Crochemore et al., 91]

Crochemore, M., and Perrin, D., Two-way string-matching, *J. ACM*, 38, 3, pp. 651–675 (1991).

[Davies et al., 86]

Davies, G., and Bowsher, S., Algorithms for pattern matching, *Softw. Pract. & Exper.*, 16, 6, pp. 575–601 (1986).

[Duval, 83]

Duval, J.P., Factoring words over an ordered alphabet, *J. Algorithms*, 4, pp. 363–381 (1983).

[Galil et al., 83]
   Galil, Z., and Seiferas, J., Time-space-optimal string matching, *J. Comput. Syst. Sci.*, 26, pp. 280–294 (1983).
[Galil, 79]
   Galil, Z., On improving the worst case running time of the Boyer-Moore string matching algorithm, *C. ACM*, 22, 9, pp. 505–508 (1979).
[Galil, 85]
   Galil, Z., Optimal parallel algorithms for string matching, *Inf. and Contr.*, 67, pp. 144–157 (1985).
[Galil et al., 91]
   Galil, Z., and Giancarlo, R., On the exact complexity of string matching: Lower bounds, *SIAM J. Comput.*, 20, 6, pp. 1008–1020 (1991).
[Galil et al., 92]
   Galil, Z., and Giancarlo, R., On the exact complexity of string matching: Upper bounds, *SIAM J. Comput.*, 21, 3, pp. 407–437 (1992).
[Gonnet et al., 90]
   Gonnet, G.H., and Baeza-Yates, R.A., An analysis of the Karp-Rabin string matching algorithm, *Inf. Proc. Lett.*, 34, 5, pp. 271–274 (1990).
[Guibas et al., 80]
   Guibas, L.J., and Odlyzko, A.M., A new proof of the linearity of the Boyer-Moore string searching algorithm, *SIAM J. Comput.*, 9, 4, pp. 672–682 (1980).
[Guibas et al., 81a]
   Guibas, L.J., and Odlyzko, A.M., Periods in strings, *J. Combin. Theory Ser. A*, pp. 19–42 (1981).
[Guibas et al., 81b]
   Guibas, L.J., and Odlyzko, A.M., String overlaps, pattern matching, and nontransitive games, *J. Combin. Theory Ser. A*, 30, 2, pp. 183–208 (1981).
[Horspool, 80]
   Horspool, R.N., Practical fast searching in strings, *Softw. Pract. & Exper.*, 10, 6, pp. 501–506 (1980).
[Iyenger et al., 80]
   Iyenger, S., and Alia, V., A string search algorithm, *Appl. Math. Comput.*, 6, pp. 123–131 (1980).
[Karp et al., 87]
   Karp, R.M., and Rabin, M.O., Efficient randomized pattern-matching algorithms, *IBM J. Res. Develop.*, 31, 2, pp. 249–260 (1987).
[Kedam et al., 89]
   Kedam, Z., Landau, G., and Palem, K., Optimal parallel suffix-prefix matching algorithm and applications, *SPAA'89* (1989).
[Knuth et al., 77]
   Knuth, D.E., Morris, J.H., and Pratt, V.R., Fast pattern matching in strings, *SIAM J. Comput.*, 6, 2, pp. 323–350 (1977).
[Li, 84]
   Li, M., Lower bonds on string-matching, Technical Report TR-84-636, Dept. of Comput. Sci., Cornell Univ. (1984).
[Li et al., 86]
   Li, M., and Yesha, Y., String-matching cannot be done by a two-head one-way deterministic finite automata, *Inf. Proc. Lett.*, 22, pp. 231–236 (1986).
[Liu, 81]
   Liu, K.-C., On string pattern matching: A new model with a polynomial time algorithm, *SIAM J. Comput.*, 10, 1, pp. 118–140 (1981).
[Lyndon et al., 62]
   Lyndon, R. C., and Schutzenberger, M.P., The equation $a^M=b^N c^P$ in a free group, *Michigan Math. J.*, 9, pp. 289–298 (1962).
[Miller et al., 88]
   Miller, W., and Myers, E.W., Sequence comparison with concave weighting functions, *Bull. Math. Biol.*, 50, 2, pp. 97–120 (1988).

[Moller et al., 84]
   Moller-Nielsen, P., and Staunstrup, J., Experiments with a fast string searching algorithm, *Inf. Proc. Lett.*, 18, pp. 129–135 (1984).
[Naor, 91]
   Naor, M., String matching with preprocessing of text and pattern, *18th Inter. Conf. Automata, Lang., and Prog.*, pp. 739–750 (1991).
[Pirkldauer, 92]
   Pirkldauer, K., A study of pattern matching algorithms, *Structured Programming*, 13, 2, pp. 89–98 (1992).
[Raita, 92]
   Raita, T., Tuning the Boyer-Moore-Horspool string searching algorithm, *Softw. Pract. & Exper.*, 22, 10, pp. 879–884 (1992).
[Rivest, 77]
   Rivest, R.L., On the worst-case behavior of string-searching algorithms, *SIAM J. Comput.*, 6, 4, pp. 669–674 (1977).
[Rytter, 80]
   Rytter, W., A correct preprocessing algorithm for Boyer-Moore string, *SIAM J. Comput.*, 9, 3, pp. 509–512 (1980).
[Schaback, 88]
   Schaback, R., On the expected sublinearity of the Boyer-Moore algorithm, *SIAM J. Comput.*, 17, 4, pp. 648–658 (1988).
[Semba, 85]
   Semba, I., An efficient string searching algorithm, *Inf. Process.*, 8, 2, pp. 101–109 (1985).
[Slisenko, 80]
   Slisenko, A., Determination in real time of all the periodicities in a word, *Sov. Math. Dokl.*, 21, pp. 392–395 (1980).
[Smit, 82]
   Smit, G. de V., A comparison of three string matching algorithms, *Softw. Pract. & Exper.*, 12, pp. 57–66 (1982).
[Smith, 91]
   Smith, P.D., Experiments with a very fast substring search algorithm, *Softw. Pract. & Exper.*, 21, 10 (1991).
[Sunday, 90]
   Sunday, D.M., A very fast substring search algorithm, *C. ACM*, 33, 8, pp. 132–142 (1990).
[Takaoka, 86]
   Takaoka, T., An on-line pattern matching algorithm, *Inf. Proc. Lett.*, 22, pp. 329–330 (1986).
[Viskin, 85]
   Viskin, U., Optimal parallel pattern matching in strings, *Inf. and Contr.*, 67, pp. 91–113 (1985).
[Waterman, 84]
   Waterman, M.S., General methods for sequence comparison, *Bull. Math. Biol.*, 46, 4, pp. 473–500 (1984).
[Yao, 79]
   Yao, A.C., The complexity of pattern matching for a random string, *SIAM J. Comput.*, 8, pp. 368–387 (1979).
[Zhu et al., 87]
   Zhu, R.F., and Takaoka, T., On improving the average case of the Boyer-Moore string matching algorithm, *J. Inf. Process.*, 10, 3, pp. 173–177 (1987).

Chapter 2: Matching sets of keywords

[Aho et al., 74]
   Aho, A.V., Hopcroft, J.E., and Ullman, J. D., *The Design and Analysis of Computer Algorithms*, Addison-Wesley, Reading, Mass. (1974).

[Aho et al., 75]
Aho, A.V., and Corasick, M.J., Efficient string matching: An aid to bibliographic search, C. *ACM*, 18, 6, pp. 333–340 (1975).

[Aho et al., 86a]
Aho, A.V., and Lee, D., Storing a dynamic sparse table, *27th IEEE Symp. Foundations of Comput. Sci.*, pp. 56–60 (1986).

[Aho et al., 86b]
Aho, A.V., Sethi, R., and Ullman, J.D., *Compilers: Principles, Techniques, and Tools*, Addison-Wesley, Reading, Mass. (1986).

[Aho et al., 88]
Aho, A.V., Kernighan, B.W., and Weinberger, P.J., *The AWK Programming Language*, Addison-Wesley, Reading, Mass. (1988).

[Aho et al., 89]
Aho, A.V., Ganapathi, M., and Tjiang, S.W.K., Code generation using tree matching and dynamic programming, *ACM Trans. Prog. Lang. and Syst.*, 11, 4, pp. 491–516 (1989).

[Aho, 90]
Aho, A.V., Algorithms for finding patterns in strings, in Leeuwen, J., ed., *Handbook of Theoretical Computer Science*, Elsevier, New York, pp. 257–300 (1990).

[Aoe et al., 84a]
Aoe, J., Yamamoto, Y., and Shimada, R., A method for improving string pattern matching machines, *IEEE Trans. Softw. Engr.*, SE-10, 1, pp. 116–120 (1984).

[Aoe et al., 84b]
Aoe, J., Yamamoto, Y., and Shimada, R., A practical method for reducing sparse matrices with invariant entries, *Int. J. Comput. Math.*, 12, 2, pp. 97–111 (1984).

[Aoe et al., 85]
Aoe, J., Yamamoto, Y., and Shimada, R., An efficient implementation of static string pattern matching machines, *IEEE Int. Conf. Supercomput. Syst.*, 1, pp. 491–498 (1985).

[Aoe, 89a]
Aoe, J., An efficient implementation of static string pattern matching machines, *IEEE Trans. Softw. Engr.*, SE-15, 8, pp. 1010–1016 (1989).

[Aoe, 89b]
Aoe, J., An efficient digital search algorithm by using a double-array structure, *IEEE Trans. Softw. Engr.*, SE-15, 9, pp. 1066–1077 (1989).

[Aoe, 91a]
Aoe, J., A practical method for implementing string pattern matching machines, *Inf. Sci.*, 64, 2, pp. 95–114 (1991).

[Aoe, 91b]
Aoe, J., A practical method for compressing sparse matrices with variant entries, *Int. J. Comput. Math.*, 36, 1, pp. 163–173 (1991).

[Aoe et al., 92]
Aoe, J., Morimoto, K., and Sato, T., An efficient implementation of tree structures, *Softw. Pract. & Exper.*, 22, 9, pp. 695–721 (1992).

[Arikawa et al., 84a]
Arikawa, S., and Shinohara, S., A run-time efficient realization of Aho-Corasick pattern matching machines, *New Generation Comput.*, 2, 2, pp. 171–186 (1984).

[Arikawa et al., 84b]
Arikawa, S., and Shiraishi, S., Pattern matching machines for replacing several character strings, *Bull. Inf. Cybern.*, 21, 1–2, pp. 101–111 (1984).

[Arikawa et al., 88]
Arikawa, S., Shinohara, T., Shiraishi, S., and Tamakoshi, Y., SIGMA—An information system for researchers' use, *Bull. Inf. Cybern.*, 20, 1–2, pp. 97–114 (1982); RIFIS-TR-CS-4, Kyusyu Univ. (1988).

[Apostolico et al., 83]
Apostolico, A., and Preparata, F.P., Optimal off-line detection of repetitions in a string, *Theoret. Comput. Sci.*, 22, pp. 297–315 (1983).

[Apostolico et al., 85]

Apostolico, A., The myriad virtues of subword trees, in Apostolico, A., and Galil, Z., eds., *Combinatorial Algorithms on Words*, Springer, Berlin (1985).

[Ben-Yehuda et al., 89]

Ben-Yehuda, S., and Pinter, R.Y., Symbolic layout improvement using string matching based local transformations, *Decennial Caltech Conf. VLSI*, MIT Press, Cambridge, Mass., pp. 227–239 (1989).

[Berry et al., 86]

Berry, G., and Sethi, R., From regular expressions to deterministic automata, *Theoret. Comput. Sci.*, 48, 1, pp. 117–126 (1986).

[Bloch, 89]

Bloch, M., Experimental Evaluation and Optimization of Aho-Corasic Pattern Matching Machine, PhD thesis, Czech Technical Univ. (1989).

[Blumer, et al., 84a]

Blumer, A., Blumer, J., Ehrenfeucht, A., Haussler, D., and McConnell, R., Building a complete inverted file for a set of text files in linear time, *16th ACM Symp. Theory of Computing*, pp. 349–358 (1984).

[Blumer et al., 84b]

Blumer, A., Blumer, J., Ehrenfeucht, A., Haussler, D., and McConnell, R., Building the minimal DFA for the set of all subwords of a word on-line in linear time, in Paredaens, J., ed., *11th Int. Coll. Automata, Lang. and Prog.: Lecture Notes in Comput. Sci.*, Vol. 172, Springer, Berlin, pp. 109–118 (1984).

[Blumer et al., 85]

Blumer, A., Blumer, J., Ehrenfeucht, A., Haussler, D., Chen, M.T., and Seiferas, J., The smallest automaton recognizing the subwords of a text, *Theoret. Comput. Sci.*, 40, 1, pp. 31–56 (1985).

[Blumer et al., 87]

Blumer, A., Blumer, J., Haussler, D., McConnell, R., and Ehrenfeucht, A., Complete inverted files for efficient text retrieval and analyses, *J. ACM*, 34, 3, pp. 578–595 (1987).

[Chen et al., 85]

Chen, M. T., and Seiferas, J.I., Efficient and elegant subword tree construction, in Apostolico, A., and Galil, Z., eds., *Combinatorial Algorithms on Words*, Springer, Berlin (1985).

[Cherry, 82]

Cherry, L.L., Writing tools, *IEEE Trans. Comm.*, C-30, 1, pp. 100–105 (1982).

[Commentz-Walter, 79]

Commentz-Walter, B., A string matching algorithm fast on the average, in Maurer, H.A., ed., *Proc. 6th Int. Coll. Automata, Lang., and Prog.*, Springer, Berlin, pp. 118–132 (1979).

[Crochemore, 81]

Crochemore, M., An optimal algorithm for computing the repetitions in a word, *Inf. Proc. Lett.*, 12, 5, pp. 244–250 (1981).

[Crochemore et al., 90]

Crochemore, M., and Rytter, W., Parallel computations on string and arrays, *7th Symp. Theoretical Aspects of Comput. Sci.*, pp. 109–125 (1990).

[Crochemore, 86]

Crochemore, M., Transducers and repetitions, *Theoret. Comput. Sci.* 45, pp. 63–86 (1986).

[Dietzfelbinger et al., 88]

Dietzfelbinger, M., Karlin, A., Mehlhorn, K., Meyer, F., Heide, Rohnert, H., and Tarjan, R.E., Dynamic perfect hashing: upper and lower bounds, *29th Ann. IEEE Symp. Foundations of Comput. Sci.*, pp. 524–531 (1988).

[Fan et al., 93]

Fan, J.-J., and Su, K.-Y., An efficient algorithm for matching multiple patterns, *IEEE Trans. Knowledge and Data Eng.*, KDE-5, 2, pp. 339–351 (1993).

[Farber et al., 64]

Farber, D.J., Griswold, R.E., and Polonsky, I.P., SNOBOL, a string manipulation language, *J. ACM*, 11, 1, pp. 21–30 (1964).

[Fredman et al., 84]

Fredman, M., Komlos L.J., and Szemeredi, E., Strong: A sparse table with O(1) worst case access time, *J. ACM*, 31, 3, pp. 538–544 (1984).

[Galil, 76]
   Galil, Z., Two fast simulations which imply some fast string matching and palindrome recognition algorithms, *Inf. Proc. Lett.*, 4, pp. 85–87 (1976).

[Galil et al., 78]
   Galil, Z., and Seiferas, J.I., A linear-time on-line recognition algorithm for "Palstar," *J. ACM*, 25, pp. 102–111 (1978).

[Galil et al., 80]
   Galil, Z., and Seiferas, J.I., Saving space in fast string matching, *SIAM J. Comput.*, 9, 2, pp. 417–438 (1980).

[Galil, 81]
   Galil, Z., String matching in real time, *J. ACM*, 28, 1, pp. 134–149 (1981).

[Galil et al., 83]
   Galil, Z., and Seiferas, J., Time-space-optimal string matching, *J. Comput. Syst. Sci.*, 26, pp. 280–294 (1983).

[Garey et al., 79]
   Garey, M.R., and Johnson, D.S., *Computers and Intractability: A Guide to the Theory of NP-Completeness*, Freeman, San Francisco (1979).

[Gonnet, 83]
   Gonnet, G.H., Unstructured data bases for very efficient text searching, *2nd ACM SIGACT-SIGMOD Symp. Database Syst.*, pp. 117–124 (1983).

[Hartmanis, 80]
   Hartmanis, J., On the succinctness of different representations of languages, *SIAM J. Comput.*, 9, 1, pp. 114–120 (1980).

[Hoffmann et al., 82]
   Hoffmann, C.W., and O'Donnell, M.J., Pattern matching in trees, *J. ACM*, 29, 1, pp. 68–95 (1982).

[Huet et al., 80]
   Huet, G., and Oppen, D.C., Equations and rewrite rules, in Book, R., ed., *Formal Language Theory, Perspectives and Open Problems*, Academic Press, New York, pp. 349–393 (1980).

[Hume, 88]
   Hume, A.G., A tale of two greps, *Softw. Pract. & Exper.*, 18, 11, pp. 1063–1072 (1988).

[Julian et al., 82]
   Julian, D., and Davies, M., String searching in text editors, *Sofw. Pract. & Exper.*, 12, 8, pp. 709–717 (1982).

[Kanbayashi et al., 79]
   Kanbayashi,Y., Nakatsu, N., and Yajima, S., Hierarchical pattern matching algorithm for strings, *Trans. Inst. Electron. & Comm. Eng.*, E-62, 5, p. 359 (1979).

[Karp et al., 72]
   Karp, R.M., Miller, R.E., and Rosenberg, A.L., Rapid identification of repeated patterns in strings, trees, and arrays, *4th ACM Symp. Theory of Computing*, pp. 125–136 (1972).

[Kemp et al., 87]
   Kemp, M., Bayer, R., and Guntzer, U., Time optimal left to right construction of position trees, *Acta Inf.*, 24, pp. 461–474 (1987).

[Knuth, 73]
   Knuth, D.E., *The Art of Computer Programming, Vol 3: Sorting and Searching*, Addison-Wesley, Reading, Mass. (1973).

[Lee et al., 90]
   Lee, Y.-C., and Jea, K.-F.J., Feature extraction based design retrieval, *1st Inter. Conf. Syst. Integration*, pp. 23–26 (1990).

[Lesk, 75]
   Lesk, M.E., LEX—A lexical analyzer generator, *Comput. Sci.*, TR39, AT&T Bell Laboratories, Murray Hill, N.J. (1975).

[Main et al., 84]
   Main, M.G., and Lorentz, R. J., An $O(n \log n)$ algorithm for finding all repetitions in a string, *J. Algorithms*, 5, 3, pp. 422–432 (1984).

[Main et al., 85]
Main, M.G., and Lorentz, R. J., Linear time recognition of square-free strings, in Apostolico, A., and Galil, Z., eds., *Combinatorial Algorithms on Words*, Springer, Berlin (1985).

[Majester et al., 80]
Majester, M. E., and Reisner, A., Efficient on-line construction and correction of position trees, *SIAM J. Comput.*, 9, 4, pp. 785–807 (1980).

[Manacher, 75]
Manacher, G., A new linear-time on-line algorithm for finding the smallest initial palindrome of a string, *J. ACM*, 22, pp. 346–351 (1975).

[McCreight, 76]
McCreight, E.M., A space-economical suffix tree construction algorithm, *J. ACM*, 23, 2, pp. 262–272 (1976).

[McIlroy, 86]
McIlroy, M.D., ed., *UNIX Time-Sharing System Programmer's Manual*, Vol.1, 9th ed. AT&T Bell Laboratories, Murray Hill, N.J. (1986).

[Meyer et al., 71]
Meyer, A.R., and Fischer, M.J., Economy of description by automata, grammars, and formal systems, *IEEE Symp. Switching and Automata Theory*, pp. 188–190 (1971).

[Meyer, 85]
Meyer, B., Incremental string matching, *Inf. Proc. Lett.*, 21, pp. 219–227 (1985).

[Morrison, 68]
Morrison, D.R., PATRICIA—Practical algorithm to retrieve information coded in alphanumeric, *J. ACM*, 15, 4, pp. 514–534 (1968).

[Pennello, 86]
Pennello, T.J., Very fast LR parsing, *SIGPLAN Notices*, 21, 7, pp. 145–150 (1986).

[Perrin, 90]
Perrin, D., Finite automata, in Leeuwen, J. van, ed., *Handbook of Theoretical Computer Science*, Vol. B, *North-Holland*, Amsterdam, pp. 1–57 (1990).

[Rabin, 85]
Rabin, M.-O., Discovering repetitions in strings, in Apostolico, A., and Galil, Z., eds., *Combinatorial Algorithms on Words*, Springer, Berlin (1985).

[Rodeh et al., 81]
Rodeh, M., Pratt, V.R., and Even, S., Linear algorithms for data compression via string matching, *J. ACM*, 28, 1, pp. 16–24 (1981).

[Scolnicov, 92]
Scolnicov, A., Structured pattern matching, *Forth Dimensions*, 14, 2, pp. 21–25 (1992).

[Seiferas et al., 77]
Seiferas, J., and Galil, Z., Real-time recognition of substring repetition and reversal, *Math. Syst. Theory*, 11, pp. 111–146 (1977).

[Shinohara et al., 86]
Shinohara, T., and Arikawa, S., Pattern matching machines for Japanese texts, RIFIS-TR-CS-10, Kyusyu Univ. (1986).

[Slisenko, 83]
Slisenko, A.O., Detection of periodicities and string-matching in real time, *J. Soviet Math.*, 22, 3, pp. 1316–1386 (1983).

[Smith, 91]
Smith, P.D., Experiments with a very fast substring search algorithm, *Softw. Pract. & Exper.*, 21, 10 (1991).

[Sridhar, 90]
Sridhar, M.A., Augmenting the Aho-Corasick pattern matching machine, *Int. J. Comput. Math.*, 32, 3–4, pp. 149–153 (1990).

[Takeda, 89]
Takeda, M., An efficient multiple string replacing algorithm using patterns with pictures, *Advances in Softw. Sci. and Tech.*, 2, pp. 131–151 (1989); RIFIS-TR-CS-11, Kyusyu Univ. (1989).

[Tarjan et al., 79]
    Tarjan, R.E., and Yao, A.C., Storing a sparse table, *C. ACM*, 22, 11, pp. 606–611 (1979).

[Thompson, 68]
    Thompson, K., Regular expression search algorithm, *C. ACM*, 11, 6, pp. 419–422 (1968).

[Tsuda et al., 92a]
    Tsuda, K., and Aoe, J., A method of text-reducing for text proofreading systems, *First Inter. Conf. Intelligent Systems*, pp. 537–542 (1992).

[Tsuda et al., 92b]
    Tsuda, K., and Aoe, J., An efficient string pattern matching algorithm: The application of reducing texts, *IEEE 7th Inter. Symp. Comput. and Inf. Sci.*, pp. 471–474 (1992).

[Tsuda, et al., 94]
    Tsuda, K., Iriguchi, H., and Aoe, J., A method for constructing dynamic string pattern matching machines, (in Japanese), J77–D,4, to be published in *Trans. IEIEC of Japan* (1994).

[Weiner, 73]
    Weiner, P., Linear pattern matching algorithms, *14th IEEE Symp. Switching and Automata Theory*, pp. 1–11 (1973).

[Zhu et al., 89]
    Zhu, R.F., and Takaoka, T., A technique for two-dimensional pattern matching, *C. ACM*, 32, 9, pp. 1110–1120 (1989).

Chapter 3: Approximate string matching

[Abrahamson, 87]
    Abrahamson, K., Generalized string matching, *SIAM J. Comput.*, 16, 6, pp. 1039–1051 (1987).

[Aho et al., 76]
    Aho, A.V., Hirschberg, D.S., and Ullman, J.D., Bounds on the complexity of the maximal common subsequence problem, *J. ACM*, 23, 1, pp. 1–12 (1976).

[Aho, 90]
    Aho, A.V., Algorithms for finding patterns in strings, in Leeuwen, J., ed., *Handbook of Theoretical Computer Science*, Elsevier, New York, pp. 257–300 (1990).

[Allison et al., 86]
    Allison, L., and Dix, T.I., A bit-string longest-common-subsequence algorithm, *Inf. Proc. Lett.*, 23, pp. 305–310 (1986).

[Angell et al., 83]
    Angell, R.C., Freund, D.E., and Willett, P., Automatic spelling correction using a trigram similarity measure, *Inf. Proc. Manage.*, 19, pp. 255–261(1983).

[Apostolico, 86]
    Apostolico, A., Improving the worst-case performance of the Hunt-Szymanski strategy for the longest common subsequence of two strings, *Inf. Proc. Lett.*, 23, pp. 63–69 (1986).

[Apostolico, 87]
    Apostolico, A., Remark on the Hsu-Du new algorithm for the longest common subsequence problem, *Inf. Proc. Lett.*, 25, pp. 235–236 (1987).

[Apostolico et al., 87]
    Apostolico, A., and Guerra, G., The longest common subsequence problem revisited, *Algorithmica*, 2, pp. 315–336 (1987).

[Baeza-Yates et al., 92]
    Baeza-Yates, R., and Gonnet, G.H., A new approach to text searching, *C. ACM*, 35, 10, pp. 74–82 (1992).

[Baeza-Yates et al., 89]
    Baeza-Yates, R., and Gonnet, G.H., A new approach to text searching, *12th SIGIR*, Cambridge, Mass. (1989).

[Berghel et al., 90]

Berghel, H., and Roach, D., Approximate string matching and the automation of word games, *Symp. Applied Computing*, pp. 209–213 (1990).

[Bickel, 87]

Bickel, M.A., Automatic correction to misspelled names: A fourth-generation language approach, *C. ACM*, 30, 3, pp. 224–228(1987).

[Bocast, 91]

Bocast, A.K., Method and apparatus for reconstructing a token from a token fragment, U.S. Patent Number 5,008,818, Design Services Group, Inc., McLean, Va. (1991).

[Boivie, 81]

Boivie, R.H., Directory assistance revisited, *AT&T Bell Labs Tech. Mem.* June 12, 1981.

[Bradford, 90]

Bradford, J.H., Sequence matching with binary codes, *Inf. Proc. Lett.*, 34, 4, pp. 193–196 (1990).

[Bunke et al., 92]

Bunke, H., and Csirik, L., Inference of edit costs using parametric string matching, *11th IAPR Conf. Pattern Recognition*, pp. 545–552 (1992).

[Chang et al., 90]

Chang, W.I., and Lawler, E.L., Approximate string matching in sublinear expected time, *31st Symp. Foundations of Comput. Sci.*, pp. 116–124 (1990).

[Chang et al., 92]

Chang, W.I., and Lampe, J., Theoretical and empirical comparisons of approximate string matching algorithms, *Third Symp. Combinatorial Pattern Matching*, Springer-Verlag, New York, pp. 175–184 (1992).

[Cherkassky et al., 90]

Cherkassky, V., Rao, M., and Wechsler, H., Fault-tolerant database retrieval using distributed associative memories, *Inf. Sci.*, 46, pp. 135–168 (1990).

[Cherkassky et al., 91]

Cherkassky, V., Fassett, K., and Vassilas, N., Linear algebra approach to neural associative memories and noise performance of neural classifiers, *IEEE Trans. Comput.*, C-40, 12, pp. 1429–1435 (1991).

[Cherkassky et al., 92]

Cherkassky, V., Vassilas, N., Brodt, G. L., and Wechsler, H., Conventional and associative memory approaches to automatic spelling checking, *Eng. Appl. Artif. Intell.*, 5, 3 (1992).

[Church et al., 91a]

Church, K.W., and Gale, W.A., Probabilistic scoring for spelling correction, *Stat. Comput.* (1991).

[Church, et al., 91b]

Church, K.W., and Gale, W.A., Enhanced Good-Turning and cat-cal: Two new methods for estimating probabilities of English bigrams, *Comput. Speech Lang.*, (1991).

[Chvatal et al., 75]

Chvatal, V., and Sankoff, D., Longest common subsequence of two random sequences, *J. Appl. Probab.*, 12, pp. 306–315 (1975).

[Dahl et al., 90]

Dahl, P., and Cherkassky, V., Combined encoding in associative spelling checkers, tech. report, Univ. of Minnesota (1990).

[Damerau, 64]

Damerau, F.J., A technique for computer detection and correction of spelling errors, *C. ACM*, 7, 3, p p. 171–176 (1964).

[Deerwester et al., 90]

Deerwester, S., Dumais, S.T., Furnas, G.W., Landauer, T.K., and Harshman, R., Indexing by latent semantic analysis, *JASIS*, 41, 6, pp. 391–407 (1990).

[Deheer, 82]

Deheer, T., The application of the concept of homeosemy to natural language information retrieval, *Inf. Proc. Manage.*, 18, pp. 229–236 (1982).

[Deloche et al., 90]
Deloche, G., and Debili, F., Order information redundancy of verbal codes in French and English: Neurolinguistic Implication, *J. Verbal Learn. Verbal Behav.*, 19, pp. 525–530 (1980).

[Dunlavey, 81]
Dunlavey, M.R., On spelling correction and beyond, *C. ACM*, 24, 9, (1981).

[Durham et al., 83]
Durham, I., Lamb, D.A., and Saxe, J.B., Spelling correction in user interfaces, *C. ACM.*, 26, 10, pp. 764–773 (1983).

[Fischer et al., 74]
Fischer, M.J., and Paterson, M.S., String matching and other products, in Karp, R.M., ed., *Complexity of Computation*, SIAM-AMS, Vol. 7, Amer. Mathematical Soc., Providence, R.I., pp. 113–125 (1974).

[Fredman, 75]
Fredman, M.L., On computing the length of longest increasing subsequences, *Discrete Math.*, 11, 1, pp. 29–35 (1975).

[Galil et al., 86]
Galil, Z., and Giancarlo, R., Improved string matching with k mismatches, *SIGACT News*, 7, pp. 52–54 (1986).

[Galil et al., 88]
Galil, Z., and Giancarlo, R., Data structures and algorithms for approximate string matching, *J. Complexity*, 4, 1, pp. 33–72 (1988).

[Gonzalez et al., 91]
Gonzalez, A.J., Myler, H.R., and Kladke, R.R., Identification of unconstrained item descriptions using string match heuristics, *Int. J. Expert Syst. Research and Applications*, 4, 3, pp. 337–364 (1991).

[Gorin, 71]
Gorin, R.E., SPELL: A spelling checking and correction program, online documentation for the DEC-10 computer (1971).

[Grossi, 91]
Grossi, R., A fast VLSI solution for approximate string matching, *VLSI J.*, 13, 2, pp. 195–206 (1991).

[Hall et al., 80]
Hall, P.A.V., and Dowling, G. R., Approximate string matching, *ACM Comput. Surveys*, 12, 4, pp. 381–402 (1980).

[Hawley, 82]
Hawley, M.J., Interactive spelling correction in Unix: The METRIC Library, *At&T Bell Lab. Tech. Mem.*, 31 (1982).

[Hirschberg, 75]
Hirschberg, D.S., A linear space algorithm for computing maximal common subsequences, *C. ACM*, 18, 6, pp. 341–343 (1975).

[Hirschberg, 77]
Hirschberg, D.S., Algorithms for the longest common subsequence problem, *J.ACM*, 24, 4, pp. 664–675 (1977).

[Hirschberg, 78]
Hirschberg, D.S., An information theoretic lower bound for the longest common subsequence problem, *Inf. Proc. Lett.*, 7, pp. 40–41 (1978).

[Hunt et al., 76]
Hunt, J.W., and McIlroy, M.D., An algorithm for differential file comparison, *Comput. Sci.*, TR41, AT&T Bell Laboratories, Murray Hill, N.J. (1976).

[Hunt et al., 77]
Hunt, J.W., and Szymanski, T.G., A fast algorithm for computing longest common subsequences, *C. ACM*, 20, 5, pp. 350–353 (1977).

[Ibarra et al., 92]
Ibarra, O.H., Jiang, T., and Wang, H., String editing on a one-way linear array of finite-state machines, *IEEE Trans. Comput.*, C-41, 1, pp. 112–118 (1992).

[Ivanov, 85]

Ivanov, A.G., Recognition of an approximate occurrence of words on Turning machine in real time, *Math. USSR-Izv.*, 24, 3, pp. 479–522 (1985).

[Jokinen et al., 91]

Jokinen, P., and Ukkonen, E., Two algorithms for approximate string matching in static texts, *16th Int. Symp. Math. Foundations of Comput. Sci.*, pp. 240–248 (1991).

[Jong et al., 92]

Jong, J.P., Eun, W.K., and Won, K.C., A study on 1-D bit serial processor design for code string matching using a MWLD algorithm, *J. Korean Inst. Telematics and Electronics*, 29B, 2, pp. 1–8 (1992).

[Kashyap et al., 81]

Kashyap, R.L., and Oommen, B.J., An effective algorithm for string correction using generalized edit distances, *Inf. Sci.*, 3, pp. 123–142 (1981).

[Kashyap et al., 83]

Kashyap, R.L. and Oommen, B.J., The noisy substring matching problem, *IEEE Trans. Softw. Engr.*, SE-9, 3, pp. 365–370 (1983).

[Kernighan et al., 90]

Kernighan, M.D., Church, K.W., and Gale, W.A., A spelling correction program based on a noisy channel model, *COLING-90*, pp. 205–210 (1990).

[Kim et al., 92]

Kim, J. Y., and Shawe-Taylor, J., An approximate string matching algorithm, *Theoret. Comput. Sci.*, 92, 1, pp.107–117 (1992).

[Kohonen, 80]

Kohonen, T., *Content Addressable Memories*, Springer-Verlag, New York (1980).

[Kukich, 90]

Kukich, K., A comparison of some novel and traditional lexical distance metrics for spelling correction, *INNC-90-Paris*, pp. 309–313 (1990).

[Kukich, 92a]

Kukich, K., Spelling correction for the telecommunications network for the deaf, *C. ACM*, 35, 5, pp. 80–90 (1992).

[Kukich et al., 92b]

Kukich, K., Techniques for automatically correcting words in text, *ACM Computing Surveys*, 24, 4, pp. 378–439 (1992).

[Kuo et al., 91]

Kuo, S., and Cross, G.R., A two-step string matching procedure, *Pattern Recognition*, 24, 7, pp. 711–716 (1991).

[Landau et al., 85]

Landau, G.M., and Vishkin, U., Efficient string matching in the presence of errors, *26th Ann. Symp. Foundations of Comput. Sci.*, pp. 126–136 (1985).

[Landau et al., 86a]

Landau, G.M., and Vishkin, U., Introducing efficient parallelism into approximate string matching and a new serial algorithm, *18th ACM Symp. Theory of Computing*, pp. 220–230 (1986).

[Landau et al., 86b]

Landau, G.M., and Vishkin, U., Efficient string matching with k mismatches, *Theoret. Comput. Sci.*, 43, pp. 239–249 (1986).

[Landau et al., 88]

Landau, G.M., and Vishkin, U., Fast string matching with k differences, *J. Comput. Syst. Sci.*, 37, 1, pp. 63–78 (1988).

[Lowrance et al., 75]

Lowrance, R., and Wagner, R.A., An extension of the string-to-string correction problem, *J. ACM*, 22, pp. 177–183 (1975).

[Majester et al., 80]

Majester, M.E., and Reisner, A., Efficient on-line construction and correction of position trees, *SIAM J. Comput.*, 9, 4, pp. 785–807 (1980).

[Manber et al., 91]

Manber, U., and Baeza-Yates, R., An algorithm for string matching with a sequence of don't cares, *Inf. Proc. Lett.*, 37, 3, pp. 133–136 (1991).

[Masek et al., 80]

Masek, W.J., and Paterson, M.S., A faster algorithm for computing string-edit distances, *J. Comput. Syst. Sci.*, 20, 1, pp. 18–31 (1980).

[Megson, 90]

Megson, G.M., Efficient systolic string matching, *Electronics Lett.*, 26, 24, pp. 2040–2042 (1990).

[Miller, 87]

Miller, W., *A Software Tools Sampler*, Prentice Hall, Englewood Cliffs, N.J. (1987).

[Miller et al., 85]

Miller, W., and Myers, E.W., A file comparison program, *Softw. Pract. & Exper.*, 15, 11, pp. 1025–1040 (1985).

[Mor et al., 82]

Mor, M., and Fraenkel, A.S., A hash code method for detecting and correcting spelling errors, *C. ACM*, 25, 12, pp. 935–938 (1982).

[Muth et al., 77]

Muth, F.E., Jr., and Tharp, A.L., Correcting human error in alphanumeric terminal input, *Inf. Proc. Manage.*, 13, pp. 329–337(1977).

[Myers, 86]

Myers, E.W., An O(ND) difference algorithm and its variations, *Algorithmica*, 1, pp. 251–266 (1986).

[Myers et al., 89]

Myers, E.W., and Miller, W., Approximate matching of regular expressions, *Bull. Math. Biol.*, 51, 1, pp. 5–37 (1989).

[Nakatsu et al., 82]

Nakatsu, N., Kambayashi, Y., and Yajima, S., A longest common subsequence algorithm suitable for similar text strings, *Acta Inf.*, 18, pp. 171–179 (1982).

[Needleman et al., 70]

Needleman, S.B., and Wunsch, C.D., A general method applicable to the search for similarities in the amino acid sequences of two proteins, *J. Molecular Biol.*, pp. 443–453 (1970).

[Nemhauser, 66]

Nemhauser, G.L., *Introduction to Dynamic Programming*, Wiley, New York (1966).

[Okuda et al., 76]

Okuda, T., Tanaka, E., and Kasai, T., A method of correction of garbled words based on the Levenshtein metric, *IEEE Trans. Comput.*, C-25, pp. 172–177 (1976).

[Pinter, 85]

Pinter, R.Y., Efficient string matching with don't-care patterns, in Apostolico, A., and Galil, Z., eds., *Combinatorial Algorithms on Words*, Springer, Berlin (1985).

[Pollock et al., 84]

Pollock, J.J., and Zamora, A., Automatic spelling correction in scientific and scholarly text, *C. ACM*, 27, 4, pp. 358–368 (1984).

[Quong, 92]

Quong, R.W., Fast average-case pattern matching by mutiplexing sparse tables, *Theoret. Comput. Sci.*, 92, 1, pp. 165–179 (1992).

[Riseman et al., 74]

Riseman, E.M., and Hanson, A.R., A contextual postprocessing system for error correction using binary n-grams, *IEEE Trans. Comput.*, C-23, 5, pp. 480–493 (1974).

[Sankoff et al., 83]

Sankoff, D., and Kruskal, J.B., *Time Warps, String Edits, and Macro-Molecules: The Theory and Practice of Sequence Comparison*, Addison-Wesley, Reading, Mass. (1983).

[Sellers, 80]

Sellers, P.H., The theory and computation of evolutionary distances: pattern recognition, *J. Algorithms*, 1, pp. 359–373 (1980).

[Takahashi et al., 90]
  Takahashi, K., Yamada, H., and Hirata, M., A string search processor LSI, *J. Inf. Process.*, 13, 2, pp. 183–189 (1990).
[Tarhio et al., 90]
  Tarhio, J., and Ukkonen, E., Boyer-Moore approach to approximate string matching, *2nd Workshop Algorithm Theory*, pp. 348–359 (1990).
[Taylor, 81]
  Taylor, W.D., GROPE—A spelling error correction tool, *AT&T Bell Lab. Tech. Mem.* (1981).
[Tenczar et al., 72]
  Tenczar, P., and Golden, W., CERL Report X-35, Computer-Based Education Research Lab., Univ. of Illinois (1972).
[Tichy, 84]
  Tichy, W., The string-to-string correction problem with block moves, *ACM Trans. Comput. Syst.*, 2, pp. 309–321 (1984).
[Ukkonen, 85a]
  Ukkonen, E., Algorithms for approximate string matching, *Inf. and Contr.*, 64, pp. 100–118 (1985).
[Ukkonen, 85b]
  Ukkonen, E., Finding approximate patterns in strings, *J. Algorithms*, 6, pp. 132–137 (1985).
[Ukkonen, 92]
  Ukkonen, E., Approximate string matching with g-grams and maximal matches, *Theoret. Comput. Sci.*, 92, 1, pp. 191–211 (1992).
[Ullman, 77]
  Ullman, J.R., A binary n-gram technique for automatic correction of substitution, deletion, insertion and reversal errors in words, *Comput. J.*, 20, pp. 141–147 (1977).
[Veronis, 88]
  Veronis, J., Computerized correction of phonographic errors, *Comput. Hum.*, 22, pp. 43–56 (1988).
[Wagner, 74]
  Wagner, R.A., Order-n correction for regular languages, *C. ACM*, 13, 5, pp. 265–268 (1974).
[Wagner et al., 74]
  Wagner, R., and Fischer, M., The string-to-string correction problem, *J. ACM*, 21, 1, pp. 168–178 (1974).
[Wagner et al., 78]
  Wagner, R., and Seiferas, J.I., Correcting counter-automaton-recognizable languages, *SIAM J. Comput.*, 7, 3, pp. 357–375 (1978).
[Wang et al., 90]
  Wang, Y.P., and Pavlidis, T., Optimal correspondence of string subsequences, *IEEE Trans. Pattern Analysis and Machine Intelligence*, PAMI-12, 11, pp. 1080–1087 (1990).
[Wen-Tsuen et al., 92]
  Wen-Tsuen, C., and Tzren-Ru, C., A hierarchical deformation model for online curve script recognition, *11th IAPR Conf. Pattern Recognition*, pp. 195–199 (1992).
[Wong et al., 76]
  Wong, C.K., and Chandra, A.K., Bounds for the string editing problem, *J. ACM*, 23, 1, pp. 13–16 (1976).
[Wu et al., 92a]
  Wu, S., and Manber, U., Fast text searching allowing errors, *C. ACM*, 35, 10, pp. 83–91 (1992).
[Wu et al., 92b]
  Wu, S., and Udi, M., agrep—a fast approximate pattern matching tool, *Winter USENIX Conf.*, pp. 153–162 (1992).
[Zamora et al, 81]
  Zamora, E.M., Pollock, J.J., and Zamora, A., The use of trigram analysis for spelling error detection, *Inf. Proc. Manage.*, 17, 6, pp. 305–316 (1981).

Chapter 4: Multidimensional matching

[Aho et al., 76a]
  Aho, A.V., Hirschberg, D.S., and Ullman, J.D., Bounds on the complexity of the maximal common subsequence problem, *J. ACM*, 23, 1, pp. 1–12 (1976).
[Aho et al., 76b]
  Aho, A.V., and Johnson, S.C., Optimal code generation for expression trees, *J. ACM*, 23, 3, pp. 488–501 (1976).
[Aho et al., 77]
  Aho, A.V., Johnson S.C., and Ullman, J.D., Code generation for expressions with common subexpressions, *J. ACM*, 24, 1, pp. 146–160 (1977).
[Aho et al., 85]
  Aho, A.V., and Ganapathi, M., Efficient tree matching: An aid to code generation, *12th ACM Symp. Principles of Prog. Lang.*, pp. 334–340 (1985).
[Aho et al., 86]
  Aho A.V., Sethi, R., and Ullman, J.D., *Compilers: Principles, Techniques, and Tools*, Addison-Wesley, Reading, Mass. (1986).
[Aho et al., 89]
  Aho, A.V., Ganapathi, M., and Tjiang, S.W.K., Code generation using tree matching and dynamic programming, *ACM Trans. Prog. Lang. and Syst.*, 11, 4, pp. 491–516 (1989).
[Amir, 92]
  Amir, A., Two-dimensional dictionary matching, *Inf. Proc. Lett.*, 44, 5, pp. 233–239 (1992).
[Baeza-Yates, 90]
  Baeza-Yates, R., Fast algorithms for two dimensional and multiple pattern matching, *2nd Workshop Algorithm Theory*, pp. 332–347 (1990).
[Baker, 78]
  Baker, T.P., A technique for extending rapid exact-match string matching to arrays of more than one dimension, *SIAM J. Comput*, 7, 4, pp. 533–541 (1978).
[Ben-Yehuda et al., 89]
  Ben-Yehuda, S., and Pinter, R.Y., Symbolic layout improvement using string matching based local transformations, *Decennial Caltech Conf. VLSI*, MIT Press, Cambridge, Mass., pp. 227–239 (1989).
[Bird, 77a]
  Bird, R.S., Two dimensional pattern matching, *Inf. Proc. Lett.*, 6, 5, pp. 168–170 (1977).
[Bird, 77b]
  Bird, R.S., Improving programs by the introduction of recursion, *C. ACM*, 20, 11, pp. 856–863 (1977).
[Blumer et al., 85]
  Blumer, A., Blumer, J., Ehrenfeucht, A., Haussler, D., Chen, M.T., and Seiferas, J., The smallest automaton recognizing the subwords of a text, *Theoret. Comput. Sci.*, 40, 1, pp. 31–56 (1985).
[Chase, 87]
  Chase, D.R., An improvement to bottom-up tree pattern matching, *14th ACM Symp. Principles of Prog. Lang.*, pp. 18–177 (1987).
[Cortelazzo et al., 92]
  Cortelazzo, G. M., Deretta, G., Mian, G.A., and Zamperoni, P., On the application of geometrical form description techniques to automatic key-sections recognition, *11th Int. Conf. Pattern Recognition*, pp. 420–424 (1992).
[Crochemore et al., 90]
  Crochemore, M., and Rytter, W., Parallel computations on string and arrays, *7th Symp. Theoretical Aspects of Comput. Sci.*, pp. 109–125 (1990).
[Dinstein et al., 90]
  Dinstein, I., and Landau, G.M., Using parallel string matching algorithms for contour based 2-D shape recognition, *10th Int. Conf. Pattern Recognition*, pp. 415–419 (1990).

[Dinstein et al., 91]

Dinstein, I., Landau, G.M., and Guy, G., Parallel (PRAM EREW) algorithms for contour-based 2D shape recognition, *Pattern Recognition*, 24, 10, pp. 929–942 (1991).

[Eilan-Tzoreff et al., 88]

Eilan-Tzoreff, T., and Vishkin, U., Matching patterns in strings subject to multilinear transformations, *Theoret. Comput. Sci.*, 60, 3, pp. 231–254 (1988).

[Eyal et al., 91]

Eyal, K., Hastie, T., and Wolfson, H., 3-D curve matching using splines, *J. Robotic Syst.*, 8, 6, pp. 723–743 (1991).

[Fischer et al., 92]

Fischer, D., Nussinov, R., and Wolfson, H.J., 3-D substructure matching in protein molecules, *Third Symp. Combinatorial Pattern Matching*, Springer-Verlag, New York, pp. 136–150 (1992).

[Fischetti et al., 92]

Fischetti, V.A., Landau, G.M., Schmidt, J.P., and Sellers, P.H., Identifying periodic occurrences of a template with applications to protein structure, *Third Symp. Combinatorial Pattern Matching*, Springer-Verlag, New York, pp. 111–120 (1992).

[Flammia, 92]

Flammia, G., Dynamic programming solves approximate planar matching, *Theory and Applications of Image Analysis*, pp. 99–109 (1992).

[Fu et al., 73]

Fu, K.S., and Bhargava, B.K., Tree systems for syntactic pattern matching recognition, *IEEE Trans. Comput.*, C-22, 12, pp. 1087–1099 (1973).

[Futatsugi et al., 85]

Futatsugi, K., Gogun, J., Jounnaud, J.A., and Meseguer, J., Principles of OBJ2, *12th Symp. Principles of Prog. Lang.*, pp. 52–66 (1985).

[Gen-Huey, 92]

Gen-Huey, C., An O(1) time algorithm for string matching, *Int. J. Comput. Math.*, 42, 3–4, pp. 185–191 (1992).

[Guttag et al., 76]

Guttag, J., Horowitz, E., and Musser, D., Abstract data types and software validation, Inf. Sci. Report ISI/RR-76-48 (1976).

[Hashiguchi et al., 92]

Hashiguchi, K., and Yamada, K., Two recognizable string matching problem over free partially commutative monoids, *Theoret. Comput. Science*, 92, 1, pp. 77–86 (1992).

[Hoffmann et al., 82]

Hoffmann, C.W., and O'Donnell, M.J., Pattern matching in trees, *J. ACM*, 29, 1, pp. 68–95 (1982).

[Karp et al., 72]

Karp, R.M., Miller, R.E., and Rosenberg, A.L., Rapid identification of repeated patterns in strings, trees, and arrays, *4th ACM Symp. Theory of Computing*, pp. 125–136 (1972).

[Kedem et al., 89]

Kedem, Z.M., Landau, G.M., and Palem, K.V., Optimal parallel suffix-prefix matching algorithm and applications, *Symp. Parallel Algorithms and Architectures*, pp. 388–398 (1989).

[Kosaraju, 89]

Kosaraju, S.R., Efficient tree pattern matching, *30th Symp. Foundations of Comput. Sci.*, pp. 178–183 (1989).

[Knuth et al., 70]

Knuth, D.E., and Bendix, P., Simple word problems in universal algebras, in Leech, J., ed., *Computational Problems in Abstract Algebra*, Pergammon Press, Oxford, pp. 263–297 (1970).

[Knuth, 73]

Knuth, D.E., *The Art of Computer Programming, Vol. 3: Sorting and Searching*, Addison-Wesley, Reading, Mass. (1973).

[Kuo-Liang, 92]

Kuo-Liang, C., A randomized parallel algorithm for string matching on hypercube, *Pattern Recognition*, 25, 10, pp. 1265–1268 (1992).

[Lang et al., 80]
  Lang, H.-W., Schimmler, M., and Schmeck, H., Matching tree patterns sublinear on the average, tech. report, Univ. of Kiel, West Germany (1980).

[Lin et al., 90]
  Lin, C.-K., and Jeng, B.-S., On-line recognition of handwritten Chinese characters and alphabets, *Int. Conf. Acoustics, Speech and Signal Processing*, pp. 3–6 (1990).

[Maes, 91]
  Maes, M., Polygonal shape recognition using string matching techniques, *Pattern Recognition*, 24, 5, pp. 433–440 (1991).

[Morita et al., 90]
  Morita, S., Kawashima, T., and Aoki, Y., Pattern matching of 2D shape using hierarchical description (in Japanese), *Trans. IEICE*, J73D-II, 5, pp. 717–727 (1990).

[O'Donnell, 85]
  O'Donnell, M.J., *Equational Logic as a Programming Language*, MIT Press, Cambridge, Mass. (1985).

[Powell, 90]
  Powell, P., Serial and parallel algorithms for rapid sequence similarity determination, *4th Parallel Processing Symp.*, pp. 119–131 (1990).

[Ramesh et al., 92]
  Ramesh, R. and Ramakrishnan, I.V., Nonlinear matching in trees, *J.ACM*, 39, 2, pp. 295–316 (1992).

[Salomaa, 88]
  Salomaa, K., Deterministic tree pushdown automata and monadic tree rewriting systems, *J. Comput. Syst. Sci.*, 37, 3, pp. 367–394 (1988).

[Schreiber et al., 90]
  Schreiber, I., and Ben-Bassat, M., Polygonal object recognition, *10th Int. Conf. Pattern Recognition*, pp. 852–859 (1990).

[Selkow, 77]
  Selkow, S.M., The tree-to-tree editing problem, *Inf. Proc. Lett.*, 6, 6, pp. 184–186 (1977).

[Snyder, 82]
  Snyder, L., Recognition and selection of idioms for code optimization, *Acta Inf.* 17, pp. 327–348 (1982).

[Steyaert et al., 83]
  Steyaert, J., and Flajolet, P., Patterns and pattern-matching in trees: An analysis, *Inf. and Contr.*, 58, pp. 19–58 (1983).

[Tai, 79]
  Tai, K.-C., The tree-to-tree correction problem, *J. ACM*, 26, 3, pp. 422–433 (1979).

[Tucci et al., 91]
  Tucci, M., Costagliola, G., and Shi-Kuo, C., A remark on NP-completeness of picture matching, *Infor. Proc. Lett.*, 39, 5, pp. 241–243 (1991).

[Vishkin, 90]
  Vishkin, U., Determistic sampling—A new technique for fast pattern matching, *22nd ACM Symp. Theory of Computing*, pp. 170–180 (1990).

[Vishkin, 91]
  Vishkin, U., Deterministic sampling—A new technique for fast pattern matching, *SIAM J. Comput.*, 20, 1, pp. 22–40 (1991).

[Wolfson, 90]
  Wolfson, H.J., On curve matching, *IEEE Trans. Pattern Analysis and Machine Intelligence*, PAMI-12, 5, pp. 483–489 (1990).

[Wu et al., 90]
  Wu, C.H., and Whitson, G.M., Artificial neural system for gene classification using a domain database, *18th Comput. Sci. Conf.*, pp. 288–292 (1990).

[Zhu et al., 89]
  Zhu, R.F., and Takaoka, T., A technique for two-dimensional pattern matching, *C. ACM*, 32, 9, pp. 1110–1120 (1989).

[Zhu et al., 92]
Zhu, X.Y., and Cahill, L.W., A self-supervised dynamic time-warping algorithm, *J. Electrical and Electronics Engr.*, 12, 3, pp. 300–307 (1992).

Chapter 5: Hardware matching

[Ahuja et al., 80]
Ahuja, S.R., and Roberts, C.S., An associative/parallel processor for partial match retrieval using superimposed codes, *7th Ann. Symp. Comput. Architecture*, pp. 218–227 (1980).

[Amir et al., 92]
Amir, A., Farach, M., and Matias, Y., Efficient randomized dictionary matching algorithms, *Combinatorial Pattern Matching, Third Symp.*, Stringer-Verlag, New York, pp. 262–275 (1992).

[Bird et al., 77]
Bird, M.R., Tu, J.C., and Worthy R.M., Associative/parallel processors for searching very large textual data bases, *Third ACM Workshop Comput. Architecture and Nonnumeric Processing*, pp. 8–16 (1977).

[Burkowski, 82]
Burkowski, F., A hardware hashing scheme in the design of a multiterm string comparator, *IEEE Trans. Comput.*, C-31, 9, pp. 825–834 (1982).

[Cheng et al., 87]
Cheng, H., and Fu, K., VLSI architectures for string matching and pattern matching, *Pattern Recognition*, 20, pp. 125–141 (1987).

[Christodoulakis et al., 84]
Christodoulakis, S., and Faloutsos, C., Design considerations for a message file server, *IEEE Trans. Softw. Engr.*, SE-10, 2, pp. 201–210 (1984).

[Ciaccia et al., 93]
Ciaccia, P., and Zezula, P., Estimating accesses in partitioned signature file organizations, *ACM Trans. Inf. Syst.*, 11, 2, pp. 133-142 (1993).

[Curry et al., 83]
Curry, T., and Mukhopadhyay, A., Realization of efficient non-numeric operations through VLSI, *VLSI'83*, pp. 32–336 (1983).

[Faloutsos, 85]
Faloutsos, C., Access methods for text, *ACM Comput. Surveys*, 17, pp. 49–-74 (1985).

[Faloutsos et al., 84]
Faloutsos, C., and Christodoulakis, S., Signature files: An access method for documents and its analytical performance evaluation, *ACM Trans. Office Inf. Syst.*, 2, 4, pp. 267–288 (1984).

[Faloutsos et al., 87]
Faloutsos, C., and Christodoulakis, S., Description and performance analysis of signature file methods for office filing, *ACM Trans. Inf. Syst.*, 5, 3, pp. 237–257 (1987).

[Foster et al., 80]
Foster, M.J., and Kung, H.T., The design of special purpose chips, *IEEE Comput.*, 13, pp. 26–40 (1980).

[Grandi et al., 92]
Grandi, F., Tiberio, P., and Zezula, P., Frame-slice partitioned parallel signature files, *ACM SIGIR'92*, pp. 286–297 (1992).

[Halaas, 83]
Halaas, R.L., A systolic VLSI matrix for a family of fundamental search problem, *Integration VLSI J.*,1, pp. 269–282 (1983).

[Harrison, 71]
Harrison, M.C., Implementation of the substring test by hashing. *C. ACM*, 14, pp. 777–779 (1971).

[Haskin, 81]
Haskin, R.L., Special-purpose processors for text retrieval, *Database Eng.*, 4, pp. 16–29 (1981).

[Haskin et al., 83]
   Haskin, R.L., and Hollaar, L.A., Operational characteristics of a hardware-based faster matcher, *ACM Trans. Database Syst.*, 8, 1 (1983).
[Hollaar, 79]
   Hollaar, L.A., Text retrieval computers, *IEEE Comput. Mag.*, 12, 3, pp. 40–50 (1979).
[Hollaar, 83]
   Hollaar, L.A., Architecture and operation of a large, full-text information-retrieval system, in Hsiao, D.K., ed., *Advanced Database Machine Architecture*, Prentice Hall, Englewood Cliffs, N.J., pp. 256–299 (1983).
[Isenman et al., 90]
   Isenman, M.E., and Shasha, D.E., Performance and architectural issues for string matching, *IEEE Trans. Comput.*, C-39, 2, pp. 238–250 (1990).
[Larson, 83]
   Larson, P.A., A method for speeding up text retrieval, *ACM SIGMOD Conf.*, (1983).
[Lee, 82]
   Lee, L.G., Designing a Bloom filter for differential file access, *C. ACM*, 25, 9, pp. 600–604 (1982).
[Lee, 85]
   Lee, D.L., A distributed multiple-response resolver for valued-ordered retrieval, *12th Int. Conf. Data Eng.*, pp. 352–359 (1986).
[Lee, 86a]
   Lee, D.L., A word-parallel, bit-serial signature processor for superimposed coding, *2nd Int. Conf. Data Eng.*, pp. 352–359 (1986).
[Lee, 86b]
   Lee, D.L., Alterp-A cellor processor for high-speed pattern matching, *New Generation Comput.*, 4, pp. 225–244 (1986).
[Lee et al., 85]
   Lee, D.L., and Lochovsky, F.H., Text retrieval machines, in Tsichritzis, D.C., ed., *Office Automation*, Stringer-Verlag, New York, pp. 339–375 (1985).
[Lee et al., 89]
   Lee, D.L., and Leng, C., Partitioned signature files: Design issues and performance evaluation, *ACM Trans. Inf. Syst.*, 7, 2, pp. 158–180 (1989).
[Lee et al., 90]
   Lee, D.L., and Lochovsky, F.H., HYTREM—A hybrid text-retrieval machine for large databases, *IEEE Trans. Comput.*, C-39, 1, pp. 111–123 (1990).
[Mak et al., 91]
   Mak, V.W.-K., Lee, K.C., and Frieder, O., Exploiting parallelism in pattern matching: An information retrieval application, *ACM Trans. Inf. Syst.*, 9, 1, pp. 52–74 (1991).
[McIlroy, 82]
   McIlroy, M.D., Development of a spelling list, *IEEE Trans. Comm.*, COM-30, 1, pp. 91–99 (1982).
[Mead, et al., 76]
   Mead, C.A., Pashley, R.D., Britton, L.D., Yoshiaki, T., and Snado, S.F., Jr., 128-bit multicomparator, *IEEE J. Solid State Circuits*, SC-11, pp. 692–695 (1976).
[Mooers, 49]
   Mooers, C., Application of random codes to the gathering of statistical information, Bulletin 31, Zator Co., Cambridge, Mass. (1949).
[Mullin, 87]
   Mullin, J.K., Accessing textual documents using compressed indexes of arrays of small Bloom filters, *Comput. J.*, 30, 4, pp. 343–348 (1987).
[Ogawa et al., 92]
   Ogawa, R., Kikuchi, Y., and Takahshi, K., Recent developments in full text database technologies (in Japanese), *Joho Syori*, 33, 4, pp. 404–412 (1992).
[Pramanick, 86]
   Pramanick, S., Performance analysis of a database filter search hardware, *IEEE Trans. Comput.*, C-35, pp. 1077–1082 (1986).

[Roberts, 79]
Roberts, C.S., Partial-match retrieval via the method of superimposed codes, *IEEE Trans. Proc.*, 67, 12, pp. 1624–1642 (1979).

[Sacks-Davis et al., 83]
Sacks-Davis, R., and Ramamohanarao, K., A two level superimposed coding scheme for partial match retrieval, *Inf. Syst.*, 8, 4, pp. 273–280 (1983).

[Sato, 90]
Sato, T., Fast string pattern matching by using compressed data files (in Japanese), *Trans. IEICE*, J73D-I, 4, pp. 451–452 (1990).

[Schefter, 87]
Schefter, J., Super searcher, *Popular Sci.*, 231, pp. 60–61 (1987).

[Severance et al., 76]
Severance, D.G., and Lohman, G.M., Differential files: Their applications to the maintenance of large databases, *ACM Trans. Database Syst.*, 1, 3, pp. 268–275 (1976).

[Stanfill et al., 86]
Stanfill, C., and Kahle, B., Parallel-free text search on the connection machine, *C. ACM*, 29, 12, pp. 1229–1239 (1986).

[Stellhorn, 77]
Stellhorn, W.H., An inverted file processor for information retrieval, *IEEE Trans. Comput.*, C-26, 12, pp. 1258–1267 (1977).

[Takahashi, et al., 87]
Takahashi, K., Yamada, H., and Hirata, M., Intelligent string search processor to accelerate text information retrieval, *Fifth Int. Workshop on Database Machines*, pp. 440–453 (1987).

[Thap et al., 82]
Thap, A.L., and Tai, K.-C., The practicality of text signatures for accelerating string searching, *Softw. Pract. & Exper.*, 12, 1, pp. 35–44 (1982).

[Tsichritzis et al., 83]
Tsichritzis, D., Christodoulakis, S., and Economopoulos, P., Faloutsos, C., Lee, D., Vandenbroel, J., and Woo, C., A multimedia office filing system, *Conf. VLDB* (1983).

[Wakabayashi et al., 85]
Wakabayashi, S., Kikuno, T., and Yoshida, N., Design of hardware algorithms by recurrence relations (in Japanese), *Syst. and Comput.* 8, pp. 10–17 (1985).

[Zezula et al., 91]
Zezula, P., Rabitti, F., and Tiberio, P., Dynamic partitioning of signature files, *ACM Trans. Inf. Syst.*, 9, 4, pp. 336–369 (1991).

About the author

Juni-ichi Aoe is an associate professor at the Department of Information Science and Intelligent Systems at the University of Tokushima, Japan. He is the author of 51 journal papers and 23 proceedings papers. His research interests include compiler construction and verification, design and analysis of algorithms, and natural language processing. He received the Best Author Award from the Information Processing Society of Japan in 1993.

He received the BE and MS degrees from the University of Tokushima, Japan in 1974 and 1976, respectively, and the PhD degree from the University of Osaka, Japan in 1980.

He is currently leader of three projects in his subject area. He served as chair of a panel session on AI Techniques and Systems for COMPSAC '88. He is a member of the IEEE Computer Society, the Association for Computing Machinery, the American Association for Artificial Intelligence, the Association for Computational Linguistics, the Institute of Electronics, Information, and Communication Engineers of Japan, the Japan Society for Software Science and Technology, the Information Processing Society of Japan, and the Japanese Society for Artificial Intelligence.

Note: The author can be reached on the Internet as aoe@j-aoe.is.tokushima-u.ac.jp

Other titles from
IEEE Computer Society Press

Advances in ISDN and Broadband ISDN
edited by William Stallings

Provides a comprehensive introduction to ISDN and B-ISDN and explores key topics related to their architecture and standards. It also details the architecture that exploits the emerging application of digital technology to integrate voice and data transmission and to provide structured interfaces and transmission services for the end user.

Sections: ISDN Overview, ISDN Protocols and Network Architecture, Frame Relay, Broadband ISDN, ATM and SONET/SDH.

288 pages. 1992. Hardcover. ISBN 0-8186-2797-2. Catalog # 2797-01 — $45.00 Members $35.00

Computer Communications:
Architectures, Protocols, and Standards, 3rd Edition
edited by William Stallings

This third edition is a major revision providing a comprehensive survey of the motivating factors and design principles for a communication architecture. It contains 29 papers, including 24 new articles, that provide a broad overview of communication protocols and highlight the important design issues for a communication architecture.

Sections: Communication Architectures, Physical and Data Link Protocols, Network Access Protocols, Internetworking, Transport and Session Protocols, Presentation and Application Layers.

360 pages. 1992. Hardcover. ISBN 0-8186-2712-3. Catalog # 2712-01 — $55.00 Members $40.00

Systems Network Architecture (SNA)
edited by Edwin R. Coover

Introduces the reader to the design, operation, and management of IBM's Systems Network Architecture. It examines the principal components of an SNA network and their functions, development of SNA and its current capabilities, and operational and maintenance aspects of SNA.

Sections: Introduction, The Beginnings: The Early "Star" Network and SNA Terms, Extending the Network, SNA Operations and Maintenance, SNA and the Office, SNA Network Management, The Future of SNA.

464 pages. 1992. Hardcover. ISBN 0-8186-9131-X. Catalog # 2131-01 — $58.00 Members $45.00

Broadband Switching: Architectures, Protocols, Design, and Analysis
edited by Chris Dhas, V. K. Konangi, and M. Sreetharan

Investigates the latest information and research on broadband switching and provides insight into the correlated areas of networking, performance analysis, and alternate technologies. It covers a number of architectures and performance modeling techniques, describes multistage interconnection networks, and discusses trends in network architectures for users with high bandwidth requirements.

Sections: Network Architecture; Interconnection Networks; Experimental Architectures; Switch Fabric Design and Analysis; Switch Architectures; Broadcast Switching Networks; Bandwidth Allocation, Flow, and Congestion Control; Performance Modeling; Photonic Switching Systems.

528 pages. 1991. Hardcover. ISBN 0-8186-8926-9. Catalog # 1926-01 — $65.00 Members $50.00

X.25 and Related Protocols
by Uyless Black

Explains X.25 operations, the advantages and disadvantages of its use, the concepts and terms of packet networks, and the role other standards play in the operation of X.25. It contains all original material and is complete with six appendices, over 100 illustrations, and more than 50 tables.

Sections: The X.25 Network, Layered Protocols, OSI and X.25, X.25 and the Physical Layer, X.25 and the Data-Link Layer, The X.25 Network Layer, X.25 Facilities, X.25 Companion Standards, Internetworking X.25 with Other Systems, The PAD Standards, X.25's Future, Examples of Packet Networks, Link Protocols, Diagnostic Codes.

304 pages. 1991. Hardcover. ISBN 0-8186-8976-5. Catalog # 1976-04 — $60.00 Members $45.00

▼ **To order call toll-free: 1-800-CS-BOOKS** ▼

▼ **Fax: (714) 821–4641** ▼

10662 Los Vaqueros Circle   Los Alamitos, CA 90720-1264   Phone: (714) 821–8380

Other titles from
IEEE Computer Society Press

VLSI Algorithms and Architectures: Fundamentals
edited by N. Ranganathan

Introduces basic approaches to the design of VLSI algorithms and architectures and provides a reliable reference source for advanced readers. It provides a variety of useful reference material for researchers and students seeking information on the design of hardware algorithms and architectures for VLSI implementation.

Sections: An Overview of VLSI Algorithms and Architectures, Systolic and Wavefront Arrays, Data Structures and Sorting, Matrix and Algebraic Computations, Pattern Matching and Text Retrieval, VLSI Processor Designs.

320 pages. 1993. Hardcover. ISBN 0-8186-4392-7. Catalog # 4392-01 — $40.00 Members $32.00

VLSI Algorithms and Architectures: Advanced Concepts
edited by N. Ranganathan

This companion volume features an in-depth examination into the latest designs of VLSI algorithms and architectures. Contains many new studies exposing various computationally intensive problems requiring VLSI solutions, discusses design issues, and describes special-purpose architectures for a wide-range of computationally intensive problems.

Sections: VLSI Architecture Design Issues; Advanced Topics in Systolic Arrays; Image, Speech, and Signal Processing; Artificial Intelligence and Computer Vision; Dictionary Machines and Data Compression; Iterative Algorithms.

320 pages. 1993. Hardcover. ISBN 0-8186-4402-8. Catalog # 4402-01 — $40.00 Members $32.00

Software Metrics:
A Practitioner's Guide to Improved Product Development
by Daniel J. Paulish and Karl-Heinrich Möller
CO-PUBLISHED WITH CHAPMAN & HALL AND IEEE PRESS

A collection of practical suggestions for implementing and managing with metrics within industrial organizations. It contains summaries of successful metrics implementation techniques, and describes the benefits that result in better, higher quality products developed with more productive resources within a shorter time frame.

Sections: Introduction, Origins of Software Metrics, Software Quality Productivity by Quantitative Methods, Metrics Introduction Program Approach, Common Implementation Problems, Metrics Characteristics, Example Metrics, Best Practices and Benefits Experience (Siemens, Data Logic, ETNOTEAM), VERIDATAS Code Inspection Metrics, RW-TÜV Process Monitoring System Testing, CRIL User Satisfaction Measurement, Tools, Conclusions.

272 pages. 1992. Softcover. ISBN 0-7803-0444-6. Catalog # 3035-04 — $39.95 Members $32.00

Distributed Mutual Exclusion Algorithms
edited by Pradip K. Srimani and Sunil R. Das

This collection presents 11 papers detailing the major approaches for solving the problem of distributed mutual exclusion, discussing assumptions and the validity of those assumptions, and featuring a detailed performance evaluation of the algorithms under examination.

Papers: Introduction, The Mutual Exclusion Problem, The Information Structure of DMEAs, A Tree-Based Algorithm for DMEAs, A Resilient Mutual Exclusion Algorithm for Computer Networks, Fault-Tolerant Mutual Exclusion Algorithms, An Efficient and Fault-Tolerant Solution for Distributed Mutual Exclusion, A Distributed Algorithm for Multiple Entries to a Critical Section.

168 pages. 1992. Softcover. ISBN 0-8186-3380-8. Catalog # 3380-05 — $35.00 Members $25.00

▼   **To order call toll-free: 1-800-CS-BOOKS**   ▼

▼   **Fax: (714) 821–4641**   ▼

10662 Los Vaqueros Circle   Los Alamitos, CA 90720-1264   Phone: (714) 821–8380